Corel**DRAW**®X4
The Official Guide

Gary David Bouton

New York Chicago San Francisco
Lisbon London Madrid Mexico City
Milan New Delhi San Juan
Seoul Singapore Sydney Toronto

30131 04431255 8

London Borough of Barnet

The McGraw·Hill Companies

Cataloging-in-Publication Data is on file with the Library of Congress

London Borough of Barnet	
Askews	Oct-2008
006.686	£27.99

McGraw-Hill books are available at special quantity discounts to use as premiums and sales promotions, or for use in corporate training programs. To contact a special sales representative, please visit the Contact Us page at www.mhprofessional.com.

CorelDRAW® X4: The Official Guide

Copyright © 2008 by The McGraw-Hill Companies. All rights reserved. Printed in the United States of America. Except as permitted under the Copyright Act of 1976, no part of this publication may be reproduced or distributed in any form or by any means, or stored in a database or retrieval system, without the prior written permission of publisher, with the exception that the program listings may be entered, stored, and executed in a computer system, but they may not be reproduced for publication.

1234567890   FGR FGR   0198

ISBN   978-0-07-154570-9
MHID   0-07-154570-0

Sponsoring Editor	**Copy Editors**	**Composition**
Megg Morin	Jan Jue, Julie Smith	International Typesetting
Editorial Supervisor	**Proofreader**	and Composition
Janet Walden	Susie Elkind	**Illustration**
Project Editor	**Indexer**	International Typesetting
LeeAnn Pickrell	Rebecca Plunkett	and Composition
Acquisitions Coordinator	**Production Supervisor**	**Art Director, Cover**
Carly Stapleton	George Anderson	Jeff Weeks
Technical Editor		**Cover Designer**
Peter W. Cooper		Pattie Lee

Adobe Systems, Corel Corporation, Microsoft, PostScript, and other brand names and trademarked items referenced in this book are the copyrights of their respective owner.

Information has been obtained by McGraw-Hill from sources believed to be reliable. However, because of the possibility of human or mechanical error by our sources, McGraw-Hill, or others, McGraw-Hill does not guarantee the accuracy, adequacy, or completeness of any information and is not responsible for any errors or omissions or the results obtained from the use of such information.

This book is dedicated to students everywhere who realize that the quest for information is a never-ending one. And this includes authors.

About the Author

Gary David Bouton is a seasoned author and illustrator with over 20 books to his name, covering programs such as CorelDRAW and Adobe Photoshop and topics such as digital video editing, content creation for the Web, and 3D modeling. Gary has been drawing and painting both traditionally and electronically for close to 40 years and has been writing books and articles on art since 1992. He has received four international awards for design and desktop publishing and was a finalist in the CorelDRAW World Design Contest. In his spare time, Gary composes and records music and works on CGI special effects for music videos.

About the Technical Editor

Peter W. Cooper has served as technical editor beginning with *CorelDRAW 10: The Official Guide*. Having earned a BS in Chemistry and an MS in Systems Engineering, he has been employed as a water systems chemist and a process engineer. His various endeavors over the years include software development for computer-aided mammography. Peter has been published in the *JWPCF* and is co-inventor of the U.S. Patent titled *Visual environment simulator for mobile viewer*. He knows firsthand how the misplaced jot or title in a technical exposition can be a most unwelcome source of headache.

CONTENTS AT A GLANCE

CONTENTS

FOREWORD

Over the years, CorelDRAW has developed into a full-featured, professional suite of graphics applications for users of all skill levels to create illustrations, design professional layouts, and work seamlessly between pixel-based and vector graphics, with powerful editing tools in a completely integrated, easy-to-use bundle. The team at Corel continues to strive to provide products that both delight and inspire users around the world with the release of CorelDRAW Graphics Suite X4 and this new *Official Guide*.

With a redesigned look and feel, **CorelDRAW Graphics Suite X4** fuels the creative process by making it simple to manage project elements through integration with desktop search engines. Professionals and aspiring designers alike will appreciate our latest product offering, a redefined standard for creating exceptional designs. New to X4 is support for camera Raw file formats, MS Publisher, and Adobe CS3 applications, creating an optimized workflow for both individual and workgroup designers. With powerful text and layout enhancements such as Live Text Preview, Tables, and Layers per Page, comprehensive file compatibility, and updated high-quality content, **CorelDRAW Graphics Suite X4** gives the user the confidence to tackle a wide range of projects, from attention-getting logos and slick commercial signage to multi-page brochures and other business-driven collateral needs. With integration into online services such as CorelDRAWConceptShare.com, there is now a top-to-bottom collaboration solution throughout the design process and robust communication opportunities with other members of the CorelDRAW.com online community. The route from a white page to a finalized and approved creation has never been easier or faster.

CorelDRAW X4: The Official Guide is the product of a valued partnership between Corel Corporation and McGraw-Hill. The author and contributors have worked closely with the product team at Corel to ensure that every user who owns our product has the information needed to turn inspiration into stunning results.

We're exceptionally pleased to welcome veteran computer graphics author Gary David Bouton to this edition of the *Official Guide,* for providing documentation, real-world tutorials, example files, and bonus content to make your adventures in

CorelDRAW X4 stimulating and artistically rewarding. Gary has been a CorelDRAW user since 1991. He has worked with Corel engineers on previous builds, and he has written several other CorelDRAW books throughout the years. As you work through each chapter, I'm sure the *Official Guide* will be an invaluable resource for users of every skill level and style of personal and professional expression.

Gérard Métrailler
Sr. Director, Product Management, Graphics
Corel Corporation
Ottawa, Ontario
July 2008

ACKNOWLEDGMENTS

As warm and fuzzy as it feels when an author sees his or her name on the cover of a freshly printed book, any good book is a *collaborative* effort. Without the help of the following kind and gifted individuals who helped tease the meat from the rind of my original manuscript, the book you'd be reading would not have the cohesiveness, the impact, and ultimately its usefulness you.

- To Megg Morin for her ready acceptance of my ideas for this new edition of *The Official Guide,* for her unflagging encouragement while reviewing the chapters, and for being a good sport and letting me get silly here and there in the tutorials.

- To Carly Stapleton, Organizational Wizardess Supreme, who made it simple for me to do *my* part of this book. Thank you, Carly, for your patience and guidance through the process, which at times seemed to me like the warehouse scene in *Indiana Jones*.

- Project Editor LeeAnn Pickrell. A good developmental and copy editor is going to fix things an author broke, but also has the insight to leave "what ain't broken" as it *is*. LeeAnn, you're indeed a good editor and I thank you from the bottom of my non-parallisms!

- Copy Editor Jan Jue for flagging me when I went out to the ozone with a few of my explanations and for catching and correcting some gaffs that the rest of us didn't notice.

- Technical Editor Peter Cooper. Thanks to Peter, we're all confident that this book is technically accurate down to the punctuation in the tutorials! A lot of time and diligence went into Peter's review of my work, and it's all for the benefit of our readers. Thanks, Peter!

- Steve Bain and Nick Wilkinson for portions of their original manuscript.

- Lyssa Wald for her outstanding work on the color signature. I never thought my work could look as good in CMYK! Thanks, Lyssa.

- Production Supervisor George Anderson. Thanks to George and his expert team for the crisp layout of this book's interior and for the hours spent working with me on getting the figures and illustrations looking their best.

- Gérard Métrailler at Corel Corporation. Thank you for your support of the *Official Guide* and for creating the fine subject of this book!

- Kelly Manuel at Corel Corporation. Without your help, I wouldn't have been able to pore through the beta versions of X4; my deepest thanks.

- John Falsetto at Corel Corporation. Thanks, John, for your timely feedback during the writing of this book. When I had a question, the answer was in my mailbox, usually before my daily spam!

- Tony Severenuk at Corel Corporation. Thanks to Tony, this book is as accurate as Peter and I tried to make it. Thanks in particular for all the advice on CorelDRAW's handling of camera Raw, Tony.

- Barbara Bouton, my wife and best friend, who did far too much grunt work on this book and managed to find time to make dinner, put up with my (occasional) moods, and take me out to the movies once or twice between paragraphs.

INTRODUCTION

There is a tradition from my childhood—which seems to have gone away in recent years—but that I'd like to restore with this book. It's called the "Prize in Every Box"; remember when you bought a box of candy or cereal and there was a bonus—something really cool inside you didn't expect?

CorelDRAW X4: The Official Guide is your handbook to the most feature-filled drawing application you could hope for, and as you'd rightly expect, the chapters contain comprehensive explanations of what tools, pop-up menus, commands, dockers, and other elements do. But the *prize* in this book is that you'll learn not only the *value* of the features, but also what they're good *for*—how each tool, command, option, and feature can be used to best serve a design problem you want to solve. Knowledge is fine—you can get facts from Wikipedia and around every corner on the Web, the bookstore, and your friends and family. When you put facts to *use*, however, you eventually gain skill you can tap into in the future, build upon, and eventually your knowledge becomes *wisdom*—something an ambitious, expressive designer has an affinity for—right up there with water and oxygen.

This book is divided into eight parts plus an appendix listing keyboard shortcuts that'll speed up your work in CorelDRAW. As you might expect, the parts follow a progression, from a very basic introduction to later chapters that delve into special effects and even photo editing. If you're the type of reader who likes to begin at the beginning and make a linear voyage to finish at the appendix, you won't be surprised. However, the chapters are structured and fairly compartmentalized to address a specific topic; if you want fast solutions for specific areas within CorelDRAW, you can also "pick and choose." One of the wonderful things about books is that you can skip ahead and rewind—just as you do with DVD movies!

■   Part I starts you off with the new features in CorelDRAW X4, a must-read for users who've made the upgrade. Also in this part you'll be guided through CorelDRAW options, thoroughly pore through the menus and palettes (including CorelDRAW dockers), and you'll learn how to set up the workspace to make you feel right at home. New users are encouraged to set aside some quality time for this part—you'll save a lot of time later when you want to get to the Fun Stuff.

- Part II focuses on navigating and measuring the workspace and your document, and on how to size things up, from measuring objects to moving and rotating them. You'll also learn how to set up a multi-page document, create brochures and flyers, and you'll see that each page can be a unique size and orientation.

- Part III gets you up and running with two of the most important tools used in designing original artwork, the Pen Tools and the Shape Tool. You'll also get a handle on creating shapes using various presets CorelDRAW has to offer. Once you have your object created and edited to your liking, it's only natural to make more of them; this part shows you how to arrange, group, duplicate, clone, and perform other tasks in your document to make laying out what you've created an inspired effort.

- Part IV dives into typography, working with Artistic and Paragraph Text, spelling and other CorelDRAW proofing tools, and some special effects you can create for fancy headlines. Sometimes it's better to just say it instead of show it; CorelDRAW has the ideal tools for both the text and graphic message, and this part of the book also shows how to blend the two vehicles artistically for what you want to communicate.

- Part V puts the meat on the bones of the objects you design; in these chapters you'll learn everything you need to know about object fills, outline properties, and most importantly, about digital color. Learn how to define and apply uniform fills, bitmap fills, and colors from different color *models* to your work so they'll print exactly as you intend them to. And if you need a map or schematic drawing, check out this part for the lowdown on creating dashed lines, lines with arrowheads, and more.

- Part VI is a truly special part; CorelDRAW comes with a boatload of special effect features, and these chapters take you through the steps to distorting, blending, and creating photorealistic effects such as object transparency and soft, life-like shadows. If you've ever been stuck at a point where your design needs that "special something," look into this special part of the book. Learn how to create shading as you've seen in airbrush illustrations, design chrome and glass-like objects, and create a seamless integration between what you draw and the digital photos you can place in your document.

- Part VII shows you that 3D object and scene creation doesn't require a megabuck modeling program—you'll find what you need to make scenes in camera-perfect perspective with CorelDRAW's Effects menu. You'll also learn how to extrude objects, letting CorelDRAW perform calculations to create a side view of the front of objects you draw. It's fun, and the result can have the visual impact you need to create new worlds and sell your ideas.

■ Part VIII (that's "8" if you're tired of reading Roman numerals) is truly an advanced section of the book, but it's accessible to readers of all skill levels, and its contents take you through working with photographs, getting your prints looking their best, and more. See how to work with CorelDRAW's extensive host of print options and features, learn the techniques for output to paper, film, transfer materials, and get to know CorelDRAW's pre-flight options so your time and the expense of professional printing are on your side. You'll also see how to get the best look out of imported bitmaps, beginning right with CorelDRAW's Raw Lab. Learn how to work with image resolutions, and see how to export your vector drawings to bitmap file format. You'll also want to pore through CorelDRAW's HTML publishing features—make that print ad you've designed into a Web banner with only a few clicks. Finally, Visual Basic for Applications (VBA) is documented. See how to write simple scripts without actually writing a line of code (it's visual; you record cursor movements), and speed up your work by automating common tasks with VBA.

■ The Appendix to the book is full of shortcuts you can use in CorelDRAW. Find a task you need to perform faster and the Appendix lists the combinations of keys you can press to get you where you need to go.

Tutorial and Bonus Content: Where to Find It

One of the new things about this edition of *CorelDRAW Official Guide* is that there are formal tutorials, laid out in steps, along with explanations as to why you're asked to do something. You can't miss a Tutorial section: it's marked with the Educated Lightbulb icon shown here. Many of these Tutorials will go better and smoother, and better demonstrate a technique or principal if you have a working file loaded in the drawing window, so we've provided you with several. Before many Tutorials, you'll see a Download icon in the margin (a down-arrow icon); that's your clue to go to the following URL and download the content before starting the related Tutorial.

The Tutorial files can be found at www.mhprofessional.com. From this page, click the Downloads link and locate this book's title to get to the tutorial files.

DOWNLOAD

Additionally, www.theboutons.com mirrors the Tutorial files that McGraw-Hill provides, plus we have some Bonus Content up there—goodies for our readers that have nothing to do with this book's Tutorials, but *everything* to do with your continuing adventures in CorelDRAW. As you can see next, The Boutons are offering original seamless tiling textures—perfect for web page backgrounds, custom object fills, and backgrounds in your CorelDRAW documents. You'll also find high-resolution images of indoor and outdoor scenes with blank signage. Because so many CorelDRAW users create billboards, package designs, and vinyl signs for vehicles, we thought it would be nice if you could previsualize a logo or other signage; for example, put your logo on a layer on top of the image of the truck, use the Effects | Perspective command (see Chapter 24) on the logo to match the camera angle, and you can then show your design to clients and coworkers before you go through the expense of commercial printing.

The Boutons also offer original typefaces and some content that we want to remain a surprise. Just visit TheBoutons.com, and then click the CBT button (Corel Bonus Things) on the navigation bar.

I know I speak for the entire group who helped make this book happen that we're excited about this new version of CorelDRAW. So much so that we were highly motivated to make this *Official Guide* reflect all the creative possibilities you'll truly have a fun time learning, exploring, and building upon. So *enough* with Introductions! Turn the page and get to the Good Stuff!

—Gary David Bouton

PART I
CorelDRAW X4 Quick Start Guide

CHAPTER 1

What's New in CorelDRAW X4?

From the features you work with, to the *way* you work, CorelDRAW X4 offers significant enhancements over previous versions. Page layouts can be refined and redefined more quickly, revised interface buttons make finding the tools you need a snap, you can import camera Raw images after correcting for exposure and color temperature—all in all, current users offered advice and Corel engineers did some serious listening.

Whether you're new to CorelDRAW or an old hand, you should take a few moments and review the new features covered in this chapter. You'll discover that "working smart" can also be a lot of *fun*.

Page Layout Enhancements

Many users have grown comfortable using CorelDRAW for page layouts; it handles text formatting as well as desktop publishing programs such as Ventura and Adobe InDesign, with the added advantage of CorelDRAW's sophisticated drawing tools. The good news in version X4 is that you now have control over layers on a page-by-page basis, the creation of tables in a document can almost be performed in your sleep, font previewing—as applied within the document—is new, and there are other DTP features worthy of exploration here. Chapter 14 is packed from column width to column width on page layout details.

Independent Layers

Pages in a multi-page document can be any size and orientation you like in CorelDRAW, but the big news is that drawing layers can be defined on a page-by-page basis, as can guidelines. This means that you can create a *bundle*—letterhead stationery, envelopes, and other promotional material for a project all within one CorelDRAW document, as shown in Figure 1-1. You'll most certainly have your own use in mind for independent layers; projects are just one creative use of this new feature.

Local, independent guidelines can be added for individual pages, and master guidelines can be added for the entire document. You can also set master guidelines and create a Master layer for objects you want repeated across a range of document pages, such as a masthead or logo. You can access everything through the familiar Object Manager Docker.

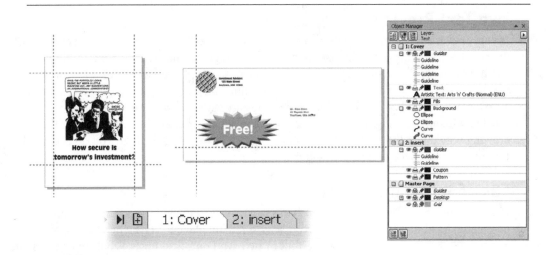

FIGURE 1-1   You can create different layers for different pages in X4.

Interactive Tables

You'll find a new Table Tool on the Toolbox in version X4. Not only can you import tables, but for simple, neat additions to a design, you can enter and format data right after you've defined a table with this tool. Once you've built a table, it's easy to align, resize, and edit the tables and table cells so your tables are visually compatible with the overall design. Figure 1-2 shows an example of a table that uses reversed coloring for the cells, individual cells have custom color applied, and the border width is thickened from the default table border using the options on the Property Bar. You can use any font you like for table entries, so your design can look like a formal spreadsheet or an elegant indexed list. Part IV in this book takes you through table creation and the ins and outs of good typography.

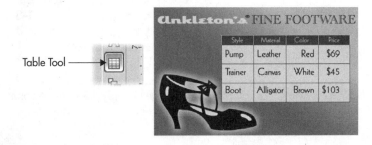

FIGURE 1-2   The Table Tool makes quick work of perfectly aligned and formatted cells.

Live Text Preview

If you've ever needed to experiment with a choice of fonts for size, appeal, and page color, the new Live Text Preview can display how your Paragraph and Artistic Text will look *before* you apply the change. In Figure 1-3 you can see a split screen: at left the text is hard to read because script fonts are intended for headline and not paragraph text, while at right, a new, cleaner typeface is previewed by choosing from the selector on the Property Bar. Finally, without applying the text change, you can see the text as it *might* appear in the drawing window in the document. If you like what you've previewed, all you do is click the font name in the selector and you're done.

Easy Font Identification

If you haven't been there yet, MyFonts.com is one of the largest clearing houses for commercial and independent digital typefaces, a terrific place to start when you have a new assignment that demands a distinctive font or two. MyFonts also hosts WhatTheFont—a site that can identify a screen capture of a typeface sample with surprising accuracy. You can access the WhatTheFont page directly within CorelDRAW, using the built-in screen capture utility. See lucky Chapter 13 for the details and instructions on this feature.

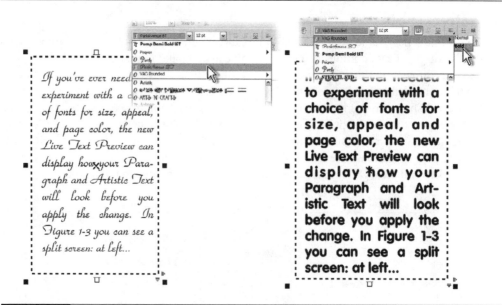

FIGURE 1-3   Live Text Preview lets you pick and choose and only asks you to commit to a font change once you're happy with your choice.

Mirroring Paragraph Text

If you need to reverse Paragraph Text for output to a T-shirt transfer or have a special printing job that requires a reversed plate, Paragraph Text can now be mirrored horizontally and vertically. To do this, you just drag a bottom or side bounding box handle using the Pick Tool and the Paragraph Text flows to the width of your needs. You also have the option to automatically mirror Paragraph Text using the buttons on the Property Bar.

Quotation Marks Support for Different Languages

You can now edit the quotation mark styles within the text and choose the styles that are automatically inserted when you type in different languages.

New Fonts

Enhanced language support for Latin, Greek, and Cyrillic now comes with an extended selection of new fonts in the CorelDRAW CDs (the boxed set only, not the downloadable version) and includes single-line engraving fonts and OpenType cross-platform fonts.

Camera Raw and Third-Party Application Support

Whether you're working in an enterprise or a small collaborative group, you'll need to process high-fidelity camera Raw images and, occasionally, open a graphics file that wasn't created using CorelDRAW. With version X4 you have a camera Raw processing lab you can access from right within the application. Additionally, CorelDRAW now imports media from many Adobe CS3 products, Microsoft Word 2007 documents, and a host of other applications.

Camera Raw File Support

CorelDRAW X4 has a top-to-bottom solution for camera Raw images that you need to use in a page layout or other design. When you choose to open a Raw image directly from your camera's memory or from hard disk, CorelDRAW's Camera Raw Lab loads the image before placing it in your document. Then, within this applet, you can process the photo for exposure, color temperature, shadow recovery, white balance, and all other aspects to make your photograph flawless. CorelDRAW sports a comprehensive list of Raw file formats from over 80 models and from 20 different manufacturers, including Hasselblad, Contax, Canon, Leica, Kodak, Nikon, and Minolta. You'd be hard-pressed not to find your camera in the list of supported cameras. CorelDRAW also supports Adobe's DNG Raw exchange file format.

Figure 1-4 shows the Camera Raw Lab; unprocessed, this image was terribly underexposed.

FIGURE 1-4   CorelDRAW's camera Raw support includes a processing Lab for unprocessed Raw images.

Enhanced Color Management Support

Color accuracy is a mandate in today's commercial world, and support has been added to CorelDRAW for the Adobe Color Management Module (CMM). On the Windows Vista operating system, you can also use the Windows Color System CMM. You can specify a color profile for exported bitmaps (this is called *color-tagging* an image) and the tagged image will appear on everyone else's calibrated monitors the way you see it on yours.

Compatibility with Today's Applications

CorelDRAW can now import (and in most cases export) the following commercial applications:

- Adobe Illustrator CS3 (AI) files
- Photoshop CS3 (PSD) images
- Acrobat 8 (PDF 1.7 and PDF/A, including PDF comments) Portable Document Format

- AutoCAD (DXF and DWG) files
- Microsoft Word 2007 (DOC or RTF, import only)
- Microsoft Publisher 2002, 2003, and 2007 (PUB, import only)
- Corel Painter X RIF files with layers intact

Corel Painter X is a natural choice for artists who want to simulate the look of traditional media such as oils, pastels, chalks, and textured artistic canvases. In Figure 1-5 you can see the creation of a multi-layer painting—the background is a separate layer from the foreground fellow. This is called preplanning; let's suppose the coworker who receives this file doesn't own Painter X and needs a replacement for the background layer, visually striking as it might be.

The user who owns X4 has absolutely no problem opening the Painter RIF file. It imports as a group, which can then be ungrouped, and in this example, the foreground character is on a layer with transparency, as shown in Figure 1-6. CorelDRAW reads the transparent regions accurately and in no time, a substitute background can be drawn and perfectly integrated with the Painter layer.

FIGURE 1-5   Corel Painter X offers natural media and can write multiple layer image files.

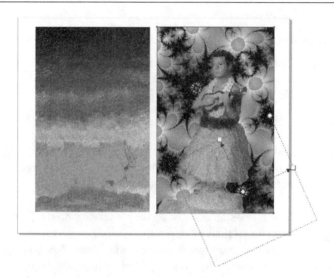

FIGURE 1-6 Integrate bitmap images from Painter with CorelDRAW fills and drawings.

Simplified Searches and Print Merging

If you use CorelDRAW as a workhorse, you'll find the new search capabilities to be invaluable, and the Print Merging feature makes mass mailings a thing that even a user without any spreadsheet knowledge (or interest) can do with speed and style.

Extended Search Functions

Now you can use keywords, notes, file type, date, and specific text when you search for CorelDRAW X4 files from Windows Explorer. You can also add or edit file properties within the application, or from Windows Explorer, Windows Search, Windows Desktop Search, or Windows Vista Search.

Search Capability When Saving and Opening Files

You can organize your projects with ease and a little preplanning by adding keywords and notes when saving your files. When opening and saving files, Windows Vista users can search by author, subject, file type, date, keywords, and other file properties.

Improved Print Merging

Easily create scores of personalized invitations, labels, envelopes, you name it, all using the same CorelDRAW design. Create and edit merged data in a record editor that operates much like a spreadsheet, but without the hassles. See Chapter 28 to learn the mercifully few steps it takes to gain mastery of this powerful new feature.

Templates and Extras

For those who purchased the X4 boxed set, there's a wealth of new goodies. In particular, the templates now are fully searchable.

Templates and Search Capability for Templates

Get a head start on a project with professionally laid out templates. You can easily find the template that's best suited for an assignment, including templates you've created and saved on your computer or removable media. You can browse, preview, and search for templates by name, category, keywords, and notes. The new templates that ship with X4 are conveniently arranged by category and style.

Extras

The CorelDRAW Graphics Suite X4 disc contains 4,000 new clipart designs. Saved in CorelDRAW's CDR file format, the clip art is simple to customize and the collection is fully searchable by keyword and category.

New Corel PowerTRACE Features

New within CorelDRAW is centerline tracing—this feature is ideal for architectural illustrations, tracing signatures (your *own* signature, hopefully; this thing is *accurate*), and any time you need a path instead of an object traced from an image. Here you can see PowerTRACE in action; in this example the toy yo-yo's string would make an excellent path for running text along.

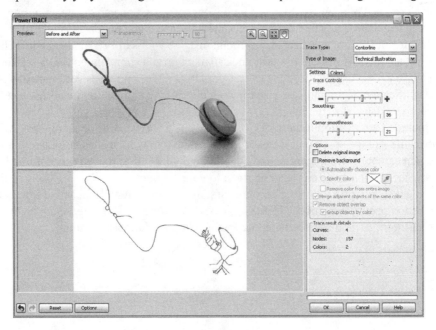

FIGURE 1-7   Trace an outline or a shape without ever leaving CorelDRAW.

Naturally, object tracing is still supported, with options for varying degrees of object smoothness and level of detail depending on the source material you need to trace. In Figure 1-7, the Text|Fit Text to Path command has been used after two sessions of PowerTRACE; once for the string, and a second time to accurately trace the yo-yo.

CorelDRAW ConceptShare: Collaborating Online

With CorelDRAW's new partnership with ConceptShare you can create an online workspace where you and those you invite can review, mark up, and comment on a CorelDRAW document in real time. It's sort of a dedicated chat room; imagine your surprised and delighted clients who can see their job as a work in progress and can mark up and comment on the piece. Your guests don't have to own CorelDRAW to view a CorelDRAW file, smooth as vector art, at any degree of magnification. Communicate visually with clients on different continents and get feedback on your work as fast as the Internet.

Included with your purchase of CorelDRAW is a forever-free account that gives you 5mb of file storage space and the capacity to set up two workspaces, each containing three files that can be viewed, commented on, and marked up. If you need more storage space or workspaces, you can purchase an upgrade to your account.

To get set up with your free account, first make sure you have an active Internet connection open. Then choose Window | Dockers | Concept Share and click on the Sign Up Now! Button. As you can see here, the free account is in the left column.

1

CorelDRAW
ConceptShare

Home   Feature Tour   **Sign up & Pricing**   Support   Language: English ▾

We have a package for you

Get started with no hassles: upgrade, downgrade or cancel at anytime.

Currency: USD ▾	Free Try it out	Solo $19.00 / month	Team $49.00 / month	Business $99.00 / month	Enterprise $199.00 / month
Active Workspaces	2	25	50	100	250
Account Managers	1	1	5	10	25
File Storage	5 MB	500 MB	1 GB	2 GB	5 GB
Custom Branding	✔	✔	✔	✔	✔
SSL Security	—	✔	✔	✔	✔
Users per Workspace	Unlimited	Unlimited	Unlimited	Unlimited	Unlimited
Concepts per Workspace	3	Unlimited	Unlimited	Unlimited	Unlimited
	Sign Up!	Sign Up!	Sign Up!	Sign Up!	Sign Up!
NEW! Annual Billing Get 12 Months for Price of 11	—	Go Annual $209.00 / year	Go Annual $539.00 / year	Go Annual $1,089.00 / year	Go Annual $2,189.00 / year

Follow the prompts and enter the information required to create your account. The CorelDRAW ConceptShare site will send you email with a link you must click to confirm your registration. Clicking on the link will take you to a thank-you screen, followed by your private workspace management screen.

To set up a WorkSpace, click on the Add WorkSpace icon in your browser window. This launches a wizard that takes you through the process of adding a workspace and inviting participants. Once you have a workspace set up, you can go back to CorelDRAW and add the files you want to exchange comments on. Here's a mini-tour of ConceptShare: in Figure 1-8 you can see a fictitious health spa's logo. To share the piece, click Publish Page on the docker, and then click Launch. By default, ConceptShare launches Windows Internet Explorer; you can copy and paste (and then save) the URL from Explorer to the web browser of your preference.

In Figure 1-9 you can see the workspace. Two fictitious clients are online (their avatars are at left) and one of the clients feels there aren't enough Blend steps in the illustration when he zooms in. The Markup Tool lets you and your guests highlight areas of interest and a message box pops up so you can explain your markups among the invited group. The tools are fairly self-explanatory and as owner of the workspace you can erase comments and restore the project to an untouched state if you like. Guests can edit their own comments, but can't edit yours or comments from other guests.

FIGURE 1-8 Take a graphic you want to share with guests to your ConceptShare workspace by clicking Publish Page. Then click Launch to load the workspace in your web browser.

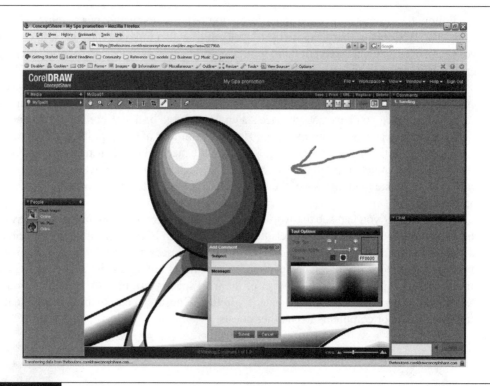

FIGURE 1-9 Invite guests to comment on your work in ConceptShare's workspace.

Here you can see what a completed comment looks like; you can hide comments, increase the font size in case you're running a high screen resolution, and as the proprietor of your workspace, you can certainly *delete* comments!

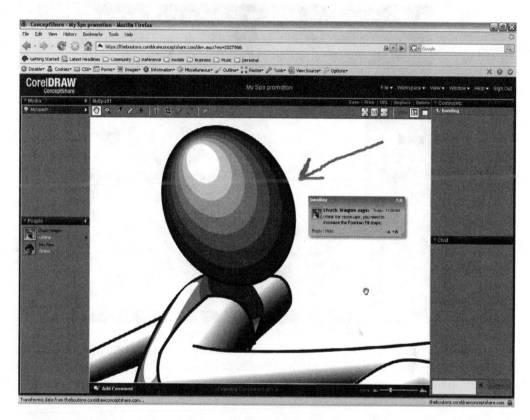

Navigation around a document can be performed with the Zoom Tool or by using the slider, shown here at the bottom right. When a graphic is zoomed in larger than the extent of the page, you can use the Hand Tool to pan the window and you can also use the navigation control near the zoom slider at bottom right. Remember, this workspace is displaying bitmap versions of your vector artwork that is updated on-the-fly, so when you or a guest zoom, all the details in your work are crisp, but smooth and legible.

You could call this chapter the tip of the iceberg, if your idea of a fun time is an iceberg (Leonardo DiCaprio didn't think so). Kidding aside, there are a lot of pages under your right thumb, and it's all good stuff. Bring along some curiosity and a design idea or two and move into second gear.

CHAPTER 2

Exploring Your Workspace

When working in CorelDRAW X4, you'll find yourself using an assortment of interface elements that offer control over everything you do. There are many areas that make up the interface because the program offers an abundance of creative tools to use so that you can create compelling graphics and documents. Certain areas of the interface such as the Property Bar are context sensitive: your available options change as you choose different Toolbox tools. Other interface areas, like the Toolbox, are always visible in the workspace. And then there are Dockers, which are displayed only if you specifically open them. Exactly which elements—and where these elements appear in the program interface— is not a set piece; you have to have ultimate flexibility and customization control so you can *personalize* CorelDRAW. You can choose between a predesigned workspace, CorelDRAW's default, add, remove, and rearrange options to suit your work needs and even make the interface look like Adobe Illustrator. The important thing is that you should feel at home working in CorelDRAW; this chapter shows you where everything is, and how you can make it suit your work style.

The CorelDRAW X4 Workspace

CorelDRAW X4 sports a sleek and handsome new look—past users will notice new icons, new menus, and other interface elements. This makeover is *not* just eye candy; it has been carefully revamped to make it easier for you to find and work with the tools you need to use, when you need to use them.

CorelDRAW workspace elements can be divided into two categories:

■ Global and program control elements, such as measurement scales, backup files, and memory use.

■ Design or complete document features, such as Guidelines, Styles, and nudge distances.

If you're new to CorelDRAW or just new to this version, you *will* want to take a look at this detailed roadmap to the new CorelDRAW interface herein.

CorelDRAW X4's Application Window

The application window is mainly what you see when CorelDRAW X4 is open. It is the stage that surrounds and contains the drawing windows. *Drawing windows* (sometimes called document windows) contain the drawing page or pages that hold the graphics and other content you create. Even if no drawing windows are open, the application window provides access to certain command menus, toolbars, the Toolbox, dockers, Status Bar, and the Color Palette. Figure 2-1 identifies the application window parts.

You can have more than one drawing window (sometimes called a *document window* in other applications) open in the application window, but only one can be active at a time. The specific settings you see displayed on the toolbar, Property Bar, dockers, and other

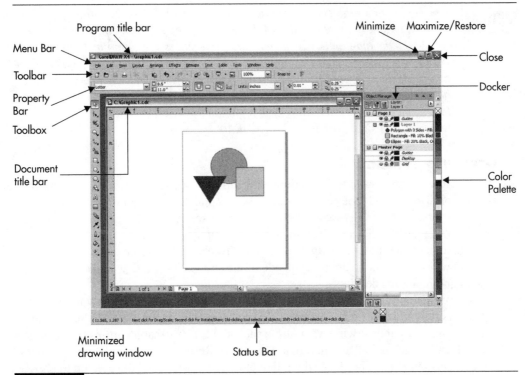

FIGURE 2-1 CorelDRAW X4's application window features these interface areas.

application windows interface elements are those that are assigned to the currently active drawing window. They change if you make another drawing window active, by clicking on the desired drawing window.

As in all standard Windows applications, clicking the Close button at the top right side of the application window's title bar closes CorelDRAW X4; clicking the Minimize or Maximize/Restore button shows or hides CorelDRAW X4, and changes the size of the application window itself quickly. Clicking on a drawing window's Close button closes the drawing window, removing it from the application window while clicking on a drawing window's Minimize or Maximize/Restore button minimizes it to a document title bar near the bottom of the application window or restores it to size within the application window.

TIP *With CorelDRAW open and all documents closed, you can still perform many necessary tasks. You can use File commands and open suite applications such as Corel CAPTURE, Corel BARCODE WIZARD, Corel PHOTO-PAINT, and even another copy of CorelDRAW with the Application Launcher. You can also use some of Corel's tool managers, work with macros, view Help Topics, and access Corel's online Web resources through the Welcome screen.*

CAUTION *The Application Launcher on the application window's toolbar allows you to open another, unique copy of CorelDRAW, but simply because you can doesn't mean you should. Depending on how your memory preferences are set up in Tools | Options | Workspace | Memory, you could potentially throttle your computer's system RAM and lose valuable work; the only reason you'd do this would be to copy objects between documents. You can achieve the same result much more simply and with less chance of a system halt by copying and moving objects between drawing windows in a single session of CorelDRAW.*

Drawing Windows

When a drawing window is fully maximized it fills the dark gray space in the center of the application window and looks as if it is *part* of the application window. When a drawing window is open but *not* fully maximized, it is easy to see that it's a separate window element with its own interface elements that are unique to that drawing window.

Unlike the Menu Bar, Property Bar, Toolbar, Toolbox, Color Palette, and dockers, a drawing window cannot be dragged outside of the application window and onto the desktop or a second monitor's desktop.

Not surprisingly, the interface elements that are contained within a drawing window report on or control that specific drawing window. Like the application window, a drawing window also has standard window controls such as a title bar that identifies the document's file path and name, as well as Minimize, Maximize/ Restore, and Close buttons. Drawing windows also have page borders, which like other windows can be dragged on to change the size of the window. They also have scroll bars that are used to change your view of the document's contents.

Interface elements special to drawing windows include Rulers, the Document Navigator, which is used to add, delete, and move between pages in a multi-page drawing window (see Chapter 6), the Drawing page, which contains what can be printed, and the Navigator which helps you move around a drawing without having to zoom out.

Parent and Child Window Buttons

A document's Minimize, Maximize/ Restore, and Close buttons are not located in the drawing window frame when a drawing window is maximized in the application window. The Minimize, Maximize/ Restore, and Close buttons for the current drawing window are grayscale, smaller in size, and placed just below the Minimize, Maximize/ Restore, and Close buttons that belong to the application window.

If you want to close a document window, but your attention is wandering a bit and you are running on autopilot, it's easy to make a mistake and click on the larger, more colorful Close button that belongs to the entire CorelDRAW application.

So save your work often and try to remember that the big, red button is for the whole application and the smaller, gray one is for the document at hand.

CorelDRAW X4 is compliant with the Microsoft Windows standard for Multiple Document Interfaces, meaning you can have more than one document (drawing) window open at a time. To switch between drawing windows, choose Window | *document name* (where *document name* is the actual name of your CorelDRAW X4 document). In Figure 2-2, you can see a basic and very useful drawing window technique: Suppose you have an object in one document window and want a copy of it in a different one. You choose Window | Tile Horizontally (you can do this manually if you're skilled manipulating Windows windows), and then move the object by just dragging it into the other window using the Pick Tool. To copy the object, hold the modifier key CTRL as you drag from one window to the other.

CorelDRAW uses a default naming system of Graphic1, Graphic2 and so on, incrementing the number for each new document you open in the current CorelDRAW session. You are

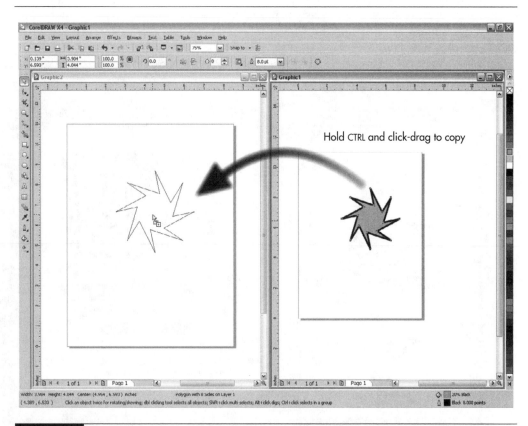

FIGURE 2-2 Working between drawing windows is accomplished by click-dragging, using the Pick Tool.

given the chance (and you should take it) to give your drawing a more meaningful name when you save the document by choosing File | Save or pressing CTRL+S.

You can also open more than one document window showing the *same* document, enabling you to work on one document in multiple windows. This is a particularly useful feature when you need to zoom in close to work on a small area of a graphic, but you also need to be able to see how your work on that area affects the whole composition.

Both windows are "live," so that you can edit in either of them and all the changes you make editing in one window will also appear in both windows because these windows represent different *views* of the same document *not* two independent files that can be saved as different versions.

To open another view of the active drawing window, choose Window | New Window. To make one of the open views the active window, you can click on that window or you can also use the menu, Window | *document name:N* (where *N* is the automatically applied view number) Open as many windows as you need—this feature is limited only by your available system resources.

Specifying Toolbar and Dialog Values

When working in CorelDRAW there are many times when you need to enter measurements or numeric values, choose options and states, and control the behavior of interface elements on toolbars, in dialogs, and so on. CorelDRAW uses a wide variety of standard input fields and controls to make the specific kind of data you need to enter or tweak easy to accomplish. This section guides you through the ways data can be entered and alerts you to some of the extra power and usability Corel engineers have endowed upon these interface work horses.

- **Num boxes**   To specify values, you'll find *num* boxes—short for *numeric* boxes. Usually there is already a value in the box, such as the page width in the following illustration. Just highlight the existing value using a click-drag action and then retype a new value. Alternatively, you can double-click to select the entire value in the num box before typing the value you want. If you insert the cursor at any point in the existing value, you can use your keyboard arrow keys to move within the value and then Backspace to remove, finally adding the value you need. Finally, you need to confirm the value you entered by pressing…ENTER. Press TAB to quickly move your cursor from one num box to the next in the group, or press SHIFT+TAB, to move to the previous box. In dialogs, clicking the Apply button applies the new options and leaves the dialog box open; OK closes the dialog and applies the new values or options. On toolbars, pressing ENTER after typing the value does the same thing, as shown here.

Highlight existing value, then type in the value you need

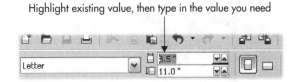

> **TIP**   *Here's an unexpected convenience: you can perform calculations in num boxes using simple math equations to arrive at a value you need. Type symbols between values to create the equation sequences. Use your plus (+) and minus (−) keys for adding and subtracting, and your asterisk (*) and forward slash (/) keys for multiplying and dividing. Pressing ENTER performs the calculation. Naturally, you can't enter invalid keystrokes in a value box, such as alphabetical letters—you'll just get a system beep after pressing ENTER and the previous, proper, numerical value will reappear.*

- **Combo boxes**   *Combo* (short for *combination*) is a num box with a clickable selection button for access to preset values. You can either enter a specific value in a combo box by typing, or by choosing a preset value from the selector. Toolbar and docker combo boxes often require pressing the ENTER key to apply the new value you type in, while clicking Apply or OK in dialogs does the same thing.

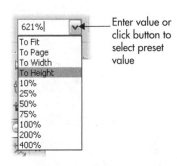

Enter value or click button to select preset value

■ **Flyout option menus and popouts**   On certain toolbars and dockers you're going to find flyout and popout menus, which are often accessed by clicking a button that has a small, triangular-shaped, flyout arrow pointing to the right. *Popouts* are usually selectors in which you can choose a nonnumeric option, and they can contain text and even mini-controls, depending on the operation or tool that is chosen. You can spot a tool on the Toolbox, for example, that has extended options you access straight from the tool button by a tick mark on the button's lower right. *Flyouts* often contain ways to change behavior states, apply commands, and access options. Some apply options immediately, while others require that they be closed first using the small X symbol usually found at the upper-right corner. Examples of each are shown in the following:

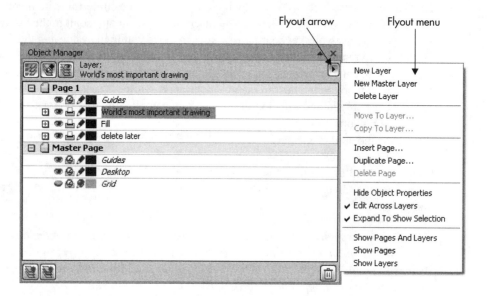

Flyout arrow

Flyout menu

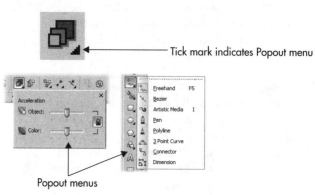

Tick mark indicates Popout menu

Popout menus

■ **Color selectors** *Color selectors* often appear in dialogs or toolbars as a clickable button that has the secondary function of displaying the currently selected color, as shown here. Clicking opens a selector to display the current color palette and requires that you to click once to specify a color. Most color selectors also include the Other button, which is a shortcut to Color models, mixers and palettes (covered in Chapter 19).

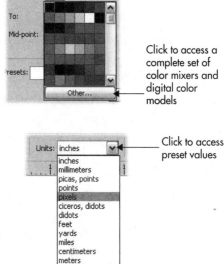

Click to access a complete set of color mixers and digital color models

■ **List selectors** *List selectors* differ from combo boxes in that you cannot enter a value, but instead pick from a predefined list of values or graphic samples that show the way that a style or arrow (or similar) will be applied or created. Clicking on one of the entries in the list chooses and applies a value, size, state, mode, or style to the currently selected object. These lists are occasionally called drop-down lists in other applications and pull-down lists on the Macintosh.

Click to access preset values

■ **Radio buttons and option boxes** These two interface devices are slightly different, not just in shape, but also in the choices they offer, as shown next. *Radio* buttons are round, come in groups, and only allow you to select one of the options in the group. *Option* boxes are square and let you choose an option or state to be either on (with a check mark) or off (without a check mark). You'll find in many areas of the Options pages, you can choose more than one option (more than one box can be checked).

Click to activate option

Click to choose between options

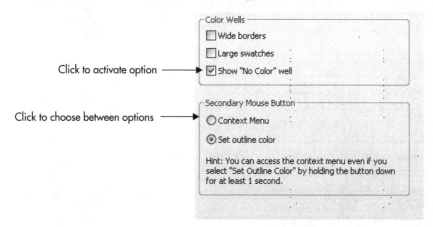

■ **Buttons**   Buttons appear throughout CorelDRAW and can do one of several things. *Command* buttons perform commands instantaneously, but *toggle* buttons control (and indicate) a specific feature's On and Off states, using a pressed or not pressed appearance. Generally, a *pressed* state indicates On, while the *not pressed* state indicates Off. *Shortcut* buttons open dialogs to further options, while *selector* buttons open lists of preset selections.

Off (inactive) ──▶ ◀── On (active)

■ **Spinners**   *Spinners* (also known as *spin boxes*) are similar to combo boxes, in that they can be used to specify values by typing *or* using mouse actions. Single clicks on the up and down arrow buttons increase or decrease the values incrementally, but you can also click-drag on the divider between the two arrow buttons, up to increase or down to decrease the value.

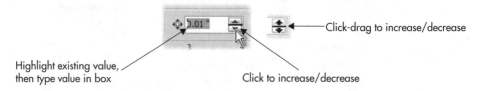

Click-drag to increase/decrease

Highlight existing value, then type value in box

Click to increase/decrease

■ **Sliders**   These enable you to specify values within a given range—often between 0 and 100 and often based on percent—by entering values, or by dragging a control slider, which is intuitive and provides the anticipated results. To manipulate a slider value, use a click-drag action to move the slider either right (to increase) or left (to decrease), as shown here on the Property Bar after the interactive Transparency Tool has been used.

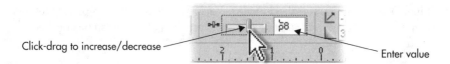

Click-drag to increase/decrease

Enter value

■ **Pop-up menus**   To access pop-up menu commands and options, click your right mouse button (instead of the typical left-click) on any given point. The pop-up menu appears at the tip of your cursor and closes automatically after a selection is made or by clicking elsewhere in the interface. Pop-up menus are sometimes called contextual menus, and a right-facing arrow next to a pop-up menu item indicates that there's a submenu with still more options, usually relating to the main menu option.

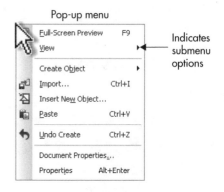

Pop-up menu

Indicates submenu options

NOTE | *Left-handed artists are not uncommon; if you're a southpaw, the order of your mouse buttons is not defined in CorelDRAW, but instead in the operating system's Control Panel | Mouse. Just mirror the instructions in this chapter: if a step tells you to left-click, it's the right mouse button, and vice versa.*

Working with Dockers

Dockers are panels or palettes, where many different commands and controls that relate to specific tasks are grouped together in one handy location. Dockers put more of Corel's power right at the tip of your cursor without forcing you to dig through lots of dialog boxes or flit between various toolbars and menus.

What's great about dockers is that these controls can be anchored to the edge of the screen and reduced to tabs or title bars, allowing you to tear them off and float them right next to where you are working in the interface. You can resize them to make your own groups of commonly-used dockers. And, if you have a multimonitor setup, you can even drag them out of the application window and stick them on a different monitor so that you have the maximum amount of space for your drawing windows.

If you don't find a docker that fills your needs after looking through the list of 26 dockers on Window | Dockers menu, dust off your programming skills and make your own *custom* docker. If you're not a programmer, check the Internet for any third-party developers who are taking advantage of CorelDraw X4's capability to use third-party dockers.

Opening, Moving, and Closing Dockers

Dockers can be opened using shortcut keys, menu commands, or through toolbars. Most dockers are found on the Window | Dockers menu, but some such as dockers dealing with text formatting are found on the Text menu and the text-related Property Bar. For example, to open the Contour Docker, choose Window | Dockers | Contour, or press CTRL +F9. To open the Character Formatting docker you can choose Text | Character Formatting from the menu, or press CTRL+T; additionally you can click on the Character Formatting button on the Property Bar *after* you've chosen the Text Tool on the Toolbox. Again, the Property Bar is contextual.

Dockers open to their last-used screen position and state, either docked or undocked, open or rolled up. While *docked,* they are by default attached to the right side of your application window. Alternatively, dockers can be positioned on the left side of the screen or anchored on both sides of the screen with your document window in the middle, if that suits you best.

While *undocked,* dockers float above the document window and can be positioned anywhere on your monitor screen(s). Docked or floating is *not* an all or nothing choice; you can have some dockers docked and some floating—at the same time. The only situation you *can't* have is more than one copy of a specific docker open at one time. Figure 2-3 shows examples of docked and floating dockers.

Floating or not, dockers feature a common look. Each has a title bar, a Close Docker group button which closes only that specific docker, and a Roll-up/Roll-down Docker button, which is used to toggle the display between the title bar-only state and a fully

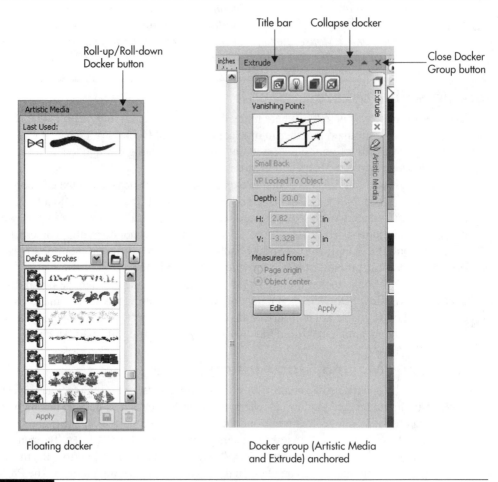

FIGURE 2-3 Examples of floating docker and anchored docker group.

open one. While undocked, floating dockers can be resized by click-dragging at the sides or bottom edges.

To move a floating docker, click-drag anywhere on its title bar. Rolled-up (minimized) floating dockers appear only as floating title bars on your screen. Minimized, docked dockers appear as vertical title tabs on the right side of the docker area.

Nested (Grouped) Dockers

When more than one docker is open, they often appear *nested,* meaning that multiple dockers overlay each other on the right side of your application window. While dockers are nested, clicking their individual title bars or name tabs brings them to the front of the interface.

Floating nested docker

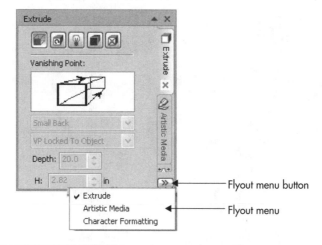

Flyout menu button

Flyout menu

FIGURE 2-4   Nested dockers can float and you can resize them and access individual dockers from the flyout menu.

Floating nested dockers, depending on how you've sized the group, might or might not feature a flyout button at bottom right (see Figure 2-4); if you've sized the group so that the tabs cannot show, you can easily access the docker you need through the flyout menu. It's fairly intuitive stuff.

Although nesting dockers (anchored or floating) are likely the best way to work with multiple dockers, you can quickly separate them (sort of kicking them *out* of the nest if you prefer). To do this, click-drag the name tab identifying the docker (or anywhere within the fully open docker pane) and then drag away from the nested docker arrangement. As you do this, you see an outline preview of the frame of your selected docker as you drag, indicating its new screen position when the mouse button is released. You can also float single-anchored dockers by dragging them from their docked position by their title bars. To *nest* multiple dockers together, click-drag on the title bar (while floating) or on the name tab of the docker and then drag it to a position inside the boundaries of another floating docker.

   To set whether title bars in floating dockers are visible, open the Options dialog (press CTRL+J) to the General page of the Workspace section, where you'll find an option called Show Titles on Floating Dockers.

Finally, if you want to maximize your drawing window area but still keep docked and nested dockers handy, you can click on the Collapse Docker arrow on the title bar of the docker group. Collapsing the docker reduces the nested dockers to a thin vertical set of tabs that correspond to the currently open dockers, as shown here in the collapsed state:

Using the Toolbox

All dockers and virtually everything that's a sub-window of an interface, by Microsoft Windows convention, is called a *child window*. Corel leverages this definition of the user interface to make just about everything detachable and capable of floating (if not flying!). The Toolbox is a component of the application window and is where you'll find all the tools in CorelDRAW X4; there are tons of features in CorelDRAW, but *tools* are found only on the Toolbox. The Toolbox itself may be altered in different ways. By default, the Toolbox is docked, but you can *un*dock it to float over your document window, which is often a handy way to quickly choose tools if you haven't memorized the shortcut keys for tools. To detach the Toolbox from its docked position, click-drag just above the "no skid" design at the top of the docked Toolbox and away from the edge of your screen, as shown here:

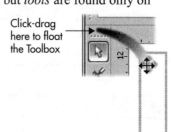

Click-drag here to float the Toolbox

An undocked Toolbox, shown next, includes a title bar and a Close button. When floating, you can move it around by click-dragging on its title bar. Double-clicking the title bar redocks the Toolbox. Clicking the Close button hides the Toolbox from view. Right-click anywhere in your document window and choose View | Toolbox from the pop-up menu to bring it back.

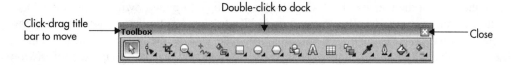

TIP *The Toolbox can feature larger icons, text labels (which are useful when just learning any program), and the orientation of the Toolbox can be vertical or horizontal (as shown in the previous illustration). To customize the Toolbox, press CTRL+J to open the Options dialog and then open the Workspace | Customize | Command bars section in the tree on the left. Individual tools on the Toolbox can be customized by opening the Workspace | Toolbox section and then clicking on the tools listed.*

You can access groups of tools by clicking buttons that feature flyout buttons. A single click selects the visible, "top" tool from the group, while a click-and-hold action opens the tool flyout. You can also separate individual flyouts from the Toolbox and have them float independently. To do this, click-hold to open any group of tools, and then when your cursor turns into a four-headed arrow, use a click-drag action by clicking the top of the flyout and dragging away from the Toolbox. The result is a *duplicate* of the tool flyout (there's still the original flyout group on the Toolbox) as a floating Toolbox group that can be treated as any floating toolbar, as shown here. To hide the duplicate mini-Toolbox group from view, click the Close button. This hides the duplicate toolbar group without affecting the Toolbox version of the same group.

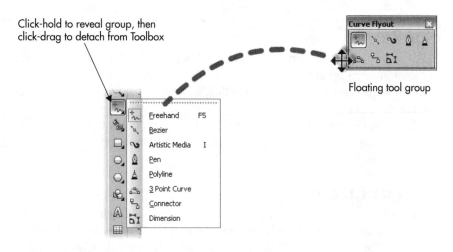

Working with Toolbars

Like other interface devices, toolbars can also appear docked or floating. This doesn't just include standard and custom toolbars, but also the Menu Toolbar, the Standard Toolbar, and the Property Bar. While docked, you'll see a small marking on the toolbars themselves. To undock any docked toolbar, click-drag the area outside of the tiny "no skid" divider away from the edge of the window. Undocked toolbars each feature their own title bar and Close button, as shown next. Usually, it's not a good idea to close the toolbars, but to return them instead. However, if you've closed a toolbar you need, such as the Property Bar, you can easily retrieve it by right-clicking over any other toolbar, and then choosing the toolbar from the pop-up menu, with any tool chosen.

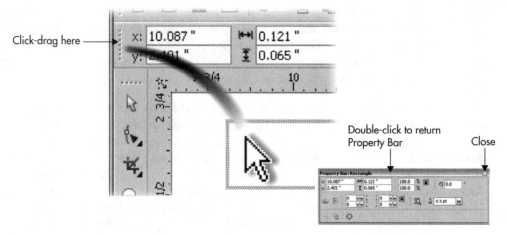

Floating Property Bar

Using the Color Palette

The *Color Palette* is by default, the vertical strip docked to the right of the workspace, and is the most convenient place to get colors for filling in your document's objects. By default, a single column of colors is shown, you can change this, and it has scroll buttons to advance and rewind the colors visible in one row. Like all Windows child windows, the Color Palette comes undocked, you can resize the floating palette, and you can dock it to any side of the application window, in any toolbar location, above or below the Status bar and to either side of the Toolbox or a docked docker.

Viewing Palette Colors

The tiny squares of color you see in this palette are referred to as *wells*. Hover over a color well to display a tooltip containing that color's name (by default, Tooltips are enabled; if you turned them off, go to Tools | Options | Workspace | Display). To scroll the Color Palette color well collection, click the Up or Down arrow buttons at the top and bottom of the palette. Single clicks using your left mouse button on these arrow buttons fast-forwards and rewinds the palette, one color well at a time. Single clicks with your right mouse button produce a Page Up and Page Down effect, scrolling the visible color selection a complete row up or down. Clicking the bottom button expands the palette to show all the color wells (it retracts after you click to make a color selection), and at top is the options flyout button for loading different color palettes, saving, renaming, and so on.

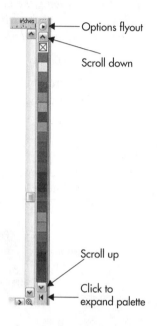

Options flyout

Scroll down

Scroll up

Click to expand palette

> **TIP** *You can rearrange the order of colors on any Color Palette by click-dragging up or down on any color well.*

You float the Color Palette exactly as you do with other interface child windows: by dragging above the little markers, into the drawing window. While the Color Palette is floating (shown next), click-drag its title bar to move it around your window or click the Close button to hide it from view. Choose View | Color Palettes and select a palette to display any palette in its last used state. Double-click the title bar to return the floating Color Palette to its original docked location in the workspace.

Double-click to return the Color Palette to its default docked location

Click-drag to move

Close Palette

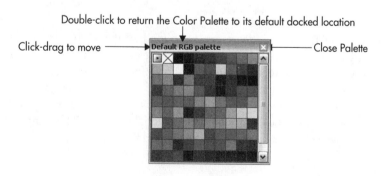

As with other day-to-day child windows, it's best not to close the Color Palette, particularly if you're new to the program, because it's a hassle to restore it. If you've by chance closed the Color Palette, the quickest way to restore it to the workspace is by right-clicking in the drawing window to get a pop-up menu. Choose View | Color Palettes, choose any palette you like from the submenu, and life is good again.

Hovering over any of the Color Palette's scroll buttons or the Expand button produces a tooltip that displays the name of the Color Palette collection you are using, for example, Default: Default CMYK palette.

Changing Palette Options

The Options flyout button (shown next) on the Color Palette features several important commands, enabling you to apply fill and outline colors (as opposed to using left and right mouse button clicks to apply colors to objects) and control how the palette itself is viewed.

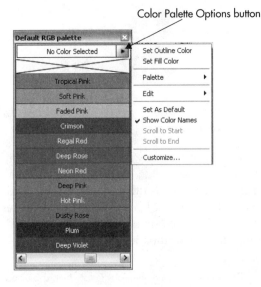

Color Palette Options button

Using the Options flyout provides some, but not all, of the options available to you for getting and using colors. CorelDRAW has an extensive color library including PANTONE and TRUEMATCH from onscreen simulations of printing press colors, as well as others for Web work. However, as mentioned at the beginning of this chapter, some workspace elements in CorelDRAW are tool-specific, while others belong to global elements—and the color library that appears on the Color Palette is a global resource. Therefore, with the Pick Tool and nothing selected in the drawing window, you right-click to display the pop-up menu, and then choose View | Color Palettes; then choose from the submenu, which also features the Color Editor dialog (see the following illustration). Displaying the child window called Color Palette and choosing a collection with which you populate the Color Palette are two different things and require different commands.

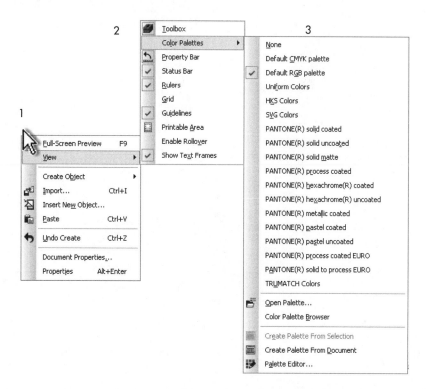

When an artist creates art, the most successful pieces are drawn from a generalization to the specifics, from a coarse outline to filling in the details. Similarly, CorelDRAW deserves a coarse examination, as covered in this chapter, but as you progress to later chapters, the details are filled in. You've got a general idea of how to navigate in this chapter; it's time to move from interface-centric coverage, to the more important document-centric coverage! Chapter 3 starts you out in a very good and wise place—how to work with files, different file types, and getting the stuff you need in and out of CorelDRAW.

CHAPTER 3

Examining the Palettes, Cruising the Menus

One of the very first things you learn as a new computer user is how to open and close files and how to use the Clipboard to copy data from one document window to another. There is nothing new or exotic you have to do when working with CorelDRAW X4 to accomplish these basic tasks. But CorelDRAW X4 has *additional* functions and options, related to file handling and data import and export, to handle your graphics workload efficiently and professionally. In this chapter you'll learn about file-saving options that ensure that your work can be used by coworkers who are using previous versions of CorelDRAW and about how to use timesaving specialty files such as templates. You'll also see how to protect your work with CorelDRAW's automatic backup feature, how to make the Clipboard work overtime for you, as well as how to store and retrieve scrapbook items and symbols and how to import and export graphics, text, and data into and out of CorelDRAW X4.

CorelDRAW X4's Welcome Dialog

When CorelDRAW opens, the Welcome/Quick Start tabbed dialog appears, where you can quickly open a new or existing drawing file, access learning tools, check for program updates, and set automatic checks for program updates. You can also find inspiration in a gallery of art created by fellow CorelDRAW customers. This launch pad is shown in Figure 3-1.

The first tab along the right edge, Quick Start, is your jumping-off point for opening a file. Here you are presented with a list of the last five files you opened and closed in

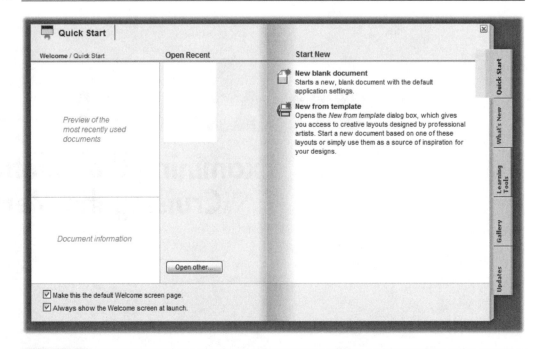

FIGURE 3-1   CorelDRAW welcomes you with this dialog after launching.

CorelDRAW X4. Hovering over the name of one of these files causes a thumbnail preview and the document information for that file to appear. Click on the name of the file, and the Welcome dialog closes and the file you selected opens. If you want to open an existing file that is not among the five most recent files you've opened, click the Open Other button to close the Welcome screen page and to open a standard Open Drawing dialog.

To start a new drawing document, click on the New Blank Document link in the Start New section of the Quick Start tab, or click on the New From Template link if you want to create a document from one of the special design layouts that ship with CorelDRAW or from a template you previously created.

The other tabs lead you to the following areas of interest:

- From the *What's New* tab, you can click your way through the CorelDRAW New Features Tour slideshow.

- The *Learning Tools* tab contains links to launch documentation from your hard disk such as CorelTUTOR and Insights From The Experts as well as a link to Corel's online Learning Resources page.

- The *Gallery* tab displays a changing selection of artwork created in CorelDRAW. It also contains a link to the CorelDRAW.com Community page, where you can create an online gallery of your artwork for the world to see and enjoy, participate in online forums, and download helpful files like custom media strokes, textures, and macros.

- The last tab is the *Updates* tab. At the top of the tab window is the word "Settings." If you click on this link, the Update Settings dialog opens as shown. It contains two options that are turned on if the box next to the option is checked, or turned off if it is unchecked. Your choices here are Notify Me Of Available Product Updates, News And Tutorials, and Automatically Download Product Updates And Ask Me Before Installing. These are useful and helpful functions that help you keep your copy of CorelDRAW and your knowledge of things related to CorelDRAW up to date.

If these boxes are checked (they are by default), every time you start CorelDRAW it will access your Internet connection in the background and check in with the Corel website to see if any updates or files should be downloaded for you. So don't be alarmed if your computer's firewall software pops up a notice that CorelDRAW is trying to access the Internet. If CorelDRAW pops up a message that says that it could not find an Internet connection, it is likely that you will have to open your firewall software and give CorelDRAW permission to access the Internet. If you don't want CorelDRAW checking the website every time you start CorelDRAW, uncheck both of these boxes and then click the close box in the corner of the Update Settings dialog to apply the changed Update option settings.

If you don't want to use the features offered by the Welcome screen, click the Close button. To *never* see the Welcome dialog again, click to uncheck the Show This Welcome Screen At Startup check box. To open the Welcome screen at any time, choose the Help | Welcome Screen.

Opening Your First New Document File

If you are not using the Welcome screen, choosing File | New (CTRL+N) or clicking the New button on the Standard Toolbar, shown here, opens a new graphic document window.

Click to open a new document
according to default settings

If you choose to begin a new document, CorelDRAW automatically applies a default name using the sequential naming pattern of *Graphic1* for the first file opened, *Graphic2* for the second new file opened, and so on, as each new file in the current CorelDRAW session is opened. The next time you open CorelDRAW, the first new file you open will be named *Graphic1*, so you really should give your files new names when you save them to avoid having tons of files named *Graphic1* and running the risk of overwriting a different, previously saved graphic with the same default name of *Graphic1*.

Each open document, whether it is new or is a previously created document, is listed at the bottom of the Window menu. If you've opened several documents, you might notice that each document window is maximized, but only the most recently opened document appears in view, indicated by the document default name in CorelDRAW's application title bar. This is because while document windows are maximized, only the document in the forefront is visible. Any other opened documents are hidden from view. To navigate between document windows in the maximized state, choose Window | *Filename,* as shown here.

TIP *To see all open document windows and automatically arrange them in your CorelDRAW application window, choose Cascade, Tile Horizontally, or Tile Vertically from the Window command menu.*

Opening Document Files

To open an existing document, choose from one of these three actions: click the Open Other button from the Welcome screen, click the Open button in the Standard Toolbar, or choose File | Open (CTRL+O). In each case, the Open Drawing dialog appears as shown in Figure 3-2. Notice that the Open Drawing dialog, as a standard Windows convention, supports the Thumbnails view of documents, and CorelDRAW files do indeed display graphical

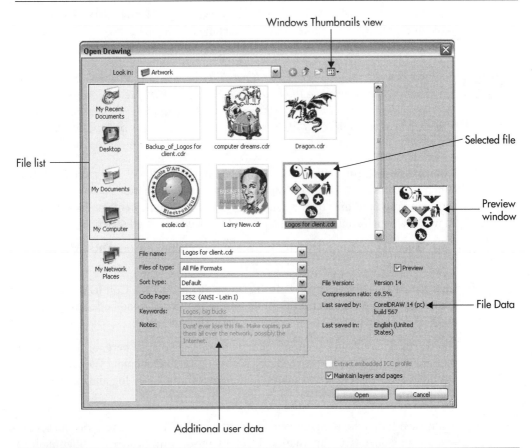

FIGURE 3-2 The Open dialog in CorelDRAW provides you with thumbnail views and document information.

thumbnails of your saved work. You can also see the version of CorelDRAW in which the file was saved plus other file information, and even see user data (covered in this chapter) when you or a coworker has entered keywords and/or other data in these fields.

To help you find the exact file you want to open, the Open Drawing dialog displays, in the lower right of the dialog, some information about the file you have selected and shows the first page of the file (CorelDRAW documents can consist of several pages) if the Preview check box is checked.

- **File Version** "File Version" refers to the version of the CDR file format the file was saved in. CorelDRAW X4 opens only files that are saved in CorelDRAW 7 or later CDR file format. CorelDRAW X4's native version is called version 14. If the file version displayed here is between 7 and 14, a file should open. If it is below 7, it will not open in X4 and you'll have to find an older copy of CorelDRAW to open the file. For example, a file created in CorelDRAW 3 could be opened in a copy of CorelDRAW 7 and then saved in CorelDRAW 7 to a version 7 file that then could be opened in X4. CorelDRAW X4 can save files of any CDR file from version 7 through 14.

 In a work environment where users have different versions of CorelDRAW, it's a good idea when you save a file to also save a copy of the file in Corel's CMX (Corel Media Exchange) file format. CMX is covered later in this chapter, and it's your gateway to saving copies of files from version X4 that users of CorelDRAW version 5 can open.

- **Compression Ratio** When a file is opened in CorelDRAW, it is stored in RAM. When a file is saved, CorelDRAW compresses the information so it takes up less space on your hard disk than when it was in RAM. The percentage displayed here shows how much smaller it is when stored in its compressed state.

- **Last Saved By** This entry tells you the exact version of CorelDRAW software that was used to save the file.

- **Last Saved In** This entry details the language used by the CorelDRAW software that saved the file. This is useful for determining if a different Code Page should be used.

- **Keywords** and/or **Notes** section Entries that are displayed here, or that are visible (but grayed out) if they were made by accessing File | Document Properties when the file was last saved, were entered in the Save Drawing dialog and can help you find the file you want to open.

Once you have found the file you want to open, you have check boxes you can set or clear to extract embedded ICC (International Color Consortium) profile information or to preserve the document's original layering structure as the document opens.

When to Change the Code Page

If you are working with files that were created in a version of CorelDRAW that uses a different language than your copy does, or possibly if you are upgrading from a version previous to version X4, you may need to change the Code Page when you open the file. Code Pages control *mapping*: which character in a typeface is used when you press a specific key on your keyboard. If you have a lot of square boxes displayed where you know you should have text (and you have the document's typeface installed), you should try reopening the file using a different Code Page.

The Code Page chosen in the drop-down list should match that used when the file was created. For example, if you are using a copy of CorelDRAW that uses US English, the Code Page that is used by default is 1252 (ANSI – Latin 1). However, if the file you are opening was created in the Korean language edition of CorelDRAW, then you should choose 949 (ANSI/OEM—Korean) from the Code Page drop-down when you open that file.

TIP   *To open your most recently accessed documents, go to File | Open Recent, where the five most-recent files are listed.*

NOTE   *While multiple files are selected, only the filenames of the selected files are displayed.*

In the Open Drawing dialog, locate and select your document file, and click the Open button (or double-click the filename) to open it. CorelDRAW supports multiple file-opening using modifier keys. You can open files that neighbor one another on the directory list, in the same folder, by holding SHIFT while selecting your files. Open files *not* in sequence in the file list (in the same folder) by holding CTRL while clicking to select the filenames, and then click the Open button.

NOTE   *Although the Open dialog automatically lists all file formats that are in your current folder, you can limit the types of files you are* viewing *to actual CorelDRAW files only, which can be more convenient. To do this, choose CDR—CorelDRAW from the Files Of Type drop-down menu in the Open Drawing dialog.*

Opening Files from Other Applications

Of course, you can open many other native files from other applications, such as Adobe Illustrator or Microsoft PowerPoint in CorelDRAW X4, using selections under the Files Of Type drop-down menu. When a file originally created in a different application is open, CorelDRAW automatically converts its contents to CorelDRAW format. If you look at the title bar of the drawing window, you will see that CorelDRAW has opened the file, preserved the filename, but has given it a .CDR extension. The original application file remains on the hard disk unchanged.

When opening nonnative application files supported by CorelDRAW's Import filters, the graphics and text objects contained in the file are converted as closely as possible to compatible equivalents supported in CorelDRAW. Although the Open command is essentially an Import operation, certain file formats may not open flawlessly, depending on their type and contents. You might get better results if you import the files as objects into an open CorelDRAW document by pressing CTRL+I (File | Import). If CorelDRAW is unable to interpret a file's contents while trying to open it, an alert dialog appears.

Warning Messages

When opening files—especially older files or files created on a different system or using a third-party application—warning messages may appear before the file actually opens. For the most part, these messages aren't meant to cause alarm, but merely to advise. Two of the most common messages are the version compatibility and font warnings.

While the Version Compatibility Warning merely serves as a reminder that the file you are opening was created in a substantially older version of CorelDRAW, the Font Substitution For Missing Fonts dialog enables you to view a list of the fonts used in the document and provides options for substituting new ones. CorelDRAW X4 supports backward compatibility only for versions 7 through 13. If you're looking to save files as far back as version 5, you'll need to use CorelDRAW 11 or earlier.

Pantone and Basic Font-Matching

Font-matching sounds good in theory, and in the Font Substitution For Missing Fonts dialog, you have the option to let CorelDRAW try to match a missing font, to locate a compatible font manually (click the Substitute Font With button and then choose from the drop-down list), or choose the Use The Panose Suggested Match. Usually, you're best off noting the name of the missing font, canceling the Open dialog, finding a similar font yourself, installing it, reopening the document, and choosing the font you just installed.

You'll soon notice a problem with letting any computer program try to match a font. It doesn't use its eyes (it doesn't have any), but instead relies on *metadata* (data about data) that is written into the header of a typeface. The problem isn't with CorelDRAW: if someone who created a digital typeface didn't bother to write the correct metadata into the file, you indeed will get suggested matches of Arial for Windsor Condensed. CorelDRAW can't *find* a match, there's no file information listed for the missing font, and it's as simple and as frustrating as that. The good news is that if you point the Font Substitution box to an installed font you want to use, CorelDRAW remembers it for this and all other documents with the missing typeface.

Saving and Closing Documents

Saving files is another basic and essential operation you'll perform in CorelDRAW. Whether you save often (pressing CTRL+S frequently is a good idea) or you're saving your document for the first time, you'll want to define some file information for it and practice good hard-drive housekeeping by saving to user-defined folders. When you know you'll want to retrieve a document in the near future, setting a save location, applying a name, setting thumbnail and version preferences, and other options go along with the job.

Saving Your First Document

Typically, you can save an *existing* document simply by clicking the Save button on the Standard Toolbar or by choosing File | Save (CTRL+S), which causes your most recent changes to be saved immediately without opening any dialogs.

CorelDRAW X4's Save Drawing dialog contains more than just options on where to save and what name to use when saving the file. For a practical exercise that explores the additional options you have when saving, follow these steps.

Saving Files with User Info

1. If you've just started a new document and want to save it, click the Save button in the Standard Toolbar, use the CTRL+S shortcut, or choose File | Save. Each results in opening the Save Drawing dialog, as shown in Figure 3-3.

2. With the Save Drawing dialog open, use the dialog options to set a location for your document, and type a unique name in the File Name box. If you're saving your document to a format other than CorelDRAW's native CDR format, choose a file format from the Save As Type menu.

3. Depending on the file type you chose in the Save As Type drop-down, you may need to choose a version from the Version drop-down. Unless you *must* save to an older file format to allow the saved file to be used with legacy software, always choose the most recent (highest number) version. If you choose an older file version, some of the work you did in your file may not save as you expect, because an effect or other feature used may not have existed in the file version you selected.

4. If saving your document in CorelDRAW or other Corel-supported formats, enter optional Keywords and Notes to include as part of the file's metadata. Some Search programs can use Keywords you assign to a file to locate or catalog the file. Notes are great places to leave information and reminders for yourself and your coworkers on what project a file belongs to, whether it is a final approved version, or other similar info. Keywords and Notes appear on the Open dialog and can also be added or edited from File | Document Properties dialog.

FIGURE 3-3   The Save Drawing dialog can save a file with user information and other options.

5. If you only want to save the object(s) you currently have selected, check the Selected Only check box. Everything that is not selected will not be saved to the file.

6. Decide if you want to check the Embed Fonts Using TrueDoc™ check box. Checking this check box will increase the saved file size because the font(s) will be included in the file. This can be a useful feature when you're working with fonts you don't have loaded every day or if you are giving the file to a coworker who does not have the font. TrueDoc embeds the entire font so you or anyone else can make changes and print the file using the correct font.

7. If you have recorded and saved a macro in this file or any other VBA project, you will probably want to check the Save With Embedded VBA Project check box. Your VBA script, macro, or project will be saved with your document and may be viewed, copied, or used by whoever reopens the document. If you want to preserve your scripts as your own intellectual property, you might want to leave this option unselected, but then you would have to find a different way to distribute your work.

3

Advanced Save Drawing Options

The Save Drawing dialog sports even more tweaks and refinements you can make. Clicking the Advanced button opens the same Options dialog that you can navigate to at any time by choosing Tools | Options (CTRL+J), expanding the tree directory under Document, and then clicking the Save item. In this section you can make choices about File optimization, Textures, and Blends and Extrudes. These options are set on a document basis, *not* a global one, so you can make different choices for each file you save.

- ■ *Save Presentation Exchange (CMX).* Check this box if you want to place or edit the file in other applications that accept this file format, such as Corel WordPerfect or Xara Xtreme, and even much older versions of CorelDRAW. For example, CorelDRAW5 can't open an X4 CDR file, but version 5 can open a CMX file. The CMX file format is a metafile format and can hold both bitmap and vector data. It is a subset of the CDR format and as such is not as capable of rendering advanced features, but it is a good way to use graphics created in CorelDRAW in other applications. X4 supports CMX files created in versions 5 through 14.

- ■ *Use Bitmap Compression.* Bitmaps and bitmap effects in a drawing can really plump up the final file size of a document. To save precious hard disk storage space, put a check in this box. The compression used is *lossless,* so you don't have to worry that choosing this option will degrade the quality of your file onscreen or when printed.

- ■ *Use Graphic Object Compression.* Checking this box reduces saved file sizes by compressing the vector elements in the file.

- ■ *Save Textures With The File or Rebuild Textures When Opening The File.* Select the radio button next to one of these mutually exclusive options. Saving the textures increases the file's size and uses more hard disk space. Rebuilding the textures saves hard disk space, but it then takes longer to open and save a file. Your choice here is between maximizing your hard disk space or your time.

- ■ *Save Blends And Extrudes With The File or Rebuild Blends And Extrudes When Opening The File.* As with saving or rebuilding textures, here your choice is really between maximizing hard disk space or your time. Click the radio button next to the choice that suits you best.

After you've made your selections, click the OK button to be returned to the Save Drawing dialog. With all your options for this file spent, go ahead and click the Save button, or the Cancel button to abandon the save.

Save As Command

The Save As command (CTRL+SHIFT+S) is useful for saving copies of your document using the same or different Save command settings. The Save As command is often used to save a file at regular intervals throughout the creation of a graphic—so you can go back to an earlier version of the file or see what different color schemes or layouts look like. Using the Save As command in combination with the Selected Only option (available only while objects are selected) is a truly useful option; if you've been working with a lot of objects you won't need later, you don't have to delete them all to tidy up, you simply use Selected Only. Otherwise, the options available in the Save As command dialog are identical to those in the Save dialog.

Although using the Save As command may seem similar to using the Export command in some ways, the two are quite different; in some cases it may be better to use one command instead of the other. Generally speaking, the Save As command is the best technique to use when saving native CorelDRAW files.

The Export command (File | Export) is best for saving your document or selected objects as any *other* type of file format, particularly bitmap formats like CPT, GIF, JPEG, PNG, or a wide variety of text formats as well as other specialized vector formats such as EPS and SVG. In CorelDRAW X4 you can save—but not export—files in CorelDRAW (CDR), Corel Pattern file (PAT), and CorelDRAW Template (CDT) format.

Using File Backup Options

Countless hours of work can be saved using CorelDRAW's Backup feature. When it comes to saving and backing up your document files, CorelDRAW X4 lets you take full control over *how, where,* and *when* backup files are created. *Backup files* let you retrieve recent changes made to documents should something unfortunate (such as a power failure) occur while you're working. Backup files created automatically are named AUTOBACKUP_OF_ *FILENAME*.CDR, where *FILENAME* is the name of your original CorelDRAW document. By default they are stored in Documents and Settings*YourUserName*\\Local Settings\\Temp. You can specify another location if you prefer.

 If CorelDRAW closes unexpectedly, the next time you open CorelDRAW, the File Recovery dialog prompts you to open the Auto-Backup file that it found. Click OK to open the file. If you click Cancel and do not open the file, the Auto-Backup file will be deleted when you exit CorelDRAW. So open and save the file when you can—you won't be prompted to do so again.

At your command, backup files can be created every time you save a file. The naming convention for these files is in the form of Backup_of_*filename*.cdr, and these backup files are stored in the same folder location as the file you saved. You can open backup files the same way as with any CorelDRAW X4 document file, by using the File | Open command (CTRL+O).

To access CorelDRAW X4's backup controls, use the Workspace | Save page of the Options dialog (shown in Figure 3-4). Choose Tools | Options | Workspace | Save.

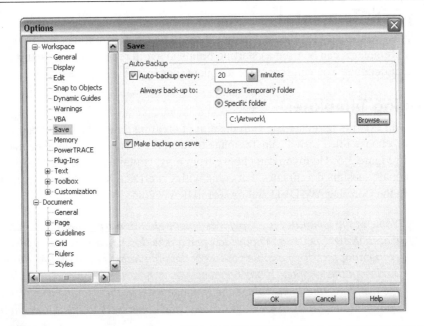

3

FIGURE 3-4   Use these options to control where and when backup files are created.

This list should help you decide which options to choose:

- **Auto-Backup Every**   While this option is selected (the default), your document files are backed up at specified time intervals. The default is 20 minutes and can be set to anywhere between 1 and 60 minutes (or never).

- **Always Back Up To**   Specify the location of the backups to be saved in your temporary folder (the default), or choose Specific Folder and use the Browse button to specify a drive and folder location.

- **Make Backup On Save**   Activating the Make Backup On Save option (selected by default) causes CorelDRAW to update the backup file to match your original document file each time you use the File | Save command (CTRL+S). This backup system is in addition to the Auto-Backup feature and complements it, because the files are in a more accessible location and *are not* automatically deleted (although they are overwritten each time you save a file), which leaves you with a backup of the most recent version of the file. It is handy to have this kind of backup file because you can revert to the last saved version of the file if you should make a mistake while editing a file—or if you just want to start over.

Working with Templates

Templates are special files that can be saved based on existing settings and/or document content. Templates can be used as starting points to avoid repetitive page setup and document defaults. You can recognize template files by the .CDT file extension.

Opening Templates

To open an existing template file with the aim of creating a new document based on the template, choose File | New From Template to open the New From Template dialog, as shown in Figure 3-5. Here you can choose from a list containing many categories of professionally designed templates that came with CorelDRAW. Additional templates are found on the CorelDRAW DVD and on CorelDRAW.com.

NOTE   *Some of the templates use typefaces you might not have installed from the CorelDRAW CD. If you choose to open a new document based on a template containing text, it's possible you'll get the Font Substitution dialog, discussed earlier in this chapter. If this happens, you can certainly open a new file based on the template, and then replace the typeface used in the document. Alternatively, you can install the fonts listed in this dialog and come back to the document later.*

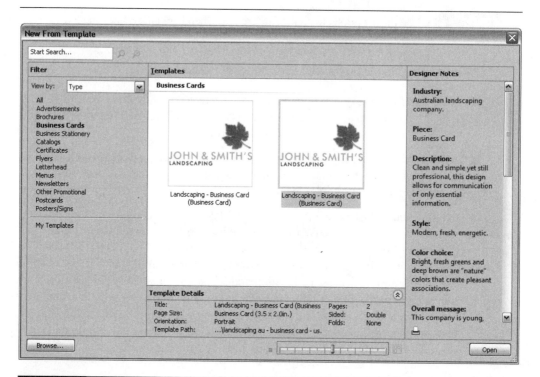

FIGURE 3-5   Choose from these template categories to begin your new document.

Templates are organized in two general groups: Type and Industry. Choose Type in the View By drop-down to see a list of template categories that is broken down by kind of document produced—a catalog, a flyer, a letterhead, and so on. Choose Industry to see the templates arranged in categories that correspond to various industries such as Hospitality, Retail, or Services. To use any templates you've created and saved, either search the list in the My Templates section on the left side of the dialog, or, if you didn't specify the Type or Industry of your own template, choose All, and then scroll to the bottom of the list to Not Specified.

Clicking on a category, such as Business Cards or Brochures in the list on the left opens (in the center of the dialog) thumbnail views of the templates available. Click once on a thumbnail to load information about the template into the Template Details section at the bottom of the dialog and into Designer Notes on the right of the dialog. To increase the size of the thumbnail for a better view or to decrease the size of the thumbnail to view more thumbnails, click-drag the slider at the bottom of the dialog.

While a template is selected, the preview window displays a thumbnail of the first page of the template. Click OK or double-click the file to open a new (unsaved) document using the template's content and page layout.

The Browse button opens a Windows standard file Open dialog that you can use to locate, select, and open a new document based on a template somewhere on your computer or network other than CorelDRAW's default location for templates.

The Search box at the top of the dialog uses Windows XP's Desktop Search or Vista's Instant Search to scour your computer system to find CorelDRAW CPT template files wherever they may be. See Windows XP or Vista Help for how to fine-tune what locations are searched.

 Preformatted template files included with your CorelDRAW X4 application are stored in the X:\Program Files\Corel\CorelDRAW Graphics Suite X4\Languages\ EN\Draw\Template folder.

Opening and Saving Templates

You can open any template file that has a .CDT extension you've saved from X4 or from any previous version for editing, and change its actual template format and/or its content. Use the File | Open command and choose CorelDRAW Template (CDT) as the file type. Before the file opens, a dialog will ask whether you want to open the template as a new document, or for editing. If your aim is to open a new document based on the template content and structure, leave New From Template (shown at left) selected in combination with the With Contents option. If your intention is to edit the template file itself, choose Open For Editing.

When saving an edited template file, performing a Save command automatically saves the file as a template without opening any dialogs—and without the need to re-specify the file as a CDT template file in the Save dialog. Additionally, a CDT file you opened will appear on the File | Open Recent list, and if you choose it, it will simply open without the dialog shown in the previous illustration.

Clipboard Commands

As many users will already know, the *Clipboard* is a temporary "place" that's capable of storing the last objects copied and is a feature of your computer's operating system. While the data you copied or cut is stored in your system's RAM, you can "paste" duplicates of the data into your document. The three most common Clipboard commands you'll likely use are Copy, Cut, and Paste—each of which is accessible either from the Edit menu or from the Standard Toolbar, as shown. Cut, Copy, and Paste are also standard Windows commands, so you can indeed use the keyboard shortcuts CTRL+C (Copy), CTRL+V (Paste), and CTRL+X (Cut) to speed up your work.

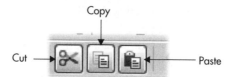

Copying vs. Cutting

Each time an object is copied to the Windows Clipboard, the previous Clipboard contents are overwritten. To copy selected objects onto your Clipboard, choose Edit | Copy. Better yet, click the Copy button on the Standard Toolbar, or use the standard CTRL+C shortcut. The older Windows CTRL+INSERT shortcut also works. After copying, the items you copy remain unaltered in your document.

 If you find clipbrd.exe in Windows/System32 (under Windows XP), you can see what's on the system's Clipboard, and this is a hedge against accidentally removing your CorelDRAW with a screen capture or some text you copied to it.

The *Cut* command automatically deletes the selected items from your document and puts a copy on the Clipboard. To cut items, click the Cut button in the Standard Toolbar, choose Edit | Cut, or use the standard CTRL+X shortcut. The older Windows SHIFT+DELETE shortcut also applies.

 To create duplicates of your selected objects immediately, press the + key on your keyboard's numeric keypad. Copies immediately are placed in front of the selected objects in the document and in exactly the same page position. This action works independently of the Clipboard, meaning that your current Clipboard contents remain intact.

If what you've copied to the Clipboard is something that you will use again in this document or that might be useful in future creations, consider saving it to the Scrapbook covered later in this chapter, or as a Symbol, which is covered in Chapter 12.

Paste vs. Paste Special

Copies of items on your Clipboard can be placed into your current document by using the Paste command. Each time you use the Paste command, more duplicate copies are pasted. When an item is pasted into CorelDRAW, it is placed on the very top or front of the active layer. To paste Clipboard contents, perform one of these actions: click the Paste button in the Standard Toolbar, choose Edit | Paste, or use the CTRL+V shortcut. The standard Windows SHIFT+INSERT shortcut also applies.

Occasionally you'll find data you need to copy into a CorelDRAW document that the Paste command doesn't support, or the data pastes with incomplete or damaged areas. This is frequently the case with data copied from web pages, office documents, or other graphics applications. Use Paste Special when you are trying to bring in data from an application whose native file format does not have a CorelDRAW X4 import filter or for additional choices on how the data will be managed by CorelDRAW. To use the Paste Special command, choose Edit | Paste Special, which opens the dialog shown next.

 Paste Special does not have a keyboard shortcut assigned to it by default. It can be incredibly handy to assign it one yourself by using the Customization | Commands section of the Options dialog.

Paste Special usually offers several different ways the copied item can be brought into CorelDRAW. These functions are controlled by Windows Object Linking and Embedding (OLE). Depending on what options are available for the kind of non-CorelDRAW file you are trying to import, and the options you choose with Paste Special, the object might be placed into your drawing, embedded in your CorelDRAW document, or the object might be linked.

To edit embedded or linked media, you can choose as follows:

- Double-click on the object with the Pick Tool.

- Select the object with the Pick Tool, and choose from the right-click pop-up menu.

- Choose the entry that corresponds to the selected object from the bottom of the Edit menu.

Embedded objects appear in the menu as, "*Application Name That Created the File* Image Object." For *linked* objects, the entry appears as "Linked *Application Name That Created the File* Image Object." Additionally, all linked files in a drawing can be managed and updated by choosing Edit | Links from the menu. There are a number of caveats about OLE placing and editing—among them, system problems that can occur if the application associated with the linked or embedded object is no longer installed on your system. For detailed documentation on OLE, go to Microsoft.com's knowledgebase.

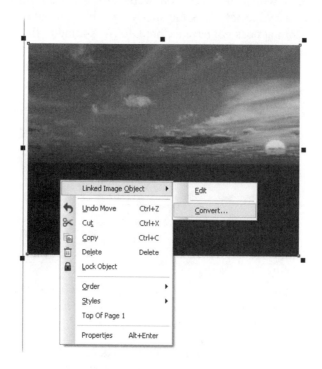

Undoing and Redoing Editing Changes

If you're accomplishing a task by trial and error, there's nothing better than the Undo command for backing out of a multi-step operation. This little lifesaver provides all kinds of ways for you to reverse your last action.

3

Basic Undo Commands

Choose Edit | Undo or use the standard CTRL+Z shortcut. To reverse an Undo command, choose Edit | Redo or use the CTRL+SHIFT+Z shortcut. CorelDRAW X4 takes both of these commands further by offering Undo and Redo buttons in the Standard Toolbar; they can be used either to Undo or Redo single or multiple commands. The buttons themselves are fashioned into buttons and popout menus. Clicking the toolbar button applies to the most recent action, and clicking the popout reveals a brief listing of recent commands, shown next. To reverse either an Undo or Redo action by using the popouts, click one of the available commands in the list. Doing so reverses the selected action back to the point you specified in the popout. Undo and Redo popouts show your most recent actions at the top of the listing.

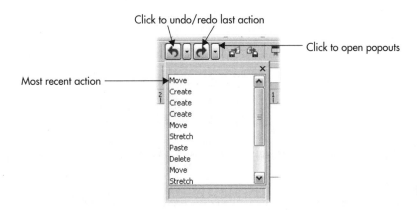

Click to undo/redo last action

Click to open popouts

Most recent action

| NOTE | *You can customize the number of Undo levels CorelDRAW performs. The default setting records your 20 most recent actions, but this value can be set as high as 99,999 actions (provided your system has the available resources). To access Undo options, open the Options dialog (CTRL+J), and click General.* |

Using the Undo Docker

For even more control over your most recent actions, you might try the Undo docker opened by choosing Window | Dockers | Undo. The Undo docker, shown in Figure 3-6, provides different views of your drawing as it appeared before certain recent actions. The Undo docker can also be used to save your recent actions as a Visual Basic for Applications (VBA) macro, which is terrific when you want to apply, for example, a dozen complex edits to different objects in different documents (on different days!).

The Undo docker displays your most recent actions in reverse order of the Undo and Redo popout menus, with recent actions placed *at the bottom* of the docker list. Selecting a command on the list shows you a view of your document as it appeared before your most recent actions were performed.

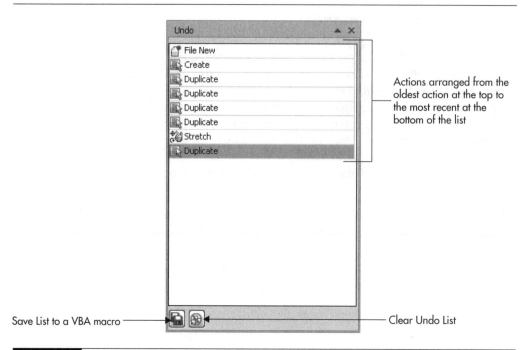

Actions arranged from the oldest action at the top to the most recent at the bottom of the list

Save List to a VBA macro

Clear Undo List

FIGURE 3-6 The Undo docker features all sorts of ways to undo or redo recent actions.

Clicking the Clear Undo List icon clears the entire list of actions in the Undo docker list, providing you with a clean slate. You cannot clear or delete *some* of the actions; clearing is an all or nothing decision. By default, the alert dialog shown next appears, warning you that clearing the Undo list can't be undone. Having a robust Undo list can be a much-needed safety net, so don't clear the list unless you have so many undos in the list that it is bogging down your system resources.

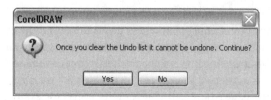

When you save and then *close* a file, the Undo docker list is automatically cleared—you will be starting fresh when you reopen the document. If you Save the document but don't close it, and continue to work on the file, the actions in the Undo docker remain, and your new actions continue to be added to the list.

As hinted at earlier, the Undo docker is also a great way to create VBA macros. Clicking the Save List To A VBA Macro button in the docker opens the Save Macro dialog, where you provide a name and description for the new macro and store it either with your open document or to CorelDRAW X4's main Global Macros list. Keep in mind when naming your macros that spaces are not valid characters, but underscores are.

Scrapbooks, An Old Favorite

If you are a longtime user of CorelDRAW, you may also be a fan of the Scrapbook docker, which can be used to store and retrieve drawings, photos, text, or floating photo objects. Many users have found it useful for searching through vast collections of clip art. The Scrapbook docker is still available for you to use, but is no longer installed by default—the Symbol Manager docker is proving to be a better feature for storing work because in X4, all the Corel clip art and your own work can be searched for using XP and Vista's native search engines.

But it's natural to stick with what works for you; if you want to use the Scrapbook, you can use CorelDRAW's customization options to bring the Scrapbook out into the open. Here's how.

 ## Revealing the CorelDRAW Scrapbook

1. Choose Tools | Customize from the menu or open the Options dialog (CTRL+J).

2. Choose Customization and then Commands in the tree on the left.

3. Click on the Search icon (the one with the binoculars on it) next to the drop-down box in the center of the dialog.

4. In the Find What field of the Find Text dialog, type in **Scrapbook** and then click the Find Next button. The Scrapbook command is highlighted in the list of commands. Click the Find Text close box.

5. Click-drag the Scrapbook command out of the list, and drop it on the toolbar or menu of your choice. The end of the Standard Toolbar is a good location if you use the Scrapbook often. Alternatively, you can group it with the other dockers on the Window | Dockers menu—toward the bottom is a logical place to put the Scrapbook docker command.

6. Click OK to close the Options dialog and apply the customization.

Importing and Exporting Files

CorelDRAW X4's Import and Export filter collection is one of the most complete and powerful available in any graphics application. X4's new, additional import and export filters make working between applications easier than ever.

Support for new File formats:

- Microsoft Publisher (versions 2002, 2003, and 2007)

- Microsoft Word 2007

- AutoCAD DXF

- AutoCAD DWG (versions R2.5 to 2007)

- Corel Painter X

Enhanced export options when working with Adobe products, including:

- Adobe Photoshop CS3

- Adobe Illustrator CS3 (you can now choose to export text to Illustrator as Curves or as Text; compressed Illustrator files are not currently supported)

- PDF 1.7, PDF/A (a ISO-approved format for long-term document archiving)

- Adobe Acrobat 8

Filters are essentially data translators for files created in other applications or in formats not native to CorelDRAW. *Import filters* take the data from other applications and translate that data into information that can be viewed and edited from within CorelDRAW. *Export filters* translate data from your CorelDRAW document to a format recognized by a different program or publishing medium. As with Import filters, Export filters frequently contain dialogs where you set up options to export the precise data you need for the target application or publishing medium.

 When you export a file, the new file format may not support all the features that CorelDRAW's native file format (CDR) supports. For this reason, even when exporting work, you should always save a copy of your work in CorelDRAW's native file format.

Importing Files and Setting Options

You can import a file by clicking File | Import, clicking the Import button on the Standard Toolbar, or using the CTRL+I shortcut. All actions open the Import dialog (see Figure 3-7), which features options enabling you to locate and select the file you want to import, specify the file type, and obtain information about the file you're about to import. The Import dialog looks similar to the Open Drawing dialog, but it has a few more check boxes and options that are available depending on the kind of file you are importing. If any option is grayed out, it means that it is not an available option for the kind of file that's currently displayed in the Files Of Type drop-down box.

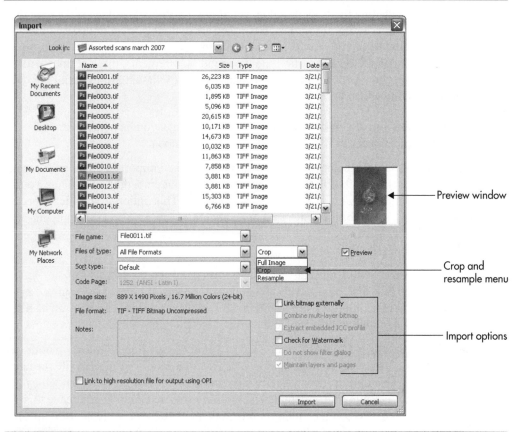

Preview window

Crop and resample menu

Import options

FIGURE 3-7 The Import dialog includes options for cropping images, provides details about images, and offers ICC color profile options.

CorelDRAW X4 features a comprehensive selection of import filters for getting various file formats into your document. Of these, Corel provides support for all its own formats, including CorelDRAW (CDR), Corel Symbol Library (CSL), Corel Painter (RIFF), CorelDRAW Compressed (CDX), Corel Presentation Exchange (CMX), Corel CMX Compressed (CPX), Corel R.A.V.E. (CLK), Corel WordPerfect (WPD and WPG), Corel Quattro Pro (WB, WQ), Corel/Micrografx Designer (DES, DSF, and DRW), Corel Picture Publisher (PP5, PP4, and PPF), Corel Paint Shop Pro (PSP), and Corel PHOTO-PAINT (CPT).

You'll also find filter support for importing files from third-party products such as Adobe Photoshop (PSD), Adobe Illustrator (AI), Adobe Acrobat (PDF), Macromedia Freehand (FH), Visio (VSD), and other Microsoft Office products. Other filters support popular PostScript, CAD, bitmap, text, and word processor file formats, and a selection of specialty file formats.

While you're visiting the Import dialog, certain options may become available in the dialog when you select a file for import. Basically, the options pertain to how the file will be *handled* by the import filter that will be used to import the file; you may have more success with one filter over another. For certain file types and requirements, these options will significantly affect how your resulting file is handled. The following brief definitions will help in determining which options to choose:

- **Crop, Resample**   When importing a bitmap image, you have the Crop and Resample choices available from the drop-down menu.

- **Link Bitmap Externally**   Choose this option when importing bitmaps to create a filename and a path link to the imported file without embedding the file in your document. By default, this option is not selected. This option is significant because externally linked bitmap files cannot be altered in any way, such as applying CorelDRAW bitmap effects. Linking keeps file sizes small, but limits what you can do in CorelDRAW with the bitmap.

  If you want to use almost any of Corel's commands on the Bitmaps menu, you must break the link first. Commands and options for controlling externally linked bitmaps, including breaking links, are found in the Link Manager docker. You can also select the bitmap with the Pick Tool and then choose Bitmaps | Break Link from the menu.

- **Combine Multi-Layer Bitmap**   Corel Painter and Adobe Photoshop both write image files that can contain layers. When you're importing bitmap file formats, choosing this option automatically combines (flattens) image data on all layers of the imported bitmap. By default, this option is not selected. If you leave this option unchecked, you can ungroup the layers of such a composite bitmap and work with each layer separately. You can also reorder the layers in the Object Manager docker and perform many other editing options on the file as a whole, or just individual layers.

- **Extract Embedded ICC Profile**   Choosing this option saves a copy of any ICC profile contained in the image to the Documents and Settings*UserName*\\ Application Data\\Corel\\CorelDRAW Graphics Suite X4\\User Color folder on the *drive where Windows is installed*.

- **Check For Watermark**   By default, this option is not selected. DigiMarc watermarks can be embedded directly in CorelDRAW X4 by selecting the bitmap, choosing Bitmaps | Plug-ins | DigiMarc | Embed Watermark, and entering specific creator and/or date information in the dialog that appears. The Status Bar displays a © symbol in front of a selected imported bitmap's filename when the bitmap contains a DigiMarc watermark.

3

- **Do Not Show Filter Dialog**   For a few import file formats, a secondary dialog may appear, offering further options for handling inherent properties in the imported file. Choosing this option kills the display of this secondary dialog and is particularly useful for uninterrupted importing of multiple images. By default, this option is not selected.

- **Maintain Layers And Pages**   If the file you are importing contains multiple pages and/or multiple layers, this option becomes available. By default, this option is selected. As the file is imported, additional pages are automatically added to your current document and/or layers are automatically added. Layers are controlled using the Object Manager docker.

- **Link To High Resolution File For Output Using OPI**   Although this option seems relegated to the opposite corner of the Import dialog, it involves a complex and powerful capability that can be used to link specially prepared TIF or CT files to your document using OPI (open prepress interface) technology. The skinny on this technology is that it creates placeholder low-resolution images that contain internal links to high-resolution digital separation files. When printed, these external separations can be set to replace the imported placeholder. The goal is to offer you the option to incorporate high-resolution images into your document while maintaining reasonable document file sizes. By default, this option is not selected.

| TIP | *You can import multiple files if they are stored in the same folder. Click one of the files you want to open, and then hold the CTRL key while clicking additional files. You can open an entire folder's contents: click the first file, then hold the SHIFT key, and finally, click the last file in the folder.* |

| NOTE | *The OPI option flags an image as a low-resolution OPI image. The high-resolution image doesn't even have to be on your computer. When you print the file, OPI comments get injected into the PostScript printing data stream. The high/low resolution swap happens on the OPI server.* |

Exporting Files and Choosing Options

Exporting your CorelDRAW work, depending on the assignment, is an operation often performed after the images or documents you have created are complete. Often these operations come at the end of a project deadline when time is critical. However, rushing through an export is incredibly *unwise*, because your export should be tailored to the application that will be using the exported file. Choosing the best export options affects your design's appearance, quality, and compatibility with other applications.

From the File menu, CorelDRAW X4 offers a general-purpose Export command that is used to export your work to almost all other applications, plus a special Export For Office command for when your work will be used in a Corel WordPerfect Office application or in a Microsoft Office application. First, let's look at the Export command that offers the greatest variety of export formats.

Export

The Export command is found on the File menu. It contains all of the export filters you chose to install during the installation of CorelDRAW. If you installed the recommended set of import/export filters, you'll find over 40 different file formats available in the Export dialog. If you need or just want to, you can always run the CorelDRAW installation program again to install additional export filters—the Secondary Import/Export File types: CUR, EXE, FMV, ICO, PCD, PCX, SCT, VSD, XCF, XPM, and/or the Tertiary Import/Export File types: GEM, HTM, IMG, MET, NAP, PIC, SHW, MOV, and QTM.

The options available to you in the Export dialog (shown in Figure 3-8) vary depending on your document's properties, such as whether you have anything selected, how many pages are in your file, and what type of file format you have chosen in the Save As Type drop-down. Secondary dialogs may also appear depending on the export file format.

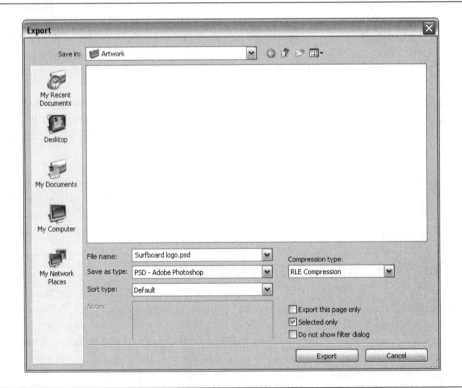

FIGURE 3-8   The Export dialog is the first step to exporting your current document page or selected objects.

The following Export dialog options are available:

- **Compression Type**   This drop-down menu becomes available while a file format supporting multiple compression types is selected (such as bitmap formats). Choosing a compression type enables you to control which compression technique is applied and how much or how little compression is used.

- **Export This Page Only**   If your document consists of multiple pages, this option becomes available when exporting to EPS or to any file format supporting text as characters (such as text or word processor formats). Choosing this option causes only your current page to be exported.

- **Selected Only**   Choose this option to export only your currently selected object(s) instead of your entire page or document.

- **Do Not Show Filter Dialog**   Choose this option to export your file immediately using the options currently set in some secondary filter dialogs; this can be useful when exporting multiple individual files in identical ways. If you are exporting vector graphics to a bitmap format, the secondary dialog, Convert To Bitmap, will display even if Do Not Show Filter Dialog is checked. See Chapter 26 for more information on exporting vector artwork to bitmap file formats.

If you're unfamiliar with a typical export operation, the following brief exercise will help familiarize you with a typical export process.

Exporting a Design

1. Have a document open in the application window. If it is a new, unsaved document, it's a wise idea (but not required) that you save it first to CorelDRAW's CDR format.

2. If you want to export only specific objects of your document, select the object(s) you want to export using the Pick Tool. Do this *before* proceeding with your Export operation.

3. Choose File | Export (CTRL+E) or press the Export button in the Standard Toolbar to open the Export dialog.

4. Select a folder and/or location, and enter a unique name for your exported file, or accept the current name—by default, the current CorelDRAW X4 document name.

5. Choose a format type for your exported file from the Save As Type drop-down menu.

 To control the order of available file formats in the Save As Type listing, use options in the Sort Type drop-down menu. For example, if you choose Bitmap from the Sort Type drop-down menu, all of the available bitmap export file options are moved to the top of the drop-down list, making selecting a bitmap format easier. Non-bitmap file formats can still be chosen—they're just below the divider in the list.

6. If you intend the file you are preparing for export to contain only the objects you currently have selected on your document page, click the Selected Only option.

7. If you choose, enter any comment information to attach to the exported file in the Notes box. Some file formats such as PSD do not support notes, so the field is dimmed (unavailable). However, the CMX file format and several others do support Notes.

8. Click Export to proceed with your export operation.

Once the Export dialog has closed, you might not be finished yet. Exporting operations often involve one or more additional dialogs that appear as you narrow the export file format properties.

Choosing Export File Formats

You're basically covered when you use CorelDRAW. You can export your work not only to other Corel product file formats, but also to third-party application file formats, as discussed earlier in this chapter. The downside is perhaps that you're now like a kid in a candy shop: they all look good—where should you begin? The following is a brief summary of the available export filters:

- **Bitmap formats**   When exporting to Bitmap formats, the general Convert To Bitmap dialog (shown in Figure 3-9) will be the first to appear. It's where you choose the Size, Resolution, Color, and specific properties for your exported bitmap file. Depending on which bitmap format you select, another dialog appears offering more options. Specific bitmap types—such as BMP (Windows and OS2), CALS, GIF, JPEG (JPG, JP2), PCX, PNG, TGA, TIF, WI—feature their own filter dialogs, custom tailoring your export for the application that receives the work.

- **Metafile formats**   Metafile formats such as CGM, EMF, FMV, and WFM *can* contain both vector and bitmap information, but *in practice* they commonly only contain vector *or* bitmap information. It is usually better to choose a dedicated bitmap or vector format.

- **Text formats**   When exporting to text formats (such as native word processor or simple text formats), no additional dialogs appear. Choose from ANSI Text (TXT), Rich Text Format (RTF), or virtually any version of Microsoft Word (DOC), WordPerfect (WPD), or WordStar 7 and 2000 (WSD).

- **Font formats**   You have the choice of exporting to TTF to create a True Type Font or to PFB to create an Adobe Type 1 font format to create your own font. A secondary dialog opens where you specify the properties for the font and character you are exporting. See Chapter 15 for more on how to use CorelDRAW to create fonts.

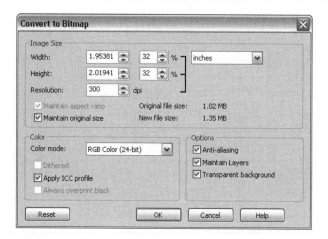

3

FIGURE 3-9   This dialog provides options for preparing exported bitmap formats.

- **Vector formats**   CorelDRAW X4 includes the following vector graphics filters: Frame Vector Metafile (FMV) and a Scalable Vector Graphics filter (SVG and SVGZ compressed), as shown in the SVG Export dialog in Figure 3-10. Each filter features its own specific property options and includes a preflight tab for correcting incorrect option choices (such as ICC color profiling; note the "1 Issue" remark in this figure) and options to create saved presets.

- **CAD/Plotter formats**   CorelDRAW X4 enables you to export files to AutoCAD (DXF and DWG), as well as to HPGL 2 Plotter files (PLT). These filters include their own specific dialog filter options.

- **EPS formats**   When you choose to export to Encapsulated PostScript (EPS) format, CorelDRAW X4's filter offers a comprehensive set of PostScript-related options, organized into General and Advanced tabbed areas in the EPS Export dialog, as shown in Figure 3-11. EPS files are the coin of the realm in desktop publishing, and CorelDRAW can write an EPS graphics file that is Mac and Windows compatible.

- **Native application formats**   Export to Adobe Illustrator (AI), Adobe Photoshop (PSD), Macromedia Flash (SWF), or Kodak FlashPix Image (FPX)—each of which opens a dialog filter with specific options. The Macintosh OS native file formats, MACPaint Bitmap (MAC) and Macintosh PICT (PIC), are also available.

- **Corel native formats**   Export to any of Corel's own native formats: Corel WordPerfect Graphic (WPG), Corel PHOTO-PAINT (CPT), Picture Publisher (PPF or PP5), or Corel Presentation Exchange 5.0 (CMX)—each of which features its own filter dialogs.

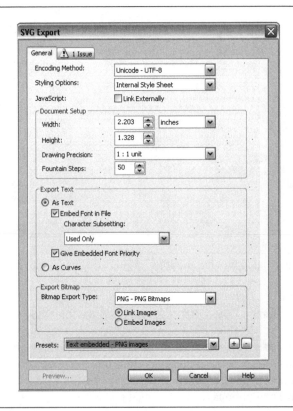

FIGURE 3-10 The improved Scalable Vector Graphics filter enables you to set property options such as embedding a subset of fonts used and compression schemes for bitmaps in your document.

Export for Office

Corel WordPerfect Office and Microsoft Office are used by tens of millions of people every day to produce letters, reports, charts, and presentations. These people often do not have graphics training or graphics software, but want and need graphics in their documents. To address these needs, Office suites not only accept graphics for placement in documents, but also provide simple tools to create and edit graphics within the suite. The tools are limited and the file formats that work best with office suites are also limited when compared with graphics applications.

CorelDRAW X4's Export For Office feature makes it easy for you to be sure that any graphics you supply for use in WordPerfect and Microsoft Office are optimized for their use in an Office document. Export For Office also helps you and your client avoid delays, bum documents, and other migraine-inducing issues.

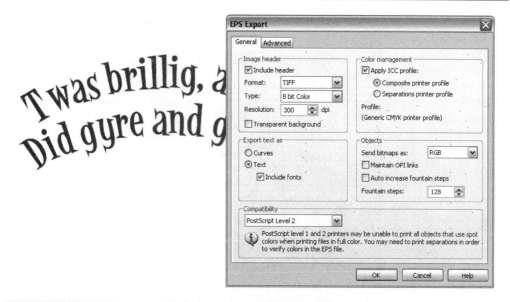

FIGURE 3-11   The EPS Export dialog offers full control over all aspects of your exported graphics and images.

Choose File | Export For Office to display the Export For Office dialog and kick off the process of creating a file for your customer that's Office-suite optimized. As you can see in Figure 3-12, the Export For Office dialog has a large preview window in the center that shows what will be exported. You can navigate around the preview window and zoom in and out by clicking on the appropriate Zoom or Hand Tool icon on the side of the dialog.

Export For Office cannot export multiple pages; it only works with the page you have active at the time you opened the dialog. If you have a multi-page document that you want to export, you'll need to do this page by page. And unlike with the Export dialog, there is no Selected Only check box; however, you can, indeed, export only a selected object. In the Export For Office process, if you have any object(s) selected before you open the dialog, only the objects you had selected appear in the preview window. On the other hand, if you have nothing selected, everything you have on the page and *partially* on the page is what is saved by the Export For Office process.

The gray checkerboard background to the preview area corresponds to areas of transparency. Vector objects and text have no background, but any bitmaps you created from vector objects will have a white background around them unless you explicitly checked the Transparent Background check box in the Convert To Bitmap dialog when converting the object for export. Bitmaps you imported into your original document that contained transparent backgrounds will retain the transparent areas.

FIGURE 3-12   Use the Office Export dialog to see exactly what an Office user can import.

The drop-down boxes at the top of the dialog are where you make some preparations for the intended use of the exported graphic. To make good choices here, you really need to know what your customer is likely to do with the file. First, you need to know which office suite they will be using the graphics file with: Corel's or Microsoft's. The answer to this question determines which file format you choose in the Export To drop-down list. Also, ask yourself (and your coworker receiving the file): Will you edit this file using the Office suite's tools, or will you just place it in their document as finished work? You also should know what the final destination for their document will be: an onscreen presentation or on the Web, printing to a low-resolution desktop printer or to a professional, commercial printer.

If your customer is using Corel WordPerfect Office, choose that in the Export To drop-down box, and all other options gray out. Your exported file will be saved as a WordPerfect Graphics (WPG) file. The Estimated File Size of the saved WPG file appears at the bottom of the dialog. Click OK and the now-familiar Save As dialog appears with Corel WordPerfect Graphic already selected in the Save As Type drop-down. Navigate to where you want to save your file, give it a name in the File Name field, click Save, and you are done.

3

If your customer uses Microsoft Office, choose that in the Export To drop-down. Next, choose either Compatibility or Editing in the Graphic Should Be Best Suited For drop-down. If you choose Compatibility, your exported file will be saved as a bitmap in the PNG file format. As a bitmap your graphic will look just as you see it onscreen, but it can no longer be edited using vector tools.

If you choose Editing, the file will be saved in the Extended Metafile Format (EMF), which can retain some (but not all) vector information and some CorelDRAW effects. EMF files can be easily edited in Microsoft Office, but fancy effects such as Distort may not travel well or at all, so you will want to open the document yourself in Microsoft Office to see how it looks. As a measure to ensure that the export looks like the original does in CorelDRAW, you might want to make a copy of the graphic, particularly if it has dynamic effects such as Envelopes or Extrude. Then use Arrange | Break Apart and similar commands on the Arrange menu to "genericize" the vector information, adding to the saved file size, but also adding to your chances that an elegant graphic displays in a Word document as you intend it to.

If you choose Compatibility, which will save your work as a bitmap, the Optimized For drop-down needs your attention now. If you choose Editing, the Optimized For drop-down will be grayed out. Here your choices are Presentation, which basically means it will be displayed on a monitor and not printed, or from one of the two print options on the list—Desktop Printing or Commercial Printing. The PNG format bitmap file saved with the Presentation setting saves at 96 dpi; the Desktop Printing setting saves at 150 dpi; and Commercial Printing saves at 300 dpi.

As you make your choices, you will notice that the Estimated File Size changes. As when you selected WordPerfect Office as your export option, click OK to open the Save As dialog where the file type is already selected in the Save As Type drop-down. Navigate to where you want to save your file, give it a name in the File Name field, click Save, deliver the goods, and ask for a (large) check!

Saving, importing, and exporting might not be the most captivating of topics, but they're essential skills that are a prerequisite to your rewards as a CorelDRAW designer. Compare it to the ennui of learning how to use a knife and fork—they're essential to being able to savor the meal that comes after learning Silverware 101! If you've read Chapter 2, you now know where a lot of the Good Stuff is in CorelDRAW's interface, and how to save anything you've created using the Good Stuff. It's logical (and only fair) to take a dip in the deep end of the pool in Chapter 4 with a little supervision and to test-drive this program. We think you'll surprise yourself at what you can accomplish by clicking here and going there; uphill rides can actually be fun, educational, and relaxing when you have this book doing some of the steering for you.

CHAPTER 4

The X4 Test Drive

There are very few guides to software applications where you'll read, "Okay, are you all ready to get going?" in Chapter 4. The *CorelDRAW Official Guide* is one of them: this chapter takes you through the steps you can take to create a *finished* design and print it!

This chapter builds upon what you now know from Chapters 1 and 2 and also serves as a bridge between understanding CorelDRAW's features and putting them to practical use. As a new user of a graphics program, it's only natural for you to poke around tools and palettes to get a feel for what you've purchased: this chapter is a supervised "poking around session." You get hands-on experience with some of the advanced features used to create some basic commercial designs, and learn how to integrate the features to put together a T-shirt logo for a fictitious company—after which you'll probably have the knowledge to apply these techniques to your own company logo.

But overall, this chapter is all about the fun you'll have designing with CorelDRAW. Everyone owns at least one manual that's dry documentation from cover to cover. This book gets your feet wet without going over your head.

Begin a Design with a Concept

One of the most basic rules for creating a good design is to begin with a concept. This might sound strange, and you might be scoffing, "Of course I have a concept! I want to design a logo!" Designing a logo isn't a concept; it's a *need*. To address this need, you'd be best served by visualizing the logo. In this chapter's example, we have a fictitious machine parts company, Gears Depot, and they want all five of their employees to proudly wear the company's logo on T-shirts. The company has a name, but not a logo; therefore, it's thinking-cap time before moving on to CorelDRAW's tools.

One of the simplest and most effective approaches to logo design is through the use of an iconic representation. For example, if you ran an ice cream stand, a very simple and effective logo would be a drawing of an ice cream cone. Don't let the simplicity of this approach put you off: Apple, Inc. has done very well through the years with a logo of you-know-what! What sets apart a logo from every other logo that's a drawing of the vendor's product is the artistic treatment of the design. You can visualize an ice cream cone—it's basically a ball with a triangle beneath it. In CorelDRAW you can draw a circle and a triangle and then apply Artistic Media strokes to the paths to make the drawing look like a child's crayon rendering or a Victorian oil painting. You can copy and paste a dozen copies of the ice cream cone and then use the Arrange | Align And Distribute commands to pepper a page with all 14 flavors the ice cream stand sells. You can extrude the simple shapes and make a 3D ice cream cone; you can apply Fountain Fills to the objects…see how the treatment of a simple geometric shape offers you dozens of logos to choose from?

Along these lines of thinking, Gears Depot would probably visually communicate their logo on a T-shirt with a drawing of a gear. That's the concept; read on to learn how to draw a gear, create a visually stunning *treatment* for the gear design, add some fancy text, and *realize* a concept.

Setting Up the Page for the Logo

Although CorelDRAW can open a new document by default when you launch the program, you're going to need to set up guidelines on a default page so the T-shirt logo design will print edge to edge on a sheet of inkjet transfer paper. If you measure an average T-shirt, you'll see that about 7 inches is a good width for a logo. T-shirt transfer paper you can pick up at an office supply store or even at the supermarket measures full-page letter: 8½ × 11 inches. So you're in luck twice: CorelDRAW's default document size is the same as most T-shirt transfer paper, and the maximum width of the logo will fit the horizontal measure.

The following steps show you how to set up nonprinting guidelines on a default page: T-shirt transfer paper needs about ½ an inch in the clear on all sides so you can peel the transfer from the T-shirt (which still gives us 7½ inches for the maximum design width).

 ## Setting Up Guidelines

1. Launch CorelDRAW, and then from the Welcome Screen, choose New Blank document.

2. You'll probably want to zoom in to the ½-inch tick on the Rulers for precise placement of the guides. Most of us have a scroll wheel on our mouse, and by default CorelDRAW uses the wheel as a zoom feature. Put your cursor at the top left of the page you see in the drawing window, and then push the wheel away from you to zoom into this area. If your mouse doesn't have a scroll wheel, choose the Zoom Tool from the Toolbox (or press Z), and then click-drag an imaginary rectangle around the corner of the page; you drag diagonally (this is called *marquee-dragging* and *marquee-selecting*).

3. You can use any tool to drag guidelines from the Rulers. Place your cursor first over the horizontal Ruler at the top of the drawing window. Click-hold, and then drag from the Ruler onto the page, at the vertical ½-inch tick. If you didn't get it quite right, you need to switch to the Pick Tool (press the SPACEBAR) and then click-drag the guideline to the ½-inch tick mark.

4. Similarly, drag a guideline to the bottom ½-inch margin you'll need, and then drag vertical guidelines out of the vertical Ruler to create vertical margins at ½ an inch inside of the page. Your screen should look like Figure 4-1 now.

5. Click the Save button on the Standard Toolbar. Save the file as **Gears Depot.cdr** to a location on your hard drive you can find later. Don't close the document; we're not having enough fun yet.

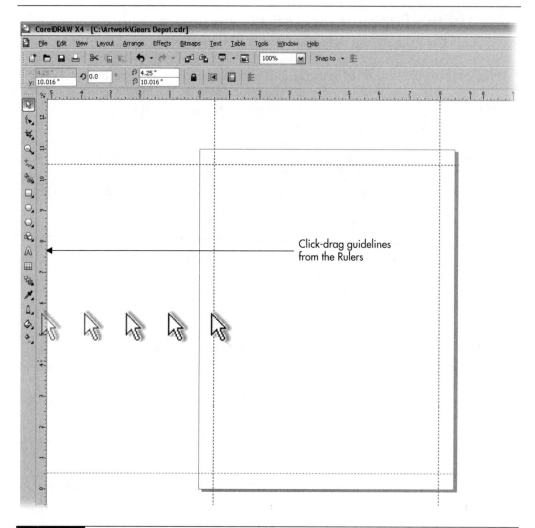

Click-drag guidelines
from the Rulers

FIGURE 4-1   Set up your page so there is a ½-inch margin on all sides for printing to inkjet transfer paper.

Using the Polygon Tool to Design a Gear Shape

The Polygon Tool might not seem like it has features to automatically create a gear shape and this is partially true. The Polygon Tool produces symmetrical shapes that can be dynamically edited; they can be dramatically modified and still keep a special base property.

And gears are symmetrical. The trick to creating a complex-looking gear is to slightly modify a polygon so it becomes a multi-spoke star shape first. Then a control node is added to the outline, and you drag the node to reposition it. This is one of those things it's easier to see while you do, but in the following steps, you'll modify a polygon you create so that the spokes end in a blunt, straight edge instead of a point. This gets you 90 percent of the way to creating an elegant gear shape (the other 10 percent is demonstrated in the following sections).

Creating and Modifying a Polygon

4

1. Choose the Polygon Tool from the Toolbox (it's just below the Ellipse Tool).

2. On the Property Bar, set the number of sides to 16. This will produce a polygon with 16 control points and control points in-between.

3. Hold CTRL (this constrains the shape to equal width and height), and then click-drag on the page until the width and height fields on the Property Bar (the second-from-left fields) tell you the shape you're creating is about 5½ inches. At this point, release CTRL and your mouse button. Your polygon should look like the illustration here.

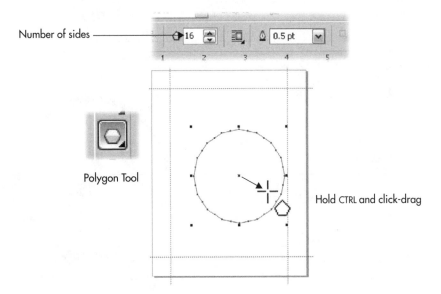

Number of sides

Polygon Tool

Hold CTRL and click-drag

4. Choose the Shape Tool; hold CTRL, click on one of the control points along the path of the polygon, and then drag until the result is a star shape, shown here. The reason for holding CTRL as you drag is that it keeps the control point from drifting to the

left or right as you move it. Otherwise this would produce a radial saw blade shape and not a star whose path segments mirror each other.

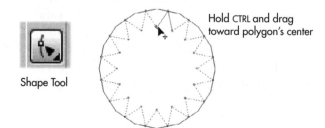

Shape Tool

Hold CTRL and drag toward polygon's center

5. With the Shape Tool still active, click a point on the path, as shown in Figure 4-2. Then click the Add Node(s) button on the Property Bar. You've created a change in the property of the path, although it doesn't look like a change yet. The polygon can still be dynamically reshaped. Look closely at the polygon path—you added a control node, but there are actually 16 added control nodes, because you made a change to a dynamic object.

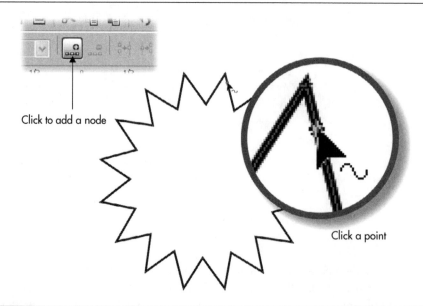

Click to add a node

Click a point

FIGURE 4-2   When you add a node to a polygon object, additional nodes are created symmetrically around the shape.

6. Take your time on this step: with the Shape Tool, drag the top control node a little to the left and then a little down. Stop when you have the shape shown here. The polygon looks very much like a 16-tooth gear now, doesn't it?

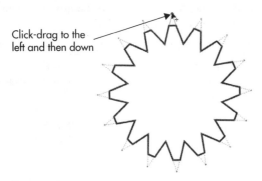

Click-drag to the
left and then down

4

Using Shaping Operations to Massage the Design

At present, no one is going to want this drawing of a gear to go into *any* piece of machinery: there's no hole for a shaft, and those teeth need a deeper groove in-between them. These two minor manufacturing defects are easily solved through the use of CorelDRAW's Shaping operations, available from the Arrange menu but also from the Property Bar when two or more objects are selected. In the following steps, you'll use two Shaping operations—Weld and Trim—that you'll definitely use in future assignments of your own.

Shaping the Polygon

1. Choose the Ellipse Tool from the Toolbox.

2. Try to position the cursor in the center of the polygon object; you'll see how to perfectly align the new shape to the polygon in a moment, so don't sweat precision.

3. Hold SHIFT+CTRL and then drag away from the polygon until the circle intersects the teeth of the polygon, as shown here. Pressing CTRL in this step constrains the ellipse to a circle, and using SHIFT creates the circle from the center outward.

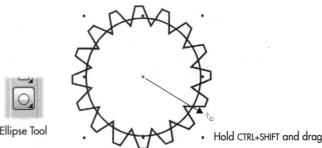

Ellipse Tool

Hold CTRL+SHIFT and drag

4. Press CTRL+A to Select All (in this case, "all" consists of two objects).

5. Press P. This command is the keyboard shortcut to Arrange | Align And Distribute | Center To Page. Your objects are aligned to each other's centers, and if you enjoy digging through application menus as much as you enjoy root canal work, remembering this keyboard shortcut is a good idea.

6. Choose the Pick Tool from the Toolbox. With both objects selected, click the Weld button on the Property Bar, as shown here. You have a single shape now, and the teeth on the gear look more pronounced and don't need root canal work.

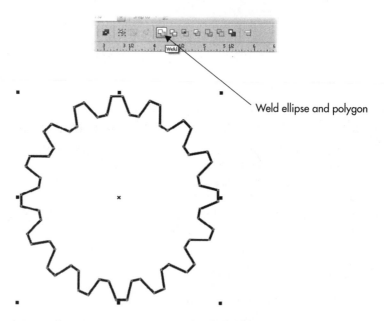

Weld ellipse and polygon

7. Let's put a hole in the gear now; a circular hole would make the gear work best. With the Ellipse Tool and nothing selected on the page, hold SHIFT+CTRL and then drag, starting at the center of the gear shape, and then stop when you feel this new circle is large enough to serve as a hole in the gear. If you designed the gear as recommended earlier to about 5½ inches, a 2½-inch circle will work.

8. Press CTRL+A and then press P; the gear and the circle are now centered relative to each other, and both are centered on the page.

9. While both objects are selected, it might be a good idea to give the objects a fill so you can see them better. On the Color Palette, left-click on a light color swatch: these are called *color wells* in CorelDRAW. Your objects are now filled with the same color.

10. On the Property Bar, click the Trim button, as shown in the following illustration. The Trim Shaping operation removes sections of an object that is underneath/behind another object on the page, and leaves the circle, commonly called the Source Object. With the Pick Tool, select the shape you no longer need and then press CTRL+X to delete it. This means you can use Trim to remove only parts of an underlying object by arranging a top object to only slightly overlap it; however, in this example, because the new circle is completely on top of the polygon, it's completely "drilled through" the polygon.

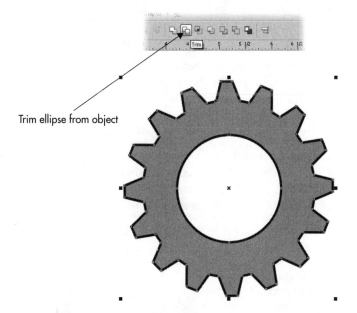

Trim ellipse from object

A Brief Excursion into Gradient Fills

You've probably seen some slick logos whose shapes have a metallic appearance, with really smooth color transitions reminiscent of traditional airbrush work. In CorelDRAW, the effect is accomplished through the use of Fountain Fills, and you're going to apply one next to the gear shape. Fountain Fills come in many different styles: they make a transition over an object's shape from one color to a different color, black to white, for example. Fountain Fill color transitions can move across an object in a linear style, circularly, and in a host of other directions. For this example, let's stick to the default of Linear—all the features covered in this Test Drive are cross-referenced at the end of this chapter.

Follow these steps to get hands-on experience with the Interactive Fill Tool.

Creating a Metallic Finish Using Fountain Fills

1. Choose the Interactive Fill Tool from the Toolbox.

2. Click the gear shape to select it, and then click-drag down and to the left (drag toward about 7 o'clock on the gear shape); then release the mouse button. By default, the end of the Linear Fountain Fill (the place where you released the mouse) is white, so whatever color you chose in the previous example to fill the shape in the gear makes a transition to white.

3. Let's say you're not thrilled with the *From* color, the beginning color of the Fountain Fill. To change the color, while the Interactive Fill Tool is still selected and you can still see the control handles for the fill above the gear drawing, click on the tiny From color marker—it's marked with the color you chose in the previous tutorial. Now the color is highlighted and available for editing. Click a color on the Color Palette that you really like for the beginning of the Fountain Fill.

4. Now let's say that the color transition between From and To in the Fountain Fill isn't dramatic enough, but you do like the two colors. Adjust the midpoint of the fill by dragging on the midpoint control, shown in Figure 4-3. You drag it toward the From color marker to emphasize the To color in the fill, and vice versa.

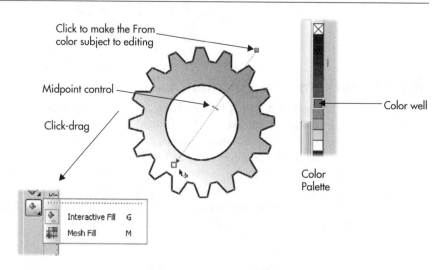

FIGURE 4-3 Use the Interactive Fill Tool to embellish your illustration.

5. The gear is looking terrific now (and it's going to look *more* terrificer by the end of the chapter), but the outline width is a little on the meek side. Press the SPACEBAR to switch to the Pick Tool, and then on the Property Bar you can see on the right side there's a Pen icon and a width drop-down box; this is the outline width control for single objects on the page. You won't see this box when two or more objects are selected, but today you're in luck: choose 3 (points) from the drop-down selector to add heft to your illustration.

 Pressing the SPACEBAR toggles your current tool to the Pick Tool; a second press of the SPACEBAR toggles you back to the last tool you were using.

6. Press CTRL+S to save your work up to this point. In fact, just make it a practice to save your work every 10 minutes or so; it's only two keystrokes.

Going 3D

Although CorelDRAW is a drawing program and not a modeling application such as 3D Studio, you can indeed get dimensional effects with the Extrude Tool to make a simple drawing such as this gear pop off the page (or off a T-shirt). The following sections take you through a basic and then an advanced editing technique that will make your audience wonder how on Earth you accomplished this logo by reading one chapter in a book!

Using the Interactive Extrude Tool

The Interactive Extrude Tool is a basic tool for defining edges that appear to extend into the third dimension of space, adding depth to the height and width of the object to which you apply this tool. However, once you've added depth to a selected object, it might not be apparent to you or your audience that this is a 3D shape because of the way it's "posed" on the drawing page. By default the Interactive Extrude Tool creates edges that appear mostly behind the extruded shape, because of an optical principle known as a vanishing point. A *vanishing point* (tell your friends you know that da Vinci discovered vanishing points) is the point in 3D space where, if you drew lines marking the angles of an object with depth, the lines would converge. You see vanishing points all the time: say you're standing on train tracks when a train isn't coming, and you look straight down the tracks. Where the rails converge is the vanishing point.

Similarly, to get the most out of the Extrude feature in CorelDRAW, you want to view an extruded shape off-axis, not straight-on, because looking at objects directly face-front removes the *perspective* from the object, flattening it in appearance. CorelDRAW has additional features after you've made a shape into an extruded shape, one of which is a rotation feature—yes, you *can* rotate a 3D object on your drawing page—to show off all three angles of the extruded shape. An object viewed in ¾ view shows off the most visual detail (this is why portrait photographers try to get customers to point their head off-camera), and the following tutorial takes you through object extruding, rotating, and how to interactively adjust the depth of the object you extrude.

TIP · *Extruded sides of an object by default inherit the fill from the parent object. Therefore, because the gear in this example has a Fountain Fill, do the objects that make up the sides of the gear. This is a good trick to quickly shade a 3D object, adding more dimension.*

Making a Logo into a 3D Logo

1. With the gear selected on the drawing page, click-hold on the Effects group button on the Toolbox to reveal the flyout that has the Extrude Tool. This group is just above the familiar-shaped Eyedropper Tool. Select the Interactive Extrude Tool from the group on the Toolbox.

2. Click-drag *just a little,* straight down on the object, as shown in Figure 4-4. *Just a little* does the trick—you're establishing an extruded object and setting a *vanishing point* for the object at the same time. *Resist* the temptation that accompanies the natural thought, "the more I click-drag, the more extruded the gear will be." Nope—the more you drag, the farther the vanishing point is defined relative to the object, and it's very easy to set the vanishing point clear off the page, and possibly extend it to the Theophilus crater on the moon.

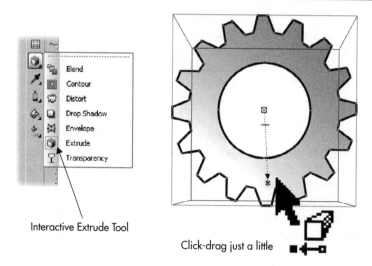

Interactive Extrude Tool

Click-drag just a little

FIGURE 4-4 The Interactive Extrude Tool is used to set a third dimension for your object. Other features help you set an angle of rotation and the depth of the object.

3. Look at the Property Bar now. There's one button that is divided into its own group by the vertical dividers; this is the Extrude Rotation option—click the button and a palette extends that features a *3* that you can click-drag to rotate the gear. Rotate the gear now by dragging up and to the right, aiming at about 2 o'clock. You can see the result in Figure 4-5. Most likely, the gear is a little too deep, too thick to fit into most gearboxes; this is what the Depth control marker, which you'll use in the next step, is for.

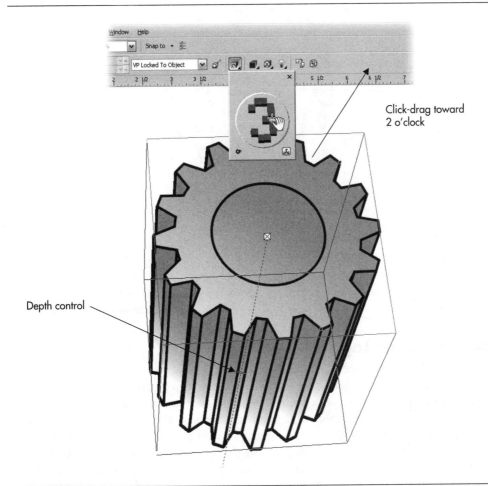

FIGURE 4-5   Use the Extrude Rotation feature on the Property Bar to make the gear truly three-dimensional in appearance.

4. Click-drag the marker shown in the following illustration toward the gear to decrease its depth. Dragging it away from the gear makes it deeper, and although this is illuminating advice, you will probably never need to make an extruded shape fatter. Also note that the vanishing-point line, the light blue dotted line, extends way off the page. This is of absolutely no consequence in your design work. The vanishing point does not print, and if your gear illustration looks fine right now, it is fine, regardless of onscreen guides.

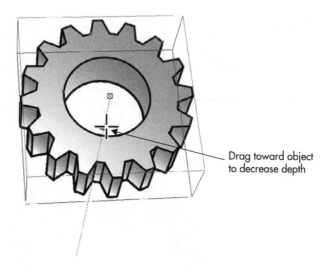

Drag toward object
to decrease depth

 At any time in the future, you can change the rotation of the extruded shape, as well as the depth—it's a dynamically editable object. To quickly display the Property Bar options and the depth control marker on the object, and switch to the Interactive Extrude Tool, you double-click on the object with the Pick Tool.

Adding Text to the Logo

We might call this assignment finished, since you now have a stunning 3D gear in the document. But this assignment is for a logo, not for an icon that really would serve an advertising purpose only if it were painted on a shingle above a store in a hamlet in the 1600s. You need *text* to accompany the graphic: a fancy Artistic Text title above the graphic will serve the purpose of a logo quite well, and in smaller text the address of the store will lessen the need of the viewing audience to ask the person wearing the T-shirt for directions.

In the following sections, you'll use another effect, the Envelope feature, which can mold a headline around an object, creating an integrated design and catching an equal amount of audience attention. Then you'll put this Test Drive into full-gear by trying out the Fit Text On Path feature—taking a string of text and making it run circles around a graphic.

Creating an Envelope Shape

The first pit stop during the Test Drive is to get the Text Tool, which operates very much like a word processor's text tool, to create a headline to apply an envelope to. CorelDRAW's Envelope feature is dynamic, just like Extrude and the Polygon Tool, so you can shape and reshape an object until you're happy with the result. However, for this assignment, a shape needs to be created into which the headline "Gears Depot" will be poured. This part of the Test Drive is called "building upon what you've learned." You'll use the Trim Shaping feature in the next steps to create a shape for headline text out of a rectangle and an ellipse.

Making a Headline/Enveloping the Headline

1. Choose the Text Tool from the Toolbox, the button with the *A* on it.

2. Click an insertion point on the page, just above the gear.

3. Type in all caps (hold SHIFT): **GEARS DEPOT**. By default, Artistic Text is created and Artistic Text is editable, but basically it's a malleable object, just like the gear. It's also by default 24 points in height and Arial, which is not an exciting font compared with the marvelous gear for the logo, shown in Figure 4-6.

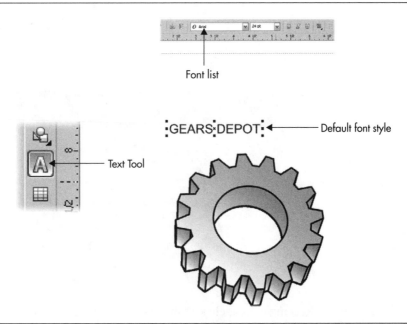

Font list

Text Tool

Default font style

| FIGURE 4-6 | Default Artistic Text is always Arial 24 point. But you can easily change text to any font you have installed on your system. |

4. Choose the Pick Tool; the text remains selected and you can see the font choice and the point size up on the Property Bar. (Unlike with a word processor, to change the font used in text you have typed, you don't need to first highlight a whole word with the Text Tool; highlighting is done to change only a word in a string of text or a character in a word.) Choose a bold, condensed font from the Font selector drop-down list; any font you have installed on your system is fine for this Test Drive. As you can see in the following illustration, Gothic 821 Cn BT, which is on the CorelDRAW CD (the one with Photos and fonts) works well at about 75 points. To increase the size of the text, you can type 75 in the Size field and then press ENTER, or you can drag a corner bounding-box handle that surrounds an object selected using the Pick Tool. To increase the size of an object, you drag the corner bounding-box handle (one of the black squares) away from the shape, and to decrease the size, you drag toward the shape.

5. With the Rectangle Tool, click-drag a rectangle, beginning at the left side of the text, ending at the right side, and bisecting the gear so what you see onscreen is a rectangle slicing the top half of the gear.

6. With the Ellipse Tool, start at the left edge of the gear; click-drag so you have a wide ellipse whose top sort of outlines the top of the gear and so the ellipse intersects the rectangle.

7. With the Pick Tool, SHIFT-click the rectangle, the text, and the ellipse. You now have a new button displayed on the Property Bar; a shortcut to the Arrange | Align And Distribute command. Click it, and to keep these objects tidy and aligned vertically, click the Center button as shown in Figure 4-7; then click Apply. While holding SHIFT, click the text to deselect it. Now only the ellipse and the rectangle are selected, they're aligned vertically, and you're all set to create an envelope shape for the text.

8. Click the Trim button, as shown in Figure 4-8. With the Pick Tool, select the spare ellipse that is kept on the page after the Trim operation, and then delete it (CTRL+X). The new shape will serve as the shape for the text when you envelope it.

9. One entry above the Extrude Tool in the Effects group on the Toolbox is the Interactive Envelope Tool; choose it and then select the text with your cursor. You'll see a faint dashed blue outline around the text now.

Align And Distribute

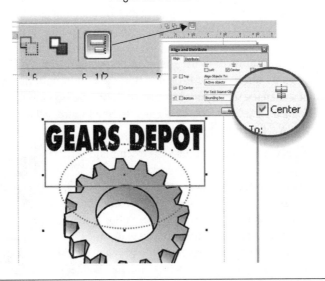

FIGURE 4-7   Align the objects so they're vertically centered using Align And Distribute.

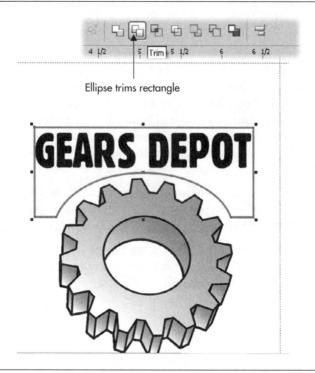

Ellipse trims rectangle

FIGURE 4-8 Subtract a partially overlapping shape to create the envelope template for the text.

10. To make the text conform to the shape you created in step 8, click the Create Envelope From button on the Property Bar, the button with the eyedropper icon. Your cursor changes to a really large arrow, and you now click on the shape you created by trimming the rectangle in step 8. See Figure 4-9 as a reference for all the stuff going on with your logo work.

11. As you can see, the shape you used as a template for the Envelope effect is still in the workspace—the Create Envelope effect doesn't actually use the shape, but instead copies the shape. And the Envelope effect might or might not have taken hold; if you don't see the effect immediately, but only a preview outline, click on a node or a path segment of the preview (the blue dashed outline) and give it a little nudge. The text should look like that shown in this illustration. The envelope can be edited using the Shape Tool now; you can click-drag any of the control nodes to modify the shape of the text, if needed.

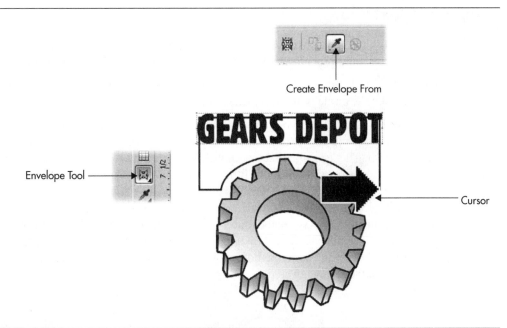

Create Envelope From

Envelope Tool

Cursor

| FIGURE 4-9 | Envelopes can be copied from existing envelopes, and they can be based on existing shapes. |

The shape on your drawing page has served its purpose; you can delete it by clicking on it with the Pick Tool and then pressing CTRL+X. Also, you might want to move the enveloped text closer to the gear illustration. To do this and get your hands on another feature in CorelDRAW during this Test Drive, select the text with the Pick Tool and then press the arrow keys on the keyboard. This is called *nudging* an object, which can be more precise than click-dragging an object to move it.

Fitting Text to a Path

To polish off the design, let's add a fictitious address and telephone number to the T-shirt logo. As mentioned earlier, you can fit text to a path in any CorelDRAW design: all you need is some text…and a path. For this logo, it would look nice to put the address and phone number in an arc along the bottom of the gear; you'll create a circle as the path. Here's how to take what you already know and apply a new effect in a creative way that reinforces the integration of the different elements in the logo.

Running Text Along a Circle

1. With the Ellipse Tool, position your cursor over the center of the gear illustration: the address should probably, artistically, revolve around the "hero" of the logo.

2. Hold SHIFT+CTRL and then drag away from your starting point. Release the mouse button when the circle is about 6 inches in size.

3. With the Text Tool, hover your cursor (move it around, but don't click) over the bottom of the circle until it turns into an I-beam with a tiny *A* with a curved line underneath it. This is a sign that CorelDRAW has detected a shape on the page and that it rightly assumes you want to fit text along the path. You could use the Text | Fit Text To Path command in CorelDRAW to fit selected existing text to a selected existing object, but it's not necessary when you can work live here. Click an insertion point and then type any address and telephone number. The text flows along the path of the circle, as shown in the illustration below, but it's upside-down because you're fitting text to the bottom and not to the top of the circle, which is easy to fix in the following steps.

Fit Text To Path cursor

4. On the Property Bar you can clearly see the Mirror Text buttons. If this text was scooted to the top of the circle, life would be great; however, as is, the text is both upside-down and backwards, from a reading point of view. Click the Mirror Vertically button, and then click the Mirror Horizontally button. As you can see in Figure 4-10, the address looks fine now.

5. There's no real need to delete the circle from the document; all you need to do to complete the logo is to assign the circle no width. Geometrically, you can have a shape with no attributes, and this can be done very quickly by right-clicking the "X" color well on the Color Palette. Since *left*-clicking assigns *fills,* and *right*-clicking assigns *outline colors,* and that empty well above black on the default Color Palette assigns emptiness, left-click for no fill; right-click for no outline.

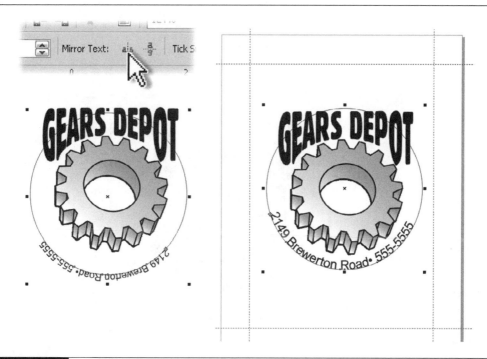

FIGURE 4-10   Flip your text along a path to make your message read correctly.

Align, Group, Scale, Flip, and Print

You're already familiar with most of the techniques covered in the upcoming tutorial that shows how to do one or two minor things to the finished logo to make it print-worthy. Yes, you're coming up to home base and concluding the X4 Test Drive, but let's make this assignment a top-to-bottom, complete excursion. Follow these steps to brush up the logo design a little, and to set it up for output to an inkjet printer.

Getting Your Logo Design into the Real World

1. You currently have the text on the (invisible) path, the gear illustration, and the headline on the page: that's three objects you want to print (it's always good to take a tally periodically). Marquee-select the object using the Pick Tool. The Status Bar at the bottom of the interface should say "5 Objects selected on Layer 1": the Extruded gear is actually two objects—the control shape and the extrusion, grouped so this is okay—the invisible path the address is fitted to, the text itself, and the headline. Press CTRL+G to group all the selected shapes.

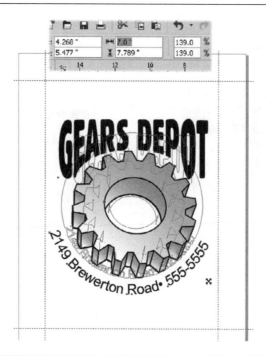

FIGURE 4-11 Make the grouped objects fit to maximum page safety, and then center the group.

2. Let's get our money's worth out of the print by making the logo that 7 inches maximum that was agreed upon at the beginning of the chapter (okay, you might not have actually agreed, but play along here). With the group selected, type **7** in the horizontal width field on the Property Bar and then press ENTER, as shown in Figure 4-11. Then press P to center the design relative to the page.

3. T-shirt transfers need to be printed as the reverse of the imprint; that is, the text needs to be mirrored so that when the inkjet page is ironed onto the shirt, it reverses back again to legibility. Click the Mirror Horizontally button on the Property Bar, which is easy enough to undo later if your logo is needed for a promotion other than T-shirts. See the next illustration.

4. Put a piece of *regular paper* in the inkjet printer and print a copy of the design. Press CTRL+P, choose the correct printer, and then click Print. This is a "proof of concept" print—T-shirt transfers cost about a dollar each while plain paper costs significantly less, cheaper still if you print on the backside of a page that has already been printed with something expendable. If everything seems to be satisfactory with the test print, do it for real with the T-shirt transfer paper.

With the exception of that all-night pizzeria around the corner, all good things must come to an end. You've passed the Test Drive; you're home safe and didn't dent a fender; and the best part is: you get to pocket the keys. You're going to need them when you take this high-performance Model X4 out on your own and take the bends and curves in the chapters to come!

The Test Drive Cross-Reference

You haven't really broken in all the features and tools covered in this chapter, so here are the signposts to learn more about the editing and transforming you performed in this chapter:

- Aligning and Distributing Objects: Chapter 12
- Extruding Objects: Chapter 25

- Guidelines and Rulers: Chapter 6

- The Envelope Tool: Chapter 20

- Working with Text: Chapters 13 and 14

- Filling Objects: Chapter 17

See Chapters 2 and 3 for the basics on the Color Palette, and for saving and opening documents. But you probably already know this stuff.

PART II

Getting Started with CorelDRAW X4

CHAPTER 5

Working with Single- and Multi-Page Documents

You have an idea for promoting your product or service; you have your graphics and you have some body copy and a snappy headline in mind. The next logical step is defining the space within which you express your promotional idea. Do you need a flyer? Or perhaps a four-page booklet? This chapter covers one of the most important aspects of any project: setting up pages in CorelDRAW. You'll learn about layout styles, page dimensions for your screen and for printing, page reordering, and in the process, gain a good working knowledge of what you need to do—and what you can have CorelDRAW do—to create a page that suits your ideas.

Setting Up Your Document Page

Every new file you create, every file your coworker shares with you, and every CorelDRAW template you use has its own set of *page properties* that have two attributes: physical properties and display preferences. The *physical properties* refer to the size, length, and color of each page. *Display preferences* control how page values are viewed. Let's begin with the most common options and then move on to the more specialized features.

Page Viewing Options

With CorelDRAW at its default settings, when you choose File | New, you'll see a rectangle in the workspace. This rectangle represents your document page in height and width. However, what you *won't* see are two other page display features, which have to do with how your page will be printed to a personal printer or to a commercial press. These features are called the *Printable Area* and the *Bleed Area*. You certainly want these features visible when designing for print; pages don't print edge-to-edge, and you don't want your designs or text to be partially cropped out. To set visibility of these Page properties, in the Options dialog choose Layout | Page Setup to display the Size page. Then click Page in the tree directory on the left side of the dialog to reveal your page display options as shown.

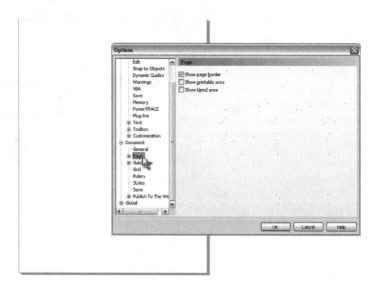

Show Page Border

You can show the edges of the page by checking the Show Page Border box. The printable area and bleed area options are for showing safety margins for printing your document.

Show Printable Area

The Show Printable Area check box in the Options dialog toggles the display between two key things—the area onto which your currently selected printer is capable of printing and the size of the printing material your printer is currently set to use. Both are represented by dotted lines.

The printable area for a personal inkjet or laser printer is typically defined by a margin inside the page border, and its placement is dependent upon how the printer physically puts pigment or toner on a page. For example, a laser printer can usually print up to ¼ inch inside the paper fed through it; however, it's not a good idea to plan your page designs to this margin (because there's always a margin of error). If you are printing to a borderless photo printer, your printable area will be the same size as your page border.

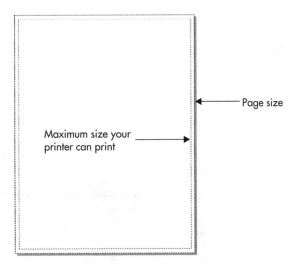

Commercial printing presses can print to material or paper stock sizes much larger than the letter size most personal printers use, as shown by the dotted lines in Figure 5-1. But like personal printers, commercial printers *won't* encompass an area as large as the material or paper stock sheets themselves because the press needs a bit of space to grip and move the paper through the press.

These two unique boundaries, printable area and the size of the printing material, can appear inside or outside your document page, depending on whether your current page size is larger or smaller than what your printer and printing material (paper, perforated business-card stock, T-shirt transfer paper, and so on) are capable of reproducing. The properties of

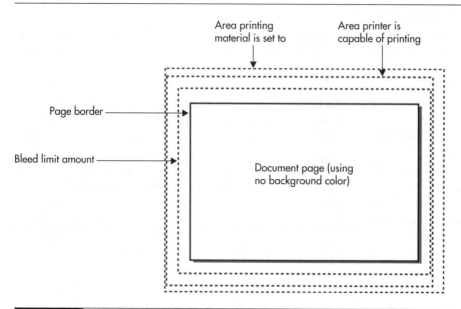

FIGURE 5-1 The Show Printable Area command toggles between page size and your printer's maximum printing margin.

these two sets of dimensions are defined and displayed by the printer options you choose in the Print Setup dialog, opened by choosing File | Print Setup, as shown.

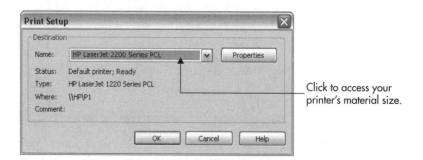

Show Bleed Area

Bleed is a printer's term for the margin between the outside edges of your design and the dimensions of what you're printing on. Bleed is frequently used to contain an unimportant excess amount of a design that is later trimmed to the final dimensions of what you need printed. If you've chosen to add a page background or have objects overlapping the edge of your document page, increasing the bleed amount enables you to include more of these areas on the printed output material. To toggle display of the currently set bleed amount, click the Show Bleed Area option in the Options dialog. If the bleed area displayed on your page looks wrong—for example, it's wide and your page is tall—you need to go to Print Setup and change the orientation of the page your printer is set up to use, Portrait (tall) or Landscape (wide), usually.

 Setting the bleed amount is done using the Size area of the Options box, under Page options, using the Bleed option num box. The bleed amount can be defined anywhere between 0 (the exact edge of your page) and 900 inches.

 ## Tutorial: Creating Your Own Bleed Designs Using Your Home Printer

5

Suppose you have a need for an elegant No. 10 envelope whose design bleeds at the left side. With the knowledge you now have about bleeds and the printable page size, you can create a bleed envelope using your home laser or inkjet printer.

1. Choose File | Print Setup; then choose Properties, Advanced. In the Paper Size drop-down list, choose Envelope #10. Click the OK buttons until you're back in CorelDRAW. Then in File | Print Setup | Properties, choose Landscape Orientation.

2. While the Pick Tool is selected (but no objects on the page are selected), choose Letter from the Page Size drop-down list on the Property Bar, and then click the Landscape Orientation button.

3. Place your design within the page border, but overlapping the printable page area in the position in which you want the design to bleed to the left, as shown in Figure 5-2.

4. Add an address and then choose File | Print (CTRL+P).

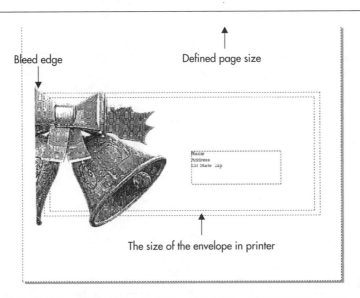

FIGURE 5-2 Creating the bleed design on the envelope

Controlling Page Size and Orientation

The default size whenever a new document is created is U.S. Letter, 8 1/2" by 11", but this can be changed in a number of ways. The quickest method is via the Property Bar while the Pick Tool—and no objects—are selected. The Property Bar features options for setting your page to standard-sized pages, custom sizes, and orientation, as seen in Figure 5-3. In case you have a multi-page document, the Property Bar also has ways to change all pages at once, or only the currently visible page.

The Paper Type/Size and orientation options control the format for your document. When you have a specific format for a design you need to print, the following sections cover the options available to you in CorelDRAW X4.

Paper Type/Size

To choose a standard page size, clicking a Paper Type/Size option in the Property Bar is the quickest method; from the drop-down box you have Letter, Legal, Tabloid, and so on. If you have a limited need for different paper sizes, click the Edit This List button at the bottom of the drop-down list, and you can delete seldom-used sizes by clicking Delete Page Size in the

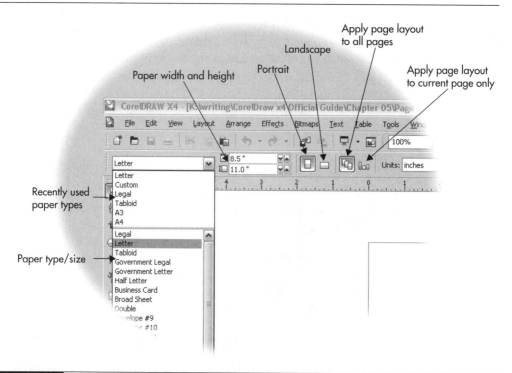

FIGURE 5-3   You change page size and orientation by using the Property Bar.

Options box. Once you've made a selection, the dimensions are automatically entered as values into the Page Width and Height boxes in the Property Bar.

- **Page Width and Height**   For a custom page size, type specific values directly into the Page Width and Height boxes, and then press ENTER. Both page width and height values can be between 0.00333 and 1,800 inches.

- **Landscape/Portrait Orientation**   Clicking either Portrait or Landscape in the Property Bar while using the Pick Tool (and no objects selected) sets the page orientation. If the page width you enter is smaller than the page height entered, the orientation is automatically set to Portrait, and vice versa for Landscape. Changing from Portrait to Landscape (or vice versa) automatically switches the values in the Page Width and Height fields.

- **Set For All Pages/Set For Current Page Only**   In CorelDRAW X4, you can create a document up to 999 pages long, with different pages set to any size or orientation. The Set For All Pages and Set Current Page Only buttons operate in "either/or" fashion like the orientation buttons, enabling you to set the page size either for all pages in your document at once (the default) or only for the current page. To set only the current page to be different from the others in your document, click the lower of these two buttons and set your new page size and orientation as needed. Other pages in the document aren't resized when you choose this option.

Controlling Page Background Color

To specify a page background color for your document, choose Layout | Page Background (CTRL+J) to open the Options dialog to the Background page.

- **Solid**   Choose this option and a color from the selector to specify any uniform color as the page background. Click Other in the color selector to use a color picker in different color models (RGB, CMYK, and so on), a mixer, or a specific color palette. Once a color has been chosen, the page background is set to that color, but the bleed area and the workspace are not.

- **Bitmap**   Choose this option to use a bitmap as the page background. Click the Browse button to open the CorelDRAW Import dialog, and locate and choose a bitmap. Background bitmaps are tiled as many times as needed to fill the page. You can also scale the number of repeating tiles by clicking the Custom Size radio button and entering values. The best bitmaps to use for patterns are ones that have been designed to tile seamlessly. In Figure 5-4, you can see an application of a Background Bitmap that is muted in tone (and therefore is suitable for white headline text) and that was designed to seamlessly repeat. The Bitmap option is terrific for creating several different signs or stationery that contain different text but must be tied together in a theme. You might, for example, create different text on layers such as "Autumn Clearance," "Autumn Sales," and "Autumn Harvest," and then print different signs by hiding all but one layer for printing. You can't accidentally move the Background, and this technique is quick to set up when you have 12 different messages that need a common background.

- **Source** The Source options let you establish an external link to the bitmap file or store a copy of it internally with your CorelDRAW X4 document file. Choose Linked to maintain an external link or Embedded to store the bitmap with your document. While Linked is selected, the file path to the bitmap is displayed, and the bitmap itself must be available to CorelDRAW during printing. This option is very useful when you need to conserve on saved CorelDRAW file sizes; additionally, you can modify the Background bitmap in PHOTO-PAINT or Painter, and then reload the edited bitmap in the future.

- **Bitmap Size** This field contains "either/or" radio buttons. If you choose Default Size, the Background appears on the page because the bitmap's original dimensions allow it to tile as many times as needed to fill the page. However, if you want a smaller bitmap as the Background (more tiles), you click the Custom Size button.

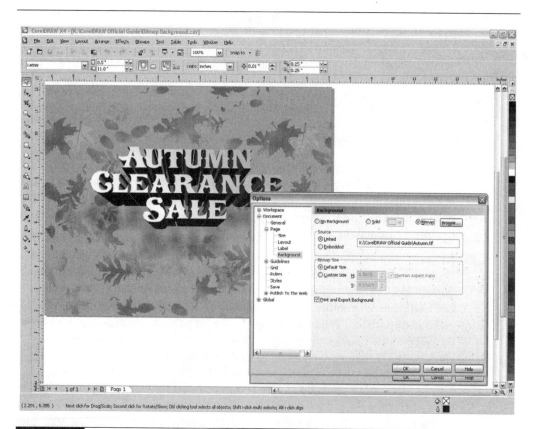

FIGURE 5-4 Use a bitmap as a Background for your design and text.

The Maintain Aspect Ratio option is checked by default; you probably don't want the bitmap Background to look smooshed or stretched—with Maintain Aspect Ratio turned on, all you need to do is enter one value in either the H or V field, and CorelDRAW automatically fills in the remaining field. Note that bitmaps are resolution dependent, unlike vector drawings. Thus, you can usually scale a bitmap down, but don't try to enlarge it because the bitmap will go through something called resampling, and blurriness is often the result. Scale down = yes; scale up = no.

- **Print and Export Background**   Use this option to control whether the page background you've added to your document page is included when exporting your drawing files or when you print the document. It's available when either Solid or Bitmap is selected for the page background; by default it's active.

Using Layouts and Labels

The Property Bar is used to set up the basic page and paper sizes and orientation. But designers often need to lay out designs for items such as labels, booklets, tent cards, and greeting cards that are printed on standard size paper, but that are definitely *not* laid out like a single-page flyer. So you don't have to sit at your workstation all day folding paper to try to figure out exactly where the fold lines are and where the text needs to be upside down. CorelDRAW X4 provides specialized layouts that are just a few clicks away. These timesavers are not on the Property Bar—you need to open the Options dialog to select the one you need from the Layout drop-down box.

Choosing Specialized Layouts

On the Layout page of the Options dialog, you can choose from seven specialized layouts for your document, including Full Page, Book, Booklet, Tent Card, Tri-Fold Brochure, Side-Fold Card, and Top-Fold Card.

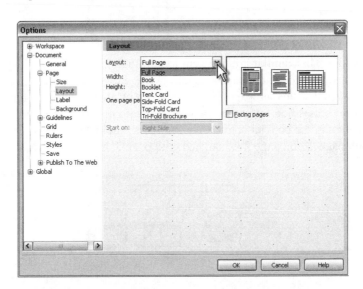

Choosing one of these layout styles instantly divides the current document page size into horizontal and vertical pages, based on the preview supplied in the dialog.

■ **Full Page** This layout style is the default for all new documents, and it formats your document in single pages, like those shown here.

■ **Book** The Book layout format, shown right, divides your document page size into two equal vertical portions, and each portion is considered a separate page. When printed, each page is output as a separate page.

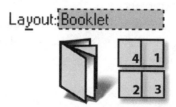

■ **Booklet** In a similar arrangement to the Book layout, the Booklet layout format divides your document page size into two equal vertical portions. Each portion is considered a separate page. However, when printed, pages are paired according to typical imposition formatting, where pages are matched according to their final position in the booklet layout. In a four-page booklet, this means page 1 is matched with page 4, and page 2 is matched with page 3, as shown at right.

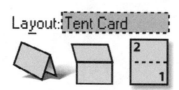

■ **Tent Card**   The Tent Card layout format, shown at right, divides your document page size into two equal horizontal portions, while each portion is considered a separate page. Because tent card output is folded in the center, each of your document pages is printed in sequence and positioned to appear upright after folding.

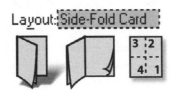

■ **Side-Fold Card**   The Side-Fold layout format divides your document page size into four equal parts, vertically and horizontally. When printed, each document page is printed in sequence, and positioned and rotated to fit the final folded layout. Folding the printed page vertically, then horizontally results in the correct sequence and orientation.

■ **Top-Fold Card**   Like the Side-Fold layout, the Top-Fold layout format also divides your document page size into four equal parts, vertically and horizontally. When printed, each document page is printed in sequence, and positioned and rotated to fit the final folded layout.

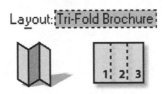

■ **Tri-Fold Brochure**   Set your page orientation to Landscape using File | Print Setup, and you then have the ideal layout for travel brochures and restaurant tabletop stand-up menus. You can print both sides for a total of six panels, with live space measuring about 3 1/2" wide and 8" high on the end panels.

After you choose a layout style and return to your document, each subdivision of the layout can be viewed individually. You can also view pages in pairs by choosing the Facing Pages option in the Layout page of the Options dialog for several layout styles. When Facing Pages is selected in the dialog, you also have the opportunity to start your document on either the Left side or Right side for some layout styles by making a selection from the Start On menu.

Using Preformatted Labels

CorelDRAW X4 has a comprehensive collection of label formats for preformatted paper stock, from vendors such as Avery, Ace, and Leitz. To use most of these label formats, your document page should be formatted to *letter-sized portrait*; otherwise, the Labels option in the Size page of the Options dialog is unavailable. Once you've clicked the Labels radio button, the Size page turns into the Label page, offering access to the label collection. After you've selected a specific label format, the preview window shows its general layout and indicates the number of rows and columns available as shown in Figure 5-5.

After you choose a label format and return to your document, each of your document pages will represent an individual label. You'll need to add the exact number of pages to accommodate all of your labels. If you don't see the exact manufacturer for your specific label type, you can create your own from scratch or base it on an existing label format (see Figure 5-5). Choose an existing label from the Label Types menu; click Customize Label; set the number of Rows and Columns; and set the Label Size, Margins, and Gutters

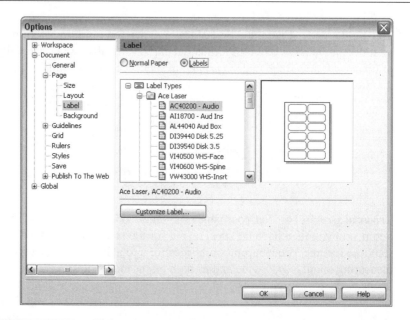

FIGURE 5-5 CorelDRAW X4 has just the preformatted label template you need.

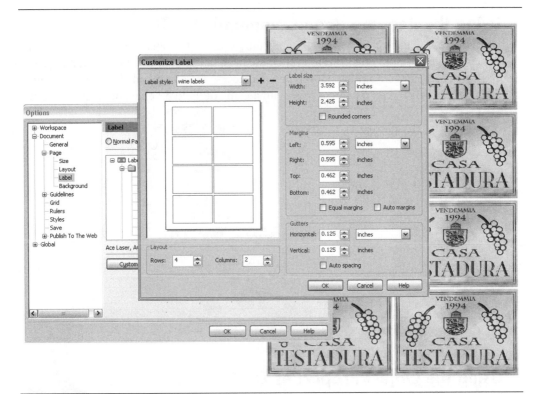

FIGURE 5-6 If you don't find the label you need, modify an existing label using the options.

according to your own label sheet. Once the format is created, you may save your label by clicking the plus (+) button next to the Label Style drop-down list or delete a selected label from the list by clicking the minus (–) button.

Naming Pages

Whenever a new document is created, CorelDRAW X4 automatically creates the names, such as "Page 1," "Page 2," and so on. These page names are only for your reference as you navigate your multi-page document. However, you can customize your page names using several different methods.

When creating Web page documents—where each document page is a *separate* Web page—adding a unique name to the page creates a title for the exported page. When your document is printed, page names can also be printed in the margins, can indicate the contents of the page, and can provide other page-specific information.

  To quickly display the previous or next page in your document, you can press PAGE UP *(previous page) or* PAGE DOWN *(following page).*

Using the Rename Page Command

Use the Rename Page command to assign a unique name to pages. Choose either Layout | Rename Page or (more quickly) right-click the page tab of your document window and then choose Rename Page from the pop-up menu to access the command. The Rename Page dialog, shown right, can rename a page with a name of up to 32 characters, including spaces.

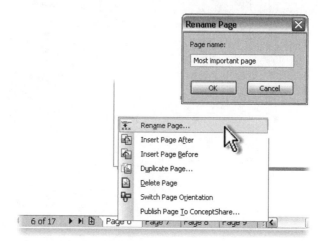

Using the Object Properties Docker

You can also edit page names in the Page tab of the Object Properties docker. Right-click a blank space on your page and choose Properties or choose Edit | Properties (or press ALT+ENTER) while no objects are selected. Either way, the Object Properties docker opens with several tabbed areas available, as shown in Figure 5-7. Click the Page tab to access page-related options, one of which is the Page Title box.

To go to different pages in a document, click a page icon at the lower left of the document window. If the page isn't in view, you can scroll to locate it, or (for lengthy documents) open the Go To Page dialog, shown next, by clicking between the Next Page and Previous Page buttons at the lower left of your document window. This dialog enables you to move quickly to a specific page in your document.

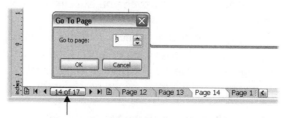

Click here to open the Go To Page dialog box.

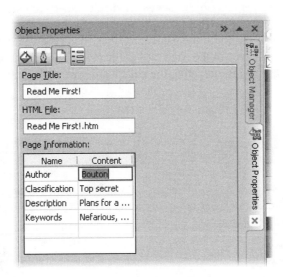

FIGURE 5-7   Click the Page tab of the Object Properties docker.

Using the Object Manager

The Object Manager docker offers the advantage of mass-editing page names from within a single docker, for editing page names. To open the Object Manager, choose Tools | Object Manager. Once the docker is open, click to ensure that the docker is set to show Object Properties by deselecting the Layer Manager view button state, shown here:

Click two times on the page title to name or rename a page.

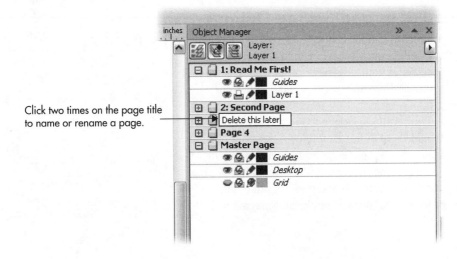

In this view, all page and object names are displayed. To rename any page (or any object), click once directly on the page title to select the page you want to name or rename, click a second time to highlight the page name text, then type a name, and finally press ENTER. Page names appear in the page tabs at the lower left of your document window, accompanied by a numeral indicating the page's order in your document:

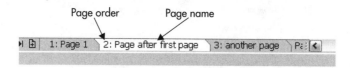

Page order   Page name

TIP   *To see more (or less) of the pages of your document in the page tab area of your document window, click-drag on the vertical divider between the page tabs and the horizontal scroll bar.*

Click-drag to expand/reduce page tab area.

Page Commands

There are several ways to add and delete pages from a document; using menu commands, shortcuts while holding modifier keys, and using certain page views are three. However, quick is best and in this section, you see the most convenient way as well as methods that are easiest to remember. You can decide for yourself which best suits the way you work.

Inserting Pages and Setting Options

From the main menu, choose Layout | Insert Page to open the Insert Page dialog, shown here, which features a host of options for specifying your new page properties and where you would like to add the new page in relation to your existing pages.

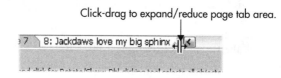

Enter the number of pages needed in the Insert box, and choose to add them either Before or After your current page, or between specific pages in your document using the Page box. You are not limited to the orientation or size of your current page when you add pages, unlike the constraints of traditional printed books and magazines!

To quickly add a new page to the beginning or end of your document, go to the first or last page and click the plus (+) symbol on the left or right of the page buttons at the lower left of your document window. To add a page before or after your current page, right-click the page tab to the right of these buttons, and choose either Insert Page Before or Insert Page After from the pop-up menu.

Deleting Pages

Deleting document pages can be done by choosing Layout | Delete Pages from the main menu; you can delete one or more of the existing pages in your document. By default, the dialog opens to display the current page as the page in the Delete Page box, shown at right, but you may select any page before or after your current page if you choose. To delete an entire sequence of pages, click the Through to Page option, which enables you to delete all pages in a range between the page specified in the Delete Page box through to any page following your current page.

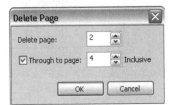

Moving and Duplicating Pages

You're going to create such fantastic content in CorelDRAW that you might never want to delete it, but instead you might want to move and/or copy pages. To move a page, use a click-drag action on the page tab to drag it to a new position. To copy a page—*and all its contents*—thus creating a new page order, hold CTRL while click-dragging the page tab, dragging the page to a new position. CorelDRAW does not duplicate the name of a user-named page; you'd wind up with an organizational nightmare if it did, so it's a good practice to name a duplicate page after you've created the copy.

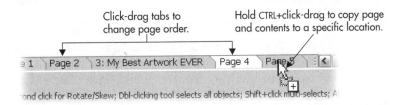

Using the Page Sorter

Page Sorter is a view that provides you with a broad look at your document and all its pages. In this view, you can add, delete, move, or copy pages in a single view. You can also change the Paper/Type Size and the page orientation of all the pages or just selected pages. A CorelDRAW document can contain pages of different sizes, which can be very handy when you are designing matching business cards and letterhead or other similarly related materials.

To open your document and all its pages in Page Sorter view, choose View | Page Sorter. The Page Sorter displays all pages in your document.

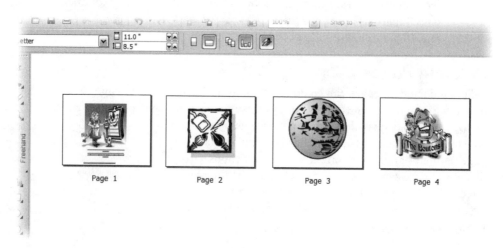

TIP *Using Page Sorter, you can export either your entire document or only selected pages quickly. Click to select the page(s) you want to export and choose File | Export, or click the Export button in the Standard Toolbar to open the Export dialog. To export only specific pages, click the option to Export This Page Only, which by default is not selected. Exporting is not to be confused with saving; exporting pages is usually done to get your work into bitmap format, Adobe Illustrator file format, or CMX (Corel Media Exchange) for sharing with users who have a compatible application. See Chapter 28 for details on exporting, saving, saving as; what these commands are used for; and which is best for a specific need.*

In Page Sorter view, a single click selects a page. Holding SHIFT while clicking pages enables you to select or deselect contiguous multiple pages. Holding CTRL while clicking enables you to select or deselect noncontiguous pages. The following actions enable you to apply page commands interactively to single or multiple page selections as seen in Figure 5-8.

- **Move Page(s)**   To move a page and change its order in your document, click-drag the page to a new location. During dragging, a vertical I-beam appears, indicating the insertion point for the page or the first page of the selected sequence of pages.

- **Add Page(s)**   To add pages to your document, right-click any page and choose Insert Page Before or Insert Page After from the pop-up menu to insert a page relative to the selected page.

- **Copy Page(s)**   To copy pages—and their contents—hold CTRL while click-dragging the page to a specific location. During dragging, a vertical I-beam appears,

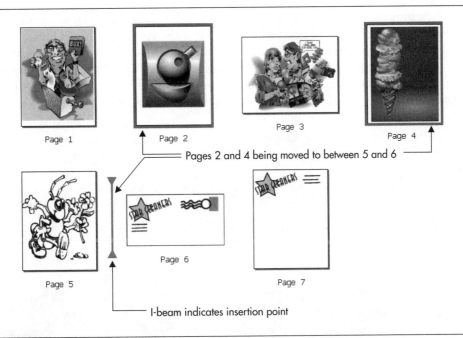

Page 1

Page 2

Page 3

Page 4

Pages 2 and 4 being moved to between 5 and 6

Page 5

Page 6

Page 7

I-beam indicates insertion point

FIGURE 5-8   Page Sorter enables you to manage your document pages interactively while viewing all page properties.

indicating the insertion point for the page copy or the first page of the selected sequence of pages.

- **Name or Rename Page**   To add a new name or change an existing page name, click the page name below the page to select it; click a second time to highlight the page title, and enter a new name; then press ENTER. You can also rename a page by right-clicking a specific page and choosing Rename Page from the pop-up menu to highlight the page name for editing.

- **Change Page Size/Orientation of All Pages**   In Page Sorter view, the Property Bar displays typical page property options for applying standard or custom page sizes and changing the orientation between Landscape and Portrait.

  If you want to change the orientation of *all* of the pages in the document, click on the Apply Page Layout to All Pages button on the Property Bar and *then* click either the Portrait or the Landscape button to change all pages to that orientation.

- **Change Page Size/Orientation of Selected Pages**   If you only want to change the orientation of some of the pages, click on the Apply Page Layout to Current Page button. Then select the pages you want to change, and click the Portrait or Landscape button to change the page(s) to the desired orientation, as shown.

Changing the orientation in the Page Sorter not only changes the view, but also changes how the pages themselves are oriented in the document. As you can see in Figure 5-8, the first and last pages have drawings that look better in Portrait view; you CTRL-click pages 1 and 4 in this example, click Apply Page Layout to Current Page Only, and both the Page Sorter view and the pages themselves are re-oriented. If you want to rethink this dynamic change, repeatedly pressing CTRL+Z (Edit | Undo) restores your document.

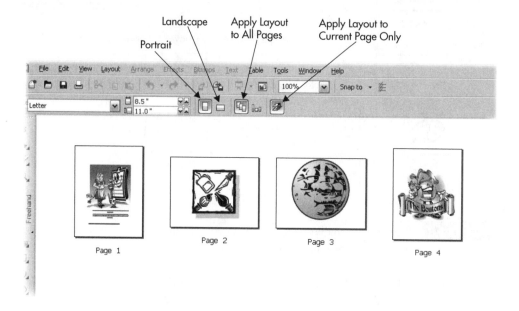

Exiting Page Sorter View is easily done; click the Page Sorter View button, or click any tool on the Toolbox. Any changes applied while in the Page Sorter are applied to your document.

 TIP *To exit the Page Sorter and immediately go to a particular page in your document, double-click the page.*

Page definition, sorting pages, margins, bleeds, and enough other options have been discussed to fill a book! Now that you know how to set up a page, how large do you want that drawing you just created on the page? And how do you precisely move the drawing if you want it perfectly centered on the page? Fortunately, the answers are on the next page, as measuring and drawing helpers are covered in the next chapter.

CHAPTER 6

Measuring and Drawing Helpers

117

More than likely, a project you are beginning is composed to a specific page size. Within the design you've envisioned, you have graphics, blocks of text, and headlines that need to be aligned, spaced, and proportioned to exact dimensions. Today is your lucky day: CorelDRAW not only has more ways of measuring objects than you can shake a stick at, but it also makes it easy for users of all skill levels to turn out professional, tightly composed pieces. In this chapter, you'll learn how to measure, scale measurements, align objects, work with guidelines, create your own guidelines, and get objects to snap to other objects with pinpoint precision. Leave "a smidgeon," "a pinch," and "just a touch to the left" behind as you enter the world of CorelDRAW accuracy and layout perfection.

Using the Ruler

Although Property Bars and toolbars offer information about the size and position of an object (to three decimal places), something about using rulers bounding a page has tangible and easy to understand qualities. Additionally, CorelDRAW Rulers are a resource for pulling nonprinting guidelines; traditional layout artists only *wish* that non-repro blue pencil marks were as nondistracting as these digital equivalents! Later in this chapter, guides and guidelines are covered; now let's look at how rulers are configured, manipulated, and how they invaluably assist in your design work.

Accessing Rulers and Ruler Properties

Straight out of the box, CorelDRAW displays Rulers on the top and left side of the page window. However, if someone experimented with your installed copy and turned Rulers off, it's easy to restore their visibility. You can choose View | Rulers from the main menu, but a quicker way is via the pop-up menu, as shown in Figure 6-1. With any tool chosen except the Zoom Tool, right-click over a blank area of the page (or outside of the page), and then choose View | Rulers from the pop-up menu.

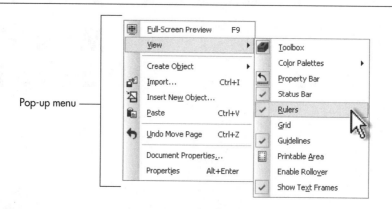

FIGURE 6-1   Rulers are displayed along the drawing window just by using the pop-up menu.

Naturally, rulers in CorelDRAW look like physical rulers with major spacing (inches, for example) and minor spacing (the ticks between whole number amounts, such as ⅜, and ¼). CorelDRAW detects when a mouse scroll wheel is active, and if you zoom the page in and out, you'll see an additional ruler nicety—the ruler ticks between major spacing have labels for fractional amounts when your zoom level is large enough to display them.

CorelDRAW Rulers (see Figure 6-2) can be broken down into three components: the Vertical Ruler, the Horizontal Ruler, and the Ruler origin. If you ever need the location of your cursor onscreen, you'll see a dotted line on the Rulers, and the numerical value is right at hand on the Property Bar. CorelDRAW uses the standard convention of displaying horizontal position values as X values on the Property Bar, and vertical values as Y. For example, you create a rectangle using the Rectangle Tool, and you're not sure you put the rectangle in the center of an 8½×11" page. A quick glance at the Property Bar will tell you that if the rectangle's X position is 4.25" and the Y position is 5.5", its center is at the center of the page.

The *origin* is the intersection of the vertical and horizontal rulers at the top left of the workspace. The origin is the page position reference where all measurements begin, but it does *not* represent the zero point for measuring the page. By default, the *lower-left corner* of your page represents the Ruler origin 0 position. Try this: create a shape near the center of the page. Then with the Pick Tool move the shape up and to the right, while watching the X, Y position values on the Property Bar. The values increase; conversely, if you move the shape down and to the left, the values decrease—eventually, if you move the shape off the page (down and left), you'll see negative X, Y values on the Property Bar, as the shape travels beyond the origin.

As with a physical ruler, you can move Rulers in CorelDRAW to assist you in your design needs; additionally, you can leave the Rulers where they are and just move the origin of the Rulers. This is something that cannot be done with a physical ruler, and working with these features is covered in the sections to follow.

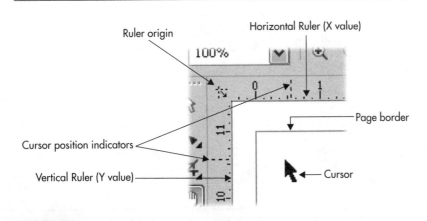

FIGURE 6-2   Elements of CorelDRAW's Rulers

Setting the Ruler Origin

There are at least two practical advantages to changing the zero origin for the Rulers. Say, for example, you're uncomfortable with measuring from the bottom left and prefer a more conventional set of Rulers that start at the upper-left corner of a page. Click-hold your cursor on the origin, and then drag to a point at the upper-left corner of the page. Doing this thwarts the ability to use the Property Bar for easy-to-read X, Y positions for objects because by convention (in drawing applications, CAD applications, and most advanced design programs), Y, the vertical measurement of space, always travels up in a positive direction. However, moving the origin not only can make the rulers suit your intuitions, but it's also a handy technique for measuring relative distance between objects, measured against each other and not as an absolute measurement against the page.

Two Inches to the Right, Please

1. Create two shapes; any shapes will do.

2. Move the shapes using the Pick Tool so that they're horizontally aligned, and, say, 5 inches from each other.

3. You need the centers of the objects to be 2 inches apart. You click-drag the origin so that it's horizontally centered on the first object. The zero horizontal point is now at the center of the first object.

4. You move the second object so that its center is at the 2-inch major mark on the horizontal Ruler.

5. With this shape still selected, take a look at the X, Y fields on the Property Bar. If the X value is not exactly 2.000, type **2.000** in the X field, and then press ENTER. See Figure 6-3.

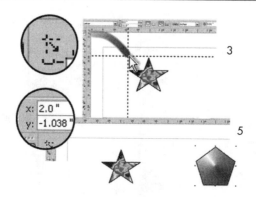

FIGURE 6-3   Specify a different origin for the Rulers to measure relative distances between the centers of objects.

It's very easy to undo what you've done: to restore the origin of the Rulers to the default setting, you double-click the origin.

A more dramatic change you can make to the Rulers is to actually reposition them in the workspace, not merely change where the units appear. To undock the Rulers (they come as a set; you cannot undock only one Ruler), hold SHIFT and then drag the Ruler origin to where you want the Rulers to begin. You'll see a dashed-line preview onscreen for the intended new location of the rulers; release the mouse button and the rulers move to this position. To restore the Rulers (to dock them), you hold SHIFT and then double-click the Rulers origin. See Figure 6-4.

Once the Rulers are undocked, you're free to move them as needed, by holding SHIFT while dragging the origin. Regardless of where you place the Rulers in the workspace, the zero for the increments on the Rulers remains constant. To see this, move the view of the page by using the scroll bars at the right and bottom of the screen or use the Hand Tool (H); the increments on the undocked Rulers move as you move your view. When you zoom in and out of the page, the Rulers behave accordingly. If you need to move the origin while the Rulers are undocked, drag the origin. CorelDRAW's Rulers accommodate your diverse needs.

Setting Unit Measure

Objects you uncover in the real world come in units: quarts, acres, yards, and so on. In the virtual world of drawing, you have unit measurements as well: the name of the setting in CorelDRAW is *unit measures,* whose appearance on the Rulers increases and decreases in frequency with your view magnification setting. The actual unit measures are specified according to the Drawing Units currently defined on the Property Bar. To set the Drawing Unit measure, choose the Pick Tool (click an empty area on your page to make sure nothing is selected), and then use the Units drop-down list on the Property Bar to specify anything from picas to kilometers, as shown at left.

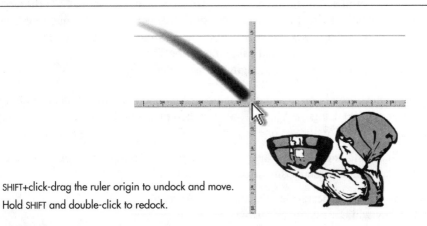

SHIFT+click-drag the ruler origin to undock and move.
Hold SHIFT and double-click to redock.

FIGURE 6-4   Rulers can be repositioned on the page.

Drawing Units control the units displayed on Rulers and also for other areas of CorelDRAW X4 where dimensions are displayed: page size, shape size, and nudge and duplicate offset commands. Drawing Units is a handy feature for any number of design assignments, from desktop publishing to architectural plans.

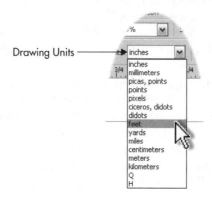

Setting Ruler Options

Options for measuring in CorelDRAW can be found in Tools | Options; to get to this dialog quickly, you double-click a Page Ruler. Alternatively, you can right-click a Ruler and choose Ruler Setup from the pop-up menu. In the Rulers area of the Options box, you'll find useful options in addition to the increments displayed on Rulers. See Figure 6-5.

Nudging

At the top of the Rulers page are Nudge options, worth covering first here, although indirectly related to the page rulers themselves. When we nudge things in the real world, our intention is to move an object by a small, but fairly arbitrary distance—and we estimate the measurement. In CorelDRAW, however, nudging objects is precise, not at all arbitrary, and on the Rulers page you can set the distance for normal, Super, and Micro nudging. Nudging can be performed on a shape, several shapes at the same time, and even a node or several nodes on a path when they are selected using the Shape Tool.

Once you've specified values for nudging in the Rulers area:

- You set the normal nudge distance of a shape by choosing the shape(s) with the Pick Tool or node(s) using the Shape Tool, and then pressing the keyboard arrow keys to nudge up, down, or across; one keyboard stroke equals one nudge distance.

- Super-nudging is performed the same way as normal nudging except you hold the SHIFT key while pressing any arrow key.

- Micro-nudging is performed the same way as regular nudging, except you hold the CTRL key while pressing any arrow key.

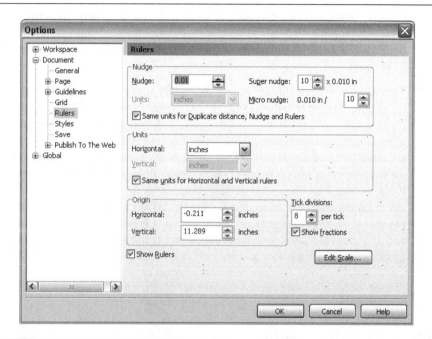

FIGURE 6-5   The Rulers area of Options is where you can set units, the independent display of units on Rulers, nudge distance, and more.

There is an upper limit of 600 inches for nudge distance, which is fair enough, because, for example, nudging a shape 600 inches to move it is more easily accomplished by simply entering the intended position in the Property Bar's X and Y fields (then you press ENTER to apply the move).

TIP   *There's an easy way to remember some modifier keys. In many applications, CTRL means "constrain," to limit, while SHIFT often means "to add to" or "to extend." So super-nudging can be thought of as an extension to normal nudge distances (you hold SHIFT while pressing arrow keys), and micro-nudging is a constrained version of normal nudging (you hold CTRL).*

Specifying Units, Origin, and Tick Divisions for Your Rulers

In the fields below Nudge options, you'll find all the controls for what appears, and where, on the rulers displayed on your drawing page. Here's how each option lets you control Ruler appearance:

- **Units**   Units are measurement values. Choose a Horizontal unit measure to specify unit measures for all Drawing Units in your document. To specify different unit measures for Vertical Ruler and Drawing Units, click to deselect the Same Units For Horizontal And Vertical Rulers option, shown in Figure 6-5.

■ **Origin**   Although you can manually set the origin as described in the previous section, you can also perform precise origin definition using this field. The origin point can be set anywhere from –50 to 50 yards in precise increments as small as 0.001 inch.

■ **Tick Divisions**   *Tick divisions* are the evenly spaced numeric labels seen bracketing the smaller increments displayed by your Ruler—for example, if you are using inches as the unit, the tick divisions are 1, 2, 3, and so on. Tick divisions are automatically set according to the type of unit measure selected. For example, standard measure displays a default of eight divisions per tick, whereas metric measures display ten divisions. Desktop publishing and printing units such as didots, picas, points, and ciceros are displayed using six divisions per tick. An option to Show Fractions is also available and set by default while a unit measure is selected. Figure 6-6 shows two divisions per tick; below it is the standard eight subdivisions, and at bottom the Show Fractions check box is unchecked in the Rulers area of Options; decimals are now shown for ticks.

 To set the Spacing and Frequency of your Ruler, see "Setting Grid Properties," later in this chapter.

Editing Drawing Scales

Scale drawing is used when the dimensions involved in drawing actual sizes are either too large or too small to be practical; for example, a world atlas at 1-to-1 (1:1) scale would be hard to carry around, and almost as hard to print. Drawing using a scale representation is used for tasks in medicine, drafting, architecture, electronics, engineering, astronomy, and in other fields.

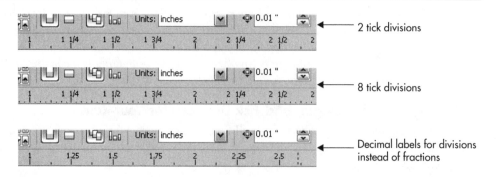

FIGURE 6-6   Choose tick divisions and whether fractions or decimals display on Rulers.

You can set up a drawing scale by clicking the Edit Scale button in the Rulers page of the Options dialog. In the Drawing Scale dialog, you can quickly apply a scale ratio, or specify your own custom scale, as shown next.

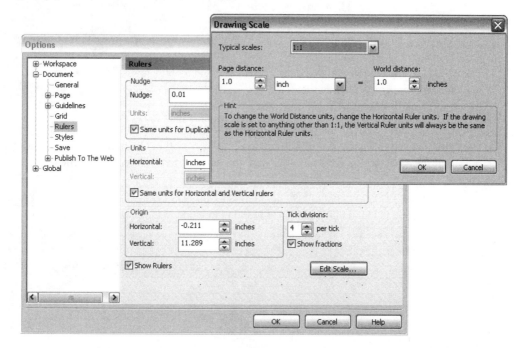

The Typical Scales drop-down menu includes a selection of the most commonly used drawing ratios ranging from 100:1 to 1:100, with the most common standard measure scales included. When selecting ratios, the first number represents the object *Page Distance*; the second number represents the *real world* distance, labeled "World Distance." Usually small objects such as circuitry and clock parts are illustrated using ratios where the Page Distance is larger than the World Distance. Conversely, the best setup for a technical drawing of a skyscraper is to set Page Distance much smaller than World Distance.

The moment you change either the Page Distance or the World Distance, the Typical Scales selection in the drop-down list turns to *Custom.* "Page Distance" refers to the measured distance on your document page, while "World Distance" refers to the distance represented by your Ruler and Drawing Units in your CorelDRAW document. Either setting can be set independently of the other and to different unit measures to an astounding range between 1,000,000 and 0.00001 inches in increments of 0.1 inch.

Drawing a Building to Scale

1. You want to draw a structure with several floors, the average height being about 10 feet.

2. Press CTRL+J to display Options; then choose Rulers. Set the Horizontal Units to Feet.

3. Click the Edit Scale button. Let's represent a page inch as 10 feet to make it comfortable to draw on a default-size page. There are 12 inches to the foot, times a scale of 10 to 1, so first set the Page Distance to 1.0 per foot; then type **120** (12 times 10) in the World Distance box, as shown in the following illustration.

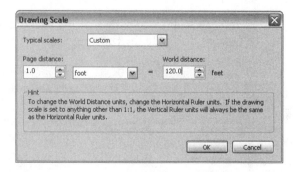

4. Set the zero origin to the point where you want to start building, and then go to it. As you can see in Figure 6-7, a Dimension line (covered in Chapter 10) clearly indicates that the story on the structure it bounds measures about 10 feet in height.

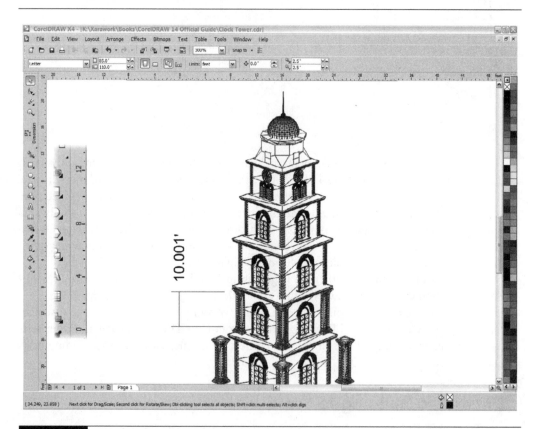

FIGURE 6-7   Use the World Distance in combination with the Units feature in Rulers to set up a page in which you can accurately design anything.

Calibrating Ruler Display

You buy a Lamborghini Gallardo (about $200,000); you pull into a gas station, and you want to put Regular in the tank? No, and similarly you can't expect precision when you use CorelDRAW on an uncalibrated monitor. Fortunately, CorelDRAW provides a very simple way to ensure what you see on your monitor screen matches real-world measurements. Occasionally, your display might not show perfectly square pixels, and as a result your 5-inch line in a very important drawing might measure 4.88" when you print it. To calibrate the Rulers in CorelDRAW to match your screen, to match real-world output, you'll need a plastic foot-long ruler (clear is better than solid, about $1 at a stationery store), about 30 seconds, and the following steps:

1. In a new document create a 5"-wide square. With the Rectangle tool, hold CTRL (constrains proportions to 1:1), and then drag while watching the size fields on the Property Bar. If you're close but not precisely 5", type **5.0** into either field with the Lock Proportions icon clicked (see following illustration), and then press ENTER.

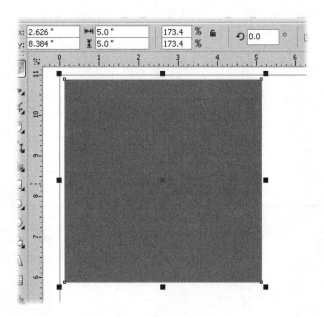

2. Using the Zoom Tool Property Bar options, set your view magnification to 100 percent.

3. Using your physical $1 ruler, measure the object you created on your screen. If both CorelDRAW's rulers and your physical ruler agree it's a 5" square, your Ruler display is accurate. If the measurements *don't* match, CorelDRAW's Toolbox Options has the fix.

4. Open the Options dialog (CTRL+J).

5. Click to expand the tree directory under Workspace and Toolbox, and then click Zoom | Hand Tools. This displays the Zoom, Hand options on the right of the dialog. First, click to select the Zoom Relative To 1:1 option.

6. Click Calibrate Rulers to display the Ruler calibration reference rulers and Resolution options, shown in Figure 6-8. Notice the vertical and horizontal ruler bars that intersect at the center of your screen. This represents your current Ruler Drawing Units. By default, your Horizontal and Vertical resolution are set to 72.0 pixels per inch.

7. Using your ruler, measure both the vertical and horizontal rulers on your screen to see that they match. If they don't match, increase or decrease the Horizontal and/or Vertical options using the spin boxes until the onscreen rulers match your $1 ruler. See Figure 6-8.

8. Click OK to close the calibration dialog, and then click OK again to close the Options dialog. Your Rulers are now calibrated.

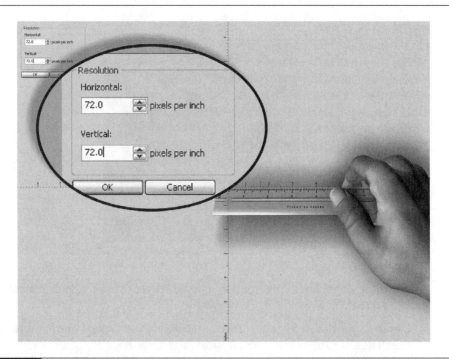

FIGURE 6-8 Clicking on Calibrate Rulers displays reference rulers and Resolution options.

Introducing the Indispensable CorelDRAW Grids

A page Grid is a customizable, by default nonprinting overlay that extends beyond the printable page onto the pasteboard area at all viewing resolutions and viewing qualities. It's not only an excellent visual reference for scaling and aligning objects vertically and horizontally, but it also can be used in combination with CorelDRAW's Snap To Grid option. To make the grid visible, right-click with the Pick Tool over an empty area of the page, and then choose View | Grid from the pop-up menu. To modify the Grid, right-click over either Ruler or the Ruler origin, and then choose Grid Setup.

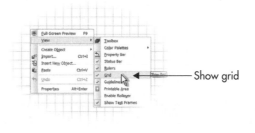

Show grid

Grid Setup (right-click)

Setting Grid Properties

You're going to have a variety of designing needs, which will certainly call for different appearances of Grids, which is why they're customizable. Changing grid-line frequency and spacing is often needed. You can use options in the Grid page of the Options dialog to tailor your grid just the way you need it to appear. To open this page, as shown next, choose View | Setup | Grid And Ruler Setup from the command menus, or right-click your Ruler and choose Grid Setup.

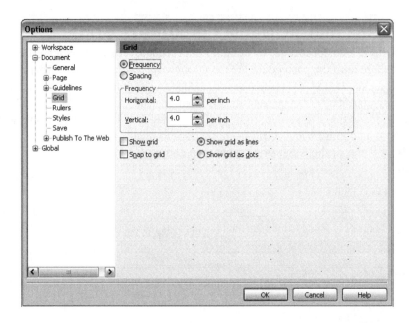

TIP   *Use the Object Manager to set all grid properties, including visible, printable, and/ or editable states. Grids are controlled by the Grid layer properties, which is a layer on the Master Page. To open the Object Manager, choose Window | Dockers | Object Manager (see Chapter 11).*

The following illustration shows the available Frequency and Spacing options; they might look similar, but there's an important distinction. *Frequency* options give you control over the grid appearance according to the number of lines that appear within a given distance. *Spacing* options control the physical space between the grid lines based on distance. Both are set according to the current Drawing Units choice, and you choose Frequency *or* Spacing; choosing both would be impossible. You can also set the horizontal and vertical spacing independently of one another, which is very useful when you have an object, such as a tall fluted glass, that you want to put etching on. You'd use more horizontal than vertical grid lines, and your design would turn out flawlessly.

○ Frequency
○ Spacing

Frequency

Horizontal: 4.0 per inch

Vertical: 4.0 per inch

☐ Show grid   ⦿ Show grid as lines
☐ Snap to grid   ○ Show grid as dots

○ Frequency
⦿ Spacing

Spacing

Horizontal: place a grid line every 0.25 inches

Vertical: place a grid line every 0.25 inches

☐ Show grid   ⦿ Show grid as lines
☐ Snap to grid   ○ Show grid as dots

TIP *When illustrating or drawing based on a specific unit measure—such as inches—formatting your grid to match the Ruler unit measure can help a great deal. For example, if Rulers are set to display inches using a Tick Division of 8 per inch, setting the grid to a Frequency value of 8 vertical and 8 horizontal lines per inch causes grid lines to appear every eighth of an inch while using a Drawing Scale ratio of 1:1 (actual size).*

Display Grid as Lines or Dots

Also on the Grid page of the Options dialog, you control how your grid appears—either as lines or as dots.

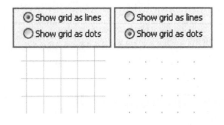

By default, new documents are set to the Show Grid As Lines option. However, a design of a checkerboard, for example, might make the grid fairly invisible and as a consequence useless; you'd opt for the display of the Grid as dots. Conversely, you're going to lose a solar system or two if dots are chosen for Grids when you're drawing an astronomy chart (use lines)!

Using Snap To Commands

Snapping is a feature in CorelDRAW that helps you move a shape to an exact location when it's in proximity to grid lines, guidelines, and other objects. Magnetism is a good analogy for the effect of snapping: you hold an object that has magnetic properties close enough to a magnet and eventually it snaps to the magnet. The Pick Tool and Shape Tool are two common tools you use to get snapping in CorelDRAW, and the *Snap To* commands available on the drop-down menu on the Standard Toolbar are your ticket to defining what snaps to what on your drawing page.

Snapping is a feature that you might not use all the time: it can be irritating, for example, if you're trying to create a random distribution of several objects. In this case, the snapping to objects feature wants your work to be orderly when *you* don't! However, you'll find that snapping is one very quick route to precise manual aligning and distribution of table callouts, symmetrical patterns, and just about any design that requires some regularity to placed shapes.

- **Snap To Grid** To have your drawing shapes snap and align to the document Grid, click the drop-down on the Standard Toolbar, or press the shortcut CTRL+Y to toggle the feature on and off. When objects snap to a grid, they snap to the grid lines, and you'll feel an even stronger attraction when you move an object close to grid *intersection* points.

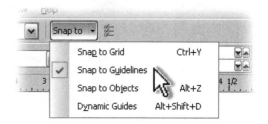

- **Snap To Guidelines** Guidelines are covered later in this chapter. To cause your objects to snap to any type of guideline, choose this option from the drop-down list.

- **Snap To Objects** To have shapes snap to and align with other objects, choose Snap To Objects from the drop-down list; it's faster to remember the shortcut ALT+Z. When objects are set to snap to each other, they can use snap points on either the source (the magnet) or target (the object that's attracted) shape. Snap points are set using options and modes in the Snap To Objects page of the Options dialog (see the later section, "Setting Snap Behavior").

- **Dynamic Guides** This feature in CorelDRAW X4 is akin to *object* snapping. Press ALT+SHIFT+D or use the drop-down menu to toggle the dynamic guides on or off. This feature is covered in detail in the next section.

 ## Snapping To It

1. You have a Web page to design, with six 1-inch squares, three across, two down, with a ½-inch space between them. Don't get out a pocket calculator and don't resort to colorful language—at their defaults, Snap To Grid and Snap To Objects make this task go like a charm. Enable Snap To Grid and Snap To Objects from the Snap To drop-down list and make sure Grids are turned on.

2. With the Rectangle Tool, begin close to a Grid intersection, and then drag down and to the right until the Property Bar tells you either the height or width of the rectangle is very close to 1". Release the mouse button when your cursor is over a Grid intersection.

3. Choose the Pick Tool.

4. Drag the rectangle over to the right until you see one vertical grid separating it from the original square, but don't release the mouse button yet. There are two spaces sidling this line that represent half an inch.

5. Right-click while the left mouse button is still depressed, and then release both buttons. What you've done is duplicate the original square to a new position. This is an important, quick technique for duplicating shapes.

6. Repeat steps 4 and 5 to build the array of evenly spaced squares, as shown in Figure 6-9. Notice that when an object's edge is on, or even close to, the Grid when Snap To is turned on, you'll see a tiny blue label indicating the snap to point. You're not limited to shape edges as the origin of a snapping point; setting behavior for snapping origins is covered later in this chapter.

> **TIP** *Snapping and snapping behavior (discussed in the following section) aren't limited to the Grid. In fact, you don't even have to have the Grid turned on to snap objects to one another; you press ALT+Z and then all your objects are sticky.*

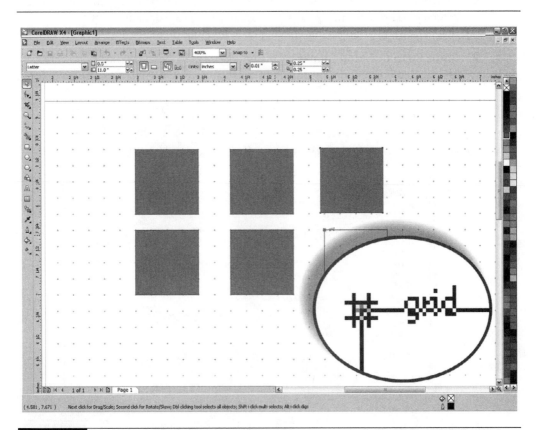

FIGURE 6-9 Duplicating and aligning shapes makes accurate composition of a design a breeze.

Setting Snap Behavior

On the Snap To Objects page of the Options dialog, you can control snapping behavior in precise detail when moving *and* drawing lines or objects. You choose Tools | Options (CTRL+J), click to expand the tree directory under Workspace, and then click Snap To Objects, shown in Figure 6-10.

The snapping feature naturally requires that you have a shape and a different object (or guideline or Grid intersection) to which it snaps. Proximity to the "magnetic" snapping object is important—you can't have an object snap to a different object that is miles away. However, in the Snap To Objects page, you have control over the *strength* of the magnetism, which by default is set to Medium.

To customize snapping behavior to suit the type of drawing you're building, you enable or disable the following features on the Options page:

- ■ **Snap To Objects On**   Clicking this check box turns the Snap To Objects feature on or off. You can also do this from the Snap To drop-down list on the Standard Toolbar.

- ■ **Snapping Threshold**   Use this drop-down list to set snapping sensitivity, based on screen proximity to snap points. Choose Medium (the default), Low (weak magnetism), or High (akin to having chewing gum on the bottom of your shoe).

- ■ **Show Snap Location Marks**   This option is on by default. Snap points are highlighted when your cursor is held over the precise points of a selected object or a

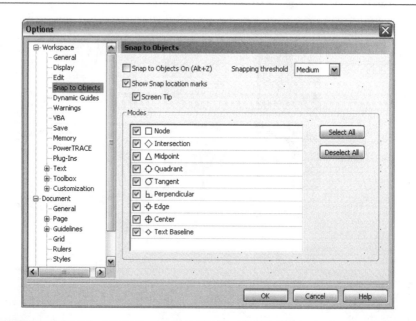

FIGURE 6-10   You can control snapping behavior in detail with the Snap To Objects option.

target object while moving objects or drawing. When it is activated, you can also choose the Screen Tip option, which identifies the snapping point, highlighted with a text label. The following illustration shows an enlarged view of Screen Tips turned on. The blue icons preceding the text labels represent some of the modes you've chosen. The types of snapping are covered next.

 When you reposition a shape by dragging it with the Pick Tool, before you release the mouse button to finalize the move, the shape remains in the original position, but a blue, outline version of the shape appears at the intended new location. Use this feature as a visual guide for repositioning objects; this preview of a move offers positioning precision because you can "see through" to objects beneath the chosen object before you release the mouse button.

Choosing Object Snapping Modes

The Mode list includes nine object snap points you can define. You can toggle them on or off using the check boxes. Symbols beside each of the modes identify the current snapping points on different object types. Use the Select All and Deselect All buttons to quickly activate or deactivate all the options in the list.

At times you might want snapping to occur at certain object points but not others—you can turn specific snap points on or off. Choose options from the modes list to have objects snap to precise points on other objects in the following ways:

- **Nodes**   Use this mode to snap where nodes exist on objects or lines. A node is a break point along the path of a shape, and it's indicated by a very small (but noticeable) black outlined square.

- **Intersection**   Choose this mode to activate snapping where the outline paths of two objects cross, including the original position of an object you're moving.

- **Midpoint**   This mode snaps to a point equidistant between any two nodes on an object or path.

- **Quadrant**   This mode should only be used with ellipses and circles. It causes snapping to one of the four nodes that were created using the Ellipse Tool (F7).

Below these modes are Tangent and Perpendicular; they work only in combination with dynamic guides, covered in the following section:

- **Tangent**   This mode shows a guide at a *tangent* (a straight line that touches a curve at a point) to a Quadrant snap point. This mode applies only to ellipse objects.

- **Perpendicular**   Choose this mode to show a dynamic guide at right angles and to snap to the midpoint between object and segment nodes.

Finally, the following modes apply snapping regardless of whether other, additional snapping points are checked in this Options page:

- ◼ **Edge** Choose this mode to have the outline path of an object act as a dynamic guide for snapping to.

- ◼ **Center** This mode displays the center point (origin) of closed-path objects.

- ◼ **Text baseline** When snapping, all text objects take on the characteristics of a normal object such as a rectangle and have snapping points for edges, centers, corners, and so on. Additionally, the *text baseline* (the hypothetical line each character appears to rest on) is included in the snapping action.

Working with Guidelines, Dynamic Guides, and Guide Layers

If you're old enough to remember the blue pencil used to rough in nonprinting guides on a physical piece of paper you'd send to a printer, you'll appreciate CorelDRAW guide features all the more. The analogy is a fair one: like blue pencil marks, CorelDRAW's page guides, dynamic guides, and objects you put on a guides layer don't print, and you don't need an eraser for cleanup, but here the similarity ends. Regardless of whether you use one or all of the guide features in your work, you're assured the precision only a computer application can offer, plus the same speed and ease with guides as you experience with the Toolbox tools.

The following sections are the operator's manual for guides: how to use them and how to customize them.

Using Guidelines

Guidelines placed on your document page extend between the top, bottom, left, and right edges of the document window. Guidelines appear as vertical and horizontal dashed lines, but guidelines can also be rotated… "slanted." In CorelDRAW, *guidelines* are considered unique objects—they have their own properties and are manipulated in many ways like objects you draw.

To view and hide the display of guidelines in your document window, right-click with no object selected and then choose View | Guidelines. By default, a new document doesn't have any guidelines—you need to create them, the subject of the section to follow. To have objects *snap* to the guidelines you create, choose from the drop-down list, Snap To, on the Standard Bar, right where you found Snap To Grid earlier in this chapter.

Manipulating Guidelines

The best teacher is an example; the following steps walk you through the tasks you'll need most often when working with guides:

■ Make sure the Rulers are visible; they're where a lot of the guides live. With the Pick Tool chosen, and no objects selected, right-click and then choose to View | Rulers. Then, using any Toolbox tool you like, click-drag beginning on a Ruler, and release the mouse button anywhere in the workspace. Although dropping a guide on the page is most useful, you can certainly create a guide on the pasteboard area to measure and align objects not currently placed on the page.

■ To move a place guide, you need the Pick Tool selected. Then hover the cursor over the guide you'd like to move; when the cursor turns into a double-headed arrow, you're all set and all you need to do is drag the guide.

■ If you want to eliminate a guide, hover over it with the Pick Tool until you see the double-headed arrow cursor (to indicate you've selected it), click the guide to confirm the guide is "in focus" in the interface, and then press DELETE or CTRL+X.

■ If you need a guide that travels up- or downhill, you create a guide first. Next click it to select it, and then click a second time, and you'll see a center and rotation handles. One of the neat things about rotating a guideline is that you can move its center point before dragging on the rotation handles to, for example, rotate a guide around the corner of a shape you have on the page. You move a slanted guideline exactly as you do with a perfectly horizontal or vertical guide—you click-drag it to reposition it. See Figure 6-11, where the design needs shafts of light emanating from a center point that is not the default center of a guide that's put into slant mode. No problem; you change the center of rotation, then drag a rotation handle clockwise or counterclockwise.

| **TIP** | *You can move and rotate several guidelines at once by pressing SHIFT to select or deselect them, then click-dragging to move them. To rotate one or more guidelines while selected, click one of the guidelines a second time to display rotation handles, and drag one of the rotation handles in a circular direction.* |

Controlling Guideline Properties

If you need several guidelines placed at an exact spacing, you manage all guidelines via the Options dialog (CTRL+J). Separate dialog pages are here for controlling the vertical, horizontal, and slanted guidelines. To see these dialogs, right-click either of the Rulers and then choose Guidelines Setup. Additionally, while a guideline is selected in a document, you can open this dialog by clicking the Guidelines Options button on the Property Bar, shown to the right.

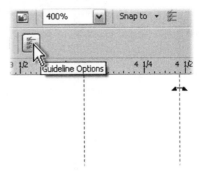

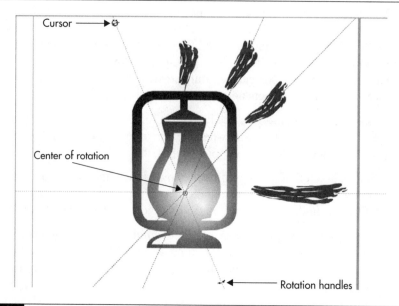

Cursor

Center of rotation

Rotation handles

FIGURE 6-11   Make your guides perform at the angle you need for a design piece.

The Options dialog lists each of the guideline types individually on the left side of the dialog. Click one to select it in the tree directory under Guidelines; here's what the Vertical page looks like when some guides have been defined at 1-inch intervals:

Guideline list   Guideline command buttons

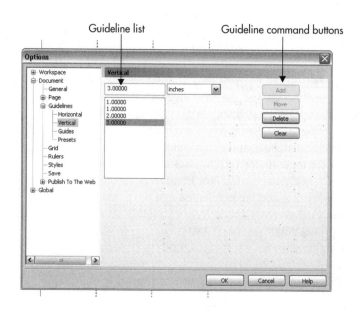

By default, guidelines are a medium blue when added to the workspace, and their highlight color when they're selected is red. However, on the main page for Guidelines in Options, you can change the color of a guide as well as the color for preset guides. This is quite handy, for example, if you're designing a series of medium blue rectangles—naturally, you'd want to choose a contrasting color for the guides!

Adding, Deleting, and Moving Guidelines

You can adjust guides en masse from the Guidelines "console" in Options in very similar ways using the dialogs. Each dialog contains a listing of the existing guidelines on your document page. Take a guided tour of guides by following these steps:

1. To create a new guideline, enter a value in the top-left num box according to the position where you want the new guideline to be created. Then click the Add button. A new guideline is created where you want it.

2. To move an existing guideline, click on it in the list, enter a new value in the top-left num box, and then click Move. The selected guideline has moved, and on the list you can see it's been thoughtful and left a forwarding address.

3. To delete a specific guideline, select it in the list and then click the Delete button. The selected guideline is gone from the page, and as you see the page from your current view, your document is immediately updated.

4. To remove all guidelines in the list, click the Clear button. All guidelines are deleted.

Locking and Unlocking Guidelines

All guidelines are editable by default; you can move or delete them using the Pick Tool. But occasionally a guide that can move accidentally is as welcome as a friend who is holding your ladder moving accidentally. You can lock it using Property Bar options:

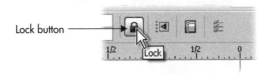

1. To lock an *individual* guideline, click the guideline to select it using the Pick Tool.

2. Using Property Bar options, click the Lock button. The selected guideline is locked, and the guide-specific Property Bar options become unavailable. You can also choose Lock Object from the pop-up menu when you've selected a guide using the Pick Tool.

3. To unlock a locked guideline, right-click the guideline and choose Unlock Object from the pop-up menu. Your guideline is now unlocked and the guide-specific Property Bar options become available again.

Working with Dynamic Guides

Dynamic guides are a novel way to increase the accuracy of drawing and moving shapes, even when their position and degree of rotation might make this act otherwise a challenge. Dynamic guides are guides that you first set up with axes of rotation (0°, 15°, and so on), and then when you want a guide at a specific angle for aligning or drawing, it appears onscreen. It can snap the object you're positioning, and dynamic guides offer onscreen information about the result of a moving or drawing action. When using dynamic guides, drawing or moving your cursor over active object snap points will cause guides to temporarily appear to aid in placement of objects and nodes. You can move your cursor along these "sticky" guides, and view snap points, angle values, and distance measurements relative to object snap points (as shown in Figure 6-12). You can also have your cursor snap to specific points along the guide path, based on a customizable tick value. To activate this feature, choose View | Dynamic Guides (ALT+SHIFT+D), or click the Dynamic Guides button in the Property Bar while the Pick Tool or Shape Tool (and no objects) is selected.

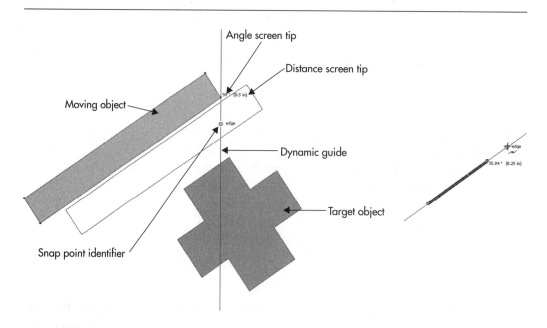

FIGURE 6-12   From the "sticky" guides, you can view snap points, angle values, and more.

Dynamic guide behavior works in combination with your selected Snap To Objects modes (see "Setting Snap Behavior" in the previous section), but has a unique set of options that control their behavior. To access these options (see following illustration), choose Tools | Options (CTRL+J), and click Dynamic Guides under Workspace in the tree directory.

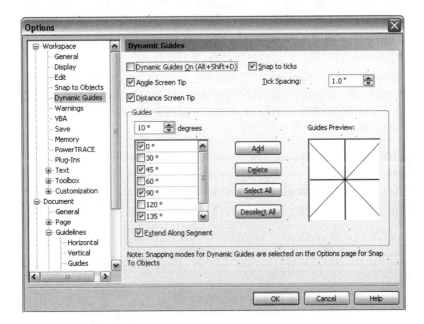

Here's how choosing each option will affect the behavior of your dynamic guides:

- **Dynamic Guides** Click this check box to turn dynamic guides on or off.

- **Angle Screen Tip** Choose this to display angle values relative to snap points on your object.

- **Distance Screen Tip** Choose this to display the distance between your cursor position on a guide and the current snap point. Unit measure is based on your currently selected drawing units.

- **Snap To Ticks** This option offers to snap your cursor position to points along the guide according to the value you enter.

- **Guides** This area opens up a whole world of choices for angles at which dynamic guides appear relative to the active snap point. Clicking a check box activates each of the default angles, which are preset at 30° increments from 0° to 150°, for a total angle of 180°, which effectively covers all possible angles (because Dynamic Guides appear bi-directional). The angle of each guide is displayed in the Guides Preview window on the right of the dialog. Enter a degree value in the num box above the list, and click the Add button to add a new guide. To remove a dynamic guide, click a guide either in the list or the preview window, and then click Delete. When a new guide is added, it appears in the list; conversely, when you delete a guide, it's permanently removed from the list.

- **Extend Along Segment** Choose this to display a guide at the same angle as straight line segments. This option is useful for Bézier and freehand drawing because this makes it easy for you to add new portions to straight lines at a constant angle (as shown in Figure 6-13).

Figure 6-13 shows a logo nearing completion by setting up dynamic guides at 45° increments. Using the Pen Tool, the dynamic guides (set to snapping) show exactly when the tool has reached a 45° angle as well as a 90° angle. Try this feature for yourself; this illustration was accomplished using 25 clicks—precision has seldom been achieved so easily.

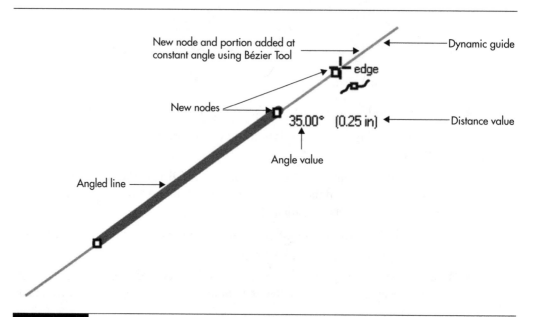

FIGURE 6-13 The Extend Along Segment option is useful for both Bézier and freehand drawing.

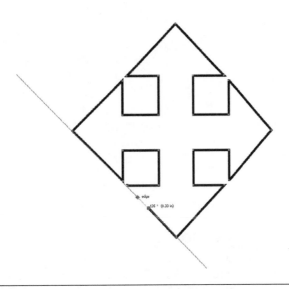

FIGURE 6-14   Use dynamic guides to assist in alignment and drawing when Rulers don't suit the assignment.

Controlling the Guides Layer

Guides belong to a special layer, named Guides on the Object Manager, reserved just for these assistants. To view the layers in your document, open the Object Manager by choosing either Tools | Object Manager or Window | Dockers | Object Manager. The Guides layer is a Master Page layer; you'll find it with other layers controlling your Desktop and Grid. By default, all guidelines on the Guides layer are set as Visible, Non-Printable, and Editable. If you want, you can change any of these by clicking the symbols to the left of the Guides layer in the Object Manager docker, as shown here:

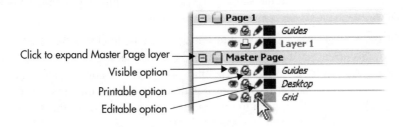

To set all options for a layer at once—including the display color of objects on the Guides layer in the Object Manager docker—right-click the layer name, for example, the Guides layer, and then choose Properties from the pop-up menu. Doing this opens the Guides Properties dialog to reveal further options, as shown here:

Make an Object a Guideline

When a straight or slanted guideline doesn't get you where you want to go, you can make almost any drawing shape into a guideline; in fact, you can also turn a guide into a drawing object. To do this, you use the Object Manager docker to move objects between layers. Moving any object to the Guides layer makes, for all intents and purposes, a guideline, with all the same properties as a typical guideline, except you might call it a guide-curve or a guide-spiral! After an object becomes a guideline, objects and anything you draw in its proximity snap to it, as long as the Snap To Guidelines option is active. You owe it to yourself to check out this feature; think of the artwork you can clean up and refine when you're tracing over the original with a drawing tool that snaps to the original.

Traveling in the opposite direction, moving any guideline to a different layer automatically makes it a printable object. To move an object to the Guides layer, use these steps:

1. Create or select at least one drawing shape that you want to use as a guideline.

2. Open the Object Manager docker by choosing Tools | Object Manager.

3. Expand the tree directories in the Object Manager docker to locate both the Guides layer on the Master Page and the shape you want to make into a guideline so both are in view.

4. In the Object Manager docker, click-and-drag your shape icon (not the shape on the page) from its current page and layer to any position under the Guides layer on the Master Page. As you drag, notice a horizontal I-beam cursor appears, shown next, indicating the shape's current position as it is dragged. When your cursor is over a layer—ideally, the layer you want to move the shape to—you'll see the default

cursor replaced with a horizontal arrow "holding" a symbol of graphics content. The following figure also shows a "before and after" of a star shape when it's moved to the Master Page Guides layer. Unlike guidelines you drag from Rulers, the look of a user-defined guide doesn't have the dashed lines; it's a solid line with no fill.

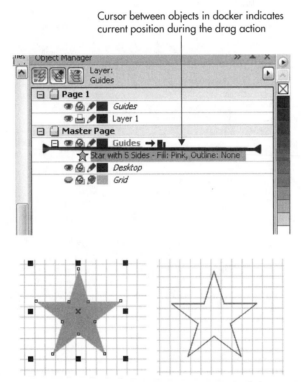

Cursor between objects in docker indicates current position during the drag action

Generally, after moving a shape to the Guides layer, it's a good practice to lock the layer, as described earlier. A guide that moves when you don't intend it to is as useful as a crèpe paper umbrella in a storm.

Using Guideline Presets

CorelDRAW's Guidelines feature comes with a group of presets that generate scripts to instantly add guidelines to your document. To use these scripts, press CTRL+J (Options); click to expand the tree directory under Document, Guidelines; and then click Presets, shown here. Click Apply Presets (you can add as many as you like in one fell swoop), and you have instant preset guides on the page. Basic Grid is a very useful preset because unlike the Grid feature, you can move, and thus customize, any of the guidelines.

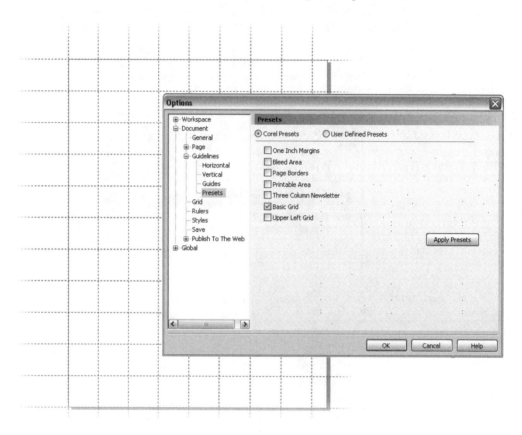

Many of the presets are page margins, many are timesavers, but you can also create your *own* preset. To define guidelines that automatically populate the page, choose the User Defined Presets option in the Presets page of the Options dialog. This displays a collection of options for you to create your own custom Margins, Columns, or Grid Guidelines. To activate any or all of these preset guideline effects, click the corresponding options and customize the associated preset values (see Figure 6-15).

 TIP *To open the Options dialog quickly to the Presets page while you currently have an unlocked Guideline selected, click the Preset Guidelines button on the Property Bar.*

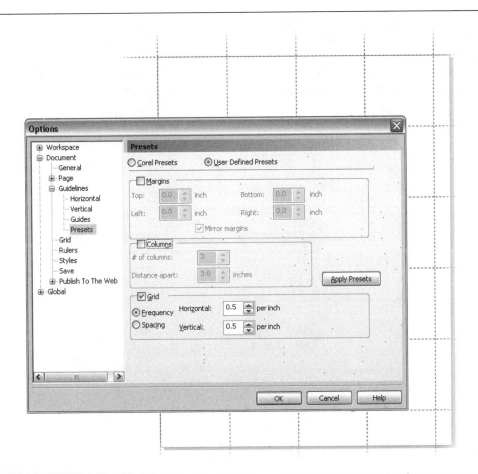

FIGURE 6-15   To apply your own guidelines according to custom options, click to activate any or all of these User Defined Presets options in the Presets dialog.

Altering Preset Guides and Saving Guides in a Template

Although preset guidelines behave like guidelines you drag from the Rulers, if you want to alter the preset arrangement by dragging one with the Pick Tool, the action triggers an *attention box*. This attention box is equivalent in seriousness to the tag you get on new pillows—it's for your own safety and is simply telling you that you're modifying a preset, your own or a Corel preset for guidelines. You can check the "Don't show warning again" box (shown below) to avoid it in the future. Basically, you cannot destroy or modify a Corel guideline preset by moving one of the guides on the page—the option is always there from session to session. And there's really nothing to mess up by altering a user preset guideline on the page after you've created one. There is no saved list of user presets; if you've created a user preset of grids, margins, or columns and want to save the modified or the original arrangement, you choose File | Save As Template. In the future, you can load a fresh new document based on the template, and your guides are all in place.

CHAPTER 7

Views, Zooming, Navigating Your Work

Artists who have embraced digital media enjoy not only new tools, but also new ways to *look* at our artwork. Because your CorelDRAW designs can be extremely large in final print size, right now is a good time to familiarize yourself with the ways you can zoom in and out of a design to get a better perspective as you work and examine and edit fine details. This chapter covers the different ways you can view dimensions of the drawing page and the level of detail displayed on your screen as you preview and work. Let the understanding you'll gain in this chapter provide you with a way to work smarter and more efficiently; these are qualities that are of value regardless of your skill level. Who knows? Learning the ins and outs of CorelDRAW document navigation might just be your ticket to better artwork in less time!

Setting View Mode

Because the type of artwork you usually design in CorelDRAW is vector artwork, the objects you create need to be written to screen from moment to moment: the process is called *rasterizing*. Realistically, with today's video cards and computer processors, the response time between changing an element in a file and seeing the change can usually be measured in a fraction of a second. CorelDRAW has always supported different levels of detail with which you view your CorelDRAW work; oddly enough they're accessed through the View menu, and these View modes serve more of a purpose than cranking down the level of detail if you're working on a 386 machine with 512K of RAM!

View modes can be used to specify how your drawing appears onscreen. They offer feedback as to how a design will print or export, and, for example, low detail modes can also save your skin if you've misplaced an object among hundreds of the same color. Switching between view modes can be done using the View menu or via keyboard shortcuts. The *View menu* itself indicates the current view using a button indicator.

You have the option of choosing from one of six display qualities: Simple Wireframe, Wireframe, Draft, Normal, Enhanced, and Enhanced with Overprints (which is the default view). The following section explains how these display modes render to screen paths and objects that have different fills and effects. Here you can see the list of View commands:

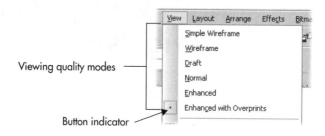

Wireframe and Simple Wireframe

The organization of views listed makes a top-to-bottom progression from low to high detail. At the top, Simple Wireframe and Wireframe provide the least detail and refresh onscreen almost immediately when you make edits or change the zoom level of your document. In Simple Wireframe viewing mode, all you see is the silhouette of vector objects: a thin black outline with no fill. This is a very useful view mode for locating a shape on the page when you don't have the time to perform a search in CorelDRAW (covered in Chapter 12). Simple Wireframe mode provides no view of object fills, but it does reveal the structure of effects objects such as Extrudes and Blends. Figure 7-1 is a visual comparison of Simple Wireframe, Wireframe, and the default viewing mode in CorelDRAW. Clearly, you're not going to apply fills to objects in Wireframe mode while you work, however, these different modes indeed provide user information about objects you don't usually see, and you can edit paths, copy objects, and perform most other necessary design tasks in any of these view modes.

Getting a Draft View

Draft view is the middle-ground of view quality between Wireframe and Enhanced modes. In Draft viewing mode, the objects in your drawing are rendered with color fills, but only Uniform fills are displayed with any accuracy. Outline properties such as dashed lines, width, and color are displayed. The two greatest visual differences between Draft and Enhanced views are that there is no anti-aliasing in Draft mode (so object edges look harsh and jaggy) and bitmaps and Fountain fills do not display as you'd expect them to.

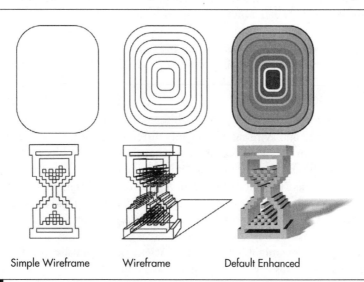

Simple Wireframe   Wireframe   Default Enhanced

FIGURE 7-1   View modes can help you see the structure of complex objects, and provide you with "unseen" clues where editing might be desired.

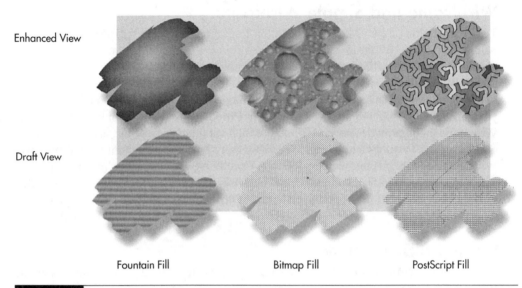

Enhanced View

Draft View

Fountain Fill   Bitmap Fill   PostScript Fill

FIGURE 7-2 Draft view provides Uniform color fill views and outline colors, but not more advanced object fills.

Figure 7-2 shows a Fountain Fill, a bitmap fill, and a PostScript fill viewed normally at the top and then at the bottom in Draft mode. There is a subtle visual indication that you can use to tell the difference between a bitmap and a Fountain Fill in this mode, but it's hardly worth the challenge. Draft mode is best used to evaluate basic color schemes in a vector drawing and for quickly navigating incredibly dense and complex illustrations such as CAD architecture designs and a single page containing 45,000 Extrude effect objects.

Using Normal View

Normal view displays all object properties—bitmap fills, Fountain fills, and PostScript fills—correctly, unlike Draft and Wireframe. The only difference between Enhanced and Normal view modes is that Normal mode does not anti-alias the edges of objects. *Anti-aliasing* is part of the rasterization process because visual data is written to the screen that creates a smooth transition whereas image areas have very different colors and brightness. This is usually done by adding pixels to the color edge of an object whose color is a blend between the neighboring, contrasting areas. The effect of anti-aliasing is particularly evident along edges of objects that travel diagonally across the page, and in curved areas such as circles and ellipses. Without anti-aliasing, the Normal view might remind you of Microsoft Paint back in 1991 when the best monitor you could buy was a VGA and you ran Windows 3.*x*.

Normal view mode will appeal to users whose video card doesn't have a lot of RAM, and to artists who create thousands of objects on a page. Screen refreshes are quicker, and if you don't mind the stair-steppy edges of aliased object edges, you can pick up some speed using Normal mode.

 Bitmaps—whether they're imported photos or bitmap fills you define using the Interactive Fill Tool— do not change their screen appearance if you switch from Normal to Enhanced view mode. Bitmaps do not update or refresh in CorelDRAW because the pixel color definitions are set within the image or fill.

Using Enhanced View

Enhanced view is similar to Enhanced with Overprints (see the following definition). In this view mode, all vector objects (text is a vector object too) are anti-aliased around the edges. It's your best view of your work, but not the default view. If you never create overprint objects, you might want to use this as your default view—the difference between Enhanced and Enhanced with Overprints is trivial to many users.

Enhanced with Overprints

Enhanced with Overprints is a print production preview mode, and it's the default view mode upon installing X4. Overprinting (see Chapter 28 for more details) is part of the standard commercial printing process used to prevent visible gaps between adjoining printed objects due to printing registration error, to accomplish proper color trapping, and to compensate for physical ink characteristics when applied to a surface. Imported bitmaps, bitmap fills, and PostScript fills are displayed onscreen as closely as possible to match printed output.

TIP   *To quickly switch between your current view mode and the last-used view mode, press SHIFT+F9.*

Zooming and Panning Pages

There are at least two meanings in CorelDRAW for the term *"view"* and the previous sections have covered only one of them: *view quality*, the level of detail with which you see your work. *Zooming*—increasing and decreasing the resolution of a page—and *panning* (sliding your view without zooming, similar to using the scroll bars on the edge of a document window) are the topics of the sections to follow. In the real world, evaluating the progress of a design from different perspectives is a chore when compared to CorelDRAW's workspace; you back into a ladder in your artist's loft, you can't find your favorite magnifying glass, and you wear the carpet thin moving toward and away from your canvas! These days, one way to work faster (and usually smarter) is through a digital design program such as CorelDRAW. Another good way is to master all the features for zooming your view, as I'll cover next.

Using the Zoom Tool and Property Bar

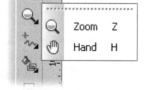

The Zoom Tool is the fourth tool located on the Toolbox, is clearly marked by its magnifying glass icon, and can be used to zoom in and zoom out of a page.

When you've chosen the Zoom Tool, the Property Bar (see Figure 7-3) displays buttons plus a drop-down selector that provides just about every common degree of magnification you could ask for (if you're currently not comfortable manipulating the Zoom Tool's cursor manually).

The following list describes the purpose of these options on the Property Bar:

- **Zoom Levels** To increase your current view by a preset magnification, use the Zoom Levels drop-down selector from the Standard Property Bar when the Zoom Tool is not chosen. When the tool is chosen you'll want to use the Zoom Tool Property Bar. You'll find selections ranging from 10 to 400 percent, and some quick views for zooming based on page size. You can also type a value directly in the Zoom Levels combo box and then press ENTER, however the Zoom Levels always increase and decrease beginning at the center of the drawing window. The option to "zoom in to 400 percent, but zoom toward the lower left of the window" isn't an option. Views saved in the View Manager (discussed later in this chapter) are also included on the drop-down list.

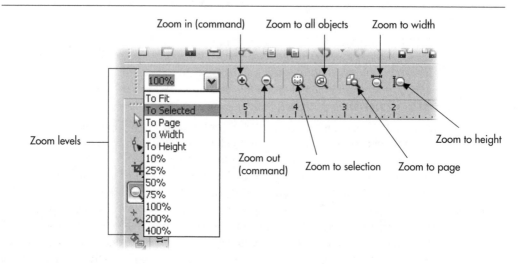

FIGURE 7-3 Here are all the Property Bar options you'll need to navigate a magnified CorelDRAW document.

■ **Zoom In**   Zoom In is the default state while the Zoom Tool is selected. Clicking once in the drawing window increases your view magnification by twice the current percentage of zoom—100 percent goes to 200 percent with a click, then to 400 percent with another click in the window. Here's an important point: when you zoom in this way, using the tool and not the Zoom Levels selections, *you zoom in centered relative to the tool's cursor location onscreen.* You direct the final point of your zoom by centering it with your cursor. You can also use the Zoom Tool to perform *marquee* zooming, visually described in Figure 7-4. You place your cursor at the corner of the area you want to magnify, and then click-drag diagonally to the opposing corner of an imaginary bounding box that defines the area to which you want to zoom. You can target any two opposing corners, but most users tend to diagonally drag from upper left to lower right of an area.

TIP   *CorelDRAW X4's zooming extent runs from a minimum of 1 percent to a maximum of 405,651 percent. You'd be hard-pressed to need a greater magnification range. The Royal Observatory in Edinburgh is currently looking into CorelDRAW X4— they downloaded the trial version.*

■ **Zoom Out**   To decrease your view magnification using the Zoom Tool, click the right mouse button anywhere on or off your document page, or hold Shift in combination with the left mouse button (in case your right mouse button is broken). Alternatively, click the Zoom Out button on the Property Bar. Doing so decreases your view to your last-used magnification or by a power of 2, similar to zooming in, and the center of the zoom out is the center of the drawing window. Identical to

Begin at a corner   Click-drag to the opposing corner   Zoomed-in area

FIGURE 7-4   Marquee-dragging is the easy way to pinpoint a location and zoom in.

Zoom in (normal
tool state, click left
mouse button)

Zoom out (hold SHIFT
while using Zoom
Tool, or right-click)

zooming in, zooming out while using the Zoom Tool is directed by the location of the Zoom Tool cursor onscreen. If you want, for example, to zoom out to the upper right of a page, you put the cursor at the upper right of the page and then right-click. To zoom out while any tool is selected, press F3.

- **Zoom One-Shot** The Zoom One-Shot command is for selecting the Zoom Tool momentarily for a single Zoom In or Zoom Out command while you are using any tool. Once the zoom has been accomplished, your previous tool reappears. This zoom command is available in CorelDRAW X4, but you won't find it on any toolbar or the Property Bar. Instead, it's an unassigned feature that you can access only through customization using a button. If you're a keyboard shortcut sort of CorelDRAW user, F2 is your key. To make the Zoom One-shot appear as a button in a logical and convenient place, the Property Bar is ideal—the Zoom One-Shot can be seen there whenever the Pick Tool is chosen. Open the Options dialog (CTRL+J), click Customization | Commands to display the command customization page, and choose View from the drop-down menu. Then, find the Zoom One-Shot button, drag the button to the Property Bar (right after the Apply Layout to Current Page button is good), and release the button, though only after you see a horizontal I-beam to confirm that you're adding the button to the desired location, as shown here.

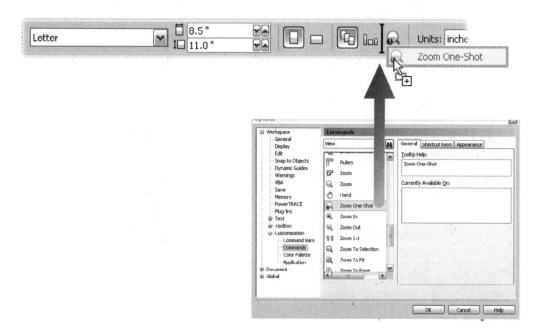

■ **Zoom To Selection**   When you have one or more objects selected in the drawing window, choosing this command changes your view magnification and viewing position of the page to show the entire selection in the window. Choose Zoom To Selection from either the Zoom Property Bar or the Zoom Levels drop-down selector list. You can also Zoom to a selected object while *any* tool is selected by pressing SHIFT+F2.

■ **Zoom To All Objects**   Zoom To All Objects changes your view magnification to display all objects visible in your document window, regardless of whether the objects are on or off the current document page. Choose Zoom To All Objects from either the Zoom Property Bar or the Zoom Levels drop-down menu. Alternatively, use the F4 shortcut while any tool is selected.

■ **Zoom To Page**   This changes your view to fit your current page size completely within the document window. Choose Zoom To Page from either the Zoom Property Bar or the Zoom Levels drop-down menu, or press SHIFT+F4 while any tool is selected.

■ **Zoom To Width/Height Of Page**   These two commands enable zoom your view to the entire width or height of the current page. You'll find these tool buttons located in the Zoom Property Bar or the Zoom Levels drop-down menu.

Using the Mouse Wheel for Zooming

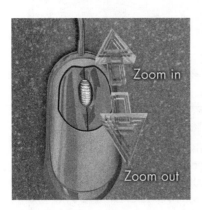

Zoom in

Zoom out

Affordable, high-quality input devices such as the mouse and even some styli for graphics tablets have had a combo wheel/button between the left and the right since the 1990s. Applications (when the engineers wrote the feature in) can scroll a document window and also zoom a document window. Happily, Corel engineers built this capability in for zooming (it's enabled by default). To zoom into a page, push the scroll wheel away from you; zooming out is done by dragging the mouse (or stylus) wheel toward you, as shown here. If you don't care for this feature, you can restore mouse wheel action to scrolling by choosing Options (CTRL+J) | Workspace | Display, and then choosing Scroll from the Default Action for Mouse Wheel drop-down list.

NOTE   *If your zooms feel jerky when you're using the scroll wheel, this is not a CorelDRAW problem, but rather that of the physical wheel (the way it was designed). But you may be able to fine-tune the scroll action using the manufacturer's mouse driver options. The best place to check for mouse options is in Windows Start Menu | Control Panel |* Whatever icon you see for your mouse (if any). *If there's no icon for your mouse (or other input device) in the Control Panel, check Start | All Programs.*

Customizing View Shortcuts

Many of the Zoom and Hand Tool commands in CorelDRAW have preassigned
shortcut keys that can be changed. To access these shortcut key commands for
viewing, follow these steps:

1. Open the Options dialog (CTRL+J) or choose Tools | Options.

2. On the left side of the dialog, click to expand Customization, and then click
   Commands to view the Commands page.

3. Choose View from the drop-down menu at the top-left corner of the right side
   of the dialog box and notice that a list of view items appears below it. In this
   list, click to select the tool or command to change, as shown next.

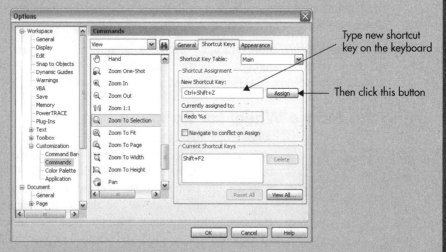

4. Click the Shortcut Keys tab at the top of the right-most section of the dialog
   box to display the Shortcut Key options. Click to make an insertion point in
   the New Shortcut Key box, and then press the key combination (or single key)
   that you want to assign as the new shortcut. If, as shown in this example, you
   want Zoom To Selection to be CTRL+SHIFT+Z instead of the default SHIFT+F2,
   you press SHIFT and CTRL and Z at the same time (you *don't* type "Shift" or
   "Ctrl"). If a conflict appears in the Currently Assigned To field, you can re-
   think your custom keyboard combo, or dismiss (overwrite) the default key
   assignment by just clicking Assign. Click the Assign button when you've got
   the keyboard key combo of your dreams entered.

5. To delete a shortcut that has already been assigned, click the shortcut in the
   Current Shortcut Keys box and then click the Delete button.

6. Click OK to close the dialog box and apply the shortcut key changes.

TIP *You can quickly Zoom To All Objects on or off your document page by double-clicking the Zoom Tool button in the Toolbox.*

Using the Hand Tool

The Hand Tool is a convenient alternative to using document scroll bars; it's your avatar for your physical hand while in CorelDRAW. The Hand Tool's keyboard shortcut is H (an easy mnemonic!) and it works exactly as you'd expect it to. To use it, you click-drag in the drawing window and your view will travel in the same direction. The principle advantage to using the Hand Tool over the document window scroll bar "thumbs" (that screen element in the center of a scroll bar you use to click-drag) is one of economy; you don't have to put in several "mouse miles" to change your view, and the Hand Tool is great for adjusting your document view by a fraction of an inch, with precision.

The Hand Tool's cursor looks like a hand (Corel engineers gave a lot of consideration to the cursor), and with a click-drag, you can scroll your view in any direction (often called panning) as you would do with a camera. As you do this, the scroll bars and Document Rulers move in unison to reflect the new position.

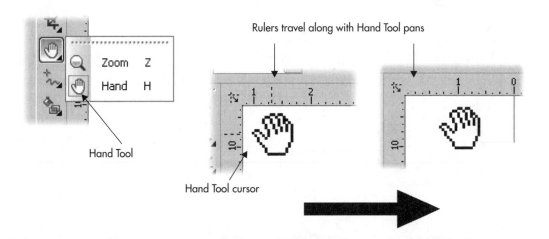

 TIP *Double-click the Hand Tool button in the Toolbox to instantly center your page view.*

Several shortcuts are available while using the Hand Tool, some of which relate to zooming, not panning. A right mouse click using the Hand Tool takes you to the Zoom Out command, and a double-click action causes a Zoom In command. You can also use

Controlling Zoom and Hand Tool Behavior

The Options dialog is where you can customize certain actions when using the Zoom and Hand Tools. Right mouse button clicks, by default, trigger Zoom Out for both the Zoom and Hand Tools. However, you might want to reassign right-clicking for the Hand and Zoom Tools to be more consistent with the right-click behavior—in other words, to display a pop-up context menu like the other Toolbox tools do.

If this is your preference, you can change your right mouse button clicks by opening the Options dialog (CTRL+J) and clicking to expand the tree directories under Toolbox | Zoom | Hand Tool, as shown here. In this dialog, you may set the behavior of the right mouse button clicks, using either tool to open the pop-up menu instead.

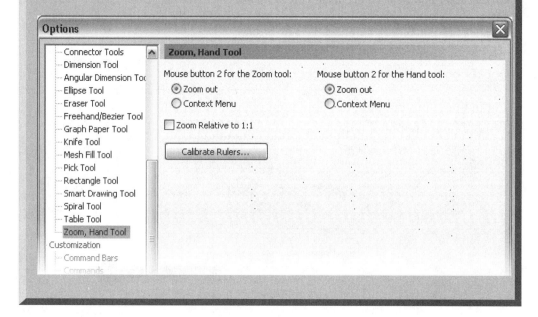

the keyboard to pan the view of your document while any tool is selected using these shortcuts:

- **Pan left**   Press and hold ALT+LEFT ARROW
- **Pan right**   Press and hold ALT+RIGHT ARROW
- **Pan up**   Press and hold ALT+UP ARROW
- **Pan down**   Press and hold ALT+DOWN ARROW

Special View Modes

There are *other* types of "views found" in CorelDRAW. In addition to viewing quality and resolution, you might have the need to change the page order in a multi-page document for a tidier presentation. Hey, you could certainly do with a preview setting that eliminates the workspace and puts the focus on your artwork, too!

The following sections explore these features, how to work with them, and how to provide views of your work you might not even have considered. You're going to *love* this stuff.

Page Sorter View

CorelDRAW X4's Page Sorter view (covered in detail in Chapter 5) becomes available as a special View mode when your document has at least one page; two or more pages will be more useful, because it's silly to try to sort one page (and impossible if you have less than one page). To go into Page Sorter View mode, choose View | Page Sorter View. While viewing a document in the Page Sorter, you can browse several pages at one time and manage their properties as a collection instead of thumbing through single pages. While using this view, your pages and all their contents are displayed in miniature, but no other view in CorelDRAW can show you a complete document page flow and offer you the chance to reorder pages and their properties in one fell swoop. The Pick Tool is the only available tool in this view, and the Property Bar displays several options unique to this document view. You can reorder pages by dragging them to different locations in the current order or right-click specific pages to rename, insert, and delete them (see Figure 7-5).

When a specific page is selected in the Page Sorter, a number of Property Bar options are available for changing its orientation or size to defaults or to a preset page size. You can also change it to a specific measure by changing the values in the page width and height boxes.

To exit Page Sorter view and return to your original document View mode, click the Page Sorter View button as shown in Figure 7-6.

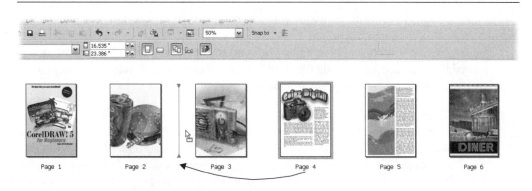

Page 4 is being scooted in front of Page 3

FIGURE 7-5   Page reordering in a multi-page document is as easy as drag and drop.

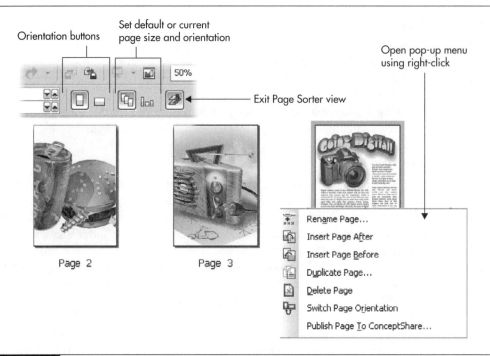

FIGURE 7-6 You have options on both the Property Bar and the pop-up Context menu for changing pages.

 To navigate to a specific page in your document quickly and simultaneously close the Page Sorter view, double-click any page's thumbnail.

Full Screen Preview

To fill the entire screen with a view of your current document page at the current zoom level, use View | Full Screen Preview, or press the F9 shortcut key. This view hides all of CorelDRAW X4's interface —including your cursor—and shows only the current view rendered in Enhanced View mode (the Full Screen Preview default view). To return to your view back to Normal, click any key or either mouse button.

NOTE *Depending on any desktop utilities you might have installed, there might be a conflict between the F9 shortcut to get to Full Screen Preview and something such as a desktop calendar or local weather applet. There are a number of remedies: you can define a different keyboard shortcut, use the View menu or the pop-up menu instead of a keyboard shortcut, or remove the desktop utility (it probably doesn't tell you the correct weather in Kazakhstan anyway).*

While using Full Screen Preview, the View mode and Page Border View appearance is set according to preferences in the Options dialog. To access these options, choose Tools | Options (CTRL+J) and click Display under the Workspace category on the left side of the dialog to access the Display options. Full Screen Preview options, located in the lower part of the dialog, let you choose either Draft or Enhanced view (the default) as the View mode and to enable or disable viewing of the page border.

Previewing Selected Only

The Preview Selected Only command, available from the View menu, lets you preview only what's selected on the page before entering this mode. This option works using the Full Screen Preview preferences and takes a toggle state either On or Off when selected. There are two caveats to using this command: if no objects are selected, the Full Screen Preview offers a nice, energy-wasting white blank screen and you'll also get similar views of all-white if the selected object is not in view before entering this mode. The result you get with Preview selected only depends entirely on what's framed in the document window at what viewing resolution you have defined before using the command.

Using the View Navigator

The *View Navigator* is a pop-up viewer that is indispensable for navigating your entire document page when you've zoomed in to 10,000 percent and need to quickly move to a different design area without zooming out to get your bearings. The View Navigator pop-up window is at the point where the vertical and horizontal scroll bars meet at the lower-right corner of the document window. To open the View Navigator pop-up, click-hold action on the button itself, the magnifying glass icon.

Click-holding causes a pop-up thumbnail to appear, which represents the outermost region of the page and the application's desktop. The preview frame—the tiny rectangle with the crosshairs through it— within the View Navigator window indicates the viewing limitations according to your current Zoom settings. Click-drag within the View Navigator pop-up window to pan around your drawing in the document window; it's panning by proxy. As you drag, releasing the mouse button ends the navigation.

In Figure 7-7 you can see the View Navigator put to the test. Let's say there's a need to edit the 6-point text in this drawing of a tabletop jukebox. At 100 percent viewing resolution this would be a true hassle; luckily, by zooming in it's easy to see the text, edit it, and then edit the next Top 40 tune title by panning the window using the View Navigator.

7

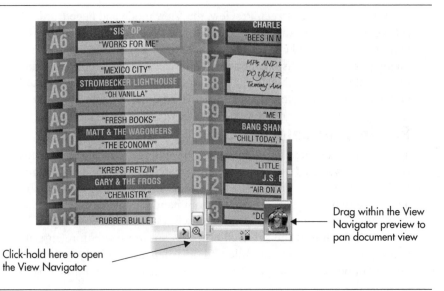

Drag within the View Navigator preview to pan document view

Click-hold here to open the View Navigator

FIGURE 7-7 The View Navigator steers you in the right direction for precise editing in very tight views.

Using the View Manager Docker

Imagine a bookmark feature in CorelDRAW that takes you to a location and viewing resolution on one or more pages just by clicking the link. This is what the View Manager does: you can define zoom levels and page locations, you can browse to any number of pages in the same document, and your document is not only better organized for future edits, but View Manager is a darned good presentation tool as well!

To open the View Manager, choose Window | Dockers | View Manager or press CTRL+F2. Figure 7-8 shows a practical use (one of many) for the View Manager: here you can see an architectural drawing. All the different parts of the building have been "viewed," and different pans and zooms have been defined for the atrium, the front entrance, and so on. Now the illustrator or client can click around the structure (and become so impressed the building is immediately approved for zoning and construction) and get a composite view from one drawn piece.

Exploring View Manager Commands

When a view is saved, its page number, position, and view magnification are recorded and become a new view in the View Manager docker window. The View *mode* isn't saved—such as Simple Wireframe, Draft, Normal, Enhanced and so on—but this is trivial because you

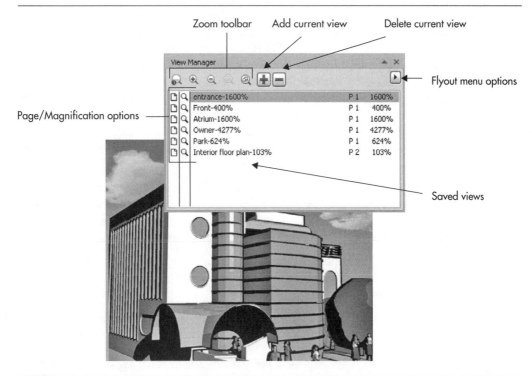

FIGURE 7-8   When working with complex drawings, the View Manager provides a quick way
of saving and recalling views.

learned earlier in this chapter how to manually define View quality with any document at
any time.

This sort of feature calls for a hands-on review, tutorial style. There are no "right" or
"wrong" steps you can make—this is just an exploration by-the-numbers!

Making and Taking a Structured View
of a Document

1. Open an existing document containing a drawing, either completed or in progress
   and the more complex the better, and then open the View Manager docker window
   (CTRL+F2).

2. Using page navigation commands and the Zoom Tool, the Zoom command buttons
   on the Zoom Toolbar, and/or the View Navigator feature, go to a specific part of
   your drawing in the document window.

3. To create and save your current view, click the Add Current View button in the docker. Notice that a new item appears in the View Manager docker. By default, the new view is automatically named View-*nn-nnnn%*; the first numbers after "View" represent a sequence in which you save views, while the last digits before the percent symbol tell you the magnification level of the saved view. At the right on the docker is the page number for the saved view and the zoom percentage again. The zoom percentage is an important label at the right of each saved zoom and cannot be edited. However, you'll definitely want to replace the first zoom percentage with an evocative name for the zoom—this first zoom percentage field is just a default name for the saved zoom.

4. To name the view, click once on the name to select it and then type a name to enter the new view name. Your view is now saved. If you want, save more new views using the same procedure; change the view display in your document window each time, and then click the Add Current View button each time to save each view.

5. To go to a view, click either the page number or the view magnification title of the saved view on the docker's list. Your view is then changed to the exact point at which it was saved.

6. To delete a specific view in the View Manager docker, click to select the view and then click the Delete Current View button. The view is immediately deleted.

 In addition to the interactive methods you can use to save, name, recall, and delete saved views, the same operations can be accomplished by choosing commands on the flyout menu located on the View Manager's docker window.

Using Page and Zoom Options

To the left of each saved view in the View Manager, two options will appear. These options enable you to control how your saved views are recalled and restored. For each view saved, you can toggle display of the Page Only and the Magnification Only to On or Off. Single-clicks activate or deactivate these options; grayed-out options indicate an inactive state.

When the page symbol is deactivated, recalling the corresponding saved view causes only the magnification to be recalled; when the zoom symbol is deactivated, only the page display is recalled. While both are deactivated, the saved view does absolutely nothing.

Hopefully, this chapter has shown you the way—both as an allegory and literally—to better get a fix on what it is you've drawn, what you *want* to draw, and what appears to need an edit or two. Thanks to zoom features that let you hone in on a fly's eye or zoom out to a scaled drawing of Chicago, you now have a handle on the magnifying glass and other tools for panning, navigating, and recalling areas of interest in your work.

Selection techniques are the focus of Chapter 8, which is only natural because this chapter taught you how to look—and it's no fun to look and not touch!

CHAPTER 8

Moving, Scaling, Rotating: Basic Transformations

Most of the time when you create or import an object, it's not exactly where you want it on the page. It might be an inch away from where you want it, or a little too large, or rotated a few degrees off from where you want it to be—you get the picture. This chapter covers the common, and not so common, methods you can use in CorelDRAW for transforming objects, from the manual approach to pin-point precise numerical entry. After reading this chapter, you'll have the skills and techniques for composing elements on a page the way you want them, and you can stop cursing at the cursor!

Basic Object Selection

To select an object for repositioning or applying some other transformation, you choose the Pick Tool from the Toolbox and then click on it; the easiest way to select more than one object is by holding Shift, which performs selection additively. With one or more items selected, you'll notice that information about the selected shapes is displayed in two key areas on the interface: the Property Bar (see the top illustration) and the Status Bar (see the bottom illustration). Also, many of the dockers display object information when they are open onscreen.

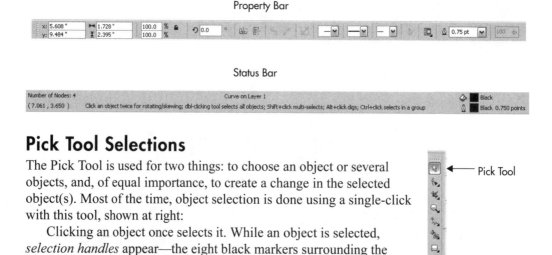

Property Bar

Status Bar

Pick Tool Selections

The Pick Tool is used for two things: to choose an object or several objects, and, of equal importance, to create a change in the selected object(s). Most of the time, object selection is done using a single-click with this tool, shown at right:

Pick Tool

Clicking an object once selects it. While an object is selected, *selection handles* appear—the eight black markers surrounding the object, as shown in Figure 8-1. Additionally, depending on the type of object, you'll see nodes at various areas around the object, which indicate breaks in the path (when a vector object is selected) or the edge of an object (when a bitmap is selected). A small *X* marker appears at the centermost point of the object, indicating its center origin. This origin can be moved and it's quite useful for defining a center of rotation for an object, and will be discussed later in this chapter.

Occasionally you or a coworker will create a shape with an outline stroke that's very narrow and, as a result, the object has no fill. If you're having trouble selecting the darned

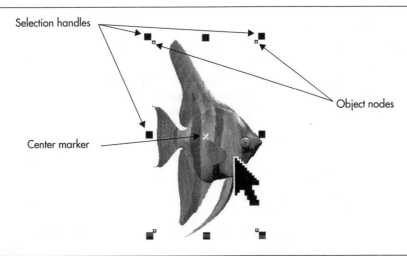

Selection handles

Object nodes

Center marker

FIGURE 8-1   Select any object with a single click using the Pick Tool.

thing with the Pick Tool, it's quite understandable, and you might want to activate the Treat All Objects as Filled option. Open the Options dialog (CTRL+J) and choose Workspace | Toolbox | Pick Tool from the tree at left. Click the Treat All Objects As Filled check box and then click OK to close the dialog, as shown in Figure 8-2.

Click this option to treat all selected objects as though they have a fill.

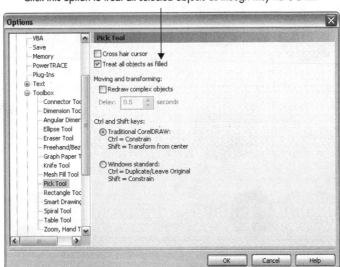

FIGURE 8-2   Choosing this option lets you select unfilled objects by clicking anywhere on them.

Object Selection Techniques

You can use a number of tricks while navigating through a selection of objects or for selecting more than one object at a time using the Pick Tool. Most of these techniques involve holding modifier keys while clicking or click-dragging to select more (or fewer) shapes or objects. Many of these object-selection techniques can also be used in combination with each other. Here's how you can make a selection of more than one object in one fell swoop.

- **SHIFT-Clicking to Select** Holding the SHIFT key while clicking an unselected object adds it to your current selection. This also works in the reverse: holding SHIFT while clicking a selected object deselects the object.

- **Marquee-Selecting Objects** To select all objects in a specific area, click-drag diagonally with the Pick Tool to surround the objects; a dashed blue outline representing the rectangular area of select appears until you release the mouse button. While doing so, all object shapes completely within the area you define become selected, as shown in Figure 8-3. The complete object's shape must be surrounded for it to become selected. Holding SHIFT while using the marquee-selection technique causes unselected objects to be selected and it also causes selected objects to become unselected.

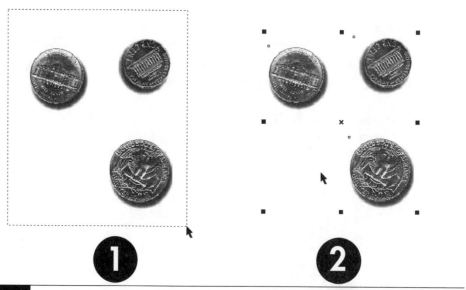

FIGURE 8-3 A click-drag with the Pick Tool in any direction marquee-selects the objects that are completely surrounded.

■ **Holding ALT While Marquee-Selecting**   If you come to CorelDRAW from Adobe Illustrator, you can use the convention of selecting objects that are only tangentially selected in a marquee selection technique. Holding the ALT key as the modifier while click-dragging to marquee a specific area causes all objects within—and even those whose *edge* you touch—to become selected. Holding SHIFT+ALT while marquee-selecting causes the reverse to occur, deselecting any objects that are already selected.

■ **Pressing TAB to Select Next Object**   Suppose you have a bunch of objects in a document, but some of them overlap, and you're getting nowhere by attempting to click the one you need. Pressing the TAB key alone while the Pick Tool is active selects a shape and causes the next single object arranged directly behind your current selection to become selected (whether or not it overlaps the current object). Holding SHIFT while pressing the TAB key causes the single object arranged directly in front of your current selection to become selected. This Tabbing action works because each new object created is automatically ordered in front of the last created object—no matter how the object was created (for example, using various Duplicate, Repeat, Transformation, or Object Effect creation methods). Tabbing cycles through single object selection on a page, whether you have a current object selected, or none at all. The key is to begin Tabbing after you've chosen the Pick Tool.

■ **ALT+click to Select Objects Covered By Other Objects**   To select an object that is ordered in back of and hidden by other objects, hold the ALT key while the Pick Tool is selected and then click where the object is located. Each time you ALT+click with the Pick Tool, objects that are ordered further back in the stack are selected, enabling you to "dig" to select hidden objects.

8

The Pick Tool's Shape Tool State

If you're getting an idea that the Pick Tool has a host of hidden features, you're right. One of these is its alternate state—the temporary Shape Tool state. There's a close relationship shared by the Pick Tool and the Shape Tool, hinted at by the fact that these two tools are relatively close in their appearance and in their interconnected uses. As shown in the next illustration, the Pick Tool can temporarily act like the Shape Tool while a single object is selected and when held over object nodes, but this isn't its normal behavior.

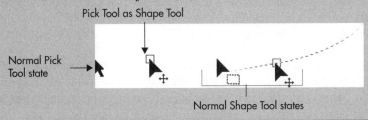

Pick Tool as Shape Tool

Normal Pick Tool state

Normal Shape Tool states

Typically, the Pick Tool is used for selecting and transforming objects, while the Shape Tool is used for editing curves and selecting object nodes. The temporary Shape Tool state enables you to alter the "path shape" of objects at the node level without changing tools.

To use this feature, be sure the *Enable Node Tracking* option is selected in the Display page of the Options dialog. (To access this, choose Tools | Options and click to select Workspace | Display in the tree directory.) This enormous convenience enables you to edit single nodes or control points and applies to any single object selected type, including open and closed paths, Ellipse, Star, Polygon as stars, Graph Paper objects, and even bitmaps. The next illustration shows this temporary state in action; you'll see in your work that when the Pick Tool is outside of a shape it looks like an arrow cursor. However, after an object is selected and the tool is positioned inside a shape, the tool presumes you want to perform an operation such as moving the selected shape, and it becomes a four-headed arrow:

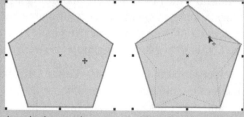

Pick Tool selecting object   Pick Tool in Shape Tool state selecting object with object node selected and moving node

TIP   *Although you can select nodes with the Pick Tool when Enable node mapping is active, you can't perform editing operations other than moving a node. To create all the different attributes a node can have and to create curves from straight path segments, you need to use the genuine Shape Tool.*

Selecting Objects by Type

So far, you've learned to select any objects on or off your page. But you may also select objects by their type (such as Text objects, Guidelines, or path nodes) using commands from the Select All menu, shown in Figure 8-4. Each time you use a command, a new selection is made (and any current selection of objects becomes *not* selected).

Here's how each of the commands is used.

- **Select All Objects**   Choosing Edit | Select All | Objects causes all objects in your current document window to become selected. Quicker is the CTRL+A keyboard shortcut, which accomplishes the same result, and is easy to remember; it's used by many professional software programs.

FIGURE 8-4 Select items in your document by using the Select command.

8

> **TIP** *Double-clicking the Pick Tool button in the Toolbox instantly selects all visible objects in your current document window view.*

- **Select All Text** Choosing Edit | Select All | Text instantly selects all text objects both on and off the current document page. Both Artistic and Paragraph Text objects become selected after using this command (unless they have been grouped with other objects, in which case they are ignored). Text objects applied with effects (such as Contour or Extrude effects) also become selected using this command.

- **Select All Guidelines** Guidelines are actually a class of document page objects, different from objects you draw, but objects nonetheless. To select all Guidelines on your document page, choose Edit | Select All | Guidelines. Selected Guidelines are indicated by a color change (red, by default). To select guidelines, they must be visible and cannot be locked; use the Tools | Object Manager to edit the properties of guidelines before you try to select them. If guidelines you've placed aren't currently visible on your page, choose View | Guidelines.

> **TIP** *Guidelines can be created using a click-drag action from your Ruler onto your document page. Choose View | Rulers to display CorelDRAW X4's Ruler feature.*

All nodes selected by ALT+clicking a node

FIGURE 8-5 Select all the nodes on an object quickly with the Shape Tool and an ALT+click.

- **Select All Nodes** You must have both the Shape Tool and an object selected (closed or open paths qualify) to use this Select command. Choose Edit | Select All | Nodes to select all the object's path nodes. For a quicker method in the same situation, use the CTRL+A shortcut, or hold ALT while clicking any node, shown in Figure 8-5. (Special objects, such as Rectangles, Ellipses, and Polygons, are not eligible for the Select All Nodes command because their shapes are defined dynamically by "control" points instead of nodes.)

 Shapes are often made up of two or more paths that have been combined. To select all the nodes on a combined path, first select the object and then double-click the Shape tool on the Toolbox.

Moving Objects

When moving objects, it's important to lift using your legs and position yourself carefully to avoid back injury. However, when moving objects in *CorelDRAW*, it's a lot less stressful and you basically have two options: to move objects directly by using the Pick Tool and dragging and by using the keyboard arrows to precision nudge objects in any of the four possible directions.

 For information on moving and transforming objects, see the section "Applying Precise Transformation," later in this chapter.

Using the Pick Tool

Holding the Pick Tool over certain areas of a selected object will cause the tool's positioning cursor to become active, as shown in Figure 8-6. This means a click-drag action on the area will move your selected object(s) in any direction. As you drag your object, you'll see a preview outline, indicating its new position. When the mouse button is released, the move is complete.

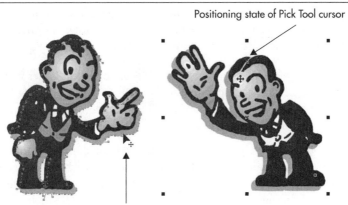

Positioning state of Pick Tool cursor

Positioning state of Shape Tool cursor

FIGURE 8-6   These two cursors show the positioning state of the Pick Tool and the Shape Tool.

 If you're having difficulty selecting and/or moving an object because it's too small, you can increase your view magnification using the Zoom Tool or use the keyboard nudge keys, covered next.

Using Nudge Keys

As an alternate to using the Pick Tool, you can also move selected objects incrementally with your keyboard arrow keys—a technique called *nudging*. To nudge a selected object, press the UP, DOWN, LEFT, or RIGHT arrow key. Your object will be moved by the nudge value specified in the Rulers page of the Options dialog. You can customize the Nudge distance by opening the Options dialog (CTRL+J), clicking to expand the tree directory under Workspace and Document, and clicking to display the Rulers options page, as shown here:

Nudge increment options

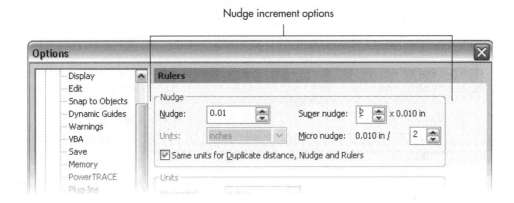

Using nudge keys, you can perform moves according to this value or by larger or smaller values. These are referred to as *Super* and *Micro nudges*. Like "normal" nudges, these values are set in the Ruler options page. Here are the techniques for using Super and Micro nudges:

- **Super Nudge** This action moves a selected object in larger increments than a normal nudge. To use Super Nudge, hold SHIFT while pressing the UP, DOWN, LEFT, or RIGHT arrow key on your keyboard. By default, this causes your selected object to move by 0.2 inch.

- **Micro Nudge** The pint-sized version of a typical nudge is the Micro Nudge, which moves your object in smaller increments. To use Micro Nudge, hold CTRL while pressing the UP, DOWN, LEFT, or RIGHT arrow key on your keyboard. By default, Micro nudges cause the selected object to move by 0.05 inch.

Transforming Objects

A *transformation* is any type of object shape or position change, short of actually editing the object's properties. This includes changing its position, size, skew, and/or rotating or reflecting it. Dragging on an object directly in a document is more intuitive than precision transformations—but both approaches to transformation have their own special advantages. In this section, you'll learn how to apply transformations using both techniques.

Transforming Objects Using the Cursor

For the intuitive method, the Pick Tool is what you need to transform objects by the simple act of click and dragging. Depending on the type of transformation you need to apply, you can click-drag any of the four, black, square selection handles that surround the selected object or group of objects to change an object's size *proportionally*, by width only and by height only. Dragging any middle selection handle or side handle scales the object disproportionately— "smush" and "stretch" are the more common terms for disproportionate scaling, as shown in Figure 8-7.

During transformations, CorelDRAW keeps track of the object's transformed size, position, width, height, scale, and rotation angle. If you master these basic transformation operations, you'll be well on your way to becoming a highly skilled digital designer.

 CorelDRAW X4 remembers your object's original shape from the time it was created, regardless of how many transformations have been applied to it. The advantage is that you can remove all transformations and restore the object to its original state in a single command. To remove transformations from your object, choose Arrange | Clear Transformations to return your object to its original shape immediately.

Original   Proportional scaling   Disproportional scaling

FIGURE 8-7   Dragging these handles changes the size of an object proportionately or otherwise.

8

While transforming objects, you can constrain certain shape properties by holding modifier keys. Here are the effects of holding modifier keys for constraining a transformed object's shape:

- **To Change Object Size (Scale)**   Click-drag any corner handle to change an object's size *proportionally,* meaning the relative width and height remains in proportion to the original object shape. Hold ALT while dragging any corner selection handle to change an object's shape *disproportionally,* meaning width and height change, regardless of original proportions.

- **To Change Width or Height Only**   Click-drag any side, top, or bottom selection handle to change the size of the object in the drag direction. Hold SHIFT while doing this to change the width or height from the center of the object, or hold CTRL while dragging to change the width or height in 200-percent increments.

TIP	*When transforming an object using the Pick Tool, click the right mouse button during the transformation to have the active object you're dragging become a copy, applying the transformation to a duplicate, not the original.*

You can also rotate or skew an object using Pick Tool states that become available after you click a selected object a second time. This action causes the selection handles to change to Rotation and Skew handles, as shown in Figure 8-8.

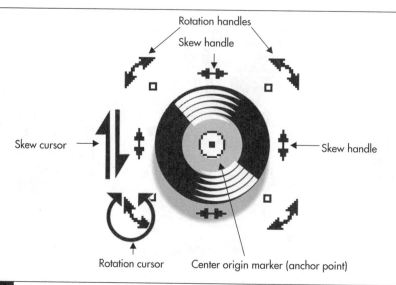

Rotation handles

Skew handle

Skew cursor

Skew handle

Rotation cursor   Center origin marker (anchor point)

FIGURE 8-8   Clicking on a selected object will cause these Rotation/Skew handles to appear.

You control the point around which objects are rotated or skewed, by moving the center origin marker or anchor point of an object or group of objects. Your cursor will change to display either the rotation or a skew cursor when held over a corner or side handle. A good creative example of offsetting the original center of an object is shown in the following illustration. The spade shape is a simple extrusion, and by putting its origin at the crosshairs in this illustration, rotating, and then right-clicking to transform a duplicate, a wonderfully intricate pattern can be made in less than a minute.

 TIP   *To flip a selected object quickly, either vertically or horizontally, use the Mirror Vertical and Mirror Horizontal buttons in the Property Bar while using the Pick Tool.*

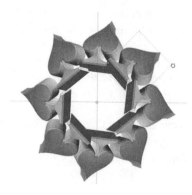

Using the Free Transform Tool

The *Free Transform* Tool offers a certain degree of redundancy with other tools but, nonetheless, it has certain interactive advantages in that it offers a live preview of the new shape of the object(s) being transformed. You'll find it grouped together with the Shape, Knife, and Eraser Tools, as shown here.

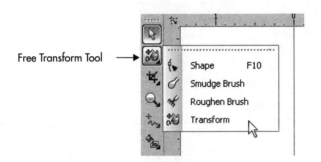

When you use the Free Transform Tool, you'll notice the Property Bar offers four modes of transformation: Free Rotation, Free Angle Reflection, Free Scale, and Free Skew, as shown here.

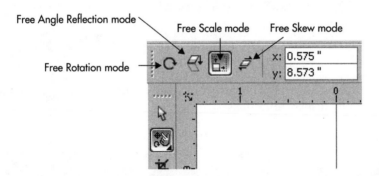

To transform a selected object in one of these four modes, click to select the mode, and then use a click-drag action on your object. As you drag, a live preview of the new object's shape appears. While using Rotation or Angle Reflection modes, a reference line appears as you drag to indicate the object's angle transformation from its original state, as shown next.

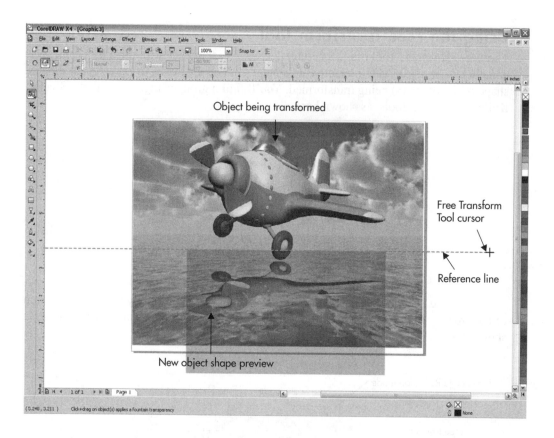

Using free Transformation, plus a little transparency, gives you the artistic opportunity to design images that faithfully display reflections.

Copying Effects with the Eyedropper and Paintbucket Tools

In CorelDRAW X4, you can copy applied effects (including applied transformations) between objects using the Eyedropper and Paintbucket tools. To do this, choose the Eyedropper Tool, have both the objects in view, and use these steps:

1. Click the object currently applied with the transformation you want to copy using the Eyedropper Tool cursor to sample its properties.

(Continued)

2. Using Property Bar options, choose Object Attributes, click the Transformation button, click the check box next to the transformation type you intend to copy in the list (shown next), and then click OK. You can choose Size, Rotation, and/or Position as the transformation to copy.

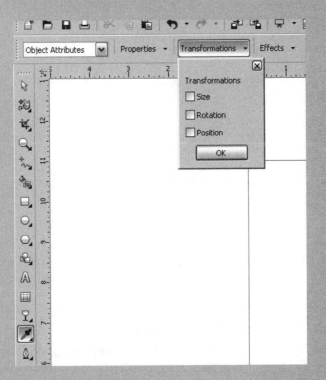

8

3. Hold SHIFT as your modifier key to temporarily switch to the Paintbucket Tool and click the object you want to copy the effect to. The effect is immediately copied to the new object.

Applying Precise Transformation

The Transformation docker enables you to apply multiple transformations with a single command. The docker has five Transformation buttons: Position (Move), Rotation, Scale and Mirror, Size, and Skew, as shown in Figure 8-9. To open the Transformation docker, choose Window | Dockers or choose Arrange | Transformations, and then click the button that applies to your task.

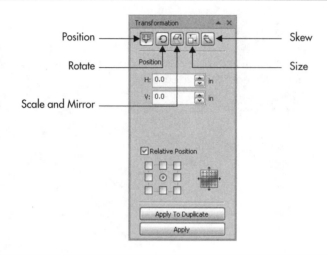

Position — Skew
Rotate — Size
Scale and Mirror

FIGURE 8-9 The Transformation docker offers precision over position, rotation, size, and skew changes.

For all transformations, the procedure is the same: click the button for the type of transformation, enter your desired values, and click the Apply button in the docker to transform your selected object(s). In this section, you'll learn what each area enables you to do and the options offered for each.

Using the Transformation Docker

Options in the Transformation docker vary by transformation type. In the illustrations shown in the next few pages, examples show only the specific transformation being discussed. If you need to, you can apply several transformations in a single command if values throughout each of the five docker modes have been selected.

Positioning (Moving) Objects

Options for the Position page enable you to move your object selection a specified distance, either *vertically* (*V*), *horizontally* (*H*), or to a specific point on your document page, as shown in Figure 8-10.

While the Relative Position option is selected, entering new values and clicking the Apply button causes your objects to move by a specified distance. While the Relative Position option is not selected, new values determine your object's page position or move it to a specified point.

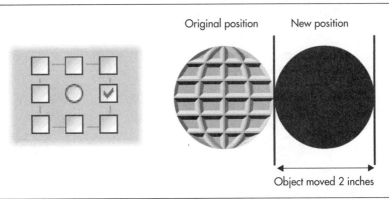

FIGURE 8-10   This object was precisely moved by applying a Position transformation.

Rotating Objects

You can enter exact angles of rotation based on degrees and in increments of 5, using Rotation, as shown in Figure 8-11.

Entering negative values rotates an object clockwise, while positive values cause counter-clockwise rotation. Selecting the Relative Center option lets you to rotate objects either *V* or *H*, according to the object's center marker position, and the position of which is specified as either *V* or *H*. Changing the existing value in the Horizontal and Vertical boxes allows you to specify a new center origin position for your object's rotation. While Relative Center is not selected, your object is rotated according to a position relative to the page center.

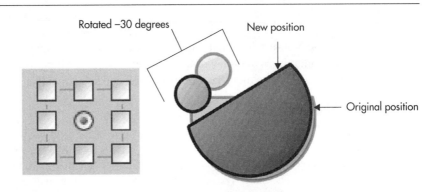

FIGURE 8-11   A precise angle change was applied to this object using a Rotation transformation.

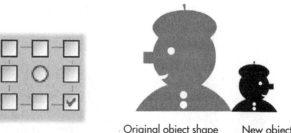

Original object shape   New object scaled 50 percent
                               and mirrored horizontally

FIGURE 8-12   Both Scale and Mirror changes were applied to this symbol.

Scale and Mirror Objects

The Scale and Mirror transformation has features for entering precise changes in object size. You can also cause the object to be flipped either *V* or *H,* and/or simultaneously, by clicking one of the two mirror buttons, as shown in Figure 8-12.

While the Non-proportional option is selected, your object's new horizontal and vertical scale values are unlinked, meaning you can apply scaling commands to either the width or height, independent of each other. While the Non-proportional option is unselected, width and height scaling operations are locked to each other. This means that scaling the width or height by a given percentage value causes the adjacent value to be calculated automatically to preserve your selected object's original proportions.

Sizing Objects

This transformation type gives you the option to change either the *V* and/or *H* measure of an object selection based on the values entered. For example, entering two inches in the Width box and clicking the Apply button causes the selected object to be scaled to a width of two inches. While the Non-proportional option is selected, the width and height values can be changed independently. While they're not selected, width and height values are linked and calculated automatically to alter the size of the object proportionally.

Precision Skewing

The term *"skew"* refers to changing the position of two sides in parallel fashion, while leaving the adjacent sides alone; "slanting is a more common term for "skew." A vertical or horizontal skew applied to a rectangle object causes its corners to become nonperpendicular—they are no longer at 90 degrees. The Skew Transformation also gives you the chance to apply both vertical and horizontal skew independently or simultaneously by entering degree measures, in turn, transforming the object either *V* or *H*. As with rotation commands, negative degree values cause clockwise skews, while positive values cause counterclockwise skews. Choosing the Use Anchor Point option enables you to specify left, center, right, top, bottom, sides, or corner points as the

Object horizontally skewed 45 degrees using bottom-right origin

Original object

FIGURE 8-13   A precision Skew changes both the angle and the size of this object in a single command.

point around which your objects are skewed, as shown in Figure 8-13, which should give you a creative idea for one of the many uses for skewing a duplicate. The skewed copy more or less looks like a cast shadow of the original symbol, doesn't it?

Common Transformation Options

You'll notice check boxes on the Transformation docker (shown in the previous figures) that are available during all transformations. These enable you to apply your transformation according to the relative areas of your selected object(s) or to apply the new transformation to a new duplicate of your object.

Relative Position Grid

Typically, the object origin grid enables you to transform your object based on a specific reference point. Points on the grid represent the top, center, bottom, left, or right side, as well as the corner points of your selected object's bounding box. Clicking one of these points causes the transformation to originate from a given point. For example, clicking the center option and then scaling an object by 200 percent causes the new object shape to double in size but remain centered with its original position. A representative diagram accompanying each docker state indicates the results of positive and negative values.

 When applying transformation using the Transformation docker, the default values displayed represent your object selection's current size, position, rotation, scale, and skew settings. For a transformation to take place, these values must somehow be changed or the applied transformation will seem to have no effect.

Applying Transformation to Duplicates

Clicking Apply To Duplicate causes your transformations to be applied to a new copy of the selected shape or group of shapes, preserving your original. The new duplicate object is automatically ordered in front of your original.

Shapes do not have to be grouped to be transformed around a central anchor point; they just need to be selected as a group, using marquee-selection or another technique. This means, for example, that if you have three triangles in a particular arrangement on the page, and want the group rotated, they will do so relative to a central anchor—they won't go spinning independently of the selected group.

Controlling the Order of Things

How your objects are ordered is another consideration when organizing drawing objects in a composition. The order of objects determines whether an object appears in front of—or behind—another object. The relative reference points to remember when ordering are your view of the page while looking at it on your monitor and your page surface. Your page surface and the pasteboard (the area surrounding your document page) are always the *backmost* point, while your screen is always the frontmost point. All objects are layered between these two points.

When overlapping objects are ordered, they appear in front of or behind each other, according to their order. As you create each new object, it is ordered in front of all existing objects on the current document layer. Changing the object order lets you rearrange overlapping objects without changing their position on the page. To do this, CorelDRAW X4 has a series of order commands that let you "shuffle" the order of objects in various ways. You'll find them in the Arrange | Order submenu, but you can also apply them using shortcut keys or using buttons available in the Property Bar while objects are selected.

NOTE *Be sure not to confuse the* hierarchy *of object ordering with* object layers. *Although layers each have their own collections of objects that can be ordered in a sequence, the layers* themselves can *also* be ordered. *This means that if you're trying to control the ordering of two or more objects, check the Status Bar to make sure they're on the same layer. For information on using CorelDRAW's Layers feature, see Chapter 12.*

Here's how each of the object order commands works:

- **To Front** This command shuffles your selected object(s) to the very front of the current layer. Press SHIFT+PAGE UP or choose Arrange | Order | To Front to apply it. The To Front command is also available as a Property Bar button when an object is selected.

- **To Back** This command shuffles your selected object(s) to the very back of the current layer. Press SHIFT+PAGE DOWN or choose Arrange | Order | To Back to apply it. The To Back command is also available as a Property Bar button while an object is selected.

- **Forward One** This command shuffles your selected object(s) forward by one in the object order of the current layer. Press CTRL+PAGE UP or choose Arrange | Order | Forward One to apply it.

■ **Back One**   This command shuffles your selected object(s) backward by one in the object order of the current layer. Press CTRL+PAGE DOWN or choose Arrange | Order | Back One to apply it.

■ **In Front Of**   This command enables you to shuffle your selected object and place it directly in front of any object you specify in the current layer order. A targeting cursor will appear, enabling you to choose which object to shuffle your selection in front of. Choose Arrange | Order | In Front Of to apply it.

■ **Behind**   This command also causes a targeting cursor to appear, enabling you to specify which object you want your object selection to be shuffled behind in the object order on the current layer. Choose Arrange | Order | Behind to apply it.

■ **Reverse Order**   This command effectively shuffles the order of your selected object so that it's in the reverse of its current order on the layer. Front objects become back objects and vice versa, as shown in Figure 8-14. For example, if your objects were numbered 1, 2, 3, and 4 from front to back, applying this command would cause them to become reordered to 4, 3, 2, and 1. Choose Arrange | Order | Reverse Order to apply it.

8

TIP	*When changing object order using the Reverse Order command, grouped objects are considered a single object, meaning their relative order in the group will be preserved. To reorder objects within a group, you'll need to Ungroup (CTRL+U) the objects first before applying the command.*

Original order   Order after using Reverse Order command

FIGURE 8-14   You can quickly change the order of objects within a layer using Reverse Order.

Hopefully this chapter has provided you with the most common solutions to hurdles you might face when tackling a full-featured design program. You now know how to move, scale, rotate, and perform other operations on page objects and their duplicates. You also know how to both manually transform and use the dockers and other features for precise moving and alignment of the elements you need for a terrific design. Chapter 9 takes you into creating these shapes that you now know how to move; you put Chapters 8 and 9 together and your family's going to start missing you because you'll be having too much fun designing to sit down for regular dinners!

PART III

Working with Object Tools

CHAPTER 9
Creating Basic Shapes

This is the "You have to begin *somewhere*!" chapter: drawing vector paths with CorelDRAW is all about creating objects that you then customize and refine through fancy fills and elegant outlines. Therefore, it's important to know the techniques for creating simple—and not so simple—geometric shapes, and to know how to edit your drawings to create exactly the shape you want to fill and stroke.

CorelDRAW X4's Smart Drawing Tool

Even if you use a graphics tablet and stylus, you're still drawing freehand, and using a mouse introduces even less precision when it comes to vector drawing. Fortunately, the Smart Drawing Tool takes the guesswork out of drawing polygonal and rounded objects—in a nutshell, you sketch an approximation of what you intend, tune the options for the Smart Drawing Tool a little, and in a jiffy you have a precise object of the proportions you need. Pictured here on the Toolbox, the Smart Drawing Tool instantly translates rough drawings into shapes you'd usually consider drawing with the Rectangle Tool or Ellipse Tool—or with other tools that require more effort and skill.

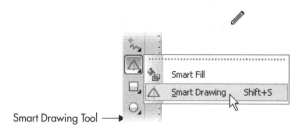

When the Smart Drawing Tool is chosen, the Property Bar displays Shape Recognition Level and smoothing options (shown next) for setting the sensitivity CorelDRAW uses in translating your roughs into precise shapes.

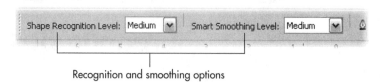

Recognition and smoothing options

You control how precisely your sketch shape is translated into shapes by setting these options:

- **Shape Recognition Level** This option sets how precisely your sketched shape is matched to a recognizable shape and can be set to one of five levels ranging from Lowest (sketched shapes are not easily recognized) to Highest (sketched shapes are easily recognized), with Medium being the default; None turns the feature off.

■ **Smart Smoothing Level**   After you've completed a sketch by releasing the mouse button, a level of node smoothing is applied to make object recognition more, or less, precise. This option gives you total control over the smoothing action, much in the same fashion as using the Reduce Nodes spin box on the Property Bar when a path is selected with the Shape Tool. Choose from five options ranging from Lowest (less smoothing applied) to Highest (more smoothing applied), with Medium as the default; None turns the feature off.

TIP   *You can control the delay time interval between the moment you release the mouse button and stop drawing to the moment DRAW X4 determines a recognizable shape. By reducing the delay time, you can sketch several separate lines or shapes one after the other, and DRAW then recognizes them as a single compound path. To get to this delay option, double-click the Smart Drawing Tool icon on the Toolbox to open Options. The Drawing Assistance Delay slider can be set between 0 and 2.0 seconds. The higher you set the delay time, the more time you'll have to keep drawing before CorelDRAW steps in to assist you.*

To experience the drawing power the Smart Drawing Tool offers, try the following steps:

CAD: CorelDRAW-Assisted Drawing

1. Choose the Smart Drawing Tool and use a click-drag action to sketch the shape of a square or rectangle. Try to keep the sides of the shape vertical and horizontal as you draw; if the square shape looks like a melted ice cube, don't worry! When you release the mouse button, CorelDRAW X4 automatically translates your sketch into a rectangle shape.

2. Choose the Pick Tool next and check your Status Bar display. The shape you sketched is specified as a Rectangle, and the Property Bar shows options associated with shapes created with the Rectangle Tool, including the rounded-corner options.

3. Choose the Smart Drawing Tool(s) again, and sketch the shape of an oval or circle. Try to keep the shape parallel to the page orientation, but CorelDRAW can also intelligently refine a sketch of an oval that's rotated. On releasing the mouse button, CorelDRAW X4 translates your sketched shape into an ellipse shape.

4. Choose the Pick Tool and check your Status Bar. The shape you sketched is specified as an Ellipse, and the Property Bar shows options associated with shapes created with the Ellipse Tool, such as the Ellipse, Arc, and Pie properties.

TIP   *You can alter your sketched shapes on-the-fly using the Smart Drawing Tool to backtrack and erase the path you're drawing. Hold SHIFT as the modifier key to reverse and erase. Release the SHIFT key to resume sketching normally.*

The shapes you draw can also be recognized as Perfect Shapes such as isosceles triangles, trapezoids, parallelograms, and so on, as shown in Figure 9-1. *Perfect Shapes* are a special category of CorelDRAW objects and they have special properties. They feature "glyph" nodes (by default a red-filled diamond)—which are different from regular nodes along a path—and the nodes can be manipulated to modify the shape without destroying any of its unique geometric properties.

Now that you've created at least one Perfect Shape and know how to make others, try these next steps to create variations on the basic appearance of a Perfect Shape:

Reshaping a Perfect Shape

1. Using the Smart Drawing Tool, sketch the shape of a trapezoid (refer to Figure 9-1; two sides are parallel, the other two sides converge). Upon releasing the mouse button, CorelDRAW translates your sketch into a Perfect Shape.

2. Choose the Pick Tool and then look at the Status Bar. The shape is identified as a Perfect Shape, a special category of shape. Use the Shape Tool next to click-drag the glyph node. You'll see that the parallel sides remain parallel, and the converging sides slope away and toward each other. By duplicating this Perfect Shape, you can edit with the Shape Tool and create an array of trapezoids, all different in appearance but all editable indefinitely, and all retain the geometric structure of a Perfect Shape.

 To learn more about creating Perfect Shapes and manipulating glyph nodes, see "Using Perfect Shape Tools," later in this chapter.

The Smart Drawing Tool helps you quickly draw and translate a variety of sketched shapes into different, geometrically flawless shapes more efficiently than using multiple tools. Each of

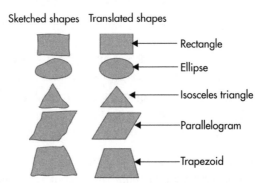

FIGURE 9-1 Perfect Shapes retain their properties even when you extensively edit their appearance.

the translated shapes has its own special properties, which you'll learn in detail in the sections that follow.

Using the Rectangle Tool and Property Bar

The Rectangle Tool is simple enough to use, but it doesn't just create a four-sided, right-angle polygon—it creates a rectangle that has *special properties* in CorelDRAW. You'll find it in the Toolbox, as shown next, or you can quickly select it by pressing the F6 shortcut key.

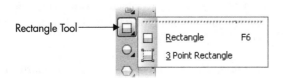

Rectangle shapes offer you the option to apply corner "roundness," based on a percentage value. Roundness can be set either manually by dragging a corner with the Shape Tool, or by using the Property Bar Corner Roundness option available while a rectangle is selected, as shown here:

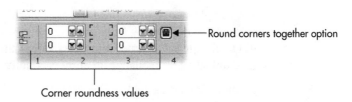

Corner roundness values

Round corners together option

 You can also choose the Rectangle Tool while any shape creation tool is selected (the Ellipse Tool, for example) by right-clicking a blank space on the document page and choosing Create Object | Rectangle from the pop-up menu.

Drawing a Rectangle

To create a rectangle, choose the Rectangle Tool from the Toolbox, and click-diagonal drag in any direction to define its corner positions, as shown here. The act of click-dragging begins by defining the first two corners; as you drag, the corner positions can be redefined, depending on where your cursor is on the page; and then before you release the mouse button, you've defined the position for the remaining two rectangle corners.

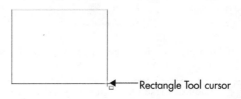

Rectangle Tool cursor

While the Rectangle Tool is selected, notice that the cursor is a crosshair with a small rectangle shape at its lower right. As you click-drag using the cursor, you'll also notice that the Status Bar and Property Bar show coordinates, width, and height properties of your new object shape.

Setting Rectangle Corner Roundness

Corner roundness is based on percentages from 0 to 100, and you can set the value a number of ways. The Corner Roundness options can be changed anytime, while the shape remains a native rectangle; that is, it has not been converted to curves. Corner roundness can be set uniformly for all corners (the default) or independently when the Round Corners Together lock option is in the unlocked state.

 Double-clicking the Rectangle Tool button in the Toolbox instantly creates a rectangle border around your current document page.

While a rectangle is selected, use any of the following operations to change corner roundness according to your needs:

- Use Property Bar Corner Roundness options to enter a percentage value.

- Set your rectangle's corner roundness manually using the Shape Tool, by dragging any corner control point away from its corner (toward a side that makes up the rectangle) to change each corner roundness value individually while the corner options are unlocked or to change all corners equally while the options are locked.

- Use the Object Properties docker, opened by right-clicking the rectangle shape and choosing Properties.

Options to apply corner roundness appear in each of these areas. Figure 9-2 shows a rectangle in differing degrees of corner roundness.

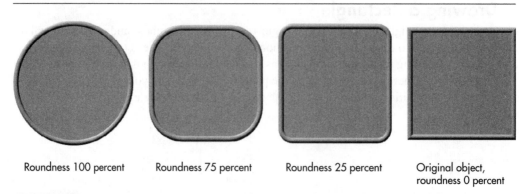

Roundness 100 percent   Roundness 75 percent   Roundness 25 percent   Original object, roundness 0 percent

FIGURE 9-2   Each of these rectangles uses a different corner roundness setting.

Constraining Shapes While Drawing

Just like most Windows applications, CorelDRAW takes advantage of keyboard modifier keys you can use to modify shapes as you draw them. Holding modifier keys as you click-drag various tool cursors makes drawing your new object shape easier, you get more options at your cursor tip, and you work faster. These shortcuts are worth committing to memory:

■ Hold CTRL while drawing new objects to constrain their shape to equal width and height.

■ Hold SHIFT while drawing new objects to draw their shape from the center outward. This is particularly useful, for example, when you need a rectangle whose center is positioned at a specific point on the page.

■ Hold CTRL+SHIFT while drawing new objects to constrain their shape from the center origin, *and* to equal width and height simultaneously.

It helps to mentally associate CTRL with "constrain" and SHIFT as "additional or added feature."

Creating 3-Point Rectangles

The *3-Point Rectangle Tool* enables you to create angled rectangles more quickly than drawing and rotating a new one. You'll find it grouped with the Rectangle Tool in the Toolbox, as shown here:

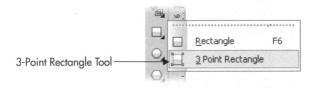

3-Point Rectangle Tool

Using this tool, you can draw new rectangles at precise angles, as shown in Figure 9-3. The rectangle you create is a native rectangle shape, meaning you may round its corners and manipulate it as any other shape.

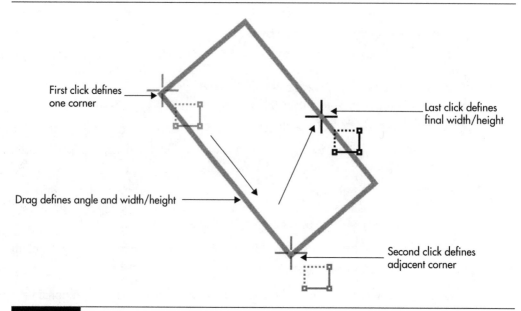

First click defines one corner

Last click defines final width/height

Drag defines angle and width/height

Second click defines adjacent corner

FIGURE 9-3 Draw new rectangles at precise angles with the 3-Point Rectangle Tool.

To create a Rectangle using the 3-Point Rectangle Tool, use these steps:

1. Select the 3-Point Rectangle Tool, click to define the corner endpoint of one side of your rectangle, and then drag to define its width/height. As you drag the cursor, the angle of the line changes freely, enabling you to set the precise angle of the new rectangle. Release the mouse button to define the opposite side of the rectangle.

2. As you move your cursor now, an angled rectangle preview shape is built on either side of the two points you defined. Your next click will define the final dimensions of your rectangle.

Using the Ellipse Tool and Property Bar

Ellipses are a staple of commercial design work, and essentially an ellipse is a circular shape that is not perfectly circular. The Ellipse Tool can be used to draw both perfect circles and ellipses, but in CorelDRAW an ellipse shape has additional, special properties, just like a rectangle can be a round-cornered rectangle. Ellipse shapes can be edited to create dramatically new shapes while retaining their elliptical properties. In contrast, an oval shape drawn with, for example, the Bezier Tool, always remains an oval.

Ellipses are easy enough to draw with the Ellipse Tool and can be set in several different states: as oval or circular closed-paths, pie wedges, and arcs. Pie wedges are the portions of an ellipse—like a single slice of a pie, or conversely, a whole pie with a slice removed. Arc shapes are the open-path equivalent of pies.

To create an ellipse, choose the Ellipse Tool, shown at left, from the Toolbox or press F7, followed by a click-drag in any direction.

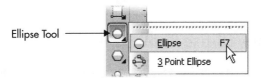

While the Ellipse Tool is selected, the Property Bar shows ellipse-specific options, shown next, that enable you to control the state of your new ellipse shape before or after it has been created. Choose Ellipse, Pie, or Arc. A complement is reserved for Pie and Arc shapes: for example, if you specify a 15° pie wedge, clicking the Complement icon changes the shape to a 345° wedge. Additionally, if you want a Pie or Arc to travel in a different path direction, double-click the Ellipse Tool icon on the Toolbox, which takes you to Options, where you can choose clockwise or counterclockwise path directions.

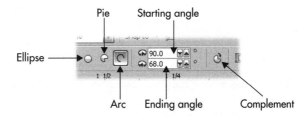

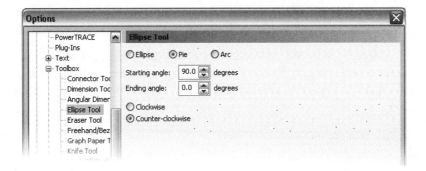

TIP *You can also choose the Ellipse Tool while any tool is selected by right-clicking in an empty space on your document page and choosing Create Object | Ellipse from the pop-up menu.*

Drawing an Ellipse

Let's walk before running; before creating pie and arc shapes, let's begin with circles and ovals. Start with these brief steps:

Round One with the Ellipse Tool

1. Choose the Ellipse Tool (F7) and use a click-diagonal drag action in any direction. As you drag, an outline preview of the shape appears, as shown here. An ellipse shape has two overlapping control nodes (so onscreen it looks like only one node); if you drag down and left or right, the nodes will be located at 12 o'clock. Conversely, if you drag up and left or right, the control nodes will be located at 6 o'clock.

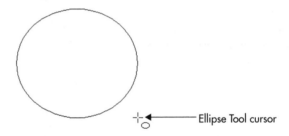

Ellipse Tool cursor

2. Release the mouse button to complete your ellipse shape creation.

Controlling Ellipse States

All ellipses have two control points (*nodes*—a start and an end) that overlap each other and are visible when the ellipse is selected. When these control points are separated, they create either a pie or an arc state, and each control point determines either the *starting* or *ending* *angle* of the pie or arc.

You can separate these control points either by using Property Bar options or by dragging the points using the Shape Tool. Dragging *inside* the ellipse's shape creates the Ellipse Pie state. Dragging *outside* the shape creates the Ellipse Arc state, as shown in Figure 9-4.

 Even though pies and arcs appear as if sections or path parts are missing, the portions are still there. They're just hidden from view.

To draw a new pie or arc without drawing an oval-shaped ellipse first, click either the Pie or Arc button in the Property Bar before you start drawing. You can also switch any selected ellipse between these states using these buttons. By default, all pies and arcs are applied with a default Starting Angle of 0° and a default Ending Angle of 270°. Starting and Ending Angles are based on degrees of rotation from –360 to 360°.

Dragging inside creates the pie shape

Dragging outside creates the arc shape

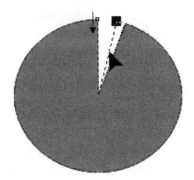

FIGURE 9-4 Dragging the points using the Pick or Shape Tool creates different states.

To set the default properties for all new ellipse shapes, choose the Ellipse Tool from the Toolbox, and choose options in the Property Bar before you start drawing. Each new ellipse shape will then be created according to the options you select, including the state of the new ellipse—Ellipse, Pie, or Arc—and the starting and ending angles for each.

Creating 3-Point Ellipses

The *3-Point Ellipse Tool* is the key for creating ellipses while setting a rotation angle (perfect circles show no possible rotation angle; we're talking ovals here). You'll find it grouped with the Ellipse Tool in the Toolbox, as shown at left.

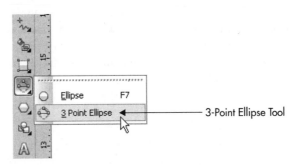

This tool enables you to create ellipses at precise angles without the need to create and then rotate an existing one, as shown in Figure 9-5. The shape you create is still an ellipse with all associated properties, such as optional pie and arc states.

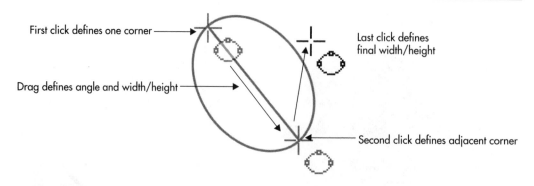

First click defines one corner

Last click defines final width/height

Drag defines angle and width/height

Second click defines adjacent corner

FIGURE 9-5 The 3-Point Ellipse Tool enables you to create ellipses at precise angles.

To create an ellipse using the 3-Point Ellipse Tool, use these steps:

1. Choose the 3-Point Ellipse Tool, click to define the midpoint of one side of your ellipse, and drag your cursor to define its radius. As you drag the cursor, the angle of the line changes freely. Release the mouse button to define the opposite side of the ellipse.

2. At this point, an angled ellipse preview shape is built on either side of the two points you defined. Your next click will define the final dimension of your ellipse.

Using Polygons and the Property Bar

The *Polygon Tool* is unique to the category of vector drawing software; competing applications offer a polygon tool, but CorelDRAW's Polygon Tool produces shapes that can be edited to create dynamic changes, just like CorelDRAW rectangles and ellipses. The shapes you create with the Polygon Tool can have as few as 3 or as many as 500 points and sides; by default, all polygon sides are straight paths. You'll find the Polygon Tool, shown at left, together with the Spiral, Graph Paper, and other group tools. To quickly select it, the shortcut is to press Y.

Polygon Tool

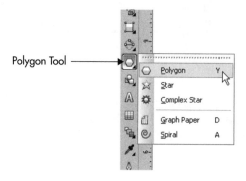

While the Polygon Tool is selected, the Property Bar offers the number of sides for the polygon you'll draw; the default value is 5.

Drawing and Editing Polygons

Most of the trick to creating symmetrical, complex shapes with the Polygon Tool lies in the editing of them. Read Chapter 11 before getting too involved with the Polygon Tool, because you really need to know how to use the Shape Tool in combination with the Property Bar to edit a polygon shape.

To create a default polygon, you use the same click-diagonal drag technique as you use with the Rectangular and Ellipse Tools. This produces a symmetrical shape made up of straight paths. Because you'll often want a shape more sophisticated in appearance than something that looks like a snack chip, it helps to begin a polygon shape by holding SHIFT and CTRL while dragging: doing this produces a perfectly symmetrical (not distorted) polygon, beginning at your initial click point traveling outward. Therefore, you have the shape positioned exactly where you want it and can begin redefining the shape.

In the following illustration, you can see the Polygon Tool cursor and a symmetrical default polygon. Notice that the polygon shape has control points, and these control points have no control handles because they connect straight path segments. However, in the following tutorial you'll get a jump start on Chapter 11's coverage of paths and the Shape Tool, and really get down in very few steps to creating a dynamite polygon shape through editing.

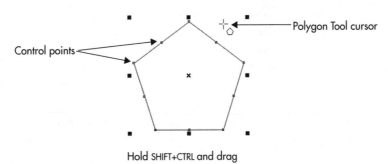

Control points ——

Polygon Tool cursor

Hold SHIFT+CTRL and drag

Here is a taxi driver's tour of how to create and then edit a polygon to design any symmetric object you can imagine (and a few unimaginable ones):

Reshaping a Polygon

1. Choose the Polygon Tool from the Toolbox, and before you do anything else, set the number of sides to 12 on the Property Bar.

2. Hold CTRL to constrain the shape to a symmetrical one, and then click-diagonal drag on the page. Release the mouse button after you have a polygon that's about 3" wide.

3. To better see what you're doing, left-click over the color palette with the polygon selected to fill it. By default, polygons are created with a small stroke width and no fill.

4. Choose the Shape Tool from the Toolbox. Click any of the control points on the polygon to select it, but don't drag yet. Hold CTRL and then drag outward, to constrain the movement of the cursor so that the polygon doesn't take on a lop-sided appearance (although you can create interesting polygons by dragging in any way without holding CTRL). You should have a star shape now, as shown here.

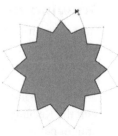

5. Notice that on the Property Bar you now have a lot of icons that control how line segments pass through nodes and whether the segments are straight or curved. Click on any line segment that makes up the polygon; your cursor should have a wiggly line at lower right, as shown here, signifying that you've clicked on a line. Then the Convert Line To Curve icon can be clicked on the Property Bar, converting not only the line, but all the lines in the polygon that are symmetrical to the chosen line, to a curve.

6. Drag the line you converted to a curve. Doing this, as you can see here, creates a very interesting and complex symmetrical shape, and you can now see the control lines for the curves segment and can manipulate the control handles to further embellish your creation.

Figure 9-6 shows but a few creative examples of polygon editing: from gears to those vinyl flowers you put over shower stall cracks, you have immense design power at your disposal with the Polygon Tool.

 After editing a polygon, you can change the number of sides. For example, you've created a 12-petal flower polygon, and your client wants only 8 petals. You select the edited shape with the Pick Tool and then decrease the number of sides using the spin box on the Property Bar.

Stars and Complex Stars

You have variations on polygons at the ready in CorelDRAW, in the same group as the Polygon Tool. The Star Tool can be used to create pointy polygons with anywhere from 3 to 500 points. The Complex Star Tool creates a number of combined polygons to make a star shape; you can create interesting symmetrical shapes by filling a complex Star—the result contains both filled and vacant polygon areas.

| FIGURE 9-6 | Shapes you can edit using a basic Polygon object |

Working with the Star Tool

As with most of the shape tools, the Star Tool produces objects by the use of click-diagonal dragging; CTRL constrains the shape to symmetry, SHIFT lets you drag from the center outward, and CTRL-SHIFT dragging creates symmetrical stars beginning at the initial click point traveling outward.

On the Property Bar, when the Star Tool is chosen, you have options for the number of points for the star and the "pointiness" (sharpness) of the resulting object—how severe the indents are between points. At a setting of 1, the star object becomes pointy not at all— you'll see that it looks quite like a Polygon Tool object. So, if you can make a star using the Polygon Tool, why would you ever choose the Star Tool? The answer is because the geometric structure of a star shape is always perfectly symmetrical. Although you can use the Shape Tool to manually tune the sharpness of a Star Tool object's points, the angle between points is always consistent. In the illustration below, you can see a Star Tool object compared with a Polygon Tool object that has been clumsily edited. You can't perform this goof with the Star Tool; its interior angles are always mirrored and symmetrical.

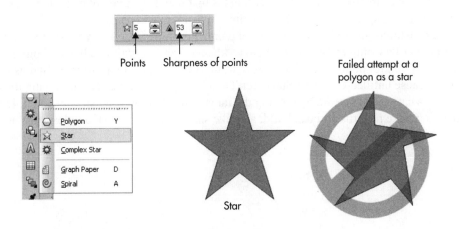

Using the Complex Star Tool

Think of the kaleidoscope images you enjoyed as a child (or still do!) when you choose the Complex Star Tool, because with only an edit or two using the Shape Tool, you can create mesmerizing symmetrical shapes, unlike with any other tool in CorelDRAW.

To use the tool, you know the drill if you've read this far! You click-diagonal drag to create a shape; by default the Complex Star has 9 points of a value of 2 on a 1- to 2-point sharpness scale (available to define on the Property Bar; see the following illustration).

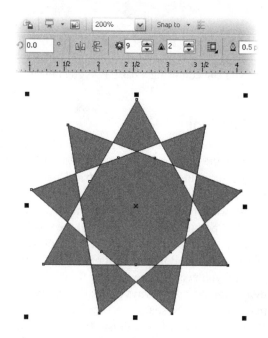

CTRL, SHIFT, and CTRL+SHIFT perform the same modifiers as they do with other shapes. One unique characteristic of Complex Stars is that they have two control points: one for the inner, negative space, and one for the points. When you edit using the Shape Tool, holding CTRL constrains your edits on the control points to symmetry, but if you want a spiral treatment of a Complex Star, don't hold CTRL and drag any way you like on both the inner and outer control points. You'll probably want to assign a fill to a Complex Star as your first edit because unfilled Complex Stars aren't as visually interesting. The following illustration shows what you can create by moving the inner control point to outside the outer. Imagine the snowflake patterns you can build; and like snowflakes, no two Complex Stars are alike!

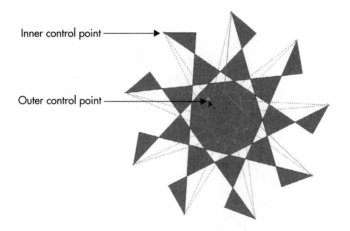

Figure 9-7 shows other examples of simply playing with the Shape Tool on a complex Star object. Also try assigning a wide white outline property to a Complex Star to create further variations.

FIGURE 9-7   Complex Stars are fast to create, fun to look at, and can serve many design purposes.

Using the Spiral Tool

With the Spiral Tool, you can create circular-shaped paths that would be tedious if not impossible to create manually. Spiral objects are composed of a single open path that curves in a clockwise or counterclockwise direction, growing larger toward the exterior of the object or smaller toward the center. You'll find the tool, shown at left, in the Toolbox, grouped with the Polygon and Graph Paper Tools.

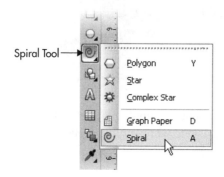

Spiral Tool options share space in the Property Bar (shown next) with options for the Graph Paper Tool and include Spiral Revolutions, Symmetrical, and Logarithmic Spiral modes, and a Spiral Expansion slider.

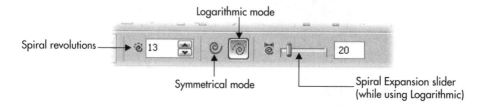

The objects you can create can have between 1 and 100 revolutions, each of which is equal to one complete rotation around its center point. The direction of the revolutions is set according to the click-diagonal drag action during creation of the initial shape, as shown in Figure 9-8.

 Spiral objects are nondynamic; no special editing or redefining is possible once the spiral has been created. This means you must set their properties before they are created. Other than your using the Pick or Shape Tool to edit its size or shape, spiral objects are a "done deal."

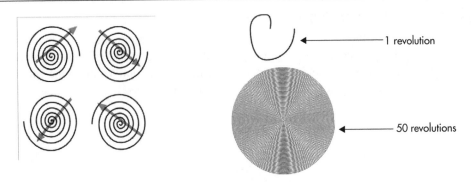

FIGURE 9-8   The direction of your spiral revolutions is determined by your initial click-drag direction.

By default, all new spiral objects are set to Symmetrical. If you choose Logarithmic, the Spiral Expansion slider becomes available. Here's how the modes and options affect the spiral objects you can create.

- **Symmetrical vs. Logarithmic**   A symmetrical spiral object appears with its spiral revolutions evenly spaced from the center origin to the outer dimensions of the object. To increase or decrease the rate at which the curves in your spiral become smaller or larger as they reach the object's center, you may want to use the Logarithmic method. The term *logarithmic* refers to the acceleration (or deceleration) of the spiral revolutions. To choose this option, click the Logarithmic Spiral button in the Property Bar before drawing your shape.

- **Logarithmic Expansion option**   While the Logarithmic Spiral mode is selected, the Logarithmic Expansion slider becomes available, enabling you to set this rate based on a percentage of the object's dimensions. Logarithmic Expansion may be set from 1 to 100 percent. A Logarithmic Expansion setting of 1 results in a symmetrical spiral setting, while a setting of 100 causes dramatic expansion, as shown in Figure 9-9. If you need a shape that is reminiscent of a nautilus, increase the Logarithmic Expansion to 50 or so.

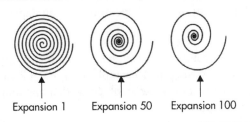

Expansion 1   Expansion 50   Expansion 100

FIGURE 9-9   The Logarithmic Expansion option results in varying-power functions of distance from the start point.

Using the Graph Paper Tool

The Graph Paper Tool is used to create a grid containing hundreds (even thousands) of rectangles—an emulation of graph paper. Graph paper is one of those materials technical illustrators, chartists, and engineers often can't do without. You find the Graph Paper Tool, shown at left, grouped with the Polygon and Spiral Tools.

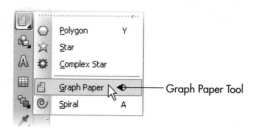

This tool's options on the Property Bar let you set the number of rows and columns for your new graph paper object. As with the Spiral Tool, you must set options *before* drawing your graph paper object; a Graph Paper object cannot be edited dynamically.

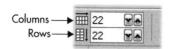

Let's explore one of the many creative ways to create and use the group of rectangles the Graph Paper Tool builds for you.

Power-Drawing a Grid with Graph Paper

1. Choose the Graph Paper Tool from the Toolbox or press D to select it.

2. Using Property Bar options, set the number of rows and columns you want to have in your new graph paper object.

3. Using a click-diagonal drag action, drag to create the new object. Holding CTRL while you drag constrains the shape of the Graph Paper object, but not the cells in the graph.

The rectangles in the group are, in fact, *native rectangles*—meaning each separate object is the same as those created using the Rectangle Tool. Each Row and Column option can be set from 1 to 99, enabling you to create an object with a maximum of 9,801 grouped rectangles, as shown in Figure 9-10.

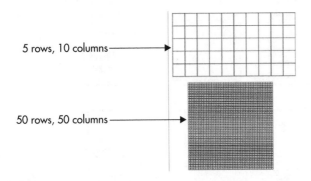

5 rows, 10 columns ⟶

50 rows, 50 columns ⟶

FIGURE 9-10 "Native rectangles" means that each object is the same as those created with the Rectangle Tool.

One of the many uses for Graph Paper is for backgrounds that need to look "high tech." The illustration below was created using a Graph Paper object with no fill, a white outline, and the Effect | Perspective command, which was used to give the impression of a plane beneath the sphere extending far into space.

9

Using Perfect Shape Tools

CorelDRAW X4 enables you to create objects called *perfect shapes*. This group of tools (see following illustration) helps you to draw shapes, many of which would be a challenge to draw manually and some of which can be dynamically edited.

Perfect Shapes often feature one or more control points called *glyph nodes*. These nodes enable you to edit specific parts of a specially formatted object dynamically, according to the shape's design. For example, the shape representing a dog-eared page features a single glyph node that enables you to set the diameter of the inner ellipse, leaving the outer diameter unchanged, or a glyph on a beveled rectangle shape enables you to set the bevel depth, as shown in Figure 9-11.

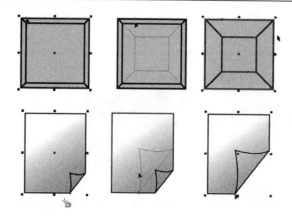

FIGURE 9-11 Glyph nodes can be used to control specific parts of these specially formatted objects.

Once a specific Perfect Shape Tool is selected, a collection of shapes becomes available on the Property Bar. Choose a specific type of shape from the Property Bar Perfect Shapes flyout selector, shown next, *before* drawing.

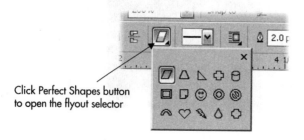

Click Perfect Shapes button
to open the flyout selector

Creating Perfect Shapes

Creating a Perfect Shape is very simple.

Creating Perfect Objects

1. Choose a Perfect Shape Tool by clicking on the Toolbox flyout and selecting a category.

2. In the Property Bar, click the Perfect Shape selector and choose a symbol. Use a click-drag action to define a size and position. For all symbol types except Callout, the direction of your click-drag won't matter because the symbols are created using a fixed orientation. For Callout shapes, the direction of your click-drag determines the object's orientation.

3. Once your shape has been created, you may notice it includes one or more glyph nodes that control certain symbol properties. In cases where more than one glyph node exists, the nodes are color coded. To position a glyph node, use a click-drag action directly on the node itself.

4. Once your object has been created and any glyph node editing is complete, your other basic shape properties (such as outline and fill) may be changed in the usual way. For example, you can change the width or height of your new shape using the selection handles available.

Editing Glyph Nodes

Glyph nodes are edited in ways similar to the control points on a polygon. As they are moved, the glyph nodes often have the effect of resizing, changing proportion, or dynamically moving a certain part of an individual symbol. Complex symbols can include up to three color-coded glyph nodes.

To explore glyph node editing, take a moment to try this:

1. Choose the Banner Perfect Shape Tool.

2. Choose the second style from the left on the Property Bar.

3. Using a click-diagonal drag action, create a new shape on your page. Notice the shape includes two glyph nodes—one yellow, one red.

4. Click-drag the yellow glyph node up or down to reposition it several times. Notice its movement is horizontally constrained; as it is moved, the vertical width of each portion of the banner changes.

5. Click-drag the red glyph node left or right to reposition it several times. Notice its movement is vertically constrained; as it is moved, the horizontal width of each portion of the banner changes to match your movement, as shown in Figure 9-12.

Converting Shapes to Curves

Any of the shapes discussed in this chapter can be converted to curves by using the Arrange | Convert To Curves command (CTRL+Q). Using this command removes any dynamic-editing properties. For example, an ellipse shape many be converted to a pie or arc (and vice versa); but after it is converted to curves, you'll no longer have the option of turning the object into a pie wedge. The same applies to rectangles, polygons, and so on. With the exception of the Undo command, once an object is converted to curves, there is no way to return the object to its dynamically editable state.

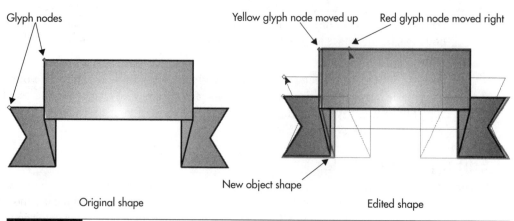

Glyph nodes

Yellow glyph node moved up   Red glyph node moved right

New object shape

Original shape   Edited shape

FIGURE 9-12 When movement is vertically constrained, the width of each portion of the banner changes.

Glyph nodes can be edited using both the Perfect Shape Tool you used to create the shape and the Shape Tool (F10). You can also edit glyph nodes by using the Object Properties docker for a selected Perfect Shape, shown in Figure 9-13. To open this docker, right-click your shape and choose Properties from the pop-up menu or press ALT+ENTER.

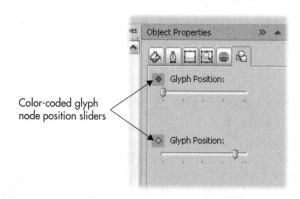

Color-coded glyph node position sliders

FIGURE 9-13 Use the Object Properties docker to edit glyph nodes.

Using the Convert Outline To Object Command

A lot of the shapes covered in this chapter, the spiral in particular, are shapes that have outline properties but no fill. So what do you do, for example, if you want a gradient-filled spiral? The Convert Outline To Object command converts any shape's outline properties to a closed path. To apply the command to a selected object, choose Arrange | Convert Outline To Object, or use the shortcut: CTRL+SHIFT+Q. Once the outline is converted, the resulting closed path looks exactly like the shape of the original except it can be filled because it's not an outline, but rather a closed path object whose shape is based on an outline.

When an object is converted to an outline, CorelDRAW X4 performs a quick calculation of the Outline Pen width applied to the object and creates a new object based on this value. When applying this command to objects that include a fill of any type, a new compound-path object is created based on the outline width. If the object includes a fill of any type, the fill is created as a new and separate object applied with an outline width and color of None. When you're converting open paths, only the path itself is created as a single outline object of the path according to the Outline Pen width applied. Figure 9-14 shows a spiral shape with a thick black Outline Pen width that is converted to outline using the command.

Things are certainly shaping up now, aren't they? You've learned how to create basic shapes, smart shapes, and how to edit them to create scores of original and visually interesting items: think of how your next brochure will look with prices framed in elegant banners, fancy stars, and rounded-corner rectangles. This isn't the half of it; in Chapter 10 we move on to using CorelDRAW's Pen Tools, which provide you with scores of options for hand-drawing freeform objects. You'll be wondering why your downstairs woodshop doesn't have the same organization and efficiency as your drawing program!

9

Original with 16-point outline applied   New fountain-filled object based on the outline

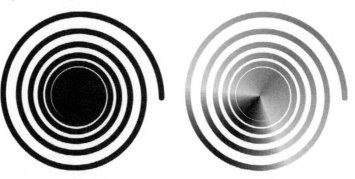

FIGURE 9-14 When an object is converted to an outline, CorelDRAW X4 performs calculations that create a new object.

CHAPTER 10

Using the Pen Tools

I f you thought learning to create basic and smart shapes in Chapter 9 was fun and a good learning experience, get ready: documenting the ways to make shapes is actually a superficial survey of the powerhouse of CorelDRAW's path-building and editing tools. The Line Tools group on the Toolbox has specific tools for drawing paths of any shape you can imagine, and some that you can't! Additionally, the Line Tools are made up of specialized tools for connecting shapes in flowcharts, and even a Line Tool for measuring and labeling what you've drawn, which is terrific for architectural sketches and maps. This chapter also takes you through the editing process of lines and their nodes, so there's no reason to draw something that's *close* to what you need. You'll have the power to draw exactly what fits the situation.

Introducing CorelDRAW X4's Line Tools

The most basic shape you can draw by and in CorelDRAW (and in any vector drawing program) is a *line*; a line is a path that passes through at least two points, called *nodes* in CorelDRAW. A line is actually a mathematical equation, and as such doesn't necessarily *have* to have an outline color or a width. It also doesn't even have to be a straight line, but it *does* have a direction; the direction in which you draw the line. Actually, this is where the fun begins because there are scores of different properties to which you can assign a line: arrowheads, a dotted look for coupons, colors, and varying widths galore. Joining the beginning and end points of a line (a *path*) closes the paths; if the beginning doesn't meet the end point, the shape is called an *open path*.

CorelDRAW X4's Line Tools are a group of eight virtual pens, shown next, and located between the Zoom/Hand and the new Smart Drawing Tool.

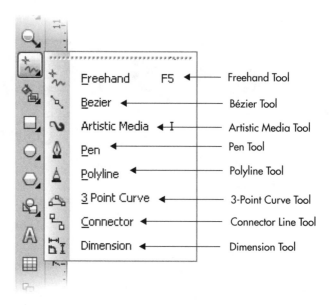

Freehand Tool   Artistic Media Tool   3-Point Curve Tool

Pen Tool   Bézier Tool   Polyline Tool

FIGURE 10-1 Each of the different drawing tools has a unique cursor look.

The Line Tools you'll work with most often are the Freehand, Polyline, Bézier, 3-Point Curve, Artistic Media, and Pen tools. The more specialized pens are the Dimension and Connector Tools, also documented in this chapter. Some of these tools are closely related in function, so it's best to become acquainted with the cursors of the most common ones, as shown in Figure 10-1.

How to Fill an Open Path

Depending on how your CorelDRAW X4 options are currently selected, open-path objects—in which the beginning and end points are not joined—might not be available to apply a fill color to the inside area of the path, mostly because it has no inside. This might seem an inconvenience if you're accustomed to using other applications such as Adobe Illustrator that, by default, normally assign open paths a solid fill. In CorelDRAW X4, you can fill an open path, but this option is not turned on by default. However, you can change this if you so choose.

Unfilled   Filled

(Continued)

To change CorelDRAW X4's drawing behavior to specify that all open paths are filled—without the need to close the path first—follow these steps:

1. Open the Options dialog by choosing Tools | Options (CTRL+J).

2. Click to expand the tree directory under Document and then click General to display the associated options on the right side of the dialog.

3. Click the Fill Open Curves option so that it is selected and then click OK to close the dialog.

After choosing this option, the open paths you draw will have an interior area.

Using the Artistic Media Tool

The Artistic Media Tool treats a path as though it's a skeleton to which you can apply a very wide variety of skins. There are five different types of Artistic Media "brushes," and a number of variations in every category. It helps to get your mind around a "paint brush"

Artistic Media Tool

metaphor; by click-dragging stokes, you get anything from complex filigree strokes to elegant calligraphic handwriting. The underlying path to Artistic Media strokes can be changed at any time, resulting in new artwork—and you can see the dynamic changes which provide fast and visually exciting feedback. You can draw while an Artistic Media effect is enabled and you can also apply these painterly strokes to existing lines. The Artistic Media Tool, shown to the left, is located in the Toolbox with other line-drawing tools.

With the Artistic Media Tool selected, the Property Bar offers five different line-drawing modes to choose from (shown next), each of which has its own unique options. You have additional options on the Property Bar, directly to the right of your choice of Artistic Media, and the options will change depending on the media type you choose.

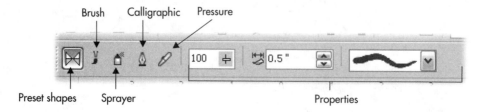

Applying Presets to Lines

Artistic Media is an evolution of CorelDRAW's Powerlines feature; veteran users will be the most comfortable with the improvements over Powerlines, while *every* user will be delighted with the new diversity of Media types. While *Presets* is selected in the Property Bar, the Artistic Media Tool lets you draw lines using specific preset vector shapes, which are dynamically linked to the underlying path. The smoothness and width of the applied effect is set according to the Freehand Smoothing and Width options in the Property Bar, as shown here:

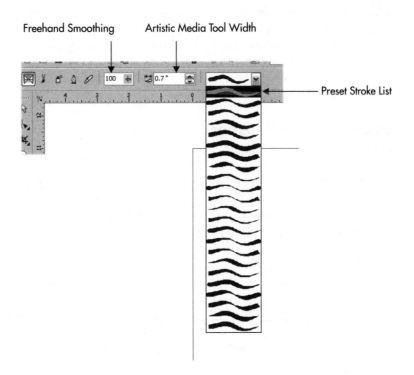

Set the shape using one of the styles in the Preset Stroke List. Smoothing is based on percent values between 0 (no smoothing) and 100 (maximum smoothing). Width can be set on a unit measure within a range of from 0.03 to 10 inches. As you draw, a path is created in freehand style and immediately applied to your line.

Are you ready to take the Artistic Media Tool out for a spin?

Painting with a Drawing Program

1. Choose the Artistic Media Tool and then use Property Bar options to choose a width for your new line effect.

2. Click the Preset Stroke List selector and choose a style.

3. Use a click-drag action to draw a line of any shape on your document page. As you drag, a preview of the full width of your new line effect appears. When you release the mouse button, the path you followed is instantly applied with a line effect.

4. Choose the Shape Tool (F10). Click the shape to select it and then edit its shape by adjusting the Freehand Smoothness. Do this by changing property Width settings or by choosing a different stroke or arrowhead style.

 Experimenting is fine, but if you turned the Freehand smoothing down to 0 while painting with the Artistic Media Tool, the result might be a stroke that has more nodes than you'd like, making it hard to create a smooth arc or straight line. If this happens (or at any time), you can choose the Shape Tool, click the stroke to reveal its nodes, and then marquee-select all the nodes. Then use the Reduce Nodes spin box on the Property Bar to remove non-essential nodes along the path that is driving the Artistic Media stroke.

Drawing with Brushes

In Brush mode, you can simulate the look of traditional, natural media that looks very similar to the brushes in Corel Painter, with a notable exception. Because a skeleton path lies beneath an Artistic Media stroke, the strokes you make can be edited *ad infinitum*; in contrast, bitmap paint programs such as Corel Painter and Adobe Photoshop feature brush strokes that can't be edited after you make them—it's a done deal after you paint a stroke. Like the Presets category, Artistic Media Brushes extend the full length of every path you create.

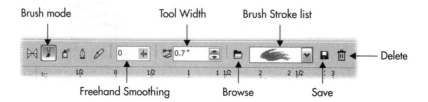

The Brush Stroke styles selector offers a variety of different styles, only six of which are shown in Figure 10-2. Freehand Smoothness and Tool Width options are used to change the appearance of the graphical object—the "skin"—applied to the underlying path.

You can draw using a Brush style or alternatively, apply one to an existing line. To draw using a Brush stroke, choose the Artistic Media Tool, use Property Bar options to choose a Brush style, and then begin drawing by click-dragging on your page in a stroking motion. To apply a new brush stroke to an existing line, select the line using the Artistic Media Tool, choose the Brush mode, and use Property Bar options to choose a width and Brush Stroke style. You can load saved brushes by clicking the Browse button in the Property Bar, save your own objects as brush strokes, and then add them to the existing Brush Stroke list.

FIGURE 10-2 These are a few of the Brush styles available in CorelDRAW X4.

 ## Creating and Saving your Own Brush Stroke

1. Take a look at how some of the Brush presets are designed to give you a better idea of what to draw. Try drawing a straight path, apply a Brush stroke, and then press CTRL+K to simplify the stroke to its vector components. Natively, a Brush stroke does not reveal its structure until you use the Arrange | Break Artistic Media Apart command.

2. Create a shape you think would make a handy Brush stroke and then give it an interesting fill. You can use gradient fills; you can also try grouping objects.

3. Select the shape(s) and then choose the Artistic Media Tool. Click the Brush button on the Property Bar.

4. Click the Save icon. Save the stroke to the folder CorelDRAW points to (so it's easy to find later), give the stroke a name, and then click Save. Brush objects are saved using Corel's standard presentation file format (CMX). The next time you choose the Artistic Media Tool's Brush, a thumbnail preview of your custom brush appears on the drop-down list.

Applying the Sprayer

The Artistic Media Tool's Sprayer mode creates a more complex effect than the other modes, but it's just as simple to use. Using Sprayer, a number of different options are available on the Property Bar, shown in Figure 10-3. This Artistic Media mode has the effect of repeating a graphical image along a drawn (or existing) path, based on spray options chosen—it's quite like the Image Hose in Corel Painter, except changes to the underlying path and the objects

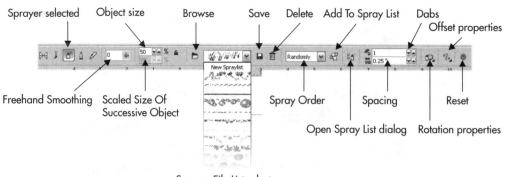

Sprayer selected Object size Browse Save Delete Add To Spray List Dabs Offset properties

Freehand Smoothing Scaled Size Of Successive Object Spray Order Spacing Reset

Open Spray List dialog Rotation properties

Sprayer File List selector

FIGURE 10-3 The Sprayer mode of the Artistic Media Tool offers a huge number of design variations.

used in a spray can be dynamically changed at any time. The Sprayer objects repeat uniformly or randomly across the full length of a path. The Size/Scale, Spray Order, Dabs, Spacing, Rotation, and Offset values can be set using the Property Bar.

Here's what the Sprayer Property Bar options gives you control over:

- **Object Spray Size/Scaling** These two options control the initial object size of the Sprayer style (the objects that make up a specific Spray type) based on a scaled percentage of the original spray object you selected. While the Size/Scale option is unlocked, you can set the scaling objects of successive objects to be increased or reduced in scale relative to the size of the first object in the Sprayer style. Some preset Sprays offer scaling, while some do not, due to their construction. The Snowflakes preset, for example, offers successive scaling, while the Footprints preset does not.

- **Spray Order** This option lets you set the ordering of the Sprayer objects: Randomly, Sequentially, or By Direction. If the Sprayer style features only one object to vary, changing this option has no effect. Try the Mushrooms preset; the Spray preset contains several different objects of different sizes and you can get different looks by choosing Randomly and By Direction.

- **Dabs and Spacing** These two values set the *number of objects* to be placed along a drawn or existing path and *the distance between* the centers of each object. *Dabs* are the individual objects in the Sprayer style; *Spacing* controls how many objects appear within a given distance. Think of Spacing as how sparsely or densely you want areas over which you stroke to be—Spacing is artistic "population control."

- **Rotation** This option is used to set the angle for the first object of the Sprayer style. The *Increment* option is used to compound rotation values for each subsequent object.

Rotation angles and increment values can be based on the degree measure relative to the page or the path to which the objects are applied. If you need a circular pattern whose objects are oriented toward the center of the circle, for example, the rotation option is the ticket.

- **Offset**   This option sets the distance between the center origin of the Sprayer objects and the path to which they are applied. Offset can be set to be active (the default) at settings between 0.014 and 13.875 inches. The direction of the offset can also be set to Alternating (the default), Left, Random, or Right. To deactivate the Offset options, uncheck the Use Offset option in the selector, which sets the Offset measure to 0.

- **Reset**   Clicking this button returns all Sprayer style settings in the Property Bar to their original default settings.

 To delete a style from the Sprayer File List, click to select the style from the list and then click the Delete button in the Property Bar. Doing this immediately deletes the selected style from the list.

As with other Artistic Media Tool modes, you can draw while applying this effect, or apply an Artistic Media stroke to an existing line.

 ## Working with Artistic Media

1. Choose the Artistic Media Tool (I); then choose Sprayer as the tool mode, a Tool Width, and a style from the Sprayer File List.

2. Using a click-drag action, drag to define the shape of your path. When the mouse button is released, the Sprayer style is applied to the path.

3. To apply a different Sprayer style to your selected line, choose a new style from the Sprayer File List in the Property Bar.

With a Sprayer style applied and the line selected, you can use Property Bar options to edit the effect. Doing this edits the style *only as it is applied to your line* and *not* the original style in the Sprayer File List selector. Figure 10-4 shows a sampling of the available Sprayer styles applied using default settings.

Calligraphy and Pressure Pens

Choosing either Calligraphy or a Pressure Pen as your Artistic Media Tool mode results in vector objects that look like a traditional calligraphic pen with expression as though you applied pressure with a physical pen to a piece of paper. While Calligraphic is selected, you can control the Tool Width and Nib Angle of lines. Once a calligraphy effect has been drawn

FIGURE 10-4 These are a few of the Sprayer styles available in CorelDRAW X4.

or applied to a line, you can use the Property Bar options to change its appearance. While drawing in Pressure mode, only the Tool Width can be changed. Pressure mode mimics the effects of drawing with a pressure-sensitive pen; the best results can be had if you use a digital stylus and drawing tablet.

Drawing with Freehand and Polyline Tools

The *Freehand* and *Polyline tools* share a common function, giving you the freedom to draw as if you were sketching by freehand on a physical sketch pad, but the tools work in slightly different ways. Sketched lines can create a single open or closed vector path. Both tools are located in the Toolbox grouped with other line-creation tools, as shown here:

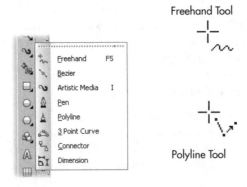

The most natural way to draw using either the Freehand or Polyline Tool is with a digital tablet and stylus, but click-dragging using a mouse is also the preferred method for thousands of CorelDRAW users. To draw lines with the Freehand Tool using a mouse:

1. Begin by selecting either the Freehand or Polyline Tool. Your next step depends on which tool you choose.

2. If you chose the Freehand Tool, you can create a continuous line by click-dragging a path shape. As soon as the mouse button is released the line is complete, as shown next. To draw a straight line between two points, click once to define the start point and a second time somewhere else to define the end point. As soon as the mouse button is released, the line is complete.

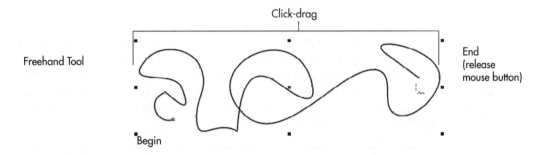

3. If you chose the Polyline Tool, the technique is slightly different. Use a click-drag action to create a continuous line, but after releasing the mouse button, your cursor will still be active. This enables you to continue drawing a straight or curved Bézier line using additional clicks, as shown next. A double-click action on your final point defines it as the end point.

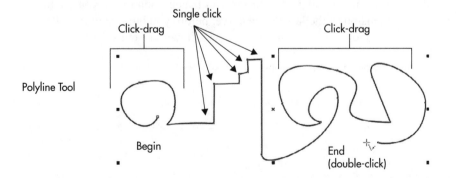

4. Both tools produce "bare bones" paths, without fancy strokes or elegant calligraphic varying widths. This means you can use the Property Bar options to make your path begin with an arrowhead, make the line a dashed line, and change the stroke width.

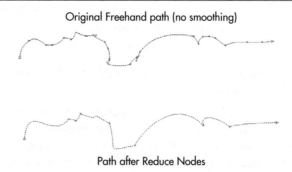

Original Freehand path (no smoothing)

Path after Reduce Nodes

FIGURE 10-5 Freehand smoothing and Reduce Nodes can change a crude drawn line into smooth curves.

Using either of these tools, you have control over the smoothness of path shapes drawn using click-drag actions by adjusting the Freehand Smoothing option in the Property Bar *before* drawing your path. You can control smoothness after *drawing* a path by selecting nodes with the Shape Tool and then using the Reduce Nodes spin box. Reduce Nodes has a range between 0 and 100 percent; lower values apply less smoothing, and higher values apply more smoothing, as shown in Figure 10-5.

Drawing Arcs with the 3-Point Curve Tool

The *3-Point Curve Tool* is used to build perfectly smooth arcing line segments, with complete control over the direction and steepness of the curve between two points. Making a smooth arc is accomplished in three steps.

You'll quickly discover that part of the power of the 3-Point Curve Tool is its use in building a series of connected arcs; you can design French curves and ornamental borders by designing a 3-Point Curve, positioning your cursor over the end point until you see the cursor signifying an extension of the last-drawn curve, before you build another 3-Point Curve. This is how the smooth, complex horn shape was drawn in Figure 10-6.

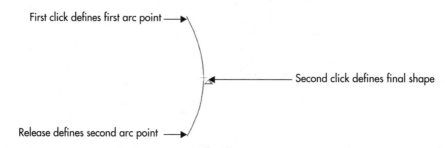

First click defines first arc point ⟶

Second click defines final shape

Release defines second arc point ⟶

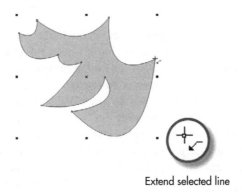

Extend selected line

FIGURE 10-6   Use the 3-Point Curve Tool when you need perfectly smooth curves to connect
at a cusp node.

Using the Bézier and Pen Tools

The *Bézier Tool* and the *Pen Tool* are variations on
the same theme of drawing connected curves and
straight segments (unlike the 3-Point Curve Tool),
through the action of first clicking to set a path
point, and then by either dragging to define a curve
behind the click point or by clicking (not dragging)
to define a straight path segment behind the click
point. You'll find these tools grouped together with
other line-drawing tools, as shown here.

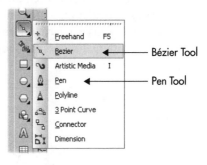

One of the less obvious differences between the two tools is that the Pen Tool offers a
"look ahead" point when you draw with it; before you click or click-drag a point, the
proposed path between the point *before* you click and the previous (already defined) point
on the path is shown in light blue. When you're just beginning with CorelDRAW, the choice
between these tools should be based on the following:

- ■ The Pen Tool provides intuitive results when you want a path that has both straight
  segments and curves.

- ■ The Bézier Tool excels at creating curved segments that are joined smoothly, and
  straight segments are not your design goal.

Both tools are used as artists gain experience with the program, and even seasoned
CorelDRAW pros tend to make these same choices when faced with a design opportunity.

The Science of Béziers

Bézier curves (pronounced *bezz-ee-aye)* were named after French engineer Pierre Bézier, who published papers on their use after seeing the need for a mathematical description of very smooth and easy-to-manipulate curves for the design of automobile bodies. A Bézier curve is a *parametric* curve, which means it *approximates* a curve through 2D space. The curve uses a convex control hull that can be described by two points on a curve and two points off the curve (called *control handles* in CorelDRAW) for intuitively reshaping the curve. The Bézier Tool, by its nature, creates smooth connections between path segments through the action of click-dragging to set a path point. At the same time, it's defining the slope of the curve segment that is created behind the newly created point; when control points are on a curve, they are called *nodes* in CorelDRAW. You can also create straight path segments between curves using the Bézier Tool; it's a matter of technique. Click-dragging creates smooth curves that have smooth connections between segments, while the act of clicking without dragging sets a path point that is not smooth—if you click again in a different location, a straight path segment is the result.

Because the Bézier Tool can produce both curved and straight path segments, there is almost no distinction between the terms *line* and *curve* in the discussions in this chapter. The shapes of Bézier lines are controlled in part by node properties and the position of curve handles. Two paths can have nodes in the same relative page position, but they may have completely different shapes (as shown in Figure 10-7).

Same node positions

FIGURE 10-7   These two paths each have the same relative node positions, but node properties make them appear completely different from each other.

Nodes and Control Points

Depending on the type of math used to describe a vector path, *nodes* (points) connect a beginning and end point. Each of the nodes has *control handles*, at the end of which are *control points*; this is the screen element you use to manipulate curves. The number of control handles and points depends on the segment connected by each node. For example, an arc (a curve) connected to a straight line segment has one control handle visible and it controls the slope of the curve segment. When two curve segments are connected, you'll see two control handles if you click the connecting node with the Shape Tool. This node can have different connection properties (cusp, smooth, and so on—described later in this chapter). A straight path segment can be described as two nodes connecting the segment and the control handles for the nodes coincide in position with the node itself. For all intents and purposes, the control handles can't be seen; they become visible when the segment is changed to a curved segment: the control handles appear on the segment and you can move them away from the launch point of the curve and then freely manipulate the slope of the curve by dragging the control points.

10

Nodes can be defined as Cusp, Smooth, or Symmetrical, as shown in Figure 10-8. *Cusp* nodes can be used to create a discontinuity in direction between two line segments; in English, this means that the two segments connect in a non-smooth fashion. Think of the moon being on the cusp: it's in a crescent shape, which is the sort of shape you can create using cusp node connections. *Smooth* nodes cause the path slope and direction to align on either side of a node (their relationship is in 180 degree opposition), which has the effect of creating a smooth transition at the node point itself. Control handles surrounding a Smooth node may be unequal distances from the node. *Symmetrical* nodes are not only smooth, but

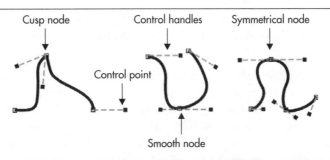

FIGURE 10-8 These paths use different node connection properties.

the control handles are of equal distance from the node. You'll immediately appreciate the effect of a symmetrical node; when you drag one control point away from a node, the opposing control handle moves an equal distance from the node in exactly the opposite direction. The artistic effect is that the two joined path segments take on an almost circular appearance, which is very useful for technical illustration work.

Drawing with the Bézier and Pen Tools

Both of these tools are used to create compound paths (segments connected by a common node) by combining a series of clicks or click-drags, but each is used in slightly different ways for different results. Single-clicks define new node positions joined by straight segments for either of these tools. Curve segments are created by clicking to define the node position, and then *dragging* to define the curve shape. Click-dragging in succession creates a continuous curved path shaped by multiple nodes and off-the-curve control handles. While using the Bézier Tool, each click-drag defines and completes the curve segment. Alternatively, while using the Pen Tool, the cursor remains active and a preview of the next curve segment appears. This means that you can define both the curve shape and the next node point. Double-clicking ends the series of path segments.

 When drawing with the Bézier Tool, holding CTRL *as you click to create new nodes constrains their position to align vertically, horizontally, or within constrained angles relative to the last created node position. Holding* CTRL *while dragging curve handles constrains their angles to 15-degree increments relative to the last node created.*

Let's try out a new drawing method:

Drawing curves and Straight Line Segments

1. Choose either the Bézier Tool or the Pen Tool and then use a single-click action to define the first node position of your path. Click again to define a second point somewhere else on your page. The two nodes are now joined by a straight line.

2. Using the click-drag mouse technique, click to define your next node position, but continue dragging in any direction. As you drag, the second and third nodes are joined by a curved line.

3. If you chose the Bézier Tool, you'll notice that two control handles appear joined by a dotted line. The point you are dragging is the control point, which steers the control handle. The farther you drag the control point from the node, the larger the arc of the curve becomes. Release the mouse button and notice that the control handles remain in view and that your path is complete unless you'd like to move a node or refine the position of its control points some more.

4. If you chose the Pen Tool, you'll notice that a preview of your next curve appears as you move your cursor, which remains active until the next node is defined. To specify a node as the last in the path, use a double-click action to define the current node as the last point.

5. Using either tool, click your cursor directly on the first node you defined. This action closes the path and automatically joins the first and last nodes.

Editing Bézier Paths

All lines are controlled by properties of the nodes they include, which are edited using the Shape Tool (F10). You'll find this tool, shown next, grouped with the Smudge Brush, the Roughen Brush, and the Transform Tools.

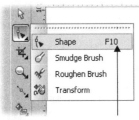

Shape Tool

Using the *Shape Tool,* you can change node positions and curve shapes by click-dragging the nodes, their control points, and by directly click-dragging on a path segment. While using the Shape Tool, icons appear on the Property Bar when one or more nodes are selected; you can select several nodes to change by marquee-dragging them or by SHIFT-clicking a few. These icons are used to set node attributes to Cusp, Smooth, and Symmetrical, to join node and break nodes to create individual path segments, and to create straight lines from curves (and vice versa) when you've selected a segment or a node connecting segments. There are additional options and a bevy of functions on the Property Bar providing exceptional control and flexibility in your design work. In short, get to know the functions for the Shape Tool! The options are called out in Figure 10-9.

Each of these buttons changes the selected nodes, lines, and curves in specific ways. The following is a description of what the icons do and what they're called.

■ **Add/Delete Nodes**   These buttons give you the power to add new nodes to a curve or delete selected nodes after you've drawn a path; you can do this by using the Shape Tool and clicking at specific points on a path. To add a node, click any point on a line to highlight the new position and then click the Add Node button. You can also add a new node to a line by clicking on one or more nodes and then clicking the Add Node button to add a node midpoint between the selected node and the next node on the path. (Pressing the plus (+) key on your numeric keypad achieves the same thing, and you might find this a quicker method.) To delete a node, click to select it with the Shape Tool and then click the Delete Node button. You can also marquee-select (drag diagonally with the Shape Tool to create a rectangle surrounding the nodes) and then delete all the selected node in one fell swoop. Pressing the minus (–) key on your numeric keypad or your DELETE key also deletes selected nodes.

10

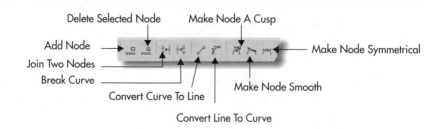

Delete Selected Node

Make Node A Cusp

Add Node

Make Node Symmetrical

Join Two Nodes

Break Curve

Convert Curve To Line

Make Node Smooth

Convert Line To Curve

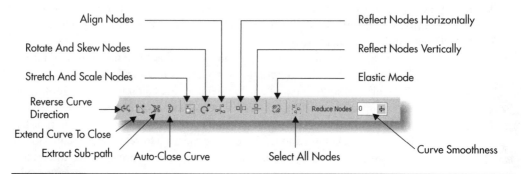

Align Nodes

Reflect Nodes Horizontally

Rotate And Skew Nodes

Reflect Nodes Vertically

Stretch And Scale Nodes

Elastic Mode

Reverse Curve
Direction

Extend Curve To Close

Extract Sub-path

Auto-Close Curve

Select All Nodes

Reduce Nodes

Curve Smoothness

FIGURE 10-9   The Property Bar offers comprehensive control over path and node properties.

- **Join Nodes/Break Curve**   When two unconnected nodes on an open path are selected (for example, when the start point is close to the end point), pressing the Join Nodes button connects them to create an unbroken path. On single paths, only the unjoined, beginning and ending nodes may be joined. On compound paths (paths that aren't necessarily close to one another, but have been joined using the Arrange | Combine command), the beginning and ending nodes selected on two existing—but separate—paths can also be joined. While a single node is selected or while a specific point on a segment is clicked, pressing the Break Curve button results in two nodes becoming unjoined, in turn breaking a closed path into an open path.

 TIP   *Unjoined paths are not the same as separate objects. Two paths, for example, can be located nowhere near each other on a page and yet still be path of a single path. If you want to break a path into its component sub-paths, you first select the nodes using a marquee-selection technique with the Shape Tool, click the Break Curve button, and then choose Arrange | Break Curve Apart. CTRL+K is the shortcut, and it's one of a handful of essential CorelDRAW shortcuts you'll want to commit to memory.*

■ **Line To Curve/Curve To Line**   These two buttons are used to toggle the state of a selected straight line to a curve state and vice versa. A single click with the Shape Tool selects a line or curve indicated by a round black marker on the line. When curves are converted to lines, the path they follow takes on a shortcut (as in the shortest distance between two points); when converting a straight line to a curve, the path remains the same shape, but control handles appear directly on the line, so that the quickest way make the control points visible is to drag on the line to force it into a curve shape. When a curve is selected, you can also adjust the shape of the curve using a click-drag action at any point on the curve and dragging to reposition the path followed by the curve.

■ **Extend Curve To Close**   For this command to be available, you must have both the beginning and ending nodes of an open path selected (marquee select the points or SHIFT+click to select them both). Under these conditions, clicking the Extend Curve To Close button joins the two nodes by adding a straight line between them and closes the path.

■ **Auto-Close Curve**   While an open path is selected, clicking this button joins the beginning and end nodes to form a closed path by adding a new straight line between the two nodes. It's a similar command to Extend Curve To Close, but depending on the closeness of the start to the end path nodes, you might not even see a visible straight line connection. You can also join the end points of a selected curve using the Close Curve option in the Object Properties docker opened by pressing ALT+ENTER.

■ **Reverse Curve Direction**   While a curve path on a line is selected, clicking this button has the effect of changing the direction of the path. By doing this, the start point of the path becomes the end point (and vice versa). The results of using this command button are most noticeable when the start or end of the line or path has been applied with an arrowhead, meaning the arrowhead is applied to the opposite end of the line or path. You may also notice subtle changes in the appearance of line styles applied to a path after using this command button.

10

TIP   *In addition to making arrowheads point in the right direction, Reverse Curve Direction is also a handy way to enforce PostScript conventions when you print to a PostScript printer. Adobe Systems' PostScript language is a page description language that has very fixed and definite rules about the direction of paths in a compound shape, which can be demonstrated with the letter "o." If your compound path "o" appears to be filled and not hollow, it's not "speaking" PostScript language. To change this, click the sub-path of the compound path, reverse the path direction using this button, and you'll find that the "o" will then print properly.*

■ **Extract Sub-path**   This option becomes available only when a compound path is selected. After clicking the Extract Sub-path button, the selected path is separated from the compound path, converting it to a separate path. Using this command on a compound path, composed of only two different paths, is essentially the same as using the Break Apart command. It's more useful when you need to extract a specific path from a compound path made up of three or more paths.

■ **Stretch And Scale Nodes**   This is a very powerful CorelDRAW feature and it isn't available in competing drawing programs. When at least two nodes on a path are selected, clicking the Stretch And Scale Nodes allows the transformation between nodes using their relative distance from each other (vertically, horizontally, or from the center). Eight selection handles become available, just as with the object selection when using the Pick Tool, and you can use a click-drag action from any corner or side selection handle toward or away from the center of the node selection. Holding SHIFT constrains the stretch or scale operation from the center of the selection.

■ **Rotate And Skew Nodes**   Similar to Stretch And Scale Nodes, when at least two nodes on a path are selected, clicking the Rotate And Skew Nodes button lets you rotate and skew the selected nodes. This is a great feature for refining a shape just a little, and also for creating more dramatic appearance changes (as shown next). Eight selection handles become available, enabling you to use a click-drag action from any corner selection handle to rotate the nodes in a circular direction either clockwise or counterclockwise. Dragging from any side handle enables you to skew the node selection either vertically or horizontally.

■ **Align Nodes**   When two or more nodes are selected, clicking this button opens the Node Align dialog, from where you can choose from the Align Vertical or Align Horizontal options that automatically align your node selection. In addition to these options, while only the beginning and ending nodes of an open path are selected, you can also choose to align control points. This has the effect of moving the two end points of the line so that they overlap each other precisely. This is a wonderful command for quickly sketching a zigzag (for an illustration of a saw blades, perhaps), and then, in one step, aligning the nodes to create a precise illustration.

■ **Reflect Nodes Horizontally/Vertically**   These two buttons become available when two or more nodes are selected. You use these options to move nodes using nudge keys (the UP, DOWN, LEFT, and RIGHT arrow keys on your keyboard) or click-drag actions in opposite directions.

 TIP   *To quickly access the same eligible Shape Tool node and curve command using buttons in the Property Bar, right-click the nodes or segments of a path and then choose commands from the pop-up menu.*

■ **Elastic Mode**   With this command, you move selected nodes according to their relative distance from each other; the effect is like experimenting with a rubber band. For example, while a collection of nodes is selected, dragging one of the nodes causes the others to be dragged a shorter distance in relation to the node that is being dragged. While Elastic mode is off, all the selected nodes are moved equal distances. Try this option to add a more organic and natural feeling to a drawing you might feel looks a little too studied and stiff; it adds expression to a path.

■ **Reduce Nodes**   When you use this command, CorelDRAW evaluates the overall shape based on the nodes you've selected, deletes nodes that deviate from a predictable course along the path, and then repositions the remaining nodes—the effect is to smooth the curve. For past CorelDRAW users, this was called The Curve Smoothness slider. To use this feature, select the nodes controlling the segments you want to smooth and drag the Reduce Nodes slider control position toward 100. As you drag the slider, the shape of the curves become smoothed and you'll notice superfluous nodes disappear from the curve. This option is useful for smoothing lines drawn using the Freehand Tool with either the mouse or a digitizing tablet stylus.

■ **Select All Nodes**   This button selects all the nodes in a path (or compound path) with one click. It's a great feature for users who aren't expert with the marquee-selection dragging technique yet. You may also select all the nodes in a path with the Shape Tool by holding CTRL+SHIFT and clicking any node on the path.

 TIP   *To select noncontiguous nodes on a path (nodes that do not neighbor each other along the path), hold ALT while dragging the Shape Tool cursor to surround the nodes in "lasso" style. Any nodes located within the area you lasso are selected.*

Are you ready to text drive the Shape Tool? Follow along here:

 ## Editing Paths with The Shape Tool

1. Choose the Ellipse Tool (F7) and create an ellipse of any size. Convert the ellipse shape to Curves (CTRL+Q) to create a closed path with four nodes joined by four curved lines.

2. Choose the Shape Tool (F10). Notice that the Property Bar now features all the line and node command buttons. Click the Select All Nodes button to select all nodes on the path.

3. With the nodes still selected, click the Add Node button (or press the + button on your numeric keypad). Notice that four new nodes are added midpoint between the four original nodes.

4. Click any of the segments once and then click the Convert Curve To Line button. You'll see that the curve is now a straight line and that the curve handles have disappeared.

5. Click a node on one of the other existing curves, drag either of the curve handles in any direction, and then notice the ways they change the shape of the path.

6. Using a click-drag action, click near the middle of the curve segment and drag in any direction. As you drag, the curve handle positions at either end will move and the shape of the curve is changed accordingly.

7. Click any node on the path to select it and click the Make Node A Cusp button. Notice that the lines on either side of the node can be curved in any direction, independently of each other. Select the cusp node you've just created, click the Make Node Smooth button, and then perform the same action. Notice that the curve handle may be dragged, but only in a single direction.

8. With this node still selected, click the Break Curve button to split the path at this point. Although it may not be obvious, two nodes now exist where the original node used to be. Drag either of these nodes in any direction to separate their positions. The nodes are now control points because they break the path to form beginning and end points.

9. Select one of these nodes, hold SHIFT while clicking the other, and then click the Extend Curve To Close button. Notice that the curve is now closed again, while the two nodes have been joined by a straight line.

10. Undo your last action (CTRL+Z) to unjoin the nodes and, while they remain selected, click the Align Nodes button to open the Align Nodes dialog. If they aren't already selected, click to select all three options (Align Horizontal, Vertical, and Control Points) in the dialog and then click OK to align the points. Notice that they are positioned to overlap precisely. Click to select both nodes and then click the Join Two Nodes button in the Property Bar. Your path is now closed and the nodes are joined.

11. Hold SHIFT and click to select two or more nodes on your path. With your nodes selected, click the Stretch And Scale Node button and then notice that eight selection handles appear around your node selection. Hold the SHIFT key (to constrain movement from absolute to relative change) and then drag one of the corner handles toward or away from the center of the selection. All node positions are scaled relative to each other's position, and the lines joining the unselected nodes also change shape.

12. With the nodes still selected, click the Rotate And Skew Nodes button in the Property Bar. Notice that eight rotate and skew handles appear around your selection. Drag any of the corner rotation handles either clockwise or counterclockwise to rotate the nodes. Notice that they are rotated relative to their current position and that the lines joining the unselected nodes also change shape.

The preceding tutorial is only a sampling of what can be accomplished when editing nodes using the Shape Tool. You'll want to invest some quality time practicing your editing skills using all the available node-shaping command buttons. Why go to all the trouble, you ask? Because the payoff is better artwork, artwork that's closer to what you have in your head, and in the long run, you'll save time while still creating wonderful pieces.

 To set the drawing behavior of the Freehand and/or Bézier tools, double-click either of their tool buttons in the Toolbox to open the Options dialog to the Freehand/Bézier Tool page. Options are discussed in the next section.

Controlling Freehand and Bézier Tool Behavior

The settings for controlling Freehand and Bézier Tools to create the curves and lines you want to draw are set using a series of options in the Freehand/Bézier Tool pane of the Options dialog, shown next. To access these options, choose Tools | Options (CTRL+J), expand the tree subdirectory under Toolbox, and then click Freehand/Bézier Tool. The quick way to get to this box is to double-click the Freehand or Bézier tool buttons after choosing them from the Line Tool group.

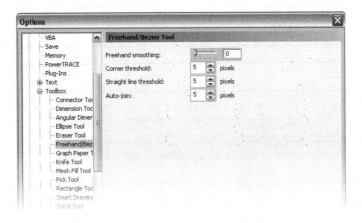

10

Here's how the options work:

- **Freehand Smoothing**   The Freehand Smoothing option enables you to set the default value of the Freehand Smoothing option in the Property Bar while drawing with the Freehand Tool. Smoothing may be set based on a percent, within a range between 0 (minimum smoothing) and 100 (maximum smoothing). This option is largely redundant, with the Freehand Smoothing option available in the Property Bar when a curve and the Shape Tool are selected.

- **Corner Threshold**   This option is for setting the default value for corner nodes when drawing with the Freehand or Bézier Tool. Lower values cause nodes to be more likely set to Cusp nodes, and higher values cause them to more likely be Smooth nodes. The range may be set between 1 and 10; the default is 5.

- **Straight Line Threshold**   This option pertains to the way that the shapes of lines or curves are created when drawing with the Freehand Tool. Lower values cause nodes to be more likely set to straight lines, while higher values cause them to be curved more frequently. The range may be set between 1 and 10; the default is 5.

- **Auto-Join**   This option sets the behavior of the Freehand or Bézier Tool while drawing closed-path objects. This value represents the distance in pixels that your cursor must be when clicking *near* the first node of a newly created path to close the path automatically. Auto-Join can be set anywhere within a range between 1 and 10 pixels; the default is 5 and is probably the best overall choice for large screen resolutions that are run today.

Working with Compound Paths

Compound paths have at least two separate paths (either open or closed), composing a single shape. To examine an example of a compound path, use these steps:

1. Choose the Text Tool (F8), click once to define a text insertion point, and then type an uppercase *Q* character. You can assign the character any typeface you like; the more ornamental the character, the more obvious the compound path will be. This character shape, shown in Figure 10-10, has two combined paths: one represents the "positive" space and one represents the "negative" space shape.

2. While the text object is selected, convert it to curves (CTRL+Q). The Status Bar now indicates the object is a Curve on Layer 1.

3. Change your view to Wireframe by choosing View | Wireframe.

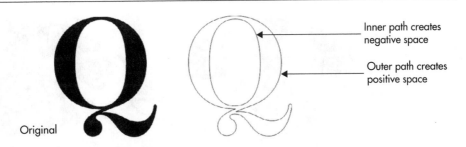

Inner path creates
negative space

Outer path creates
positive space

Original

FIGURE 10-10 In vector artwork, "holes" in objects are achieved through compound paths; paths that are combined to create a single object.

4. Press CTRL+K (Arrange | Break Curve Apart). With the Pick Tool, click on one of the shapes and drag it to move it; clearly the two paths are now separate. You have just converted a compound path featuring two sub-paths into two individual objects, as shown in Figure 10-11.

Combining Objects

When separate objects are combined, they behave as a single object. While two or more closed paths are combined, they form positive and negative spaces within the object. Applying a fill to this type of object causes the positive shapes to be filled, and the negative shapes remain clear, as shown in Figure 10-12. The Combine command does this: choose Arrange | Combine or use the CTRL+L shortcut. You can also click the Combine button in the Property Bar, or choose Combine from the pop-up menu.

Combining objects that normally feature unique properties—such as rectangles, ellipses, polygons, and perfect shapes—permanently converts them to curves.

10

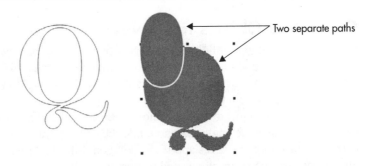

Two separate paths

FIGURE 10-11 Break a compound path apart to work with the component objects.

Original objects   Combined objects

FIGURE 10-12   The Combine command enables you to make two or more separate objects into a single compound path.

NOTE   *If you intend to output to PostScript, it might not be a good idea to combine paths that overlap each other. Again, it's one of the limitations of the PostScript page description language—in human terms, a PostScript printer or image-setting device gets "confused" when a single closed path intersects itself; the device doesn't know which areas to fill and which to leave empty. If you have a design need for a shape that looks like it self-intersects and you have to have proper PostScript output, don't fret. You can use the Shaping docker (or the buttons on the Property Bar when multiple shapes are selected, using the Pick Tool) to create the illusion of a self-intersecting shape.*

Breaking Paths Apart

You can separate the individual paths in a compound path using the Break Curve Apart command (CTRL+K). This command is available when a compound path composed of at least two sub-paths is selected. (Using the Extract Sub-path command button in the Property Bar also does this, but only for the *selected* path.)

Converting Objects to Curves

Converting special types of objects to curves frees them to be manipulated with the Shape Tool as if they were ordinary paths. Choose Arrange | Convert To Curves, press CTRL+Q, click the Convert To Curves button in the Property Bar, or right-click the object and choose Convert To Curves from the pop-up menu.

Converting an object to curves removes any special editing properties; text loses its editability and rounded rectangles can no longer be edited to refine the curvature of the rounded corners. Converting to Curves applies to Polygon, Ellipse, Artistic Text objects, and certain effects objects such as envelopes and perspective effects.

Using the Dimension Line Tool

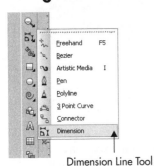

Dimension Line Tool

If the document you are creating requires that you indicate linear or angular distances or degree values, you might consider using dimension lines. These lines enable you to indicate sizing and/or angles automatically and are created using the Dimension Line Tool (shown next and located in the Toolbox grouped with other line-drawing tools). This tool may be of interest to users creating precision diagrams that require an accurate display of sizes.

Once a dimensioning line has been created, you can edit its line, text, and reference point properties. Figure 10-13 shows a catalog piece with Dimension lines calling out details and measurements.

Using Dimension Tool Modes

Six Dimension Line Tool types are available, each of which creates a different type of line with a specific purpose. When the Dimension Tool is selected, the Property Bar shows six different tool modes that may be selected for specific purposes. These six modes, shown in

FIGURE 10-13   One of the many purposes for dimension lines.

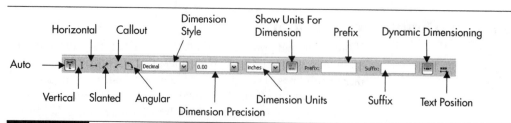

FIGURE 10-14 The Dimension Tool has six different modes, each with a common set of options.

Figure 10-14, are Vertical, Horizontal, Slanted, Callout, Angular, and Auto. You may also specify the style, precision, and unit values of your displayed dimensions, and control the display and appearance of the labeling text.

To help you choose which of these Dimension Tools is best suited for a particular need, the following list describes their functions:

- **Auto Dimension Tool** This tool creates either Vertical or Horizontal dimension lines defined by your initial click-drag direction while creating your dimension line.

- **Vertical/Horizontal Dimension Tools** These two modes limit your new dimension lines to a specific orientation. By default, the text labels associated with Vertical dimension lines are oriented at 90 degrees to your page orientation, while the Horizontal mode creates horizontally oriented labels.

 You can apply arrowheads and line styles, as well as change the outline width value applied to dimension lines, by using the Outline Pen dialog (F12). For information on controlling Outline Pen properties, see Chapter 18.

- **Slanted Dimension Tool** This tool creates dimension lines that measure distances at an angle. By default, the text labels applied to Slanted dimension lines are read upright, from left to right.

- **Callout Tool** This tool creates lines attached with labels at various positions. The resulting text label displays the text you enter, but does not measure distances.

- **Angular Dimension Tool** Choose the Angular Dimension Tool to measure an object or space where angles are based on degrees, radians, or gradients.

Creating a dimension line is usually a three-step operation: your first mouse click defines one end or side of the line, the next click defines the other side or end, and the final click enables you to define the position for the dimensioning text label.

Measuring with Dimension Lines

1. Press CTRL+J to go to Options. Choose Document | Rulers, and then click on Edit Scale. From here, set up your page to accurately reflect the scale of the object you'll add Dimension Lines to. Refer to Chapter 6 for the details on World distance and other page and Ruler settings.

2. Choose the Dimension Tool and then use Property Bar options to select a Dimension Tool mode. Choose the mode that best suits your needs.

3. Click to define the first reference point for your dimension line and then release the mouse button. Notice that as you move your cursor around the screen, the Dimension Tool cursor remains active and the dimension line changes to reflect the cursor position.

4. Position your cursor at the second side or end of the area for which you want to display measurements and click again to define the point. With this point defined, the area you are measuring has been defined, but your cursor still is active and it now includes a rectangular-shaped box. This cursor remains active until you complete the next step.

5. Click a point between the first two points to define where your dimension line text label will be placed. Notice that the measured distance between the first two points is immediately displayed, and that the text label is formatted using your default text format properties.

 After creating a dimension line, you can format text labels by clicking directly on the text object using the Pick Tool and by using Property Bar options to set its font, size, and so on.

Dimension Tools and the Property Bar

The Property Bar is where you set options depending on your selected Dimension Tool mode. It features various selection menus, custom text boxes, and command buttons for controlling the display of angles or distances measured by your dimension lines. Here's how each of these Property Bar options works:

- **Dimension Style**   This option enables you to choose among decimal, fractional, or standard measuring conventions, the default of which is decimal. These styles are available only while Auto, Vertical, Horizontal, or Slanted mode is selected.

- **Dimension Precision**   This option enables you to choose a level of precision. While using Decimal as the measuring style, precision may be specified up to ten decimal places. While using Fractional, precision may be specified using fractions up to 1/1024 of a selected unit measure.

10

Double-clicking the text portion of a dimension line using the Pick Tool automatically displays the Linear Dimensions Docker, which includes options identical to those found in the Property Bar while using the Dimension Tool.

- **Dimension Units**   Use this option to specify the measurement unit with which to display your text labels. You may choose any of the unit measures supported by CorelDRAW X4.

- **Show Units For Dimension**   This option may be toggled on or off to display the units associated with your dimension line.

- **Prefix/Suffix For Dimension**   These options enable you to enter your own text so that it appears before and after the text label for your dimension line. Prefix and Suffix text may be any character you want and may be applied before or after the dimension line has been drawn.

- **Dynamic Dimensioning**   This option allows you to specify whether your measurement values are updated automatically as the size of the dimension line is changed. By default, this option is turned on for all new dimension lines. If you plan on resizing or changing the drawing scale of your drawing after creating the dimension lines, disabling this option essentially "freezes" the values being displayed so that they remain fixed, whether your dimension lines are resized or not.

 If, for some reason, resizing a drawing applied with dimension lines causes the measured values to change, you can right-click the dimension line and choose Break [mode] Dimension Apart from the pop-up menu as a workaround.

- **Text Position Drop Down**   To specify a position for the text labels applied to your dimension line, choose one of the options available from the Text Position option. Choose from top-centered, middle-centered, or bottom-centered for Auto, Vertical, Horizontal, or Callout dimension lines. Text labels applied to Slanted dimension lines may also be oriented upright and/or centered within the line.

 The best way of controlling the format of dimension lines is to set their default properties before you begin your dimension process.

Setting Dimension Tool Defaults

To set the default properties for specific dimension lines, use the Options dialog, shown next. To access specific dialog pages controlling dimension lines quickly, choose the Dimension Tool button in the Toolbox and then double-click on it. Once the options are set, your new dimension lines are created according to your preferences.

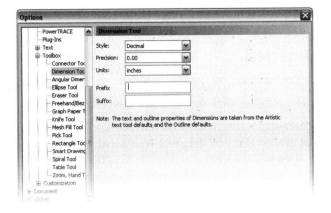

Using the Connector Tool

Connector lines are for drawing lines quickly between objects. Once these lines are created, you can reposition the parent shapes without breaking the connection, which is indispensable for technical drawings such as charts, schematics, and diagrams. You find the Connector Tool in the Toolbox grouped with other line-drawing tools, as shown to the left.

Connector Tool

Creating connector lines is relatively straightforward, as are the options that set the appearance and behavior of these lines. While using this tool, the Property Bar features properties, shown next, that apply to typical open curves, as well as two basic tool modes: Angled Connector and Straight Connector. After you've created a connector, you can choose to modify its style (dashed lines, dotted lines, and so on), whether the connector has an arrowhead or other head, and the width of the connector. You can also, for example, color a connector line. Suppose you're working with a black background design; a right-click over the color line on a white swatch makes your connector visible against the contrasting background.

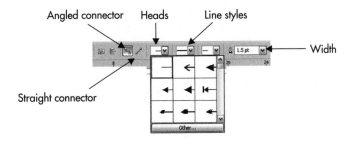

For a little experience using the Interactive Connector Tool, follow these steps:

Getting Connected

1. Create several objects to connect and then choose the Connector Tool. Using Property Bar options, click the Angled Connector button.

2. Using a click-drag action, click your Interactive Connector Tool on an object to define the start of the line and then drag to a separate object and release the mouse button. As you drag, snap points appear either inside or at the edge of your objects. Notice that the Angled connector lines include vertical and horizontal lines, as shown here:

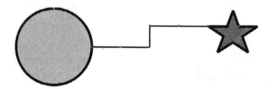

3. With the line still selected, click the Straight Connector button. The Angled Connector is now a Straight Connector. Click the Angled Connector button to change it back again.

4. Choose the Pick Tool and click-drag either of the connected objects in any direction. Notice that the connector line remains connected to both objects and changes its connection point on the object to maintain the connection.

5. With the connector line selected, use Property Bar options to customize its appearance if needed.

While a connector line joins two objects, the connecting shape is controlled by a Threshold option found on the Connector Tools page of the Options dialog, as shown here:

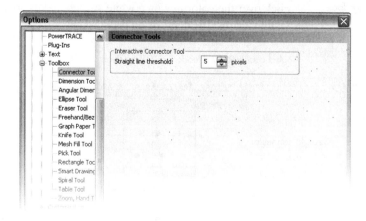

To quickly access these options, double-click the Connector Tool on the Toolbox or choose Tools | Options (CTRL+J), and then choose Toolbox | Connector Tools. This option enables you to control the likelihood of a connector line taking the shape of a straight line, as opposed to a stair-step sort of line composed of a sequence of vertical and horizontal lines. Threshold may be a value between 1 and 10; the default is 5.

Editing Angled Connector Lines

Angled Connector lines are composed of both vertical and horizontal lines, but they also feature control points at the center of the path segments. These points act as "hinge" points, so you can edit the line, add vertical or horizontal segments, and/or change the vertical and horizontal direction between two objects.

To edit an Angled Connector line, use the Shape Tool (F10). To reposition connector line end points, click to select the point and drag it along the edge of the object. By default, the connector line snaps to the boundaries of the object's edge. Figure 10-15 shows the action of editing an Angled Connector.

Changing the actual path of the connector line is accomplished by either dragging the center points or the corner points. To add a new segment to the line, drag the center points

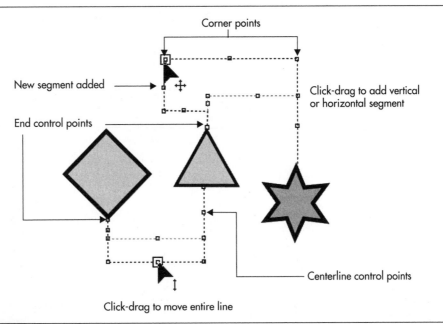

FIGURE 10-15   The center point on connector lines enable you to edit their path shape.

closest to either end point. To delete a segment, drag any corner point over its closest corner point. Dragging either the center points or corner points of an Angled Connector line lets you manipulate the path; the best teacher, as always, is experience.

You've seen in this chapter that there are two different types of paths you can create in CorelDRAW: the types used for designing art and the Connectors and Dimension Lines for labeling and organizing objects. You've also learned how to edit paths using the Shape Tool. You'd be well served to bookmark this chapter; there's an awful lot of power in CorelDRAW's drawing and editing tools, and this chapter can be a good reference in the future. After all, the program isn't called CorelFILL or CorelRECTANGLE—*drawing* is what good vector design is all about.

CHAPTER 11

Editing Objects

Let's say you've drawn an object and you're fairly pleased with it, *except* for that little corner that you couldn't draw *just* right. Editing objects is the theme of this chapter, where you'll learn various techniques to massage that almost-perfect shape into *exactly* the shape you've envisioned. Because every object you draw on a page can be broken down into rectangles, ovals, path segments, and so on, this chapter covers the tools and features for doing exactly this: breaking down shapes, combining them, subtracting a little of this, adding a little of that. Often, arriving at a design of your dreams can be most quickly accomplished by creating an approximation of the shapes you need. Then with a pull and a tug here and there, erasing a tiny area perhaps, you'll get quicker results than if you had built the object from scratch. You'll see in this chapter that editing objects not only provides you with the best results, but that you can also add visual complexity and embellishments that would be hard to achieve using other methods.

Reshaping Things Up

You have a choice of two places to begin when you want to edit an object: you can use operations (commands you make with the click of a Property Bar button), or you can use the hands-on approach; both are covered in this chapter. Both approaches will serve you well, and your choice largely depends on what you need to edit, what type of operation is required.

Shaping and Reshaping Object Shapes

Drawing shapes from scratch is often a tedious and time-consuming process, but CorelDRAW has great shaping commands to speed the process. Shape commands such as Trim, Weld, and Intersection make creating complex shapes quick and painless. You'll also find three other shape commands at your disposal: Simplify, Front Minus Back, and Back Minus Front. In this next section, we'll examine exactly how you can use these commands to shape and reshape your objects. Before we get into the specifics of each type, though, let's take a look at where you can find them in CorelDRAW X4.

Shaping Commands and the Property Bar

CorelDRAW X4's Property Bar provides shaping command buttons that enable you to shape selected objects instantly. These Property Bar options become available only while at least two objects are selected—and they make shaping commands available, whether or not the objects are positioned to overlap. Property Bar shaping buttons are shown here:

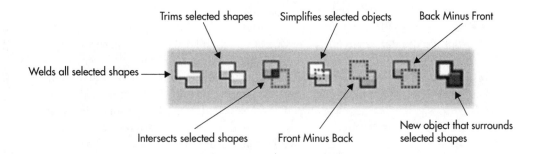

Welds all selected shapes

Trims selected shapes

Simplifies selected objects

Back Minus Front

Intersects selected shapes

Front Minus Back

New object that surrounds selected shapes

> **TIP** *When using Property Bar shaping buttons, shapes are subtracted, added, and so on, but the original objects go away. To keep your original objects, use the Shaping docker, which offers options to specify that the Source Object (the one performing the operation—the "scissors") and/or Target Object (the object receiving the operation—the "paper") should remain after shaping.*

Now that you know where to find the buttons to launch these commands quickly, let's examine what they enable you to do. The following section explains the results of applying each command to at least two selected objects:

■ **Weld** The *Weld* command creates a new shape based on the outline shape of two (or more) overlapping objects, as shown at right. Original objects are automatically deleted.

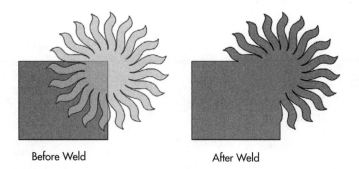

Before Weld

After Weld

This illustration shows a polygonal, sun-like shape with partial transparency applied to better show the order of objects on the page: the rectangle is behind the sun shape. Not only did the Weld operation create a single object from the two, but it also gave the result object the *color* of the *bottom* object. This is an important thing to know when welding objects.

Boolean Shaping

This tidbit will interest anyone who wants to look under the hood and see what's actually happening when you use shaping operations in CorelDRAW. Users are insulated from the mind-boggling math; all you need to do is click here and go there, but the history of the Shaping features is an intriguing one. The proper mathematical name for "shaping" is "Boolean operations," named after the 19th century mathematician George Boole, who invented a logic system in algebra for describing certain functions in plain English terms, similar to Visual Basic and Python scripting, in which mere mortals can fathom what the code is doing.

Boolean operations extend a typical digital data set from elements such as "true" and "false" to include operations such as "and," "not," "or," and so on. When these operations are applied to geometry, we make the leap from "A is a rectangle, B is an overlapping circle" to "show me A and B together," or "include in the new shape A but not B." This is the basis for the operation CorelDRAW performs when you use one shape as a target and a different one for the source in a shape operation.

- **Trim** The *Trim* command removes any overlapping areas of the object in front from the object(s) in back, as shown here—the rectangle in front is partially transparent to make the effect more obvious. The original objects are automatically deleted, and no color change takes place (the back object does not inherit the front object's color, transparency, or any other trait).

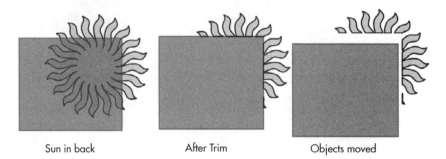

| Sun in back | After Trim | Objects moved |

- **Intersect** The *Intersect* operation creates a new object based on the overlapping areas of two or more objects. The original objects remain on the page, and the result is not obvious because the new object is in the same position as the overlapping parts of the original objects. In the following figure, the sun shape was on the bottom, and the result shape takes on the color of the bottom object. Intersect is a great operation for creating difficult crops of complex objects (the new sun shape will make a nice logo for a tanning salon!).

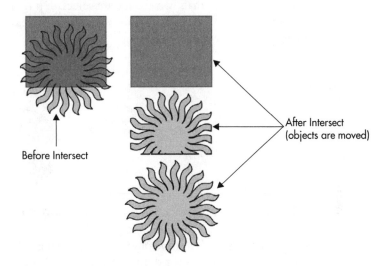

Before Intersect

After Intersect (objects are moved)

■ **Simplify** The *Simplify* command removes all hidden areas of objects that "underlap" foreground objects, as an example shows here. This command is great for uncomplicating an intricate drawing, and it can also make a design that otherwise might not print to PostScript correctly print just fine. As you can see in the middle example, there is no apparent change to this simple design, but at right, you can see that when the objects are moved, overlapping areas of the sun in back have been erased, similar but not identical to the Trim command. Different order and arrangements of objects will result in slightly different results.

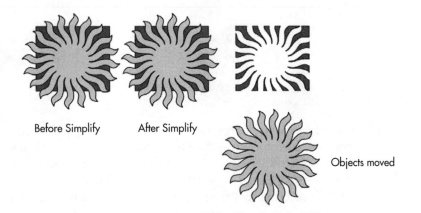

Before Simplify   After Simplify

Objects moved

11

■ **Front Minus Back** When two or more shapes are selected, applying the Front Minus Back command removes the hidden area of the object in back from the shape in front. When more than two shapes are selected, it removes all portions where the shapes in back are overlapped by the object in front, leaving only the object in front remaining, as shown here:

Before Front Minus Back

After Front Minus Back

Front Minus Back is a trim operation, "A but not B" in Boolean terminology, and the advantage to using this operation to trim objects is that it removes the guesswork of, "Gosh, what's the order of the objects in this design?" Front Minus Back is an unambiguous, straightforward trim operation.

■ **Back Minus Front** This shaping command works in reverse of Front Minus Back. While at least two shapes are selected, applying the Back Minus Front command removes the portions of the shape layered in front from the shape in back. When more than two shapes are selected, it will remove all portions where the shapes in front overlap the shape in back, leaving only the shape in back remaining, as shown here:

Before Back Minus Front

After Back Minus Front

■ **New Object That Surrounds Selected Objects** This is similar to the Weld operation, except it leaves the Target objects on the page. Below is an example of several objects selected and below them, the resulting shape. By default, the new object has no fill and is ordered on top of the Target objects. It's usually a good idea to fill the object; after the operation, the new object is selected. Just click a foreground color on the color strip, and the new object will become immediately apparent.

Before New Object That
Surrounds Selected Objects

After New Object That Surrounds
Selected Objects (moved)

 Shaping commands work on vector objects in CorelDRAW X4, but do not apply to bitmap objects. If a bitmap is selected as part of a collection of selected objects, the shaping commands are not available.

Using the Shaping Docker

Under the Arrange menu, you'll find all the shaping commands except Creates A New Object That Surrounds Selected Objects. Also, the Shaping command is on this menu, which opens the Shaping docker in the workspace. As with all dockers, you can detach (undock) this palette so it floats near your work (demanding fewer "mouse miles"), and this docker offers more options than when you use the shaping operations from the Property Bar. Because of their operation, the Simplify, Front Minus Back, and Back Minus Front commands have no additional options.

The first three shaping commands in the selector are applied in slightly different ways from the last three. To Weld, Trim, or Intersect, you must have at least one object selected and another unselected (but still in view) for the commands to be available. Once Weld, Trim, or Intersect is selected, the docker will display available options, as shown next. Clicking the docker command button begins the action.

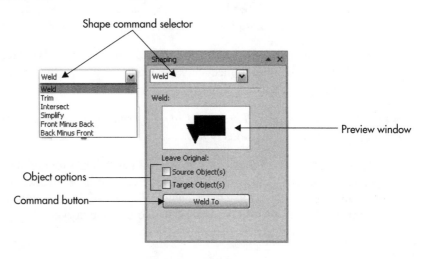

The preview window on the docker doesn't actually change; it's an illustration that shows the result of using each operation. The Object options check boxes are what you use to set what object, if any, remains after an operation. Leave Original is equivalent to "make a copy so I don't lose my originals," and the options mean:

- **Source Object(s)** When this option is selected, the object you selected before the shaping operation remains after the command has been applied.

- **Target Object(s)** With this option selected, the object you Trim, Weld to, or Intersect with remains after the command has been applied.

Let's give this docker a spin. First, create two shapes; the Rectangle Tool is fine to make shapes you won't need later, so they're expendable in this example:

1. If you haven't already done so, create the objects on which you want to base your new shape, and position them in such a way that the shape created by their overlapping portions represents your new shape.

2. Select one of these overlapping objects, and open the Shaping docker by choosing Window | Dockers | Shaping.

3. Choose Weld, Trim, or Intersect from the selector at the top of the docker.

4. Choose which original object(s) you want to remain after the command has been applied by clicking Source Object(s) and/or Target Object(s), and then click the command button at the bottom of the docker to apply the command. Notice your cursor has changed to one of three targeting cursors, shown next, depending on your shaping operation.

Weld targeting cursor   Trim targeting cursor   Intersect targeting cursor

5. Click the object you want your selected object to Trim, Weld to, or Intersect with. Your new shape is immediately created based on the overlapping area of your existing objects.

> **TIP** *The outline and fill properties of newly shaped objects are determined by the properties of the target object.*

Choosing Simplify, Front Minus Back, or Back Minus Front requires that at least two objects are selected. If only one object is selected, you'll get an attention box politely telling you so and asking if you'd like to try again. With any of these commands, the shaping is applied when you click the Apply button in the Shaping docker.

Working Examples of Object Shaping

If you've seen some stunning CorelDRAW artwork on the Web (or in this book!) and say to yourself, "Wow, that must've taken that artist ages to do all that work," nope, it probably didn't: the artist put object shaping to work. The following examples show just three of thousands of creative possibilities for shaping operations; these are just a few examples to kindle your efforts.

Figure 11-1 shows an example problem and a solution using the Trim operation. The chicken came first, then the need to make the chicken drawing look as though it's peeking through the broken eggshell. The chicken drawing is composed of several sub-objects grouped; the Trim operation trims all objects in a group. First, you trace the jagged edge of the eggshell, close the path at the bottom, and then position the chicken drawing in the appropriate area relative to the jagged Source object. The Source object should be on top; you use the keyboard shortcut of CTRL+PAGE UP to reorder the jagged Source object. Then you use the Trim operation on the Shaping docker—making sure to check Leave Original: Target Object(s) so the chicken illustration isn't ruined. Then with the jagged-edge object selected, you click the Trim button. You're then prompted with the large arrow cursor to point to the Target object; you click the chicken, move the original to a convenient location, and then reposition the trimmed chicken to complete the illustration.

Figure 11-2 shows a combination Weld and then a Trim, although Back Minus Front would work as the second step, too. The problem is that a specific font is needed in stencil style, but the artist doesn't have such a typeface. So Arial is first used, and then several rectangles are drawn over areas that need to be removed from the text to create the stencil effect. Right-drag then clicking was used to drop duplicates of one narrow rectangle, to keep consistency between areas to be removed from the text. After all the rectangles are in position, the rectangles are marquee-selected, and in this example the text was selected as

Original art (wireframe view)
and Source object for Trim

Trimmed chicken in front of egg objects

FIGURE 11-1   Trimming grouped objects can help illustrate the illusion that one object is behind or inside another one.

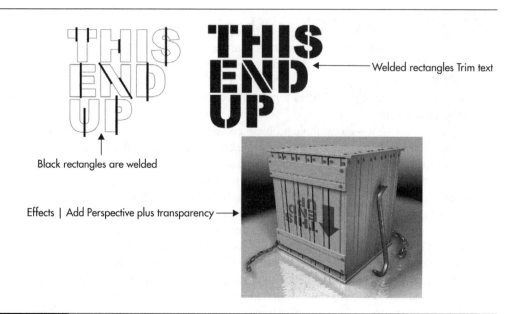

Welded rectangles Trim text

Black rectangles are welded

Effects | Add Perspective plus transparency

FIGURE 11-2 Weld and then Trim are used to make a stencil treatment out of the text.

well, but by holding SHIFT and then clicking the text, it is removed from the selected shapes. The Weld command is then used to make a single object out of the rectangles, and then the single shape is used as the Source object in the Trim operation. The text is trimmed and finally Effects | Add Perspective is used to make the text appear as though it's on the 3D crate. The text probably could use some rotation, but you get the idea.

Figure 11-3 uses Back Minus Front, Weld, and an Arrow Shape (covered in Chapter 9) to create a complex-looking design for a corporate logo. First, a circle is drawn using the Ellipse Tool in combination with holding CTRL (to constrain ovals to perfect circles). Then, to put a smaller circle centered inside the first, you hold SHIFT, drag the original circle's corner-bounding box handle toward the center, then right-click before releasing the left mouse button to create a scaled duplicate. Back Minus Front is chosen on the Shaping docker with both objects selected; click Apply and you have a perfect doughnut object. The Arrow Shapes come in all four directions on the Property Bar; four arrows are dragged to create with this tool, they're arranged, and then all four arrows are selected. The Weld operation is chosen on the Shaping docker. Then with the large arrow cursor, the doughnut is clicked on to indicate it's the Target object. This could be the end of the story, but in only a few clicks, the resulting shape can be extruded and rotated. See Chapter 25 for the complete details on object extrusion—3D is yours to experiment with within CorelDRAW.

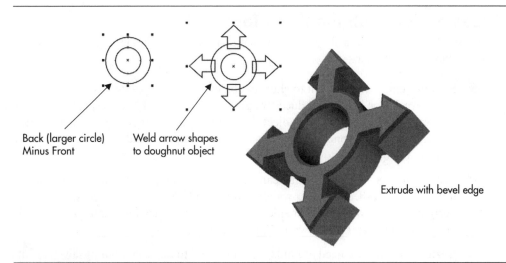

Back (larger circle)
Minus Front

Weld arrow shapes
to doughnut object

Extrude with bevel edge

FIGURE 11-3   Complex illustrations don't need to take a lot of time. Get to know the Shape
Tools, and what you envision is only a few clicks away.

The Knife Tool

The Knife Tool functions like a knife you'd use in the real world and feels quite natural to
use. You begin by hovering over an object area where you want to begin the cut, your cursor
changes its appearance to signify it is ready, and then you click-drag to the end of the cut,
the other side of the object. The result is two separate closed objects. As with many of
CorelDRAW's tools, SHIFT and CTRL can be used as modifier keys as you work with the
Knife, and in the case of the Knife Tool, these modifier keys add precision to your cuts.
You'll find the Knife Tool in the Toolbox grouped together with the Crop, Eraser, and
Virtual Segment Delete Tools.

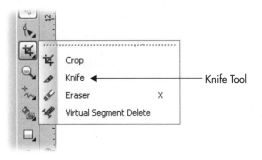

Knife Tool

Types of Cuts with the Knife Tool

There are three ways to cut a shape with the Knife Tool, and each one requires a different keyboard/mouse technique.

- **Straight cuts** If you want to slice an object into two separate shapes as you'd do with a workshop saw, to produce straight lines on sides of both objects, you aim the cursor on the near side of the object, hover until you see it change from an angled cursor to an upright one, click, release the mouse button, and then click on the far side of the object, as shown in Figure 11-4.

- **Freeform cuts** This technique can be used, for example, to quickly create an illustration of a sheet of paper roughly torn in half. You hover the cursor until it turns upright, click-hold on the near side of the object, and then drag until you reach the far side of the shape, as shown in Figure 11-5.

- **Bézier cuts** If you need to guide the Knife tool to make smooth jigsaw-like cuts, you hold SHIFT, and then click-drag points, beginning at the near side and completing the cut at the far side, as shown in Figure 11-6. Notice that not only do the cut result objects inherit the original shape's fill, but this applies to all types of fills, including gradients. The shapes in this figure each have a gradient start and end point inherited from the original shape, and if you choose the Interactive Gradient Tool, you can adjust each object's gradient directly and come up with a visually interesting jigsaw puzzle composition or other complex drawing.

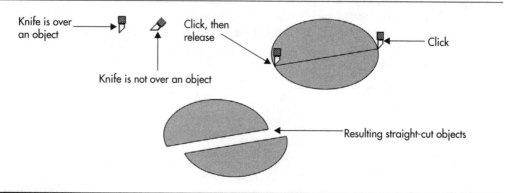

FIGURE 11-4   Click, release, then click to create a Knife Tool straight cut.

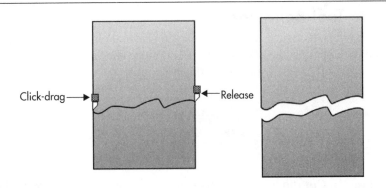

FIGURE 11-5   Click-drag to create a freeform cut.

Naturally, if you have a specific cut in mind, you'll get the best results using the shaping operations, and you cannot edit a Bézier cut's path as you make the cut, but the Knife Tool does provide fast and easy results.

 If you hold both SHIFT and CTRL while click-dragging to make a Bézier cut, doing so constrains the direction of the path to 15° increments for more predictable results making the edge of the cut.

11

Hold SHIFT and drag.

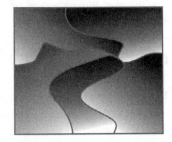
Cut objects inherit the original object fill and outline.

FIGURE 11-6   Bézier cuts guide the Knife Tool with the precision of using a digitizing tablet and stylus.

Setting Knife Tool Behavior

Using the Knife Tool results in just what you'd expect—several objects out of a single one. However, you do have options, the two Property Bar options shown here. Each of these options toggles on and off to suit a specific cutting requirement.

Leave As One Object ———————— Auto-Close On Cut

- **Auto-Close On Cut mode**   This option, on by default, sets the Knife Tool to create closed-path objects following any style of Knife Tool cutting. If you turn this option off, the Knife Tool divides an object into two open paths and removes any fill. This can be a useful mode for breaking a closed shape into open paths. To use this option, you don't drag with the Knife Tool, but instead click a near point and a far point.

- **Leave As One Object mode**   This option is active by default; if you disable it, the Knife Tool cuts an object, but the result is a combined path—in other words, you don't get two separate objects. This option is useful on occasions (for creating characters in typefaces, for example), but it probably would not be an everyday mode of operation for your work.

Both the Eraser and Knife Tools can be used on imported bitmaps; you can perform a little photo retouching with these tools exactly as you would with vector objects. The only restriction is that a bitmap (BMP, TIFF, JPEG, and so on) has to actually be imported to the document; if it is externally linked, the tools can't be used on this reference to bitmap images.

Using the Eraser Tool

The Eraser Tool, shown next, completely removes areas of selected objects you click-drag over—just like a real art eraser, but without the stubble landing in your lap. The Eraser comes in two different shapes, and you can define the size by using the Property Bar. You'll find it in the Toolbox grouped with the Knife, Virtual Segment Delete, and Crop Tools.

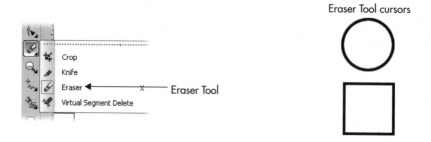

Working with Eraser Operations

With this tool, you can remove portions of shapes in four ways:

- **Double-clicking**   When you double-click a selected shape, you remove an area that is the shape of the cursor. Therefore, if you double-click a lot with the circular cursor chosen, you can quickly design a slice of Swiss cheese.

- **Single-click two points**   If you single-click, move your cursor, and then click a second time, the Eraser Tool erases a straight line through the selected object.

- **Click-drag**   This is the most common method of erasing, and the results are totally predictable. If you click-drag, you erase the area you've dragged over on a selected object.

NOTE *Grouped objects do not qualify for use with the Eraser Tool. However, if you CTRL-click an object in a group to temporarily isolate it, you can indeed erase part of the object.*

- **Hovering and pressing TAB**   This technique creates several connected straight-line segments, and after you get the hang of it, it will feel like you're painting with an eraser, and you'll be able to quickly produce phenomenally expressive and complex drawings.

Walk through the following tutorial to see the power of this hover-TAB erasing technique and make it your own:

 Power Erasing

1. Create a shape. In the figure to follow, a square with rounded corners is the target object for an illustration of an international "Put Litter Here" sign.

2. With the object selected, single-click anywhere to define the first point. Move your cursor over the next point you want to define, but don't click. Notice as you move the Eraser Tool that a path preview follows the cursor.

3. Press TAB, but *don't click* your mouse button. Notice that a new erasure appears between the first single-click point and the point where you pressed TAB.

4. To define a third point, move your cursor to a new point (without clicking the mouse button) and then press TAB again. A third point is defined, and the path between the second and third points is erased. See Figure 11-7, where the finished illustration at right uses a combination of the hover-TAB, double-clicking, and other erasing techniques.

11

Single-click

Pressing TAB defines points; single-clicking defines end

FIGURE 11-7 Press *tab* to define intermediate points between your first and last erase path points to create connected, straight-line erasures.

TIP *Each time the Eraser Tool cursor is clicked to erase portions of your object, CorelDRAW considers the action as a unique and separate erase session. This means that Eraser Tool actions can be reversed using the Undo command (CTRL-Z) in steps, depending on which erase technique was used. While using the single-click technique, an Undo command is needed to reverse each erase point. During a continuous erase using the click-drag action, a single Undo command reverses each continuous erasing session.*

Setting Eraser Tool Properties

The width and shape of the Eraser Tool are set using Property Bar options, as shown next. The complexity of the removed shape, the number of path segments, and the connecting nodes created during an erase session can also be controlled. These properties significantly affect the shape of erased object areas.

TIP *As with most of the Toolbox tools, you can get to the options for the Eraser in Options by double-clicking the button on the Toolbox.*

Auto-Reduce On Erase

Eraser Width ——— 0.09 "

Eraser Shape

1 3/4   2   2 1/4   2 1/2

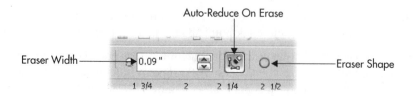

Eraser Width

Width can be set between 0.001 and 100.0 inches either by entering values in the Property Bar combo box or by pressing the UP and DOWN ARROW keys on your keyboard to increase or decrease the size. Each UP or DOWN ARROW keystroke changes the Eraser Width by 0.025 inch. Naturally, you might never need a 100-inch eraser; it makes more sense to use the shaping operations—but you do have this latitude.

| TIP | *Use the keyboard to change the cursor size while you erase. Press the UP and/or DOWN ARROW keys on your keyboard while click-dragging, and the result can be a tapered brush, as shown here. After you release the mouse button, the Eraser Tool resets to its original size, so you don't have to worry about starting out a new erase stroke with a yard-wide tip!* |

Eraser Tool Shape

The Eraser Tool shape can be set to Square or Round by using the Shape toggle button on the Property Bar. Square and Round are your choices.

Auto-Reduce Mode

Erasing continuous paths removes portions of objects to create new sides that are made up of normal vector path segments and nodes. How closely the new edges follow your erase path is determined by the number and properties of the nodes that are produced. The more nodes, the more complex and accurate the erased shape will be. While selected, the Auto-Reduce On Erase option affects the complexity of the resulting erased shape when erasing in continuous freehand-style paths.

Adding nodes to an already-complicated object, however, can create an overly complex object, something that can slow you down—the excess nodes don't contribute to the artwork and may result in inconvenient screen redraws of effects you might apply. The Auto-Reduce On Erase option lets you reduce the complexity of erased area shapes at the price of what's usually trivial inaccuracy. To activate the Auto-Reduce On Erase option, click the button to the depressed position (the default), or deactivate it by clicking it to the undepressed state.

11

Eraser Tool Auto-Reduce On Erase settings are set according to the Freehand Smoothing default setting used by the Freehand and Bézier tools, which can be set between 0 and 100 percent (the default is 100 percent). To set this option, double-click the Eraser Tool button on the Toolbox.

Using the Virtual Segment Delete Tool

The Virtual Segment Delete Tool is used to delete specific portions of objects, specifically, overlapping areas. Additionally, this tool removes portions of an object's path where they intersect paths of *other* overlapping objects.

To use this tool to delete path segments where an object intersects itself, use these quick steps:

1. With the Freehand Tool, draw a path that loops around and crosses itself.

2. Hold your cursor over the segment to delete—you don't need to have the objects selected to use this tool. You'll notice the cursor becomes upright when an eligible segment is hovered over (shown at top here).

3. Click the cursor directly on the segment you want to delete. The segment you targeted is immediately deleted.

After deleting portions of a path with this tool, what remains is either an open curve with just one path, or a compound curve with two or more subpaths. For example, if the object you're deleting segments from is a closed path, deleting one segment will result in an open curve. Deleting a segment from a rectangle, ellipse, or polygon object will convert the resulting shape to curves and remove the dynamic object properties. To delete segments that are hidden behind an overlapping object, temporarily set its Fill to None.

 If the object you are deleting segments from is a compound path (an object composed of more than one open or closed path), the Virtual Segment Delete Tool will work best if the object is first broken into individual curves using the Break Curve (CTRL+K) command.

Cropping an Illustration

The Crop Tool, located in the group with the Knife and the Eraser, brings a bitmap effect to vector drawing. If you have experience with Corel PHOTO-PAINT or another photo editing program, you already are familiar with a crop tool: you select an area within a photo, perform a command such as clicking inside the crop area, and the result is that the area outside the crop is deleted and the image is resized.

The Crop Tool in CorelDRAW behaves exactly like an image editor's crop tool. Objects do not have to be grouped; you just drag a rectangle around the area of your design you want cropped, double-click inside the proposed crop area, and all object areas outside the crop

FIGURE 11-8   The Crop Tool removes all areas of every object that lies outside the crop box.

box are deleted. In Figure 11-8 at left, you can see two objects: the goal is to leave only the comedy mask and get rid of the tragedy mask. In the middle, the Crop Tool is dragged around the desired area, which then is double-clicked. At right you can see two separate objects: the cropped gray background and the cropped mask. This is a powerful and potentially very destructive tool, but fortunately you can work with the proposed crop box before cropping: you can drag a *corner* crop box handle before cropping to proportionately resize the crop; dragging a *middle* handle disproportionately resizes the crop area. Additionally, once you've made a proposed crop, clicking, then clicking again inside the box puts the box in rotation mode, and you can actually crop a diamond shape. If you want to cancel a crop operation, press ESC and the crop box goes away.

Using the Smudge Brush

The Smudge Brush is yet another paint tool in a drawing program: this tool is not only a lot of fun to use, but you can dramatically alter shapes in a natural, painterly fashion whose results would take hours using any other method. You move areas of a vector object by dragging from a starting point inside the object, dragging outward, or starting outside and dragging inside the object. The result is a smear, but with all the crispness of a vector design. You'll find the Smudge Brush, shown next, in the Toolbox, grouped with the Roughen Brush, the Shape, and Transform Tools.

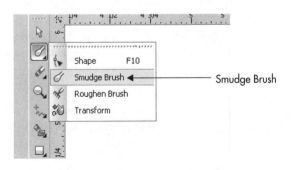

FIGURE 11-9 The Smudge Brush treats vector objects as though they're made of liquid.

Applying Smudge to Shapes

Using the Smudge Brush, you can alter the outline shapes of open or closed paths by click-dragging across the outline path, in either an outward direction (to add a bulge) or an inward direction (to create a pucker). As you drag, the path is altered according to your drag action and the shape settings of the Smudge Brush cursor. Figure 11-9 shows a creative example of using the Smudge Brush: the cartoon head has long, spiky hair now, the editing took less than 5 seconds, and the resulting path can be edited for refining using the Shape Tool and other CorelDRAW features.

 If you're trying to smudge shapes that have been applied with an effect (Envelope, Blend, Contour, Distortion, Extrude, or Drop Shadow), you'll first need to break apart the effect. If the shape is part of a group, you'll need to ungroup it first (CTRL+U). Smudging cannot be applied to bitmaps.

Choosing Smudge Brush Property Bar Options

In case you haven't noticed, the Smudge Brush works quite differently from other tools. You can control how the Smudge Brush effect is applied by varying tool properties such as the tilt, angle, and size of the nib; or by adjusting how quickly the effect diminishes; or by using optional pressure stylus settings.

While the Smudge Brush is selected, the Property Bar offers these options for controlling the shape and condition of your Smudge Brush cursor:

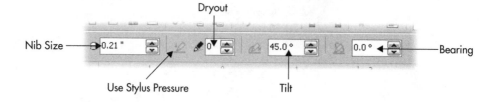

Changing each of these options has the following effect:

- **Nib Size** Nib Size can be set between 0.03 and 2.0 inches; the default is 0.1 inch.

- **Use Stylus Pressure** If you have a digitizing tablet and stylus that supports pressure, choose this option to have the Smudge Brush react to pressure you apply as increasing the width of the nib.

- **Dryout** This option sets a rate for the effect of gradually reducing the width of a smudge according to the speed of your click-drag action and can be set between –10 and 10. Higher values cause your smudge to be reduced in width more quickly (as shown next), while a setting of 0 deactivates the Dryout effect. Interestingly, negative Dryout values make your stroke begin small and eventually widen as you click-drag.

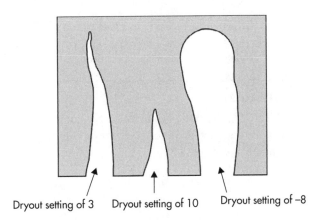

Dryout setting of 3   Dryout setting of 10   Dryout setting of –8

- **Tilt** The Tilt value controls the elliptical shape of the Smudge Tool nib. Tilt is measured in degrees set between 15 (a flat-shaped nib) and 90 (a circular-shaped nib), as shown next. Tilt and Bearing values (discussed next) work in combination with each other to control the smudge nib shape.

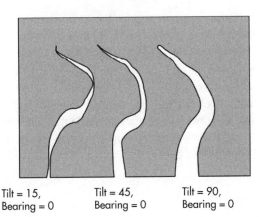

Tilt = 15,
Bearing = 0

Tilt = 45,
Bearing = 0

Tilt = 90,
Bearing = 0

11

■ **Bearing**   Bearing lets you set the angle of the cursor in circular degrees (0 to 359). The effects of changing Bearing are most noticeable at lower Tilt values—such as 15°, as shown here. It's the rotational angle of a non-circular tip…

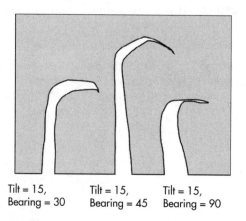

Tilt = 15,   Tilt = 15,   Tilt = 15,
Bearing = 30   Bearing = 45   Bearing = 90

Using the Transform Tool

The Transform Tool, located in the same group as the Smudge Brush, the Shape Tool, and the Roughen Brush, is your one-stop shop for performing rotations, skews, and other object transformations using an onscreen guide.

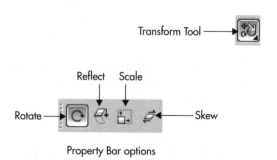

Unlike the Pick Tool for object transformations, the Transform Tool has a handle by which you steer and have precise control over the object you manipulate. To use the tool, you choose it from the Toolbox, choose a transformation type on the Property Bar, and then with the object selected, you click-drag on a control point (or any object node) to set the center of the transformation; dragging reveals a handle that also serves as a visual indicator of the amount of transformation you're creating. This preview of the transformation is in effect until you release the mouse button. As you can see in this illustration, it's obvious the rectangle is being rotated, where the center of rotation is, and the extent of the rotation before the transformation is actually made.

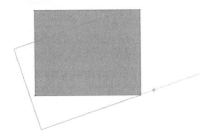

The Roughen Brush

To add a touch of character and imperfection to ultra-precise objects, you have the new Roughen Brush in the group with the Smudge Brush, shown here:

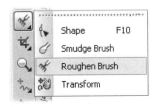

The Roughen Brush alters the course of an outline path on an object, and depending on the setting you use on the Property Bar, you can achieve effects that range from lightning bolts, to really gnarly lines, to zigzag patterns, just by dragging on the edge of a shape. The options you have when using the Roughen Brush can be seen here on the Property Bar; they're similar to those of the Smudge Brush:

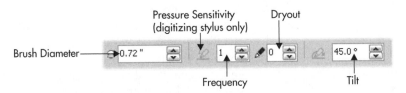

- **Brush Diameter**   This sets the size of the Roughen Brush. It's usually a good idea to scale the nib in proportion to the selected object you want to roughen. By default the scale of the nib is measured in inches.

- **Pressure Sensitivity**   If you use a digitizing tablet and stylus that responds to pressure, this option can be used to vary the nib width as you drag over object areas. The option is dimmed on the Property Bar if CorelDRAW doesn't detect a digitizing tablet hooked up to your system.

- **Frequency**   You'll see that the Roughen Brush creates irregularity on an object edge that is similar to the peaks and valleys of a mountain range—it varies the object outline in an "in and out" fashion. At low Frequency values, the roughened object outline will feature large, varying areas. At high Frequency settings, you'll attain a zigzag effect. The range of Frequency is from 1 to 10 (10 produces zigzags).

- **Dryout** Like the Smudge Brush, the Roughen Brush can "dry out" at the end of a stroke you drag with the cursor. The range of dryout effect is from –10 (the stroke tapers in the opposite direction in which you click-drag) to 10 (the stroke tapers and fades). At 0, the stroke remains consistent. The greater the dryout setting, negative or positive, the more natural a roughened appearance you can achieve.

- **Tilt** This option measures your stroke with the Roughen Brush perpendicular to the edge on which you stroke. Therefore, if you have an edge that travels straight up and down, at a 90° setting you'll achieve very little effect. In your experiments with this tool, try 45°, an overall good setting for all angles of edges on most objects. When you roughen an edge that already has roughening applied, you overwrite the previous distortion of that edge. Figure 11-10 shows two examples of the Roughen Brush; at left a small nib is used at a low Frequency, and at right a large nib is used at high Frequency.

TIP	*Shapes that have special properties, such as Rectangles and Ellipses created with the Rectangle and Ellipse Tools, need to be simplified using the Arrange	Convert To Curves command (CTRL+Q) before they can be roughened. If you try to use the Roughen Brush on such a shape, you'll get an attention box telling you that the object needs simplifying, but then CorelDRAW will automatically do the operation for you. So if you want to avoid the attention box, press CTRL+Q while a shape is selected so you can get right down to editing.*

This chapter has taken you through several processes by which you can create minor and big-time alterations to just about anything you draw; additionally, many of the operations apply to bitmaps you bring into the workspace. Use the command that best suits the task you have in mind, and use your judgment as to which operation will get you to your goal fastest. Personal computers are productivity enhancers: there's no need to labor over something when CorelDRAW and your PC can do it for you in less time.

Now that you have one, or two, or a dozen shapes on your drawing page, it would be nice to know how to group them, perhaps put some on different layers, and clone a few to create thousands of identical, intricate objects. That's what Chapter 12 is all about.

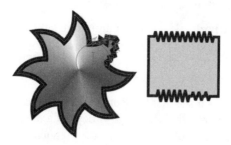

FIGURE 11-10 Use the Roughen Brush to achieve object complexity in a fraction of the time needed using other tools.

CHAPTER 12

Arranging and Organizing Objects

CorelDRAW offers plenty of arrangement functions; once you've designed scads of objects, the need to group, distribute, and align them becomes obvious. This chapter takes you through all the commands to keep things from accidentally moving apart, to lock objects to a page (and to unlock them!), to use layers so you can hide objects and print only those you want visible, and more. Additionally, one of the exclusive features of CorelDRAW is a function to search on the specific property of an object. You'll soon see that if you've drawn a needle in a drawing of a haystack, finding it later is child's play.

Using Group Commands

You've seen a group of kids, perhaps playing a sport or hanging out at the mall. They tend to follow each other when they travel, and it takes nothing less than a dinner bell to separate them. CorelDRAW objects can be arranged similarly, except the objects don't hit you up for movie money. The Group command in CorelDRAW creates an association for multiple object selections; the command is available when two or more objects are selected. A group behaves as if it were a single unit; any changes made to a group affect all objects in the group. For example, if you have three objects, each with different fills and outline widths, and you select the group, click a new color on the color palette, and then define a new outline width on the Property Bar—all objects in the group take on the new color and outline property. Call it peer pressure.

 TIP *CorelDRAW X4 indicates on the Status Bar that a group is selected.*

Grouping is a convenient and simple way to organize a collection of objects at a very basic level in CorelDRAW (more complex methods are demonstrated later in this chapter). Each object in a group is called a *child*. Groups of objects can also include other groups; it's very easy and sometimes a desired thing to create groups of groups.

To group objects together:

■ Select them using the Pick Tool, and then click the Group button in the Property Bar, shown here.

■ Alternatively, you can use the CTRL+G shortcut.

■ The command is also available on the pop-up menu when you right-click a multiple selection of objects. However, you need to make certain that your cursor is *over one of the several selected shapes* to get the Group command on the pop-up menu.

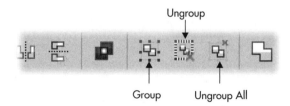

> **TIP**   *Selecting several objects in the workspace can be accomplished by SHIFT-clicking with the Pick Tool, but it's often more convenient to marquee-select objects. Marquee-selection is performed by click-diagonal dragging on the page to create an imaginary rectangle that completely surrounds the objects you want to select and then group.*

Ungrouping a group returns the objects to their original, isolated state. It's also one of the most frequently used CorelDRAW commands, so you can Ungroup a selected group in several ways:

■ Click the Ungroup button in the Property Bar.

■ Or use the CTRL+U shortcut.

■ Alternatively, choose Ungroup from the pop-up menu after right-clicking a selected group of objects.

Ungroup works with a single group and also with several groups you might select at one time.

Because a group is treated as a single entity in CorelDRAW, you can easily make groups of groups. Groups within groups are called *nested groups.* To Ungroup a group and any groups it already contains in a single command, you can use the Ungroup All command. Choosing Ungroup All undoes the group relationship for *all* grouped, nested items in the group. However, be cautious using this command; if you've nested groups within groups with some planning, all the planning goes to waste when you use Ungroup All. Think of nuts, bolts, and washers, each category grouped in a little drawer, and all the drawers grouped in a cabinet. Ungroup All performs the equivalent of pouring all the nuts, bolts, and washers onto the table.

You *can* edit and make changes to the properties of a grouped object; the trick is to temporarily pick out the member of the group while the group is still together. You choose the Pick Tool, hold CTRL as a modifier key, and then click a specific object in the group to specify that child object as a selection. If the child object is part of a nested group itself, holding the CTRL key and clicking a second time selects a child in the group. While a child object is selected, the selection handles surrounding it are circular instead of square, as shown at right:

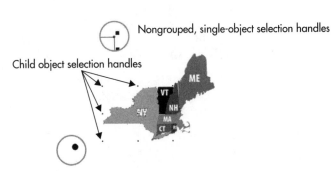

Nongrouped, single-object selection handles

Child object selection handles

| NOTE | *Only one child object in a group can be selected at a time, which means you can't marquee-select or SHIFT-select multiple objects when selecting child objects. For changes to several objects in a group, you need to ungroup the group.* |

Knowing the *child group* terminology will help you down the road, as you select objects within a group. When a child object is selected, the Status Bar tells you the current layer, that the object is a child object, and the color and outline width of the selected child object. You'll see the Status Bar indicate properties such as "Child Curve," "Child Rectangle," "Child Ellipse," "Child Artistic Text," and so on. Groups that are objects themselves within a group are referred to as *child groups.* Within a group, items that are dynamically linked to effects are called *child control* objects such as "Child Control Curves" and "Child Control Rectangles." Child objects for an effect are named *child effect* groups, such as "Child Blend Group."

Locking and Unlocking Objects

Locking objects in the workspace is a very good precaution against unintended changes and is performed using the Lock command, available when single or grouped objects are selected, and when an object is on or off the document page. While objects are locked, they are visible, they can be printed and even selected, but they can't be moved, edited, or have any properties changed.

As with the group commands, locking involves three operations: Lock, Unlock, and Unlock All. All three commands are available from the Arrange menu and from the pop-up menu when you right-click while using any tool other than the Zoom Tool. Additionally, the command can be found under Arrange | Lock Object. CorelDRAW X4 indicates an object is currently locked in two ways: by visually displaying lock handles around the object, as shown at left, and on the Status Bar, which, for example, describes a selected rectangle as "Locked Rectangle."

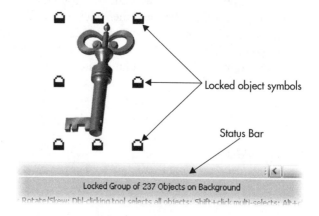

Locked object symbols

Status Bar

Locked Group of 237 Objects on Background

When importing Corel Designer files into CorelDRAW X4, objects created with unsupported effects will automatically be locked; an alert dialog appears during the import operation to notify you of this. These objects will display, print, and export correctly, but to edit them as CorelDRAW objects, you will need to first unlock them. If they are left locked, the effects will be preserved if the CorelDRAW file is then imported back into Corel Designer.

To unlock a locked object, choose Arrange | Unlock Object. To unlock all locked objects in a drawing, choose Arrange | Unlock All.

NOTE *While an object is locked, you won't be able to select it as part of a multiple selection. So if you're trying to select a number of objects on your document page and only one remains unselected, there's an excellent chance that it's locked, and you'll need to unlock it before proceeding.*

Copying, Duplicating, and Cloning Objects

There's absolutely no reason why you can't reuse an object you toiled over; you've drawn an elegant gear, for example, and your assignment is to illustrate a clock. You create duplicates of the gear for the clock to save time, and there are several ways and techniques to make copies of objects and object groups, the topic of this section. Copying, duplicating, and cloning result in different object types; here you'll see how each type works and how to make it.

Creating Quick Object Copies

CorelDRAW can use the clipboard to copy and paste, but there's a much faster way that doesn't require the clipboard.

■ **Using the Right-Click Method**   Click your right mouse button before you release the left mouse button (then release both buttons) when transforming, rotating, or moving an object with the Pick Tool to "drop a copy." The object being dragged, rotated, or scaled becomes the copy, leaving the original object unchanged. The small + symbol beside the cursor indicates that a copy has been created, as shown here.

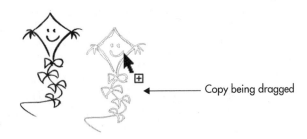

Copy being dragged

12

NOTE *Using the right-click technique to copy an object as you transform it applies only when using the Pick Tool.*

■ **Using the SPACEBAR Method**   Press the SPACEBAR while transforming, rotating, or moving an object with the Pick Tool to create a copy. Doing this causes a copy to be created *in situ,* meaning a copy is "dropped" each time the SPACEBAR is pressed, as shown next. You have to start the click-drag before pressing or holding the SPACEBAR; if you don't, by default you switch to the Zoom Tool (which is not the intention here, that's a different shortcut key combo). Pressing and *holding* the SPACEBAR causes your key-repeat action to create multiple copies as long as the SPACEBAR is held. As you can see here, by holding instead of clicking the SPACEBAR, you can make hundreds of copies of the selected object, creating a sort of motion-blur effect, particularly when an object or object group contains semitransparent objects. The other use for the SPACEBAR technique to create multiple copies is for the Distribute command, shown later in this chapter.

Each time the SPACEBAR is pressed, a copy is "dropped."

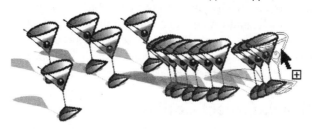

■ **Pressing Numeric + Key**   Pressing the + key on your numeric keypad creates a copy of the selected object in exactly the same position as (and copied in front of) the original. After you press the + key, the copy becomes the selected object. You can create as many copies as you want using this method, but be aware that each additional copy will hide the original (or the copy) behind it.

Using the Duplicate Command

The Duplicate command creates a precise and orderly series of copies of a selected object (or group of objects) through the use of Offset values. To apply this command to a selected object, choose Edit | Duplicate or press CTRL+D.

There are two locations where you can specify the Offset values in CorelDRAW, and one is the simple way: *with no objects selected,* the Offset fields can be seen toward the right on the Property Bar (labeled in the following illustration). The other place you can set Offset values is in Tools | Options, then Document | General, Duplicate Offset. By default, duplicates are placed 0.25 inch above and to the right of the selected original. Both vertical and horizontal offsets can be set between –600 and 600 inches (in increments of 0.05 inch). Negative values place duplicates below and to the left of your original; positive Offset values put duplicates up and to the right of the original.

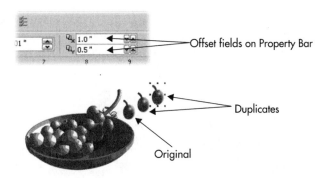

Offset fields on Property Bar

Duplicates

Original

Cloning Objects

Clones are special object copies that are dynamically linked to their original objects in a sort of master-slave relationship. Clones imitate any property changes made to their master, which offers the nicety of editing one master to change the properties of any number of linked clones. Linked clone properties include object Fill, Outline, Path Shape, Transformations, relative position of objects in a group you clone, and Bitmap Color Mask properties. With any object or group of objects selected, choose Edit | Clone from the main menu.

Clones are created and placed using the same offsets as duplicates. Let's take a short trip into the world of cloning:

 ## Creating Clone Objects

1. Create and/or select an object. Choose Edit | Clone to create the clone of your object. Your original object is now the master of the clone. Try clicking on the master and then on the clone while watching the Status Bar to confirm what you've created.

2. Select the master object and change its fill or outline color. Notice that the clone properties also change. Experiment changing other properties, such as rotating and scaling the master object; notice that the changes are reflected in the clone.

3. Select your master object and choose Edit | Clone a second time to create another clone. Select the master control object and change one or more of its properties. Notice the master and the properties of both clones also change.

NOTE *Once your first clone has been created, a hierarchy is created. You can create additional clones from the master control object, but you can't create clones from clones—that would be silly and confusing.*

Locating Clones and Their Master Objects

Because clones and masters often have the same appearance, it's difficult to distinguish one from the other. Let's say you've created several master objects and scores of clones; the Status Bar tells you the clones from the masters (called *control objects*), but doesn't sort out

12

which clone belongs to which master. To locate a cloned object or select its master clone, right-click an object. If the selected object is a master or a clone, one or more of the following commands is available on the pop-up menu, shown here.

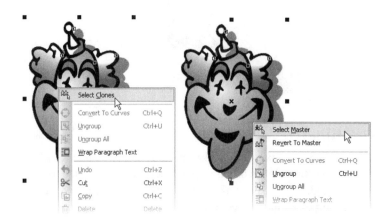

- **Select Clones**   Choose this command to select all linked clones on your current page.

- **Select Master**   If your selected object is a clone, choosing this command causes the linked master object to be selected. If the master is located on a different page, CorelDRAW X4 automatically changes your page view and then shows you the master object(s).

- **Revert To Master**   The Revert To Master command becomes available if the clone you've selected has been edited after being created. Choosing this command opens the Revert To Master dialog (shown next), which offers to restore some or all properties of the original master object. Only those properties that have changed are available; properties include Clone Fill, Clone Outline, Clone Path Shape, Clone Transformations, and Clone Bitmap Color Mask.

If you'd like to break the master-clone linking, the clone is converted to a standard CorelDRAW object, and there are several commands to do this, all having to do with simplifying the object. CTRL+Q (Arrange | Convert To Curves) does the trick; also, if the clone is made up of a group of objects, ungrouping them breaks the relationship between master and clone.

NOTE   *All of the preceding methods for copying objects create real, editable copies. As you read on, other methods create* references *to the original object; these clones are* not *directly editable. One of the more important differences in copy making is that "straight" copies increase the saved CDR file size; clones do not appreciably increase the saved file size.*

Creating Object Symbols

The ability to define objects as "symbols" is worth investigating if you create drawings where you need lots of the same object. Symbols are related to cloning objects, but you'll soon see that clone management is simpler with symbols. By making an object into a symbol rather than duplicating it, you work more quickly and keep the saved CDR file size small. You could define an arrangement of objects as a symbol and duplicate it 100 times without significantly increasing the saved file size. Symbols can also be organized into libraries that can be shared between document files and/or between users on a network.

The Symbols feature requires that you first define objects and groups of objects as symbols. You then access the symbols and manage collections of symbols through the Symbol Manager docker (CTRL+F3). Figure 12-1 uses symbol *instances* for duplicate objects. Here, the landscape drawing was created using symbols for the trees, the picnic tables, the bicycles, and the gazebo, shown in the symbol inventory list in the Symbol Manager docker.

12

TIP   *A quick way to tell whether an object on the page is an instance or a normal object is to select it. Instances of symbols are surrounded by blue bounding box handles, not the black ones that border normal objects.*

Let's build you a library of symbols to better demonstrate the value of this CorelDRAW feature:

 Creating and Storing a Symbol

1. Create and/or select the objects (or group of objects) to save as a new symbol. Take your time; the more complex the object, the more time you'll save later doing illustrations where you need several of the same symbol.

2. Choose Edit | Symbol | New Symbol. This command defines your object(s) as a symbol and adds it to the Symbol Manager docker. In the Name field, type something easy to locate later; the preview window on the Symbol Manager doesn't provide a huge view.

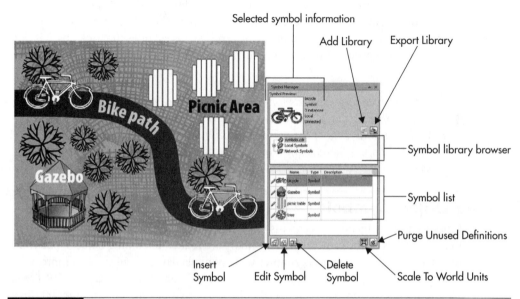

Selected symbol information

Add Library

Export Library

Symbol library browser

Symbol list

Purge Unused Definitions

Scale To World Units

Insert
Symbol

Edit Symbol

Delete
Symbol

FIGURE 12-1 The Symbol Manager is your ticket for quickly populating a scene with instances of symbols you've defined.

3. Open the Symbol Manager docker by choosing Window | Dockers | Symbol Manager (CTRL+F3). Your new symbol is listed in the docker inventory. The Symbol Manager features a preview of the shape(s) with information about it, such as its name, the number of instances (copies) in your document, and where it's stored (local or network) as well as the document the symbols are used in. The list portion of the docker displays specific information about the symbol such as its Name, Type, and Description. By default, the Description field is blank; click in the field to select it, and then click a second time to type an evocative description of your symbol.

TIP *To create a new symbol from a selected object quickly while the Symbol Manager docker is open, drag the object directly into the docker list area.*

4. With your new symbol selected in the docker list, drag the thumbnail from the list area onto the drawing page. A new instance (copy) of the symbol is added to your document, the Symbol Preview summary now indicates that two instances exist, and the Status Bar indicates the selected object is a symbol.

TIP *You can also click the Insert button to put a symbol selected on the Symbol Manager list directly in the center of the page.*

Editing Symbols

Once an object becomes a symbol, it is automatically added to your document's Symbol library; it's not saved to a library you can use on all future documents yet. Network symbols are covered later in this chapter. The library version is referred to as a *symbol definition,* and a symbol placed in your document is called an *instance.* Symbol instance properties can be changed in various ways, with one or two limitations. For example, you can group the symbol with other objects, apply transformations to it, change its order on the page (such as from back to front), and move it to any page and/or layer. The only properties you can't change are its path structure or its fill or outline properties. These properties can only be changed by editing the master symbol using the Edit Symbol command, which in turn will change all instances where they've been used, either in your current document or in any other document where the symbol has been used from the Symbol libraries.

Once an object has been defined as a symbol, the original becomes a symbol definition in a library. To edit a symbol, locate and select any of its instances, and click the Edit Symbol button in the docker, or click the Edit Symbol button in the Property Bar. Doing this opens the symbol master on its own page for editing. Perform any editing changes and click the Finish Editing Object button, shown here at the lower-left corner of your document window. The original symbol and all its instances will reflect the editing changes wherever any of its instances exist. You can also access Edit Symbol and Finish Editing Symbol from the pop-up menu when you right-click over an object instance.

Click here to end symbol editing ——————→

12

 To convert a symbol instance to a typical CorelDRAW object, right-click the instance and choose Revert To Objects from the pop-up menu. Your symbol definition in the library will be unaffected.

Working with Symbol Libraries

Symbol libraries can be stored either internally with your document or externally as exported library files. Internally stored libraries will be available only while your document is open; exported libraries can be accessed while other documents are open. In the Symbol Manager docker browse area, you'll see your current document name listed as well as a Local folder and a Network folder. To make your document's symbols available to other documents or other users on a network, you'll need to export them as a unique library. Once the library is exported, you'll be able to open it and place symbols from it into other documents. Next, you'll make a collection of symbols available as a library to all future documents.

Creating a Symbol Library

1. SHIFT+click the items on the Symbols list on the Symbol Manager you want exported as a user library.

2. Click the Export Library button. Accept the default location for the saved library, name it, and then click OK.

3. Open a new document. Open the Symbol Manager, and then click to open the User Symbols category in the browser pane.

4. Click the library you want available.

5. Drag any of your saved library symbols into the new document.

Save Library

User library available to all documents

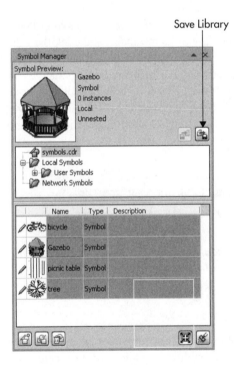

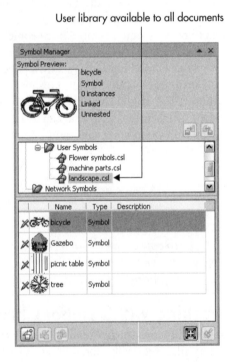

> **TIP** *You can quickly save selected symbol instances in your drawing to a separate library file by using the Save As command (meaning they must already be defined as symbols). To do this, select your objects, choose File | Save As, choose the Selection Only option (click Options to expand the dialog to access this), choose CSL—Corel Symbol Library—from the Save As Type menu, and click Save. To make your saved library file easily accessible, save it to your local or network User Symbols folder location.*

Applying Transparency to Symbol Instances

You can apply transparency effects to each individual symbol using the Object Properties docker (ALT+ENTER), shown at left, which is opened by right-clicking the instance and choosing Properties or by clicking the Object Properties button in the Property Bar.

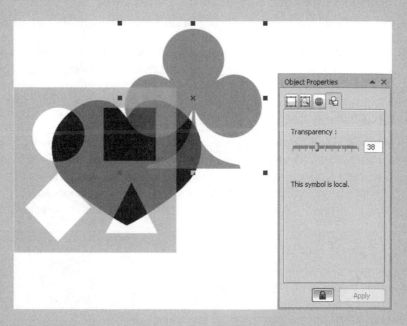

In the Symbols page of the docker, you'll see a Transparency slider. This is where you can apply a Transparency value between 0 and 100 percent to a symbol instance, where 0 applies no transparency and 100 makes the instance completely transparent. Each instance can be set to a different transparency without affecting the original symbol's properties.

Symbols placed as instances from externally stored libraries are automatically linked to the library from which you placed them. You can manage these linked symbol instances using the Link Manager, opened by choosing Windows | Dockers | Link Manager. These link commands are used in the same way as those of other types of linked objects, such as imported and linked bitmaps.

To break a link to an externally stored library definition, right-click its instance and choose Break Link from the pop-up menu. An alert dialog will warn you that this will break the link to the external symbol definition. Click Yes to proceed and convert the instance to an internally stored symbol, a symbol unique only to the current document. The symbol will now appear as a library definition stored in your document's internal library.

Purge Unused Definitions and Scale To World Units

Two other commands worth covering here you'll find on the Symbol Manager docker:

- **Purge Unused Definitions**   This command is available if symbol definitions are stored with your document but you haven't placed any instances of them in your document. Clicking this button deletes the unused definitions permanently from your document's internally stored Symbol library. Therefore, think twice before you click this button so you don't accidentally delete an object.

- **Scale To World Units**   This is a great option to use if you create drawings using *drawing scales*. (Drawing scales can be set up by clicking the Edit Scale button in the Document | Rulers page of the Options dialog, opened by double-clicking your onscreen rulers.) While this option is selected, symbol instances added to your drawing will automatically be scaled according to your document's current drawing scale.

Using the Repeat Command

The Repeat command enables you to reapply your last command on the same object—or on a different one. To use the Repeat command, choose Edit | Repeat *whatever* (where *whatever* is your last action performed), or press CTRL+R. The Repeat command applies to virtually any editing action you last performed—typically actions such as copying, scaling, skewing, and rotating objects. For example, if your last command was to copy an object while transforming or moving it, the Repeat command enables you to perform the identical operation again on the same object or a different object. In the

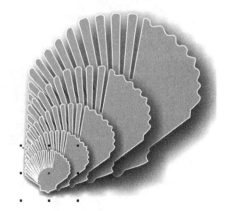

illustration here, the large seashell was scaled, and before completing the scaling, a right-click was made to duplicate the original in a scaled state. By pressing CTRL+R after performing this "drop a copy" technique, you can see multiple copies, incrementally scaled.

The Repeat command feature can also be used to edit object properties; think of Repeat as a mini-macro you might set up in a word processor or spreadsheet application. For example, if your most recent action was to fill a selected object with a specific color, you can select a different object and apply the identical fill using the Repeat command. Unfortunately, the Repeat command is restricted only to single edits; you can't Repeat several steps, but if you make a move such as scaling or rotating and dropping a copy, you can do fairly sophisticated Repeats and save a lot of time building complex designs.

 The Repeat command capabilities include object transformations but not operations such as bitmap commands, certain effects commands, or text property commands.

Step And Repeat

Think of the Step And Repeat command (CTRL+SHIFT+D) as a hybrid between the Repeat command and Duplicate. With this command, found under the Edit main menu, you can create duplicates of your original almost any number of times while specifying the Horizontal and Vertical Distance each copy is placed. To quickly make an array of identical objects, you select the object, choose the command, and a modeless dialog appears in the workspace; then you set the Horizontal Settings, which can be No Offset (the duplicates are placed horizontally aligned to the original), Offset, or Spacing. Spacing is a good option, because you can then choose to duplicate the selected object to the left or right.

The Vertical Settings are the same as Horizontal, except they define the up or down direction of the duplicates. As you can see in this illustration, Step And Repeat is a great timesaver for getting your ducks (or other objects) in a row.

Aligning and Distributing Objects

The Align and Distribute commands don't simply tidy up objects into neat little rows—the commands can be used to *align* or *evenly space out* objects in several different and convenient ways. Both types of commands can be applied using menu commands, dialog commands, or keypresses while objects are selected. To access the menu commands, choose Arrange | Align And Distribute and make a selection from the submenu, shown in Figure 12-2. It will probably fit into your workflow better, however, to open the Align And Distribute dialog, the last choice on the submenu. The floating dialog is shown here, and it's a *modeless* dialog, which means you can access the alignment and distribution commands one or a thousand times without the need to go back up to the main menu for multiple arrangements.

You may also use the dialog-based method by choosing Arrange | Align And Distribute | Align And Distribute or by clicking the Align And Distribute button in the Property Bar, shown next, which is available while at least two objects are selected. Both actions open the Align And Distribute dialog.

Click to open the Align
And Distribute dialog

Using Align Command Options

The Align tab of this dialog, shown next, enables you to align a selection of objects based on their width and height. To have your selected objects align in a specific way, simply choose

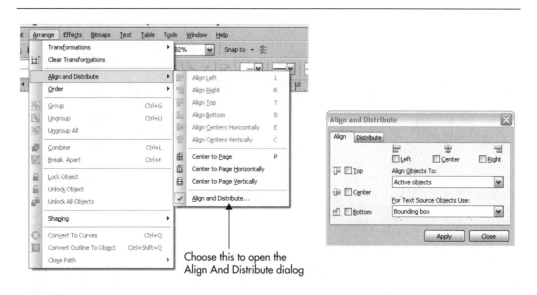

Choose this to open the
Align And Distribute dialog

FIGURE 12-2   Access the Align And Distribute dialog commands here.

a vertical and/or horizontal align option. Once an option is selected, click the Apply button to apply the alignment. Clicking Close does exactly that, it closes the dialog, which is something you don't necessarily have to do (it might be more convenient just to move the dialog out of the way while you design).

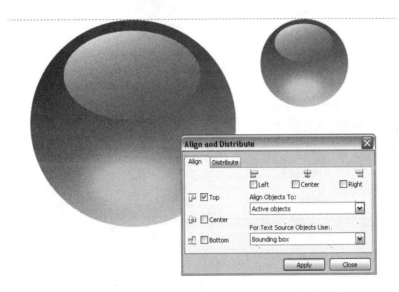

Align options are arranged into four areas: vertical (the top-right row of options), horizontal (the left column of options), page alignment options, and text options. Choose one vertical and/or one horizontal alignment option for each align operation. Here's how each of the options affects how your objects are aligned:

- **Vertical Alignment** Choose Left, Center, or Right to align your objects accordingly. Figure 12-3 shows the results of a vertical alignment of a selection of objects. In the Left and Right alignment operations, the object farthest from the center of your selection determines the point at which the objects align.

- **Horizontal Alignment** When aligning objects horizontally, you can choose the Top, Center, or Bottom portions of your selected objects. Only one of these three options can be selected at any one time. Again, the alignment symbols accompanying the options may help when deciding which to use. Figure 12-4 shows the results of the horizontal alignment of a selection of objects. While using either the Top or Bottom alignment option, the furthest object from the center of your selection determines the point at which the objects align.

Page options in this dialog take the form of a drop-down menu for objects titled Align Objects To and include options for Active Objects, Edge Of Page, Center Of Page, Grid, and

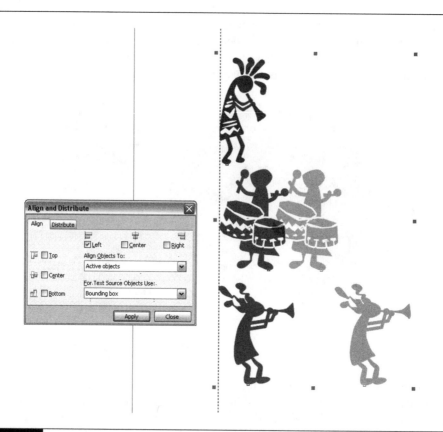

FIGURE 12-3   These objects were aligned vertically using the Left option.

FIGURE 12-4   These objects were aligned horizontally using the Top option.

Specified Point. The For Text Source Objects Use drop-down is for aligning text objects. Let's begin with object alignment options:

- **Active Objects** Use this option to perform alignments based on the area occupied by your selected objects.

- **Edge Of Page** Three options exist for aligning objects in relation to your page borders in combination with—or independently of—other alignment options. For example, to align your selected object(s) to the upper-right corner of your current document page, choose Top and Right in combination with Edge Of Page from the drop-down list. Choosing the Edge Of Page option without choosing the Top, Right, or Other check box won't change the alignment of your selected objects.

- **Center Of Page** This option centers your object(s) on your page based on its width and height. If Left, Right, Top, or Bottom is selected as the vertical or horizontal align option, the alignment is immediately changed to the center of the page.

- **Align To Grid** If you want your selected object(s) to align with the closest grid point on your page, choose Align To Grid in combination with other options. Choosing this option causes your selected objects to align to the closest grid line, based on your selection. For example, choosing Align To Grid in combination with the Bottom alignment option causes the bottom of your object to align to the closest grid line. Naturally, this option is most useful if you can *see* the grid: with no objects selected, right-click on the page (any tool except the Zoom Tool can be the active tool for this), and then choose View | Grid from the pop-up menu. To change the Grid Frequency and Spacing, right-click over a Ruler and then choose Grid Setup.

- **Specified Point** Use this option in combination with vertical and/or horizontal alignment options to specify an exact point to use as the basis for the alignment. After you click the Apply button, your cursor will become a crosshair, which you click anywhere to define the aligning point.

Text alignment options in CorelDRAW X4 enable you to use specific areas of a text object for alignment, as follows:

- **First Line Baseline** Choose First Line Baseline to have CorelDRAW use the baseline of the first line of text as a reference for the alignment action.

- **Last Line Baseline** Choose this option to have CorelDRAW use the baseline of the last line of text as a reference for the alignment action.

12

Aligning Hot Keys

To align objects quickly, use *hot keys* while at least two objects are selected and while using the Pick Tool. Here are the hot keys you can use to align objects:

Align Tops	>T
Align Left Sides	>L
Align Right Sides	>R
Align Bottom	>B
Align Horizontal Center	>E
Align Vertical Center	>C
Center To Page	>P

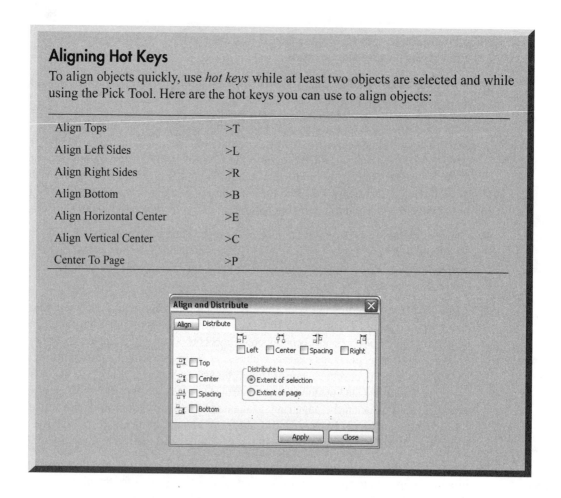

- **Bounding Box**   This option is active by default. The bounding box defines the outermost extent of text, or any object; the visual indicator on screen are the eight black markers when an object is selected. The Bounding Box option causes CorelDRAW X4 to use the bounding box of text as the source for the alignment action.

Using Distribute Command Options

The Distribute tab, shown at the top of the following page, gives you control of the spacing of a selection of objects. Distribute commands add *automated spacing* between objects based on their width, height, and/or center origins.

Begin your distribute operation by specifying which part of your objects you want to measure from. Choose Left, Center, Spacing, or Right from the top-right row of options to distribute horizontally. Choose either Top, Center, Spacing, or Bottom from the left column of options to distribute vertically. In either case, choosing Spacing creates equal spacing either vertically or horizontally between your selected objects.

Objects can be evenly spaced within one of two areas. Use the Extent Of Selection option to space objects evenly within the width and/or height of the area occupied by your selected objects.

Use the Extent Of Page option to space your objects evenly within document page dimensions. Choose a vertical and/or horizontal spacing option together with Extent Of Page to apply even spacing between the selected reference point on your objects. Figure 12-5 shows examples of choosing both Extent Of Selection and Extent Of Page options.

In Figure 12-5, Extent Of Selection is used at left and Extent Of Page is used at right; the light gray objects show the original positions of the objects.

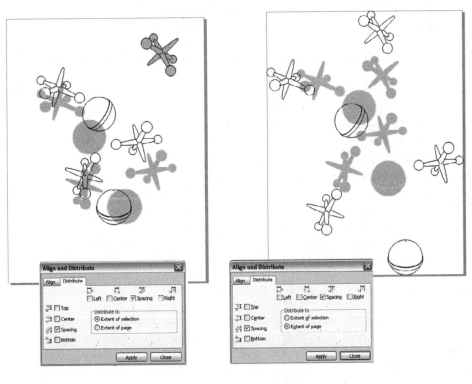

Extent Of Selection used   Extent Of Page used

FIGURE 12-5   The Extent Of Selection and Extent Of Page options space objects evenly.

Distribute Hot Keys

To distribute objects quickly, use hot keys while at least two objects are selected and while using the Pick Tool. Here are the hot keys you can use to distribute objects:

Distribute Tops	>SHIFT+T
Distribute Left Sides	>SHIFT+L
Distribute Right Sides	>SHIFT+R
Distribute Bottom	>SHIFT+B
Distribute Horizontal Center	>SHIFT+E
Distribute Horizontal Spacing	>SHIFT+P
Distribute Vertical Center	>SHIFT+C
Distribute Vertical Spacing	>SHIFT+A

Working with CorelDRAW Layers

CorelDRAW X4's layer feature provides invaluable ways to organize complex drawings. You can create several layers and move shapes between layers. You can also name layers, control their order and appearance, change object ordering within layers, group objects, and use available resources to obtain object information. One immediate advantage to adopting layers in your composition work is that you can hide layers. Suppose you have a lot of objects that need labels, and you need to print the objects with and without labels. The solution is to put all the labels on a layer. Hide the layer, print just the objects, then unhide the layer and make a second print: easy!

Exploring the Object Manager

The Object Manager docker is your main resource for controlling all layer functions. Using this docker, shown next, you can perform a whole range of actions, such as navigate document pages, create and name layers, select and move objects between layers, and set layers as editable, printable, and/or visible. To open the Object Manager docker, choose Tools | Object Manager. The Object Manager shows a listing of the layers, each accompanied by options and a flyout menu. A Master Page also appears and includes default layers for controlling guides, the desktop, and grid objects.

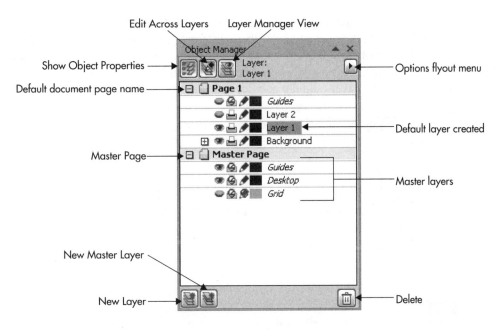

Edit Across Layers   Layer Manager View

Show Object Properties

Default document page name

Default layer created

Master Page

Master layers

Options flyout menu

New Master Layer

New Layer

Delete

Navigating Pages, Objects, and Layers

The best way to use the Object Manager docker to navigate through your document, select layers, and control Layer options is by experimenting, with the following steps as a guide. You'll learn exactly how these operations are performed; look at the next illustration, which shows a default layer structure for a new document.

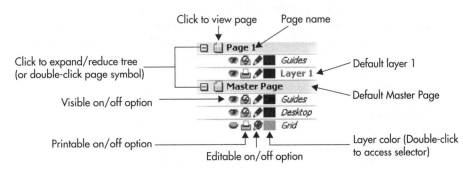

Click to view page   Page name

Click to expand/reduce tree
(or double-click page symbol)

Default layer 1

Default Master Page

Visible on/off option

Printable on/off option

Editable on/off option

Layer color (Double-click
to access selector)

Navigating and Mastering Layers

1. Open a new document and then open the Object Manager docker by choosing Tools | Object Manager. Notice that the docker lists each page of your document. Each page features a default layer named Layer 1, accompanied by three symbols and a black color indicator.

2. If your document is new and contains no objects, create an ellipse, a Perfect Shape, and an Artistic Text object and color them differently, just to prime the pump. As you create your objects, they appear as objects belonging to Layer 1 on Page 1, and they are accompanied by symbols and brief descriptions, as shown next. This is because the active layer (and the only layer that exists so far) is Layer 1.

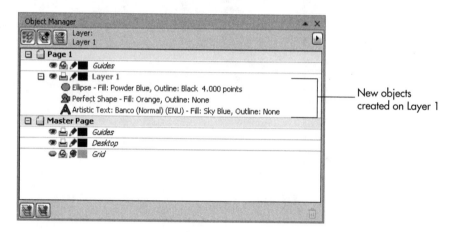

New objects created on Layer 1

3. Click the New Layer button. A new layer named Layer 2 appears above your active Layer 1. Type in a name for the new layer while it's still selected and press ENTER. Notice that Layer 2 is now your active layer and highlighted in red in the docker list.

4. In the Object Manager docker list, click to select the ellipse. Notice that the ellipse also becomes selected in your document. Click-and-drag the ellipse *within* the Object Manager docker onto the new Layer 2, and release the mouse button. Notice that the ellipse in your document hasn't changed its position on the page, but in the docker it now appears under Layer 2, as shown next. You have just moved the ellipse object from one layer to another.

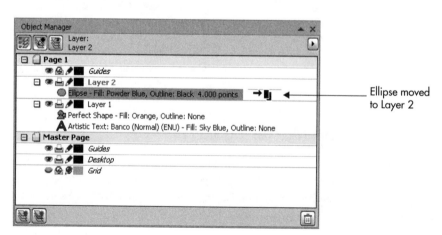

Ellipse moved to Layer 2

5. Single-click the Eye symbol beside Layer 2, so the layer closes. Notice that the ellipse you just moved to Layer 2 disappears from view on the page, although it's still listed on the docker. Notice also that the information describing the ellipse on Layer 2 now appears grayed out. This action toggles the display of all objects on a specific layer. Clicking the other corresponding symbols toggles printing and/or editing of a specific layer.

6. Add a new page to your document by clicking the + page button at the lower left of the screen, to the left of the scroll bar. Notice the page now appears in the docker, and your view is automatically changed to Page 2.

7. Click to expand the Page 2 structure to view its contents. Notice that Page 2 has the default layer (Layer 1), but not the layer you made invisible on Page 1. Layers and layer contents are *unique to each page,* except Master layers, discussed later in this section.

8. In the docker, click the page symbol beside Page 1. Notice your view immediately changes to Page 1, which demonstrates a quick, easy way to navigate pages in your document.

9. Create a third layer for your document by clicking the New Layer button. Click the new layer once on the docker to ensure that it's selected, and create a new object on your document page. Notice that the new object is automatically created on the new layer. This demonstrates that new (and imported) objects are created on the selected layer on your current page.

10. Click the Eye symbol beside Layer 2 to make the layer visible again. All four objects should now be visible on Page 1. Using the Pick Tool, drag the Artistic Text, the ellipse, and the polygon objects on your document page to overlap each other, while leaving them on their current layers. Notice that the Artistic Text and polygon objects on Layer 1 appear behind the ellipse on Layer 2. This is because Layer 2 is ordered *above* Layer 1.

12

11. Using a click-drag action in the Object Manager docker, click the text label of Layer 1 on Page 1, drag it vertically upward and just above the position of Layer 2, and then release the mouse button. Notice that the Artistic Text and polygon objects now appear in front of the ellipse. This action changes the order of your layers. As you drag, the cursor changes to indicate the new insertion point before the mouse button is released.

 To assign unique names to pages, layers, and even to objects in the Object Manager docker, click the text label of the page, layer, or object name once to select it and a second time to highlight the text for editing (this is not *a double-click action). Enter the text for the new name and then press ENTER.*

Using Object Manager Editing and View States

Objects can indeed be on different layers, and you can edit across layers in CorelDRAW. Create a new file document that has objects on, let's say, three layers, to better understand about the editing and view states of CorelDRAW layers. Open the Object Manager docker. You'll see three view state buttons at the top of the docker where information about viewing and editing behavior are set. Clicking each button toggles its state on or off. Each button has the following effects:

 You can use Combine, Group, or Convert To Curves commands on objects in the Object Manager docker by selecting the objects, right-clicking them, and choosing a command from the pop-up menu.

■ **Show Object Properties**   Click the Show Object Properties button to set whether properties associated with each object are listed in the docker.

■ **Edit Across Layers**   Clicking the Edit Across Layers button to set whether objects can be selected, moved, and copied between layers. While cross-layer editing is disabled, objects appear grayed out, allowing only objects on your current page layer and/or the desktop to be selected or edited. While cross-layer editing is enabled, you can select, move, or edit any object on an unlocked layer.

 Use the Object Manager to PowerClip—change object order, copy object properties, and group objects by right-click-dragging one object onto another. After you have done so, the pop-up menu lists the available commands. Grouping and PowerClip commands apply only when right-click-dragging objects within the same layer. PowerClip is discussed in detail in Chapter 22.

■ **Layer Manager View**   The Layer Manager View button toggles your view to show only your document's layers. When working with complex drawings that have many pages, layers, and objects, using this view can make managing layer properties a lot easier. In this state, all page and object information is omitted.

To delete a layer in your document, right-click the layer and choose Delete. Keep in mind that the objects *on the layer you delete will also be deleted.*

Controlling Layer Properties

Using the Layer Properties dialog, shown next, you can control specific properties for each layer. To access these options, right-click a specific layer in the Object Manager docker, and choose Properties from the pop-up menu. As you can see here, you can access properties directly from the pop-up menu or display a modeless dialog for defining the properties of a specific layer. There is a minor difference between using the dialog and the pop-up: the pop-up (right-click) menu has the Rename command, grouped with Delete, Cut, Copy, and Paste. Although this command is clear and easy to locate, basically what it does is open the name field on the Object Manager, and you type in a new layer name. This can also be done just by clicking to select the field and then clicking a second time on the layer field to open it so you can type a new name in it.

 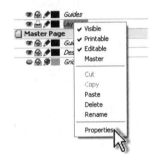

Options in this dialog control the following layer properties:

- **Visible** This option enables you to toggle the view state of a layer between visible or hidden. You can also control the visibility of objects on a layer by clicking the Eye symbol to the left of the layer name.

- **Printable** This option toggles the printing state of objects on the layer on or off. You can also set whether layer objects are printable by clicking the Printer symbol beside the layer in the Object Manager docker to toggle the printing state of objects on the layer.

Nonprinting layers will also not export. If you need objects selected on a nonprinting layer to be included when exporting, you'll need to turn on the layer's Printable option.

12

- **Editable** Use this option to lock or unlock all objects on a layer. While a layer is locked, its objects can't be edited (or even selected), which is a little different than the Lock (object) command. You can also set whether layer objects are editable by clicking the Pencil symbol beside the layer in the Object Manager docker to toggle the editing state of objects on the layer.

- **Master Layer** This option is only available after you've dragged a layer on the Object Manager onto the Master Page icon. Changing a layer to a master layer causes it to become part of the Master Page structure. Any objects on a Master Page appear on all pages. For details on working with master pages and master layers, see the next section.

- **Layer Color** This selector sets the color swatch as it appears in the docker listing directly to the left of a layer name, for easy recognition. Layer Color also determines object colors when viewed using Normal or Enhanced views while the Override Full Color View option is selected. You can also set the color coding for a layer by double-clicking the color indicator next to a layer name to open a typical color selector menu and then clicking any color from the drop-down color picker.

- **Override Full Color View** Use this option to control how the objects on the layer appear when viewed using either Normal or Enhanced view. While selected, it has the effect of displaying all objects in wireframe style, using the layer color specified.

Working with Master Page Layers

Whenever a new document is created, a *Master Page* is automatically created. The Master Page isn't a physical page in your document, but instead a place where document objects can be placed so that they appear on every page of your document. Objects on a Master Page layer are visible and printable on every page in your document, making this an extremely powerful feature. For example, a text header or footer, or a company logo on a Master Page layer becomes a quick and easy way to label all the pages in a pamphlet or brochure.

Moving any object onto a layer on the Master Page makes it a Master Page object and causes it to appear on each page. Let's try this feature:

Working with Master Page Items

1. Open the Object Manager docker by choosing Tools | Object Manager.

2. Click the New Master Layer button at the lower-left corner of the docker and press ENTER. When a new document is created, a Layer 1 is placed on Page 1. When the New Master Layer button is clicked, the default name of the new master layer is "Layer 2." The default name is "Layer 1" only if Layer 1 on Page 1 is deleted beforehand.

3. With this new Master Layer as your current layer, create the object(s) you wish to appear on every page in their final position and appearance. By creating the object while the Master Layer is selected, you automatically make the object a Master Layer object. You can also move objects from other pages onto the Master Layer by click-dragging them in the docker list from their position under a layer name to the Master Layer name.

4. Click to select the new Master Page object(s) on your document page. Notice that you can still select, move, and edit it. To toggle the lock or unlock state of your Master Layer object(s), click the Edit button (the Pencil symbol) beside the Master Page in the docker. Locking prevents any accidental editing of the Master Page object(s).

5. Add pages to your document by clicking the + button at the lower left of the workspace. As you browse through the pages, you'll see the same object on all pages.

Several default layers already exist on your document's Master Page for controlling special items that appear in your document such as Guides, Grids, and Desktop. These layers have the following purposes:

■ **Guides Layer**   This is a global layer for guides you create; if you click the Master Guides entry on the Object Manager to select it, and then drag a guide onto the page, all pages in the document will display this guide. If you need a guide on only one page, you choose that Guides entry on the page you're working on, drag a guide from the Rulers, and that guide belongs to the page and is not a Master item.

| TIP | *You can move a local guide, a guide you created on a page, to the Master Guides entry on the Object Manager to make it global—it will then appear on every page of your document.* |

12

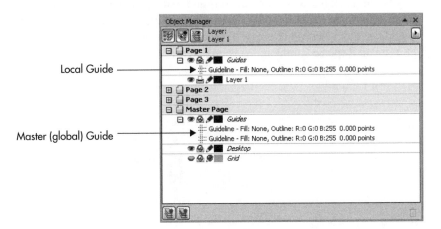

Local Guide ——

Master (global) Guide ——

■ **Grid Layer** This controls the appearance of grid lines. You can control the grid color and visibility, but you can't set the Grid Layer to be printable, nor can you change its editable objects or add objects to that layer. Options in the Grid Layer Properties dialog enable you to control the grid display color and to gain quick access to the Grid page of the Options dialog by clicking the Setup button in the dialog. To open the Grid Layer Properties dialog, right-click the Grid Layer under the Master Page in the Object Manager docker and choose Properties from the pop-up menu.

 The Grid Layer visibility can be toggled on or off by clicking its Eye icon on the Object Manager.

■ **Desktop Layer** This is a global Desktop, the place outside of your drawing page. If you want to keep objects handy but don't want to print them on your page, drag the object to this entry on the Object Manager. If you put an object on the Desktop from a layer, you can hide it or keep it from printing by the using the respective "visible" and "printable" Layer Properties.

Finding and Replacing Objects by Their Properties

You don't need to hunt to locate and change objects in documents with scores of design elements. CorelDRAW X4 will conduct object searches and/or object replacement according to the object's properties. This is done using a *wizard,* a feature that guides you through a search and/or replace operation using a simple question-and-answer sequence in a series of progressive dialogs.

CorelDRAW X4 includes two separate wizards: one for *finding and selecting* objects and another for *replacing* object properties. Wizard dialogs can be navigated forward or in reverse, so you can back out of your selections and make changes to your search as you go. Once a search or replace operation has been performed, you can also save the parameters of the search and use them again later. You'll find the commands for starting these wizards in the Edit | Find And Replace submenu, as shown here:

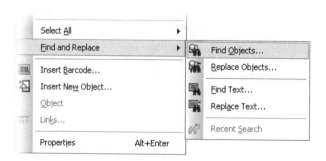

Finding Objects and Selecting Objects

The Find Wizard enables you to specify exact object properties either by choosing a nonspecific object property or by specifying the exact object and property to find. Let's create an Artistic Text object and a few different colored shapes such as an ellipse in Pie mode and a rectangle to experiment with the Find And Replace Wizard using the following steps:

 ## Finding Objects

1. Open an existing document and choose Edit | Find And Replace | Find Objects. This launches the Find Wizard and the first dialog appears. Choose either Begin A New Search or Load A Search From Disk (only if you've previously saved a search), and then click the Next button. If you currently have an object selected, you can also search for similar objects by choosing Find Objects That Match The Currently Selected Object. Choosing Load A Search From Disk opens the Open dialog, and then you search for the saved search. Click Next to proceed to the next page. The selected variables from previously saved searches are automatically specified as the selected wizard options.

2. In the next page, shown in Figure 12-6, choose Object Types, Fills, Outlines, or any applied Special Effects by clicking each of the dialog tabs and selecting the options. In this figure, we're looking for an ellipse that is in Pie shape mode among dozens of shapes on the page. Unchecked variables are omitted from the search. Selecting options within each of the tabbed areas of this dialog causes the Find Wizard to display additional editing dialogs for each object type, fill type, outline, and special effect, and enables you to narrow the parameters further. After confirming or further specifying your choices, proceed to the next dialog by clicking Next. In Figure 12-6 you can see the dialog that results if you check the Look For Object Names Or Styles box. One very easy way to locate an object involves forethought: you know in advance you're going to build a design with a huge number of objects. You name the object you know you'll need later. To do this, you select the object in the Object Manager, click a second time on its listing to open the field for typing, and then type in a unique name. As a result, The Find Wizard can easily and quickly track down a rectangle named "Fred" or any other object on the page.

3. When conducting a search for objects based on their properties, you click Next; the next wizard page, shown in Figure 12-7, displays a listing of the objects you selected for your search, in this case a single ellipse. You then refine your search by clicking on the Specify Properties For (object) button. As mentioned in step 2, we're not looking for just any ellipse, but one that's in Pie mode. Once you've narrowed all possibly ellipses on the page to a pie-shaped one, you click Next.

12

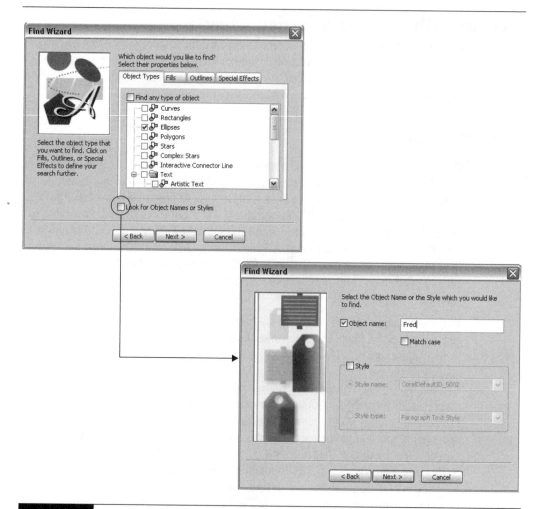

FIGURE 12-6   Select the properties of the objects you would like to find.

4. The following dialog of the wizard shows you the narrowed list of object(s) to find; this dialog is also where you can save search criteria to file for future searches. An FRW file with the *fin file extension is a small file CorelDRAW writes to save a search; save it to a location on hard disk you don't have to try to find later!

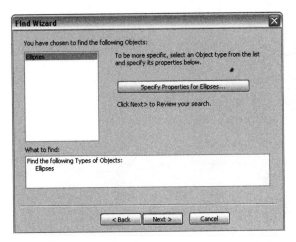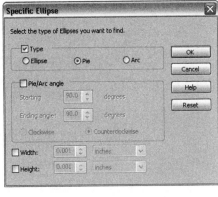

FIGURE 12-7   You will see a listing of the objects and have the opportunity to refine the search.

5. After you click Finish, the last step in the process opens the Find dialog, shown next, and automatically selects the first search object found. If more objects are found to match your search criteria, the Find dialog offers several command buttons: click Find Previous to return to the previous object (if any), Find Next to proceed to the next object (if any), Find All to instantly select all search objects on your document page, and Edit Search to return to the Find Wizard.

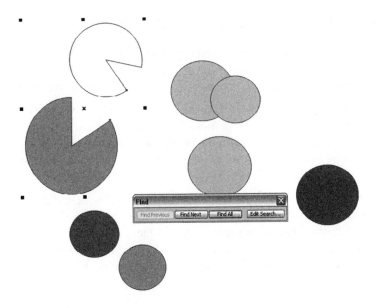

12

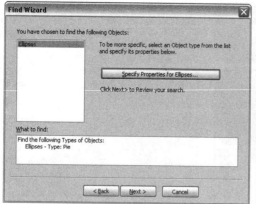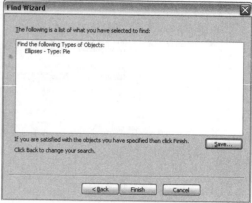

FIGURE 12-8 The final dialog of the wizard gives a summary of your objects.

Replacing Object Properties

The Replace Wizard is an extremely powerful tool for changing specific object properties in an entire document. The wizard guides you through the process using a series of questions and answers, which begins with defining which properties to replace. You can replace objects by color, color model, palette, outline pen properties, and/or text properties.

To explore this feature, use these steps:

 ## Changing Object Properties with the Wizard

1. Open a document containing object properties you want to change. Launch the Replace Wizard by choosing Edit | Find And Replace | Replace Objects. The Replace Wizard opens to reveal the first set of options, as shown in Figure 12-9.

2. Select a property to replace. Choose from Color, Color Model Or Palette, Outline Pen Properties, or Text Properties. By default, the replacement properties you specify apply to all objects in the document. However, you can choose the Apply To Currently Selected Objects Only option to limit the range. What dialog appears next depends on which option you select here. Click the Next button to proceed.

3. Depending on your choice in the previous dialog, the next dialog to appear will present choices for choosing specific properties to replace, so you'll see one of four different dialogs. In general, each of these dialogs enables you to choose the properties you wish to find with corresponding properties to replace them with. After making your selection, click Finish to close the wizard and proceed to the next page.

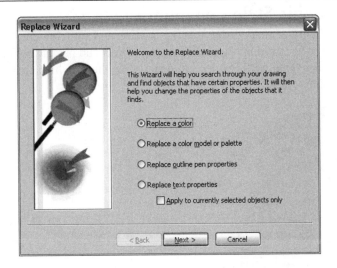

FIGURE 12-9   The Replace Wizard reveals the first step of options.

4. If the Replace operation locates multiple objects having the properties you specified, the Find And Replace dialog features several active buttons: Find Previous, Find Next, Find All, Replace, and Replace All. Clicking Find Previous or Find Next enables you to navigate backward or forward through the search. Clicking Find All selects all the relevant objects in the document without performing the replacement operation. Clicking Replace or Replace All replaces the selected objects with the specified replacement properties or simply replaces all relevant objects in the document with the replacement properties without any further prompting.

Additionally, you can find and replace text. However, this wizard is for finding and replacing the content of text, what the audience reads. It does not automatically change a font or color. If you need to find and replace a font selection, conduct a regular Replace (object), and then choose Replace Text Properties, as shown in Figure 12-9.

Using Graphic Styles

Using styles to format text can be a huge timesaver. Although styles are often associated with text, CorelDRAW X4 has the capability to create, save, and apply styles to *objects* as well. These are known as *graphic* styles. Once a graphic style has been created, the style itself can be edited to affect all the objects to which it's applied.

Using Graphic Style Commands

The best way to use commands for creating, saving, and applying graphic styles is through the pop-up menu accessed by right-clicking any object and navigating a series of submenus. The pop-up menu features the Styles submenu, shown next, which enables you to Save and/or Apply graphic styles.

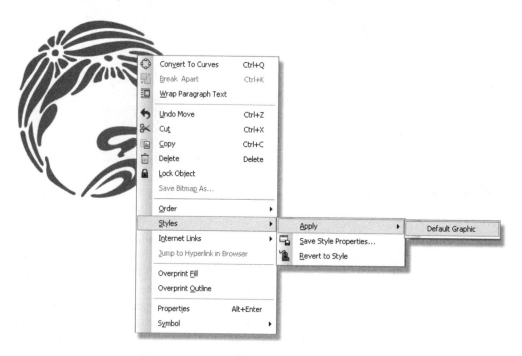

For a hands-on experience using graphic styles, follow along here:

Applying Object Styles

1. Create several objects on your document page, and apply different fill and outline properties to them. Right-click one of the objects and choose Styles | Save Style Properties to open the Save Style As dialog. Enter a name for the style, accept the fill and outline properties as they are, and then click OK.

2. Right-click a different object on your document page and open the Style | Apply submenu. Notice that the style you just saved now appears in the list. Choose this new style as your style for the second object by selecting it from the list. Your style's fill and outline colors are applied to the second object (see the following illustration).

3. With the second object still selected, change either its fill or outline properties to something else. With the object properties now changed, right-click the object again and choose Styles | Revert To Style. This will reapply the original style properties.

4. Right-click the same object and choose Properties from the pop-up menu to open the Object Properties docker (or press ALT+ENTER). Click the General tab. Notice that the Style drop-down menu shows that the new style you saved earlier is applied to the object. As mentioned earlier, you can conduct a search based on object Style.

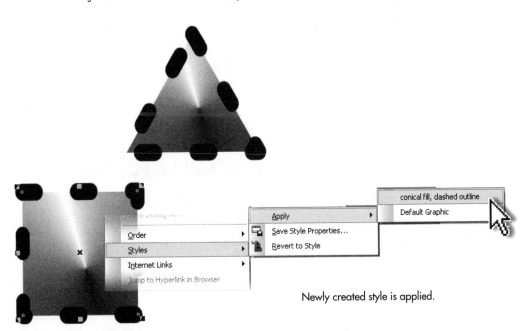

Newly created style is applied.

Using the Graphic and Text Docker

For a complete inventory of the graphic styles saved with your document, open the Graphic And Text docker by choosing Tools | Graphic And Text Styles or press CTRL+F5. The Graphic And Text docker, shown next, lists all the Graphic, Artistic, and Paragraph Text styles available in your document, including default styles. Thumbnails mimic each style's Fill and Outline Pen properties and include the style name.

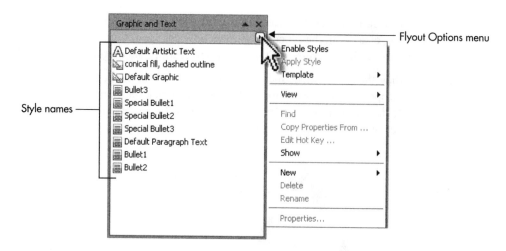

Style names ——

Flyout Options menu

Let's experiment with the docker now.

Experimenting with the Graphics And Text Docker

1. Create any object, apply unique fill and outline properties to it, and open the Graphics And Text docker (CTRL+F5).

2. To hide nongraphic styles, click the Options flyout menu, choose Show, and uncheck Default Artistic Text Styles and Default Paragraph Text Styles. If you know that your document includes *only* Graphic Styles, choose Show | Auto-View.

3. Choose New | Graphic Style from the flyout menu to add a new default graphic style named New Graphic to the list. Click its name slowly two times, enter a suitable style name, and press ENTER. This creates a new graphic style applied with graphic defaults.

4. Choose View | Large Icon from the flyout menu to view Graphic Styles properties visually. This provides a very nice visual reference for styles in your document.

5. Click-drag the object you created into the docker. Notice another new style is created using the object's assigned fill and outline properties. This action enables you to quickly create styles based on an object's current properties.

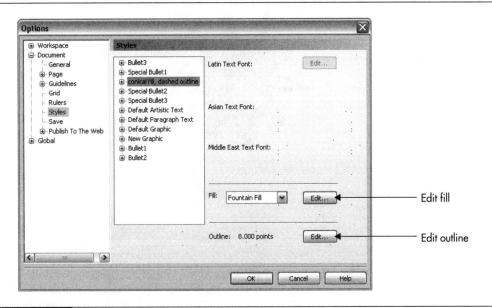

Edit fill

Edit outline

FIGURE 12-10 The Options dialog opens to the Styles page.

6. To change a style's properties, right-click the style and choose Properties from the pop-up menu. The Options dialog opens to the Styles page, shown in Figure 12-10. To edit the properties, click the Edit button beside the Fill and/or Outline values at the lower right to access the Fill and/or Outline property dialogs. After editing, click OK to return to your document. Any changes you make to the style are immediately updated in both the style and any objects applied with the style.

7. Return to the object on your document page and change either of its fill or outline properties. Right-click-drag the object onto the new Graphic Style in the docker. Doing this causes the pop-up menu to appear, as shown next, offering command options to modify the Style, Style Fill, Style Outline, Style Element, or to Cancel. Choose one of these to update your new graphic style with the selected properties of the object dragged. You can also click-drag any object onto an existing style to overwrite the style's current properties automatically.

12

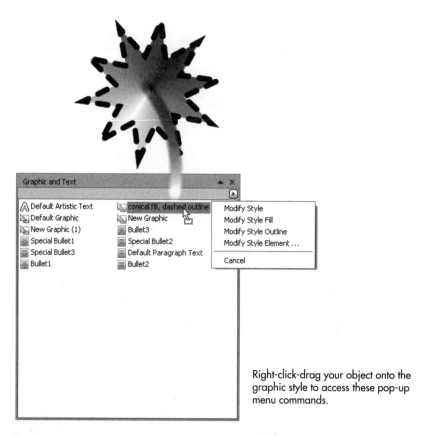

Right-click-drag your object onto the graphic style to access these pop-up menu commands.

8. Create a second object using default fill and outline properties. With the object selected, double-click your new graphic style in the docker. Your Graphic Style properties are applied to the object.

9. To locate objects in your document that were applied with a specific graphic style, right-click any style in the Graphic And Text docker, and choose Find from the pop-up menu. Doing this locates and selects the first found object applied with the graphic style. To apply the same style to more objects, right-click the style again and choose Find Next.

Using Graphic And Text Docker Options

The Graphic And Text docker has options for viewing and copying graphic styles, loading styles from templates, and applying or editing custom style shortcut keys. These commands (and others) are available from the Graphic And Text docker flyout menu or from the pop-up menu accessed by right-clicking in the docker.

■ **Loading Styles From Saved Templates** The Graphic And Text docker flyout menu includes a Template submenu enabling you to choose from one of three commands: Load, Save As, and Save As Default For New Documents. Choosing the *Load* command from the flyout menu opens the Load Styles From Template dialog, which lets you select and load styles from any templates you saved. Choosing *Save As* from the flyout menu opens the Save Template dialog, which enables you to save all the styles in your current document to a new template document, including Artistic and Paragraph Text styles. Your styles are saved to a separate template document with (or without) the content of your document. Once the template has been saved, you can use the Load command from this same flyout menu to load your styles into a new document. Choosing *Save As Default For New Documents* takes this one step further by automatically saving all currently saved styles to be available to all newly created CorelDRAW X4 documents. Doing this adds your document's styles to the default *Coreldrw.cdt* file, which includes default styles available whenever a new document is created.

■ **Views** Use the Views submenu to control how styles are displayed. Choose Large or Small icons, List (strictly a text-based view), or Details to view both the style names and a brief description of each style's properties. Using either the List or Details view can be handy if the document you're working with contains a lengthy style collection.

■ **Copy Properties From** Choose this command to update a selected style using the fill and outline properties applied to a specific object in your document or from another existing graphic style. After you choose this command, your active cursor becomes a targeting cursor used to click the object from which you want to copy properties.

■ **Edit Hot Keys** To apply your most frequently used styles quickly, assign hot keys to them. *Hot keys* are keyboard shortcuts that instantly apply the style. To assign or edit a hot key, click to select a graphic style, and choose Edit Hot Key from the flyout menu. Doing this opens the Options dialog to the Shortcut Keys page, shown in Figure 12-11. To assign a hot key after choosing this command, click your cursor in the New Shortcut Key box, press the actual keyboard shortcut you want to apply as the new hot key assignment (just press your keyboard keys, *don't type* "Ctrl" if you want CTRL as part of the key combo), click the Assign button, and then click OK to close the dialog.

■ **Delete/Rename** Choose the Delete command (or press DELETE) to delete any selected styles. Use the Rename command to highlight the text name of a style and enter a new name, or just click its text label and type the name.

12

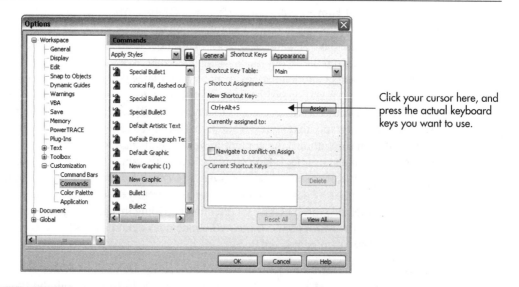

Click your cursor here, and press the actual keyboard keys you want to use.

FIGURE 12-11 The Options dialog opens to the Shortcut Keys tab.

TIP *If your document contains a large collection of styles, you can reorder the styles as they appear in the docker by click-dragging. To do this, click-drag the style thumbnails to change their order. You'll probably want your most frequently applied styles to appear near the top of the list.*

Using the Object Data Docker

Although this next feature is used only by a select few, it enables you to associate data—such as text names and/or comments, numerical and/or capital values, or measurements—to any object. This is useful for engineering, architecture, or other related industries or professions that involve evaluating or tracking a drawing's objects using numeric data. All functions of this are accomplished using the Object Data Manager docker (opened by choosing Tools | Object Data Manager) and using the Object Data Field Editor, shown in Figure 12-12, opened by clicking the Open Field Editor button in the docker.

The purpose of this docker is to assign data to each individual object in your drawing and to obtain quick summaries of the data in spreadsheet style. For example, if your drawing features the various parts of an industrial product, assign dollar values to each part, and then you can get a quick summary of the total cost of all parts. The Object Data docker does exactly this. You can also associate other nonnumeric data, such as text comments and summaries.

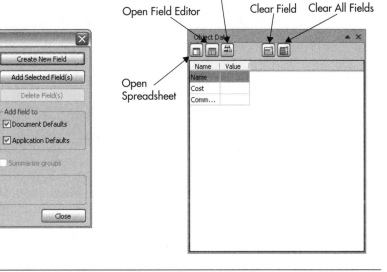

FIGURE 12-12   The Object Data Field Editor can be used to associate data to any object.

This chapter concludes Part III of this book. If you read from the beginning of this book up to this point:

- ■ Your head rightfully hurts.

- ■ You've got a good and sound working knowledge of CorelDRAW objects, how to edit them, rearrange them, and manage even a drawing with a thousand objects.

It's time now to turn to type: Part IV is your guide to typography, how to create headlines with impact, brochures that are eye-catching, and have some fun with fonts. After all, designers are supposed to be fun people!

12

PART IV
Working with Text

CHAPTER 13

Typography Rules
and Conventions

The art of typography isn't easily separated from the art of illustration—text and graphics have coexisted on the printed page for centuries. This chapter is a departure of sorts from regular documentation of CorelDRAW because before you drive CorelDRAW text engines, you need to know the rules of the road. For example, the physical appearance of text should complement an illustration. Think of a font choice as the attire in which your message appears and CorelDRAW as the boutique where you shop for accessories to dress up your message.

Like successful design work, typography has rules, such as hyphenation, punctuation, justification, line spacing, and in addition to the rules, typography is subordinate to the design it appears with. Nothing spoils a good display sign like 15 exclamations marks misused to stress a point. Give this chapter a thorough read-through before moving on to the chapters on working with text later in this part of the book. This chapter has great examples of typographic dos and don'ts, and the tips you'll learn will enhance the worth of your printed message—and at the very least this chapter has good examples of punctuation.

Font Families and Font Styles

When beginning a project, it's usually best to cruise the installed fonts drop-down list in CorelDRAW, see what you think is an appropriate typeface choice, find fonts that work harmoniously if you need more than one typeface in the design, and then, if you're drawing a blank, check out the typefaces you own but have *not* installed. It's generally a bad idea to pick the first font on the installed fonts list; Arial is a good workaday font, but it's most appropriate for text on aspirin bottles and caution signs because of its legibility at small point sizes and its authoritative, Spartan (yet clean) look.

The following sections describe the anatomy of a font, what *stroke width* means, serifs, and font characteristics and basically explain why a typeface looks the way it does and therefore becomes appropriate for a design idea. Also, the better you understand the characteristics of characters, the better you'll be able to communicate a specific need to a typographer or a pressman, and to conduct a quicker search on your drive and the Web for the typeface you need.

Styles and Types of Typefaces

There are two basic categories of typefaces a designer uses daily:

- **Roman** The characters (called *glyphs* by typographers) consist of thick and thin stems (called *strokes*) providing good contrast between characters to make long paragraphs at small point size easy to read.

- **Gothic** The characters are made up of strokes of even or almost-even widths. This makes a Gothic font an excellent choice for headlines with impact and official signs.

Within the categories of typefaces, there are two more branches: *serifs* and *sans* (from the Latin "without") *serifs*. Serifs are an embellishment at the end of a stroke in a character; their original purpose was both as a flourish when scribes would hand-copy manuscripts and, as typesetting was invented, serifs made the wooden and metal slugs easier to remove from the surface the slug was pressed into.

Typographers ages ago decided that a Gothic font could benefit from serifs and conversely, a Roman typeface could become more functional as a headline-style font by removing the serifs. Designers now enjoy the use of both Roman and Gothic type cast in serif and sans serif treatments, examples of which are shown in Figure 13-1.

> TIP | *In typographer's language, a* font *is usually part of a* family *of typefaces. Optima, for example, has normal, italic, bold, and bold-italic as part of the font family; additionally, other weights of Optima, part of the Optima* family, *are available from several vendors you can find online.* Typeface, *in contrast, is generally used to describe either a single member of a family (Optima Bold is a typeface) or a typeface that has no family members, such as Rockabilly.*

Other Types of Typefaces

The design world would be a fairly boring place today if there weren't other types of fonts designed by professionals. Variations on the traditional Roman and Gothic typefaces abound

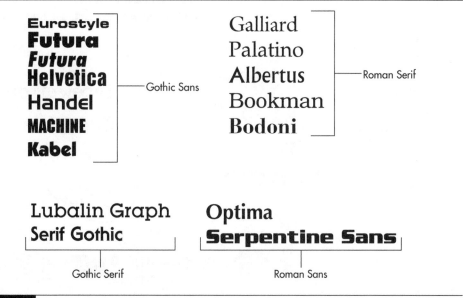

FIGURE 13-1   Examples of Gothic and Roman typefaces in serif and sans serif styles

in the desktop publishing world and many defy classification. On the CorelDRAW CD that contains objects and photos, you'll also find about a thousand typefaces, many of which would fit in the category of "designer" fonts: from classic to classy, very appropriate for packaging and logo treatments. In the world of digital typefaces, an element of playfulness has snuck in, and we have "grunge" fonts that look as though the office photocopier's having a bad hair day, elegant script typefaces that are ideal for wedding invitations, Blackletter typefaces that span usage from fairytale stories to metal band logos, fonts that look like handwriting, and Pi (picture) fonts. In Figure 13-2 you can see a small collection of different types of fonts gathered from the CorelDRAW disk and third-party vendors such as Émigré, The Font Bureau, and Stu's Font Diner.

Distant Cousins in Typeface Families

Often, font families are written for normal, bold, bold-italic, and italic variations on a typeface. However, as the need arose for specific printing purposes, typographers extended font families to include expanded versions—compressed, condensed, engraved, stenciled, and professional sets that include characters not regularly written to standard typeface sets. For example, Helvetica, Futura, and Goudy come in more than 17 "flavors" from different typeface foundries. Typeface manufacturers have retained the name "foundry" from the days when typefaces were cast from metal using a forge, much like a metal foundry that manufactures machine parts. When shopping and using Bitstream Font Navigator (included with CorelDRAW, discussed later in this chapter), it's important to know a few of the fancier variations on typeface families. Below are examples of a small caps typeface: it's appropriate for formal announcements and doesn't assault the reader as ALL CAPS does! Look for *SC* in a font name; typographers often use it to denote this

Pi (picture, symbol fonts)

FIGURE 13-2   Examples of fresh and uncommon styles of typefaces

What Is a Digital Typeface?

Fonts you use in CorelDRAW and most every other Windows application are actually applications, specifically *runtime applications* that require a "player" to display, print, and otherwise use the characters contained in the typeface. Fortunately, after you add a typeface to the Fonts folder in Windows Control Panel, you don't have to worry about the player; it's in the operating system, and most applications recognize a recently added typeface immediately.

A digital typeface has outlines that describe the shape of the individual characters. This is why you'll see a lot of picture fonts available on the Web for free: characters can be anything in a font, and it requires less skill to draw a tiny picture than to design a professional font such as Times New Roman for desktop publishing. Because the shapes are vector in nature, fonts can be small in file size, they scale smoothly to any size you might need, and CorelDRAW can simplify characters you type in a document so they become regular vector shapes that can be manipulated in any way you like. Common file extensions for digital typefaces are OTF (OpenType font) and TTF (TrueType font), and older fonts come in two parts: PostScript Type 1 fonts have the PFB file extension for the *binary* data part, which contains the outlines of the characters, and an accompanying PFM file holds header and *metrics* information (information about kerning and character width). Windows and CorelDRAW can handle all three types of digital fonts.

Later in this chapter you'll learn how to use CorelDRAW's Symbol Manager to catalogue characters you use often in a specific font that are frequently hard to locate.

special font. Also, some Roman serif typefaces have *swash* members: Bookman, Goudy, Garamond, and other popular fonts for body text can be purchased with characters that have strokes that sweep under and above neighboring characters for an elegant look. OldStyle versions of fonts contain numbers that alternate in position to make long sequences of digits easier to read, and frequently their filename is appended with *OS*.

Finally, a well-designed, professional typeface of any family member will contain extended characters. An *extended character* is one you can't directly access from the keyboard; instead you must first hold ALT and then type four digits on the numeric keypad area of your keyboard. For example, if you want to put a pause in a sentence, one way to punctuate is with ellipses (three periods when we used typewriters). However, the proper punctuation in today's typesetting is the ellipse character, which is accessed from standard-encoded typefaces by pressing and holding ALT, then typing **0133**. Some typefaces don't come with extended characters, some come with a few, and the more professional typefaces have ligature characters in the extended range of the font. Ligatures were first invented by

13

scribes several centuries ago to get more words per line on parchment and to even out the look of certain words, usually Latin. For example, (in today's English) the word "find" looks awkward in certain typefaces because of the proximity of the *f*'s extension to the right, hitting the dot in the *i*. Because today's digital typefaces can contain thousands of characters, including entire foreign-language character sets, a specific typeface might have a ligature for *fi* with the dot missing from the *i*, but this ligature is nearly impossible to look up to use. Fortunately, you can add an *fi* ligature, an *fl*, or any other extended character through the Insert Character docker (CTRL+F11), demonstrated later in this chapter. If you're into typesetting, it's a good idea to remember this keyboard shortcut.

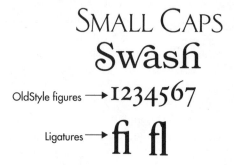

 TIP *Ligatures occasionally come as part of an Expert set of a specific typeface, making it easier to locate the ligature you need. These sets are often called "Extras" in their filename.*

The Anatomy of a Font

When looking for a font that seems appropriate for a specific design, the shape of the individual characters might or might not work out the way you intend; you want the spacing between lines of text (called *leading*) to be extremely tight, but the ascender on certain characters is too high and juts into the preceding line of text. What's an ascender? The vertical strokes in characters have names typographers use and you should, too, when describing an ideal font or when seeking one.

- ■ **Character height**   Used to describe the overall height, which includes not only the character but also the space above the character, this is usually coded in by the person designing the typeface. Character height determines how much interline spacing you'll need to make more than one line of text.

- ■ **Cap height**   This is the height of a capital letter in a typeface, which is usually not the same as character height, nor is it necessarily the height of all characters (which is called the *ascender*).

- ■ **Ascender**   This is the height of the tallest character in a font; usually it's the *f*, the *h*, or a swash if the font contains this embellishment.

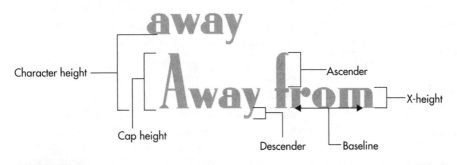

FIGURE 13-3   The heights of the strokes in a typeface

- **Descender**   This is the lowest part of a character; usually a *g* or a *y,* except when a font has swashes.

- **X-height**   The measurement of a lowercase character, traditionally measured by the letter *x* in the font.

- **Baseline**   An imaginary line where all the characters should rest.

Figure 13-3 shows all the measurements described above.

> **TIP**   *A few typographic elements have characters not found in a digital typeface, but instead are built by CorelDRAW and other applications. For example, an underscored character, used a lot in legal documents, in CorelDRAW is built from any typeface: you select the character(s) to be underscored, click the Underline button on the Property Bar, and you're done. Similarly, if you need a Superscript or Subscript character (see illustration below), CorelDRAW builds one from any font. However, a Superscript is a special treatment of a character, and you need to first choose the character's glyph node with the Shape Tool (not the Pick or the Text Tool). Then the Super and Subscript buttons appear on the Property Bar and you're home free.*

Super 1ST and Subscript H₂O

Finding the Font You Need

In this age of online transactions, you might find it hard to simply walk into a store and ask a knowledgeable person for a specific font. This is not a problem; fonts are small enough in file size to be downloaded in seconds, there are scores of places where you can find the font you need, and CorelDRAW X4 has a feature that makes it a snap to identify a font you want to own. The following sections take you through the browsing process at MyFonts.com and get you up and running with Bitstream Font Navigator for previewing fonts. Let's face it, "tt1040m_.ttf" doesn't tell you that the typeface is actually Bitstream Amazone or that it's a really cool script typeface!

Working with Font Navigator

Because the engine for displaying and printing fonts in Windows (all versions after Windows 95) was written to accommodate a hypothetically unlimited number of installed fonts, today's designer enjoys an incredibly wide selection for pamphlets, flyers, and other needs. However, just because you have 1,000 fonts at hand on the CorelDRAW CD, doesn't mean it's a wise idea to install all of them! Managing your typeface collection is similar to arranging your sock drawer: it's not a glamorous task, but you're glad you've done it when you have a 9 A.M. meeting, it's 8:30, and showing up with a blue sock and a black one is not a fashion statement.

Happily, Font Navigator comes with CorelDRAW; if you chose not to install it during setup, you might want to install it now—it's a must for previewing, organizing, and installing typefaces. Here are the simple instructions for using Font Navigator…

Launch Font Navigator exactly as you do any other application: click the Windows Start button, choose All Programs, and then choose CorelDRAW Graphics Suite X4 | Bitstream Font Navigator. Alternatively, you can double-click the Font Navigator icon in a folder window if the program doesn't show in the Programs menu. If you have the CorelDRAW CD that contains the Fonts and Photos folders in your optical drive, Font Navigator immediately recognizes the disc and offers up all the fonts on the disc for previewing and organizing. If you want to browse a different collection, you choose a different drive or folder from the drop-down list.

- If you scroll up the drop-down list, you'll see that above My Computer is the Font Catalog, an index of the fonts you decide to catalog. It's not a location for fonts on your hard drive, but rather just an index. Therefore, when you browse a CD or folder location for fonts, you've moved from the Catalog to a hard drive or CD location. To browse a folder, you navigate the drive(s) from the drop-down list; to do some indexing, you go back up the folder tree on the drop-down list and choose Font Catalog.

The four-pane interface is easy to understand, and everything you want to do can be accomplished by click-dragging. At upper left is the list of fonts available in a folder or CD; they aren't installed, so you cannot use them. At upper right is the list of fonts you currently have installed on your system. These fonts were most likely installed through Windows Control Panel | Fonts and an application that auto-installs the fonts it needs. At lower left is the Font Group area and by default there's nothing in it. At lower right is a preview panel, which can display samples of any typeface far faster than the Windows Fonts utility can. To view a font you haven't installed yet, click a name in the upper-left panel to highlight it, and instantly the preview shows at lower right. It's the same deal with an installed font; click the name in the upper-right panel to preview the installed font. Typefaces don't always have names indicative of what they look like, and occasionally you might find an installed font you don't want installed. If you want to remove a font from your system, the easy way is to open Windows Control Panel | Fonts, right-click and drag the typeface's icon out of the Fonts window. You can drop it on your Desktop of a different drive folder: when you release the right mouse button, be sure to choose Move Here—the font's no longer available on your system. You can also delete a font you're certain you never, ever want to use by dragging its icon from the Fonts window directly into the Desktop Recycle Bin.

Font groups are a handy and welcome feature. Any font that is installed can be put in a group and the group named anything you choose. At any time in the future, you can add or remove a group and the icons in that group folder. For example, let's say you had a job for a Halloween party and you needed to use bold, striking, and truly *ugly* typefaces for the project. If you put them in a group, you can now uninstall them in one fell swoop, keeping your installed fonts in tidy and useful order.

Performing operations in Font Navigator is as simple as its interface suggests:

■ To add any typeface to the Catalog for indexing, choose it from the upper-left list, right-click it, and choose Add To Font Catalog. You'll then be asked through a dialog whether you want to install the font and whether you want to copy the font file to a new location, an easy and convenient way to keep all your font files in one central location. After a font has been catalogued, its icon features a tiny yellow star tag, as shown here.

■ To install a font from the upper-left pane, drag the font name into the Installed Fonts pane, or right-click the font name and then choose Install Font.

■ To create a font group, right-click in the Font Group pane, and then choose New Group (the menu command is File | New Group). A new folder icon appears with its default name highlighted, ready for you to type a user name for the group. Organization here is key; you might like to create groups by the name of an assignment so you can install and uninstall them as the occasion calls for it. MEGATRONICS PRESENTATION, BIRTHDAY CARDS, TRUCK SIGNAGE are examples of group names…you get the idea. Alternatively, you might want to create groups by types of fonts: HEADLINES, BODY TEXT, UNUSUAL, PICTURE FONTS will help you sort out the fonts you need quite quickly.

The illustration below shows the Font Navigator interface; a font in the Catalog is being dragged into the Installed fonts list, and immediately Windows is updated and the font's ready to use in CorelDRAW and other programs with no need to reboot or restart an application.

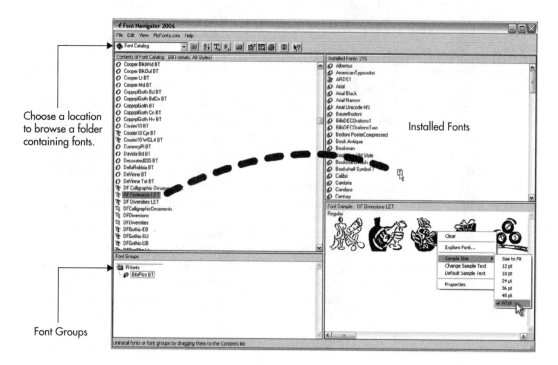

Choose a location to browse a folder containing fonts.

Installed Fonts

Font Groups

Looking Up a Font

You have a wealth of font choices on the CorelDRAW CD, and now you know how to preview them using Font Navigator. So what if you're looking for a font you've seen used in a layout or advertisement and you don't own it and you don't even know its name?

An invaluable resource for font finding and purchasing is MyFonts.com; they are probably the largest clearinghouse for type foundries ranging from large such as Linotype and Bitstream to cottage industry independent font authors. A new feature in CorelDRAW is an URL on the Text menu called What The Font?!—to use it, you need an active Internet connection and an understanding of how this command works.

What The Font?! (part of MyFonts.com's site) is an automated utility that intelligently matches a bitmap of a sample of text to a best guess at what the name of the font is. Like any software code, What The Font?! is "intelligent" up to a point, and your best chance of finding, for example, the font used on a wedding invitation, is to make sure that the bitmap you have of the invitation has the characters neatly spread apart and that the bitmap is of a pixel resolution large enough for What The Font?! to clearly "see" the outlines of the characters in the bitmap. Also have sufficient blank space surrounding the text so that What The Font?! isn't confused with surrounding text and graphics. Consider using Corel PHOTO-PAINT to edit the bitmap before using the What The Font?! command in CorelDRAW.

Here is a working example of how to use What The Font?! to find out what a specific font used on an invitation is called so it can be purchased:

1. Open the bitmap containing the invitation text in a new document; press CTRL+I, scout down the bitmap on your hard drive, click Import after you select the file, and then click the loaded cursor on a new document page to place it. Alternatively, with a new document in the workspace and CorelDRAW's interface not maximized (so you can see your desktop or a folder window), drag the bitmap file into the workspace to place it.

2. Choose Text | What The Font?! Doing this calls Corel CAPTURE from inside CorelDRAW.

3. Your cursor actually has tiny text that explains what to do now; you drag a box with your cursor to highlight the text you want to send to What The Font?! In Figure 13-4, you can see the bitmap at top, and what your screen looks like after you've "lassoed" the text. If you make a mistake, reset by clicking outside of the box you defined, and then click-drag the crosshair cursor again.

13

FIGURE 13-4   Click-drag around the text you want to send to What The Font?! as a bitmap copy.

4. After you click inside the box, What The Font?! on the Web guides you through any help it might need to identify the typeface, as shown in Figure 13-5. At left you can see that this automated routine occasionally asks you for help identifying characters; for example, 1's and exclamation marks are sometimes mistaken for one another.

5. Once you've scrolled to the bottom of the characters you captured, click Search. As you can see, What The Font?! offers a number of foundries for Beesknees, the font used in the invitation.

TIP *There is no "Cancel" command once you've launched the What The Font?! command. However, if you drag a box around an empty area of the page and then click inside it, CorelDRAW tells you that nothing worth sending to What The Font?! has been captured and the process ends.*

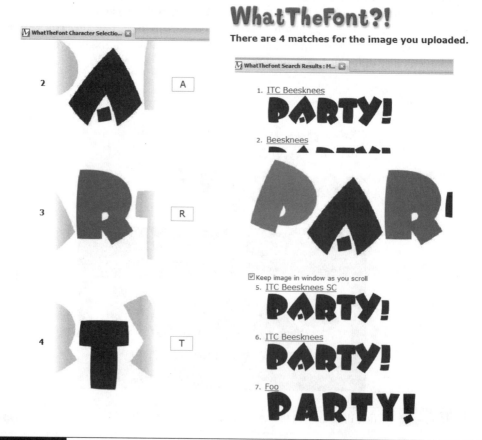

FIGURE 13-5 What The Font?! identifies a typeface you have in a bitmap version of an invitation or other printed material.

Font Foundries

Digital typeface files can be broken down into two parts: the information about the characters themselves—the vector outlines that are pure artistic design work—and the coding that allows the characters to run as a small application, so you can type using a font. Copyright issues concerning the ownership of a typeface can also be broken into two parts: what the font looks like and who owns the name. It might sound weird, but you will find several different names for what essentially looks like the same font, because the design of characters in a digital typeface isn't copyrighted, but the brand name is.

This strange legality can easily confuse a consumer: for the most part, the Bitstream typefaces on the CorelDRAW CD are trademarked by Bitstream; their names are clear and forthright and easy to look up in any traditional typeface specimen book or on the Web. You'll also see the same font name distributed or owned by different foundries and vendors. In this case, such as with Clarendon, the original character designs were sold as physical artwork ages ago, and several digital foundries traced off the characters, usually embellishing them with their unique style. Almost all the time, if you didn't own Clarendon and wanted to buy it, the smart thing to do would be to shop around and buy the best-priced version of Clarendon.

However, a foundry such as Bitstream might have licensed both the design of the font and its name to a different vendor; in this case, Bitstream still offers the typeface, using its original character designs, but offers it using a nonstandard, unique font name. This is why What The Font?! is an invaluable CorelDRAW menu command—you might own a typeface but not recognize the unique name! For example, EXOTC 350 on the CorelDRAW CD has a different industry standard name: PEIGNOT. Use Font Navigator and What The Font?! to explore what you own; your personal type case might be better stocked with workaday classic fonts than you imagine.

The Last Word on Accessing Installed Fonts

Depending on the programs you've used before working with CorelDRAW, accessing the fonts you've installed might or might not feel familiar. The steps to follow are a brief guide to getting the most out of all the fonts you've installed for your design work. Although working with text is covered in detail in chapters to come, you might like a jump start so you can get right down to business with that job that was due five minutes ago!

The Text Tool (F8) accessed from the Toolbox (the icon with the *A*) operates in two different modes: Artistic Text and Paragraph Text. Artistic Text is usually the best choice for brief headlines. Selecting, manipulating, and otherwise editing Artistic Text is accomplished differently than with Paragraph Text. Paragraph Text is intended for typesetting long blocks of text (a short story, an instruction manual) and has different properties than Artistic Text, explained in Chapter 14.

13

Finding Fonts on the Web

For a specific assignment, you might want to shop for a fresh, unusual typeface. The following URLs are reputable places where you can buy or download for free some interesting typefaces whose themes run from staples (basic fonts you can't live without) to Retro to novelty to "goth":

- **Linotype Library** http://www.linotype.com/
- **ITC** http://www.itcfonts.com/fonts/
- **Bitstream** http://www.bitstream.com/
- **URW** http://www.urwpp.de/deutsch/home.html
- **Monotype** http://www.agfamonotype.com/

Also, clearinghouses for fonts are the distributors and only occasionally the creators:

- **The Font Bureau** http://www.fontbureau.com/
- **Adobe Systems** http://www.adobe.com
- **MyFonts** http://www.myfonts.com/, probably the largest distributor

Smaller type shops also offer quality, refreshing selections:

- **Acid Fonts (http://www.acidfonts.com)** The collection is uneven; you may need to do some sifting to find quality typefaces you find useful, but you can't beat the price, and Acid Fonts is one of the largest repositories of free and shareware typefaces on the Web (about 4,700 free fonts).

- **Harold's Fonts (http://members.aol.com/fontner)** Harold Lohner advertises that he vends "homemade fonts," but they're actually clean and professional in every regard. Harold offers over 100 free fonts, including fonts designed to look like famous product logos.

- **Stu's Font Diner (http://www.fontdiner.com)** Stu offers all Retro fonts and has free downloads of some very nice pieces.

To create Artistic Text, you choose the Text Tool and then click an insertion point in your document. Then you type. By default, the font you use is Arial 24 point, justified to the left. You can change the default to anything you like: with the Text Tool selected, you choose the font, point size, and justification on the Property Bar, and CorelDRAW displays a Text Attributes box. Here you can redefine Artistic and Paragraph Text for all future default documents.

> | TIP | *A* point *is a typographic term, a measurement of the height of text. Traditionally, there are 72.27 points to the inch, but with the advent of digital fonts, this measurement has been modified to 72 points to the inch. Because typefaces are designed by hundreds of different professionals, the actual size of, for example, 24 point Arial, is not necessarily the same size as 24 point Palatino. It's always a good idea to measure the height of text cast in different fonts using Rulers in CorelDRAW to ensure consistency. Usually, paragraph text is set in anywhere from 9 to 14 points (except for aspirin labels, which seem to be set in 2 point type), while fonts used in headlines look best at 24 points to 72 points on a page that measures standard letter 8.5×11".*

Paragraph Text is entered the same way as Artistic Text and in the same way as most other Windows applications, but you define Paragraph Text by marquee-dragging a frame into which Paragraph Text flows. Marquee-dragging is accomplished by click-holding the primary mouse button and then dragging diagonally; top left to bottom right is the most common technique. Then you release the mouse button, a frame appears, and you type in the frame (or paste from the clipboard when you have copied text).

- To change the font and the point size of the font after you've entered text, you highlight the text using the Text Tool, and then choose a different font and point size from the Property Bar.

- To change a single character in text you've typed, you highlight only that character and then use the drop-down lists on the Property Bar to make the change(s). The Property Bar lists installed fonts alphabetically, with their names shown in the font style itself as a convenient preview method. A font family is listed on the flyout for a font name on the list; you click the triangle and then choose a family member. Single-member fonts have no little triangle to the right of their name. The illustration below shows two lines of text being edited to change family members. Additionally, at the top of the fonts list are the most recently used fonts, a handy way to access the same font in a document you're continuing from two hours ago.

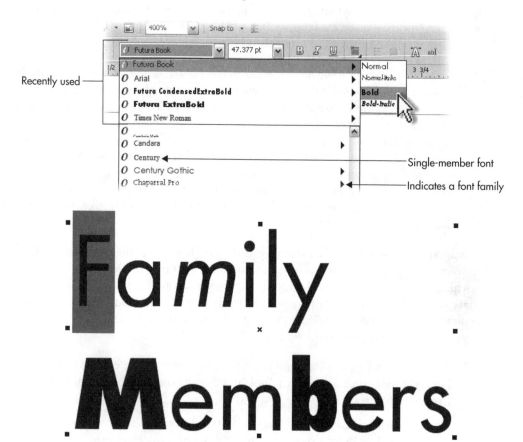

Finding and Saving Important Characters

Picture (Pi) fonts, also called Symbols, are terrific for embellishing design work, but locating a specific character within a Pi font isn't straightforward because your keyboard has letters and not very many symbols; no two font designers agree on a specific mapping for symbol sets, although occasionally there is a progression as you type across your keyboard. For example, some picture-font designers code an upper-left ornamental frame corner as "a", the upper-right frame corner as "s"; if the users are intuitive enough, they can type across the left end of the second row (a-s-d-f) on the keyboard to make a sequentially correct four-corner picture frame from such a symbol font.

Using the Insert Character Docker

CorelDRAW, via Text | Insert Symbol Character (CTRL+F11), removes the guesswork in locating a character or symbol in any font you have installed. When you choose this command, the Insert Character docker appears, and you have two ways to insert a character:

- ■ **As text**   If you need, for example, a fancy bullet that is inline in existing text in your document, you place the Text Tool cursor at the location in the text where you want the character, click the character on the docker to select it, and then you click the Insert button. You might not always want to choose this method; the advantages are that the character is editable text and stays aligned to the text that comes before it and after it. However, the disadvantage is that as a designer, you might want to move this ornamental character around on the page—but as inline text, the inserted character is bound to the line of text you added it to.

- ■ **As a collection of editable shapes**   To add a character to your document as a shape you can immediately edit with the Shape Tool, you first select the Pick Tool instead of the Text Tool. Then you drag the thumbnail of the symbol you want onto the page. It's easy to spot the difference between an inserted Symbol on a page and a Symbol added as a shape: shapes have a default black outline and no fill, so they're easy to single out in a document. The disadvantage to adding a Symbol as a shape is that you can't edit it with the Text Tool, but overall, you have an endless supply of special characters at your cursor tip with the Insert Character docker, so mistakenly adding the type of symbol you don't want to a document is corrected in a flash.

Figure 13-6 shows the process of adding a Symbol to a document by dragging a thumbnail into the document; you locate the installed font from which you want a symbol by using the drop-down list at the top of the docker, set the size of the symbol at the bottom (a symbol can be resized at any time in the future by scaling it with the Pick Tool), and then drag and drop. Notice in the enlarged inset graphic in this figure that the Insert Symbol docker provides you with the extended character key combination for the symbol you've clicked on. This feature is a great help if you're coming to CorelDRAW from a word processor such as WordPerfect. You might already be familiar with certain extended character codes; for example, standard font coding for a cents sign (¢) is to hold ALT, then type **0162**. Therefore, for any font you've chosen on the Insert Symbol docker, if the font has a cents sign and you want to choose it quickly, you type **0162** in the Keystroke field, press ENTER, and the docker immediately highlights the symbol—it's easy to locate and equally easy to then add to the document. Conversely, when you click a symbol, the Keystroke field tells you what the keystroke is; you can then access a cents sign, a copyright symbol, or any other extended character you like in any application outside of CorelDRAW. You just hold ALT and then type the four-digit keycode in, for example, WordPerfect or Microsoft Word, and you're home free.

13

FIGURE 13-6 The Insert Character docker is your ticket to quickly looking up and adding special extended characters to your designs.

Using the Symbol Manager

Now that you've located the perfect symbol for a design by using the Insert Character docker, it would be nice to save the symbol so you can reuse it in the future instead of hunting for it again! This is where the Symbol Manager (CTRL+F3) under Windows | Dockers is an invaluable resource. The Symbol Manager provides you with information about symbols contained and saved only to a document you have open and also provides User Symbols, an area on the Symbols Manager where you can duplicate a catalogued symbol into any document at any time.

Let's say you've found a great symbol for a layout, you've placed it in your document, and you decide you want to reuse it tomorrow. Here are the steps for cataloguing the symbol and for accessing an *instance* (a duplicate that takes up less saved file space in a document) of it tomorrow:

1. With an object selected, choose Edit | Symbol | New Symbol.

2. In the Create New Symbol box, type a name you'll remember later in the Name field and then click OK. As you create more and more new files using CorelDRAW, you'll definitely want to stay tidy in your cataloguing work. Cross-referencing is a good practice; in Figure 13-7, the Name of the symbol refers to the typeface it was copied from. Later, it's easy to look up the name of the symbol and use it in a program outside of CorelDRAW.

3. Open the Symbol Manager and then click on the Graphic1 title. A thumbnail of the symbol you just saved appears.

4. A tiny Export icon becomes active; click it, it's the Export Library command. This is not much of a library, but you need to start somewhere!

5. In the Export Library box, it's best to save the new library to where CorelDRAW recommends (to better allow the program to locate it in the future; User Symbols is a good location). Name the library and then click Save. You're done.

6. In any new document, open the Symbol Manager, click the User Symbols + icon to open the collection, and then click the name of the library you saved in step 5. Now all you need to do is drag the thumbnail into a document, and you have an instance of the symbol you saved.

Symbols saved to a library are always instances and as such, duplicates you add to a document cannot be edited using the Shape Tool or other shape editing features. You can apply transformations such as scaling and rotating, but you cannot edit the nodes of a shape instance. However, you can edit the original shape as saved in the Library, and all future instances you use reflect your edits. To edit a symbol in your library, you right-click over the shape thumbnail in the Symbol Manager and then choose Edit. After you've edited the shape, you right-click over the shape in the document window and then click the Finish Editing Object button to the left of the document horizontal scroll bar. Every instance in every document is updated to reflect your edits.

| TIP | *It's easy to tell the difference between an instanced symbol and one that can be edited in any document. Choose the shape using the Pick Tool. If the bounding box dots are blue, it's a shape instance. If the bounding box handles are black, it's a regular shape and you can perform any CorelDRAW operation on the shape.* |

13

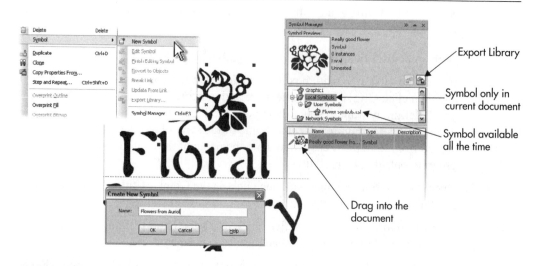

FIGURE 13-7   Define a Symbol and then save it to a Symbol Library.

Font Etiquette: Using Fonts with Style and Appropriateness

It's easy for anyone to mistype a word or use fractured grammar in an email message. However, an ad posted on the Web and a sign hanging in a store window for thousands to see is not a use of typography between friends and it's hard to retract. A badly designed sign from a typographic point of view hurts the product, the company, and your reputation as a professional. The following sections discuss common mistakes we try to avoid from the planning stage of a printed message; you'll work with CorelDRAW's type features in future chapters, but now it's time to learn to walk before you learn to fly with new talents and skills.

Font Appropriateness and Very Basic Layout Rules

When an audience looks at a printed message, they don't simply absorb what the message says, but they additionally look at the *presentation*: the choice of capitalization, emphasis through bold and italic family members, how lines of text are stacked (justification), point size, font color, and how well the printed message harmonizes with any accompanying graphic. With most digital typefaces, the artist casts a tone on the typed message. Headline, sans serif Gothic fonts, for example, are rather hard-edged and cold yet impactful, while Roman serif fonts tend to lull the audience with rounded strokes, swooping serifs, and swashes. Roman typefaces generally send a warm but clean and professional signal to the viewer, while Gothic fonts wake up the reader, perhaps even warning them—hence their appropriateness as a headline typeface.

FIGURE 13-8   Don't undercut your message with the wrong font!

Figure 13-8 has two obvious sight gags demonstrating inappropriate uses of specific fonts. At left, the use of all uppercase, Gothic, stencil contrasts extremely distastefully with both the message and the graphic behind it. At right, the choice of fonts on the page the officer is showing to someone about to be detained clashes with the message to the extent that the officer will probably have a hard time getting the cuffs on the person rolling on the pavement laughing.

A quick fix to these two bad examples would be to swap the fonts around, so the stencil font is used in the Miranda rights, and the slightly silly typeface is used for "I Love You." But better still, a quick trip to Font Navigator and the CorelDRAW Fonts CD will show you that Staccato 222BT (its industry name is Mistral) is warm, loose, and splendid for a valentine, and News 701 XBld condensed (similar to Helvetica Bold Condensed in the type world) is serious, functional, and perfect for the arresting officer. You have the choices of fonts at hand; all you need to do is apply your artistic sensibilities to the selection.

When you have more than one line of text in a headline, legibility is a concern, and this, too, is accomplished by an appropriate choice of fonts. You want a "quick read" from the audience, especially on billboards and vehicle signage that appears and disappears as the sign or the reader moves.

Let's take a simple example headline, pull it apart, examine it, and make it work hard for your money. "The best deals in town" is a common slogan. In Figure 13-9 you can see this headline cast in text three different ways, with icons beneath them to indicate their merit as a sales message.

FIGURE 13-9 From clownish to professional, your message stands or falls based on fonts and layout.

First, the sign above the clown suffers from the following abuses of typographic conventions and rules:

- The use of Times New Roman, a Roman serif font, is stale (it's a Windows default typeface used since 1991 on the PC) and artistically defeats the message. It's large yet the characters aren't bold enough to present an impactful message.

- The use of all capital characters looks particularly inappropriate; Roman typefaces have upper- and lowercase characters, and the message looks like the designer had the CAPS LOCK key enabled. Also, it's plain bad form to "shout" a message unless a typeface has no lowercase letters and the designer is firm about the choice of fonts.

- The use of several exclamation marks suggests that if the business owner shouts loudly enough, someone will buy the product. One exclamation mark is sufficient for stressing a message; often a headline is adequately emphasized with no exclamation at all. It is redundant to cast a headline in all caps followed by several exclamation marks.

- The use of quotes is for quotations, not for emphasizing a phrase. When a designer puts quotation marks around "BEST" in this example, it creates in the reader's mind the suggestion that the retailer is speaking *euphemistically*. For example, when someone writes, "Get that 'antique' out of my parking lot in 15 minutes," they aren't actually referring to your 10-year-old car as a valuable antique, but rather as a piece of junk to which they're referring euphemistically or sarcastically. The word "BEST" in quotes will surely be interpreted by anyone with writing skills as, "They really aren't the best deals; they mean something else."

■ The alignment of the headline is wrong. Although left justification is acceptable for Western language countries, the second line is much shorter than the third line. As a result, the reader has a hard time focusing to quickly read the message.

The center example in Figure 13-9 is a vast improvement and gets one star. Here's what is going right for this treatment of the slogan:

■ The use of sans serif Gothic fonts makes the headline easier to read quickly.

■ The emphasis created by using a bold, italic font to stress "BEST" makes it the first word a casual passerby will read. What this design does is create a hierarchy of importance within the message. It directs the reader to the most important, then to the second most important area of the slogan.

■ The slogan uses center justification and the lines are stacked to align well; no line is too long or short, and both legibility and neatness have been added.

The middle example is short of ideal for two reasons:

■ Because "BEST" is italicized, it might be design overkill to also make it all capitals and bolder.

■ The exclamation mark at the end is not really necessary. The message's importance is already well supported by the use of the fonts. Generally, if you've graphically punctuated a slogan, you don't need to add an exclamation mark to overdo the importance of the slogan.

The example at right, which earns four stars, works the best for the slogan. Here's why:

■ The lines of text have been stretched to fit, by using the Pick Tool and scaling horizontally, disproportionately. You can do this with CorelDRAW Artistic Text. The result is a very neatly stacked presentation of words.

■ The word "BEST" stands out through the use of a different color. In design, you don't necessarily have to use black to emphasize something, not when text surrounding a particular word is set in black. Contrast can be achieved through emphasis, or by "negative emphasis"; when objects surrounding the most important one are gray, you make the most important object black. And conversely, a gray object gets noticed when surrounded by black objects. Additionally, uppercase for

13

"THE" and "BEST" works in this example because the other words are upper- and lowercase. In art, you first learn the rules, and then when you understand them well enough, you can *break* the rules with style.

■ The hierarchy of importance of the words is proper and reads well. "BEST" is read first, then the surrounding text, and then "in town"—because a thin typeface is used, a script type font, it becomes subordinate in visual importance.

It's not hard to think up a more compelling and fresh sales slogan than "The Best deals in town." Once you have that ideal slogan, consider the good and bad points in the previous example, approach your sales message with taste and sensitivity, lean but don't push, and you cannot go wrong.

You've seen in this chapter how to define a font, how to find a font, how to find and save an individual character, and how to put the whole of your acquired knowledge into motion with some good working rules for the ambitious sign-maker. There's a lot more in store in the following chapters on working with text. It's not just about signs: you'll see how to work with the Text Tool to its fullest potential, creating extraordinary logos and headline treatments, and then work your way up to outstanding page layouts and special design needs such as reverse printing, flawless character alignment, special effects, and more.

You've *read* enough text in this chapter; let's move on and actually *work* with text!

CHAPTER 14
Working with Text

Chapter 13 covered how to load and choose typefaces and provided guides for proper punctuation and text justification in your artwork. *This* chapter shows you how to *work* with the Text Tool and other CorelDRAW type features to express your ideas in an inviting and clear fashion. Whether it's for a poster, a newsletter, a banner, or a logo, you have the tools within reach to create the text and graphics that go hand in hand in presentations.

CorelDRAW's Text Tool

All text in CorelDRAW is created (by typing or pasting from the clipboard) using the Text Tool, the tool with an *A* as its icon in CorelDRAW's Toolbox. To begin designing, click its button in the Toolbox, press F8, or double-click an existing text object. The Text Tool cursor is a small crosshair with an *A* below and to the right, which becomes an I-beam (a text-editing cursor) when it's over a text object.

 A shortcut to reselect the Pick Tool while the Text Tool is selected is CTRL+SPACEBAR—to reselect each of the other tools, you can press either SPACEBAR or CTRL+SPACEBAR.

When you use the Text Tool, you can produce two different types of text objects in a document: Artistic Text and Paragraph Text. Figure 14-1 shows a simple layout that uses Artistic Text in combination with the Text | Fit Text To Path command (the path is hidden in this illustration). The smaller body copy text uses Paragraph Text; the top paragraph wraps around the top of the image by use of a CorelDRAW Envelope (see Chapter 20).

Artistic Text and Paragraph Text have different properties, but are added to a document by use of the same Text Tool. Artistic Text, by the way it's produced in a document, is easy to reshape and distort—you'll find it simple to do artistic things with it, such as creating a company logo. Conversely, Paragraph Text is optimized for longer amounts of text, and it's a great text attribute for quickly modifying columns of, for example, instructions, recipes, short stories, and so on. In short, Paragraph Text is best used for several paragraphs of text in a composition, while Artistic Text should be reserved for headlines and just a few lines of text you might want to curve along a path, extrude, or do something else unique and fancy with.

Although there are similarities between Artistic and Paragraph Text, you're best off using one or the other depending on the type of text element you want in your design.

Entering and Editing Artistic Text

Artistic Text will serve you best for illustration headlines, callouts, and on any occasion when you want to create text that has a special effect such as extrusion, an envelope, text on a path, and so on. To add a line of Artistic Text to a document, click an insertion point with the Text Tool and then type your phrase; alternatively, after clicking an insertion point, you can press CTRL+V to paste any text you have loaded on Windows' clipboard. Creating several lines of Artistic Text simply involves typing and then pressing ENTER to put a carriage return at the end of the line; you then continue typing. By default all Artistic Text is set in Arial 24 point; later in this chapter you'll see how to change the default.

Artistic Text

Paragraph Text

FIGURE 14-1   Artistic Text and Paragraph Text have different attributes, each suited for different text treatments in a design.

Artistic Text is also easy to convert to curves so you can modify a character in a word: for example, Microsoft's logo has a tick missing in the second "o". To duplicate this effect (but not Microsoft's logo!), you'd begin with Artistic Text for the company name by pressing CTRL+Q (Arrange | Convert to Curves), and then you'd edit using any of CorelDRAW's tools. Artistic Text, as editable text, can be fine-tuned using the features on the Property Bar when the text is selected by using either the Pick Tool or the Text Tool. The options are shown in Figure 14-2.

- **Mirroring (horizontal and vertical)**   In addition to creating special effects, the mirroring buttons are also useful when, for example, you want to print a T-shirt transfer of your company name. The name needs to be reversed (mirrored horizontally) to print on the transfer paper, so that the print on the T-shirt reads correctly (or at least without the need for a mirror).

- **Type of font (file)**   To the left of the font name displayed in the drop-down box is an icon signifying what file format the chosen font uses: OpenType, Type 1, or TrueType. This is a nicety when you're sorting your fonts in Bitstream Font Navigator or Windows' Fonts utility in Control Panel.

14

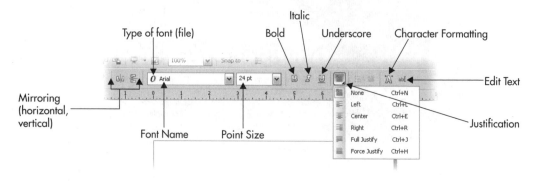

FIGURE 14-2 Use the Property Bar to get Artistic Text looking exactly the way you want.

■ **Font Name** This is the name of the typeface you choose. By default you're using Arial 24 point. You change fonts in a new document by selecting text you've typed with the Pick Tool, and then choosing a different font from the drop-down list. If a font has family members, a right-facing triangle can be seen to the right of the font name when the drop-down list is extended, and you can choose the font member by clicking the (flyout) triangle. You can also perform a speed-search by clicking the current name in the Font Name box and then typing the first few letters of the font you want. The drop-down list immediately scrolls to the neighborhood of installed fonts, making your selection a fast and effortless one. Note also that the Font Name drop-down list, at the top, above the divider bar, shows the fonts you've chosen recently from previous documents and even from previous CorelDRAW sessions.

■ **Point Size** Text has traditionally been measured in points. With current digital typeface technology, the rounded-off value is 72 points to the inch (traditionally, physically set type was 72.27 points to the inch; you can safely ignore this trivia!). Artistic Text used as a headline ideally can be anywhere from 24 points for a flyer headline, to 72 points for an impactful newspaper headline, to 300 points (over 4 inches in height) and up—for headlines that fairly shout at the reader. There's no hypothetical limit to how large Artistic Text can be.

- **Bold and Italic**   These buttons on the Property Bar are shortcuts to defining a whole line of text or only selected characters as bold and italic members of the typeface shown in the Font Name box. If a specific font has no family members, CorelDRAW doesn't "fake" a bold or italic look, and the buttons are dimmed. If you need an italic treatment of a font that has no italic family member, a quick fix is to use the Transformation docker, and then to set Skew to about –12° to apply to the Artistic Text.

- **Underline**   As mentioned in Chapter 13, an underline (sometimes called an *underscore*) is an effect available for every font you have installed—you click the button when text is selected, and CorelDRAW renders an underline. You can modify the style of the underline to your choosing by pressing CTRL+T; then on the Character Formatting docker choose from the Character Effects | Underline drop-down list. If you don't see the preset you want, choose Edit from the list, and then build the underline width and style you need. Underlines are great for professional documents, particularly legal ones, but an underline isn't the tastiest way to emphasize a phrase in an advertisement (use a bold font instead, or a colored outline, or a gradient fill to attract attention artistically). Although Underlines are effects, they're very real, and if you convert an underlined phrase to curves (CTRL+Q), the underline becomes a simple object, with corner nodes and total nodes depending on how many characters you typed.

- **Justification**   This drop-down list specifies how lines of text are aligned relative to one another. Although Justification will serve you best when using long columns of Paragraph Text, Artistic Text takes on a more polished look, too, when you apply, for example, Center justification to two or three lines. By default, there is no Justification for newly entered Artistic Text, but this is left-justified text. Full justification creates a splendid, professional look for columns of Paragraph Text, but tends to generate an awkward look for Artistic Text, because a line containing only one word with only a few characters has to take on very wide character spacing. Similarly, Right justification is not an everyday choice for audiences who read Western languages (from left to right)—Right justification is a "slow read," and hyphenations and line breaks between words usually look awkward. Right justification should be reserved for a page layout where the right edge of the text needs to align perfectly to the vertical of a graphic and the left side of the column can be flowing and freeform. *Force Justify* creates lines of text whose left and right edges are perfectly vertical, like *Full Justify,* with an important difference. Force justification gives equal emphasis to the spacing between characters; although it can sometimes create unsightly gaps in Paragraph Text (called *rivers*), it's usually a good alignment choice for correcting justified lines of text where there are too few words

14

on a line and when hyphenation is not used. Force Justify can also be used as an artistic treatment of Artistic Text, as shown in the illustration below.

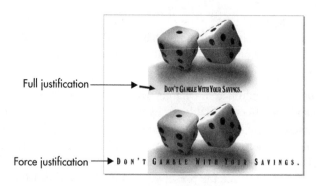

- **Character Formatting** This button will serve the greatest number of creative purposes when you have one or only a few characters highlighted (selected) using the Text Tool. You can Underline a single character, change its font type, family member, point size, and even rotate the selected character(s), all through Character Effects and Shift on the Character Formatting docker. See the following section on Character Formatting.

- **Edit Text** This button displays a text editing box, which also appears when you click on a piece of text to which is applied an Effect such as an envelope or an Extrude. CorelDRAW is designed with text editing flexibility in mind, so to transform text using just about any feature—and to allow the text to still be editable—you work in a proxy box so you don't have to start over when you make a typographic error. Here's a visual example: You've chosen a lovely font to express a lovely sentiment for a card and have extruded the font. Looking at it in the morning, you discover you've misspelled "Happy." No big deal: Using the Text Tool, you click an insertion point in the text where the fix is needed. The Edit Text box appears; you enter the additional characters and finally click OK. Occasionally, you might need to modify an envelope containing text if you're adding a lot of characters, but the Edit Text box is your friend in a jam, and as you'll see, you can even change the font of selected characters, the family members, and the point size.

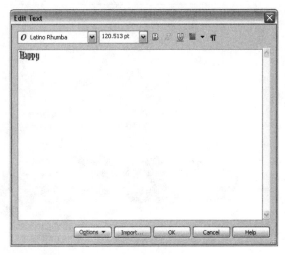

TIP	*The name of a typeface you see in the Fonts drop-down list can be anything the professional who designed the font wants it to be, and it's not necessarily the same as the font filename. Therefore, by accident you or an application could install, for example, Bookman as a TrueType font when you already have Bookman as an OpenType font installed. By default (and you can't change this), Windows "prefers" TrueType, and some applications hide a duplicate font with the same designer name. CorelDRAW will show you that in this example you have Bookman listed twice, once as a TrueType and once as an OpenType font. If, having discovered this, you prefer one font format over the other, you can remove the duplicate through Control Panel	Fonts, or have Font Navigator do it for you.*

Character Formatting

You'll often want to change the look of only one or two characters in an Artistic Text phrase in your document. Character Formatting can be accomplished using:

- The Shape Tool in combination with the Property Bar.
- The Text Tool in combination with the Character Formatting docker.

As you can see in Figure 14-3, you have some options right at hand by using the Shape Tool to select characters, but you have a more complete set of options when you highlight a character with the Text Tool and then click the Character Formatting button on the Property Bar. Therefore, for quick and simple reformatting, use the Shape Tool, and for extensive reworking of your

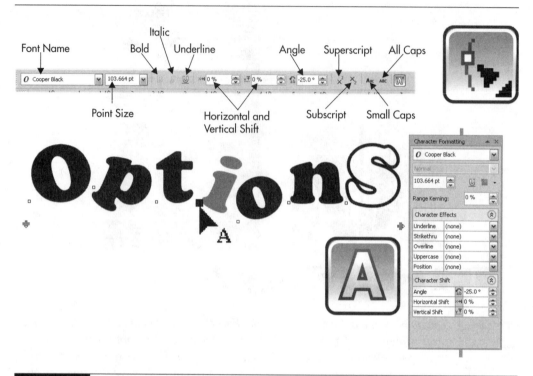

FIGURE 14-3 Format and reformat text characters using the Character Formatting box and the Property Bar.

Artistic Text, use the Text Tool. You have additional options for lines running under, over, and through selected characters. If, for example, you've used the Character Formatting docker to put a Double Thin Underline beneath your text, you can remove this underline later using the Property Bar while character nodes have been selected using the Shape Tool. Character nodes appear black when selected (as shown in Figure 14-3); your cursor is a clear indication you're editing text, not an object path node, with the Shape Tool.

Artistic Text and the Shape Tool

The Shape Tool can be used to make various changes to the text, including repositioning individual characters within the Artistic Text object, changing the horizontal and vertical spacing of all the text at once, and selecting nonconsecutive characters, so you change their properties independent of the rest of the text in the object.

Selecting and Moving Characters with the Shape Tool

To select arbitrary characters in an Artistic Text object, select the Text object with the Shape Tool (F10)—the cursor changes to the Shape Tool pointer with an *A* next to it. With the Text

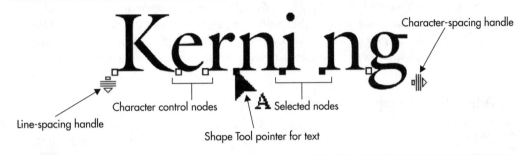

FIGURE 14-4   Set character and line spacing and reposition individual characters with the Shape Tool.

object selected in this way, a small, empty box or "control handle" appears at the lower-left corner of each character, as shown in Figure 14-4.

To select any character, click on its control handle by using the Shape Tool. To select nonconsecutive characters, hold SHIFT while clicking. You can also marquee-drag around the nodes you want to select with the Shape Tool. With the control handles selected, you can modify the text formatting, fill, outline, and position of those characters.

To move one or more characters selected with the Shape Tool, click-drag one of the selected control handles—all the selected characters will move together. Unless you're striving for a humorous effect, however, it's usually a good idea to keep the characters you move horizontally aligned: hold CTRL while dragging.

Moving characters with the Shape Tool changes the horizontal- and vertical-shift values of them, and the new values can be seen in the Character Formatting box (CTRL+T). Moving characters with the Shape Tool is useful for manually adjusting the position of characters visually to improve the *kerning,* the intercharacter spacing. Although repositioning character nodes can create fun, freeform headlines, it's also useful if you own a "bum font," a digital typeface that is coded poorly and as a result, certain characters neighboring other characters are too tight or too loose. The classic example uses the word "HAWAII"; in the illustration below, at top is the way the characters align as typed. Clearly, there is too little space between the *I*'s, and the *A* and *W,* which should tuck into each other, do not. At bottom, see that after 30 seconds' work with the Shape Tool, the word not only has a better relationship between negative and positive areas, but the word is also shorter (which is good when design space is cramped).

14

As with the Pick Tool, the Shape Tool can also be nudged after selecting character nodes and nodes along object paths. Therefore, you can create better headline kerning by first adjusting the Nudge Distance in Tools | Options | Workspace | Rulers and then using the keyboard arrows to create a professionally typeset headline.

Adjusting Spacing with the Shape Tool

When an Artistic Text object is selected with the Shape Tool, two additional handles appear at the lower-left and lower-right corners of the object, as shown in Figure 14-5. These two handles modify the line spacing and character spacing for the entire block in one go.

To increase or decrease the word and character spacing, drag the handle at the lower-right corner of the selected Text object right or left with the Shape Tool. To increase or decrease the line spacing (also the before-paragraph spacing), drag the handle at the lower-left corner of the selected Text object down or up with the Shape Tool.

All spacing values modified with the Shape Tool can be viewed and edited in the Character Formatting box.

Combining and Breaking Apart Artistic Text

You can combine several Artistic Text objects into a single Artistic Text object; you select all the Artistic Text objects with the Pick Tool, and then choose Arrange | Combine or press CTRL+L. Each Text object starts a new paragraph in the new Text object.

The Text objects are combined *in the order in which they are selected*—if you select several objects in one go by dragging a marquee around them, they will be selected from front to back. Text objects that do not contain spaces are combined onto a single line. If any of the selected objects is not a Text object, all the Text objects will be converted to curves and combined with the non-Text object.

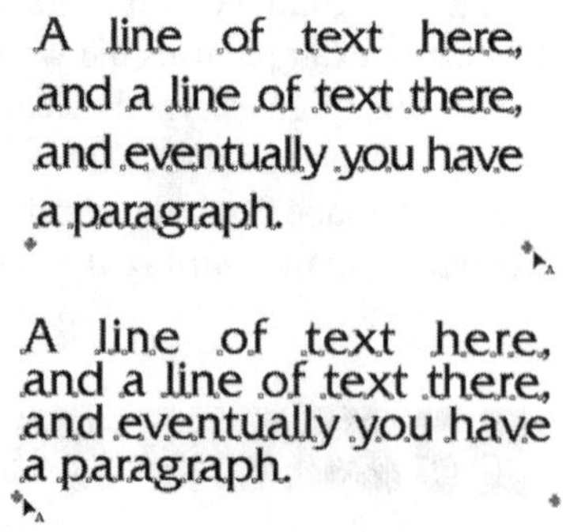

A line of text here,
and a line of text there,
and eventually you have
a paragraph.

A line of text here,
and a line of text there,
and eventually you have
a paragraph.

FIGURE 14-5 *Leading* (interline spacing), *kerning* (intercharacter spacing), and interword spacing can be tuned using the text handles.

| TIP | *If the text doesn't combine in the order you want or expect, you can reverse the stacking order of the original Text objects by choosing Arrange | Order | Reverse Order.* |

Artistic Text can also be broken apart from several lines of stacked text to individual lines, all unique objects. To break apart Artistic Text, choose Arrange | Break Artistic Text, or press CTRL+K. With multiline Text objects, the breaking apart command results in one Text object for each line or paragraph from the original object.

Also, using the breaking apart command on single-line Text objects results in one Text object for each word. And as you'd expect, breaking apart single-word Text objects results in a new Text object for each character.

Understand that this combining and breaking apart of Artistic Text does not destroy the editability of text as text. In the following section, we move into some advanced, entertaining, and quite *destructive* text editing.

Converting Artistic Text to Curves

Many effects can be applied directly to Artistic Text, but you might want to apply effects that cannot be applied as a "live" effect to editable text. To achieve the desired effect, the Artistic Text objects first need to be converted to curves: choose Arrange | Convert To Curves, or press CTRL+Q. Text that has been converted to curves is *no longer editable with the Text Tool* and must be edited with the Shape Tool instead, just like any other curve object. As mentioned earlier, text converted to a plain object with paths and control nodes is a good way to begin creating logos. The following illustration shows a treatment of Artistic Text converted to curves, and then with a push of a node here and a pull there, you have a workable party store sign.

Entering and Editing Paragraph Text

Paragraph Text is very much like the frames that text professionals work with in desktop publishing applications such as CorelVentura and Adobe InDesign; however, you'll soon see options and features in CorelDRAW that DTP (desktop publishing) applications don't provide. The largest difference between Artistic Text and Paragraph Text is that Paragraph Text is held in a container—a frame—so *you don't directly edit,* for example, the width of characters in a Paragraph Text frame simply by yanking on a bounding box handle with the Pick Tool. In Figure 14-6 at top are duplicate Paragraph frames; they're easy to spot and differentiate from Artistic Text because even when not selected, they have a dashed outline around them signifying the Paragraph Text frame. The duplicate at top right has been scaled so it's wider than at left: note that the lines of text flow differently, but the characters themselves remain unchanged, as does the spacing between characters and words. At bottom the same *greeking* (nonsense text, usually Latin, used by layout people to show a page design before the text has been finalized and entered) has been entered as Artistic Text, and then the center-right bounding box was dragged to the right using the Pick Tool. The words per line don't rearrange, but what does happen is that the characters themselves are stretched, which is often unwanted. That's the biggest difference between Paragraph and Artistic Text: if text doesn't have a frame, then you're scaling the text.

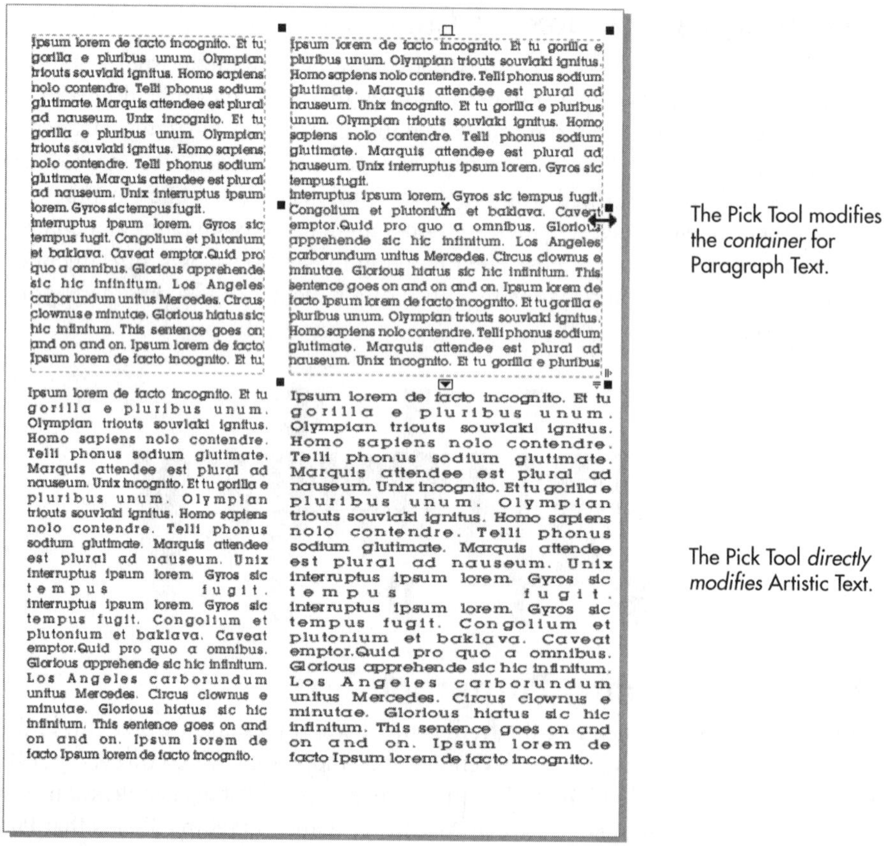

The Pick Tool modifies the *container* for Paragraph Text.

The Pick Tool *directly modifies* Artistic Text.

FIGURE 14-6 When you edit Paragraph Text with the Pick Tool, you're only changing the shape of the frame and not the text itself.

Working with Paragraph Text can be a challenge, a little more complex than riding a bike but a lot less complex than rocket science. However, once you get the hang of it (and the following sections are your guide), you'll find Paragraph Text indispensable for business designs. Those Tri-fold and Top Fold page presets you learned about in Chapter 5 will spring to life and a new purpose, and your brochures will look as slick as can be.

To create a Paragraph Text object, select the Text Tool in the Toolbox, and then click-and-drag diagonally to create a rectangle into which you'll enter the text. In the illustration below, the arrow at left shows the click-hold+diagonal-drag technique (this is commonly called a *marquee drag*), and at right you see the result. The text inside the Paragraph frame is simply a visual prompt, and it disappears after you've added text. There are resizing handles on a Paragraph Text frame and kerning and leading handles (Artistic Text features these as well), discussed later in this chapter.

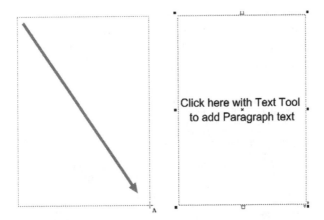

Click here with Text Tool
to add Paragraph text

Especially if you're pasting text from the clipboard, the frame you drag for Paragraph Text might not accommodate the amount of text. As a result, the text is hidden; the frame is a dashed red outline instead of black. To reveal the text, you drag down on the "window-shade handle," the small square tab at bottom center on the text frame; when there's hidden text, the handle has a down arrow in its center.

One of the most useful things you can do with Paragraph Text frames is to link them; instead of spoiling a design by increasing the size of the frame, you can create a second, third, or any number of additional frames, and flow the excess text into the new frames as you create the frames. The advantage to this is that you can move the linked frames around in your design, and the content (the printed message of the Paragraph Text) remains in perfect order. For example, if you need to break a paragraph into two frames in the middle of, "Now is the time for all good people to come," you do this, and in the future if you need to resize the first Paragraph Text frame, the excess words "pour" into the second frame, regardless of its position on the page. This is too neat to simply describe with words, so let's try creating linked text frames in the following tutorial.

14

Creating Linked Paragraph Text Frames

1. In a word processor or plain text editor, copy some existing text to the clipboard; it doesn't matter what the text is. Highlight a few paragraphs and then press CTRL+C.

2. In CorelDRAW, choose the Text Tool and then diagonal-drag to define a Paragraph Text frame. Try to make the frame smaller than the text on the clipboard (eyeball it).

3. Insert your cursor in the frame and then press CTRL+V to paste the clipboard text. If you copied from a word processor, CorelDRAW will flash you the Import/Pasting Text box, where you have the option of retaining the formatting (if any) created in the word processor—font choice, point size, justification, and tabs are all attributes of text formatting. Go with it; click the Maintain Fonts And Formatting button, and then click OK.

4. Click the bottom-center text handle (the window-shade handle), and your cursor is now loaded with all the text that was hidden from view because your frame is smaller than the text you pasted into it. Your cursor takes on a new look, shown in the following illustration.

5. Click-hold+diagonal-drag to create a new, linked text frame. The excess text from the first frame automatically flows into the new frame, shown here. A light blue line with an arrow indicates the relationship between the text in the first and the second frame (this screen element does not print, don't worry). Try repositioning the two frames now using the Pick Tool. Then try resizing the first frame. You'll see, dynamically, that the second frame takes the overflow from the first frame.

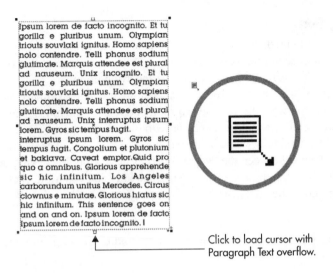

Click to load cursor with
Paragraph Text overflow.

Web-Compatible Paragraph Text

If you are designing Web pages in CorelDRAW, you should make all Paragraph Text Web compatible. *Web-compatible* Paragraph Text will be exported as real text in the final HTML Web page. Web-compatible Paragraph Text has a limited subset of normal Paragraph Text properties: font, size, bold, italic, underline, alignment, and solid color, but no tabs, bullets, or other advanced features you might find in a DTP program. All other properties are removed from the text. All text that is not Web compatible (symbol fonts, certain extended characters, and so on) is exported as bitmaps when the page is published to HTML. Bitmaps do not scale on dynamic HTML pages—they take more time to download than live text and do not render to screen as crisply as actual text.

To make Paragraph Text Web compatible, right-click the Paragraph Text object with the Pick Tool, and choose Make Text Web Compatible from the pop-up menu.

Editing Text: The Comprehensive Tour

A few of the basics of text entry and editing have been discussed to get you up and running. However, as your needs arise for more complex character formatting and fancy text layout, you'll want to become more familiar with the nitty-gritty of everyday typography and publishing. The good news is that CorelDRAW's text handling features are very similar to those of your favorite word processor or desktop publishing program. Just select the Text Tool (F8) and let's begin the exploration.

Navigating with the Insertion Point Cursor

You can use the text cursor to select text a character at a time, whole words, or even whole paragraphs, just by dragging to highlight. You can also use the UP, DOWN, LEFT, and RIGHT ARROW keys on your keyboard to quickly navigate the cursor insertion point around large amounts of text.

Selecting Text

To place the text cursor (the I-beam) in the text where you want to start typing, simply click with the left mouse button. Any text you type will be inserted at that point and will have the same style as the character *to the left* of the insertion point.

To select text with the Text Tool cursor, click-drag with the primary mouse button from the point at which you want the selection to start, and release the mouse button where you want the selection to end. Alternatively, click once to place the cursor in the text where you want the selection to start, and then, while holding down the SHIFT key, click where you want the selection to end—all the text between the two clicks is selected. Double-clicking on a word selects that word. Triple-clicking selects the entire paragraph in which you triple-clicked.

You can move the cursor with the cursor keys (the keyboard arrow keys) as well as with the mouse.

- To move left or right a word at a time, hold CTRL while moving the cursor with the LEFT or RIGHT cursor key.

- To move up or down a paragraph at a time, hold CTRL and press the UP or DOWN cursor key, respectively.

- To expand or contract the selection, hold SHIFT while moving the endpoint with the cursor keys.

- To move to the beginning or end of the current frame, hold CTRL and press the HOME or END key, respectively. Alternatively, use the PAGE UP or PAGE DOWN key to move up or down a frame.

Moving Text

You can move a selection of text with the mouse by dragging-and-dropping; select the word or phrase you want to move, and then click-drag the text to its new location in the current text object—or in any other text object—with the primary mouse button. A vertical bar indicates the insertion point at the new location; the cursor becomes the international "no" sign (a circle with a slash through it) if it is not possible to drop the text at the current location.

Dragging with the *right* mouse button causes a pop-up menu to appear when you drop the text, with options for what to do with the text. The options are Copy and Move, and this special editing gesture puts the copied or moved text outside of the body of Artistic and Paragraph Text…it is no longer in line with the text from which you copy or move, so use this command (particularly Move) only for very good reason.

Converting Between Artistic Text and Paragraph Text

To convert a block of Artistic Text to Paragraph Text, right-click the Artistic Text object with the Pick Tool; then choose Convert To Paragraph Text from the pop-up menu. The menu command is Text | Convert To Paragraph Text, and the keyboard shortcut is CTRL+F8. All the text formatting is maintained as closely as possible each time you convert between the two text types, although some formatting, such as Paragraph Text Columns and Effects, cannot be applied to Artistic Text and is lost.

Converting Paragraph Text to Artistic Text is similarly simple. However, all the text in a Paragraph Text frame must be visible: it cannot be hidden and you cannot convert a linked Paragraph Text frame. With the Pick Tool, right-click over Paragraph Text and then choose Convert To Artistic Text (pressing CTRL+F8 works, too).

 Paragraph Text objects that are Web compatible cannot *be converted to Artistic Text. You need to first (with the Pick Tool) right-click over Web-compatible text, and then uncheck the Make Text Web Compatible check box.*

The Text Bar and Special Paragraph Formatting

Let's dig deeper into Paragraph Text options and discover new ways to embellish your printed message. Create or open a document now that contains a Paragraph Text frame. Because of large screen resolutions we enjoy today, we can view pages almost at 1:1 resolution as they would print, but this also means we might need to scroll and mouse around a document more than is healthy for the wrists. The solution in CorelDRAW is a simple one: if you're working extensively with text, you float the Text Bar close to the area of the document that you're fine-tuning. Right-click over any area of the Property Bar, and then choose Text from the pop-up menu. You can drag the Text Bar to hover over any area you like.

The Text Bar can be used to edit single characters in Artistic Text and Paragraph Text, but its real strength is in the offering of options for making Paragraph Text look polished and sophisticated. When the Pick Tool or the Text Tool is active, all the features shown in Figure 14-7 are active and at your disposal. Additional modifications to the available options are described a little later in this chapter.

TIP *The Text Bar and the Text options on the Property Bar when the Pick or the Text Tool has selected text are essentially identical. The Text Bar is simply a more portable device for working closely to text.*

14

Drop Caps and Bulleted Lists Formatting

A *Drop Cap* is, literally, a dropped capital character that goes at the beginning of a paragraph. It's much larger than the rest of the text, extending three, four, or more lines down in the paragraph…and it adds a touch of class to a document, particularly if you're illustrating a fairy tale.

Bulleted lists are a common necessity for page layouts for restaurant menus, assembly instructions, just about anything that's a list that doesn't need to be a numbered list! In the following sections you'll see not only how to create a bulleted list, but also how to choose any character you like for the bullet and even to create a hanging indent for the bulleted list for an ultraprofessional presentation.

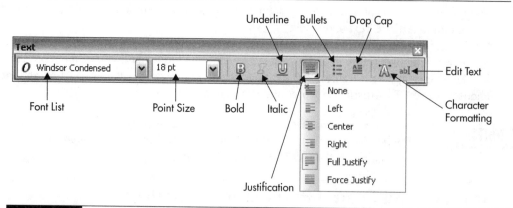

FIGURE 14-7 The Text Bar is a convenient gateway to access the text formatting you need on a daily basis.

Creating a Drop Cap

You have a lot of options, hence a lot of different design opportunities, for drop caps in a CorelDRAW document. You can decide on the drop cap's height relative to the lines of Paragraph Text it neighbors, where it nestles into the body of the text or stands to the left (called a hanging indent), and even the font used for the drop cap.

First, the Drop Cap button on the Text Bar and Property Bar is available when the Pick Tool is used to select Paragraph Text, and when the Text Tool is used to highlight a paragraph within a Paragraph Text frame. This is a show/hide *toggle* button: it turns the default attributes for a Drop Cap on and off within the selected text. Therefore, you can create a Drop Cap for Paragraph Text in one click, but if you want to add your own input, you need to additionally work with the Drop Cap options box, as demonstrated in the following tutorial:

Adding a Drop Cap to Your Paragraph Text

1. Create some Paragraph Text, as described earlier in this chapter.

2. Use the Text Tool to highlight a paragraph you want to lead off with a Drop Cap. You can create Drop Caps by simply selecting a Paragraph Text frame with the Pick Tool, but doing so will put a drop cap at the beginning of every paragraph (after every carriage return), which might be overdoing the effect.

3. On the Text Bar or the Property Bar, click the Show/Hide Drop Cap button; you'll get the default drop cap effect, as seen in the next illustration.

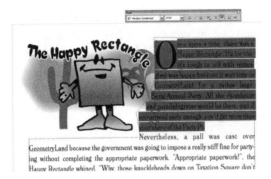

4. Change the font style of the drop cap to something ornamental you have installed: insert the Text Tool I-beam cursor just before the second character on the first line (directly after the drop cap, although it might not look this way), and then highlight backwards, to the left, to select the drop cap. Then choose a different font from the drop-down list on the Property Bar or the Text Bar. Because there's some tricky automation going on, the font list might still display the Paragraph Text font choice and not your new ornamental font choice, so trust the result you see in the drawing window and not the font list.

5. Choose Text | Drop Cap to display the options for the drop cap. The most common customizing would be to change how many lines the cap is dropped; by default it's three, but four or even five can look interesting, depending on the font you use. If you feel there isn't enough air between the Paragraph Text and the drop cap, use the Space After Drop Cap spin box to increase the space to the right of the drop cap. You also have the option to Use Hanging Indent Style For Drop Cap, which casts the drop cap to the left of the Paragraph Text while the Paragraph Text then takes on a flush-left indent. The following illustration shows the completed effect; a hanging indent was not used because the design uses Paragraph Text inside a path (discussed later in this chapter) to wrap the text around the cartoon, and an indent would spoil the overall composition.

14

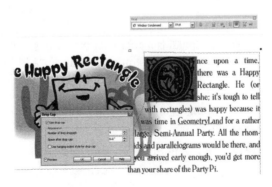

Use the Edit Text button on the Text Bar and the Property Bar if you're not getting the results you need by selecting the Drop Cap to change the font style. The Edit Text box is like Windows WordPad, a mini word processor, where you can select characters with precision and edit text very quickly, for those designs where long paragraphs of extremely ornamental typefaces are slowing you down.

Making Bulleted Paragraph Text

Like the toggling Drop Cap, the Show/Hide Bullet button can be your one-click stop for creating bulleted lists; however, you'll surely want a custom bulleted list that looks as artistic as your document layout. On the Text menu you'll find the Bullets command: it's straightforward and you'll quickly achieve great results. Find or create a list of something and follow along to see how to work the options for Bullets.

 ## Creating a Bullet Motif

1. There's no real harm in simply using the Pick Tool to select the Paragraph Text you want to make a fancy bulleted list: every line break in the list begins a new bulleted item, so select the text and then click the Show/Hide Bullets button on the Property Bar or the Text Bar. See the following illustration.

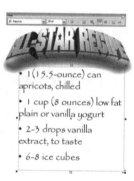

2. Choose Text | Bullets.

3. Choose a typeface that contains a character that works well with the theme of the bulleted list composition. The illustration here is an "All-Star Recipe," so a bullet shaped like a star is appropriate. Microsoft's Wingdings font is installed with every copy of Windows, and it features some nice symbols. Choose Wingdings from the Font drop-down list in this example, and then click the Symbol drop-down button and locate a good star shape.

4. Click the Use Hanging Indent Style For Bulleted Lists check box to get a polished look for the list.

5. Increase the point size by dragging upward in the center of the spin box control for Size.

6. Most likely, the baseline of the enlarged symbol won't look right compared with the text in the list (it'll be too high). Drag downward on the Baseline Shift spin box control until the bullets look aligned.

7. Optionally, if your symbol is crowding into the list text, increase the Bullet To Text spacing. Or the Paragraph Text frame might be too tight to the left of the bullet; in this case, you increase the Text Frame To Bullet amount. See the following illustration for the completed design.

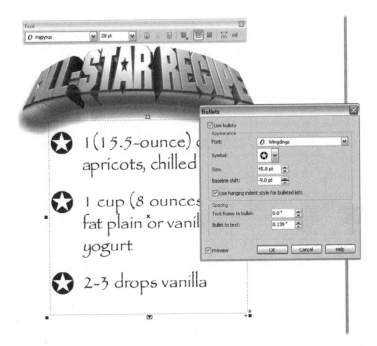

Working with Columns

Although you can manually create flowing columns of Paragraph Text, it's often less time-consuming to use the automated Columns feature in CorelDRAW. Text columns divide Paragraph Text frames into several vertical columns separated by *gutters* (margins). Multiple columns can be created only in the Text | Columns dialog box. This section describes how to manipulate columns with the mouse. You must have Paragraph Text selected with the Text Tool to work with columns: the tabs do not show on the Rulers when you're using other tools.

Select the frame in which you want to place columns, open the Text | Columns dialog, and then set the number of columns on the Columns page. It is always a good idea to keep the number of columns balanced, so each column is neither too wide nor too narrow. Here's a good rule of thumb: each line of text should be no wider than 6 inches or 16 words, but it should be wide enough to have at least 4 words per line.

14

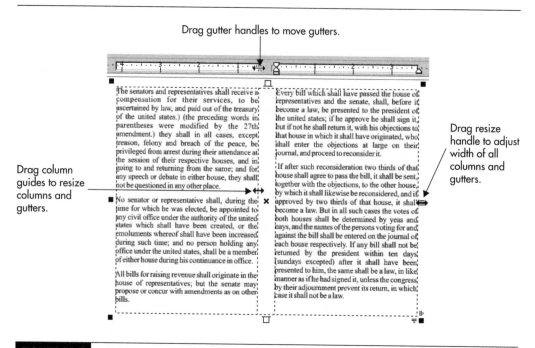

Drag gutter handles to move gutters.

Drag resize handle to adjust width of all columns and gutters.

Drag column guides to resize columns and gutters.

FIGURE 14-8 Column widths can be edited directly by dragging with the mouse.

To change the width of the columns and margins, drag the column guides, column-boundary markers, gutter handles, and horizontal-resize handles, as shown in Figure 14-8. When you're dragging the column guides or boundary markers, if the Equal Column Width option is selected in the Format Text dialog, all the gutters will be resized together; the gutter handles are available only when this option is not selected.

 Columns can be applied only to whole Paragraph Text frames and cannot be applied to individual paragraphs or to Artistic Text.

Columns Settings

The automated approach to setting the number of columns and widths for columns and gutters is done through Text | Columns, as shown in Figure 14-9.

To add extra columns, first set the Number Of Columns, and then set the Width of the columns. The Gutter value is the distance between the selected column and the next one. If Equal Column Width is selected, changing the width of any column or gutter changes the width of all columns or gutters to the same values. If Maintain Current Frame Width is selected, changing the width of any column or gutter will not change the overall width of the

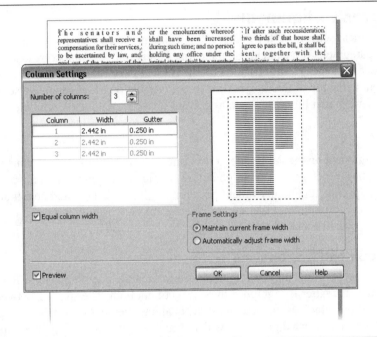

FIGURE 14-9   Use the Column Settings page of the Format Text dialog to apply columns to Paragraph Text.

frame, so the other columns and gutters will be resized to accommodate the change. A preview of the column settings is shown in the preview frame on the right side of the dialog.

Text in columns (even if only one column is used) can be justified via the Text Bar and the Paragraph Formatting dialog box.

 You can have more control over columns by laying them out as multiple text frames, each one containing a single column.

14

Formatting Paragraph Text

Stepping inside the frame and column formatting of Paragraph Text, CorelDRAW has extensive options for specifying how lines of text look compared with one another, how tightly characters and words are spaced, and how you want individual paragraphs to separate from each other. The following sections cover the use of the Paragraph Formatting box, which is accessed through the Text main menu.

 If you intend to perform a lot of Paragraph Text editing, you might want to set up a shortcut key combo, through Options (CTRL+J) | Customization | Commands.

Paragraph Alignment

The Alignment settings on the Paragraph Formatting box affect the spacing for the entire selected paragraph; you can choose the entire Paragraph Text object by using the Pick Tool or choose only pages by highlighting them with the Text Tool. Horizontal and Vertical Alignment at the top of this box pertain to the orientation of the language set of the font used; American and European users will want to use Horizontal Alignment.

Spacing

Below Alignment on the Paragraph Formatting box are controls for interline spacing (leading), how much space should go before or after a paragraph, intercharacter and interword spacing, and finally Indent preferences. It should be noted here that proper typographical form dictates that separate paragraphs are usually indicated by either a first line indent, or a line space between paragraphs, but not both.

Paragraph and Line Spacing

Depending on your layout, you might choose to separate paragraphs by using the Before Paragraph or the After Paragraph spin boxes, but not both. The spacing between paragraphs is measured by default as the percent of the character height (% Of Char. Height), the total height of a character in a digital font, which is not always easy to discern. Typically it's about 30 percent taller than a capital letter in the font. If this proves to be too time-consuming to calculate, you can always choose Points or Percentage Of Point Size from the drop-down list. In the following illustration, 200 percent of the character height is chosen to separate paragraphs: this is an option you want to experiment with, depending on the typeface you're using. Anywhere from 125 percent to 200 percent can work from an artistic standpoint.

Line spacing is used to let some "air" into Paragraph Text and is especially useful when you have a font whose ascenders or descenders are unusually tall. You can also use very wide Line spacing to create an artistic effect when starting, for example, a magazine article. It's been fashionable in layout for several years now to put about 300% line spacing in the opening paragraph: it lightens the page when you're using a bold font and also allows the reader to see more of any decorative background you've used.

Language, Character, and Word Spacing

If you're typesetting an article using an Asian font, Language spacing will be useful to space non-left-to-right sentences; otherwise, you have very little use for this option. You can set how much extra space is added to the default intercharacter space for the paragraph as a whole by using the Character spacing. The values are a percentage of a normal space character for the current font. You can also modify the interword spacing—this has the effect of adjusting the width of the space character. The following illustration shows some adjusted text at right (highlighted), and you can compare the effect to the default Paragraph Text at left.

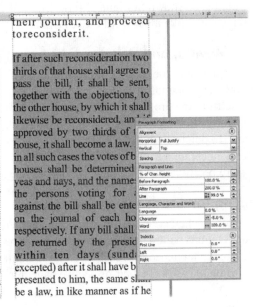

TIP *Remember the control handles on the bounding boxes of Paragraph Text. They offer less precision for character and line spacing than the Paragraph Formatting box, but they're quick to use and provide a good coarse view of how your layout is shaping up.*

Indentation and Margins of Paragraph Text

You can set the sizes of the indents of the left and right margins, as well as the size of the first-line indentation, just as you do in a word processor. These can be set precisely from the Paragraph Formatting dialog, or you can set them with a little less precision using the triangular markers on the Ruler, which are shown here:

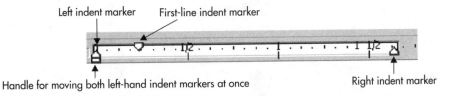

14

Formatting Tabs

Tab stops for Paragraph Text can be edited either directly in the Ruler or in the Text | Tab Settings dialog, as shown in Figure 14-10. CorelDRAW supports Left, Right, Center, and Decimal tabs, just like most word processors do.

Adding, Moving, and Deleting Tabs from the Dialog

Tabs can be added to the current paragraph in the Text | Tab Settings box by first entering a value in the Tab Location spin box, and then by clicking Add. To set the type of the new tab, you choose from the drop-down list associated with the tab. Similarly, you can adjust an existing tab by clicking its position (thus opening the value for editing) and then typing in a new value. To delete a tab, select it in the list, and then click the Remove button.

   When you create a new paragraph, unless you have modified the default paragraph style, tab stops are positioned every half-inch. To remove all the tabs, click the Remove All button.

Formatting Tab Leaders from the Dialog

You can choose whether text positioned to any tab has a leader between the tab settings. Click the Leader Options button in Tab Settings to go to the Leader Setting box. *Leading characters* are often used in tabulated lists such as tables of contents and menus to join the section titles or menu items on the left with their respective page numbers or prices on the right.

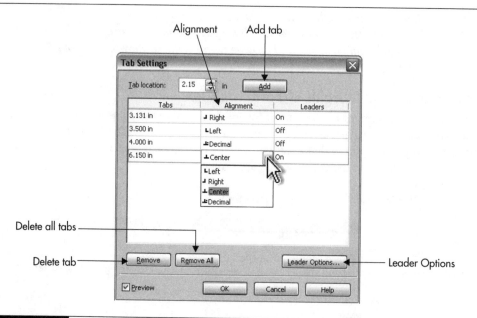

FIGURE 14-10   Edit tab stops by using the Tabs Settings dialog.

Leaders are usually displayed as a series of dots, but they can be changed to any of the characters shown in the Character drop-down list (unfortunately, you can't make a leader using a font other than the one used in the Paragraph Text). To change the leader character, select a Character from the drop-down list. The distance between the leader characters is set with the Spacing option: this value is the number of space characters to insert between each leader character. A preview of the leaders appears in the leader preview box.

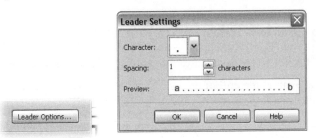

Using the Ruler to Set Tabs

To edit tab stops on the Ruler, the Ruler must be visible (choose View | Rulers). You use the Text Tool in selecting the Paragraph Text, and you click to set or edit the tab stops. To view tab characters in the body of your Paragraph Text, press CTRL+SHIFT+C (Text | Show Non-Printing Characters).

 TIP *Before creating new tabs, you should delete all the tabs that are already in place—select Remove All from the Tab Settings dialog.*

To create new tabs with the Ruler, use the Text Tool to select the paragraphs to which you want to add tabs, and then click on the horizontal Ruler where you want to add the new tab stop. The type of the tab is set with the tab-type selector at the left end of the Ruler, where you usually find the Ruler origin. Clicking the selector button cycles between the four tab states: left–center–right–decimal, as shown in Figure 14-11.

To move a tab, simply drag it to its new position on the Ruler. To delete a tab, drag it off the Ruler and into the drawing. To change the type of a tab, delete it and create a new one of

14

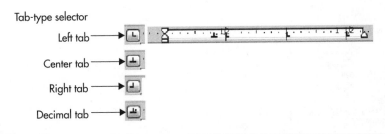

FIGURE 14-11 Tab stops can be edited directly on the horizontal Ruler when editing.

the correct type, right-click it in the Ruler and select a new type from the pop-up menu, or change its type in the Tab Settings dialog. Tabs cannot be added to Artistic Text.

Here's a practical example of the value of knowing how to set up tabs: create a folding menu design, and then create Paragraph Text with menu items and their corresponding prices on the same lines (make up anything you like; have fun here!). Here's how to create a dot leader so the guests can see the prices at far right easily, based on the menu items at far left:

Creating Leader Tabs for a Price List

1. With the Text Tool cursor inserted in the body of the text, choose Text | Tabs.

2. Create a tab at the end of the line, just short of the end of the paragraph frame; give it the Right tab property.

3. Unfortunately, you can't have a decimal leader and a regular text leader on the same line of text, but for the most part this is okay; with most typefaces, the decimal in the price column will line up fairly evenly with a leader tab in place. Click Leader Options.

4. Choose a period as the character, or if you want something fancier, you might try a guillemotright (œ) character (ALT+0156) if your font supports this character.

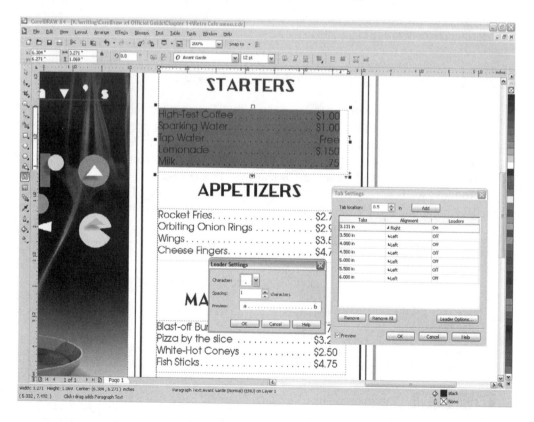

5. Set the Spacing for the leader character. Notice that your document updates live, so you can preview how your dot leader looks before clicking OK.

6. Click OK and the menu will certainly look more appetizing after applying your newfound typographer's skills.

Wrapping Text Around Other Shapes

You can apply text wrapping to shapes in CorelDRAW so that any Paragraph Text placed close to the shape will flow *around* the shape instead of over or under it, as shown in the examples in Figure 14-12.

Several types of wrapping are available.

- **Contour wrapping**   The text is wrapped a line at a time *around* the outline of the shape.

- **Square wrapping**   The text is wrapped around an imaginary rectangle that bounds the shape with the wrap (its *bounding box*).

In either case, the text can be made to flow down the left or right of the object, or to straddle it (flow down both sides). Square wrapping also supports Above/Below, where no text flows to the sides of the object.

To apply Contour Straddle, right-click the shape and select Wrap Paragraph Text from the pop-up menu. To set a different wrapping type, select it from the General tab of the

14

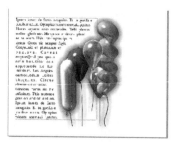
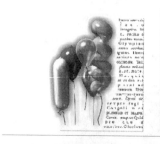
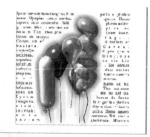
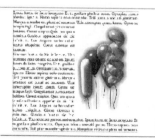

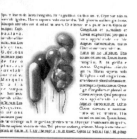

FIGURE 14-12   Six contour and square text-wrapping options are available and one nonwrapping option (None).

Object Properties docker (press ALT+ENTER). Then set the margin distance, which is the gap between the outline or bounding box of the shape and the Paragraph Text wrapped around it.

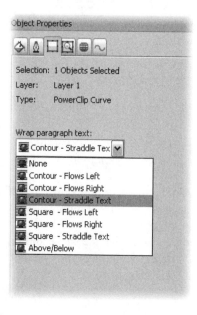

It's important to understand that text legibility can suffer when you wrap text around a highly freeform shape; it's just not good layout, for example, to create a zigzag-shaped wrap, causing the reader's head to whiplash every other line. Use wrapping text as a creative element, but use your artistic eye to avoid unnecessarily hard-to-read Paragraph Text.

Wrapping affects only Paragraph Text. Text wrapping is not applied to the wrapped text itself, only to the shapes that are wrapped by the text.

Fitting Text to Curve

Wrapping text around an object has its alter ego: putting text inside a shape, so it looks as though the text itself forms a shape. And there's a third variation called Fitting Text To Curve—you can have Artistic Text follow an arc, a freeform line, and an open or closed shape, and you have options for the style in which the text follows your line.

Pouring Text into a Shape

The simplest way to form text so it appears to have a geometry other than rectangular, is to first create a shape, copy some text to the clipboard if you don't have a message in mind, and then carefully position your Text Tool just inside the line of the shape (perhaps 1/8th of a screen inch inside) until the cursor turns into an I-beam with a tiny text box at its lower right. Then click to start typing, or click and then press CTRL+V to paste your clipboard text. Text inside a shape is Paragraph Text, and it obeys all the Paragraph Text formatting conventions covered in this chapter. Here's an example of a creative use for shaped Paragraph Text: the following mock article is about buttons, so the shape of the Paragraph Text might look appropriate if it were shaped like…a button:

Creating a Round Text Frame

1. With the Ellipse Tool (F7) selected, hold CTRL to constrain the ellipse to a circle, and then drag a shape in the document about 4" wide. Check the Property Bar if necessary to get an approximation of the 4" circle.

2. With the Text Tool, hover the cursor just inside the circle until it turns into the special cursor, and then click. The insertion point for text is inside the circle. You can start typing or paste text from the clipboard.

14

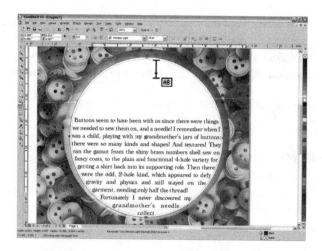

3. Format the text (Full justification works well). If you need a headline inside the circle shape, put the cursor before the first word in the paragraph, and then press ENTER a number of times until there's room for the headline.

4. In this example, there's a background photo behind the text, and the outline of the bounding circle should be invisible. You select the circle with the Pick Tool (check the Status Bar to make sure the circle and not the text is selected), and then right-click the No Outline swatch on the color line.

FIGURE 14-13 Create visual gestalt! Make your text look like the graphic.

Alternatively, one very popular treatment for text "bound" to an object is the arc of text. This is accomplished by first creating the arc shape (a circle usually works well), and then instead of clicking inside the shape, you hover your Text Tool cursor above the shape until it becomes a Text Tool with a tiny swooping curve beneath it.

Follow these steps to flow text in a semi-circle:

Text Along a Curve

1. Create a circle using the Ellipse Tool.

2. With the Text Tool, position the cursor just above the outline of the circle; then click an insertion point and begin to type. You'll see that the text follows the curve.

3. If the text isn't aligned to your liking, use the Horizontal Offset spin box on the Property Bar to correct it.

4. If you'd like the text to be a little off the curve, use the Vertical Offset spin box.

5. If you'd like a truly wild and interesting style or treatment of the text, such as a 3D ribbon look, check out the drop-down list at left on the Property Bar. Click any style to apply it. Figure 14-14 shows an example of an award; the circle still has an outline, but it takes one right-click to correct that.

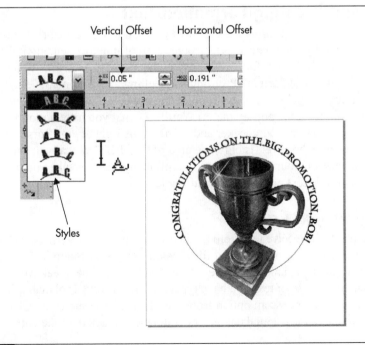

FIGURE 14-14   Use Fit Text To Curve to make your message a flowing one.

Embedding Objects into Text

Graphic objects and bitmaps can be embedded into blocks of Artistic and Paragraph Text—in the layout profession, this is called an *inline graphic*. This is great for adding special symbols to text, such as logotypes, bullet points, or horizontal separators, or for embedding instructional graphics such as mouse cursor images.

You can embed an object into text in two ways:

- **With the clipboard**   Copy or cut the object to the clipboard (CTRL+C or CTRL+X), click the Text Tool in the text where you want the object to be placed, and paste the object (CTRL+V).

- **Drag-and-drop**   Select the object with the mouse, and then drag it with the *right* mouse button to the position in the text where you want it to appear—a vertical bar between characters in the text indicates where the object will be placed. Release the mouse button and select Copy Into Text or Move Into Text from the pop-up menu.

Embedded objects are treated as "special characters"—they can be selected only with the Text Tool or the Shape Tool. To resize an object after it has been embedded, select it and set its point size on the Property Bar as if it were a typographic character.

To delete an embedded object, select it with the Text Tool and press DELETE.

Changing and Proofing Formatted Text

Once you have your text formatted the way you want it, it's still editable text, and as such, if you've entered it by hand, you should probably proof it before sending it off for printing. There's no equity in 12,000 four-color posters that proudly exclaim, "Enter The Millyun Dollar Speling Contest!", right? Proofing for spelling and grammar is easy: you select the text with either the Pick or the Text Tool, and then press CTRL+F12 (or right-click and then choose Spelling from the pop-up menu). You'll see that you have not only a spelling checker, but also a grammar checker and a Thesaurus right at your cursor tip.

Spell checking, however, is only one area of CorelDRAW that you can use to put the finishing touches on your text message; the following sections take you through other features and a little text preflight for your work.

Changing Text Case

Occasionally you'll receive text from a client who inadvertently uses the CAPS LOCK key, or you have a really, really old plaintext file created using a DOS application. In any event, all caps in a text message, unless it's a very brief headline, can be a real eyesore.

To change the case of text you have typed, insert the Text Tool cursor in text and then right-click the text: choose an option from the Change Case submenu. Changing the case of characters replaces the original characters with new characters of the correct case.

Hyphenation

It's bad form to have two or more consecutive lines of text with a hyphen at the end, and this sometimes happens when you use a specific column width or frame shaping.

■ To remove hyphenation from a paragraph, choose the text with either the Pick Tool or the Text Tool, choose Text, and then uncheck Use Hyphenation.

■ To manually hyphenate a line after hyphenation is turned off, you can put your cursor between the characters you want to break and then press CTRL+SHIFT+-. Alternatively, click the insertion point with the Text Tool and then choose Text | Insert Formatting Code | Optional Hyphen.

Converting Paragraph Text to Curves

It is possible to convert Paragraph Text to curves. By converting text to curves, the resulting shapes can be extensively modified, reshaped, and restyled. This is also a method for preventing others from making any text modifications to the document. It is also an acceptable way to prepare text-heavy illustrations for sharing when you're confident that a coworker doesn't own a font you used in the document.

To convert a Paragraph Text object to curves, select it and choose Arrange | Convert To Curves. Or right-click the Text object with the Pick Tool, and choose Convert To Curves from the pop-up menu or press CTRL-Q. Because Paragraph Text as curves can have thousands of nodes, don't perform this sort of thing capriciously, and be prepared to wait a while during the conversion of large paragraphs. CorelDRAW converts Paragraph Text to curves quite intelligently; it breaks the text into groups—groups almost never consisting of a single shape that has more than 1,000 nodes. PostScript printing language has a complexity threshold of 1,000–1,200 nodes along a single path. If you ever arrive at a single curve shape that has more than this number, you're best off breaking the shape (Arrange | Break Curve Apart, CTRL+K) and then joining shapes that should be joined (Arrange | Combine, CTRL+L). Use too many nodes, and a PostScript job will fail, and a commercial printer is not likely to thank you for your business.

14

Text and Styles

After you've created a specific look for text, it would be a shame not to be able to save it as a style so it can be reused later. You can create styles for Artistic and Paragraph Text in CorelDRAW. *Styles* store the text attributes from one object and can be used to apply those attributes to other objects at a later time in the same document (styles are by default local properties). If you edit the properties of a style, all the text formatted with that style is updated immediately.

To save a style, with the Pick Tool, choose the text, right-click, and then choose Styles | Save Style Properties, and you'll get a box that looks like the following illustration. This box is valid for objects as well. Object styles can also be applied for fill and outline settings.

Creating and Editing Styles

In the Save Style As dialog, select only those formatting options that you want as part of the style. If, for example, you select the Text option but clear the Fill and Outline options, then applying this new style to some text will only modify the type-related properties and will keep the existing fill and outline.

Give the style a new, unique name. Click OK, and the style is created and ready for use on the Graphic And Text docker, which is opened by pressing CTRL+F5 and choosing Window | Dockers | Graphic And Text Styles. With the Text Tool, you drag the title of your saved style and drop it onto a text object you want formatted. Alternatively, right-click the Text object and choose Styles | Apply in the pop-up menu; then choose the style you want from the list.

 When a Text object is selected with the Pick Tool, double-clicking a saved style on the Graphic and Text docker's list of styles will apply that style to the Text object.

Editing Text Styles

To edit a style, right-click its title on the Graphic And Text Styles docker, and then choose Properties. This opens the Options dialog at the Styles page under Document, with the style selected in the list, from where you can enable and disable features of the style. You can also edit the settings of the style by clicking the Font, Fill, or Outline Edit button in the Options dialog.

To delete a style from the docker, right-click it and choose Delete. You cannot delete default styles.

 To revert some text to its assigned style, either reapply the style or right-click and choose Styles | Revert To Style from the pop-up menu.

You have in front of you a very handy and thorough documentation of how to make a text message stand out in the marketplace—how to attract attention in a polished, professional manner. From drop caps to justification, leading to indents, these aren't just a typographer's tools, but tools for everyone who needs to communicate visually. After a while, what you used to consider an extraordinary effort to accomplish with text will feel quite natural and even ordinary. At this point, it's time to move to Chapter 15, where some *extra*ordinary techniques are demonstrated: adding special effects to text.

CHAPTER 15

Creating Your Own Font

At some point in your work as a designer, you'll need a special font—something you can't locate online, something that perfectly complements a drawing—perhaps a typeface that contains a logo that you want to distribute to employees for letterhead stationery.

You can design the characters of your dream font right in CorelDRAW and export your work as a typeface that you and others can use. In this chapter you'll learn how to set up a page layout specifically for creating fonts, design a simple but interesting typeface, discover some of the secrets to professional font-making, and construct a typeface template you can reuse. Because a digital typeface's characters actually are simple drawings, this chapter also makes it easy to make a logo font for business. Naturally, some rules are covered in this

Type 1 or TrueType?

CorelDRAW X4 can export your font design to Adobe Type 1—one of the oldest file formats for digital typefaces—and to the TTF file format, TrueType, a font format shared by Windows and Macintosh users. Which format you choose depends largely on how skilled you are in file management and how much free space you have on your hard drive(s). Type 1, invented before operating systems were capable of displaying fonts onscreen almost exactly as they appear in print, uses two separate files: a PFM (PostScript Font Metrics) file and a PFB (PostScript Font Binary) file. CorelDRAW automatically generates the PFM file for you if you choose to export to Type 1 (listed as PFB on the Save File As Type drop-down list in the Export dialog). Windows uses this file to display fonts onscreen, but the PFB file is the one that actually contains the vector information for the font so it can be printed.

As you can imagine, if a PFM file is lost or misplaced, the corresponding PFB file is pretty useless. This is the primary reason why you might want to choose TrueType as the file format for your fonts. Similarly, a PFM file without the corresponding PFB lacks the font outline information, so you're sunk. One of the advantages to writing your font to TrueType is that the outlines when you type with it are exceptionally smooth. This is because TrueType uses more nodes in the outline than a similar Type 1 version. And this is also the disadvantage to writing all your fonts to TrueType format. The more nodes it takes to describe the outline of a character, the larger the file size is: approximately 1 byte per node. This seems like a trifle, but it eventually adds up. Some symbol fonts that are more than 200K in TrueType format can be written to less than 100K as Type 1's. Another consideration is how many nodes on a character are required to describe the shape of the character. Type 1 files require that a character have fewer than 200 nodes; there is no real limit to the number of nodes in a TrueType character.

chapter for building a font that works correctly, and it's a good idea to review Chapters 10 and 11 if you're not totally comfortable yet with drawing paths and editing them. The payoff, however, is a new skill, the ability to create a font unlike anything anyone has seen on the Web, and a tool you've created from knowing the tools in CorelDRAW.

Basic Setup Rules and a Custom Template

By digital typographical convention, characters are set up on a 1,000×1,000-unit grid. The units don't actually have a label such as "inches" or "centimeters," but to get a bearing here, 1,000 points is valid and works for making the characters in a font. The characters you draw won't fill the entire height of the page, and some can extend below the page (for descenders in characters such as *q* and *y*) and occasionally to the right of the page for characters such as *W*. Ultimately, you'll export each character by using CorelDRAW's Export dialog for TrueType and/or Type 1 fonts, and in this dialog you can scale your page so characters are exported in their entirety.

The wisest approach to creating a digital font is to set up a custom page size, add guidelines, and then to create new pages for the document as you design the characters in the typeface. Probably the hardest part of designing anything is finding a place to start. Begin by creating a custom page and adding guidelines, as shown in this tutorial.

Making a Template for a Digital Typeface

1. In a new document, double-click on the Page border (or choose Layout | Page Setup). This displays the Page Setup options menu.

2. Choose Points from the Units drop-down list, and then type **1000** in both the Width and Height fields.

3. Uncheck the Apply Changes To Current Page Only box.

4. It's a good idea to save this custom page size: click Save Page Size, and then type something you'll remember in the Custom Page Type box, as shown in Figure 15-1. Click OK, and then click OK in the Options dialog to apply your changes. In the future, the Typography page size can be accessed from the Page Selector drop-down list on the Property Bar.

5. A very good question to ask now is, "How large should the upper- and lowercase letters be?" A good answer is to use a font installed on your system to size up your own font's measurements—to type an upper- and lowercase letter from, say Arial, on the page, make it the final size, and then drag guidelines from the Rulers for your own character-building. With the Text Tool, click the cursor to make an insertion point as close as possible to the lower-left corner of the page, and then type **Aa**.

15

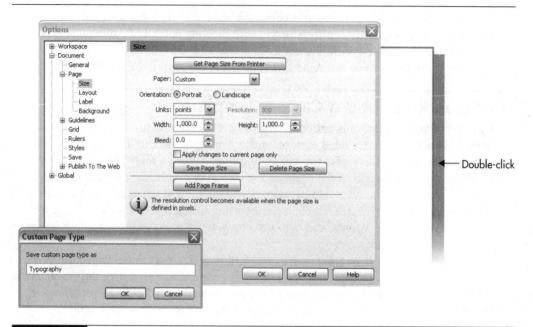

← Double-click

FIGURE 15-1 Create a custom-size page and apply special units for the Rulers to make a document suitable for building digital typefaces.

6. With the Pick Tool, select the text, and then type **1000** in the Points field on the Property Bar; press ENTER to apply the value.

7. With the Pick Tool, use your mouse wheel to zoom very close to the lower-left corner of the page, and then click-drag the Artistic Text so it exactly touches the lower-left corner.

8. From the Rulers, drag guidelines so they touch the top of the capital *A*, the left edge of the capital *A*, the bottom of the capital *A* (this is the *baseline* of the font) and the top of the lowercase *a*. You're not done with the guidelines, nor are you finished with the "stand-in" text on the page, but you do have a good working template for designing your own font now.

9. Choose File | Save As Template. Save the document in CorelDRAW's CDT file format; keep it open for further refinements. The document should look like that shown next.

Think of these color pages as an "Idea Book." They show the result of variations on techniques you'll learn in the chapters mentioned in the text.

Patterns can be created by tracing over photographs using Artistic Media brushes. Create a grouping and add the Perspective Effect, and you can pre-visualize your pattern on packaging.

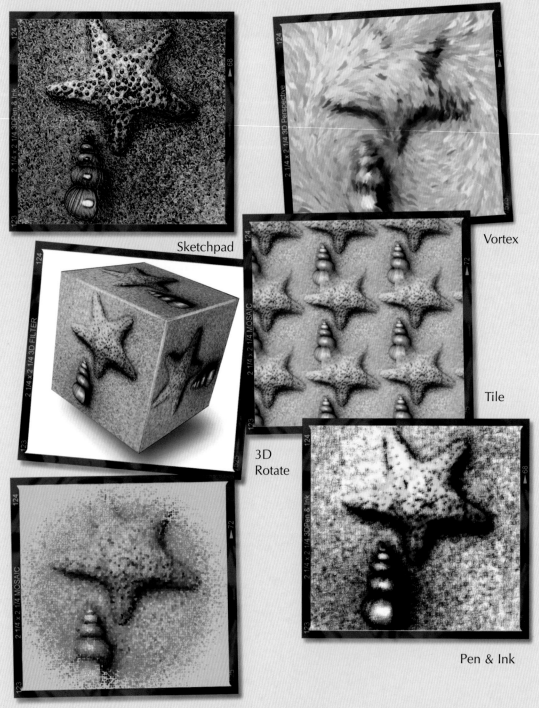

Sketchpad

Vortex

Tile

3D
Rotate

Pen & Ink

Mosaic

Choose from scores of special image effects to
apply to bitmap images. Check out Chapter 27.

Create a shape into which you "pour" Paragraph Text.

Create drop caps for the first line or all paragraphs.

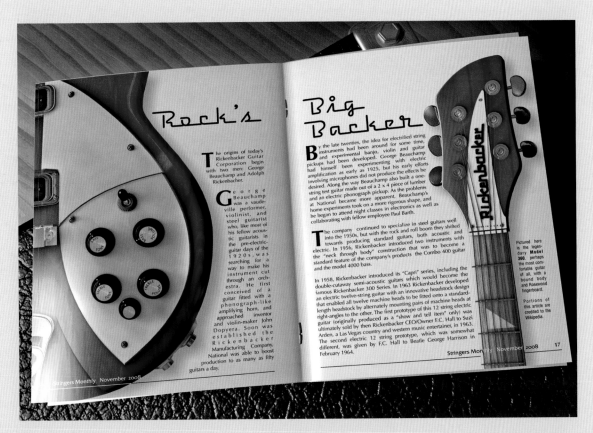

Part IV guides you through the use of typography. Create magazine layouts that command attention.

If you're handy with a pen, digitally shading your physical artwork is easy. Scan it, bring the bitmap into CorelDRAW, and then let PowerTRACE (see Chapter 27) create vector shapes to which you can apply Fountain Fills.

SILENTLY, CAPTAIN APEX SURVEYS THE SLEEPING CITY BELOW...

Your client loves your logo, but wants a "greener" color treatment. No problem. Name your colors as Styles in CorelDRAW (see Chapter 19), and then redefine your original colors.

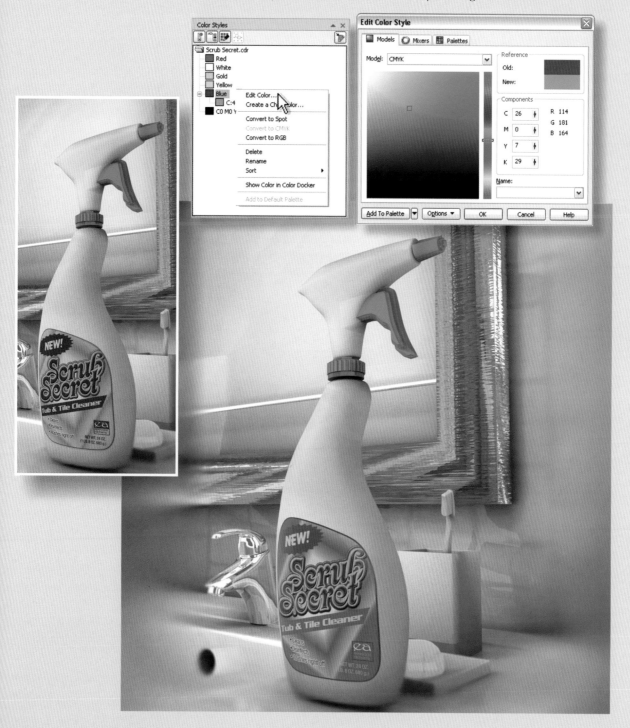

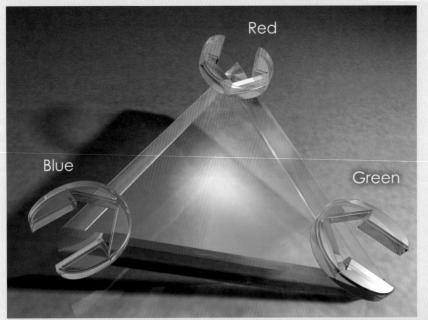

The RGB color model is additive; red, green, and blue channels add to make other colors, and at full intensity, they make white. Chapter 19 covers color models and color theory.

The CMYK color model is subtractive; cyan, magenta, yellow, and a key plate of black create the range of colors used in commercial printing.

The HSB color model is an artist-friendly arrangement of color components. See Chapter 19 for the use of this model in CorelDRAW.

Because hi-fidelity images are organized into channels, an additional channel can be made to specify transparency. See Chapter 27 on alpha channels and bitmap compositions.

A good logo design can be dimensionalized using CorelDRAW's Extrude Effect (see Chapter 25). From there, you can use and reuse your logo on shirts, flyers, business cards—you name it!

TIP	*By default, the templates that come with CorelDRAW are stored in the CorelDRAW application folder (probably C:\Program Files\CorelDRAW Graphics Suite unless you chose a different folder during installation), in CorelDRAW Graphics Suite X4\ Languages\EN\Draw\Templates. This is a good place to store your own templates. If for some reason CorelDRAW does not display your templates when you choose File	New From Template, click the Browse button in the New From Template dialog, and then choose the path to this folder.*

You'll notice something funny going on right now: although you specified 1,000-point text and the page is set up to 1,000 points in height for the imaginary font grid, the guideline you dragged to the top of the capital *A* shows that this character is only 716 points. This discrepancy occurs for two reasons:

- The gap from the top of the letter to the top of the page is for descenders of letters from the line above when you type with the font.

- The 1,000-point grid is only a reference that designers work against. You'll find some font capital letters are taller and some are shorter, as specified by the font's creator.

Refining and Resaving the Template

The template requires two more guidelines, and although in theory you'll be finished with the Arial font in the current template, it would be nice to hang onto it for reference as a custom, user-created guide. First, to create a complete typeface, you'll need a guideline for where a descender (in *g*'s, *y*'s, *q*'s) should end, and a good typeface would also contain a hyphen (-) and an em dash (—): their positions are easy to determine based on the current font on the page.

Follow these steps to finish off the template so you can get down to drawing characters for your font:

Creating More Guidelines

1. With the Artistic Text selected with the Pick Tool, press CTRL+C to copy and then CTRL+V to paste the text in exact alignment with the original text.

2. With the Text Tool, highlight both characters of the duplicate text, then type **g**, then type a hyphen.

3. With the Pick Tool and the text selected, apply a color other than black so you can see what you're doing; red is good.

4. Drag a guideline from the horizontal Ruler to the point where the descender of the *g* ends.

5. Drag a guideline to the bottom of the hyphen. Choose Window | Dockers | Object Manager for your next move. Now your screen should look like this illustration.

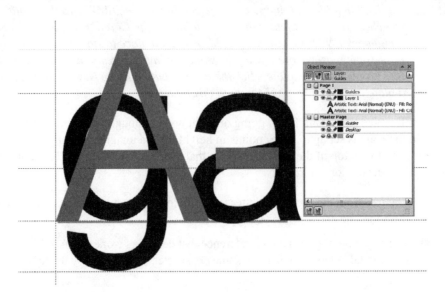

6. Click-drag the Artistic Text titles, one at a time, to a position on the Object Manager directly below the Master Guides layer, as shown here. By doing this, you'll have the characters you typed as a visual guide on all the pages you create for the different characters in your font.

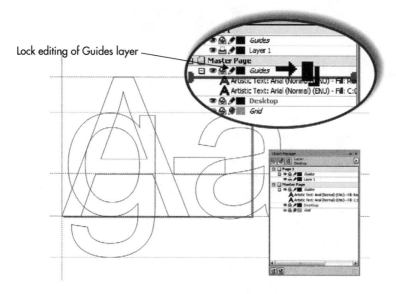

Lock editing of Guides layer

7. Lock the Master Guides layer from editing (and from accidentally moving the guide characters) by clicking its Pencil icon.

8. Save the document again as a template (File | Save As Template), overwriting this file as it existed earlier.

Drawing a Centerline, Not an Outline

The only real qualifier for characters you design for a digital font is that the shape must be one single shape, vector in format. This means as part of the font creation routine, you'll use the Shaping operations a lot to combine several objects into a single one. But that's about it: typefaces don't use fancy fills, but rather a digital typeface just has to have outline (path) information for each character.

You can take three different approaches to drawing the characters that make up a typeface:

■ If you're handy with a felt-tip pen and own a scanner, you could bring the bitmap images into CorelDRAW and then use PowerTRACE (see Chapter 27) to auto-trace every character. Using this approach, as shown in Figure 15-2, often leads to a natural style, full of little irregularities, for the typeface characters. Routinely, you'll need to manually edit the result of the tracing to eliminate superfluous nodes and to make other minor consistency corrections. Alternatively, you could bring in your scanned image, lock it on

15

FIGURE 15-2   Corel PowerTRACE is available with CorelDRAW for tracing bitmap characters to vector format.

a layer, create a new layer, and then manually trace over the characters you physically drew. This takes more time, but adds consistency as you draw.

- Drawing each character by hand. This approach often leads to gross inconsistencies between character stem widths—the strokes that make up a character are called *stems*—and even to inconsistency with a single character's parts. This is a time-consuming process, and you can't reuse the basic structure of each character, as you can by defining centerlines for the stems of each character and then giving the stems different properties.

- Making centerlines for characters, then applying outline properties. This is the way to go for speed, stem consistency, and reusability of your character designs, and it's the approach shown in this chapter. Here's the idea: you draw a "skeleton" of a capital *A*, for example, a teepee shape with a crossbar, so you have two paths, three maximum. You can now apply a wide outline to the paths, even put a round-line cap on the strokes (see Chapter 18). Then at some point, you choose Arrange | Convert Outline To Object on a copy of your paths, and before you know it, you have a character whose stem widths are completely consistent. After you combine the paths, the combined shape qualifies for export as a TrueType character. Better still, you can apply an Artistic Media stroke to your capital *A*, and then later use the Break Apart command. CorelDRAW saves your original paths, and with a little refining, the Artistic Media object becomes an elegant, intricate character perfect for exporting to a font. In the illustration here you can see three examples: a manually drawn character, a character made by increasing the outline width and then converting it to an object, and a character made with a centerline and with Artistic Media then applied.

Just drawing   Centerline with   Centerline with Artistic
                    wide outline and   Media applied
                    rounded caps

Professional Fonts

It's beyond the scope of this book to describe how commercial, professional fonts are created, not because CorelDRAW doesn't have the tools, but because typography is an art unto itself and requires many years of developing the skill and knowledge to produce such contemporary classics as Garamond, commonly credited to Tony Stan in the 1970s. The typeface you're reading in this book has serifs (the small extensions to the stroke stems on each character), and Roman-style typefaces have thick and thin stems that need to be carefully calculated for character consistency and legibility at small point sizes. Therefore, creating a commercial typeface that you could, for example, sell for $300, is not the point of this chapter. You need both an artist's skills in CorelDRAW and a typographer's skills to make the big bucks. However, you can indeed make interesting fonts for personal and in-house use and make symbol fonts. This chapter is intended as a guide to making a basic typeface and to exporting the characters to TrueType file format.

Using Artistic Media on a Centerline for Characters

As covered in Chapter 10, Artistic Media Pens can be used by click-dragging on a page with the tool, or the media that surrounds any path can be applied at any time by using the Artistic Media docker. Artistic Media presents a wonderful opportunity to make elegant characters from a "skeleton" path, and it's also a great timesaver, as you'll soon see. To qualify as a bona fide TrueType and Type 1 character in a digital font, Artistic Media strokes need to be simplified before you export them: digital fonts must consist of only paths (usually closed paths) to indicate the shape of a character, while the space outside the path is empty space (the inside of the letter *o,* for example). Artistic Media strokes, at least most of the presets that ship with CorelDRAW, can consist of several objects. Therefore, an Artistic Media character needs to become a single object before it's exported. But let's tackle first things first.

Basically, no one but you can tell you what your own typeface's characters should look like; but in English-speaking countries, you're probably best off with a capital *A* that looks like two strokes converging at the top with a crossbar somewhere in the center—you get the idea. Therefore, your best working tool is probably the Bézier Pen Tool because it handles both straight strokes and curves, and you can use the Arial font on the Master Guides layer to determine a centerline for your font creation, just to get you started. A *centerline* is necessary to provide a "skeleton" upon which you hang Artistic Media strokes. It's much easier and provides character *consistency* to first make a centerline for a character and then to apply an Artistic Media stroke than to go click-dragging with an Artistic Media brush from the get-go.

15

Let's cut to the chase: in the illustration here you can see an alphabet composed of paths. Notice that this skeleton for a typeface is a little unusual: it's narrow and the crossbars for characters are lower than you might expect. It's also not a complete alphabet: there are no lowercase letters and only the essential punctuation marks. There are two reasons for presenting this example. First, you'll be able to get through the tutorials in this chapter faster if you have fewer characters to create, and second, a typeface doesn't necessarily need lowercase letters; plenty of commercial typefaces such as Banco (ITC) are uppercase only, because certain fonts are used primarily for large headlines. However, it's a good idea to *map* the uppercase characters you create to both upper- and lowercase keystrokes; this is done during the export process and saves the frustration of having to type with the CAPS LOCK key on! This example typeface, Odyssey, is used in the following examples. You might want to base your own font on these characters; they're very easy to draw.

Let's create the first character now.

Creating the Centerline Characters

Keep in mind when drawing the centerlines of the characters that the center of the lines needs to end before you reach the top and bottom guidelines you created earlier. If you don't end a path, for example, about 30 points (using the 1,000-unit grid you set up earlier) above the baseline, when you apply an Artistic Media stroke, the media will extend below the baseline. Fortunately, because Artistic Media strokes and their underlying paths can be dynamically edited, this is not a big problem.

Follow these steps to create a few characters and to add pages to the document:

 ## Drawing the Characters

1. Choose File | New From Template, and then load the template you set up earlier.

2. The Bézier Pen is probably the best tool for drawing both curve and straight segments, so choose it from the Toolbox.

3. Drag a guideline to about 30 points above the baseline guideline; this will be the baseline for the skeleton of the character. Artistic Media will extend your strokes to meet the actual font baseline at the bottom of the page. You might not even want the Arial font as a guide in this document if you're following the structure of the Odyssey typeface for your own font. You can unlock the Master Guides layer and delete the Artistic Text.

4. Click-drag the upside-down *U* path, starting at the path baseline, extending up but not reaching the capital character (the *cap height*) guideline in the template, and then click-drag down to reach the path baseline guideline. You can now press ENTER to end the path.

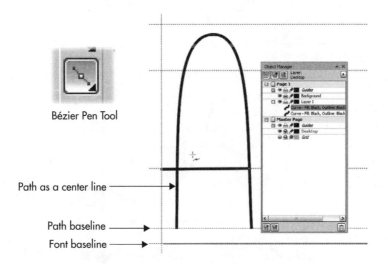

Bézier Pen Tool

Path as a center line ⟶

Path baseline ⟶
Font baseline ⟶

5. Click a start and an end point with the Bézier Pen Tool to create a horizontal crossbar for the capital *A*; press ENTER to end the stroke. The illustration here shows the two paths with an 8-point-wide outline, only so you can see it here. Eventually the path's outline will be hidden by Artistic Media, so use any width outline you like as you work.

6. Click the Add Page button at the lower left of the interface. You should have all your Master Guides in place; now, off to the character *B* in the typeface. You'll get the routine: draw the character, add a page. However, don't confine yourself to using the Bézier Pen Tool, particularly when you get to *C* and *D*. These characters can more easily be described using an arc, and arcs are quickly created by using the Ellipse Tool, then click-dragging outside of the shape on the nodes to make the arc, as shown in the following figure. As you're designing, don't forget to reuse paths by copying, going to the page where you need a path, then pasting. For example, the

15

crossbar of the *A* can (and should) be reused as the top of the capital *T* and as the crossbars of the *E* and *F*; the *O* can be reused for part of the *Q* and also works for the zero in this font. Consistency is the name of the game to ensure a good-looking typeface.

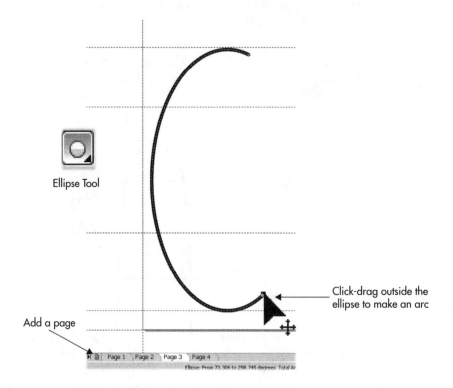

Ellipse Tool

Click-drag outside the ellipse to make an arc

Add a page

Side Bearings: Where to Position Your Characters

Even though you drew the characters according to the guidelines, there's a little bit of page relocation that needs to happen before you export the characters. The tops and bottoms of the characters are probably fine, but when you type using this font, think of where the character will begin. Characters have *side bearings*: you can set the right side-bearing when you export the character, but it's usually a good idea to set the left side-bearing (the point where the character begins) according to how you designed the font. This Odyssey typeface has crossbars that overshoot some characters such as the *A* to the left. If you were to type some words with this font, you'd see that the crossbar needs to extend beyond the left of the page just a little, thus making words you type look evenly spaced. In your own work you might not design a typeface like this, but if you do, here and now is the time to move the character so that any part of the character you want tucked into the character that precedes it, does so on the document page. In the illustration here you can see what the *A* looks like compared with the page guidelines—the crossbar extends just a little outside of the imaginary 1,000-point grid on the page—and when the *A* appears in a word and a sentence, overall the spacing looks good.

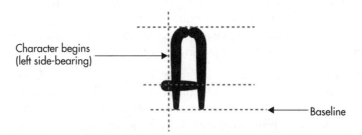

Character begins
(left side-bearing)

Baseline

The Fun Part: Applying Artistic Media

It's quite a lot of work drawing the centerlines, but here's the part where it all pays off: applying Artistic Media strokes to the characters. As mentioned before, you're *not* locked into a look for the characters—it's quite easy to separate the Artistic Media objects from your centerlines (CTRL+K), use a different Artistic Media style, and possibly get five or six entirely different-looking typefaces using the same centerlines! Consistency, however, again is important; it would be a good idea to settle on an Artistic Media style and to keep that style for all the characters.

Depending on how you drew your characters, you might or might not get exactly the look you're seeking because Artistic Media wraps itself around the entire length of a path,

Limitations and Workaround to Paths with Artistic Media

If you think a path is too long to take an Artistic Media stroke in an eye-pleasing way, you use the Shape Tool to break the path where you think it should break. You right-click and then choose the Break Apart command. But you're not done, because the broken path is still one compound object. You press CTRL+K (Arrange | Break Apart) and life is then good. However, this is a lot to remember, so here is a "worst-case scenario": once Artistic Media is applied to a path, no Break Apart command is available. You need to select the Artistic Media stroke on the page, not the underlying path; break the Artistic Media from the path (CTRL+K); delete the media object; and then work on the path and reapply the Artistic Media to the broken, individual path segments.

including bends and turns. Therefore, a stem for a character might need to be split to get exactly the detail you need—this and other techniques are covered in the following tutorial.

Stroking a Character Path

1. Choose Window | Dockers | Artistic Media. The steps you'll follow could use any type of Artistic Media, but for this example, let's just work with a Default Stroke. You can hide the Brushes and Object Sprayer categories from the selector list by clicking the flyout button and checking only the Preset.

2. Because it was recommended earlier to set a baseline for the paths above the font baseline, you're free to choose from the selector a stroke that has a round tip at its beginning. For simplicity's sake, click a path in the character with the Pick Tool, and then click the very top stroke in the list, as shown in Figure 15-3. If the stroke looks too thin, increase its width using the Artistic Media Tool Width spin box on the Property Bar. As you can see with the *W* character here, the stroke doesn't work very well; it really should break at the bottom node so both segments of the *V* shape that make up the *W* get the full tapering effect. This won't be a problem with the short crossbars to characters and with single strokes such as the capital *I*, but there's a fix for this seeming problem. Tutorials are often about problem/solution situations.

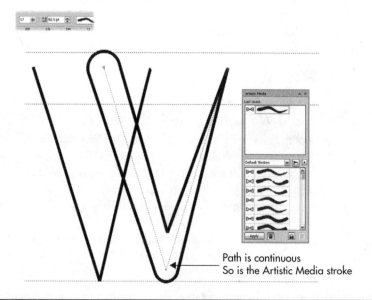

Path is continuous
So is the Artistic Media stroke

| FIGURE 15-3 | Artistic Media travels the length of a path. |

3. With the Shape Tool, right-click over the node on the centerline, which is invisible unless you go to View | Simple Wireframe, but you probably have a good idea where the path is lurking. You can right-click on the path, which then reveals itself as a faint blue line; then it's easy to spot the path node.

4. Click the Break Curve button on the Property Bar. You'll see that the Artistic Media changes; it's wrapping around two parts of one path now, so you're close to the finished character, as you can see in Figure 15-4.

5. With the Shape Tool, drag one of the bottom nodes (horizontally) away from the other until you have a good view of both unconnected bottom nodes.

6. Hold SHIFT and then click the bottom node of one of the broken path segments; then click the top node of the same segment so they are both selected.

7. Click the Reverse Curve Direction button on the Property Bar, as shown in Figure 15-5 (before reversal at left, after reversal at right). You're almost there.

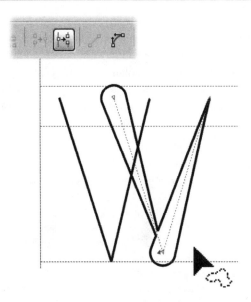

FIGURE 15-4 Break the path at the bottom node to make the Artistic Media travel along two path segments.

15

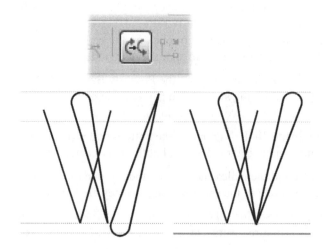

FIGURE 15-5 Reverse the path segment to reverse the Artistic Media stroke.

8. Drag the bottom node on the path segment close to, but not directly over, its original position, so the Artistic Media strokes overlap, but *don't* drag the node directly *on top* of the other segment's node. By default, CorelDRAW rejoins broken paths, and if you allow the bottom node to touch the other node, you're back to step 4! See the following illustration for the right and wrong position for the node you need to move.

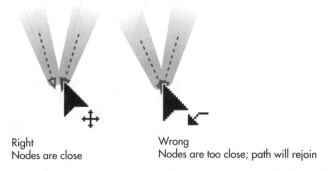

Right
Nodes are close

Wrong
Nodes are too close; path will rejoin

9. This is the biggest step: take what you've learned in this tutorial and apply Artistic Media, the same Preset, to all the characters in the typeface on all the pages. If it helps to visualize your characters, you can give them a fill and no outline property when your editing work is done. After you've applied the Artistic Media to all the path segments of your characters, it's time to detach the strokes from their paths and to export all the characters to your own typeface.

You might want to copy some of the characters to a new document window, and line them up to get a better visual idea of how your typeface will look when you actually type with it. The following illustration shows a few of the characters from this typeface; they align nicely and there's good consistency because of all the preplanning, setting up of guidelines, and use of the same Artistic Media stroke for all the letters.

Exporting your Typeface

Depending on the strokes you used on your paths, the next thing you'll want to do is review the characters to make certain the baseline of the character meets the baseline guideline; similarly, the top of the Artistic Media stroke should meet the Cap Height guideline. Some of the Artistic Media strokes begin with a butt cap (the stroke ends in a straight line, defined using the Outline Pen properties), while the one recommended in this chapter's tutorials has a round cap. Adjusting the strokes is not a big deal; because the media is dynamically linked to the paths, use the Shape Tool to move nodes until the ends of the Artistic Media strokes meet the proper guidelines.

It's time now to break the Artistic Media strokes from the paths. Follow these steps; they're easy and the process goes quite quickly:

Converting Artistic Media Strokes to Objects

1. Go to the first page of your document or wherever the first letter of your alphabet is.

2. Select an Artistic Media stroke with the Pick Tool, and then press CTRL+K to break the stroke from the underlying path. Deselect by clicking an empty space on the page. You might want to click on the Artistic Media stroke now to confirm that it's now an object and not bound to the path. The Status Bar should tell you that a Curve is selected and a number of nodes on the curve are displayed. It should also help here to choose View | Wireframe; this view doesn't show object fills, so you can see the path in the center of the (former) Artistic Media stroke, another confirmation that the Break Apart command was successful.

3. Repeat step 2 with all remaining paths until you see all your paths and the surrounding objects.

4. SHIFT-click on all the objects, and not on the paths.

5. Click the Weld button on the Property Bar, as shown in Figure 15-6.

6. You can go through all the letters in the typeface and repeat steps 2–6, but this tutorial will continue to the export process now. It's simply a choice about your workflow whether to "husk" and weld the characters in one session, or to perform this process page by page.

Exporting your Finished Font

The hard part is over; CorelDRAW's dialogs will guide you through exporting your characters to a typeface, but you'll need to understand some of the typographer's terms in the dialogs. What you need to do before exporting the characters is to break the Artistic Media from the underlying paths—you've used this command before; it's CTRL+K. Then, as mentioned earlier, every character needs to be composed of a combined path, one single object, to qualify it as a TrueType character. This, too, is a simple task: once the media is detached from the paths, they're closed path objects, and the Weld Shaping command (available on the Property Bar) makes quick work of creating one object per typeface character.

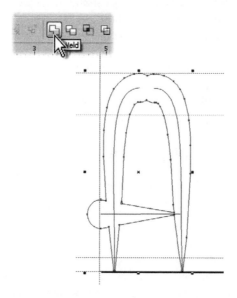

FIGURE 15-6 Use the Weld operation to make all the components of the character into a single object.

Follow these steps to export your typeface!

Exporting a Character to a Digital Font

1. With the welded object but none of the paths selected, click the Export button on the Property Bar.

2. In the Save As Type drop-down list in the Export dialog, you can choose PFB-Adobe Type 1 font, but for reasons discussed earlier, unless you absolutely must have a Type 1 font, choose TTF-TrueType Font now, check the Selected Only box, and then give the font a name you'll remember later. You can change the TrueType Font Name later the same way you rename any other file; its filename has nothing to do with the font's name as it appears in Font drop-down lists. Click Export.

3. You're greeted by the first in a series of dialog boxes, as shown in the illustration here. This one, Options, wants the name of the font (Family Name). Type the name of your typeface as you want it to appear on CorelDRAW's and all other applications' font list. Think about this one, because it's nearly impossible to change later without buying a font utility. It's not a Symbol Font, so don't check this box; the Style is Normal (not Bold, not Italic); and the grid you used is 1,000 units. Leading is a relative issue and in this example you can set the Leading to 0 because you only used about 700 of the 1,000-unit grid for the height of the characters. Finally, Space Width is the space between words—"Space" is actually a character in a typeface. This is a narrow font; usually 300 units is a good value, and perhaps 280 is best for this font, cheating a little narrow due to the characters being narrow. Click OK, click Yes to respond to "Save changes to Font File?", and it's on to the next dialog.

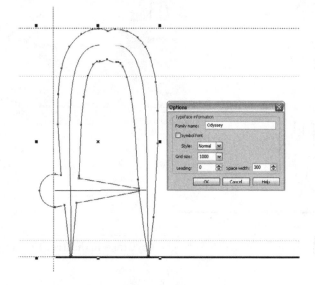

4. Here's where the show takes place. By default, Character Width is set to Auto, and usually this is a good option. However, the right vertical line in the preview window shows exactly where the character ends and where the next character you type with the finished, installed font begins. You can call this *kerning* (intercharacter spacing). Eyeball this preview window (there's really no way to judge before you use the font); if the space looks too tight, uncheck Auto, and then use the Character Width spin box controls to increase or decrease the right side-bearing for the character.

5. Click the character in the Character Number box that corresponds to the character you're exporting. In Figure 15-7 you can see the *A* is selected. Click OK, and you have one character in a new font saved.

6. Click the Export button again, and this time there's no Options box—you simply choose the TTF file where you saved it in the Export dialog.

7. Choose the lowercase *a* in the Character Number box this time; then click OK. Now you've used the same character design twice, but when you type, you'll get the same character when you press A, with or without holding SHIFT. There are few things in life as annoying as a typeface that has no lowercase CHARACTERS!

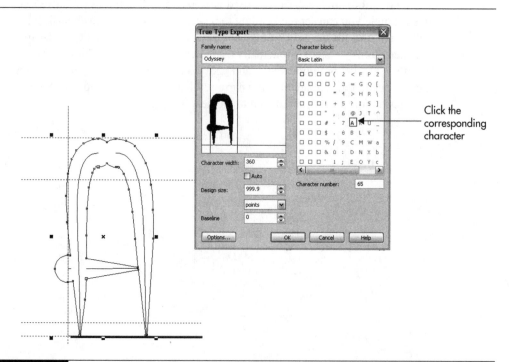

FIGURE 15-7   Assign the selected object a keystroke in the TrueType Export dialog.

8. Continue through the pages and export all the characters, numbers, and punctuation characters. If by chance you assign the wrong Character Number to a character, you can go back, choose the correct one, and CorelDRAW will ask you if you want to overwrite the existing definition. In this case, yes you do.

Under certain conditions, you can export one or more characters to an existing font. Those conditions are as follows:

- You have permission to. There is a coding in commercial typefaces that sometimes is written to prohibit users from tampering with the font. Commercial typefaces fall under the Digital Rights Management Act. They're actually little runtime programs, and unless you have a very real and pressing need to hack a commercial font, don't do it. If you do, don't share it or post it anywhere.

- The font is Type 1 or TrueType. CorelDRAW cannot export to OpenType or other proprietary font file formats.

- You know what you're doing and you have a backup copy of the font. You have to make absolutely certain that your character height, baseline, and other properties match for the characters that you want to write into this font. And this sort of thing can take quite a while to become good at.

Creating a Logo Font

Especially for small businesses, having your logo as a typeface can speed up the office workflow and serve a number of different and valuable purposes. Imagine the letterhead stationery you can generate, at any paper size, when you have a font with your logo in it. You can put that font on a keychain thumb drive and always have it available—at a print house, a convention, or a novelty manufacturer who might not have CorelDRAW on their computers.

A logo font follows the same conventions as a symbol font such as Wingdings and Zapf Dingbats: it's simply a little picture assigned to a keystroke, and you now know most of the procedure. The dimensions of your logo, however, are a consideration; many logos are very wide, and they don't fit well on the grid template you set up earlier. And it's usually not a good idea to scale down the logo to fit the grid width. The result would be a keystroke in the font that requires all your hired help to scale the logo up to 2,000 points in their WordPerfect or Word document! No problem, however: you can break up the logo into two pieces, and the tutorials in this section show you a little about perfectly aligning the pieces so that when they're typed, they create your logo without a seam. The following illustration shows a logo for a fictitious antique company copied and placed on the template you designed at the beginning of this chapter. Get out your own logo or design one now. Then align it on the grid as shown in the following illustration: the left edge needs to meet the left of the page,

15

and the bottom needs to meet the baseline guide—the logo should be about 750 points tall. Just leave the right edge dangling off the right of the page for the moment.

Cutting Your Logo in Two

In this example we lucked out, so the break in the logo can happen between the *N* and the *T* in "ANTIQUES." If your logo is similar, use the Arrange | Break Apart command (CTRL+K) in the area of the design where you need to separate the pieces, and then use the Arrange | Combine (CTRL+L) command after marquee-selecting the components of the logo that are broken apart but shouldn't be. If you have a logo that needs to be split in the middle of an illustration, use the Knife Tool (covered in Chapter 11) with Auto-Close On Cut enabled on the Property Bar and Leave As One Object disabled. Drag a guideline to the cut area to ensure that your cut is clean and perfectly vertical. In the following figure you can see (because the two objects have been recolored only to show this example) that the left side of the logo extends a little to the right of the page grid (this is okay to do), and the other part is off the page, but it will be moved onto the page shortly.

One object   One object

Exporting the Two Logo Pieces

The way it stands now, the logo can be exported to the TrueType file format as two characters, and there's really no immediate need to fill all the keystrokes in the typeface with anything else for the resulting font to be usable. You could put additional symbols or a custom typeface into this new font, but all that's really necessary is to make the alignment of the two pieces perfect when typed using the font, and to assign characters that everyone at this business will easily remember. A lowercase *l* and then a lowercase *c,* for "Lost Coral" is very easy to remember, so all that's left is to export the *l* keystroke—the part of the logo that is aligned to the template, measure the right distance between the first and second part of the logo, and then to align the second part and export it.

Follow these steps to export a logo of your own:

Exporting a Two-Part Logo Font, Part 1

1. Choose File | New From Template, and then browse for the typography template you saved at the beginning of this chapter.

2. Copy your logo to the template and then (if necessary) scale and position the logo as discussed in the previous section.

3. Zoom into the rightmost extent of the first part of the logo. Look at the horizontal Ruler, and drag a guide if necessary, but by all means you'll need to know the width. In this example, the first part of the Lost Coral logo extends a little beyond the page to 1014 points. Write down this number for your own logo font.

4. Select the left part of the logo—the part on the page—and then click the Export button.

5. In the Export dialog, choose TTF-True Type Font from the Save As Type drop-down list, and then name your font file. In this example, it's Lost Coral logo.ttf. Check the Selected Only check box, and then click Export.

6. In the Options dialog, type the name you want your users to see ("Lost Coral logo," in this example) in the Family Name field. This is a Symbol font, so check the Symbol Font check box; the Grid Size is correct at 1000, and the (word) Space width is immaterial—no one is going to press the SPACEBAR when using this logo font—so it can be set to 0, or to about 300 if you plan to add typeface characters to this font later. Click OK and then click Yes in the True Type Export confirmation box.

7. Uncheck the Auto check box for Character Width, and then type the width you saw in step 3. For the Lost Coral logo, the value is 1014; for your own logo, the width might be different.

8. For the Lost Coral logo, the lowercase *l* is a good Character Number. Choose for your own two-part logo a lowercase Character Number that's easy to remember, and then click OK to export the first character.

Here comes the tricky part: the first part of the logo ends exactly at the character width you entered during export. This means there will be absolutely no space between this first character and the next one you export. This is good most of the time, particularly when your logo needs to be perfectly joined when users type the two keystrokes that make the logo.

This Lost Coral logo is a little different, because it breaks between the *N* and the *T*. If your logo is like this one, you're in luck because the following steps show a quick manual way to keep the spacing perfect between characters if your own logo requires this.

Exporting a Two-Part Logo Font, Part 2

1. With the Rectangle Tool, click-drag a rectangle exactly and precisely where you want a gap between the first and second part of the logo font, as shown here.

Use a rectangle to measure distance

2. SHIFT-click the second part of the logo to add it to the selected rectangle.

3. Hold CTRL to constrain movement, and then drag the rectangle and the second part of the logo to the left guideline at the left of the page. Be careful to only drag left—you want the second part of the logo to align to the first part you already exported. Use the LEFT and RIGHT ARROW keys to nudge the two objects if necessary. The rectangle's left side should be touching the left guideline.

4. Select only the second part of the logo now, and then click the Export button. In the Export box make sure Selected Only is checked and that you've chosen the same font as the one you exported the first part of the logo to.

5. Choose the letter you want to represent the second half of the logo. For Lost Coral, the lowercase *c* works fine, as shown here. The user only needs to remember the initials of the place they work!

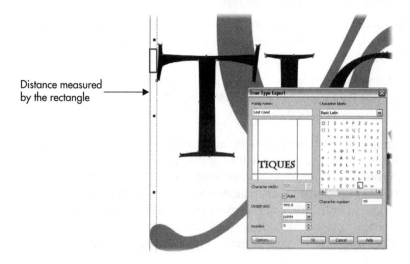

Distance measured by the rectangle

Installing Your Font

Naturally, after your hard work, you want the payoff; it's very simple to install your font right now. Go to the Start menu, choose Control Panel | Fonts. Now that the Fonts window is open, you can drag your font file from an open window where you saved it, into the Fonts window. The font is now available to CorelDRAW and every application that uses typefaces. The Fonts utility in Control Panel copies typefaces; you didn't move the font—but you might want to copy it to a safe location now.

This chapter is an integration chapter; you've seen how to use a lot of CorelDRAW's tools that are documented in previous chapters to actually make a tool of your own: a digital typeface. In Figure 15-8 you can see that some of CorelDRAW's templates were used to create a letterhead envelope, a tri-fold brochure, and even some hang tags, all using a custom font—and all the work you see here took about 15 minutes.

Now that you have a font, you're going to want to type a lot of words. Fortunately, the next chapter shows you how CorelDRAW can help you spell your words correctly, can make grammar suggestions, and can write a SIGGRAPH paper all by itself.

Only kidding about the last part!

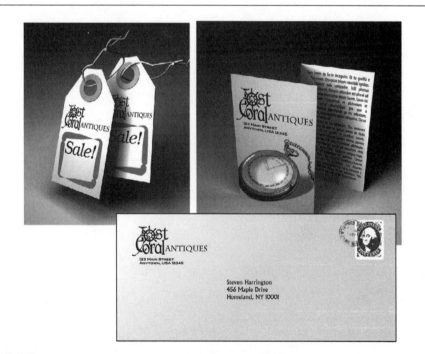

FIGURE 15-8   Use a logo font in combination with templates to make stationery, T-shirt transfers, and all your signature business needs.

CHAPTER 16

Getting Your Words
Perfect

You want your text to look as good as your drawings, and the good news is that the same powerful grammar and spelling tools offered in Corel WordPerfect Office suite are right inside CorelDRAW. Proofing tools including a spell checking system, thesaurus, and grammar checker—in 25 different languages—are at your fingertips. This means you don't have to duck out to your word processor just to proof text that you've entered on-the-fly in a CorelDRAW document.

CorelDRAW also has the same QuickCorrect feature that's in WordPerfect, for correcting common typos and spelling mistakes *as you type*. With QuickCorrect, you can also automatically replace something you've typed with something else—which is extremely helpful for words that you commonly mistype and for common extended characters such as © or ™.

Both CorelDRAW and WordPerfect use the same writing tools, dictionaries, word lists, and configurations. If you add a word to your User Word List in WordPerfect, it is there for you in CorelDRAW. Therefore, when you know how to use the writing tools in WordPerfect, you already know how to use them in CorelDRAW and vice versa. If you're a Microsoft Word user, CorelDRAW's proofing tools are as easy to learn as WordPerfect's—the dialogs and labels are a little different in appearance, but you'll soon get the idea. This chapter takes you through the steps and options you have to step up to the title of Literary Wizard in addition to CorelDRAW Design Guru.

Using CorelDRAW's Writing Tools

Frequently, small to medium businesses communicate with customers around the world; with text proofing in 25 different languages available right out of the box, CorelDRAW makes it easy for you to get your sales language proofed perfectly regardless of whether you minored in French in school. When you install CorelDRAW, choose the languages you are most likely to use (you can go back at any time and install more), and you are ready to check the spelling and grammar of anything that comes your way.

By default, CorelDRAW assigns a language code and checks all text using the proofing tools that correspond to the language your operating system uses. For example, if you use a U.S. English copy of Windows, CorelDRAW automatically installs English–U.S. proofing tools and assigns all text to U.S. English (ENU).

Assigning Language Codes

If your document contains text in a language other than the default language, you need to select the foreign language text and assign the proper language code to the text so CorelDRAW will use the appropriate proofing tools. The language currently assigned to selected text is noted by a three-letter code in parenthesis next to the font description in the Status Bar as shown, for example, by "(ENU)" here.

To change the language assignment of any character, word, or paragraph of Artistic or Paragraph Text in a document, select the text and then choose Text | Writing Tools | Language. When the Text Language dialog opens, you can choose any one of the 122 different language and language variants that appear in the list. Click OK to make the addition.

Why Language Codes Are Important

You want your text to be spelled correctly, including accent and other orthographic marks (text indicators of how a word is pronounced), regardless of what language you use. When text is tagged with the proper language codes and you've installed the corresponding proofing tools, it's as easy to check foreign language text as it is to check your native language text.

For example, suppose you're working on a package design that contains text in English, French, and Spanish on a system that uses U.S. English. To proof in multiple languages, you select each piece of French text and assign it a French language tag, select each piece of Spanish text and assign that text a Spanish language tag, and so on. CorelDRAW has already assigned the English language tag, so you don't have to do that. Now when checking the document for spelling and grammar, CorelDRAW will use English, French, and Spanish proofing tools (if you installed them) to check the text for foreign language spelling errors.

Corel's proofing engine is also capable of proofing text to meet the spelling and punctuation standards of different regional and national variations for a number of major languages. This ensures, for example, that text that has been tagged as French Canadian will be checked using the French (Canadian) proofing set and rules that reflect correct French Canadian spelling, grammar, and word choice. If the French text in the document is intended for French speakers in Belgium, France, Luxembourg, Monaco, or Switzerland, instead of Canada, you would tag the text to match French (Belgium), French (France), French (Luxembourg), French (Monaco), or French (Switzerland) so that the appropriate proofing tools would be called into use by CorelDRAW.

16

Using the Proofing Tools

To use CorelDRAW's spell checker, thesaurus, or grammar check on text in your document, select the text with the Pick Tool or the Text Tool, and then choose the appropriate writing tool from the Text | Writing Tools menu. Alternatively, you can right-click a text object with the Text Tool and then choose a proofing tool from the pop-up menu. You can also right-click with the Pick Tool and choose Spell Check, or press CTRL+F12. This opens the Writing Tools dialog to the Spell Checker tab, as shown here:

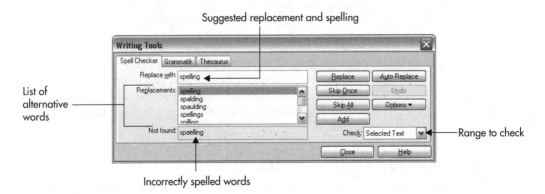

 If you have the WordPerfect Office suite installed on your computer, you will also have a Dictionary tab to the right of the Thesaurus tab in the Writing Tools dialog.

Common Buttons

The Spell Checker and Grammatik tools share common buttons in the Writing Tools dialog. These buttons perform the functions described here:

- **Start button** The Start button starts the Spell Checker or Grammatik. This button is visible only if Auto Start is off—it is on by default. To enable or disable the Auto Start option, click the Options button in the Writing Tools dialog, and make a selection from the drop-down menu.

- **Replace button** As the check is performed, when a misspelled word or grammatical error is found, the Start button changes to Replace, and the misspelled word or grammatical error is highlighted. Select the suggested correction from the list, and click Replace to apply it. You can also edit the replacement word in the Spell Checker's Replace With box, or type in a new word before replacing it. After the replacement has been made, the checker rechecks the replacement and continues checking.

- **Undo button**   The Undo button reverts the last correction to its previous state.

- **Resume button**   After you correct a mistake, if you move the insertion point—for example, to a different part of the text—the Start button changes to the Resume button. Simply click it to recheck any selected text and to continue checking from the insertion point.

- **Skip Once and Skip All**   If the word or sentence that a checker has queried is actually correct—for example, a name with an unusual spelling such as PowerTRACE—you can click one of the Skip buttons to have the checker ignore it. Skip Once causes the check to continue, but future instances of the same problem will stop the checker. Skip All tells the checker to ignore *all* instances of this spelling or grammatical error.

- **Add**   Add allows you to add a word to the current User Word List. Many unusual names and technical terms are not included in the Spell Checker's dictionary, and these can be added to the User Word List for the current language. In the future, these words will not be queried. If a word appears in the Replace With box or in the Not Found box, clicking Add immediately adds the queried word to the default User Word List. Otherwise, if no word appears in either box, clicking the Add button opens an input box, where you can type the word you want to enter into the User Word List.

- **Auto Replace**   If you choose an alternative spelling for a queried word, the Auto Replace button becomes active. Clicking this button will add the misspelled word and its replacement to the default User Word List, *and* if QuickCorrect is enabled, then the next time you type the same mistake, the correct word will be automatically substituted.

- **Options**   The Options button displays a drop-down menu that contains various settings for the current Writing Tool.

- **Range Of Text**   By using the options from the Check drop-down list, you can set the range of text for performing a spell check or a Grammatik check. The available options depend on whether text is selected with the Text Tool or the Pick Tool.

NOTE   *When Auto Start is enabled, so spelling and grammar checks are performed as soon as the dialog is opened, you cannot choose the range before the check is performed. Disabling Auto Start means that CorelDRAW does not perform the check until you click the Start button, so you can change settings before the check begins.*

16

Setting Spell Checker Options

You can click the Options button on the Spell Checker page of the Writing Tools dialog to access various settings that affect how the Spell Checker works. The Options drop-down menu is shown here:

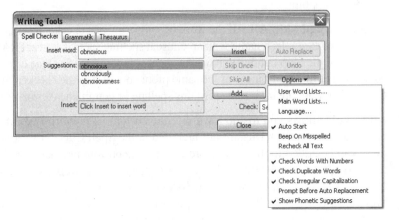

Setting the Checker's Language

The Language option sets the current language for the Spell Checker. When you click Language, the Select Language dialog appears, as shown next, in which you can select the language for the checker to use. By checking Show Available Languages Only, you reduce the list to those languages for which dictionaries are installed.

Selecting a different language and checking Save As Default Writing Tools Language causes both the Spell Checker and Grammatik to use this language by default in all future checks.

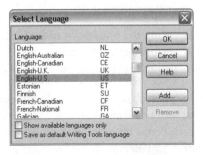

Although you can change the Language of the Spell Checker, it is much better to select the text and then to set the language of the text via Text | Writing Tools | Language, than to change the language from the Writing Tools dialog. When you change the language of the text, the checker language is automatically changed to match, but the reverse doesn't happen. Changing the Language option of the text saves the change to the file so that the proper proofing tools will be used without additional user intervention.

You can also add new language codes by clicking the Add button to open the Add Language Code dialog, as shown here:

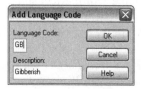

NOTE *Adding a new language code does not create or install a dictionary or User Word List to go with it. CorelDRAW does not come with a utility to create or edit main dictionaries, but if you have WordPerfect, you can use the Spell Utility that comes with it to create main and user dictionaries to use with your custom language code.*

Using Word Lists

CorelDRAW's writing tools maintain Word Lists that contain all the valid words and phrases for spelling checks. If a word in your document is not in one of the active lists, it is flagged as being incorrectly spelled. CorelDRAW has two types of Word Lists:

- **Main Word Lists**   These lists are provided by Corel and contain the most common words and spellings in each language. One Main Word List exists per language and this list is not editable.

- **User Word Lists**   These lists contain words that are not in the Corel-supplied lists but rather are made up of words you have added during a spell check by clicking the Add button. It is up to you to ensure that the words you add to a User Word List are spelled correctly! User Word Lists also contain the QuickCorrect entries for the text's language. Each language has at least one User Word List.

  You can create your own User Word Lists with the WordPerfect Spell Utility, or you can use third-party created lists. Specialized User Word Lists such as those containing medical, legal, engineering, scientific, or other words and phrases that are common to an industry are very useful to create. The Spell Checker compares each word in your text to those in the Main Word Lists and then to the User Word Lists that you have chosen for that word's language.

NOTE *You should include the User Word Lists in your regular data backups. That way, if you have to reinstall CorelDRAW, you can also reinstall the latest versions of your User Word Lists. User Word List filenames have the extension .UWL, and Main Word Lists files use .MOR. These files are found in the My Documents\Corel User Files folder.*

16

Using Main Word Lists

The Main Word Lists are predefined by Corel and cannot be edited by CorelDRAW. However, they can be edited by the WordPerfect suite's Spell Utility if you happen to have a copy. Main Word Lists contain only words used by the Spell Checker—no QuickCorrect word pairs are included. The Main Word Lists dialog is shown here.

 If you don't own a copy of WordPerfect but you'd really like to edit and create word lists, download the trial copy of WordPerfect. You'll have 30 days to use the Spell Utility and explore the merits of WordPerfect.

Which Main Word List is currently being used changes according to the Language setting. Click the Change button (Writing Tools | Spell Check | Main Word Lists), choose a different language, and CorelDRAW will use Main Word List for the new language you chose. Changing which word list CorelDRAW is currently using does not change the language code of the selected text but rather temporarily proofs that text using the new Main Word List.

You can also *add* extra Main Word Lists to a language by using the Add List button. For example, some U.S. English users might want their *U.S. Spell Checker* to include Spanish words. By adding the Spanish word list, the Spell Checker will first check words against the English lists. Then, if the words are not found in the English list, the checker compares against the Spanish list. Only if the check fails against both lists will the Spell Checker display an error. Using this method, you don't have to specifically set a language code for the Spanish text.

Setting Options in User Word Lists

To choose which User Word List is used, and to edit entries in a User Word List, open the User Word Lists dialog. From the Writing Tools dialog, click the Spell Checker tab, and then click the Options button; then choose User Word Lists from the drop-down menu. From the User Word Lists dialog, shown in Figure 16-1, you can add existing User Word Lists you might have, set the default list to which new entries are added, as well as add, delete, and edit entries in any existing User Word List. Also, you can edit the AutoCorrect entries contained in the selected list and manually add new entries to the currently selected User Word List.

FIGURE 16-1   Use the User Word Lists dialog to set options for new lists.

Setting Current Language

User Word Lists are language-dependent, and at least one list is created for each language. You can choose which language's User Word Lists to edit with the Change button, located at the top right of the dialog. The Change button opens the Select Language dialog shown in the earlier section, "Setting the Checker's Language." This does not change the language of the text or of the writing tools—it changes which language's settings are shown in the dialog. Changing the current language offers you the chance to edit the User Word List of *other* languages.

Adding User Word Lists

Clicking the Add List button in the User Words Lists dialog adds new lists to the current language; each language can have more than one list. This is useful, for example, for adding company- and industry-specific word lists to everyone's installation of CorelDRAW without having to enter the words individually on each computer.

To choose which User Word List will be the one that is used to store new words added when you spell check, choose the list you want to use in the User Word Lists field, and then click the Set Default button to the right.

16

Hacking a User Word List

If you don't have the Spell Utility, you can create a User Word List by use of a little backdoor maneuvering. Close CorelDRAW. Go to the My Documents | Corel User Files folder on your hard disk. Locate the User Word List that corresponds to the default language you use; for example, WT13US.UWL is the U.S. English User Word List file. Press CTRL+C and then CTRL+V to copy and paste the copy into the same directory. Select the copied file and rename it from "Copy of WT13US.UWL" to a descriptive name and a .UWL file extension, for example, "Aereospace.UWL." Next time you open CorelDRAW, you can use Aereospace.UWL—add it to your list, add to or delete entries from it—as you would any other User Word List.

Browsing and Editing User Word List Contents

You can browse and edit the User Word List Contents. Just scroll up and down the list to view the contents, or enter a word or the first few characters of a word into the Word/Phrase box to scroll to a certain point in the alphabetical list.

NOTE *The list contains words that you have added. It also contains QuickCorrect entries that you have added with either the Spell Checker's Auto Replace button or in the QuickCorrect section of CorelDRAW's Options dialog.*

You can scroll through the list to view any particular word. Each entry has two parts: the word or phrase for which CorelDRAW checks (Word/Phrase), and the word or phrase with which CorelDRAW replaces the incorrect word (Replace With).

Adding a New Entry   If you want to add a new word or phrase to the User Word List, enter the word or phrase that you want replaced into the Word/Phrase box. In the Replace With box, enter the text you want to use to replace the Word/Phrase, or leave the box empty if you want CorelDRAW to ignore the spelling of the word or phrase. Click the Add Entry button to add the new word to the list. For example, if you perennially type *Ive* instead of *I've*, enter **Ive** in the Word/Phrase box, enter **I've** in the Replace With box, and click Add Entry.

TIP *To add a word that is spelled correctly but that is not in any list, type the word in the Word/Phrase box and then type it in the Replace With box. If you put the correctly spelled word in both boxes, Corel will not put the red squiggle under the word. If you leave the Replace With box empty, CorelDRAW adds "<skip>" to the Replace With column, which tells QuickCorrect and the Spell Checker to ignore this word, but it will put a red underline under the word.*

Deleting Entries   If you have an entry in the User Word List that is misspelled or simply not what you want, you can delete it. Select the item and click the Delete Entry button. You'll see a confirmation box asking whether you really want to delete the word—yes, you do—just confirm it and it's history.

Editing Entries   You can also correct or edit any entry. Click the entry in the list to select it, make your changes in the Replace With box, and then click the Replace Entry button.

Setting Entry Properties   The property set for each word in your User Word List is important to consider and may need tweaking to get the results you want for the particular entry. With the word or phrase selected in the list, click on the Properties button to display the Entry Properties dialog. From here, the Entry Type can be set to Skip Word, which causes the proofing tools to ignore the word. Choose Auto Replace Entry to have CorelDRAW substitute what you typed with what you've entered in the Replace field.

Other Spell Checking Options

Some other options available from the Options drop-down menu of the Writing Tools dialog are described here:

- **Auto Start**   The Spell Checker and Grammatik start the check automatically when the Writing Tools dialog is opened or when that checker's page is opened in the Writing Tools dialog.

- **Check Words With Numbers**   Checks or ignores words that include numbers.

- **Check Duplicate Words**   Flags words that appear twice in succession.

- **Check Irregular Capitalization**   Checks for words that have capital letters in places other than the first character.

- **Show Phonetic Suggestions**   Makes *phonetic* suggestions—replacement words that *sound* like the unrecognized word.

Main Spell Checking Options

The Workplace | Text | Spelling section of CorelDRAW's global Options dialog (CTRL+J) also includes various options that modify how the writing tools work.

- **Perform Automatic Spell Checking**   Check this if you want to check spelling as you type. When it is turned on, unrecognized words are underlined with a red zigzag line while you're editing text with the Text Tool.

- **Visibility Of Errors**   Choose here to have all errors underlined in all text objects or just the text object being edited.

16

- **Display Spelling Suggestions** You set the number of suggestions to display in the pop-up menu after right-clicking a misspelled word with the Text Tool. The maximum and default number of suggestions is 10.

- **Add Corrections To QuickCorrect** When checked, CorelDRAW will add a correction pair to the User Word List based on a correction made from the right-click pop-up menu.

- **Show Errors Which Have Been Ignored** When you right-click a word, the pop-up menu includes an Ignore All command, which tells the Spell Checker to ignore this word. With this option set, CorelDRAW will still show ignored errors, but it will use a blue zigzag line to indicate that they have been ignored.

Using Grammatik

Spelling errors aren't the only proofing goof that can make your work look unprofessional. Poor grammar is a big, red flag that reflects on your education and communication skills. To make you look in print as smart as you are in person, CorelDRAW includes the Grammatik grammar checker, in many of the languages that spell checkers are available in.

Grammatik is a flexible, powerful tool for checking your work. Grammar checking is a much harder task than spell checking; no program can serve as a proxy for an educated, native speaker's judgment. What Grammatik excels at is calling your attention to parts of your text that *might be* grammatically incorrect; it second-guesses you, and it's always good to have this resource at 1 A.M. when all your coworkers are sensibly asleep at home! Grammatik encourages you to stop and think about what you've written and offers helpful suggestions to fix the problem it *thinks* is a thorn in your rosy prose.

Grammatik has different sets of rules that it uses to judge the correctness of your grammar. When you use Grammatik, you should choose the rule set that corresponds to the level of formality and complexity of your writing. You can also edit any of Grammatik's rules to suit a specific situation.

Mastering every in and out of Grammatik combined with the intricate nature of grammar for a given language is beyond the scope of this book. However, the day-to-day operation of Grammatik is not difficult to manage, as you'll witness in the next section, where the basics are covered.

Checking and Correcting Grammar

To check your grammar, select the text objects to check with the Pick Tool, or select sentences with the Text Tool; in the Writing Tools dialog open the Grammatik tab, shown in Figure 16-2, by choosing Text | Writing Tools | Grammatik. As with all of the other writing tools, you can also select text and then use the right-click pop-up menu to launch the tool you want to use. It's common to use a word that sounds like the word you want: in this figure "affects" is indeed a real word, correctly spelled, but it's a homonym—a word that sounds like the *intended* word—"effects."

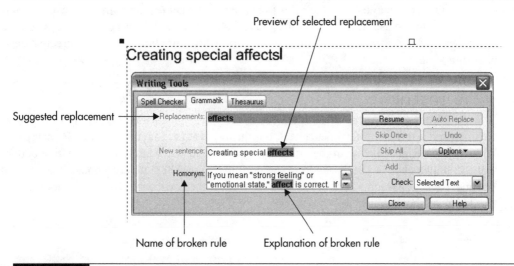

FIGURE 16-2 Grammatik catches errors in your writing that spell checking wouldn't alert you to.

Grammatik underlines potential grammar problems with a green zigzag line. Occasionally when it finds more than one space between words, the white space is underlined. This is very helpful; modern rules of good digital typography call for only one space between sentences and not the two that were required in the days of typewriters.

If Auto Start is enabled, Grammatik will immediately start checking the text; otherwise, you must click the Start button.

If Grammatik finds something that breaks the rules of grammar using the current settings, it displays an explanation of the problem next to the name of the broken rule—the "Rule Class" that has been broken. Grammatik may make one or more suggestions of better grammar, and if you click an option, the new sentence is shown so that you can decide if that's what you meant to say. Click Replace to apply the change and continue checking.

Turning Grammatik's Rules On and Off

When Grammatik finds fault with your grammar, you might not always agree with its suggestion. If you don't want Grammatik to check a certain kind of grammatical error, you can tell it to ignore it. As soon as Grammatik pops up a grammar query, the Add button in the Writing Tools dialog changes to Turn Off. If you click Turn Off, the specific grammar rule that is currently being used will be deactivated for as long as the Writing Tools dialog is open. If you want to turn it back on again, choose Options | Turn On Rules, which brings up the Turn On Rules dialog. Choose those rules that you want to reactivate and click OK. The next time you perform a check, these rules are included.

After you have pared down the rules to the one you want to keep, you can save this new "profile" for future use: Choose Options | Save Rules. The Save Rules dialog opens, and you can either click the Save button to update the current style or click Save As to create a new checking style.

Using the Thesaurus

When the word you're using doesn't convey exactly the right shade of meaning or if you've already used it three or four times, check out the available synonyms with the Thesaurus Writing Tool. Right-click with the Text Tool on the word you want to replace with a better word, and then choose Thesaurus from the pop-up menu. Alternatively, choose Text | Writing Tools | Thesaurus. The Writing Tools dialog opens with the word in the look-up word box, as shown here:

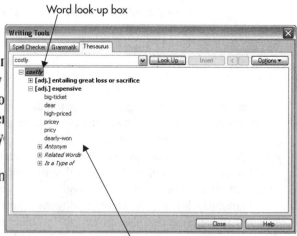

Word look-up box

It's extremely costly to put in a r
bathroom, and almost as costly
install new tiles. What makes ho
rennovation the most costly, howeve
the high-price of *towels* to put in y
new bathroom. Have you ever *seen*
price tags on even the less-costly or
You're usually better off staying **wet**!

Suggestions area: similar words and phrases, opposite meanings

The look-up word box contains the word that you want to look up. The suggestions area of the dialog contains a folder-like tree view list of alternative words and meanings for the word you are looking up. Find one that matches the message you are trying to present and click to expand the entry. If you find the word you want to use, select it and click the Replace button to insert the word into your text. You can also choose *the opposite meaning* of a word in case inverting a sentence is a style of writing you like—*antonyms* are available for the word you chose in the expandable tree in the suggestions area.

If you find a word that is close, but not exactly the right word for you, double-click on the word to automatically open another suggestion area in the dialog that makes suggestions for words that are similar to the selected word. Up to three panes of suggestions are visible at once, but you can keep clicking on suggestions and open up more panes that you can navigate through using the left and right navigation buttons at the top of the dialog. To use a word in one of the alternate panes as your replacement word, select it and click the Replace button.

Setting Thesaurus Options

You can set various options for the Thesaurus by clicking the Options button in the Writing Tools dialog and clicking the Thesaurus tab to view the drop-down menu; the most useful ones are described here:

- **Auto Look Up**   This option speeds up your work by starting the process right away.

- **Auto Close**   When turned on, it closes the dialog as soon as the Replace button is clicked.

- **Spelling Assist**   When enabled, if the word that you selected to check in the Thesaurus is not recognized, a list of similar words from the Thesaurus is shown. Click the word that best matches the correct spelling of the word you typed, and then click Look Up. The suggestions area will contain alternatives.

- **Synonyms**   This option displays synonyms of the look-up word in the list of suggested alternatives.

- **Antonym**   This option displays antonyms of the look-up—a lifesaver for those times when you can't think of an opposite for the word you want.

- **Language**   Choose this to change which language's Thesaurus is used for the current session. This does not change the language of the text in your document, but any replacements will be set to the new language. This only works with languages you have currently installed.

- **Set Data File**   Use this option to link to a different thesaurus for the current session such as a third-party-supplied one, or if you want to use a different language's thesaurus from the CorelDRAW software disc without installing writing tools for that language.

| NOTE | *CorelDRAW's Thesaurus has no alternative word or phrase for "Thesaurus," but this is okay—neither does Merriam-Webster.* |

16

Using QuickCorrect

QuickCorrect is a dynamic part of CorelDRAW's writing tools. QuickCorrect works with you *as* you type, much like Auto Spell; it replaces words that you commonly mistype or misspell with the correctly spelled versions. It can also be used to replace an abbreviation with the full-word form to save you having to type a word or phrase each time.

How QuickCorrect Works

While you are typing, every time you "leave" a word by typing a space, period, tab, comma, or linefeed, QuickCorrect compares that word with its User Word Lists. If it finds the word—or possibly a phrase in one of its lists—it replaces that word or phrase with the replacement in the list. For example, people often mistype the word *the* when typing quickly; the English word lists already include an entry to change *teh* to *the*. Similarly, *don't* is the QuickCorrect replacement for *dont*, *misspell* for *mispell*, *you're the* for *your the*, and *weird* for *wierd*.

QuickCorrect also manages other automated text-correction features, such as capitalization of the first words of a sentence and the names of days, correcting consecutive capitals, and adding typographic or "smart" quotation marks.

To remove an unwanted QuickCorrect change, choose Edit | Undo or press CTRL+Z. *The QuickCorrect change is undone without undoing any* other *typing. You then continue typing and the word that you typed is as it is. This does not work for typographic quotes, however.*

Setting QuickCorrect Options

To set QuickCorrect's options, open CorelDRAW's global Options dialog (CTRL+J) and navigate to the QuickCorrect section of the tree, as shown in Figure 16-3.

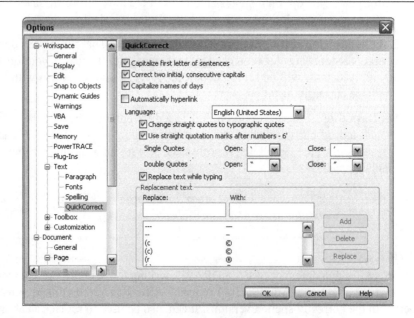

FIGURE 16-3   Use this dialog to choose your QuickCorrect settings.

The available options are listed here:

- **Capitalize First Letter Of Sentences**   Does exactly that.

 If you use a lot of symbol fonts in your text, the sentence capitalization option is notorious for capitalizing those symbols when you don't want this. In these instances, you might want to disable this feature.

- **Correct Two Initial, Consecutive Capitals**   This option automatically corrects for holding the SHIFT key down too long when typing.

- **Capitalize Names Of Days**   This option capitalizes the first letter of days of the week.

- **Automatically Hyperlink**   When this option is enabled, typing *www* (followed by the rest of the URL) creates an Internet hyperlink. You might not want this if you're creating flyers, but if you are creating Acrobat PDF documents, it's a welcome option.

This next Language section of the dialog is used to customize how a specific language deals with single-quote (apostrophe) and double-quote marks. Different languages use different glyphs to mark quotations. When you choose a language in the Language drop-down, CorelDRAW automatically displays the traditional characters that language uses if they are available. To change which characters are used when working with a specific language, choose from the drop-downs. All of the settings are language-specific, and you will need to set them for each language you use.

- **Change Straight Quotes To Typographic Quotes**   QuickCorrect changes single- and double-quotation mark characters from the plain typed form to the appropriate left or right typographic quotation mark.

- **Use Straight Quotation Marks After Numbers -6'**   Choose this if you work with measurements a lot. It looks awkward and unprofessional to denote six inches as the number 6 with a closed double-quote mark after it instead of a double-prime.

TIP   *If you need to use prime symbols for foot-and-inch measurements (such as 1' or 12"), copy the prime (or straight apostrophe) or double-prime (straight double-quote) symbol to the Clipboard from the Windows Character Map (Start | All Programs | Accessories | System Tools | Character Map) or other application. When the Importing / Pasting Text dialog opens, make sure that Discard Fonts And Formatting is checked. Click OK and the character will be inserted into your document without being intercepted by QuickCorrect.*

- **Replace Text While Typing**   When enabled, QuickCorrect replaces those words in the Replace list with the corresponding word in the With list. Entries to a language's QuickCorrect or directly into a User Word List were shown earlier in this chapter, in the section "Adding a New Entry."

16

Finding and Replacing Text and Special Characters

All too often you may find yourself in the situation of having to find a specific piece of text so you can change the font or formatting or even the content of the text itself. CorelDRAW has terrific tools for searching for and replacing text—and text attributes—regardless of whether your layout is a paragraph or a multi-page document.

Finding Text

To find a word, phrases, and other marks such as dashes, hyphens, and special characters like tabs, paragraph breaks, and spaces, open the Find Text dialog by choosing Edit | Find And Replace | Find Text. In the Find box, enter the word or exact phrase you want to find.

You can include special characters such as an Em or En Space or Dash, a ¼ Em Space, a Non-Breaking Space, a Non-Breaking Hyphen, a Column/Frame Break, an Optional Hyphen, a Space, a Tab, or a Hard Return in your search. To enter the search tag for a special character into the Find box, click on the right arrow next to the Find drop-down, and choose the character you want to include in your search.

If you know the exact character case of the word or phrase, enter it and check the Match Case check box—if the Match Case check box is cleared, all matching words will be found, regardless of the case of the characters (a case-insensitive search). The Find Text dialog is shown here:

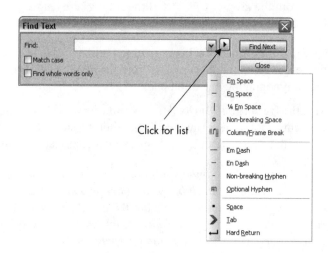

Click for list

Click the Find Next button to find the next instance of the searched text within the document. All the text objects in the document—Paragraph, Artistic, and Fitted Text—will be searched, starting with the current page and working to the end of the document. You will be asked whether you want to continue from the start of the document when you reach the end: Clicking Yes takes the search back to page 1, and it will continue through to the start position, so the whole document is checked once. If the search text is not found, CorelDRAW tells you.

Replacing Text

If you want to replace a word, phrase, or special character in the text with another word, phrase, or special character, use the Replace Text dialog, shown below, which is accessed by choosing Edit | Find And Replace | Replace Text.

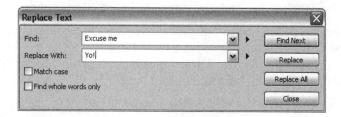

You enter the word or phrase you want to find into the Find box, and enter the replacement word or phrase into the Replace With box using the same process as described for finding text in the previous section. Click the Find Next button to find the first instance of the search text. When the search text is found, click the Replace button to replace it with the replacement text, or click the Find Next button to skip over the found text and to find the next instance to replace.

If you are sure that you want to replace *all* instances of the Find text in the current document with the Replace With text, click the Replace All button.

NOTE *The ability to search and replace special characters in addition to text is incredibly useful when you are cleaning up imported text, changing five spaces into a tab, and removing column/frame breaks (soft returns). It is also a useful feature if you want to tweak your typography; for example, you can search for a hyphen between numbers and replace it with an en dash. You can also give your text some breathing room and search for all the em dashes in your text and put ¼ em spaces on either side of the em dash.*

Finding and Replacing Text Properties

You can also find and replace text properties using the general Find And Replace Wizard interface, invoked by choosing Edit | Find And Replace and then choosing one of the two wizards that can be used, either Find Objects or Replace Objects.

Finding Text Properties

Using the Find Objects Wizard, you can find text based on its type, such as Artistic, Paragraph, or Text On A Path (Fitted); on its contents; and on its styles. To find text in the current document, use these steps.

16

A Simple Text Hunt Based on Object Properties

1. Open the Find Objects Wizard by choosing Edit | Find And Replace | Find Objects. Then choose Begin A New Search and click Next.

2. On the next page, from the Object Types tab, choose the type of text you want to find, or just check the Text box in the list, which will select all types of text. Then click Next.

3. On the next page, you must provide the settings for each text type individually. Click a type in the left box to choose it, and then click the Specify Properties For button. This will open the Specific Attributes dialog, where you choose the properties that the text must have in order for it to be found. This dialog is shown in Figure 16-4.

4. The properties shown in Figure 16-4 must all be present for the text to qualify: For example, if you type "village" and choose the font Garamond, and then choose Normal-Italic from the Weight field, the Artistic Text object containing the word "village" will be selected *only* if it is in the correct font *and* Weight (the style of the typeface); CorelDRAW will select the text object but not any words within the object.

2

3

4

FIGURE 16-4   Use this dialog to give the properties of the text that needs to be located.

5. Click Finish and use the button bar, shown below, to jump between the found instances:

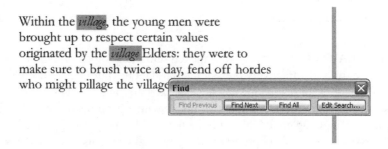

To find the occurrences of text objects containing text that uses a Text Style, check Look For Object Names Or Styles at the bottom of the first page of the Find Wizard. When this option is checked, clicking Next takes you to a page where you can choose the Style Name or a Style Type that you want to search for from a list.

Replacing Text Properties

The Replace Objects Wizard replaces one set of matching text properties with another set. When you start the wizard, you can choose whether to restrict the search to the text within the selected text objects only or to search the whole document.

In the first page of the wizard, choose Replace Text Properties and click Next. You can now set the search and replace criteria for text properties, as shown in Figure 16-5.

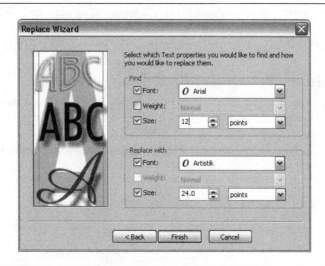

FIGURE 16-5   Set the find and replace properties for your text.

You can set the Font, Weight, and Size of the text to find, and you can replace one or all of those settings with new ones. Click Finish and use the button bar to decide whether to find each match one at a time or just to replace them all in one go.

Tables

With CorelDRAW X4's new Table Tool tucked into the Toolbox, you no longer have to struggle to neatly and attractively present tabular data in your documents. Creating data sheets or directories, or displaying spreadsheet data no longer hinges on setting up elaborate networks of guidelines, or paragraph text blocks with a generous handful of tab and column settings thrown in. Drag out a table with the new Table Tool, or import a table from your word processor or spreadsheet program, and you're all set to use CorelDRAW's tools to make the data look good.

Creating a Table

You can create a new table with either the Table Tool in the Toolbox or from the Create New Table command on the Table menu. If you use the Table Tool to create the table, you can click-drag to position and size the table exactly where you want the table to be inserted. If you create the table using the menu command, the table will be inserted in the center of the document. In either case you can drag the table to a new position or resize it just as you would any other object, such as a rectangle that you create with Toolbox tools.

Using the Proper Tool for the Job

Customization of a table takes place on several levels: the entire table, a single cell, a range of cells. The content you place inside a cell, such as text or graphics, is controlled with the same tools and settings that would affect it if it were not inside a cell. Which tool you have active, and what you've selected with that tool, if anything, determines what customization options are available to you at that moment from the Property Bar or the menus.

Table Options When the Pick Tool Is Active

With the Pick Tool, click anywhere in or on the table to select the entire table. You can use the Pick Tool to select, move, resize, stretch, skew, or rotate the entire table. When the Pick Tool has been used to select the table, the following commands and options appear on the Property Bar as shown in Figure 16-6. These options apply to the entire table.

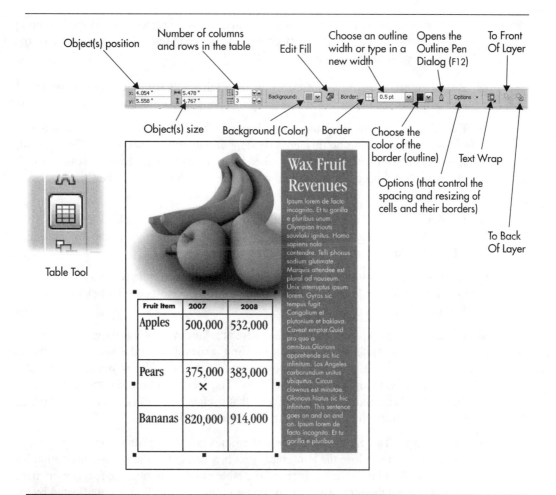

FIGURE 16-6 Use the Property Bar to customize the look of a table.

The table's position on the page and the overall dimensions of the table use the same common entry fields on the left of the Property Bar that other objects such as rectangles or polygons use. Other important options are:

- **Number of columns and rows in the table** Use the top control to enter the number of columns you want your table to have and the bottom one to enter the number of rows you require. You can change these entries at any time. For example, if a table currently has 2 columns and 2 rows, entering *4* in the column field and *6* in the row field causes the table to immediately reconfigure itself to contain the new number of columns and rows.

16

If you reduce the number of columns or rows, they are removed from the bottom up and from the right to the left. Any content you have in the columns and rows is lost, so do this with aforethought!

- **Background** Choose a uniform color for all the cells from this drop-down list. You can also accomplish the same thing by choosing a color from the Color Palette.

- **Edit Fill** If you've given the table a background fill, you can go directly to the Edit Fill dialog by clicking on this icon. By default, tables are filled with a Uniform fill. If you want your table to have any other fill type, such as Fountain or Pattern fill, you must first select the table and then change the fill type from the Object Properties docker (ALT+ENTER).

- **Border** "Border" refers to the outline of each cell and the table as a whole. You can show or hide the interior cell outlines and/or combinations of the top, bottom, left, and right sides of the table.

- **Outline width and outline color** These options control the width and color assigned to the borders you have set. For more advanced control, click the Outline Pen Dialog icon to open that dialog.

- **Options** The options that can be set here are Automatically Resize Cells When Typing and Separated Cell Borders. The first is useful when the amount of content you need to enter in each cell is not uniform. Enabling this prevents your content from overflowing and moving out of view. The second option lets you space out your cells horizontally and vertically so that each cell is still contained in the table but is not in immediate proximity to the adjacent cell.

- **Text Wrap** This important option determines how *Paragraph Text* flows around the table and how close the Paragraph Text box can get to the table—this option has nothing to do with the text content of the table. Tables are objects; text can be made to flow around them or over them or under them. Artistic Text is not affected by the Text Wrap setting.

- **To Front Of Layer and To Back Of Layer** These icons become available if another object is layered on top of or below the table. Clicking these icons changes the position of the table in the stacking order.

Table Options When the Shape Tool Is Active

When you want to select a single cell or multiple cells in a table, use the Shape Tool. To select a single cell, click in it with the Shape Tool. To select adjacent cells, click-drag across the row(s) or column(s) that you want to select. To select non-adjacent cells, hold the CTRL key and click in the cells you want to select. Diagonal blue lines shade the cells you've selected. These lines are an onscreen visual indicator and not an actual fill.

Once cells are selected with the Shape Tool, you can use the options available to you on the Property Bar, as seen in Figure 16-7, to customize the cells. The attributes you apply to cells override any you set for the table. The first control group on the left now will set the dimensions of the selected cells as opposed to those of the entire table. The Background and Border options work the same as before, but making changes with them now only affects the selected cells. New to the Property Bar are the Margins drop-down, which sets the top, bottom, left, and right margins within the cell's bounds, and a group of controls to merge or split the selected cells into fewer or more cells.

You can also use the Shape Tool to select an entire column or row. With the Shape Tool click on the left border of the table next to the row you want to select. When the cursor turns into a small arrow, click again to select that row, or click-drag to select additional adjacent rows. To select columns, click on the top table border over the column you want to select, wait for the arrow to appear, and click again to select the column, or click-drag to select additional columns.

To select non-adjacent rows or columns, follow the preceding procedure, but hold the ctrl key and then click next to or over the rows and or columns you want to select.

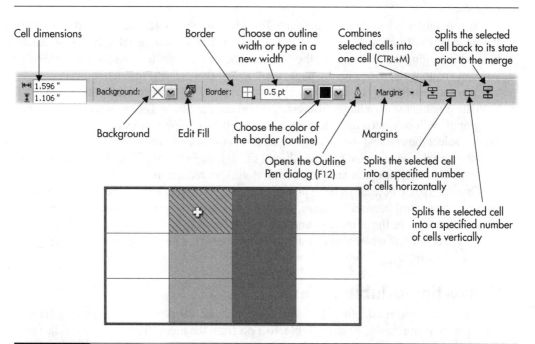

FIGURE 16-7   These options are available for table customization when the Shape Tool is active.

16

Editing a Table When the Table Tool Is Active

The Table Tool is used to create the table by click-diagonal dragging in your document, but it is *also* used to edit the table once it is created. Right-clicking in a table row, column, or cell and choosing the appropriate option from the Select menu in the context menu is a quick way to select a single row, column, or cell. To select the entire table, choose Table from the Select command on the pop-up menu.

The Table Tool can also be used in the same way the Shape Tool is used to select multiple columns and rows, but it is easier to use the Shape Tool and avoid the possibility of creating a table instead of a selection.

You can add or delete columns or rows from your table by clicking in a row or column and then choosing Delete | (Row or Column) from either the Table menu or the right-click context menu.

Working with Text and Graphics in a Table

Entering text into a table is easy; just use the Table Tool to click in a cell and enter text using any method for text entry. You can type text directly into the cell, import text from the File menu or from the Edit Text Box dialog (CTRL+SHIFT+T), or paste text into the cell from the Clipboard.

Text in tables is handled as Paragraph Text and can be proofed, edited, and formatted in the same ways. If you want to draw a Paragraph text box within the table cell, you can do so by click-dragging the Text Tool in the cell. Artistic Text cannot be *created* in a table cell, but you can create it elsewhere on the page, copy it, and then paste it into a table cell.

You can paste any graphic into a cell, but which tool you use to select the cell that will hold the graphic makes a huge difference. If you use the Shape Tool to select the target cell, the graphic will be pasted into the center of the cell as a graphic object. If you use the Table Tool to select the cell and then paste the graphic into the cell, the graphic will be pasted in as an inline graphic whose size matches that of the default or current font size being used in that cell. This operation can take some time if the size reduction is great.

Once a graphic object has been placed in a cell, you select it by clicking on it. You can then use the control handles to resize, rotate, and skew it. You can even extrude it if you like. If you want to move the graphic to another cell, select it with the Pick Tool, and drag it into a different cell in the table. You can drag a graphic *out* of a table, but you cannot drag a graphic into a table.

Converting a Table to Text

A table can be converted into a single Paragraph text box at any time by selecting the table and then choosing Table | Convert Table To Text from the menu. The Convert Table To Text dialog that appears offers you the option to separate the contents of each cell with a delimiter—a comma, a tab, a paragraph, or the character of your choice. If you choose to separate the cell contents with a comma, a tab, or one of your own choice, each row of cells will be saved to a paragraph with the individual cell contents separated in that paragraph by the delimiting character you choose. If you choose to separate cell contents by paragraph, you will get a paragraph for each cell.

 Converting a table to text sometimes produces results you don't like, so be prepared to undo the conversion. Saving a copy of your file before converting isn't a bad idea either.

Converting an Existing Text to a Table

Existing Paragraph Text can be converted into a table in a process that is basically the reverse of the process outlined in the previous section. Select the text you want to convert, and choose Table | Convert Text To Table from the menu. From the Convert Text To Table dialog choose the delimiter you've used to break up the text into the chunks that you want to go into each cell. CorelDRAW analyzes the selected text and guesses what will work best as a delimiter. Because commas and tabs are frequently used within a section of text, they might cause the creation of many more cells than you were expecting. At the bottom of the dialog it tells you how many rows and columns it is going to create. If the number sounds wrong, cancel and go back to your text. Mark the end of each piece of text you want transferred into a cell with some other character—an asterisk or a tilde, for example. Then choose User Defined and enter the character you choose as a delimiter into the field.

Importing a Table from Another Application

You don't have to create tables in CorelDRAW to use them in CorelDRAW. You or your client may have created a table in a document or spreadsheet that you want to include in a CorelDRAW document.

To import a table, choose File | Import from the menu. Use the Import dialog to navigate to the spreadsheet or word processing document. Select the document, and then click the Import button. When the Importing/Pasting Text dialog opens, choose how you want to handle importing formatted text. Your choices are Maintain Fonts And Formatting, Maintain Formatting Only, or Discard Fonts And Formatting. Then be sure to choose Tables from the Import Tables As drop-down list.

If you chose to maintain fonts and you don't currently have a font installed that was used in the table, you will have to work your way through the Font Substitution For Missing Fonts dialog. See Chapter 14 for information on font substitution.

Your cursor will be loaded with the table; you then click in your document to place the table. This is a live, editable, customizable table that you can use all of CorelDRAW table tools on to make it exactly the way you want.

16

NOTE *If the existing table looks just the way you want it to look in CorelDRAW, by all means choose one of the first two options. Although CorelDRAW is pretty good at interpreting what other applications did and mapping them accurately to CorelDRAW features and functions, the translation may not be perfect. Once the table has been imported, you may be able to make some simple fixes to make it look like it did in the other application. It may be a more effective use of your time to import your table without any formatting or fonts and to spend your time styling your table from scratch, instead of trying to fix the imported formatting.*

And this is the last word on typography in CorelDRAW! You now know how to spell check, grammar check, find and replace text, and how to create a text-driven table for your work. Our next stop is setting properties for filling objects and outline properties for paths. Let's get your Pen Tool work looking as handsome and as embellished as you'd like it to be.

PART V

Attributes for Objects and Lines

CHAPTER 17

Filling Objects

A shape without a fill on your drawing page is like a brand-new coloring book. To make a coloring book (and your CorelDRAW artwork) visually meaningful, you need to fill your shapes with colors and textures. Fortunately, CorelDRAW has more than a half-dozen different types of fills you can apply to your shapes, and these types have hundreds of different variations. In computer graphics, you have over 16 million solid shades of color at your disposal; just think what you can do with blends of colors, colors in different patterns, and colored textures! The worst part of filling CorelDRAW objects will be deciding on a style of fill; the best part, as you explore filling shapes in this chapter, is that it's very difficult to color outside of the lines.

Examining the Fill Types

Each type of CorelDRAW fill has its own special characteristics.

- *Uniform* fills apply flat color.

- *Fountain* fills make a color transition from one color to another, in different directions—sometimes also called a gradient fill. You can also make a fountain fill composed of more than two different colors.

- *PostScript* fills are good for repeating patterns; although PostScript is a printing technology, you don't need to print a CorelDRAW document to see a PostScript fill, and you can indeed export a PostScript filled object to bitmap format and the fill looks fine. PostScript fills support transparency and are ideal for exporting to EPS file format to use in desktop publishing programs. And, naturally, a PostScript fill is valid for printing to a PostScript printer.

- *Pattern* and *texture* fills can fill shapes with bitmaps, including photographs, and a large supply of preset bitmaps is included with CorelDRAW.

- *Mesh* fills take multicolored fills and present you with the option of "smearing" colors within the fill, much like finger-painting.

Every fill type is applied in a slightly different way through the use of onscreen tools, docker windows, or the Interactive Fill and Mesh Fill Tool (see Figure 17-1).

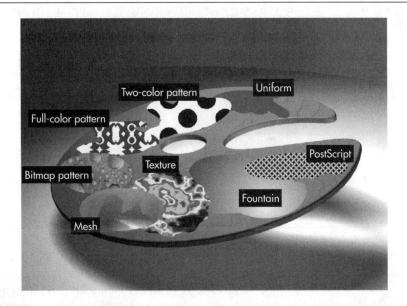

FIGURE 17-1   Fill your shapes in a composition with exactly the fill type that draws attention to your design work.

Using the Color Palette

With color selection, the Color Palette is an excellent starting point, and to apply a uniform (solid) fill to a selected object, you just left-click a color on the Color Palette. You can also drag a *well* (a color swatch) from the Color Palette, drop it onto a shape, which does not have to be selected, and the object is filled.

But perhaps one of the most interesting new features in CorelDRAW is the capability to select not only a color from the Color Palette, but a shade or a tone of that color—in color theory terms, these are called *analogous colors*. To pick a shade of a color on the Color Palette, you first select the object you want to fill (using the Pick Tool), click-hold on the well color, and a small pop-up menu of shades and tones of that color appears. While holding the mouse button, drag to the exact shade you want, release the mouse button, and the object is filled, as shown next. This pop-up features shades that vary in *hue* from top to

17

bottom, and in *brightness* as you drag your cursor from left to right. It's like having 49 possible colors at your cursor tip when you choose one color.

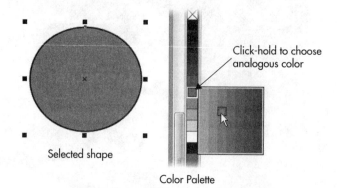

Click-hold to choose analogous color

Selected shape

Color Palette

Uniform fills can also be assigned to all objects right from the get-go, and here are the details in case you're intrigued. With no objects selected in the drawing window, left-click a color you want to use for all objects, Artistic Text, and/or Paragraph Text from now on. CorelDRAW then displays a dialog, as shown here, that asks what sort of object you want filled as it's created from now on. Naturally, you can cancel out of this operation, but as you can see, you can choose objects, text, or both.

 If you have a need to set the default fill for all documents you create in the future, go to Options | Documents, where you can check Save Options As Defaults For New Documents, then check Styles, which applies the fill you've chosen to Default Graphic (the properties for all new objects).

From Uniform to Non-Uniform Shape Filling

The quick way of applying any of the fill types in CorelDRAW X4 is by using the Interactive Fill Tool, shown here. You'll find it at the bottom of the Toolbox; to quickly select it, press G. You'll see a hint here that the Interactive Fill Tool is also a selection tool—the cursor is an arrow cursor with a paint bucket. You don't have to have the object selected that you want to fill when choosing this tool. You can click an unselected shape with the Interactive Fill Tool; it becomes selected, and then a second click-drag on the object modifies the fill type you've chosen on the Property Bar. The default fill mode is Fountain Fill.

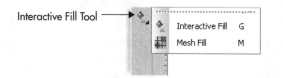

Interactive Fill Tool

Interactive Fill   G
Mesh Fill   M

Interactive Fill Tool cursor

While you're using the Interactive Fill Tool, the Property Bar displays fill options that change depending on the type of fill you choose from this drop-down list. If your selected object features no fill color at all, the selector displays the type as No Fill and the Property Bar options are unavailable. The selector, shown next, is where you can choose from any of ten fill types: Uniform Fill, four fountain fill types (Linear, Radial, Conical, and Square), two Color Pattern fill types (Two Color and Full Color), Bitmap Pattern, Texture Fill, and PostScript Fill. In this section, you'll learn to control every fill type using Property Bar options and the control handles on the Interactive Fill Tool.

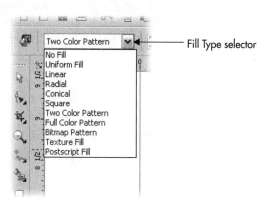

Two Color Pattern

Fill Type selector

No Fill
Uniform Fill
Linear
Radial
Conical
Square
Two Color Pattern
Full Color Pattern
Bitmap Pattern
Texture Fill
Postscript Fill

The technique you use to set angle and position (among other properties) of fills varies a little from fill type to fill type, so let's run through the basics for a moment.

Filling an Object, Setting Fill Properties

17

1. Select the object to fill and then choose the Interactive Fill Tool (G) from the Toolbox.

2. If your object already has a fill, the Property Bar automatically displays the fill type and the current properties of that specific fill.

3. Use the Fill Type selector to choose a fill type. As you do this, your object will be filled with the default fill associated with your selection, and the Property Bar shows available options. Your object will also display control handles for the direct manipulation of the current fill type.

4. Use the Property Bar to specify properties of your fill, which are instantly updated in the drawing window.

The following section covers the Property Bar options specific to the fill type when the Interactive Fill Tool is selected.

Uniform Color Fill Options

Uniform fills are like the paint chips at the hardware store; it's a solid color, no variations, and a uniform fill floods an object within the boundaries of its outline with the color you choose. As mentioned earlier, the Color Palette is a fast and easy way to assign a uniform color; however, when you choose the Interactive Fill Tool, you have several different color models from which to choose. See Chapter 19 for details on color theory, but if you're already familiar with the CMYK printing color model, the intuitive HSB color model, and others, you'll feel right at home using the Property Bar to mix up color values, and better still, entering values a client might have telephoned to you for that big advertising job. The following illustration shows the color models you can choose from the Property Bar selector drop-down list when the Interactive Fill Tool is chosen and Uniform Fill is selected.

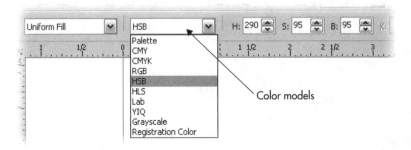

Color models

 HSB and RGB color models occupy the same color space, the extent to which a color can be expressed onscreen. Therefore, you can arrive at an identical color using either color mode. This means you can switch color models for a filled object, and between RGB and HSB there will be no real color change.

Setting Uniform Fill Options

For complete uniform fill color control, use the Interactive Fill Tool and Property Bar options, shown next. They provide access to all palette collections and include numeric entry boxes and spinner controls for setting values for each. It would be "flying blind" and ridiculously hard to "spec" a color by using the value spin boxes and then waiting to see the result color onscreen; this is why the Edit Fill button is your friend. Right after you choose a uniform fill color model on the Property Bar, click Edit Fill to put a floating Color Palette in the drawing window, as shown here:

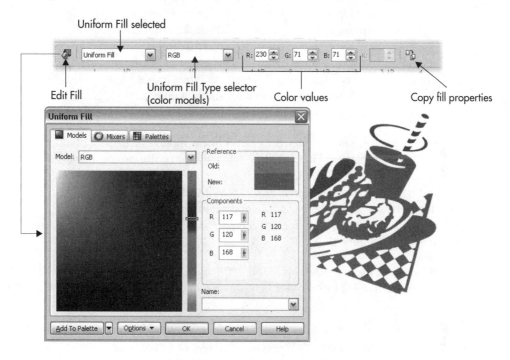

Uniform Fill selected

Edit Fill

Uniform Fill Type selector (color models)

Color values

Copy fill properties

Applying a Fountain Fill

Fountain fills fill objects with a smooth transition between two (or more) colors and come in various styles. Many commercial pieces of artwork are created today that imitate the traditional airbrush (popular in the mid 20th century) by using fountain fills. You can apply a fountain fill in different ways, and the following tutorial shows you the quickest, most artistically satisfying way.

 ## Creating Fountain-Filled Objects

17

1. Select an object and then choose the Interactive Fill Tool (G) from the Toolbox.

2. Click-drag, beginning at one side of your object and dragging to the opposite side at any angle; try dragging from 10 o'clock to 4 o'clock, for example. A default linear fountain fill is created using the object's current fill color, making a color transition from the defined color to white, indicated by settings in the Property Bar. If your object has no fill, a default black-to-white fountain fill is created.

3. For a different fountain fill type, choose Radial, Conical, or Square from the Fill Type selector. As you do this, the shape of your fountain fill (and the available Property Bar options) changes.

4. Experiment with changing the appearance of the fill by dragging to move the color markers and midpoint slider control. Notice how the position changes affect your fill. The midpoint slider is used to influence the point at which the *From* color and the *To* color in the fountain fill is exactly a 50/50 mix of the colors. So if, for example, you want to create a shaded sphere, you begin with an ellipse object, fountain fill it with the Radial fill type, and then move the midpoint closer to the white marker than the black to make a small, subtle, sharp highlight on the object: bingo, you have yourself a dimensional sphere!

Using these steps, you've created a default linear fountain fill. Your click-drag action specifies several properties. The first click sets the From color position, and the drag direction defines the angle. The length of the drag defines the distance, and the mouse release defines the To color position. A series of interactive markers shows the position of each of these values. This is important to understanding how fountain fills are applied; other fountain fill operations are variations on this theme. Next, let's examine each fountain fill type in detail (see Figure 17-2).

■ **Linear** This is the default fountain fill style, and it is most useful for shading rectangular shapes to suggest lighting on a dimensional plane or 3D object. The color marker positions mainly control its appearance.

■ **Radial** This type makes a color transition outward in a circular style, terrific for shading round objects and objects you'd like to soften in appearance. While using radial fountain fills, the center offset controls where the fill begins.

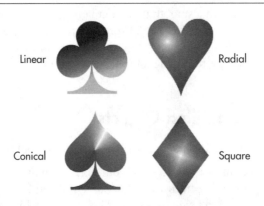

Linear   Radial

Conical   Square

FIGURE 17-2   There is a fountain fill type to bring out the dimensional qualities of almost any shape.

■ **Conical** This might not be a fill type you use every day, but if you need to simulate the look of the playing side of a DVD or an aerial view of a grain silo, Conical produces a strongly shaded and unique transition between two or more colors. The From color of a Conical fill is the beginning and the end of the conical fill, and the To color shades all the in-between blend steps. The center control handle can be used to increase the contrast of the effect by dragging it toward the From color marker along the dotted-line arc of the control handles; dragging the center toward the To marker creates less contrast and a milder effect.

■ **Square** This style produces a look like a four-pointed starburst. In fact, it is also a type for the Transparency Tool. You could overlay transparency in Square blending mode with a Fountain fill and get a truly sparkling effect. The center marker controls contrast; the To marker sets distance and direction for the fill.

> **TIP** *There's a really fast way to copy fill or outline properties between objects. Right-click-drag one object over the other until a target cursor appears, and then release the mouse button. Then choose Copy Fill Here from the pop-up menu.*

> **TIP** *When a shape is selected, double-clicking the Fill box in the Status Bar opens a corresponding dialog where you can edit the current fill of the object and also add it to a Preset list for safekeeping for future needs.*

Controlling Fountain Fills Interactively

The interactive fountain fill markers hovering on top of an object you've drawn, combined with the Property Bar, give you control over the look of your fill. Among these, you'll see color selectors, a Midpoint option, Angle and Edge Pad options, and a Fountain Step option, shown here:

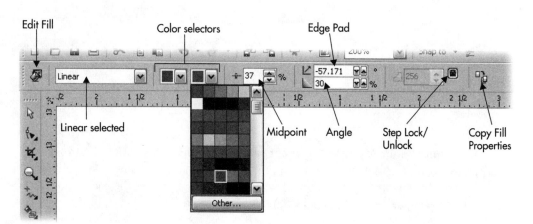

17

Sampling and Applying Fill Colors

Two special tools on the CorelDRAW X4 Toolbox help you to sample and apply fill and outline colors quickly: the Eyedropper and the Paintbucket Tools, shown here:

The tools are meant to work with each other. To sample the properties (including the Fountain Fill type) of any object in your document, choose the Eyedropper Tool and click on the object. Sample options appear in the Status Bar, and for fills the Fill Properties box is already checked by default. To apply a sampled color, hold SHIFT to toggle to the Paintbucket Tool, and then click over the object you want to fill.

While either tool is selected, holding the SHIFT key toggles your active cursor between the two tool states. Also while either tool is selected, the Property Bar has Eyedropper options to choose the object properties to sample. To sample any color area in the view, choose Sample Color from the Sample Mode menu (a mode optimized for sampling colors in bitmap images you've imported), as shown next. Choose an area size from the Sample Size menu—either 1×1, 2×2, or 5×5 pixels. Larger sample areas use an averaging of the colors surrounding the point being sampled. To sample a page background color, click the Select From Desktop button.

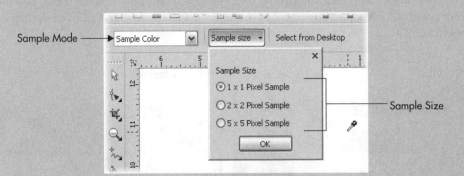

Don't underestimate the usefulness of sampling colors with a "big" eyedropper: averaging a 5×5-pixel area actually improves your chances of getting a compatible color, for example, to replace a background in a bitmap. In Figure 17-3, the background of the ceramic moon is dreadful, and a harmonious color value sampled from the moon

(Continued)

sculpture itself would be splendid. But the color at top right was taken using a "point sample," 1×1 pixel. You need to try this to realize that bitmap images have pixels that vary from neighboring pixel to pixel, especially with JPEGs that by their nature have noise—similar to film grain, random distribution of color pixels that don't belong in image areas. So at top, the 1×1 pixel Eyedropper Tool sample is a dud, even after three tries. But at bottom, when the same area in the circle is sampled using the 5×5 setting, accuracy is no longer critical and a nice average of a 25-pixel area yields a suitable color for the background on the moon.

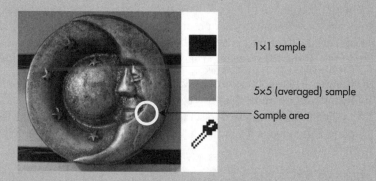

1×1 sample

5×5 (averaged) sample

Sample area

To sample and apply object outline or fill colors (either together or independently), choose the Object Attributes mode and click the Fill and/or Outline options in the Properties menu to tell the Eyedropper Tool what you want to sample, as shown here:

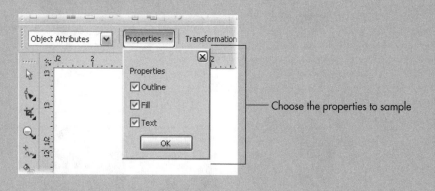

Choose the properties to sample

Many of these fountain fill Property Bar options correspond to interactive markers surrounding your object, but the marker positions can be changed to produce different looks, according to the type of fountain fill. Although the Property Bar offers precision, dragging the markers is extremely intuitive. In Figure 17-3 you can see the different interactive marker positions that appear around each fountain fill type.

Moving any of the markers will change the fill appearance in different ways. The following explains the purpose of options you'll see in the Property Bar while dragging interactive markers and what the effect is on the fill:

- **Color Markers**   Use these to set the position and colors in your fountain fill. Each fountain fill type has to have at least two colors. To change a color, click to select it and click a color well in your onscreen palette, or drag a color well directly onto a color marker. To move a marker, click-drag it in any direction, which changes the properties of the filled object, usually relocating the center of the fountain fill.

- **Midpoint**   This slider control is available only while a two-color fountain fill is applied; if you use more than two colors for the fill, the midpoint marker goes away. The midpoint marker is used to set the point at which the From and To colors are equal in value. This value is measured in terms of percentage—by default it's 50 percent.

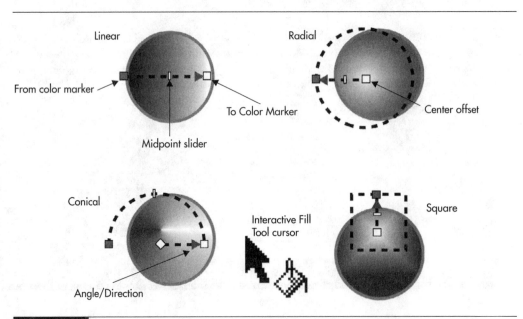

FIGURE 17-3   Interactive markers surround each fountain fill type while you're using the Interactive Fill Tool.

■ **Angle**   The Angle value applies to linear fountain fills and is set in degree values between 360 and –360 (a negative value). Positive angles rotate the fill counterclockwise, while negative values rotate the fill clockwise.

■ **Edge Pad**   This option sets the amount of contrast between the To and From colors, expressed in percentage. The default setting, 0, creates smooth, even blends at the slowest possible rate. Increasing this setting causes colors to change more abruptly, as shown next. Edge Pad can be set within a range of 0 to 49 percent, and this can also be adjusted in Object Properties (ALT+ENTER) and in the Fountain Fill dialog (F11). Moving the color markers of a Linear fill away from or toward your object's outline increases or decreases this value; try dragging the To and From color markers to positions outside of the object, for example, to decrease the Edge Pad effect.

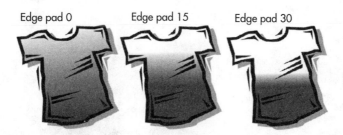

Edge pad 0   Edge pad 15   Edge pad 30

■ **Center Offsets**   Radial, Conical, or Square fountain fills feature this marker; you change the center position of the fill relative to your object's center by dragging the marker. Dragging the center marker of a Radial, Conical, or Square fill away from or toward your object's center also increases or decreases the Edge Pad value.

■ **Steps**   This setting affects both the display and printing of fountain fills. A fountain fill is actually calculated by blending neighboring bands of color in succession, but you don't see this banding effect because so many shades of intermediate colors are used between the To and From color. The Steps option is fixed at the maximum setting of 256 by default. However, you might be *looking for* a banding effect, to create shirt stripes or other geometric patterns. To lower this setting, click to unlock the Lock button. Lowered step values cause the color gradation in your fill to become unsmooth, as shown next. While 256 steps is set and locked, fountain fills will display and print using the maximum capabilities of your monitor and printer resolution.

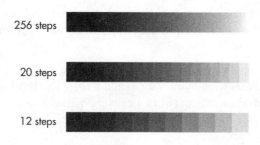

256 steps

20 steps

12 steps

17

Using Custom Fountain Fills

A default fountain fill features two colors, but you can *add* colors to make any type of fountain fill your own version. When colors are added, the appearance of your fill will change dramatically. The position of added colors is shown by node positions on the dashed line guide joining the two default colors. After you've added color markers and clicked on them to select them on the object, the Property Bar will display their Position and Color, as shown here:

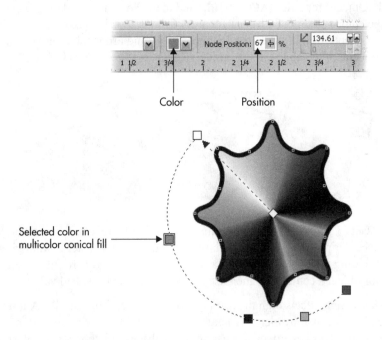

You can add, move, and delete fountain fill colors you've added to a default fountain fill type in several ways, but you *must* have both the object and the Interactive Fill Tool selected, or you'll wind up editing the filled object and not the fill itself! To explore doing this, follow the steps in this tutorial.

Editing a Fountain Fill In-Place

1. Select the object to be filled, choose the Interactive Fill Tool (G), and then apply a fountain fill by choosing Linear, Radial, Conical, or Square from the Property Bar Fill Type selector.

2. With a default fill applied, double-click a point on the guide between the two existing color markers where you want to add a color marker. Doing this adds a color that is based on an average of two existing marker colors, so your custom fountain fill probably looks the same as the default fill.

3. Decide on a new intermediate color (choose one in this example on the Color Palette), and drag a color from the color well (drag the swatch) onto your new marker. You have a three-color gradient now.

4. Try a different technique to add a color marker position and a color at the same time: drag a Color Palette well directly onto the same fountain fill guide, but at a different location.

5. To reposition an added color, click-drag it along the guide path. As you do this, the color's node position changes, as indicated by the Node Position value on the Property Bar.

6. To change any fountain fill color, click to select it, and choose a color from the Property Bar selector or click a color well on the Color Palette.

7. To delete an added color, right-click or double-click it on the guide. To and From color nodes can't be deleted, but they can be recolored.

Setting Fountain Fill Dialog Options

The interactive way is great for controlling fountain fills, but if you want deeper and more precise controls, you can use the Fountain Fill dialog, shown in Figure 17-4.

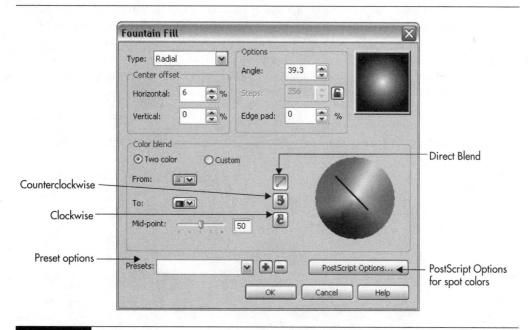

FIGURE 17-4   The Fountain Fill dialog provides some options common to the Property Bar and others unique to this box.

You can open the Fountain Fill dialog while a fountain fill is applied to a selected object and while using the Interactive Fill Tool by clicking the Edit Fill button in the Property Bar. Or, with your object selected and while any tool is in use, press F11.

The Fountain Fill dialog options that aren't available while you're using the Interactive Fill Tool Property Bar are listed and explained here:

■ **Color Wheel Rotation**   This option is available only while a two-color blend is selected. You can choose to blend directly from one color to the other (the default), more or less "jumping" the hue cycle the traditional color wheel goes through, or choose Counterclockwise or Clockwise to blend between colors while cycling through a standard color wheel's colors, traveling around the outside edge of the wheel. This might seem like a trivial option, but CorelDRAW is one of the few design programs that can shortcut through the traditional model of visible colors. For example, in other applications, a fountain fill that goes from red to blue necessarily has to travel through green, somewhat muddying the fountain fill. Not so if you choose Direct Blend here.

■ **PostScript Options**   When a two-color fountain fill is selected with both the From and To colors specified as *spot color inks,* the PostScript Options button becomes available. PostScript Options offer halftone screens of special fills to certain dot shapes. Possessing PostScript level 3 capabilities, CorelDRAW X4 features an expanded collection of screen styles including CosineDot, Cross, various Diamond styles, various Double and InvertedDoubleDot styles, various Ellipse and InvertedEllipseA and other styles, Euclidean, Grid, Rhomboid, Round, Square, and Star shapes. While any of these styles is selected, Frequency and Angle options are available in the PostScript Options dialog, enabling you to override default printing settings for your selected spot color inks, shown here:

If you're unfamiliar with spot colors, it's the printing process used to add a color to packages, for example, that cannot be reproduced using standard press inks, such as that reflective silver logo on a box of cereal. See Chapter 28 for the lowdown on spot versus process colors and a guide to commercial printing of your CorelDRAW work.

- ■ **Presets** The Presets drop-down menu includes a variety of sample fountain fill types, colors, and positions; use them as they are or edit them to suit a specific need. To select any of these, choose a name from the drop-down list. While you're browsing the alphabetical list, a preview of the highlighted preset is displayed in the fountain fill preview window in the upper-right corner of the dialog. Although the Presets list becomes available only when the Custom option is selected, a preset can contain any of the properties associated with a two-color or custom fountain fill color.

- ■ **Add/Delete Presets** The two small buttons to the right of the Presets drop-down list can save you hours of custom fountain fill creation time. First, the button labeled with the minus (–) symbol deletes your current selection from the list of preset fountain fills after presenting a confirmation dialog, just to ensure that you don't delete a factory preset by accident. The button labeled with a plus (+) symbol is for saving the current fountain fill as a preset.

To save your selected fountain fill settings, follow these steps.

 ## Saving Your Own Fill as a Preset

1. With your custom fountain fill colors and options set in the Fountain Fill dialog, enter a name in the Presets box.

2. Click the + button. Your custom fountain fill is immediately saved alphabetically in the list of available presets.

3. Click OK to apply the saved preset and close the dialog.

4. To retrieve and apply your saved preset to fill a selected object, press F11 to open the Fountain Fill dialog, click Custom to view the Presets menu, choose your saved preset from the list, and click OK to close the dialog and apply the saved fountain fill.

Applying Pattern Fills

Pattern fills are rectangular-shaped tiles that repeat vertically and horizontally to fill a closed-path object completely. They come in three different varieties: Two Color, Full Color, and Bitmap, each with its own unique qualities, shown in Figure 17-5.

17

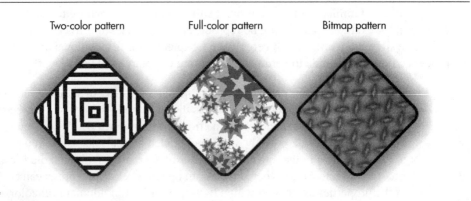

Two-color pattern   Full-color pattern   Bitmap pattern

FIGURE 17-5   Pattern fills come in three types.

While a pattern fill is applied, the Property Bar includes a host of options that can be used to apply dramatic changes to the fill's appearance, as shown here when the Two Color Pattern fill has been applied to an object, and the object is currently selected:

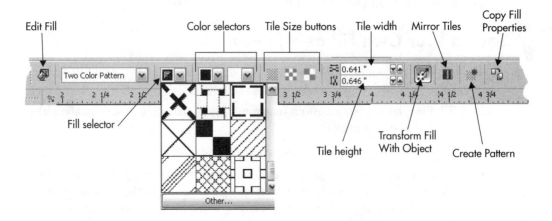

Two-color patterns are 1-bit pixel-based tiles where the two colors in the pattern may be controlled. This means that the edges of the design are harsh and somewhat jaggy at large pattern sizes; they're of the most professional use when you need a quick pattern for a Web GIF image. Full-color patterns are composed of vector shapes, but the pattern itself already has color applied and cannot be altered. Additionally, these full-color fills cannot be extracted as vector shapes from the pattern. Therefore, when making your own, save a copy of your pattern to CDR file format for editing in the future, and forget about the Break Apart and Convert To Curves commands in an attempt to reduce a full-color pattern to its vector component shapes. Bitmap patterns are carefully edited bitmaps; some of the presets are taken from photos while others are paintings, and all of them are relatively small in dimensions. The difference between a full-color and a bitmap fill is that the vector-based pattern tiles for the full-color fills can be resized without losing design detail, focus, or introducing noise, but enlarging bitmap pattern tiles carries the same caveat as enlarging any bitmap—the more you enlarge it, the better your chances are that the component pixels will eventually become visible. You can scale bitmaps down, but not up—computers are "smart," but they can't create extra visual data from data that wasn't there to begin with.

Controlling Pattern Fills Interactively

Interactive markers come into play for tailoring the pattern fill to the object containing the fill, and various Property Bar options common to all patterns become available.

The interactive handles surrounding a pattern fill help you to set the tile size, offset, skew, and rotation of the pattern. To experience this firsthand, breeze through this tutorial.

Customizing a Pattern Fill

1. Select an object to fill, and then choose the Interactive Fill Tool (G).

2. Using the Property Bar options, choose Two Color Pattern from the Fill Type selector. By default, a two-color dot-style pattern fill featuring Black as the Front color and White as the Back color is applied to your object featuring fill markers.

3. Click the Medium Tile button in the Property Bar to set the resolution of the pattern fill to medium. Notice the markers change position to match the tile size.

4. Drag the diamond-shaped handle slightly in any direction. Notice that the center origin of the pattern changes.

5. Drag either the black marker representing the Front fill color or the white marker representing the Back color in a circular motion in any direction. Notice the skew properties of the tile change.

6. Drag the circular-shaped marker in any direction. Notice that the rotational appearance of the pattern tile changes as you do this. Now drag the same handle toward or away from the diamond-shaped handle.

7. Drag a color from your onscreen Color Palette to either the black or white color markers. Notice that the Front or Back color of your two-color pattern changes.

Figure 17-6 shows the marker handles around a two-color pattern fill. Copy Fill Properties is used in this figure to add a custom pattern fill to the glasses lens at right.

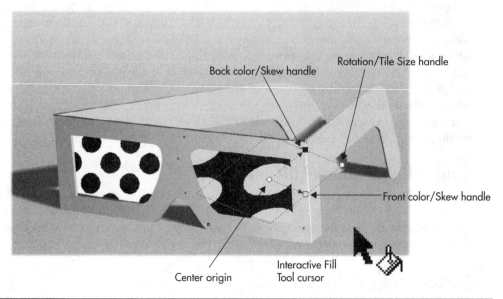

Back color/Skew handle

Rotation/Tile Size handle

Front color/Skew handle

Center origin

Interactive Fill
Tool cursor

FIGURE 17-6 The interactive markers surrounding a two-color pattern fill are there for you to control the pattern's colors, size, and skew.

In addition to altering pattern properties, the Property Bar has features to control the appearance of your pattern in the following ways:

- **Fill Selector** Use this drop-down box to choose from existing pattern fill libraries.

- **Front/Back Color Selectors** When a two-color pattern is selected, these two selectors let you set colors other than black and white for a pattern.

- **Tile Size Buttons** Use these buttons to set your pattern to Small, Medium, or Large preset width and height sizes.

- **Tile Width/Height** The Width and Height sizes of your selected pattern can be set individually using these two options, each of which can be set within a range between 0.1 and 15 inches. If you need a larger tile, use the Two-Color Fill dialog, where you can set a maximum width/height of 60 inches.

- **Transform Fill With Object** When this option is active, transformations applied to your object will also be applied to your fill pattern. This is a useful feature when you need to scale an object larger and don't want your pattern to "shrink"!

- **Mirror Fill Tiles** Using this option forces a transformed pattern tile back into a seamless pattern.

Using Pattern Fill Dialog Options

The Pattern Fill dialog offers an alternative way to control pattern fills (see Figure 17-7). To open this dialog (which is nearly identical for two-color, full-color, and bitmap pattern fills), click the Edit Fill button in the Property Bar while a pattern fill type is in effect.

Here's what each of the options in the Pattern Fill dialog controls:

■ **Origin** The X and Y Origin options enable you to offset the center of the pattern from 0 within a range between 30 and –30 inches. Positive X or Y values offset the origin right or upward, while negative values offset the origin downward or left.

■ **Transform** These options are Skew and Rotate, each of which is measured in degrees. Skew values are within a range between 89 and –89 degrees, while Rotate values can be set between 360 and –360 degrees. These options work in combination with each other to apply vertical and/or horizontal distortion to the fill pattern, as shown here:

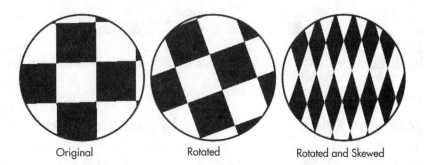

Original   Rotated   Rotated and Skewed

■ **Row and Column Offsets** By default, pattern tiles join to appear seamless. However, you can inadvertently ruin the pattern by offsetting the pattern seams through either of these two options. To apply an offset, choose either Row or Column as the offset option, and enter a value between 0 and 100 percent, as shown here:

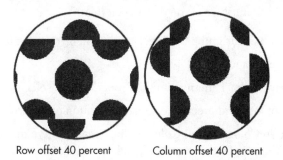

Row offset 40 percent   Column offset 40 percent

17

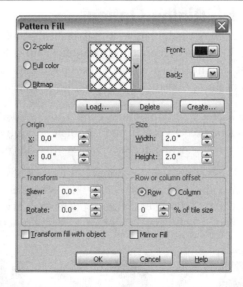

FIGURE 17-7 The Pattern Fill dialog provides an alternative method for setting pattern fill properties.

Create Your Own Two-Color and Full-Color Patterns

You can create a two-color pattern based on a selection of objects by clicking the Create Pattern button in the Property Bar while the Interactive Fill Tool and Two Color or Full Color Pattern is selected. This opens a dialog for specifying the new pattern type and resolution. After you choose the type and resolution, crosshairs will appear on your screen, enabling you to click-drag to define an area in your document to use for the new pattern; then the pattern will be added to your two-color or full-color pattern selectors.

It's important that you follow the technique exactly, or you'll accidentally call the dialog for setting fill and text attributes (you don't want this):

1. Select the object or group of objects with which you want to create the fill.

2. Choose the Interactive Fill Tool.

3. Choose Two Color Pattern from the Property Bar's selector drop-down.

4. Click the orange and green Create Pattern button on the Property Bar.

5. Choose Two Color (or Full Color) in the Create Pattern dialog that appears. Choose Low, Medium, or High Resolution, and then click OK.

6. Drag the crosshairs to create a rectangular shape around the object(s) to become the fill.

7. Release the cursor and then click OK in the confirmation box that appears.

8. Showtime! Your pattern has been saved and can be accessed from the selector on the Property Bar the next time you want to fill an object.

Understand that it takes time and experience to create a *seamless* pattern (a subject discussed in Chapter 27). However, it's very easy to drag the Make Pattern crosshairs around a single shape on the page, and then to use the Offset option to stagger the shape so it repeats in an eye-pleasing pattern.

To *manually* create and edit a two-color pattern, with the Interactive Fill Tool selected, choose Two Color Pattern from the drop-down selector on the Property Bar. Then click the Create Pattern button (the orange button, second from right on the Property Bar) to open the Two-Color Pattern Editor dialog (see Figure 17-8) and edit the pattern by choosing a tile size, a cursor size, and then left-dragging and/or clicking to set the foreground pattern; right-clicks and right-click-drags act like an eraser. Alternatively, you can click Load if you've created a bitmap image (a two-color one works best, so the Editor doesn't brute-force a tonal image to black or white); the Editor accepts TIF, BMP, and other image file formats.

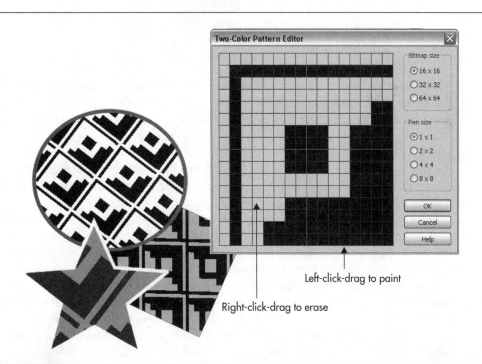

Left-click-drag to paint

Right-click-drag to erase

FIGURE 17-8 Create your own two-color pattern by clicking the Create pattern; then edit an existing preset pattern.

17

You can also create patterns by using the Tools | Create | Pattern menu command.

Applying Texture Fills

When you choose a texture fill (the Interactive Fill Tool has been chosen), the Property Bar (shown next) displays texture-related options, including a Texture Library selector, a Texture Fill selector, and options for controlling the appearance of the texture.

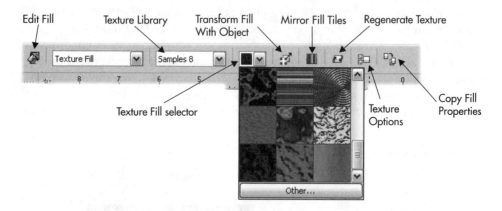

The interactive handles surrounding a texture fill are the same as those for Pattern fills; they're there for you to set the size, offset, skew, and rotation of the texture. If you have experience manipulating pattern fills by click-dragging the control handles above the object, you'll discover bitmap fills are exactly the same. However, because these are *bitmap-based* textures, you'll need to take note of some transformation limitations, covered shortly.

As you'll discover next, each texture is based on a range of variables specific to a style type. To view these core styles, you'll need to open the Texture Fill dialog (see Figure 17-9) by clicking the Edit Fill button.

You'll notice below that the same options available in the Property Bar are in the dialog—but also included when you click the Edit Fill button are the texture variables. There are settings for texture, color, frequency of properties of the textures, and so on. Don't hesitate to drag a spin box value and then click Preview; although several of the values might seem to have strange labels for the values, they'll indeed modify the texture preset (changing the Texture # is a great place to begin experimenting). Also, it's very hard to give a label to some of the properties of fractal math; they're abstract attributes and fairly difficult to write in the first place! Start by choosing a type of texture from the Texture List, and then use different values in fields such as colors (another good starting place). Click Preview, and

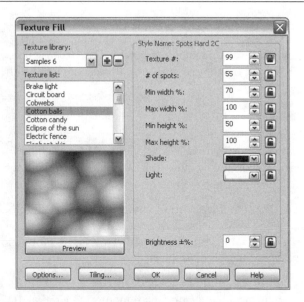

FIGURE 17-9   Texture fills are based on fractal and procedural math algorithms, which generate images based on math "recipes."

if you like what you see, save it as a Preset, click OK to apply the texture, and then use the control handles for the Interactive Fill Tool to adjust the fill as it appears in the selected shape.

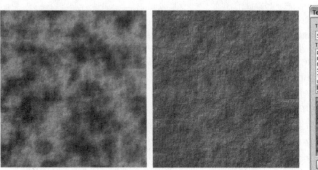

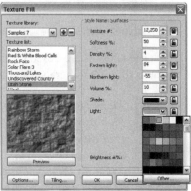

17

What Is a Fractal?

Fractal geometry is based on mathematical equations, whose core is beyond the scope of this book; however, fractal geometry usually appears to have the following visual characteristics:

- **Self-similarity** Fractal designs branch with variations set by the mathematician writing the fractal math, but typically a fractal design repeats a basic structure within itself at smaller scales, branching from a main body in the design. This is why many fractals look like organic forms such as ferns, broccoli, and seashells—these designs in nature also obey fractal math.

- **A recursive structure with irregularities** As with self-similarity, fractals repeat, with variations, as they branch. If you're familiar with Euclidean geometry, fractal math is too unpredictable when plotted to 2D space to be described in Euclidian geometric functions.

- **Exist within a domain of 2D or 3D space** Fractal math is used in several 3D programs to generate organic sculptures. KPT Frax4D, in fact, is a plug-in for PHOTO-PAINT and other bitmap programs that can generate fractal designs in 3D space. Fractals were once described by a mathematician using this analogy: if a square represents the number *2* and a cube represents the number *3*, fractals live somewhere between these two integers.

Understand that not all the Texture fills use fractal math; some use procedures (a recipe of equations), but overall, they're just *fun* to add to a design. And because they're math-based they can be rendered to the size you need—this is part of what the Regenerate button on the Property Bar is for.

The textures are based on more than a hundred different styles ranging from bubbles and clouds through minerals, raindrops, ripples, rock, and vapor.

TIP *Many of the fractal patterns in the Samples libraries do not seamlessly tile all on their own. Fractal math can be coded as nonterminating (which creates an infinite branching and can be quite processor-intensive) and terminating, which means the math ends at a certain point and you'll see a tile edge in your design once in a while. To fix this: click the Mirror button on the Property Bar when the object is selected and when the Interactive Fill Tool is chosen. Alternatively, this option is available by clicking the Tiling button on the Property Bar, to display the Texture Fill dialog, where there's a check box for Mirroring at lower right. The texture fill will then appear in your object as a seamless one, regardless of how you scale, rotate, and skew the pattern.*

Setting Texture Fill Options

Besides being able to set the appearance of your
texture fill interactively and to customize the fill
using the value fields in the Texture Fill dialog, you'll
want to be able to set other options, too. For example,
if your texture fill looks like it's been pushed through
a screen window, it means the resolution is too low, as
measured in pixels per inch (called dots per inch [dpi]
in the dialog). To increase the texture size and its
resolution, click the Texture Options button in the
Property Bar to open the Texture Options dialog,
shown at right.

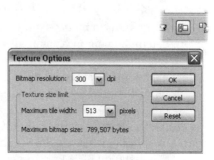

By default, texture fills are initially created at a resolution of 300 dpi and at a tile width
of 2,049 pixels. Increasing both of these settings will sharpen and add detail to your texture,
as shown here:

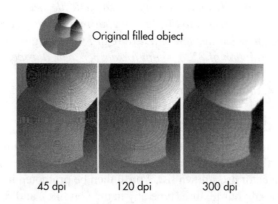

Original filled object

45 dpi   120 dpi   300 dpi

Texture options affect the appearance of your texture fill in the following ways:

- **Bitmap Resolution**   The Bitmap Resolution option sets the amount of detail in the
  bitmap image created. By default, the bitmap resolution setting is 300 dpi, but it can
  be reset to preset values ranging between 75 and 400 dpi, and to a maximum value
  of 9999 dpi.

- **Texture Size Limit**   This option should be set according to both the desired
  resolution of your texture and the size of your object. To avoid seeing seams
  between your texture's tiles (which will ruin the effect), set the tile larger than the
  object it fills *and* ensure that the tile seams are hidden from view; use the Mirror
  button on the Property Bar if necessary.

17

Calculating the Resolution of Texture Fills

If you're the ambitious, professional sort, you can use a very non-nerdy equation to determine your maximum tile width setting. Calculate the value based on twice the final line screen multiplied by the longest object dimension in inches. Line screens are what PostScript laser printers and commercial printer image-setting devices use for reproduction. You're good to go with 133 lines per inch (lpi; this value is half of 266 dpi, which is commonly used in high-quality art books); 1200 dpi laser printers can use 85 lpi. Inkjet printers don't arrange dots in a logical order (they sort of splatter ink on the page), but a ballpark estimate (if inkjets were to render lines of dots) would be about 180 lpi for inkjet printers manufactured as late as 2007. Enter this value in the Maximum Tile Width box, or choose the next highest preset value available.

NOTE *Increasing the Bitmap Resolution and Maximum Tile Width settings of your texture fill can dramatically increase your saved CDR file size and the time it takes for high-resolution textures to display on your monitor. For screen display, you can usually get an accurate view of a texture at 1:1 viewing resolution (100 percent) with a texture resolution of 72 to 96 dpi (pixels per inch, dots per inch). Coincidentally, this is also an ideal texture resolution for web graphics, because visitors to your website are also viewing your texture at 1:1 on their monitors.*

Creating and Saving Texture Samples

Once you've gone to the effort of selecting or editing a texture fill to suit your needs, you may wish to save it for later retrieval. To save a texture, click the + button to the right of the Texture Library selector drop-down list. You'll then be prompted in the Save Texture As dialog for the name of your texture (type any name you like), and for the name of the library in which you want the texture saved. Click a library name found in the drop-down list, click OK, click OK in the Texture Fill dialog, and your custom texture is ready to be applied to the selected object.

Applying PostScript Fills

PostScript fills are vector-based and use PostScript page-descriptor language to create a variety of patterns from black-and-white to full color. Each PostScript fill included with CorelDRAW has individual variables that control the appearance of the pattern, much the same way as you can customize texture fills. PostScript pattern styles come in a variety of patterns, as shown in Figure 17-10, and also come as nonrepeating fills.

While using the Interactive Fill Tool and while PostScript Fill is selected in the Property Bar Fill Type selector, very few options that relate to the individual fills are available on the

| **FIGURE 17-10** | PostScript fills come in a variety of repeating and nonrepeating patterns.

Property Bar. You need to click the Edit Fill button on the Property Bar to get access to line widths, how large the pattern elements should be, and color options, depending on the specific preset.

The image you see onscreen is an accurate representation of the actual pattern that will be printed; again, PostScript is a printing technology, but Corel Corporation has made the technology viewable in CorelDRAW and printable without the need for a PostScript printer. On that note, it should be mentioned that PostScript fills will print exceptionally well to any PostScript device; that's what the fills are intended for, but you don't necessarily have to use PostScript. However, *you must be using Enhanced View to see it* (choose View | Enhanced).

To apply a PostScript fill, use these steps:

1. Create and then select the object to apply any PostScript Texture fill, and then choose the Interactive Fill Tool (G).

2. Using Property Bar options, choose a PostScript fill from the selector by name.

3. To customize the fill, click the Edit Fill button in the Property Bar to open the PostScript Texture dialog, shown in Figure 17-11. To view your currently selected fill, click the Preview Fill option. Notice that each fill has its own set of Parameters that can be changed.

17

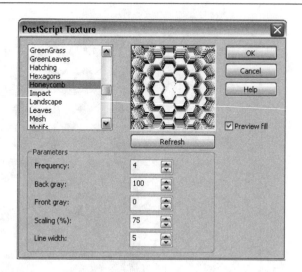

FIGURE 17-11   The PostScript Texture dialog lets you customize a PostScript fill.

4. Make any changes to your fill, and click the Refresh button to view the results of your new settings.

5. Click OK to accept the fill, close the dialog, and apply the new fill to your object. Your object is now filled with a PostScript Texture fill.

PostScript fills can be very useful in schematic and roadmap illustrations, and if you use no background color when you customize many of the fills, the fills support transparency. So you can actually apply, for example, Crosshatching over a color-filled object to enhance the shading.

Applying Mesh Fills

Mesh fills take advantage of PostScript level 3 technology and create the effect of several blending-color fountain fills over a mesh of vertical and horizontal Bézier curves. Editing a mesh grid creates a sort of fill that doesn't really look like a fountain fill but instead looks very much like a *painting*. The effect is not unlike dabbing liquid ink onto an absorbent surface such as watercolor paper or a tissue. You'll find the Interactive Mesh Fill Tool, shown on the left, in the Toolbox grouped with the Interactive Fill Tool; or press M for speedy selection.

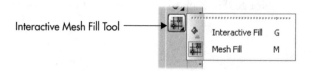

While the Interactive Mesh Fill Tool is selected, the Property Bar features a number of options, shown next, for controlling this truly unique fill type. Use these options to set the vertical and horizontal size in the mesh grid, to alter node and curve conditions, and to set the smoothness of curves.

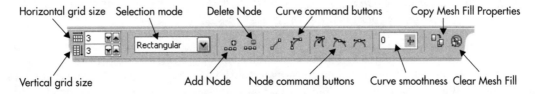

Horizontal grid size | Selection mode | Delete Node | Curve command buttons | Copy Mesh Fill Properties

Vertical grid size | Add Node | Node command buttons | Curve smoothness | Clear Mesh Fill

Applying a mesh grid to an object is a quick operation. Mesh fills are dynamic, so they can be edited and reedited at any time. Editing the shape and color of a mesh grid can be a little bit of a challenge your first time out, but to be able to smear and almost paint on a fill will make the effort worthwhile to you and your work. Node and curve editing actions to move fill areas are done exactly the same as for Bézier curves. For information on how to do this, see Chapter 10.

To apply a mesh fill to an object and add color, use these steps.

Blending Colors Using the Mesh Fill

1. Select any noncompound (no combined paths, no holes in object), closed-path shape, and then choose the Interactive Mesh Fill Tool. A default mesh fill grid is applied to the object.

2. Using Property Bar options, change the number of vertical and/or horizontal grids you think you'd like to create; higher numbers of divisions make the object easier to build complex fills within. Each time a grid change is made, the grid is updated.

3. Click one of the grid intersection points either at the perimeter of the object or within the interior area.

4. Click any color in your onscreen Color Palette. Notice that the color is smoothly and evenly blended in a circular area around the point. To use an alternative technique, click-drag a color well from your onscreen palette onto a grid point. You can also apply color to entire grid patches by using the same technique. Try lasso-selecting several grid nodes and then change their color. It's useful when working with mesh fills to undock the Color Palette and float it close to your work area so that accessing well colors requires less skill and effort.

5. Either put your cursor on a node, or lasso-select several nodes, and then click-drag. Wet media in a vector drawing program!

17

You don't have to select an entire patch to create color changes. You can select a single node, several patches, and parts of patches. Selecting a row or column of nodes and then changing their color can create an interesting effect.

 When moving nodes, don't select the outside border nodes, the ones that define the outside of your shape. Dragging on these nodes changes the shape of the object—unless this is your intention, of course!

Mesh Fill Control Handles

Applying a mesh fill immediately converts the object to a "mesh object" by converting it to curves. While a mesh fill is applied, the various parts can be manipulated and edited, often dramatically altering the appearance of the object. Figure 17-12 shows the various parts of a mesh fill.

 Mesh fill effects may be applied only to single-path objects, meaning compound objects are not eligible for this type of fill.

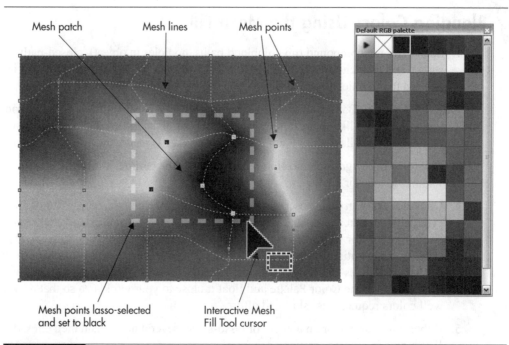

FIGURE 17-12 A mesh fill involves these different parts.

Mesh Fill Advanced Editing Techniques

A mesh fill can include up to 50 individual vertical and/or horizontal patches. Although you change these values by using the Property Bar's + or – button, you can also do it interactively by double-clicking any point on the grid or between the grid lines. Adding a new mesh point adds either a new vertical or new horizontal mesh line to the complexity of the effect. To add a single node without adding an associated mesh line, click a point on the line, right-click to open the pop-up menu, and choose Add Node. To delete a point with your cursor, double-click the point.

 To add a mesh point quickly anywhere on an existing mesh line or mesh patch, double-click anywhere on the mesh object.

While a mesh point or mesh line is selected, you change the node or curve properties using options on the Property Bar, or by right-clicking a point or line and using the options on the context-sensitive pop-up menu. Mesh line properties can be changed by choosing To Line or To Curve, and mesh points may be changed by choosing Cusp, Smooth, or Symmetrical. To delete a selected mesh point or mesh line without the Property Bar options, right-click the point or line and choose Delete from the pop-up menu, or press DELETE.

 To select all the mesh points in a mesh object instantly, double-click the Interactive Mesh Fill Tool button in the Toolbox while a mesh object is selected.

Mesh fills can be applied to vector *and* bitmap objects; however, unless the visual content of the imported bitmap is very, very simple (like a screen capture of a cursor or icon), the bitmap will be a good starting place for playing with colors, but the visual content often will resemble oatmeal after you begin editing the mesh nodes. Here's the deal: with bitmap objects, the bitmap's color is mapped to the mesh intersection points, and fountain fills are then created. Although you may clear a mesh fill effect from a vector shape and return it to its original condition, the same does not apply to bitmap objects, but don't worry—CorelDRAW imports bitmaps so your original photo of your pets or family remains unchanged.

 After a mesh fill has been applied to an object, the object cannot be filled with any other fill type unless the mesh fill effect has first been cleared. To clear a mesh fill applied to a selected object, click the Clear Mesh button in the Property Bar.

If you've had your fill, this is okay…so have your objects. You've learned in this chapter how to tap into CorelDRAW fills, and hopefully you've also seen how important fills can be to your drawings. Fills can actually be more visually complex than the shape of objects. Take a cardboard box, for example. The shape of the box isn't that interesting and takes only a few seconds to draw. But the texture of a cardboard box is where the object gets its character and mood.

Line attributes are covered in the following chapter, where you can do as much with customizing the thing that goes *around* an object as with the object itself.

17

CHAPTER 18

Outline Attributes

C hapter 17 covers only half the story about how you can flesh out a visual idea by using CorelDRAW. Although an object can usually live its life just fine without an outline, the attributes you can apply to a path can add a touch of refinement to an illustration. The right outline color can help visually separate different objects. Additionally, you can simulate calligraphic strokes without using Artistic Media when you know how to work the Outline Pen dialog; you can even make a path a dashed line, complete with arrowheads for fancy presentations and elegant maps. In fact, an outline, especially an open outline, can live its life in your work just fine without defining a filled object! You don't have to draw the line at fills and effects in your CorelDRAW artwork. This chapter shows you the ins and outs of properties you apply to your paths, from beginning to end.

Applying Outline Pen Properties

By default, when you create an open or closed path, it's given a ½-point-wide outline in black, with no fancy extras. Part of the rationale for this default is that vector paths can't really be seen without some sort of width. In contrast, bitmap artwork by definition is made up of pixels, written to screen and written to file; so when a user draws an outline, it always has a width (it's always visible). Happily, vector drawing programs can display a wide range of path properties, and unlike with bitmap outlines, you can change your mind at any time and easily alter the property of an outline.

In a number of areas in CorelDRAW, you can apply a property such as color, stroke width, and other fun stuff to an open or closed path (and even to open paths that don't touch each other but have been unified using the Arrange | Combine command). The following sections explore your options and point out the smartest and most convenient way to travel in the document window to quickly arrive at the perfect outline. When an open path or an object (which necessarily has to be described using a path) is selected on the page, the Property Bar offers a lot of options for outline properties. You can also dig into the Outline Pen Toolbox flyout (and even detach it to make it persistent in the workspace for repeated access), and there's also the Properties dialog—accessed from the pop-up menu when you right-click a path, and ALT-ENTER also gets you there. Some shortcuts for performing simple property adjustments are covered on the long and winding path through this chapter.

Outline Pen Options and the Property Bar

Although it doesn't offer all options for path properties, the Property Bar is probably the most convenient route to outline properties. It actively displays a selected path's *current* properties, which you can change when a path is selected. The Property Bar, shown here while a path is selected, has width, style, and arrowhead options—you can make an open path with a head, tail, two heads—it's up to you. Other options pertain to controlling connector lines, wrapping text around a path, and items not directly related to the look of the outline. Closed paths, naturally, can't have arrowheads, but your options for dashed lines and other attributes are available for rectangles, ellipses, all the polygon shapes, and for freeform closed curves you've drawn by hand.

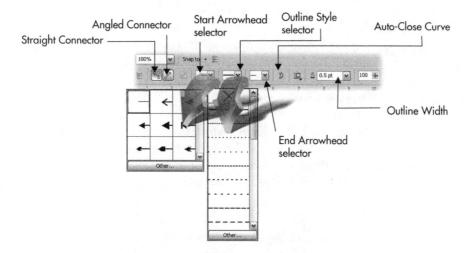

The following tutorial is intended to hone your skills when you use the Property Bar options.

Going Long and Wide

1. Using the Pick Tool, select a path by clicking it once.

2. On the Property Bar, choose a thickness using the Outline Width selector, or enter a value and then press ENTER.

3. For arrowheads (on an open path), click the Start or End Arrowhead selectors, and then choose an arrowhead style from the pop-up. The Start option applies an arrowhead to the first node of the path; the End option applies it to the last. Therefore, this might not be the direction in which you want the arrow to point. You have to perform a little mental juggling; the head of your arrow is always the *last* node on a path you create, not the first.

4. To apply a dashed or dotted-line pattern to the path, click the Outline Style selector, and then choose from one of the presets. Creating custom dashed patterns is covered later in this chapter.

5. Try increasing and decreasing the outline width, and see what happens to dashed line styles and arrowheads; they scale proportionately to the width of the outline.

As you apply outline properties from the Property Bar to your object or path, the effect is immediately visible, making this method both quick and convenient to use.

18

To quickly define the color of a shape's outline, right-click over any Color Palette color well.

Using the Outline Tool

The Toolbox method is a different way to define the properties of a path. The Outline Tool isn't really a tool at all but rather it's a flyout selector of options, shown next. If you're working on outlines a lot in a design, the Outline Tool—like all the Toolbox tools—can be floated as a palette by dragging on the tread marks at the top of the flyout into the workspace. Here you can see access points to the Outline Pen dialog, which offers options not available on the Property Bar; the Outline Color dialog (which is a one-shot deal); and the Color docker, whose options overlap the Outline Color dialog, but here it's a persistent element, always available for you to use. Also, you have seven preset widths for outlines, and an *"X,"* which removes a path's outline width, making it invisible.

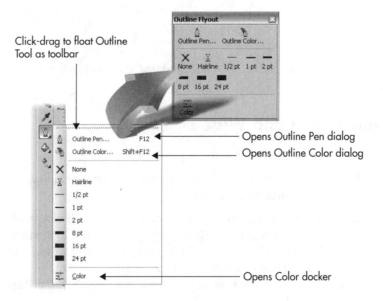

 If you're new to CorelDRAW and want to use the Outline Tool as a floating toolbar, it would be nice if the outline widths were labeled! You can display titles on the Outline Flyout (palette) by right-clicking on the palette and then choosing Customize | Outline Flyout Toolbar | Caption Below Image or Caption To Right Of Image. Also, when you apply a preset width, doing so does not change the current color of an outline—you use the Color docker or the Outline Color dialog to do this.

Exploring the Outline Pen Dialog

Use the Outline Pen dialog for total control over a single object's outline or a selected group. It includes the same set of options available in the Property Bar, plus several more.

 The Eyedropper and Paintbucket tools can be used to sample and apply outline properties between objects.

The Outline Pen dialog includes options for specifying outline color, editing arrowhead and outline styles, and setting nib shape and transformation behavior; this is the only place in CorelDRAW where you'll find all these options together. To open the Outline Pen dialog, shown in Figure 18-1, the quickest way is to double-click the Outline well on the Status Bar, but you can also choose the dialog from the Outline Flyout (pressing F12 gets you there, too).

Setting Outline Color

Using the Pen Color selector in the Outline Pen dialog, you can choose a color for your selected path(s). Pen Color affects only the color of the object's path; object fills are not changed. Outline color can be set only to CorelDRAW's Uniform colors from the drop-down palette. To access every color collection and color model for outlines, click the Other button located at the bottom of the Pen Color selector in the dialog, shown next. By doing this,

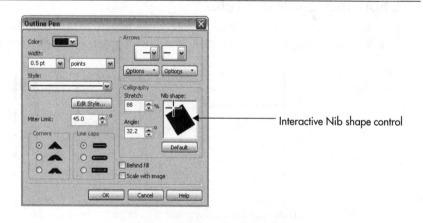

Interactive Nib shape control

Double-click on the Status Bar to open the dialog

18

FIGURE 18-1   Comprehensive options for outline properties are in the Outline Pen dialog.

you'll also have access to all CorelDRAW's color palettes, including custom swatches and the Color Mixer.

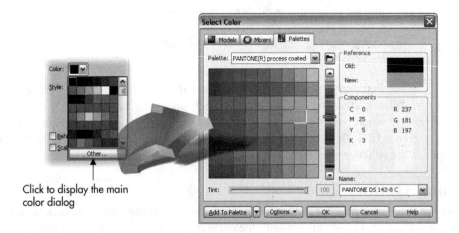

Click to display the main color dialog

If you want color control and don't need to fuss with dashed outlines, arrowheads, or other outline attributes, don't choose the Outline Pen dialog—click the Outline Color dialog button on the Outline Flyout in the Toolbox.

Choosing Outline Styles

For a quick way to apply a dashed- or dotted-line pattern to the path of a selected object, the Outline Style selector offers more than 28 different preset variations, shown here.

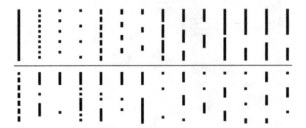

Applying an outline style causes a pattern to appear along the entire path, which is a must for anything you need to visually suggest to the reader that they should go running for the scissors: coupons, tickets, you name it. Styles are repeating patterns of short, long, and a combination of dashes that apply to the entire path. Line styles can be applied to any open or closed path object, as well as to compound paths (paths that look like two or more individual paths, but are bound using the Arrange | Combine command). The quickest way to apply a dashed style is to use the Pick Tool and the Property Bar Outline Style selector when one or more paths are selected, as shown here.

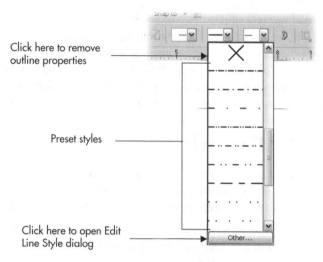

Click here to remove
outline properties

Preset styles

Click here to open Edit
Line Style dialog

> | **TIP** | *Once you have a nice custom outline set of properties defined and want to apply all the parameters to a different path, you can copy outline properties of one path to another by right-clicking and dragging one path to on top of the target path (this doesn't move your original path; it's a special editing technique). Release the mouse button when a crosshairs cursor appears over the target path. Then choose Copy Outline Here from the pop-up menu.*

Creating and Editing Outline Styles

If you're looking for a special dashed-line style, one of your own invention, you can always *build* it. Choose Other from the Style selector in the Property Bar while a curve is selected, or within the Outline Pen dialog click the Edit Style button. Both actions open the Edit Line Style dialog, shown here:

Click to draw or erase part of
the dot/dash pattern

Drag to increase blank space
between pattern dots/dashes

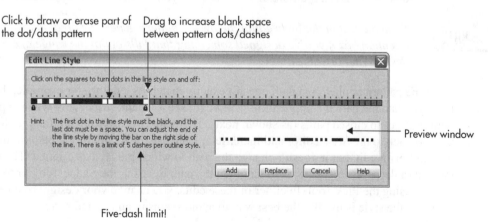

Preview window

Five-dash limit!

18

Creating a custom line style of dots and dashes is a fairly intuitive process, very similar to drawing a line in a paint program; your cursor alternately serves as a pencil and an eraser. Once you save a style by clicking Add, it becomes available throughout CorelDRAW X4 wherever outline styles are offered. Your only limitation, clearly noted in the editor, is that you can't create a sequence consisting of more than five dashes or dots; adjoining marks count as a single dash. To create and save your own custom outline style, follow these steps.

 ## Drawing a Dotted Line Style

1. Create and/or select a path to serve as a host for your new line style, open the Outline Pen dialog (F12), and then click the Edit Style button, or click the Other button at the bottom of the Outline Style selector on the Property Bar.

2. In the Edit Line Style dialog, you see a horizontal pattern generator featuring a slider control, a preview window, and a set of command buttons.

3. In the pattern generator, drag the slider left or right to change the style length. Click (or click-drag to make a long dash segment) on the small squares to the left of the slider to set the on/off states of the pattern. If you want to erase a segment, you click or click-drag on the black square(s) you've drawn. As you do this, the preview window shows the new pattern.

4. Click the Add button to add the new style to the list (or click Replace to overwrite the style currently selected in the Outline Style selector) to return to the Outline Pen dialog. New styles are added to the bottom of the selector list.

5. Verify that your new line style is available by choosing it in the selector and clicking OK to apply your new outline style; it will be at the bottom of the drop-down list, and as with the preset styles, there is no name for custom styles—you search by the look of the saved thumbnail. The line style you created is now applied to the object.

> **NOTE** *Read the text in the Style editor, below the pattern generator area, to avoid an attention box if you've designed something that falls out of the range of acceptable designs and/or values!*

If the pattern applied to a path doesn't exactly match its length—for example, the pattern is longer than the path it's applied to—you might see a "seam," especially when applying outline styles to closed paths (as shown next). There are two ways to cure the problem. One is to go back to the Style editor and increase or decrease the length of the pattern; this is a trial-and-error edit, but it doesn't change the path to which the style is applied. The other method (a desperate measure) is to lengthen the path by using the Shape Tool, or to scale the path by using the Pick Tool. In either of these edits, you change your design, so editing the length or the style is usually the best way to avoid seams in an applied style.

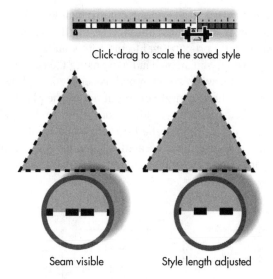

Click-drag to scale the saved style

Seam visible   Style length adjusted

Setting Outline Arrowheads

Arrowheads are both heads *and* tails on an open path, and although you have a handsome collection of preset arrows, they can be almost anything you decide to draw. Most of the preset styles are arrowheads, but some are symbols that represent a tail, as shown in Figure 18-2, and many of the tails match the visual style of the arrowheads. When applied, arrowheads can be set to appear at the start and end points of open paths, both ends, one end, or naturally (by default) neither end.

Here's a trick to defining the size of an arrowhead or tail: you increase or decrease the size of an arrowhead by adjusting the outline width, using the Property Bar or the Outline dialog. However, if you want to scale a path's width *without* scaling the arrowhead, you

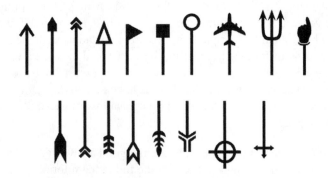

FIGURE 18-2   CorelDRAW includes these arrow styles and many more.

18

scale the path by using the Pick Tool and the control handles surrounding the selected path. Scaling a path (object) instead of increasing/decreasing the outline width is your ticket to making an arrowhead exactly proportional to the path's outline.

The quickest way to apply an arrowhead is by using the Start and/or End Arrowhead selectors in the Property Bar when an open path is selected, as shown here. The Edit Arrowhead dialog, shown shortly, might or might not be the place you want to go if you want to create your own custom arrowhead and/or tail. Procedurally, you need to draw an arrowhead, for example, define it; then the Edit Arrowhead dialog is used to position and scale an arrowhead that's already been created. The editor isn't a drawing window; when you realize this, custom arrowhead and tail creation goes like a charm!

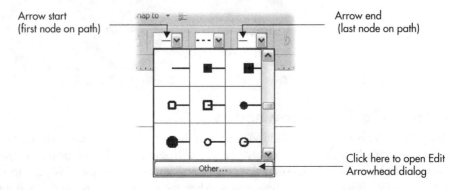

Arrow start (first node on path)

Arrow end (last node on path)

Click here to open Edit Arrowhead dialog

NOTE	*Applying an arrowhead to a closed path has no visible effect unless the path is broken at some point.*

Creating Custom Arrowhead Styles

Realistically, CorelDRAW could not have the ideal arrowhead (and tail) for your (and every other user's) assignment as a preset, or the preset selector would need a head and a tail itself, from here to the moon! That's why there's the Tools | Create | Arrow command—don't choose the command yet; you'll need to draw the arrowhead first, as covered in the following tutorial. The best arrowhead should be simple in its construction and needs to be a single or compound path—fill makes no difference in creating the arrowhead because a finished and applied custom arrow style gets its color from the outline color you use on the selected path in your drawing. The orientation of the arrowhead needs to be in landscape, too, before entering the Create command. In other words, the top of your custom arrowhead design needs to face right, not the top of the page.

To give you an idea of the shape and size of a good arrowhead and tail to design, download Shovel.cdr. You can even use it in the following tutorial.

DOWNLOAD

To create a new arrowhead and save it, follow these steps.

Drawing and Saving an Arrowhead Style

1. Give some thought and planning to what would make a good arrowhead and tail. Shovel.cdr has a drawing of the business and the user ends of a common garden shovel. This works for designs of garden planning (an arrow pointing to "dig here"), treasure hunts, and certain civil engineering diagrams. About 3" for your symbols to be used as arrowheads seems to work well and gets you around the need to edit the size later. When you've drawn your arrowhead (a tail is optional for this tutorial), rotate it so it faces the right of the drawing page.

2. With the shape selected, choose Tools | Create | Arrow, as shown here.

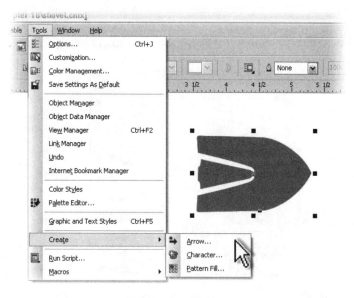

3. Answer OK to the query dialog that appears to confirm this action. Possibly you're done now. Let's check, before calling it a day, to see how the arrowhead, now saved on the arrow selector drop-down list, looks when applied to an open path.

4. With a Pen Tool (the Bézier pen is fine) click-drag a two-node path. Straight is good; a curved path can be more visually interesting for the arrowhead.

5. On the Property Bar with the path selected, choose the 10 pt. outline width so you'll have a clear view of the arrowhead you defined (or the shovel head if you used the Shovel.cdr file).

18

6. On the Property Bar, choose the arrowhead from the last node drop-down selector, the one on the right on the Property Bar. Let's continue here and open the editor whether the arrowhead looks good or not. Click the selector drop-down again, and then choose Other to go to the Edit Arrowhead dialog.

7. Here's where you can correct a number of problems with your arrowhead, outside of editing the path of the arrowhead itself. If, for example, your arrowhead is pointing the wrong way, you click Reflect In X, as shown in this illustration. The black markers are used for scaling your arrowhead; the corner marks scale proportionately, and if you want to stretch your arrowhead, you use the middle markers. The hollow markers indicate the nodes on the path that make up your arrowhead, but they cannot be directly edited; click-drag them to manually reposition an arrowhead relative to the path to which it's associated in the proxy window. If you've made a mistake drawing the arrowhead, you cannot change it in the editor, but instead need to revise your drawing and then redefine the arrowhead. Other controls are here for centering the arrowhead relative to the path. You can zoom in 4X for precision editing, and even move the path away from the arrowhead instead of moving the arrowhead's position.

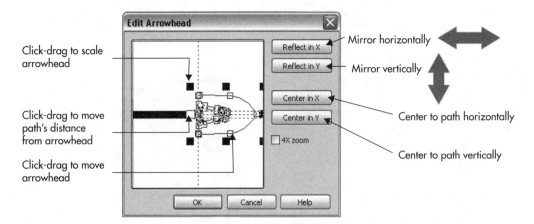

8. Click OK and changes are applied to your arrowhead. The Edit Arrowhead dialog can also be used to modify existing preset arrowheads, but only to the extent that you just modified your custom arrowhead in step 7. End of tour!

Here you can see a few uses for a shovel. Don't be hesitant to mix and match outline styles; in the middle illustration here, a dashed outline style happily coexists with a custom arrowhead.

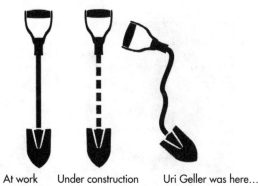

At work   Under construction   Uri Geller was here...

Setting Arrowhead Options

While an arrowhead style is applied, other convenient options are available from within the Outline Pen dialog. Just below each Arrowhead Style selector are two Options buttons. Click either the start or end buttons to open a drop-down menu that features the following commands:

- **None**   Choose this command to clear the arrow style you selected from your path. This can also be done from the document window using the Property Bar.

- **Swap**   This command switches the styles currently selected for the Start and End arrowheads. This cannot be done, at least not as easily, from the document window.

- **New**   Choose this command to open the Edit Arrowhead dialog and to create variation on a default style to add to the existing collection. New does not offer custom arrowhead creation; you need to use Tools | Create, as you learned earlier, to make a truly new arrowhead.

- **Edit**   This command becomes available only while an arrow style is currently selected and opens the Edit Arrowhead dialog to change an existing arrow style, much the same as the New command.

- **Delete**   While an existing style is applied, choosing this command permanently removes the selected style from the collection.

Setting Corner Shape

Frequently, you'll create a path whose segments join at a node in a cusp fashion; the connection is *not* smooth—for example, a crescent moon shape has a least two "sharp" cusp connections between path segments. When shapes have *discontinuous* connections—when a path abruptly changes direction as it passes through a node— you can set the appearance of the node connection through the Outline Pen dialog, the only area in CorelDRAW's interface that offers these options. Therefore, it's always a good idea to remember that double-clicking

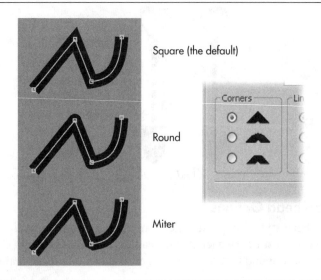

Square (the default)

Round

Miter

FIGURE 18-3   Corners can be set to one of these three styles.

the Outline box on the Status Bar is your quickest route to defining how nodes look as they join two segments. Figure 18-3 shows the visual effect of Round, Miter, and Square (the default) joints on a path that has cusp nodes. Notice that at extremely sharp node connection angles, the Square joint option produces an area of the outline that extends way beyond the path, an exaggerated effect you might not always want in a design. You can use Corner properties creatively to soften the appearance of a node connection (Round works well) and also to keep a severe cusp angle from exaggerating a connection. Miter corners can often keep a path more consistent in its width than the default Corner.

Setting Line Cap Shape

Line caps, the beginning and end of an open path, can look like their counterparts, the corners, covered in the previous section. One of the greatest visual differences you can create is that the true width of a path is extended using the Round and Extended choices—the outline width overshoots the true path's length, proportional to the width you choose for an outline. Figure 18-4 shows examples of your end cap options.

Applying line cap options to the end points of an open path affects not only the first and last nodes' appearance on an open path, but it also affects dashed and dotted line styles, as shown in Figure 18-5.

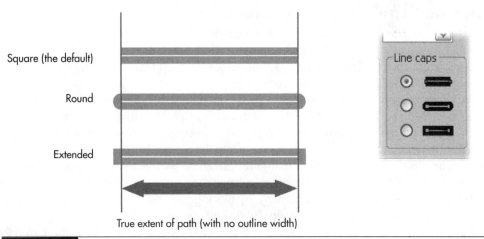

FIGURE 18-4   End caps can be set to one of these three styles.

| TIP | *Line cap options control the shape of all end points in an open path simultaneously; therefore, a compound path receives your choice of end caps at all two, four, six end points, and so on, depending on the structure of such a compound path. Also, end caps are not "mix and match"; for example, if you choose Round, both end caps in a two-node path are rounded—there is no facility in CorelDRAW for a two-node path that begins Rounded and ends Square.* |

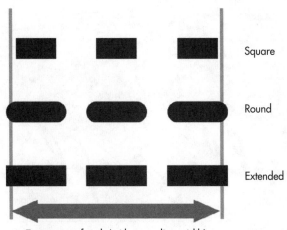

FIGURE 18-5   Applied end caps will affect the appearance of dash patterns applied to your outline path.

18

Outline Pen Calligraphic Effects

The term *calligraphy* has come to be accepted today as a handwriting craft, the result of which is text and ornaments that have a varying width along strokes due to the popular use of a flat-edged pen nib held at an angle. The same effect can be achieved using the Calligraphic options in the Outline Pen dialog.

Calligraphic options are applied using a set of options and an interactive preview window used to define the shape of the nib that affects a path you've drawn. *Stretch* controls the width of the nib using values between 1 and 100 percent. *Angle* controls the nib rotation in 360° (the minimum, −180°, produces the same "12 o'clock" stroke angle as the maximum, 360°). Click the Default button to reset these parameters to their original state. Stretch and Angle values work together to achieve the nib shape. Set them numerically by entering values or better still, interactively, by placing your cursor in the preview window and then click-dragging to shape the nib. By default, all paths in CorelDRAW X4 are created using a Stretch value of 100 percent and an Angle value of 0°. As you can see in Figure 18-6, varying the Stretch and degree of a Calligraphic nib changes the look of an outline, but the *shape* you begin with also has an impact on the final look of the design. For example, the word "Calligraphy" here looks terrific with a 45° angled nib, but looks like nothing worthy of reproducing in this book at many other angles. The lesson here is that if you have an

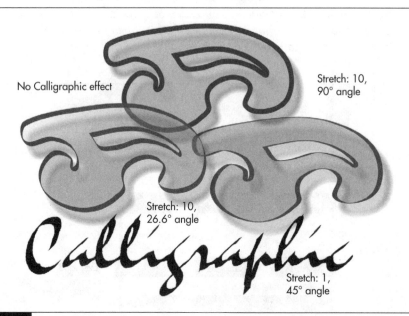

FIGURE 18-6   Calligraphic effects can be used as ornamentations to a piece of work or to imitate handwritten phrases.

object that you think will look more refined and elegant with a calligraphic stroke, keep changing the angle until you're happy with the finished artwork.

DOWNLOAD

French curve.cdr is the same drawing featured in the figures in this section. You can download this file (it's very small), and although a drawing of a French curve might not strike you as the world's most thrilling download, here's a little trivia about the shape. French curves have been used by drafting artists for over 100 years to better trace-off parabolic and other mathematically complex curves. The French curve has the reputation, in the right hands, of being able to assist in drawing almost any angled shape. Therefore, you might get a better preview of calligraphic Stretch and Angle values in one fell swoop by using this humble little CorelDRAW illustration. The drawing is a fairly accurate tracing from one of the Burmester sets, and the 3-point Curve Tool was used in CorelDRAW to ensure outline smoothness.

Scaling and Behind Fill Options

Two more options for controlling outline properties available in the Outline Pen dialog are very important for controlling how outlines display in particular design situations. The following sections explain how Scale With Image and Behind Fill work.

Scale With Image

Choose Scale With Image to increase or decrease the outline width applied to an open path or closed object when you scale the object at any time after the outline width has been applied.

For example, a 2-point outline width applied to a path will become 1 point if the object is scaled in size by 50 percent. In most illustration work, where drawings commonly change size before they are complete, choosing this option is a smart move. However, if you leave the scale constant (leave Scale With Image unchecked), you can duplicate, for example, 50 stars, arrange them on the page at different sizes, and the design looks good because the outline width is consistent from star to star. The illustration here shows copies of a pretzel shape reduced with and without the Scale With Image option selected. If this were a drawing of a *salted* pretzel, the one in the center—Scale With Image—would be less likely to cause high blood pressure and other heart risks if eaten by a drawing of a person.

Original object

Reduced using Scale With Image option

Reduced without the Scale With Image option selected

18

Behind Fill

Behind Fill sets outline properties to print and display in *back* of the object's fill. One of the many practical uses for using Behind Fill is in a sign or other simple illustration where you need rounded corners along the outline, but sharp and crisp edges along the fill, the important and recognizable part of many illustrations. Here you can see at left the ubiquitous recycle symbol with a 16-point rounded-corner outline. The arrows are lost in the design. However, at right, a 32-point outline is used with Behind Fill checked in the Outline Pen dialog. Therefore, the same outline width has been achieved (visually); however, because the outline is behind the fill, the points on the arrows are undistorted, even in weight, and will print crisply.

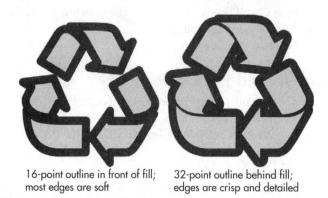

16-point outline in front of fill;   32-point outline behind fill;
most edges are soft   edges are crisp and detailed

Setting the Outline for All New Objects

Each time you create a new object, CorelDRAW X4 automatically applies a set of default outline properties, as follows:

    Width = .5 point
    Color = CMYK black (from Corel's default custom palette)
    Style = Solid line
    Corner Shape and End Caps = Square
    Calligraphy: Stretch = 100, Angle = Off
    Behind Fill, Scale With Image = Off

To change any or all of these default properties, open the Outline Pen dialog (F12) while *no objects* are selected.

By choosing Graphic, Artistic Text, or Paragraph Text, you can control the defaults for new objects. Unless you have a specific reason for changing the default outline properties of text objects, it's wise to accept Graphic as the object types to apply, and then to click OK to proceed to the Outline Pen dialog to change the outline pen defaults.

Turning an Outline into an Object

A fancy calligraphic property for an outline, arrowhead, and even for dashed outlines can be freed from being editable *outline* properties when you convert an outline to an object. Consider this: an outline is constrained to solid fills, while an object that *looks* like an outline, that was originally *based* on an outline, can have any type of CorelDRAW fill. To make an outline into a shape, you choose Arrange | Convert Outline To Object—but this will disturb your workflow less if you perform this on a *copy* of the path you slaved over! In Figure 18-7 you can see the command on the Arrange menu (the shortcut is similar to Convert To Curves; it's CTRL+SHIFT+Q). This path that has an arrowhead and tail is about to become a shape that's freely editable with Toolbox tools and will accept all of CorelDRAW's effects such as contours and distortions.

In Figure 18-8 you can see at left that the path of Figure 18-7 is now a shape that will take, in this example, a Linear style fountain fill—in contrast, you can't fill an open path. See also in this figure that the arrowhead path that's now a shape can be extruded (okay, it's an example, it's not great "Art"!). To come full circle, the path that's not an object can have an outline; in this figure the white 8-point outline is used artistically to visually separate the linear fill areas. Dashed lines are a lot of fun to play with as objects, too.

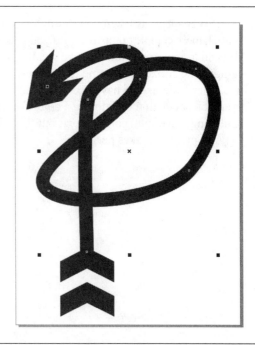

FIGURE 18-7   Convert a path to an object, and all outline properties become editable objects.

18

FIGURE 18-8 If you need to edit certain areas of a fancy outline, you can do it more easily and more precisely by first turning the outline into an object.

This chapter has taken you through the simple assignment of one property to a path, to several, more complex properties. As you gather more understanding of options in CorelDRAW, you add to your personal, creative wealth of design options. Dashed lines, arrowheads, and calligraphic strokes will come to your rescue during 11th-hour assignment crunches, just as will other features that have been covered in previous chapters. Chapter 19 takes a side-step from object creation to defining a color for that object you just created. You've probably read things on digital color *theory,* but the following chapter puts theory into *practice.*

And practice makes perfect.

CHAPTER 19

Digital Color Theory
Put to Practice

P ut away those crayons and fling that color wheel out on the front lawn. *Digital* color obeys *none* of the rules we were taught in school. Digital color models are what you use to fill objects that CorelDRAW in turn displays on your monitor, and defining colors, *period,* is an art that even professionals occasionally struggle with. The good news is that CorelDRAW X4 makes it as simple as can be to apply exactly the color you have in mind to an object, through an extensive collection of industry-standard swatches, color models that are intuitive to use, and color mixers that make color definition more like play than work.

This chapter covers color theory and how it's put to practice in your CorelDRAW work. If you've ever been faced with picking out a tie to match your shirt at 8:30 in a dimly lit closet, you have an appreciation for the importance of choosing harmonious and intriguing color schemes. Similarly, your color work is out there for the public to evaluate; this chapter guides you through the digital process of choosing colors and making certain what you print is what you see onscreen.

Digital Color Terms and Definitions

Let's say you've created a rectangle on your page; by default it has no fill and there are two quick fixes to fill it. You can left-click a color on the Color Palette, which offers a nice selection of preset colors, but let's say you want a specific color. You double-click the Fill icon on the Status Bar shown in the following illustration, and you can see (and work in) the Uniform Fill dialog, a combination of interface palettes that has tabs for Models, Mixers, and Palettes.

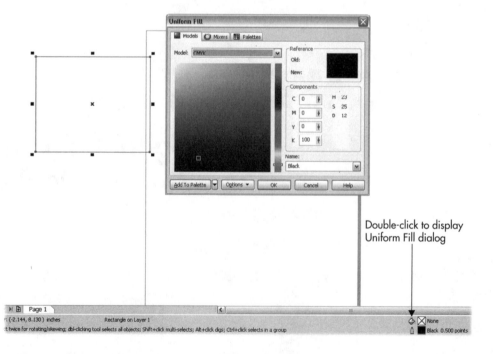

Double-click to display
Uniform Fill dialog

Palettes are predefined collections of color swatches; this one is fairly self-explanatory. Then you have Mixers; this is not a self-explanatory area and it's covered later in this chapter. Finally, you have Models, an area worth some serious documentation here.

The first terms that set the stage for color exploration in this chapter are used in digital color descriptions and also to define real-world colors you apply to paper, plastic, and so on. They'll give you a handle on a seemingly overwhelming variety of attributes that colors have. They're also somewhat interrelated; when you change a parameter in one, most of the time you change a parameter in a different class of color description.

- **Color model**   A *model* is a representation of something that's intangible or too ungainly in other respects to directly manipulate. For example, a child plays with a model airplane because this representation fits in his bedroom better than an actual airplane, and the passengers feel safer. Color models are used in CorelDRAW to make it easy to deal with the relationships between colors; without a model of the intangible qualities of the spectrum of light, it would be quite a challenge to choose the colors you need. Additionally, a color model *scales* all the available colors you have when working on CorelDRAW and other programs, in the same way a model airplane can be rotated to see all its sides—a task that's hard to do with a full-sized airplane. Today, users have at least 16.7 million possible colors from which to choose in design work; a color model makes color selection much easier than choosing colors from a palette containing 16.7 million swatches (if such a thing were possible)!

- **Color space**   Think of a color model as a piece of architecture: it's a structure. Now, if you were having a house built, your structure would need to take up space, usually on some land. A color space is that "land" for your color model "architecture." Different color models require different color spaces. To get off of this analogy kick here, let's say you have a CorelDRAW file to print from your inkjet printer. Inkjet printers use the CMYK color model as the basis for reproducing the colors you've filled objects with in your document (CMYK color is covered later in this chapter). Unfortunately, digital color, the color you see on your monitor, has its structure in a fairly wide color space; RGB colors have a wider range of expression (more possible colors) than CMYK color space. What can happen (unless you read this chapter thoroughly) is that some colors you use in your CorelDRAW document look fine onscreen, but they don't print as you anticipate. The reason is that CMYK color space is smaller than the color space of your monitor, and some of your original design's colors are *clipped* when printed. They've been arbitrarily moved to a color that's *similar* to the color you used, or they just don't print, or you get a nice splotch of muddy brown on the printed page. You certainly want more control over how a CorelDRAW design prints, and that's why CorelDRAW offers a CMYK color picker and also a Gamut Alarm. *Gamut* is a term that means the expressible range of color;

in other words, colors that fall into a specific color space. When you choose a color that falls out of the range of the color space, it's called an *out of gamut* color, and these colors won't print correctly because they're a structure that is built on a part of the land you don't own.

> **NOTE** *The K in "CMYK" indeed stands for "Black," and it's fair to ask, "Why don't we call it CMY**B** color?" The K is for "key"; the key plate in CMYK printing is the last plate that is printed. In this case, Cyan is pressed first, then Magenta, then Yellow, and finally the key, Black. In printing, a key plate is the plate that prints the detail in an image; as you can often see in a progressive proof of a print job, C, M, and Y inks don't provide much image detail. We use the term "key plate" in printing because black is not always used. For example, in two-color print jobs, the key plate is the darker of the two colors. In general, however, K means "Black" and you'll often see CMYK written as "CMY (black K)" to avoid ambiguity.*

- **File color capability** If the extent of your CorelDRAW work is to create CDR files, print them, and save them, you have no concerns about a file format that can hold all the colors you've picked and applied to objects. The CDR file format will retain the colors you've used. But if you intend to export a design to bitmap file format, you'll want to check out Chapters 26 and 27. Different bitmap file formats have different ceilings of color capability, which relates to color space in many ways. TIFF images as written by CorelDRAW, for example, can contain 16.7 million unique colors, and this file format can be written to the RGB color model, the CMYK color model, and even some color *modes* such as Grayscale, which offers no color at all but instead only brightness values. On the other hand, GIF images continue to be written for the Web, and these images can only hold 256 unique colors, pretty meager when compared with 16.7 million colors, so you need to know how to design using only 256 colors, tops.

The sections to follow are a step-by-step documentation of topics from the structure of digital color, to the space in which color resides, through how you manipulate color models in CorelDRAW to define colors you want or to match color values a client might have read to you over the telephone.

Subtractive and Additive Color Models

The world of color models has two distinct categories: *subtractive* and *additive* color models. You, the designer, use both: when you print something, you use a device that uses the subtractive color model. When you design for the Web or an onscreen presentation, you use an additive color model. How these models are similar, where their differences lie, and how you access these models in CorelDRAW X4 are the subjects of the following sections.

Subtractive Color Models

From the moment the first caveperson depicted an antelope on the family room wall, humans have been using a *subtractive color* model for painting. Subtractive color is what a lot of artists were brought up on, mixing physical pigments, and as we all know, when you mix a lot of different pigments together, you eventually get black. This is what the traditional subtractive color model is all about: you *remove* part of the visible spectrum as you overlay one color upon another. The color signature in this book shows a graphic of the CMYK color model. CMYK is a subtractive color model used in commercial printing, and in theory, if you put Cyan, Magenta, and Yellow pigments together at full intensity, you should get black—Cyan, Magenta, and Yellow are the primary colors in a subtractive color model. However, due to chemical impurities in physical pigments such as ink and paint, you get a deep brown and not true black. Hence, a black printing plate is used in addition to the C, M, and Y plates to reproduce a wide spectrum of colors available in CMYK color mode.

> **NOTE** *If you take your kids out to a family restaurant where they have crayons and menus that the kids color, notice that the crayon colors are not cyan, magenta, and yellow. More than likely, they're red, yellow, and blue, and if you're lucky, green also comes in the little box. You might rightfully wonder why commercial presses use CMYK and your kids are using red, yellow, and blue. The answer is that red, yellow, and blue have traditionally been the primary subtractive colors used by painters throughout history,* before *scientific color theory proved that cyan is more of a pure subtractive primary than blue, and that magenta describes a component of subtractive color better than red. Green was introduced as a primary subtractive because of the human mind's perceptual bias that green is a* perceptual *primary color, although it's not used at all in today's commercial printing.*

The RGB Additive Color Model

The *additive* color model describes color using *light*, not pigments, and a combination of the primary additive colors Red, Green, and Blue, when combined in equal amounts at full intensity, produces white, not black as subtractive CMYK color does. RGB is a common additive color model, and it is not at all intuitive for an artist to use; however, CorelDRAW has different views of the RGB color model that make it easy and intuitive to work with.

Because a color model only does one thing—*it shows a mathematical relationship between values that are intangible*—the visualization of the relationship between Red, Green, and Blue can use any model anyone cares to use, with the goal being to make color picking and color relationships as painless as possible to perform! Figure 19-1 shows the default view of the Uniform Fill dialog. When you first install CorelDRAW, it's optimized for print, both with your view of the drawing window, and with the CMYK color model offered on the Uniform Fill dialog. If you do Web work and zero print work, this chapter walks you through how to customize your onscreen display and your color choices for the RGB color model.

19

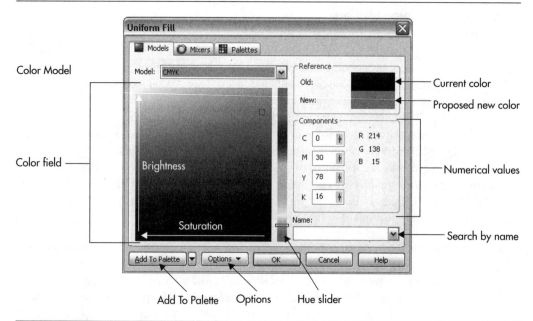

FIGURE 19-1   The Uniform Fill dialog is one of several areas from which you can pick colors
in CorelDRAW.

Let's take these controls in Figure 19-1 slowly and one at a time. It's quite likely that a
color attribute you're looking for right now can be defined in this dialog.

- **Color Model**   This selector drop-down list includes CMYK, CMY (as explained
  earlier, black is more a part of the printing process than a part of the color model),
  RGB, HSB, HSL, Grayscale, YIQ, LAB, and Registration. These models are covered
  later in this section. If you're in a hurry: CMYK should be chosen for in-gamut colors
  for printing, and RGB is the color model for doing work that won't be printed.

- **Color field and Hue slider**   Here is something tricky, a little confusing, and totally
  wonderful on the Models tab. A model is a representation of a hard-to-grasp thing or
  idea. Simply because the default color model is CMYK, there's no real reason to
  offer a CMYK color picker to accompany the color model: CMYK is an intangible
  item—a model of it is best represented by what works for the user! Therefore, by
  default, the *HSB* color-choosing field and slider are presented to you, even though
  you're not choosing HSB colors. To manipulate Brightness, you drag the little
  rectangle up or down in the color field. To manipulate Saturation, you drag left or
  right; and obviously you can navigate both Brightness and Saturation at the same
  time. The Hue slider to the right of the color field sets the predominant, recognizable
  attribute of the color you're picking. Users generally set the Hue first, and then play
  with the amounts of Saturation and Brightness.

■ **Current Color/New Color**   The color well at the top shows you the current color of the selected object on the page. The bottom color well shows you any changes you've made, and the two together provide a convenient way to compare color changes.

■ **Components**   The field at left provides a numerical breakdown of the current color, as expressed in the components of the current color model. Therefore, in Figure 19-1, you can see that the current color is an orange, and its CMYK numerical values are C: 0, M: 30, Y: 78, and K: 16. However, these values are not static; in fact when you click on the icon to the right of any value (the icon that looks like a slider), a slider does indeed pop up, and you can adjust the color you want by dragging any component value up or down. This offers a more precise adjustment of the filled object's color; you can also insert your cursor into the number field (it's a live field), double-click to select the entire value, and then type in a new value. The fields to the right of the current color model fields are a secondary, static readout that gives you the selected color's equivalent using a different color model. You set the secondary field through the Options button in this dialog.

■ **Name**   The Color Palette, the strip docked to the right of the drawing window, contains colors that are tagged with names such as Desert Blue and Mint Green. To quickly search for a preset color on the Color Palette, you can choose from the drop-down list, or begin typing a name in the Name field—as you type more characters, the dialog narrows the search. If you have a custom palette loaded, you can't search it using the Models tab of the Uniform Fill dialog; you conduct a search using the Palettes tab.

■ **Add To Palette**   This button adds the current color you've created to the Color Palette's default palette. You can then retrieve this color directly from the Color Palette at any time without visiting the Uniform Fill dialog. This is one way to save a custom color; see "Using the Color Styles Docker" later in this chapter for a more feature-filled way to save a custom color.

■ **Options**   In this drop-down, you can choose Value 2, which sets the fixed Component readout; for example, if you're working with the RGB color model and want to see a color's components expressed in CMYK values, you choose CMYK from the Value 2 flyout. The Swap Colors option switches the order of the New and Old colors displayed at the top right of this box. The Gamut Alarm feature puts a brilliant highlight color overlay in the color field to alert you when a color you're selecting can be viewed onscreen but cannot be printed to a CMYK printer with complete color fidelity. Of course, you won't see the Gamut Alarm if you're working with the CMYK color model, because all CMYK colors are CMYK-legal. Last on the Options list is Color Viewers. This flyout offers a choice of color selection interfaces for your chosen color model. This deserves a little explanation: to represent the components of color models, the various color models necessarily need to be graphically represented in their unique structure. Some color models such as HSB are blessed with a structure that is intuitive for mere mortals to use; others are less intuitive. Figure 19-2 shows the RGB model, using the "RGB as 3D" color model color-picking fields and slider. Try it, you'll hate it—although the model itself is mathematically sound, it just isn't user friendly and a slider is necessary *in addition to* the 3D picking cube because this model is hard to visualize. At top right is the RGB color model, except this time the HSB Hue Based picker has been chosen from Options | Color Viewers. This is perhaps the best all-purpose color picker from which you can choose colors in any color model. Again, try it; it's very similar to Adobe Photoshop's Color Picker and very easy to use to get the color you need very quickly. At bottom left is the RGB color model displayed as the HSB Wheel Based color viewer. A variation of this color picker is used in Corel Painter; it, too, makes defining colors a joy instead of a chore.

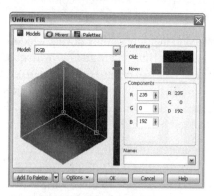

RGB as 3D color model

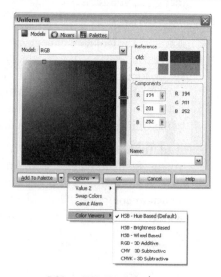

RGB as HSB Hue Based

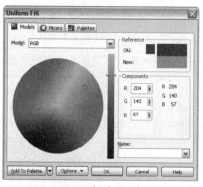

RGB as HSB Wheel Based

FIGURE 19-2 Many color pickers' views can be assigned to color models through Options in the Uniform Fill dialog.

The HSB Additive Color Model

The HSB color model is to designers what the RGB color model is to software engineers; HSB serves the nonprogramming community for intuitively choosing colors, and HSB and RGB occupy the same color space, but use different components. HSB is the acronym for Hue, Saturation, and Brightness. It's occasionally called HSV (the *V* is for "Value"), and HSL (*L* is for "Lightness"), but it all boils down to a user-friendly model for working with digital color. HSB, in fact, was modeled by Dr. Alvy Smith, cofounder of Pixar Studios, former Microsoft Fellow, and an accomplished artist. The HSB color model has the same number of colors (the same color space, discussed later in this chapter) as the RGB color model; however, HSB organizes the relationship between components of colors differently, and in a friendlier fashion, than RGB does. The components of HSB color are as follows:

- **Hue**   The distinguishing characteristic of color. When we tell a friend, "Oh, that's a very nice blue tie" and "The TV set is a little orange, isn't it?" we're describing the Hue component of the color. Hue is usually expressed in degrees on a hue wheel; technically, Hue is determined by light wavelength.

- **Saturation**   The presence of color, the purity, the predominance of a Hue. We often use the component of Saturation when we talk about how juicy the colors are in a photograph. If there's a lot of noticeable blues in a photo or a drawing, the blue hue is said to be quite saturated in that color. Conversely, colors you often see on today's household appliances, such as a toaster oven, that the manufacturer calls "Oyster," "Putty," "Ivory," or "Bisque," are neutral; they have no strong dominance of Hue, and therefore have little Saturation. You can't make out the Hue in such an appliance's color; you usually describe it as off-white or a warm gray. The pages in this chapter have no Saturation.

- **Brightness**   The amount of illumination a color has. Brightness, as described in digital color terms is somewhat elusive, but an analogy from traditional painting with pigments (subtractive color) provides some clarity here. When you mix a pure color with white, you're increasing its brightness; in industries where color description is critical (fashion design, house paints), bright colors are a *tint* of a pure color, also called a pastel color. Then there are darker colors: a *shade* is the mixture of a color with black. Mixing with white increases lightness, while mixing with black reduces it. In both digital and traditional color, mixing black, white, or a perfectly neutral value in between black and white leaves Hue unchanged.

> TIP   *X-Rite has emerged as the color industry's heavy-hitter after adding Pantone (the color-matching people) and Gretag Macbeth (proofing systems, monitor calibration hardware/software) to Munsell and other acquisitions in recent years. If you have any questions about printing, packaging, paints, plastics, or just color in general, Xrite.com is the place to visit. Their website contains not only catalog areas, but also many areas with seminar listings and free downloads of collateral material—all about color.*

LAB Color

LAB is both a color space *and* a color model. CorelDRAW offers LAB as a color model; however, LAB—the color space—is device-independent, and therefore it can be used to describe colors you see in the drawing window, on a physical plastic bottle of soda, and even on a basketball. Almost 100 years ago (this was before PCs), the Commission Internationale de l'Eclairage (the CIE, the International Commission on Illumination) was established as a worldwide organ for standardizing and exchanging color specifications. They are responsible for creating the LAB color model. It successfully replicates the spectrum of human vision, and this is why there is a disproportionately large area of green in LAB color space. This is because the human eye responds to this region of the visible spectrum more strongly than to other hues. LAB is modeled after one channel of **L**uminance, one color channel (named **A**) that runs from magenta to green, and another channel (named **B**) from blue to yellow. When you use LAB to describe a color, you're (theoretically) assured color consistency. LAB, the color space, is frequently used by software engineers as a conversion space. When you want, for example, to convert an RGB bitmap to CMYK, the LAB color space is larger than both, and as a consequence colors are not driven out of gamut when the pixels in such a bitmap are reassigned new component values.

YIQ

The YIQ color model is similar in its components to LAB color; however, its purpose is for working with designs and text that are video-legal, as defined by the National Television Standards Committee (NTSC). YIQ's components are one channel of luminosity and two of chromacity (color). Standard definition TV is brighter than PC monitors, the color range is smaller, and if you get an assignment to draw a logo for a commercial, you'd use this color model.

Grayscale

You'd use the Grayscale color model (which actually has no Hue) if you're designing for one-color commercial printing and for laser print output. You might find that a color design you've drawn doesn't look right if printed to a laser printer: blue areas seem too faint and reds look much too dark. By using Grayscale, you take the influence of Hue out of the color equation, and what you see onscreen is what you get on paper.

Registration

You do not design with this color model; it's only one color. Registration is used for an object when you want that object to be printed on all commercial press plates, including spot color plates. As the name suggests, Registration applied, for example, to hairline paths around the border of a design helps a commercial press operator to see and keep all the printing plates in registration when they review progressive proofs of the plates. Also, if your design calls for spot-color inks, you can use an object with Registration color to manually knock out (remove) areas on all other plates. For example, if you want a headline printed using a spot color on top of a photograph, a Registration-colored object can be used to knock out the exact area on the C, M, Y, and K plates where printed areas of the underlying photograph would obscure the overprinted spot color.

The following sections bring relevance to all of these explanations of color; you want to put color to *use* in CorelDRAW, so it's only fitting to move into where the palettes and other features are *located*!

Using Color-Related Dockers

If you've been doing some independent exploring, you've certainly discovered the Uniform Fill option on the Toolbox, but you've also noticed that it doesn't dock; it is not a persistent part of the interface. The good news is that it's not supposed to be. Two dockers—covered next—are used to handle almost all commands that specify color. These are the Color docker and the Color Palette Browser docker. Let's take a look at these essential features.

Using the Color Docker

The Color docker, shown in Figure 19-3, is extremely convenient to work with and essentially, it's the Uniform Fill dialog—smaller, dockable, and persistent in the workspace. When an object is selected, you can specify whether the color applies to the outline *or* fill color of the object, and any changes to colors are immediately applied. To open the Color docker, click-hold on the Fill Tool on the Toolbox to reveal the flyout group of tools—Color is at the bottom. It's also available when you choose Window | Dockers | Color. Unlike with Uniform Fill, you don't need to have an object selected to call it.

The Color docker is organized into three areas—color viewers and color sliders, the same as discussed earlier on the Uniform Fill dialog…and fixed palettes (actually, they were never broken…). You can display each area by clicking one of three buttons at the top of the docker. Each area is geared toward specifying a color using its unique parameters, and to then applying that color to the fill and/or outline of a selected object. Here's how each of the three areas is used for specifying color:

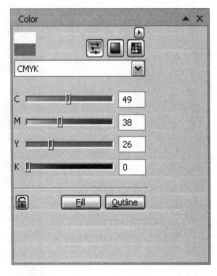

■ **Color sliders**   You can mix the components of any color model you choose from the drop-down selector at top by dragging the sliders or entering percentages in the number fields. Notice that the sliders are in color and change dynamically, instantly updating to show you how much of a component affects the overall color, and the relationship between one component and the others.

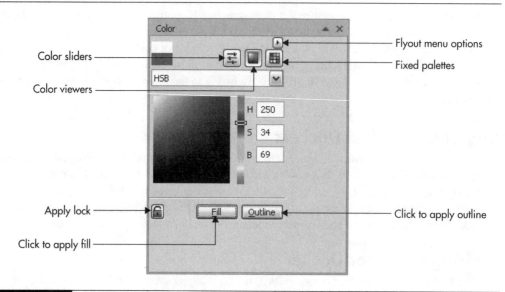

FIGURE 19-3 The Color docker is your one-stop shop for choosing by component values, by using a Color Model, and for choosing from custom predefined colors on the Palettes area.

- **Color viewers** The color viewers (occasionally called *color pickers* in other programs) on the Color docker basically offer the same options as the color viewers on the Uniform Fill dialog; the Options button is simply located in a different place so the palette is more compact onscreen.

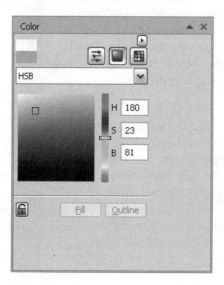

■ **Fixed palettes**   Use this area to choose a color from a swatch collection from vendors such as Pantone, Trumatch, Focoltone, and others from the palette selector. Use the flyout options menu to display a color by name; if you have Tooltips turned on (Tools | Options | Workspace | Display), the names of the swatches appear when you hover your cursor, as shown in this illustration. The slider at the bottom of this docker is dimmed if you've loaded Uniform Colors or any user or Custom palette. This slider is for creating a mathematically precise color tint of an industry-standard solid color, such as any swatches in the Pantone metallic coated collection. Solid colors can take tints, thus producing pastels, because the printer or a vendor of paints can mix white into this real-world, solid color according to numerical values. Therefore, you can use this tint slider with solid predefined colors, but not with process colors; *process colors* are created in the physical world through separate passes of C, M, Y, and K pigments, and as a consequence it's impractical to tint the four components. However, CorelDRAW professionals make spot colors for designs by applying a tint to a solid. The technique works because a spot color always requires a separate printing plate.

Using the Color Palette Browser Docker

The Color Palette Browser docker, shown in Figure 19-4, gives you the option to manage multiple palettes and palette colors. To open the Color Palette Browser docker, choose Window | Dockers | Color Palette Browser. The docker is structured as a tree directory so you can view palettes by folder as you browse, and it includes handy palette command buttons.

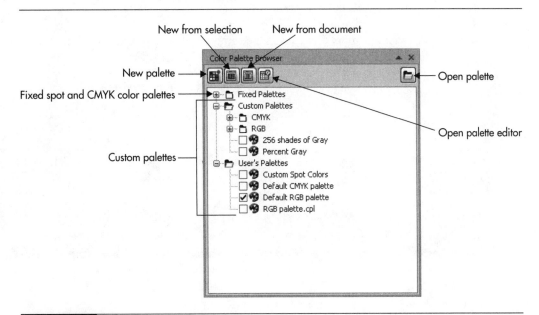

Solid Colors and Swatches

To quickly set up a tint of a solid color, you can click-hold on a swatch, release the mouse button after the flyout appears, and then choose from 10-percent increments from solid to white. You click the tint on the flyout, and then click Fill or Outline to apply the tint.

Swatches on the Color docker are "drag and drop." You can click-drag a color onto an object, selected or unselected, to instantly fill it. If you have good skills with your mouse or other input device, you can set an outline color for an object by dragging and then dropping a color swatch on the edge of an object; even if the object has no outline attributes, the action of drag-dropping a color forces the object to take on a 0.5-point outline. If you miss the edge and the object itself while attempting to apply a color, CorelDRAW lets you know this by changing the cursor's appearance, shown at right in the following illustration. If you release the mouse button over an empty area, this is the same action as redefining all object fill and/or outline properties, and you'll get an onscreen confirmation box about this action. You probably want to Cancel such an action—you might grow bored with every new object you create filled with Pale Avocado.

Drop over path to apply outline color

Drop over object to apply object color

Cursor tells you that it's not over an object or its outline

To make this docker, which you'll use frequently in your work, follow these example steps.

Accessing Color Palettes

1. Open the Color Palette Browser docker by choosing Window | Dockers | Color Palette Browser. By default, the docker displays the palettes located in CorelDRAW X4's User's Palettes folder. A check mark indicates whether a palette is currently open.

2. To open a palette, click the check box next to it. To close an open palette, uncheck the box next to it.

3. Click the Open button in the docker to access the Open Palette dialog.

4. Create several objects (seven rectangles are fine) and then fill them with different colors using the (default) Color Palette wells. Just select an object with the Pick Tool, and then left-click a color well on the Color Palette.

5. Press CTRL+A to select all, and then click the Creates A New Palette From Selected Objects button on the top of the docker. CorelDRAW prompts you for a new palette name and a location in the Save Palette As dialog. Fill in the required information and then click Save. As a result, all seven colors now appear on a Color Palette to the left of the default. This is an invaluable method for saving colors you've spent a lot of time defining, and the palette can now be used on a new or existing document any time.

Using the Color Styles Docker

Color Styles is the route in CorelDRAW to create, name, and apply colors and color *relationships* to objects.

 Because all styles are associated with individual documents, you must have at least one document open to use the color tools available in the Color Styles docker.

Color styles are managed completely from within the Color Styles docker, shown in Figure 19-5, which is opened by choosing Tools | Color Styles. The docker features command buttons for creating new styles, child colors, and shades.

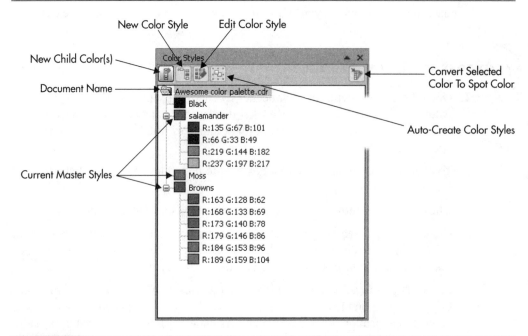

FIGURE 19-5 The Color Styles docker has commands for creating new styles and tints of Master colors.

Follow these steps for an introduction to working with Color Styles.

Saving a Color as a Style

1. Open the Color Styles docker by choosing Tools | Color Styles.

2. Click the New Color Style button in the docker. The New Color Style dialog opens. Select a color and then click OK to create the style.

3. To name your new style, select and then click on the default "Style1" text label field, enter a new name, and then click outside of the style text field to complete the naming. By default, each style you create is named by its color values. For example, a typical CMYK color would be labeled "C:18 M:45 Y:9 K:0."

4. To edit a selected style's color, click the Edit Color Style button to open the Select Color dialog. Click OK to complete the editing operation and close the dialog.

 To apply a master or child color from the Color Styles docker, drag the color directly onto an object in the drawing window. To add an object's current color as a style, drag the object into the docker window's field area below the document folder icon.

Creating Child Colors

Child colors have a dynamic relationship with a defined master color style. The child colors remain the same hue as the master color, but their brightness and/or saturation can be different. Any hue changes made to the master color are automatically updated in the child colors, which is the real power of setting up a drawing using master color—in less than 30 seconds you can recolor a drawing so it's significantly different from your original.

To explore the master/child color relationship controlled using the Color Styles docker, run through these tutorial steps.

Building a Parent-Child Relationship

1. Open the Color Styles docker by choosing Tools | Color Styles.

2. Click the New Color Style button to open the New Color Style dialog. Pick a color for your new style, and then click OK to create the style. Select and click the style name, and then enter a unique name of your own for the color.

3. With your style selected in the list, click the New Child Color(s) button in the docker to open the Create A New Child Color dialog, shown in Figure 19-6.

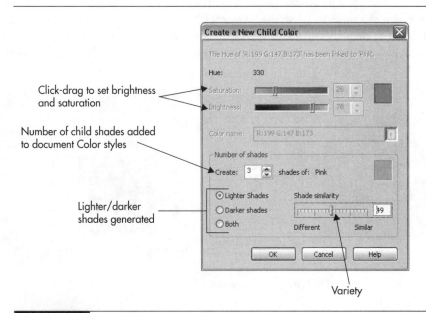

FIGURE 19-6   Control the number of child colors, the diversity of shades, brightness, and saturation through this dialog.

4. By default, the child color is based on the Hue component of the master. You can change the Brightness and Saturation of the child colors by altering the saturation and/or brightness of the child color. You can do this by dragging the sliders or by typing a value in the numeric fields.

5. Enter a name for the new style or accept its default name, and click OK to close the dialog. The new child color appears in the Color Styles docker.

6. Select the master once again and click the Edit Color Style button in the docker to open the Select Color dialog. Change the style's color to any other color, and click OK to close the dialog. Notice the style's color is updated, and so is the hue of all the child colors. This same effect applies to any of the objects that feature either the master color style or its associated child color.

TIP *As an alternative to using the docker buttons, you can right-click a color style in the docker and then select commands from the pop-up menu.*

A practical example of the usefulness of master and child colors can be seen in the following illustration (it's in color in the color section of this book). Say a client had you design a wonderful logo for a product. It really leaps off the shelf with its bright primary colors, but then the client considers the aesthetic impact of the packaging now that everyone is using natural colors to suggest an all-natural product. Your first step is to open the Color Styles docker, and then, one at a time, to select the "unnatural" color, right-click to access the Edit Color Style dialog, and then choose a Hue (and a different Brightness and Saturation if you need to do so) that looks more like it belongs in a forest instead of on a comic book superhero.

Child color   Right-click to edit master color

As shown here, because the logo was originally created using named master colors, the colors and all of their child colors magically fall into a new harmonious scheme in the logo in a matter of seconds.

Revised master and child colors reflected in illustration

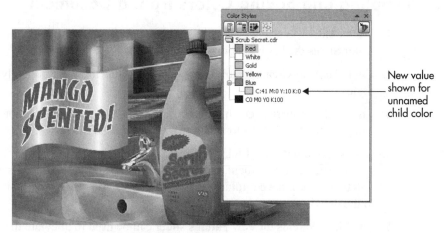

New value shown for unnamed child color

 You can create up to 20 shades of a master color in the Create A New Child Color dialog. If you need more, try creating a child of a child color. The result is that all the shades appear below the master color, so you could have, hypothetically, scores of child colors based on one master.

Creating Styles from Selections

The Auto-Create Color Styles command button in the Color Styles docker offers you the opportunity to create a collection of related color styles based on a selection in your document. Clicking the Auto-Create Color Styles command button opens the Automatically Create Color Styles dialog, shown here:

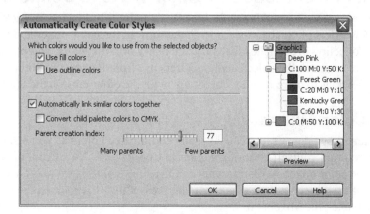

To create a collection of color styles and child color styles from a selection of existing colored objects in your document is quick and easy, as follows.

 ## Sampling and Saving Colors from a Document

1. Press CTRL+A to select everything on the page, or select individual objects. Open the Color Styles docker by choosing Tools | Color Styles.

2. Click the Auto-Create Color Styles button to open the Automatically Create Color Styles dialog.

3. Choose the properties O which you want to base your new collection of styles by choosing the Use Fill Colors and/or Use Outline Colors boxes.

4. Choose Automatically Link Similar Colors Together for flexibility in future revisions to your document, or choose Convert Child Palette Colors To CMYK if you think you'll have a future need to use only CMYK values for objects you'll add to the drawing.

5. The Many Parents Or Few Parents slider can be used to alleviate the world's overpopulation crisis. *Only kidding*—use this slider to limit the number of parent (master) colors generated, which is quite useful if you have hundreds of unique colors in the document.

6. To review the styles that will be automatically created and listed in the Color Styles docker before committing, click the Preview button. The color styles CorelDRAW X4 is about to create are listed in the preview window.

7. To accept the previewed listing and close the dialog, click OK. Your styles are automatically created.

Moving from Color Models to Other Ways to Define Color

Although color models provide the designer with an intuitive device for picking colors, CorelDRAW offers alternative methods, in the form of the color mixer and palettes—an extensive collection of swatches that simulate real-world ink, paint, and plastic colors on your monitor to match the colors manufacturers use from Pantone and other vendors. The following sections explore how to "mix it up" with the other tabs on the Uniform Fill dialog.

Using Color Mixers

Color mixers provide ways to create as many coordinated colors as you need automatically. Any time you find yourself choosing a color in CorelDRAW X4's Color dialog, you have access to the color mixers. Mixers create colors using "color harmonies" and color blend tools. Select any object in your document and press SHIFT+F11 to open the Uniform Fill dialog; then click the Mixers tab.

Mixing with Color Harmonies

Click the Options button at the bottom of the Mixers tab dialog shown in this illustration, and choose Mixers | Color Harmonies. This is the default mixing type for Mixers. The term *color harmony* means that the color spectrum is organized using *equal emphasis*—equal space is devoted—on each color of the spectrum. Think of color harmonies as *organization* in the same way that color models show *structure.* To arrive at several colors that *work well together in a composition,* well, this is a manual task; no computer program can decide which colors work well together for *you.* The harmonies mixer features a color wheel and control handles you drag to choose which Hue you want to make variations from, and which other hues, if any, should be used to create variations. Again, the Color Mixer creates variations you can choose from and can show other hues that have a math relationship to your chosen hue, and the related hues can be used to generate their own variations. However, the mixer is a mixer; it does not generate an "Oh, these colors all work together well in a drawing" color palette.

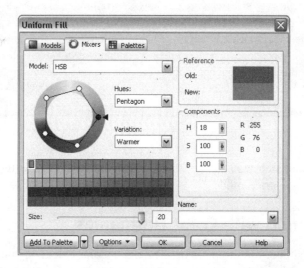

Use the Model drop-down selector to choose a color model on which to base a collection of color variations you can save. Choose one of the configurations from the Hues drop-down list, and then click-drag to rotate the color wheel markers to alter the collection of swatches displayed at bottom left. Choose from Primary, Complementary, Triangle (1 and 2), Rectangle, or Pentagon hues to create color markers that move as you change the primary Hue marker around the color wheel; the related color markers range from a single point to five points. Use the Variation drop-down selector to choose among Cooler, Warmer, Lighter, Darker, and Less Saturated "children" of the target color you've defined on the color wheel.

Color Relationships

It is through color harmonies that you can better see the relationships between primary, secondary, and complementary colors. In the additive color model, the primary colors are red, green, and blue. Complementary colors are the color opposites of primaries and lie at 180° in opposition on a color wheel of hues. For example, the complementary color of Red is Green; the opposite of Blue is Yellow; and these complements are largely responsible for the A and B color channels in the LAB model, discussed earlier in this chapter. Secondary (additive) colors are the result of mixtures of two primary colors: Red + Green yields Yellow, Green + Blue produces Cyan, and Red + Blue produces Magenta, which is the basis for the CMYK (subtractive) color model. It should be noted, however, that color harmonies, relationships that are described based on math, are not necessarily the sort of "harmony" you think of when designing a scheme, for example, for the living room. The "color explorer" utilities you can download online typically do exactly what CorelDRAW's mixer does. Usually showing only contrasting colors (color opposites, complementary colors), color mixers have no intelligence; they describe only relationships between hues, and therefore can choose, for example, college sports team colors, but you truly have to use your own mind's eye when designing an *eye-pleasing* palette of colors to use in your work.

Here is a set of steps you can use to gain experience with the features of the Color Mixer's Color Harmonies mode.

Experimenting with Color Harmonies

1. You might not want to mess up the default Color Palette in your workspace, so before exploring mixers, create a new palette; click the menu options button on the default palette, as shown in this illustration, and then choose Palette | New. When prompted for a new palette name, name it "Test" or anything you'll remember later. A new blank palette appears to the left of the default Color Palette at the edge of the drawing window.

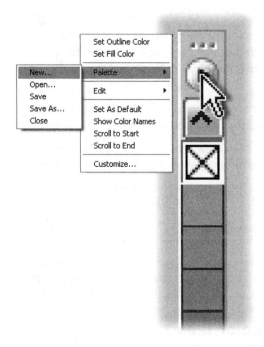

2. With an object selected on the page, open the Uniform Fill dialog (SHIFT+F11), click the Mixers tab, and choose Options | Mixers | Color Harmonies. Choose a color model from the Model drop-down menu.

3. Choose a Hue type—in the illustration shown here, Rectangle is selected. A four-pointed rectangle shape appears around the color wheel. Click-drag the black marker to change hue, and click-drag the white markers to reshape the rectangle; triangles and other multi-point harmonies can be reshaped, too. The result in this illustration, of making the rectangle wide and short, is that the range of complementary colors to red (the selected color) becomes narrow; yellows, greens, and violets are eliminated from the mixer swatches, in preference for cyans and blues.

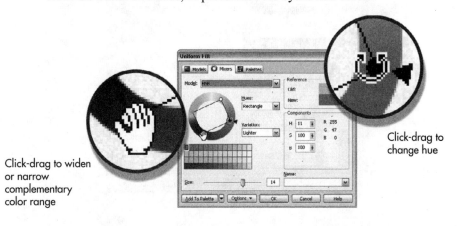

Click-drag to widen or narrow complementary color range

Click-drag to change hue

19

4. Choose a Variation type to change the swatch collection below the color model, based on the color marker positions on the model. If you choose None from the Variation drop-down list, only one color per marker appears in the collection, and the Size slider is dimmed. In the case of the Rectangle harmony, four markers appear.

5. Choose a Variation other than None, and then choose a Size for your collection using the Size slider control. Choose up to 20 different variation colors per marker.

6. Work on this color collection using different Harmonies and Variations until you arrive at something you think you'll use in the future.

7. To save the collection now to the palette you created in step 1, click the first color well (the color swatch), and then SHIFT-click the last color well to select them all. Alternatively, if you have some colors you feel are useless, CTRL-click only the valuable color wells. Highlighted color wells take on a bevel-edge highlight.

8. With your colors selected, click the down arrow to the right of the Add To Palette button, and then choose your palette, not the default palette. Now click the Add To Palette button, and your collection of colors is saved to your custom Color Palette.

Mixing with Color Blend

The Color Blend mixer (shown in the following illustration) is the other mode of the Mixer module, where you define colors almost literally by mixing them, very much like when you create a multi-stage fountain fill (Chapter 17). You can choose four different colors and then generate a collection up to 1,024 unique values, and then choose the ones you like to create your own color palette. All these color options are easier to mentally sort by task: when you want a specific color, you use the Models module. When you want a palette of colors based around your tastes, you use the Mixer module.

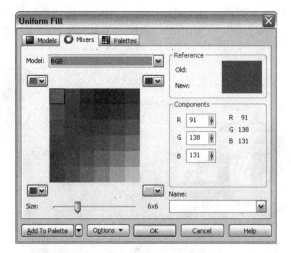

To access the Color Blend feature from within the main Uniform Fill dialog while you're on the Mixers tab, choose Options | Mixers | Color Blend.

Here's how to work the Color Blend feature to create a small collection, and then to choose the colors you want to save as a palette.

 ## Using the Color Blend Mixer

1. Create an object, select it, and then double-click the Fill Color button on the Status Bar to open the Uniform Fill dialog.

2. Click the Mixers tab and then choose Options | Mixers | Color Blend.

3. Choose four colors for your blend by clicking each of the four color selectors in view and choosing a color from the palette displayed. You do not need to blend from four colors: you can choose the same color from two or more of the flyout palettes to hone in on a range of colors, making your decisions easier. Each time a selector is changed, the color field changes, as do the available colors from which to choose.

4. Choose a Size for your collection using the Size slider control.

5. Save some of the more useful colors to a palette; let's use the palette you saved in the previous tutorial. Remember that if you've got some eye-pleasing colors in the collection, you don't have to save a huge, all-inclusive collection; you can create shades of your favorite colors on-the-fly using the child colors feature covered earlier in this chapter. CTRL-click on the color wells in the collection to select only, let's say, your 12 favorite colors. See the following illustration.

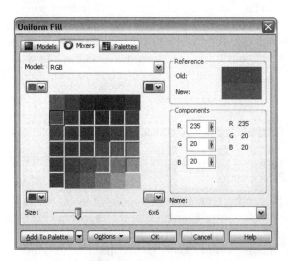

6. Choose a palette from the drop-down list, and then click the Add To Palette button. Your color blend collection is saved.

Using Fixed and Custom Palettes

A *fixed* palette is a collection of ink colors prepared by an ink manufacturer, such as a specific process or spot color. Because these color specialists have spent a good deal of time preparing combinations of inks and other pigments to match as closely as possible between your monitor's display and how the colors look on real-world packaging and other goods, you don't edit these colors as you can with Color Model colors and Mixers. However, if you choose a collection made up of one solid ink color (not a process color) such as Pantone Solid Uncoated, you can specify a Tint of this solid color (the Tint slider is below the color samples); the professional mixing the color for you simply adds white pigment. Fixed palettes are like small color catalogs. Manufacturers such as Pantone, Trumatch, and Focoltone have supplied color simulations for CorelDRAW users; you might use only one color collection, but you have a wide variety from which to settle on, and these simulations are as faithful in the "What You See Is What Will Print" arena as technology can bring you today.

Using Fixed Palettes

Some of the palettes are for use in commercial print—they provide simulations for metallic inks, inks that will be printed to coated or uncoated stock (in English: glossy and matte finishes), while other palettes you'll find in this area of Uniform fills are geared for the Web and not for print. The World Wide Web has color specifications, too. Using a specific color palette usually ensures that colors you use in a design fall within the capabilities of the reproduction or display technique used to show off your work.

To apply process color values (CMYK, usually, although Pantone Hexachrome fixed-palette inks use six values) to your work, the very first thing you do is talk with the commercial press operator. They might want to use substitution values (less expensive inks) or they might not even own the physical equipment to reproduce Hexachrome. You always work backwards when your final output is print—you find out what can be reproduced on what budget, and then you choose your colors. Here's a short tutorial on how to specify a color from the Palettes list.

 ## Choosing Predefined Colors for Print

1. With an object selected on the page, in the Uniform Fill dialog (press SHIFT+F11), click the Palettes tab.

2. Choose a palette from the Palette drop-down menu. Colors appear in the main selector window, and you can pick swatches by clicking them; their names appear in the Name list at bottom right. You can more quickly thumb through colors by choosing Options | Show Color Names; the selector window changes from swatches to larger color samples with the name in the center of the color. The vertical selector to the right of the selector window lets you navigate through the available colors *very* quickly.

If your client has given you, for example, a Pantone number to use in a design, you can get to that value pronto by starting to type the color number in the Name field. CorelDRAW narrows down your selection as you continue to type. Make sure, however, that you're choosing from the right catalog! You don't want to use, for example, a process uncoated collection when the color you need is in the process coated *collection.*

3. Click on the color you need.

4. If you've chosen a process color collection, the Tint slider is unavailable. However, if you've picked a Metallic, Pastel, or other *solid* color collection, choose a percentage value for your color using the Tint option. By default, tints of selected colors are set to 100 percent of the ink, but you can specify any value between 0 and 100 percent. However, choosing zero for a Tint just changes the chosen color to white; printing white on white paper probably won't earn you big bucks with your client!

5. Click OK to apply the palette color or a tinted value of the color.

Information about the Palettes You Can Use for Printing Assignments

Here's a quick rundown on each of the commercial palettes you can choose in the Palettes tab of the Uniform Fill dialog:

■ **SVG Colors**   This collection was designed to address the need for standardized colors for Scalable Vector Graphics (SVG), an emerging technology that allows designers to post vector images as vector images (and not bitmaps) on web pages. These colors were agreed upon by the W3 Consortium.

 For a chart featuring user-friendly names for SVG colors, visit http://www.w3c.org/TR/SVG11/types.html#ColorKeywords.

■ **Pantone**   Pantone dominates the publishing industry with its color-matching system. CorelDRAW X4 includes all of Pantone's color-matching simulations including coated, uncoated, and matte color versions for solids, as well as process and Hexachrome colors. CorelDRAW X4 also features Pantone's metallic, pastel, solid-to-process EURO, and process-coated EURO palettes.

■ **HKS (Hostmann, Kast, and Schmincke)**   This palette collection uses CMY components that occasionally (depending on the color) don't require a black plate. The HKS collections use a Euroscale color space, ISO 12647:2 2002, the FOGRA standard. If you're a Westerner, you probably won't use this color collection. HKS palettes include HKS Colors, HKS E, HKS Z, HKS N, and HKS K.

19

- **Focoltone**   This 750-color palette was designed from the ground up to be ICC-compliant. If your commercial printer supports Focoltone (an abbreviation for "Four-color tone"), if your client is insistent on color consistency between printed material and packaging, and you, the designer, need some flexibility in choosing colors and tints, you might want to try this collection.

- **Trumatch**   The Trumatch process-color palette is made up of more than 2,000 printable colors. Trumatch has specifically customized its color-matching system to suit the digital color industry using the Computer Electronic Prepress System (CEPS). The palette has 40 tints and shades of each hue. Black is varied in 6-percent increments.

- **Web Safe**   The Web Safe Palette contains the 216 colors of the Web Safe color model. Colors are defined using the hexadecimal scheme; one of six shades of each color (red, green, and blue) is combined together to create each color in the palette.

- **TOYO and DIC**   The TOYO and DIC color-matching systems are widely used throughout Asia—Japan, in particular. Each system contains its own numbering system and collection of different process colors. The TOYO collection of colors has been developed using its own process ink colors. The DIC (Dainippon Ink and Chemicals, Inc.) brand of process color inks is divided into three categories: DIC, DIC Traditional, and DIC Part II.

"Web Safe" Colors

Although the W3 Consortium publishes standards, you might feel a little confined choosing from only 216 colors that are Web Safe. "Web Safe," by definition, means that these colors can be displayed accurately on a VGA monitor without color dithering, and that the colors display somewhat consistently whether you have color management on your computer turned on or off. Realistically, three people on Earth still have a VGA monitor and a video card with less than 10MB of RAM. Additionally, designers tend to work with designers, and very few of us don't run a color management system—color management is actually at the core of CorelDRAW X4 and Windows 95 and later.

There's something commendable about "playing to the cheap seats," but in actuality, very few designers bother with Web Safe colors. Every day, millions of people post JPEG images to the Web that look just fine, and these JPEGs decidedly have colors that fall outside of Web Safe standards.

Loading and Creating Custom Palettes

Through dialogs, the Color docker, or an open Color Palette, you can manage your color collections. The fastest way is to click the flyout arrow on a Color Palette and then choose Palette | Open from the pop-up menu. This displays the Open Palette dialog, where you can browse what's available. The pop-up menu also includes Save, Save As, Close, and New palette commands.

The Palette Editor, shown in Figure 19-7, is the ideal place to rework custom palettes. In this dialog you can create, save, edit, and manage new and existing palettes using convenient command buttons. While editing palette colors, you can also access CorelDRAW X4's other color features.

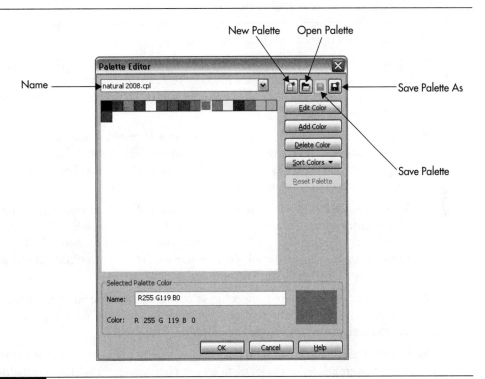

FIGURE 19-7   Manage custom palettes in the Palettes Editor.

Refining and redefining your palettes is easy, fun, and often necessary to keep palettes for client colors up-to-date. Try these steps to appreciate the ease of this powerful dialog.

Editing Color Palettes

1. Open the Palette Editor; choose Tools | Palette Editor. Choose a palette by clicking the drop-down selector; open the directory tree for Custom Palettes or User's Palettes; click a palette name to choose it.

2. To edit an existing palette color, click on a color and then click Edit Color. The Select Color dialog opens to offer color models, mixers, and palettes, exactly like the Uniform Fill dialog.

3. To begin a new palette, click the New Palette button in the Palette Editor dialog to open the New Palette dialog. Enter a name and then click Save. Your new palette is automatically opened, but there are no colors yet.

4. To add colors, click Add Color, which takes you to the Select Color dialog. Define your new color—with the Mixer module, you can choose a whole color range in one fell swoop—then click the Add To Palette button. New colors are immediately added to your new palette.

5. Once your colors have been added, click Close to return to the Palette Editor dialog. In the Name box, here's where you get to name a new color. When you use the edited color palette, the color name will appear on the Status Bar and in Tooltips pop-ups instead of the component values.

6. To remove a selected color, click Delete Color and confirm your action in the prompt that appears. To reorganize your palette colors, click Sort Colors and choose from Reverse Order, By Name, or By Hue, Brightness, Saturation, RGB Value, or HSB Value. You can also click-drag a color well (color swatch) to reorder swatches as they appear on the Color Palette.

7. To name or rename an existing color, select the color in the palette, highlight its current name in the Name box, and then enter a new name. Existing names are automatically overwritten once a new color is selected.

8. Use the Reset Palette button to restore your palette to its original state before any changes were made, or click OK to accept your changes and close the dialog.

There's one more way to make and save a user-defined palette: if you like the color of objects you have on the page, choose Window | Color Palettes | Create Palette From Selection (if you have objects selected in advance), or Create Palette From Document. This opens the Save Palette dialog, where you can name and save the colors you've used as a unique palette.

Color Transformations Through Lens Effects

Lens Effects are comprehensively documented in Chapter 22, but deserve a mention in this chapter on color. Lens Effects can be used to change object colors beneath an object that has a Lens Effect, just as though you were changing the Brightness or other property of a bitmap image. Suppose, for example, you have a very complex drawing, hundreds of objects, and several custom fountain fills, and you want to make a global color adjustment to your drawing. You'd follow these steps.

Dramatic Color Changes with Lens Effects

1. Choose Tools | Object Manager. Create a new layer and make this the active layer.

2. Double-click the Rectangle Tool on the Toolbox to put a rectangle on the new layer that's exactly the size of the page.

3. Fill the rectangle with 50 percent Gray from the Default Color Palette just to ensure there's no color influence in the following adjustments.

4. Choose Effects | Lens; ALT+F3 is the quick way to get to this docker.

5. Let's brighten up whatever composition is on the bottom layer; click the drop-down selector and choose Brighten from the list.

6. Click-drag the spinner on the Rate box, or type a value in the numerical field (then press ENTER to enter the value). This is pretty incredible stuff; you can tune a vector drawing composition as though it were a bitmap!

 You can quickly copy color properties between two objects (including groups) by holding keyboard modifiers as you right-click-drag one object onto another. Holding SHIFT copies the fill color, holding ALT copies the outline color, and holding SHIFT+ALT together copies both. With each action, the cursor indicates the property being copied.

You've seen in this chapter that color is important; color sets a mood for an illustration, and the artistic use of color can actually remedy an illustration that lacks visual interest or complexity. And you now know how to define and save not only a color you need, but an entire palette. This concludes the section on colors and fills; from here we travel to the land of very special effects—take what you've learned, take what you've drawn, and bend it, distort it, in general, make it a unique piece by learning how to sculpt vector shapes.

19

PART VI
Creating Special Effects

CHAPTER 20

Envelope and Distortion
Effects

You've probably seen an effect in stores a dozen times: the words "Fresh Fish" are shaped in the silhouette of a fish. In CorelDRAW, this is called an *Envelope effect*; with it, you can shape words and other objects (and groups of objects) to conform to a different shape. And to add to your creative effects in CorelDRAW, there's also the Interactive Distort Tool, a kissing cousin of the Envelope effect, which provides much more dramatic reshaping options, and which makes quick work, for example, of reshaping a simple flower petal shape to look more natural and intricate.

Remember when you were a child and played with that putty that came in a plastic egg? This is the theme of this chapter; in it, you'll learn how to treat apparently solid and stiff objects as though they had the flexibility of putty. In the process, you'll gather several practical and creative uses for the Envelope and distort features…and discover that work can be fun!

What Does an Envelope Do?

In CorelDRAW you can start with a fresh envelope around an object, use presets, copy a shape to use as an envelope of a different shape, and edit the envelope until the shape suits your need. Envelopes are nondestructive; your original artwork can be restored at any time (the Property Bar has a "remove envelope" button when an enveloped object is selected with the Shape Tool), and once an Envelope has been defined, you edit the envelope exactly as you would a path—you can drag on segments and nodes, and change the node control points to your heart's content.

Figure 20-1 demonstrates both the ease and usefulness of the Envelope effect. In the top illustration, the Artistic Text object is enveloped, and the envelope is based on an existing

Envelope shape copied from the object

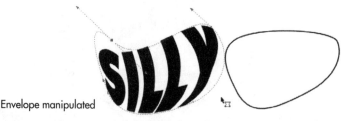

Envelope manipulated

FIGURE 20-1   In these examples, the envelope is used to create different looks.

shape seen at right. The bottom illustration shows the envelope control segments and nodes in the process of being edited. It's true: the CorelDRAW Envelope effect is just like playing with silly you-know-what!

Creating Envelope Effects

When applying envelopes, you can choose from three different methods:

- Shape your envelope from scratch by defining a default envelope and then manually reshaping it.
- Copy an envelope shape based on an object on the drawing page.
- Apply a preset.

Let's begin working with the first technique.

Using the Interactive Envelope Tool and Property Bar

Using the Interactive Envelope Tool in combination with the Property Bar options is the most intuitive way to apply envelopes. You'll find it in the Toolbox grouped with other interactive tools, as shown here.

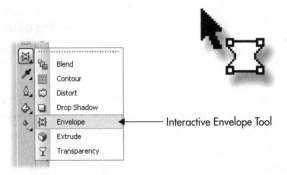

With both the Interactive Envelope Tool and an object selected, the Property Bar displays the options shown here:

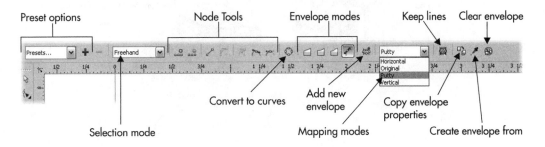

You'll get the best results from the Envelope effect if you follow a sequence of moves in CorelDRAW. Let's work through some basic maneuvers using the following steps.

The Envelope, Please

1. Create or open an object (or group of objects) that you feel would make a good target for the Envelope effect, and then choose the Interactive Envelope Tool from the Toolbox. Notice that the Property Bar shows envelope options. The more intricate the object, the more noticeable the effect will be. In general, don't choose a rectangular shape to which you want to apply a rectangular envelope; the effect would be more or less defeated.

2. Click the mode button resembling a square with one corner higher than the other—the Straight Line mode—and notice the markers surrounding your shape.

3. Drag one of the nodes on your object in any direction. Notice that the direction of movement is constrained, and the shape of your object changes shape to match the envelope as you release the mouse button.

4. Click the next mode button resembling a square with one curved side—Single Arc mode. Drag any node in any direction and notice the object shape changes, but this time you have some curvature going on with the edges of the Envelope and the object(s) inside. The Double Arc mode provides more distortion, most noticeably when you drag a center envelope node instead of one of the four corner bounding nodes.

5. Notice that you can drag an Envelope node to reshape the object, but the direction handles on either side of the node are fixed and won't budge. Click the Unconstrained mode button, the rightmost envelope mode on the Property Bar. Now try dragging nodes and then their direction handles. The following illustration shows the object group in its original state, and then at right it's been worked over a little in Unconstrained mode…it looks reminiscent of how your packages occasionally arrive on Mondays, doesn't it? In all seriousness, however, this is a prime example of the plasticity with which you can reshape objects through the Envelope feature. Nothing is hard and fixed in a CorelDRAW drawing and no changes are permanent.

Original   Unconstrained Envelope mode

You've applied a basic Envelope effect to your object, but the inherent shape of the object remains intact. Clicking the Clear Envelope button in the Property Bar will remove the Envelope, returning all to normal.

> **CAUTION** *There is a limit, particularly with grouped objects in an Envelope, to how much you can reshape before the paths that make up an object begin to self-intersect. This is usually an unwanted effect, so the remedies are to take it easy on the extent of the Envelope, ungroup the group and apply similar Envelope effects to individual objects, or to use the distort effect, shown later in this chapter.*

Using the Envelope Docker

The Envelope docker provides an alternative to using the interactive method. This docker enables you to select options before they are actually applied. To open the Envelope docker, shown in Figure 20-2, choose Effects | Envelope, or press CTRL+F7.

> **TIP** *The main difference between using the Interactive Envelope Tool and the Envelope docker is that the docker is more visual—you have a good view of presets, but the set of editing tools on the docker is not comprehensive. The docker is intended for the casual user, while using the Property Bar with the Interactive Envelope Tool and the Shape Tool after an Envelope has been created is the sport of users who want hands-on, low-level control over the effect.*

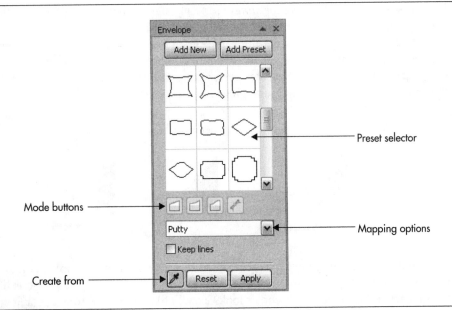

FIGURE 20-2 The Envelope docker lets you select options before they are applied.

To apply the effect using the Envelope docker, follow these steps.

Creating Envelopes via the Docker

1. Select an object and then open the Envelope docker (CTRL+F7).

2. Click the Add Preset button; notice how the Preset Selector window fills with thumbnails of the presets. Choose one (try the heart shape) by clicking the thumbnail; you can see a dashed outline preview surrounding your shape on the page. You can click Apply to apply the preset, but don't do that right now.

3. In any direction, drag a node on the envelope bounding-box surrounding your object. Depending on the preset shape, you can also drag a direction handle—straight line presets don't have node direction handles, but curved shapes such as the heart do. Notice that the Apply button is now dimmed; when you edit a preset bounding box, CorelDRAW assumes you've accepted the preset shape, so there's no fussing with the Apply button.

4. The Reset button does not reset the preset shape; instead, it calls the last-used preset. If you want to clear the envelope now, notice that the Property Bar features the Clear Envelope button and other options as long as the docker is onscreen.

Envelope Tool Cursor States

By following either of the previous tutorials, you'll have noticed your cursor changes its look, as shown next. These *cursor states* are visual signals that you're about to edit the envelope in different ways, depending on what part of the envelope your cursor is over.

While you're shaping your envelope, the cursor becomes active. But when your cursor is held over envelope nodes or segments (the dotted lines surrounding your envelope shape), the Shape Tool (see Chapter 11) takes over, letting you change the position and properties of the nodes and segments by click-dragging (see Figure 20-3).

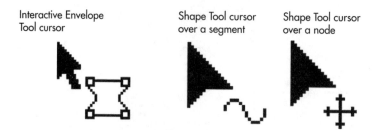

You don't necessarily have to reach for the Interactive Envelope Tool to edit an enveloped shape. You can use the Shape Tool, and as you can see in the previous illustration, the Interactive Envelope Tool's cursor looks exactly like the Shape Tool's default cursor when it's over an envelope segment or node. When you're repositioning or changing the

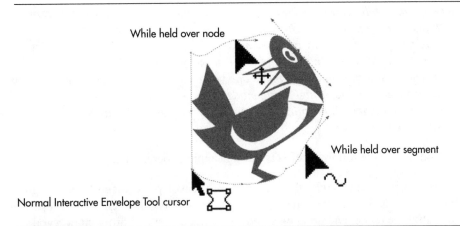

While held over node

While held over segment

Normal Interactive Envelope Tool cursor

FIGURE 20-3 The Interactive Envelope Tool has these three cursor states.

property of envelope nodes, your cursor looks like the Shape Tool's reposition cursor, indicating the node can be moved, and that you can use the Property Bar's Envelope Node Tools to convert, for example, a Smooth envelope node to a Cusp node. When held over an envelope segment, your cursor will change into the Shape Tool with a tiny curved-line symbol, indicating the segment can be edited. Using either cursor immediately alters your envelope, but editing envelope curves can be done only while the Unconstrained Envelope mode is selected.

 For speedy envelope editing, use the Pick Tool to double-click any object that has an envelope. The enveloped object is immediately available for editing, and surprise, the Pick Tool is now the Interactive Envelope Tool.

Choosing an Envelope Mode

The Envelope mode you choose has no initial effect on the envelope you apply to an object; however, as you begin to move envelope nodes around, the mode of the Envelope offers features or limitations, depending on what it is you want to accomplish. Depending on the mode, corner and segment nodes take on different properties, which result in different capabilities to edit the envelope, as seen here:

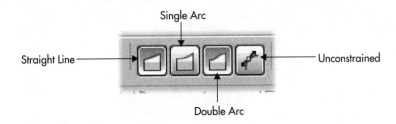

Single Arc

Straight Line

Unconstrained

Double Arc

At any time while editing an envelope, you can change its mode just by clicking a button on the Property Bar. This capability gives you control over the overall shape you're trying to create. Any previous mode limitation is inherited with existing nodes, but nodes you've not changed inherit the new node property. For example, if your envelope is in Double Arc mode and you drag a node to make a swooping arc, and then you click the Straight Line mode button on the Property Bar, the arc remains an arc, but all the other nodes can now only be edited as connectors to straight lines.

These modes have the following effects during shaping operations:

- **Straight Line**   This mode (the default) causes envelope segments to be straight lines; in effect, you're manipulating an eight-point polygon when the envelope is in Straight Line mode. Dragging on an envelope node creates a different polygon shape, and this mode will serve you well for imitating the shape of a traffic sign, a simple house shape, and other outlines you create with straight line segments. In this case, all node positioning is constrained to vertical and horizontal position changes.

- **Single Arc**   This mode sets the resulting envelope segments to curves and sets side nodes to Smooth nodes, and corner nodes to Cusp nodes; you can't change the angle of the cusp for corner nodes directly, but you do change it when you reposition a side envelope node. Using this mode, dragging corner nodes creates a curved side on the envelope, while side nodes align with the path of the resulting curve. Node movement is constrained to vertical and horizontal movement, while side nodes can be moved independently of corner nodes.

- **Double Arc**   This mode creates the effect of sine-wave-shaped sides. Behind the scenes, corner points become Cusp nodes, while side nodes become Smooth nodes. However, the curve handles of side nodes remain stationary in relation to the nodes, causing the segments to take on a double-arc shape. The same vertical and horizontal constraint restrictions as with the previous modes apply. Side nodes may be moved independently of corner nodes, but they apply a similar curve effect, as with the Single Arc mode.

- **Unconstrained**   The Unconstrained mode gives you complete control over nodes, segments, and control handles for envelope elements; it's probably the mode of choice for ambitious enveloping-type artists. You can position either side or corner nodes as if they were ordinary vector path object nodes. In this mode, the Shape Tool and Interactive Envelope Tools give you unlimited flexibility (you can *severely* reshape objects), and nodes can be dragged in any direction to shape the envelope in any way. Unconstrained mode also adds the option to add or delete nodes, change any line segment states to straight or curved, or change the properties of nodes to Cusp, Smooth, or Symmetrical using Property Bar buttons for these tasks.

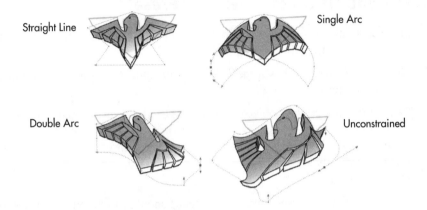

Saving and Applying Envelope Presets

The Property Bar Preset List selector (shown in Figure 20-4) contains saved presets and options for applying, adding, and deleting preset envelope shapes.

You can add a shape you've created as a new envelope shape, and delete presets from the list using the Add (+) and Delete (–) buttons. It's best to create an envelope shape from one,

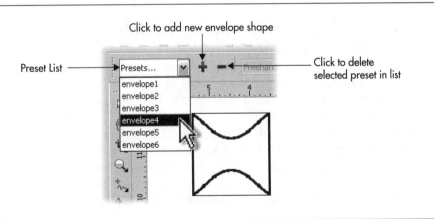

FIGURE 20-4   Use the Property Bar Preset List selector to access saved presets.

single path (no sub-paths)—an object with a hole in it, for example, will produce an envelope that's unusable except for abstract artwork. For hands-on experience, use these steps.

Creating and Using an Envelope Preset

1. Create a simple closed path you think would make an interesting envelope; an egg shape would work well, for example.

2. Choose the Interactive Envelope Tool and notice that the Property Bar now features Envelope options.

3. To add the shape of your object to the Preset List selector, click the Add (+) button on the Property Bar. The Save As dialog opens with the Save As Type drop-down menu automatically listing preset files. Enter a name for your new preset. CorelDRAW will automatically append the name with the .PST file extension; then click Save to add it to the list.

4. To apply your new preset, create an object (it shouldn't look like your new preset envelope) or a group of objects, and then choose your new preset from the list selector. The new envelope is applied.

5. To delete an envelope shape from the Preset List selector, make sure no objects are selected (it helps to switch to the Pick Tool and then back to the Interactive Envelope Tool), and then choose a saved preset from the list selector.

6. With the preset selected, click the Delete Preset button, the minus (–) button. Confirm your delete action in the prompt dialog that appears and your preset is deleted.

Choosing Envelope Mapping Options

You have envelope Mapping options both for the Envelope docker and while using the Interactive Envelope Tool and Property Bar options, which offer control over how the shape of an envelope changes your object's shape (see Figure 20-5). As you can see, Original and Putty mapping provide almost identical results for this particular group of objects and the envelope shape used here, but Horizontal and Vertical Mapping afford the design opportunity to ignore the other envelope axis (Horizontal Mapping ignores the vertical aspect of the envelope, and vice versa). This is useful when you want limited distortion of an envelope but don't have the time (or need!) to create a unique envelope for several different design purposes.

Mapping options give preference to the shape of your original object's node positions and path shapes. Four types are available: Putty (the default), Horizontal, Vertical, and Original, as shown here:

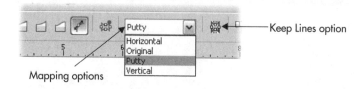

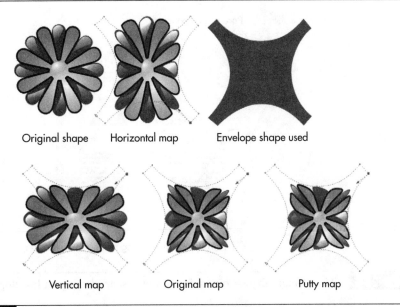

Original shape   Horizontal map   Envelope shape used

Vertical map   Original map   Putty map

FIGURE 20-5   This object group uses the same envelope but different mapping options.

The four envelope mapping options, plus a special option for text and another to preserve lines, are worthy of a little explanation here:

- **Putty**   This option (the default) distorts the shape of your object to match the envelope as closely as possible; the envelope's nodes are given priority over the nodes in your object being enveloped. The Putty option maps the envelope shape to your object and results in a smoothly mapped effect.

- **Horizontal**   This option maps the lines and node positions in your original object to match the horizontal shape of the envelope, without significantly altering the vertical shape of the original object.

- **Vertical**   This option maps the lines and node positions in your original object to the *vertical* shape of the envelope, with the horizontal shape mostly ignored.

- **Original**   This mapping type is similar to Putty. The main difference is that Original maps *only the outer shape* of your original object to the envelope shape. Corner nodes are mapped to the corner nodes of your original object's shape, while node positions and line shapes toward the inside of your object are mapped using an averaging value. The result can be less distortion. If Putty mode is too severe, try Original.

- **Text**   This option becomes available as the only mapping option when a Paragraph Text object frame is selected. Text mode applies an envelope to the *frame* properties of a Paragraph Text object; the actual text and line of text are not distorted; see Figure 20-6.

20

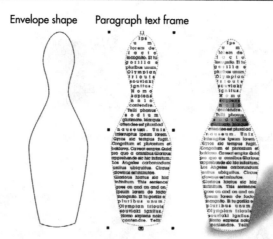

Envelope shape   Paragraph text frame

Envelope defined using Property Bar, then applied to text

FIGURE 20-6   This Paragraph Text object frame was reshaped using an Envelope effect.

- ■ **Keep Lines**   Using this option changes only the node positions in your object to match the envelope shape being applied, leaving any existing straight lines unaffected. If your object is already composed only of curved lines, choosing Keep Lines has no effect, as shown at right in Figure 20-7, which looks like Keep Lines has been turned off. While not selected (the default), all node positions and lines in your original object are reshaped to match the envelope shape—even if this means changing straight lines to curved lines.

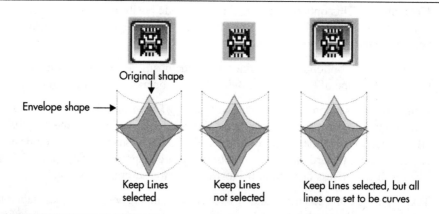

Original shape

Envelope shape →

Keep Lines
selected

Keep Lines
not selected

Keep Lines selected, but all
lines are set to be curves

FIGURE 20-7   The Keep Lines option changes node positions but not any straight lines in the target object to match the envelope shape.

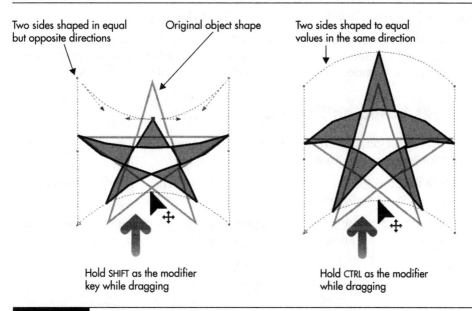

Two sides shaped in equal but opposite directions

Original object shape

Two sides shaped to equal values in the same direction

Hold SHIFT as the modifier key while dragging

Hold CTRL as the modifier while dragging

FIGURE 20-8 By holding key modifiers, you can shape two sides concentrically or simultaneously.

Constraining Single Arc Envelopes

Modifiers keys offer valuable ways to constrain the shaping of an envelope while using *Single Arc* mode. By holding key modifiers, you can quickly shape two sides concentrically or simultaneously. Hold SHIFT and drag any side or corner node to have the corresponding node on the opposite side move in the *opposite* direction. Hold CTRL to move the corresponding node on the opposite side of the shape in the *same* direction and by an equal distance, as shown in Figure 20-8.

Using Envelope Shapes Between Objects

You can copy single-path objects—and even other envelopes—that already exist in your drawing, and use them as envelopes. The commands for these operations are available from the Effects menu and by using the shortcut buttons in the Property Bar when the Interactive Envelope Tool is selected; they are shown here.

Copy Envelope Properties

Create Envelope From

Clear Envelope

20

Copying Properties from Other Envelopes

If you've taken the time to create an Envelope effect but you'll only use it a few times so it's not worth creating a preset, you can copy its properties to another object using the Copy Envelope Properties command. To copy an envelope's properties, try the following steps.

Envelopes Based on Existing Envelopes

1. Select the object to which you wish to apply the envelope shape, and choose the Interactive Envelope Tool.

2. Click the Copy Envelope Properties button in the Property Bar. Your cursor will change to a targeting cursor.

3. Click to target the object with the applied Envelope effect you wish to copy. The Envelope effect is immediately copied and applied to the new object, as shown here:

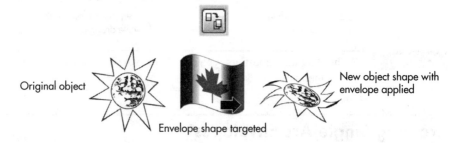

Original object
Envelope shape targeted
New object shape with envelope applied

TIP   *If the Envelope effect you need to copy from is on a different page of your document, try dragging a copy of the object onto the Desktop (the pasteboard outside the document page). You can copy envelope shapes from the Desktop.*

Creating Envelopes from Objects

Creating envelope shapes from existing objects is another common operation that enables you to create and apply new envelope shapes based on the targeted object's shape. The steps are shown left to right here:

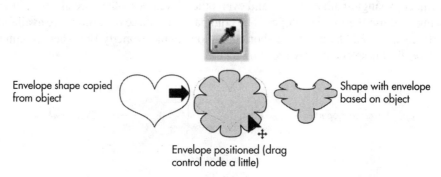

Envelope shape copied from object
Shape with envelope based on object
Envelope positioned (drag control node a little)

Unlike the Copy Envelope Properties feature, copying a shape to apply to a different shape as an Envelope requires a little additional step. First, you target the object to be enveloped using the Interactive Envelope Tool. You click the Create Envelope From button on the Property Bar, click the source object, and then a preview of the envelope shape appears around the target object. It doesn't actually transform until you drag one of the control nodes just a little, or click on an envelope path segment; then the target object transforms.

Clearing an Envelope Shape

Removing an Envelope effect from an object is a quick operation. If you applied Envelope effects in succession, all shaping can be removed at once. To remove an Envelope effect, select the object bound to the Envelope effect, and choose the Interactive Envelope Tool. Click the Clear Envelope button.

TIP *The Clear Envelope command is also available by choosing Effects | Clear Envelope.*

Copying Envelopes with the Eyedropper and Paintbucket Tools

You can copy applied effects (including envelopes) between objects by using the Eyedropper and Paintbucket tools. To do this, choose the Eyedropper Tool and have both the objects in view. Got 'em? Follow these steps:

1. Click the object currently applied with the Envelope effect you wish to copy using the Eyedropper Tool cursor to sample its properties.

2. Using Property Bar options, click the Effects button, click the Envelope check box in the list, and click OK, as shown here:

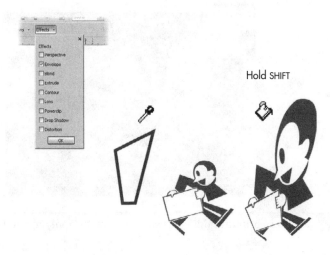

3. Hold SHIFT as your modifier key to switch temporarily to the Paintbucket Tool, and click the object you wish to copy the effect to. The effect is immediately copied.

Using the Eyedropper/Paintbucket technique, you can apply several instances of an envelope, an envelope enveloping an envelope, and so on, if you need a truly gnarly effect. After you've sampled the envelope, click the Paintbucket Tool over the target shape three or four times until your laughter subsides.

Mastering Distortion Effects

Distortion effects apply complex math to the curve paths that make up your object. But artists don't need to know what's under the hood to take advantage of these wonderfully intricate equations to produce outstanding and very naturalistic artwork. The Distort Tool and options are also *dynamic,* which means they create distortion without ruining your original. Distortion properties can be edited at any time; your custom distortions can be saved as presets; and they can be cleared from your shape, just like Envelopes.

Distortion effects also change your object without affecting its other properties such as outline width and fill. Using distortion, the curve values and node properties are dramatically changed, and the more complex your object is to begin with, the more dramatic the Distortion effect will be. Adobe Illustrator users will feel right at home; although distortions are similar to Punk & Bloat, they go beyond this effect in variety and complexity, and when you're using CorelDRAW distortions, you can restore your objects at any time. Distortion effects are great for a number of illustration challenges, including simulating organic-type effects, as shown in Figure 20-9. Believe it or not, the simple star shape at top left was used to generate the primitive cave scrawling. You can create flower shapes, zippers, swirly galaxies in space—not even the sky's the limit.

FIGURE 20-9   These primitive drawings were created by applying the Distort Tool effects.

Using the Interactive Distort Tool and the Property Bar

Apply your distortions using the Interactive Distort Tool, shown next, which is found in the Toolbox grouped with other effects tools and is used together with these Property Bar options.

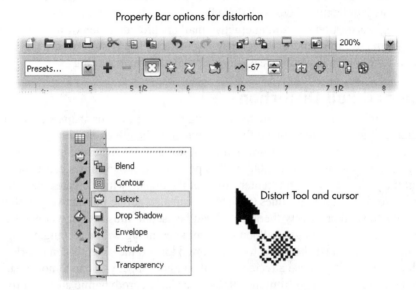

Property Bar options for distortion

Distort Tool and cursor

You'll notice three basic distortion modes: Push And Pull, Zipper, and Twister. With each mode, a different set of parameters is available. Amplitude and Frequency values can be varied in combination with certain other options (covered shortly) controlled interactively or by setting values on the Property Bar. For the moment, though, let's take a look at the Property Bar when one of the modes, Zipper distortion, is chosen. All three modes offer slightly different options; by reviewing Zipper mode, you'll get a handle on many of the options.

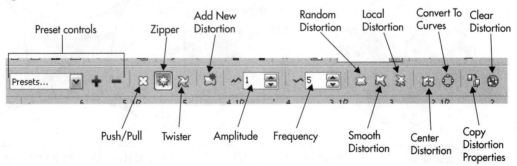

Choosing Distortion Modes

If you've tried using this effect, even just a little, you probably have a newfound appreciation for "steering" this effect—it's akin to slipping into a Ferrari right after your dad took the training wheels off your bike. However, chin up, there are examples and explanations for this powerhouse of an effect, and as you read on (and get hands-on), the Distort Tool will grow on you, and the intimidation factor will dwindle.

During a distortion session, interactive markers provide much of the control over this effect. Interactive markers vary by the mode selected. The Distort modes are covered in the sections to follow in digestible, easy-to-assimilate, fun-size servings.

Push and Pull Distortion

Push and Pull distortions can inflate or deflate the slope of your shape's curves by amplitude. The *amplitude* value affects the extent of the effect, sloping the curves of paths from an object's original path from shallow at low settings to severe at high settings.

Amplitude can be set from 200 to –200 percent. Negative values cause the effect to distort the path away from the center origin of the object, which creates the "push" condition of the distortion. Negative values (which you can also define interactively with the Distort Tool—it's fun and creatively therapeutic) can be used to illustrate flower petals, a cartoon splash into a pond, a thought balloon—all from beginning with a rectangle shape. Positive amplitude values cause the effect to be distorted toward the object's center origin, the "pull" condition. Again, if you use a rectangle as the target shape, you can almost instantly produce anything from a diner sign from the 1950s, to a sleek, aerodynamic auto or airplane, to a nice 3D visualization of a TV tube viewed in perspective. At the amplitude of 0, there is no distortion. Figure 20-10 shows the effects of both negative and positive Push and Pull amplitude settings.

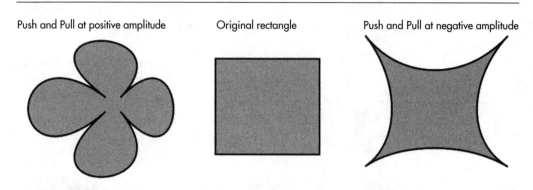

Push and Pull at positive amplitude   Original rectangle   Push and Pull at negative amplitude

FIGURE 20-10   Amplitude can be set from 200 to –200 percent. But a little goes a long way!

Zipper Distortion

Zipper mode distorts the paths in your object to resemble a zigzag or stitching pattern. Here, amplitude can be set between 0 and 100 percent and can be used together with a frequency value and options for Random, Smooth, or Local distortion, as shown here:

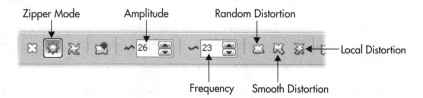

Interactive markers involve an outer marker controlling the amplitude and a slider controlling frequency, which enables you to set the number of zigzags within a given distance. Both can be set within a range of 0 to 100 percent. You can see the dramatic effects of various amplitude and frequency values while applying a Zipper distortion in the next illustration. When beginning to work with the Distortion effects, you might prefer to use only the Property Bar to define an effect, but as you grow more comfortable with Distortion you'll surely want hands-on control by dragging the control handles directly with your cursor.

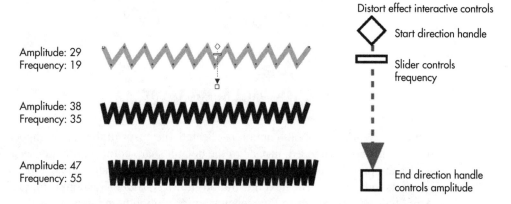

After the effect has been created, you can slant the zipper line by dragging the Start direction handle vertically, left or right, as shown here:

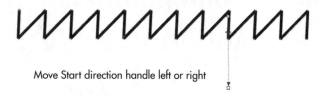

> **TIP** *You can invert the direction of the zigzags on a line or closed shape by repositioning the control handles for the effect. For example, begin by placing the start and end handles so they bisect the line that is affected. Then arrange the handles so both the start and end handles are above the line; notice where the peaks and valleys are on the line. Now move the Start and End handles so they're below the affected line. You'll see that where there were peaks there are now valleys, and vice versa.*

In addition to amplitude and frequency, three additional options are available for setting the shape and size of the zigzags. Each can be toggled on or off, so you can mix and match to create the following effects:

- **Random** Choosing the Random option causes the zigzag Zipper distortion on your object's path to vary randomly between the current Amplitude values and zero. This creates the appearance of nonrepeating frequency and varied wave size, creating an uncontrolled distortion appearance. In this illustration you can see two examples of Random set at 25 and then at 74. Notice where the interactive frequency marker is on the controls just above each object. You can slide this control instead of entering values on the Property Bar.

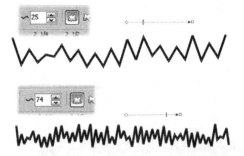

- **Smooth** While the Smooth option is selected, the cusps of the zigzag Zipper distortion become rounded, instead of the default sharp corners normally seen. This is a great option if you need to simulate sound-wave frequencies and equipment monitors in hospitals. The next illustration shows *constant* (Random is toggled off) Amplitude and variations in Frequency when the Smooth option is active.

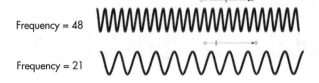

■ **Local**   Using the Local distortion option has the effect of varying the Amplitude value of your Distortion effect around the center origin. At the center of the Distortion effect, Amplitude is at its maximum value. Amplitude then tapers to 0 as the distortion emanates from the center origin of the effect. The results of applying the Local distortion option while the Frequency is varied are shown here:

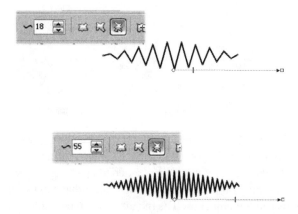

TIP   *To clear a Distortion effect, click Clear Distortion Effect in the Property Bar or choose Effects | Clear Distortion. If you've applied successive distortions, each distortion is cleared individually in order, from the last distortion applied to the first, enabling you to step out of the effect incrementally.*

To bring all this Zipper talk down to a practical level, the following illustration shows two creative, commercial uses. At left, the Zipper distortion is used as a coupon border. The only finessing needed was to apply a dashed Outline Pen Style. At right, the diagram of a sewing pattern is gussied up a little by making the cut marks look as though real pinking shears were used.

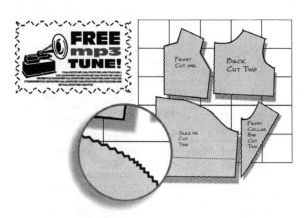

Twister Distortion

Twister distorts the outline paths and nodes of objects by rotating the outer areas around the center (which is largely undistorted), either clockwise or counterclockwise to achieve an effect much like a child's pinwheel toy. Twister options on the Property Bar include rotation direction, rotation amount, and degree of additional rotation.

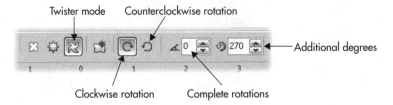

Controlling a Twister distortion is simple; rotation can be clockwise or counterclockwise, but increasing the rotation really dramatizes the effect of this mode. Whole rotations can be set to a maximum of 9; additional rotations can be added up to 359°—nearly another full rotation. Figure 20-11 shows some of the widely differing effects that can result—it all depends on the number of rotations and the object used as the target for the effect.

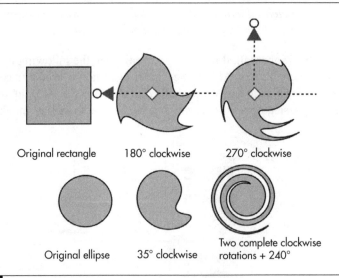

Original rectangle	180° clockwise	270° clockwise
Original ellipse	35° clockwise	Two complete clockwise rotations + 240°

FIGURE 20-11   Some of the different effects you can achieve using simple objects and the Twister mode of the distort effect

Objects applied with a Distortion effect can't be edited using the Shape Tool unless the effect is cleared. However, you can convert *a distorted shape to curves (CTRL+Q) and then edit away to get the shape you need.*

Getting Hands-On with the Distortion Tool Markers

The best way to shape a distortion is interactively, by dragging directly on the Distort Tool markers with your cursor. Depending on which distortion mode you're using, these interactive markers serve different purposes.

There are different interactive markers, depending on which mode (Push And Pull, Zipper, Twister) you've chosen, but basically you have a Start direction handle shaped like a diamond, which sets the center of the distort effect. The start direction handle is connected to the End direction handle, which is used to define the direction of the effect and also the *amplitude* (with the Push And Pull and Zipper modes). Generally, interactive markers involve a center marker and at least one other, each joined by a directional guide. When Zipper distortion is being applied, a small extra slider appears between these two markers and controls the amount of *frequency* applied. In the case of Twister distortions, the outer marker serves as a handle for determining the degree angle and amount of rotation you apply to an object.

 To realign the center marker (the Start control handle) with the center of the distortion, click the Center Distortion button in the Property Bar while the Interactive Distortion Tool and the distorted objects are selected. It's the button with the + symbol, to the left of the Convert To Curves button.

Changing Push and Pull Interactively

Push and Pull distortions are controlled using two interactive markers: a diamond shape indicates the center of the distortion, and a square marker controls amplitude. The center marker can be moved around the object, but the amplitude marker movement is constrained to left or right movement. Dragging the amplitude marker left of center changes the negative amplitude values, causing the Push effect. Dragging it right of the center marker changes the positive values, causing the Pull effect. Figure 20-12 shows the effects of typical interactive marker positions.

Working with the Zipper Control Handles

Using Zipper distortion, the movable diamond marker represents the center origin, and the square marker to the right controls the amplitude value. Use the small rectangular slider on the dashed blue centerline to set frequency by moving it left or right. Dragging it right increases the frequency, adding more zigzag shapes to your object's path, while dragging it left does the opposite. You also have the opportunity with Zipper, unlike the fixed positions

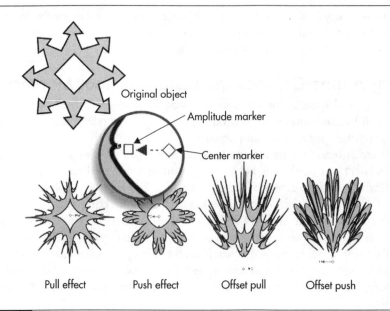

Original object

Amplitude marker

Center marker

Pull effect   Push effect   Offset pull   Offset push

FIGURE 20-12   Push and Pull distortions are controlled by a diamond shape and a square marker onscreen.

of the markers in Push And Pull mode, to move the amplitude handle to slant the zigs and zags in a direction:

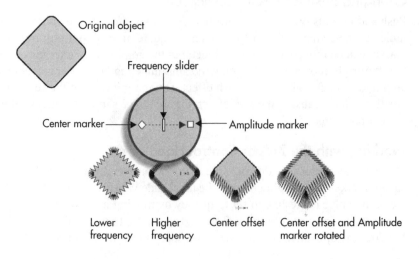

Original object

Frequency slider

Center marker ——— Amplitude marker

Lower
frequency

Higher
frequency

Center offset

Center offset and Amplitude
marker rotated

Exactly as with Envelopes, the Distortion effects can be copied using the Toolbox Eyedropper Tool. You then hold SHIFT to toggle to the Paintbucket Tool, and then click over an object to "fill" the object with the Distortion effect you copied.

Changing Twister Interactively

Controlling Twister distortions by dragging with your cursor over the markers is the most productive (and fun) way to apply this distortion mode since one click-drag enables you to set two properties at once, both of which have a dramatic effect on the distortion. The markers during a Twister distortion are a diamond-shaped center marker and a circular-shaped rotation handle. Dragging the rotation handle around the center marker causes distortion based on the angle of the guide between the center and rotation markers and the number of times the rotation marker is dragged completely around the center marker. You'll also see a dashed blue line connecting the markers, which provide a quick visual reference of the beginning angle of the Twister effect and the current angle of distortion you define. Figure 20-13 shows examples of Twister distortions and positions of the markers.

 To copy a distortion to a new object, select an object, click the Copy Distortion Properties button in the Property Bar, and use the cursor to target an existing distortion.

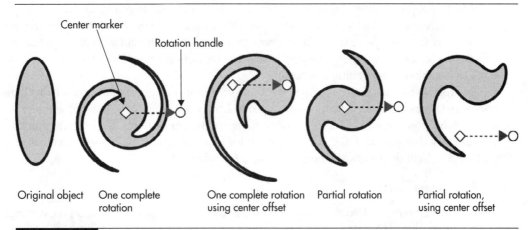

| Original object | One complete rotation | One complete rotation using center offset | Partial rotation | Partial rotation, using center offset |

FIGURE 20-13   It's best to use the control handles to create Twister distortions.

Using Distortion Presets

The Property Bar Preset options for Distortion effects give you the power to apply, save, and delete saved distortions, as shown here:

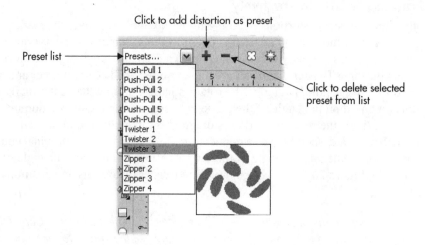

Click to add distortion as preset

Preset list

Click to delete selected preset from list

Exploring Distortion Presets

When the Distort Tool is the current tool selected, choosing a Preset from the list immediately applies a new Distortion effect to a selected object. If you've created a really awesome Distortion effect and you want to save the effect while the distorted shape in your document is selected, you can add it as a new Distortion Preset by clicking the Add button. The Delete button *permanently* removes a selected Distortion Preset from the list; therefore, think twice about ever clicking this button.

Between Distortion and Envelope effects covered in this chapter, you should be well on your way to massaging an object or object group from something close to what you like to *exactly* what you like and need. Remember, these are dynamic effects and as such, you don't permanently change that shape you've worked for hours on. And if you need to exchange data with a client or coworker who doesn't own CorelDRAW:

- Take pity on them.

- Convert *a copy* of your effects work to curves (CTRL+Q), and then export the distorted or enveloped object to any number of file formats CorelDRAW supports. Effects are proprietary to CorelDRAW, but vector information can be used in other vector design programs and modeling programs or exported as typefaces—you name it.

Blends and Contours are the topic of the next chapter, each with their own use, and you can actually take what you know now about Distortions and apply a Contour to a distorted object. Will it look weird? Yep, and *interesting*. Just think of it as building on your knowledge!

CHAPTER 21

Blends and Contours

Although they're different effects, blends and contours share the common property of creating many shapes based on a control shape; the additional shapes are dynamically linked to the control object, and the "in-between" objects will vary in size, color, and outline shape depending on how you set up the effect. Blends and contours are a boon to the designer who wants to add shading to flat color fills in a way that fountain fills do not. Additionally, blend objects can be used to illustrate the transition between two objects of similar or completely dissimilar shape. This chapter takes you through the use of blends and contours so you can add these effects to your bag of illustration tricks and create outstanding, intriguing work.

Blend and Contour Effects: Similarities with Distinctions

The Blend effects create a series of objects *between* objects in a number of steps you define— an object can be a closed path, a group of objects, and even a line (an open path). The properties of each step are influenced by the objects used in the blend. The Contour effect also creates additional objects in steps, however, only one object is required to produce a contour. When you imagine a Contour effect, think of a shape surrounded by the same shape radiating outward (or inward) in a concentric pattern, like the waves produced when you drop a pebble in a still pond. Depending on the assignment, you'll choose the contour or blend to achieve the exact look you need. The following sections reveal the properties of the effects you can manipulate, so you can decide for yourself which effect to reach for.

Blending as Illustration Shading

If you've ever tried to add depth to a drawing and found that a fountain fill didn't quite do the trick, the solution is to blend a large shape through transition objects to a smaller object inside the large one. By making, for example, the outer shape darker than the inner one, you can position a highlight wherever you need it on the face of a drawing of a hardware tool or a fork or a drinking glass…you get the picture. Similarly, a Contour can be used to create a highlight; however, the Contour object should be symmetrical to achieve the highlight effect, such as an ellipse. You'll often see Blend effects used in illustration work for creating realistic illustrations, but regardless of whether the visual content of a drawing is real-life accurate or a whimsical cartoon, through blends you add depth and suggest lighting and the type of material on an object. The left side of Figure 21-1 shows a decent drawing of a frankfurter in perspective, but you and other viewers detect that there's something missing from the illustration. At right, you can see a Wireframe view of the same drawing, except several blends and contours have been added on a new layer in CorelDRAW. You'll see how to do this stuff later in this chapter.

In Figure 21-2 you can see the finished illustration in Enhanced view in CorelDRAW's drawing window. About eight pairs of shapes were used, different sizes, and different colors, and what you see here is smooth shading and highlights that suggest lighting and a little shininess on the frankfurter, thus creating a visual impression of strength, size, and other qualities that help the audience read very quickly, "Oh, that's a *frankfurter*! It looks really large and bright! It probably has a lot of calories and nitrites, and the bun doesn't look like

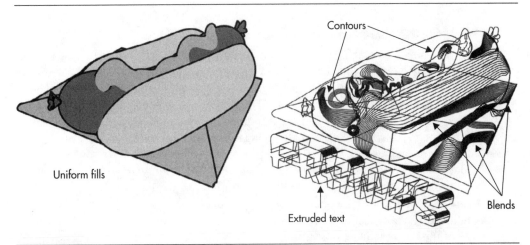

Contours

Uniform fills

Extruded text

Blends

FIGURE 21-1   A drawing, especially a perspective drawing of an object, can appear flat until you add shading with blends and contours.

whole wheat…" Seriously, the more complexity you build into an object's fill, the more you tell your visual story, and the more readily the audience will pick up on that story and fill in *more* details. And before you know it, you've *sustained your audience's attention.*

Blends can also be used to create a lot of similar objects very quickly; the trick is to blend between similar objects that are quite a distance apart on the page. Figure 21-3 shows an example of two groups of objects blended to create a bar graph; the reference lines were

FIGURE 21-2   The main difference between this illustration and that in Figure 21-1 is depiction versus illustration. Illustrations are complete visual ideas, from outline shape to interior fills.

Photorealism Is Achieved Through Complex Fills

Dr. Alvy Smith is responsible for most of Pixar's photorealistic rendering system that has produced many lifelike characters in several animated motion pictures. He once made the observation that the shape—the silhouette—of an object is usually not as visually interesting as the texture on the surface of that object. This is one of the keys to using CorelDRAW blends and contours to make drawings not only more visually interesting, but also more photorealistic in appearance. For example, just about anyone can draw rectangles that represent a box viewed in perspective; in fact, this task takes about 1 minute using the Interactive Extrude Tool. However, your audience probably won't immediately see the drawing as a box until it has shading; the side facing a hypothetical light source would be lighter than the side(s) facing away from the light. Additionally, some text or a simple drawing placed in the correct perspective on one face of the box drawing would also help convey an image of a box. Graphics inside of graphics add visual complexity to illustrations. They are the "fills" for shapes, and the more complex you make an illustration, the more closely the drawing suggests a real object: the world is a visually complex place.

The more attention you pay to fills for objects, the more quickly and successfully you'll communicate a visual idea to an audience, with the speed of today's communications. You need to make your point—a selling point or just a point about Fine Art—fast and thoroughly before someone loses interest and moves on to a different web page!

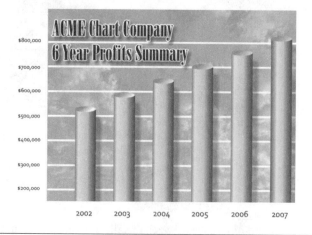

FIGURE 21-3 Objects in this chart were created using blends.

blended from two identical lines. This is a graph with an even, upward progression. However, when you need to create similar blend objects that *don't* follow an even progression, you use the Break Apart (CTRL+K) command to break the relationship between the blend control objects, then ungroup the blend group, and finally, you edit the individual blend shapes to create a more random transition from object to object.

The Interactive Blend Tool and Property Bar

The tool to use for the Blend effect is the Interactive Blend Tool; it's in the Toolbox, grouped with other interactive tools, shown here.

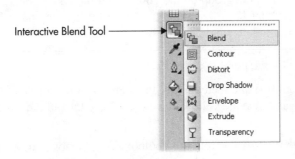

When the Interactive Blend Tool is chosen, the Property Bar offers options (shown in Figure 21-4) for customizing the effect. By default, 20 intermediate steps are created between two blend control objects.

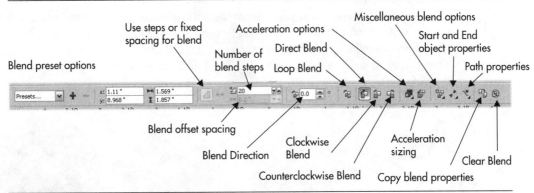

FIGURE 21-4   When the Interactive Blend Tool is used, the Property Bar has options to customize your Blend effects.

Creating a Simple Blend Effect

You might want to work with similar objects to create blends that look like repeats—rubberstamped copies of the original objects—but there's another creative use for the Interactive Blend Tool. You can morph totally dissimilar objects, and the resulting blend will probably contain a lot of interesting and useful transitional shapes. Work through the following tutorial to experiment with a basic Blend effect between a star and an ellipse object.

A Basic Blend Between Very Different Shapes

1. Choose the Star Tool; it's in the group on the Toolbox with the Polygon Tool. Click-drag a star that's about 1" in size at the top left of the drawing page. Fill it with yellow on the Color Palette, and give it a 4-point blue outline. First, choose 4 pts. from the Outline width drop-down box on the Property Bar, and then right-click any blue color well on the Color Palette.

2. Choose the Ellipse Tool (F7) and then click-drag an ellipse at the top right of the page. Fill it with blue and give it a yellow outline, but keep the outline width at the default of .5 pts.

3. Choose the Interactive Blend Tool from the Toolbox. Your cursor changes and the Property Bar's options are all dimmed because a blend doesn't exist yet on the page.

4. Click inside the star and then drag until your cursor is inside the ellipse. Once you release the mouse button, a series of new objects appears, and the Property Bar comes to life with almost all options available.

5. Twenty steps is too many for this example: type **2** in the Steps field on the Property Bar, and then press ENTER. As you can see in the following illustration, the blend shapes make an interesting progression; the outline color makes the transition from blue to yellow; the fill color transitions from yellow to blue; and the intermediate shapes are some interesting stars in stages of distortion as they become the ellipse. These types of star shapes are actually a little difficult to make using the standard drawing tools!

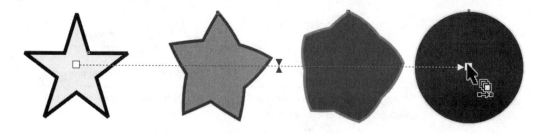

TIP	*To remove a Blend effect, click the blend portion of the effect to select it, and choose Effects	Clear Blend; or, while using the Interactive Blend Tool, click to select the Blend effect portion, and click the Clear Blend button in the Property Bar.*

Looking at the Components of a Blend

The Blend effect you built in the previous tutorial creates a fun composition, but to build on your *knowledge*—to be able to create more complex blends—it's a good idea to now examine what really went on, and what properties the objects on your page now have. A two-object blend includes several key components: the original objects become *control objects*; any changes made to either the star or the ellipse will change the blend itself. The effect portion—called a *blend group*—and the *control objects* maintain a relationship as long as the blend exists.

Each of the interactive markers around a Blend effect corresponds to an option in the Property Bar. Figure 21-5 shows the various parts of a two-object blend.

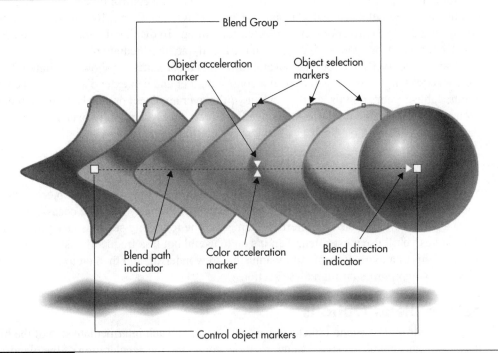

FIGURE 21-5	This blend between two shapes shows the interactive markers controlling the effect.

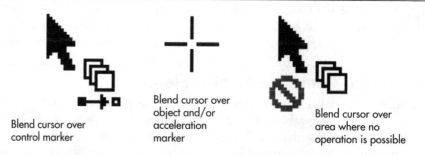

Blend cursor over control marker

Blend cursor over object and/or acceleration marker

Blend cursor over area where no operation is possible

FIGURE 21-6 The Interactive Blend Tool has several cursor states.

Editing a blend is a little more of a challenge than making dinner reservations, but significantly less challenging than brain surgery. With the Pick Tool, click the blend group to begin editing it using the Property Bar options. Single-clicking selects both the blend and its control objects. To select either control object, click only the control object itself. You'll see that the Status Bar tells you that a "Control *Whatever*" (Object, Curve, Rectangle) is selected, confirming that the correct object is selected for editing. To display the interactive control handles for the blend, you double-click on the blend, the intermediate objects.

The Interactive Blend Tool has several different cursor states, as shown in Figure 21-6. Cursor states tell you when you're over a control marker and can extend a blend to include another object (more on this shortly), when you're over an object or acceleration marker (you can then move the marker and change the effect), and when you're over an area where the tool can't do anything, such as a blank space on the page.

Editing Blend Effects

You can create a custom Blend effect by directly manipulating markers and objects with your cursor, setting specific values for options using the Property Bar, and occasionally by using a combination of the two interface elements. The following sections take you through the features you'll use most often; then it's on to useful but less frequently used options. Think of this as a journey from mildly amusing, to wonderful, and then on to totally bizarre effects as you progress through these sections.

Setting Blend Options

Options controlling a Blend effect can have an impact on each intermediate step of the blend itself. You can change the steps' value, rotation, color, and the acceleration of the blend objects, as well as save the effect you've custom-designed as a preset.

Controlling Blend Steps

The number of steps in the blend group can be set within a range of 1 to 999, as shown in Figure 21-7. To set a number of steps, enter a value in the Property Bar Blend Steps num

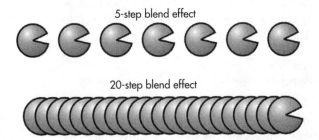

FIGURE 21-7 You can create dozens—and even hundreds—of objects and object groups by using a Blend effect.

box and then press ENTER. Notice that as you set higher step numbers, depending on the closeness of the blend control objects, they might overlap. This is an interesting effect, but if you need intermediate blend objects that don't touch one another, you can resize both blend control objects, or move them farther apart from one another.

Specifying Blend Spacing

To set spacing values between blend steps, use the Step option, which becomes available *only* if a blend has been applied to a path, as shown in Figure 21-8. This limitation is because the distance between the blend control objects must be fixed by the length of the path. Use the Blend Spacing option in the Property Bar; enter the value to a specific unit measure.

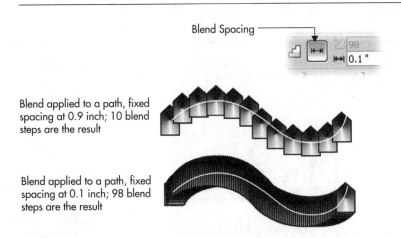

FIGURE 21-8 Fixed spacing between blend objects applied to a path can be controlled using the Blend Spacing feature on the Property Bar.

CorelDRAW automatically calculates the number of objects required to fit the path's length. Blend Spacing works within a range of 0.010 inch to 10.00 inches, in increments of 0.010 inch. To learn how to blend objects along a path, see "Assigning a Blend Path," later in this chapter.

Rotating a Blend

You can rotate the objects in a blend group by fixed degree values using the Blend Direction option, shown in Figure 21-9. Enter an angle value (based on degrees of rotation). Positive values rotate the objects counterclockwise; negative values rotate them clockwise. With a rotation value specified, the last object in the blend group is rotated the full angle, with the intermediate steps rotated in even increments starting at 0° rotation—the rotation value of the Start blend control object. This is a handy feature for suggesting action or even an animation.

When Blend Direction is set to anything other than 0° on the Property Bar, the Loop Blend option is available. Choosing the Loop Blend option has the effect of applying both rotation and path Offset effects to the blend group. Looping a blend works in combination with the Blend Direction value, offsetting the objects from their original direction and rotating them simultaneously, as shown in Figure 21-10. If you then modify a blend control object, as done in the illustration on the bottom, you can achieve a different Loop effect, sort of like one of those children's toys that never really got the hang of walking down stairs.

Changing Color Rotation

By default, the object colors in your blend group are blended *directly* from one color to the next to create a smooth color transition. However, you can change this using either Blend Clockwise or Blend Counterclockwise on the Property Bar. Ideally, if you want, for example, a rainbow effect, one control object should be red and the other filled with blue so the Blend Clockwise and Counterclockwise can cycle through the visible spectrum.

Blend Direction ────────▶

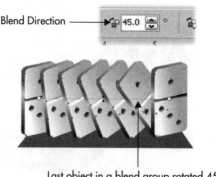

Last object in a blend group rotated 45°

FIGURE 21-9   Rotate the objects in a blend group using the Blend Direction option.

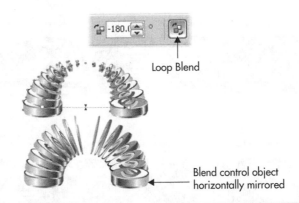

Loop Blend

Blend control object
horizontally mirrored

| **FIGURE 21-10** | The Loop Blend option applies rotation and path Offset effects to the blend group. |

Acceleration Options

Acceleration increases or decreases the rate at which your blend group objects change shape; think of it as "preferring" one control object over the other—the technical term is *bias*. When a default Blend effect is applied, both of these settings are at the midpoint of the blend; the blend group objects change in color and size evenly between the two control objects. You change object and color acceleration rates simultaneously (the default) when the two options are linked, or make acceleration changes independently of one another by clicking the Unlink Acceleration option from the Object and Color Acceleration buttons on the Property Bar, shown here.

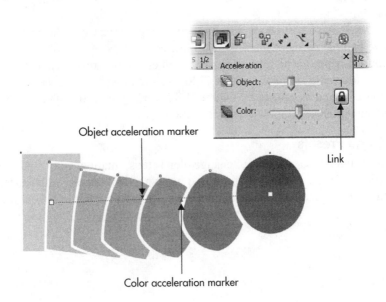

Object acceleration marker

Link

Color acceleration marker

Object Acceleration decreased, slider moved left of center

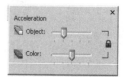

Object Acceleration increased, slider moved right of center

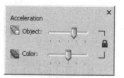

FIGURE 21-11   By modifying Object Acceleration, you can increase/decrease how many intermediate objects appear in the blend.

Moving either slider in this popout box to the left of the center position reduces (or slows) the acceleration from the Start object toward the End object of the Blend effect. Moving either of the sliders to the right increases the acceleration of your blend group objects from the Start object toward the End object of the Blend effect. Interactive acceleration markers can also be used to adjust these values. While the two rates are unlinked, changing the Object Acceleration affects only the progression of shapes in the blend group. Figure 21-11 shows the effects of increasing and decreasing the Object Acceleration.

With Object Acceleration sliders unlinked, changing the Color Acceleration affects only the change in progression of the fill and outline colors between the two objects, leaving the blend group's shapes unchanged. Moving the sliders, or the interactive markers, left or right changes the acceleration. Changing the Color Acceleration also affects the width properties applied to outline paths of objects. Figure 21-12 shows the results of changing the Color Acceleration unlinked from Object Acceleration.

Using Blend Presets

It's taken up to now to learn how to change blend steps, rotation, color, and acceleration rates of Blend effects; naturally, you want to be able to save an elegantly customized blend so you can apply it to other objects in the future. Saving your hard work as presets is

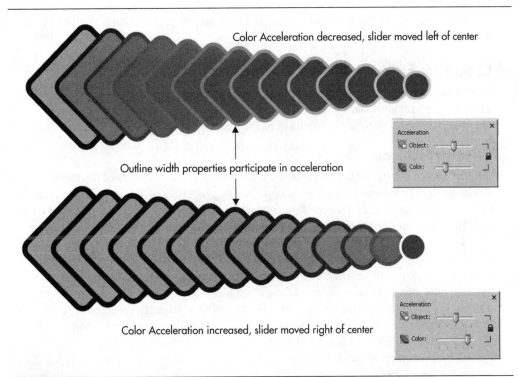

Color Acceleration decreased, slider moved left of center

Outline width properties participate in acceleration

Color Acceleration increased, slider moved right of center

FIGURE 21-12   The Object and Color Acceleration options in this blend have been unlinked. The rate at which the blend group objects are shaped remains constant.

accomplished through the Blend Preset list when a blend is selected; you can also tap into some nice *existing* presets on the list, shown here:

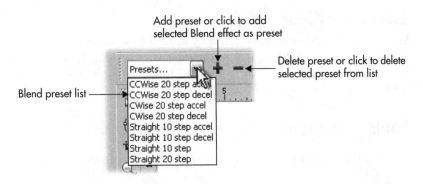

Add preset or click to add selected Blend effect as preset

Delete preset or click to delete selected preset from list

Blend preset list

Presets...

CCWise 20 step accel
CCWise 20 step decel
CWise 20 step accel
CWise 20 step decel
Straight 10 step accel
Straight 10 step decel
Straight 10 step
Straight 20 step

NOTE   *Blend paths, multipoint blends, and multi-object blends (covered later in this chapter) have to be created manually and cannot be saved as presets.*

Blend presets are used the same as other CorelDRAW preset controls and can be saved and applied to two or more different shapes.

Creating Extraordinary, Complex Blend Effects

More advanced blending can solve illustration challenges when a standard, direct blend can't. The following sections show you how to create *multipoint blends,* how to *map* blend control object *nodes,* and how to apply blends to paths. Yes, this is the "good part" of this chapter!

Creating Multipoint Blends

You can set the intermediate objects *in* the blend group as *child objects* of the blend, which causes them to behave as blend *control* objects. The properties of these child blend objects can be edited in the same way as control objects, which in turn affects the appearance of the Blend effect applied between the *original* parent control objects and/or other child blend objects.

The action is referred to as *splitting.* When split, the blend objects between the child objects and the control objects become *child blend groups.* By creating and moving child blend objects, you can have a blend follow an indirect path between its parent control objects. This affects the appearance of the child blend groups between the child and control objects. As byzantine as this sounds, the effects can be absolutely spectacular; they more than pay for your mental gymnastics, and this is as difficult as it gets for complex blends.

Child objects controlling a split blend can also be returned to their original state as blend group objects, which eliminates the split. This is called *fusing* and is done using the Fuse End command. Figure 21-13 shows in detail the before-and-after effects of a split blend; familiarize yourself with what the visual effects are of splitting and fusing a Blend effect. In splitting, two blend objects within a blend group are specified here as child blend objects and then moved, resulting in a multipoint blend. Each time the blend is split, a new set of interactive markers appears between the control and child blend objects on the path of the child blend group.

Splitting and Fusing a Blend

You can split an existing Blend effect by using the Interactive Blend Tool and Property Bar options. Fusing a split blend is done the same way as using the Fuse End command. Let's take a dip in the deep end of the pool in the following tutorial and put all these explanations to hands-on use.

Splits and Blends: The Fun Never Ends!

1. Create two objects and then use the Interactive Blend Tool to make a blend of about 12 steps.

2. Choose the blend group object whose position in the blend is the point at which you want to make a split, and then double-click this object. Your Blend effect is now split.

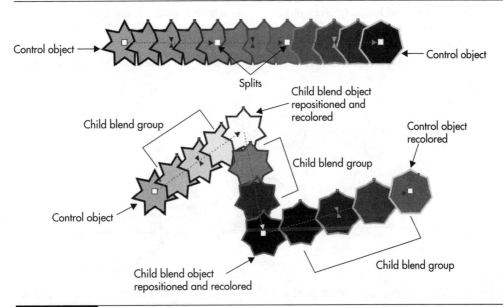

| FIGURE 21-13 | A blend between two polygons with different colors is fine. But when two of the blend group objects are split, and the child objects are repositioned and then assigned new fills, you're talking something visually complex and fascinating! |

3. While the blend control markers are visible, click-drag the object's marker to move it around on the page. The effect should remind you of editing a path with the Shape Tool—this child blend object is a "node," and you alter the path of the blend by moving this object.

4. You can also change the shape of the blend path by click-dragging the child blend object with the Pick Tool; try this now.

5. Drag a color well (a swatch) from the Color Palette, and then drop it onto the child blend object. Notice that there are two color transitions happening now in the total blend; one from the Start blend control object to the child, and a different one from the child to the End blend control object. Think of the drawings of fuzzy caterpillars that are easy to create using child blend objects.

6. Make the blend a contiguous one now by removing the child blend object's "childhood": choose the Interactive Blend Tool, click the blend to reveal the child blend object's marker, and then double-click the marker. This is called *fusing* and it can also be performed using the Miscellaneous Blend options on the Property Bar. You'll see that the blend reshapes itself to make a Direct Blend transition across the page and that the color transition you created in step 5 is removed.

You can also use Property Bar options to split a blend, which is handy when you have a lot of blend steps and a precise point in the blend is difficult to select. To do this, click the Miscellaneous Blend Options button in the Property Bar and click the Split button, as shown here. The cursor changes to a targeting cursor, and then you can click the object on the blend group where you want the split to be.

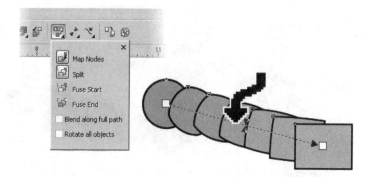

> TIP *Because a blend with child blend objects is more or less a blend within a blend, the markers between control objects and child objects also include acceleration marks for objects (their positions) and colors. You can make use of the acceleration markers with child objects to create phenomenally complex arrangements from blends, such as autumn leaves scattered on a sidewalk and a box of marbles someone carelessly dumped on the floor.*

Mapping Control Object Nodes

When a blend is applied, the blend group is built of a series of intermediate objects between the control objects. When you use two completely different shapes as control objects, the chances are that they won't have the same number of nodes connecting path segments; additionally, the position on the page of the first node you draw is usually arbitrary, depending on your style of drawing. By default, CorelDRAW blends two different objects using *node mapping*: the Blend effect makes an assumption that the blend should start with the first node on the Start object, and end at the first node on the End object, and that all objects in the blend itself make the transition based on the same node position on the page as the Start and End control objects.

Occasionally you might get a blend that looks like a parade of crumpled sheets of paper, or something similarly nasty—it's interesting, but not what you had in mind!

Fortunately, you can match the nodes of your control objects in a few clicks. To map the nodes in a blend, click the Miscellaneous Blend Options button and click the Map Nodes button. The cursor becomes a targeting cursor, your signal to click the nodes you want matched. Node mapping is a two-step operation: click on a node on the Start blend control object (the operation temporarily increases the size of the nodes so it's easy to tell what the targeting cursor wants you to do), and then click on the corresponding node on the End blend control object (see Figure 21-14).

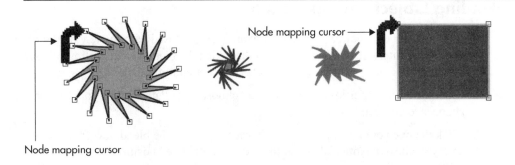

Node mapping cursor

Node mapping cursor

FIGURE 21-14 The blend is confused; you need to remove the kinks by node mapping the control objects to make a smoother blend transition.

NOTE *Node mapping is unavailable if a Blend effect has been split into a multipoint blend.*

Assigning a Blend Path

Making a blend travel along a path can produce anything from kaleidoscopic patterns, to numbers on a clock, to a handsomely illustrated directions map. Blend paths can be set to evenly space a number of objects along a path; with a little skill, you can even adjust the acceleration of the objects along the path, thus adding a little random quality to this effect. Blend objects on a path can also be rotated, offset from the path, and set to fill the full path or only part of the path.

There is a "down and dirty" way to create a Blend effect while simultaneously directing the blend along a path: with two objects on the page, you choose the Interactive Blend Tool, and then while holding ALT, click-drag a path from one object to the other. The only real disadvantage to using this technique is that the path you define probably won't show the steadiness of a path drawn, for example, with the Bézier Pen Tool, and the blend along the path might look a little shaky. The following tutorial takes you through the more studied and precise approach to binding a blend to a path, using the Path Properties pop-up, shown here:

Path Properties button

Blending Objects Along a Path

1. With a Blend effect already created and an open or closed path in view on the page, choose the Interactive Blend Tool, and then click the blend group portion of your effect to select it, not the control objects on either end of the blend.

2. Click the Path Properties button and then choose New Path. Notice your cursor changes to a targeting cursor.

3. Click the open or closed path with this special cursor; the blend now follows the path you clicked. Notice also that the blend has changed position to align with the path exactly where it's positioned. Figure 21-15 shows a Blend effect applied to a path.

Choosing New Path while a Blend effect is already applied to a path lets you assign a new and different object as the blend path. To remove a Blend effect from a path, use the Detach From Path command. If the blend includes so many steps that the path is hidden—or if the path itself is not visible because it has no outline color applied—use the Show Path command to select and highlight it for editing. Show Path is also a good command for editing a path you created using the ALT+click-drag technique described earlier. Remember: as long as the path is visible (in any View mode), you can change its course by using the Shape Tool to edit the path's nodes.

 TIP   *If you don't want a path to be visible in the final effect, set its Fill and Outline colors to None. This way you can edit the path later.*

Rotating Blend Objects

Objects set to follow a path do so using their original, unaltered orientation by default. For example, a blend involving vertical lines when blended to a path results in the centers of objects aligning with the path, but their orientation will remain vertical. If you need your blend group objects to *align* with the orientation of the path itself, choose the Rotate All

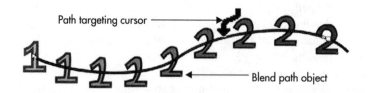

Path targeting cursor

Blend path object

FIGURE 21-15   These two objects were set to follow an open path by using the New Path command.

Objects option in the Miscellaneous Blend Options pop-up menu in the Property Bar, shown here, which is available when a blend on a path is selected.

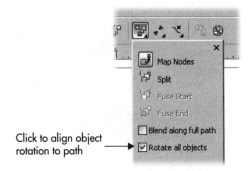

Click to align object
rotation to path

Doing this applies rotation values to each of the objects in the blend group to align with the direction of the path. In Figure 21-16, 3D stars were created using the Star Tool in combination with the Extrude Tool; the Extrude effect was simplified (Arrange | Break Extrude Group Apart), and then the objects were grouped and duplicated to make a Start and an End control object for the Blend effect. Clearly, the bottom illustration, where Rotate All Objects was used along an arc path, is more visually interesting.

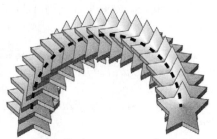

Rotate All Objects option unchecked

Rotate All Objects option checked

FIGURE 21-16   The Rotate All Objects option can create a scaling progression between blend group objects.

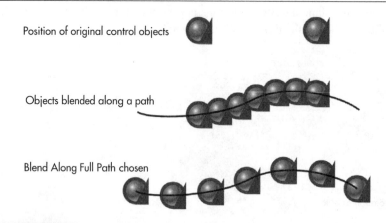

Position of original control objects

Objects blended along a path

Blend Along Full Path chosen

FIGURE 21-17 You have the option either to blend along the full length of a path or to retain the same original distance between control objects.

Blend Along Full Path

If the path you've applied your Blend effect to is the right size and length to cover your blend completely, you may automatically set the blend group and control objects to cover the entire path. To do this, choose the Blend Along Full Path option from the Miscellaneous Blend Options pop-up. Using this option, you can move the center origins of the control objects in the blend to the first and last nodes of the path. Figure 21-17 shows the effect when a blend is applied to an open path.

Once a blend group is bound to a path, you can manually space the blend objects by click-dragging the Start control object with the Pick Tool. This technique might not get you where you want to go 100 percent of the time; you cannot move the End control object. However, this is a good feature for visualizing how you want spacing to occur in a blend.

Controlling Blend Object Path Alignment

When a blend follows a path, the point at which all objects align with the path is determined by their center origin. The *center origin* is where all objects are rotated during any default rotation. Controlling how a blend aligns to a path is one of those hidden features you won't find in any dialog or Property Bar. Instead, the center origin is moved manually using the Pick Tool, with object rotation and skew handles in view. By moving the center origin, you can control how the objects align to the path.

By default, the blend aligns all objects on the path using the object's default center. If you reposition the center origin of a control object, the Blend effect aligns with the path to create a different overall composition. To move an object's center origin, select the object

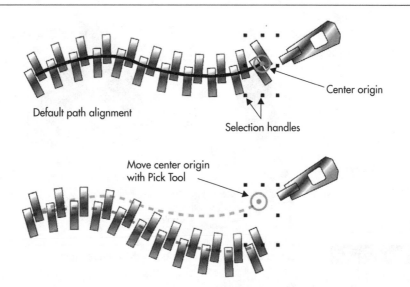

Center origin

Default path alignment

Selection handles

Move center origin
with Pick Tool

FIGURE 21-18	The center origin of these control objects was moved to change how the blend aligns with the path.

with the Pick Tool, click it a second time so the object is in rotate/skew transformation mode, and drag the center origin marker in any direction. Once the center origin is moved, the blend is updated automatically. Figure 21-18 shows an illustration of a zipper; the artist wanted the zipper to begin exactly where it begins at the top illustration, but felt it should swoop downward as it travels from left to right. The simple and quick solution is to move the End control object's center upward, offsetting its relationship to the path, and the blend group follows this change gradually and smoothly.

Working with Multi-Object Blends

Blending between *more* than two objects can produce an effect quite unlike splitting a blend, and it's just as easy to do. You click-drag between different objects on your document page. Each time you do this, a new blend group is created. The dynamic link is maintained between all objects in a multi-object blend, which means you can change control objects and the blends are instantly updated. Figure 21-19 shows two Blend effects applied to three different objects with the multi-object blend defined in different directions.

Each blend of a multi-object blend is considered a separate effect; each has its own control objects with defined Start and End blend objects. You can change the Start and End blend objects using the Start And End Properties pop-out menu commands, shown next, available on the Property Bar. The Start and End blend objects are the key to making blends that change shape all over the place in very intriguing patterns.

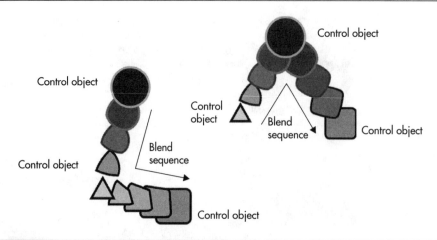

FIGURE 21-19 These three shapes are blended in different sequence.

With a blend selected, you first need to locate the Start or End blend objects—choose either the Show Start or Show End command. Choosing New Start changes the cursor to a targeting cursor, so you can then unlink the Blend effect from one object and target a different one. Doing this creates a new effect each time a different object is targeted. Choosing New End works similarly.

Start And End Object Properties button

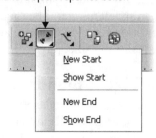

| TIP | *When working with multi-object blends, clicking any blend group in the effect selects all control objects and all blend groups. To select individual blend groups, hold* CTRL *while clicking. Blend effect properties across multiple objects can only be edited individually and only while selected.* |

After a blend has been made, you might need to dismantle it and break the link between the control objects. This is easily done, but keep in mind that it can't be reversed without using the Undo command (CTRL+Z). To dismantle a blend, choose the Pick Tool, right-click the blend group portion, and choose Break Blend Group Apart from the pop-up menu. The control objects then become separate objects, leaving the blend intermediate objects grouped. To further dismantle the arrangement, select only the blend group by using the Pick Tool, and then choose Arrange | Ungroup (CTRL+U).

Copying and Cloning Blends

You can also copy or clone from existing blends. Neither command requires that you have the Interactive Blend Tool selected as you do this, and both operations are done through command menus.

To copy a blend, at least one blend must be in view, and at least two objects must be selected. To proceed, choose Effects | Copy Effect | Blend From. Your cursor then changes to a targeting cursor—click on the blend portion of an existing blend to copy all its properties. The selected objects then adopt the Blend effect you targeted. This command can also be performed using the Interactive Blend Tool by clicking the Copy Blend Properties button on the Property Bar.

Cloning a Blend effect produces a slightly different result than copying the effect. When an effect is applied by cloning, the master clone effect object controls the new effect. Any changes made to the master are applied to the clone. However, any changes made to the clone override the properties of the master; any properties you've *left alone* with the clone still link to the master clone effect. To clone a Blend effect, you must have created at least one other Blend effect and have this in view. The options you have to clone a Blend effect to a different existing blend group are essentially limited to the properties you can set and change on the Property Bar: for example, you can remap the nodes in a master blend and the clone's mapping changes, and you can change acceleration of objects and the colors.

 If you select a blend group and then choose Edit | Clone, you might find that you have more control over changes you make in the master blend affecting the clone object. This is not the same effect as cloning a blend; however, you can change master objects colors as well as other edits and see the change in the clone.

To clone a blend, choose Effects | Clone Effect | Blend From. Your cursor becomes a targeting cursor used to target the existing blend to clone. Be sure to click directly on the blend group portion of the effect.

Copying Blend Effects with the Eyedropper and Paintbucket Tools

In CorelDRAW X4, you can now copy blends between objects using the Eyedropper and Paintbucket tools. To do this, choose the Eyedropper Tool and have both the objects in view. Try this now.

Copying a Blend Through the Toolbox

1. Using the Eyedropper Tool, click the object currently applied with the Blend effect. This is the *copy* step.

2. Click the Effects button, click the check box next to Blend in the list, and click OK, as shown here.

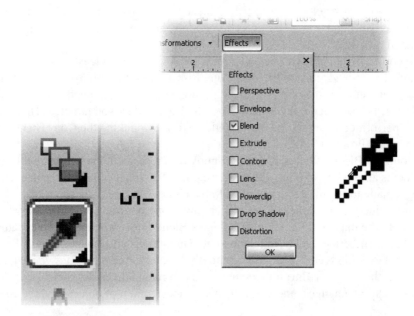

3. Hold SHIFT; it's the modifier key to switch temporarily from the Eyedropper to the Paintbucket Tool. Click the object you want to copy the effect *to*. The effect is immediately copied to the new object.

Using the Blend Docker

The Blend docker provides an alternative way to apply blends. Like all dockers in CorelDRAW, it's handy and a persistent interface element, and all the functions you can access on the Property Bar are located on this detachable palette.

Choose Effects | Blend or choose Window | Dockers | Blend to put the docker in the drawing window. Blend options in the docker are organized into four docker pages: Steps, Acceleration, Color, and Miscellaneous Options blends, shown in Figure 21-20. Unlike with the options on the Property Bar, the Blend docker lets you choose all your blend options before applying them; no changes are made to the selected objects in your drawing until you click the Apply button.

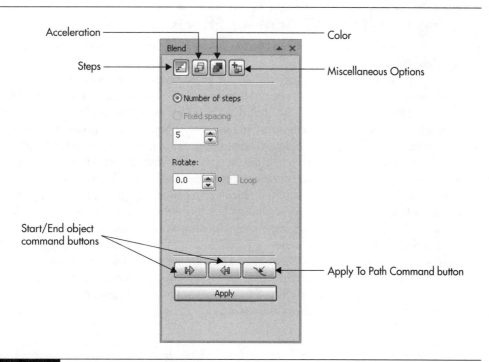

Acceleration

Steps

Color

Miscellaneous Options

Blend

Number of steps

Fixed spacing

5

Rotate:

0.0 ° Loop

Start/End object
command buttons

Apply To Path Command button

Apply

FIGURE 21-20 The Blend docker provides an alternative way of applying blends.

Tapping into Contour Effects

CorelDRAW X4's Contour effects are slightly less complex than the Blend effects but nonetheless powerful. Contour effects instantly create perfect outlines of shapes or paths by the dozens or even hundreds. The result is similar to viewing a topographical or *contour* map, hence the name.

During a Contour effect, dynamically linked shapes are concentrically created outside or inside an object's path. CorelDRAW effectively calculates the shape of each contour step and applies progressive outline and fill colors based on the original object's properties and selected contour options.

While a Contour effect is linked to an object, the object itself becomes a control object, and the new shapes created become the "contour group." Changes made to the properties of the original immediately affect the linked group. While the contour group is selected, its properties can be edited at any time—without your having to begin the effect from scratch.

Exploring CorelDRAW's Contour Effects

First, let's see what Contour effects enable you to do. One of the more popular uses is to simulate depth.

Figure 21-21 shows two illustrations of climate zones in the Urals region of Russia. At left, uniform fills (solid colors) occupy the objects; at right, the same objects have Contour effects. In the contour version, the control objects still use uniform color, but the contour uses different colors for the outermost and innermost objects. This is one of the uses of the Contour effect. As with blends, intermediate objects are generated from the beginning object; however, you don't have to draw the end—the inner object—it's part of the Contour effect function. Because a high number of steps are used in the Contour effect, you can see a smooth color transition in most of the objects. Also note that some of the objects have a low number of intermediate objects, producing banding, which can be useful in your design work. Just use a low number of steps when drawing a map of the Steppes.

Figure 21-22 shows two versions of the Contour effect applied to text. At top, a two-step Contour runs inside the word "Opera," creating an engraved look. At bottom, 25 Contour steps are used outside the word to create a glowing effect; a duplicate of "Opera" with Linear transparency was put on top of the design as an embellishment. You do not have to convert text to curves to apply a Contour effect.

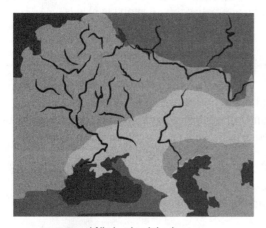
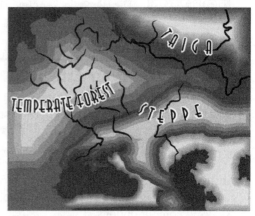

Original filled with solid colors   Finished artwork with Contour effects

FIGURE 21-21   Contour effects create a smooth color transition.

2-step Contour effect inside text

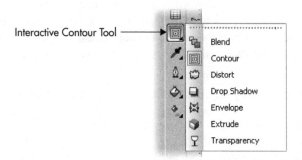

25-step Contour effect outside text with transparent overlay

FIGURE 21-22 Two different looks are achieved for the text by using different options for the Contour effect.

Using the Interactive Contour Tool and Property Bar

To apply Contour effects, you'll need to use the Interactive Contour Tool, shown here, in combination with the Property Bar. You'll find the tool in the Toolbox, with other interactive tools: Blend, Drop Shadow, Envelope, Distort, Extrude, and Transparency.

While you're using the Interactive Contour Tool, the Property Bar displays options for customizing the effect. These options include contour presets, contour direction, steps and offset spacing, color rotation, outline and fill color, and buttons for copying and clearing the effect, as shown in Figure 21-23.

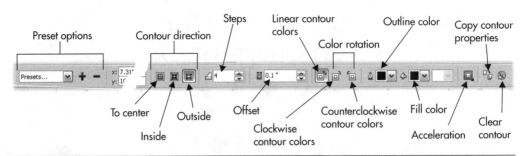

FIGURE 21-23 Use the Property Bar to make the fullest use of the Interactive Contour Tool.

Let's dig right into the use of the Interactive Contour Tool's features.

Applying a Contour Effect

1. Create an object (a polygon or Star shape is a great seed shape for contours); apply a fill and (optionally) outline properties. If you'd like to go wild with this Contour tutorial, try filling the object with a fountain fill—Contours produce interesting results with fountain fills.

2. Choose the Interactive Contour Tool. Notice that your cursor changes and the Property Bar now displays Contour options.

3. Click the object and drag (click-drag) in the direction you want the contour to be applied. Dragging from the center outward creates Outside contours; dragging in the opposite direction creates Inside contours. The angle of the drag action has no effect on the contours themselves—only inward and outward count. Notice that as you drag, a silhouette of the final size of the Contour effect appears in inverted screen colors.

4. Release the mouse button, and your effect is finished and ready for customizing.

These steps created a contour in its default state. Adjusting the effect to suit your needs takes a little more work with the Property Bar options. The contours outside or inside the object can also be controlled using the interactive markers surrounding the effect. The next section explains the use of these markers, their purpose, and how to manipulate them.

 TIP *To remove a Contour effect, click the contour portion of the effect using either the Interactive Contour Tool or Pick Tool and choose Effects | Clear Contour, or click the Clear Contour button in the Property Bar.*

Editing Contours Interactively

The easiest way to edit a Contour effect is by doing it hands-on, using the Interactive Contour Tool to change the interactive markers in combination with adjusting Property Bar options. Use them to adjust the direction, spacing, and offset values of the effect.

The black diamond-shaped marker indicates which object is the control object of the effect. The white rectangle marker indicates the final object in the contour group, and its position sets the distance between the control object and the last object in the effect. A slider between these two enables you to adjust the spacing between the contour steps interactively, which, in turn, sets the number of steps by dividing the difference. Figure 21-24 identifies the interactive markers and their purpose.

NOTE *Different types of objects are eligible for Contour effects in CorelDRAW X4. You can apply contours to closed paths, compound paths (such as a doughnut shape), and grouped objects. These object types don't have to have a fill, but obviously they'd need an outline width, or you'd be applying a contour to an invisible object. Applying a Contour effect to a group applies the effect to the entire group. Depending on how a group is arranged, if objects overlap, the contour will "trace" the silhouette of the objects as though the two shapes were combined using the Weld operation. An object applied with the Contour effect is not eligible for other effects unless it's first grouped with its linked Contour effect object.*

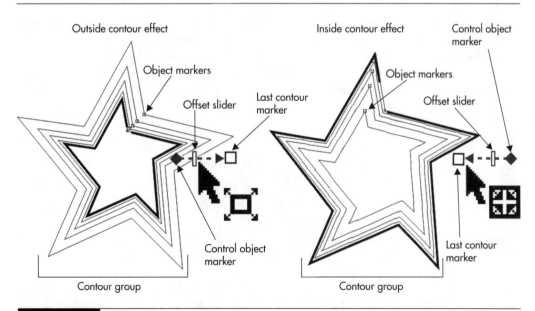

FIGURE 21-24 These two shapes have contours applied in opposite directions.

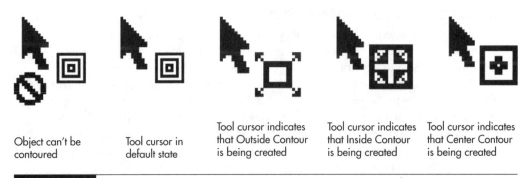

| | | Tool cursor indicates that Outside Contour is being created | Tool cursor indicates that Inside Contour is being created | Tool cursor indicates that Center Contour is being created |

Object can't be contoured   Tool cursor in default state

FIGURE 21-25   The Interactive Contour Tool cursor lets you know what's going on.

You'll also notice the Interactive Contour Tool cursor changes its appearance as you drag outside, inside, or to the centermost point of your selected object, as shown in Figure 21-25. While held over an object, the cursor will also indicate whether the object is valid for the Contour effect.

 To quickly edit a contour, double-click the effect portion of an existing contour with the Pick Tool.

Choosing Contour Direction

In addition to click-dragging a contour to set its direction, you can also use Property Bar options, shown here. Choosing To Center, Inside, or Outside causes the contours to be applied in the direction relative to the object's outline path. When Inside or Outside is selected, you can set the number of steps and the offset spacing between the steps by entering values in the Steps and Offset boxes in the Property Bar, and pressing ENTER.

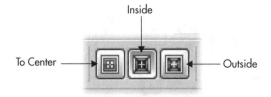

To Center   Inside   Outside

TIP   *To separate an applied contour and break the dynamic link to the original object, right-click directly on the effect (objects), and then choose Break Contour Group Apart from the pop-up menu.*

The effect's contour direction, spacing, and offset values affect one another. In the sections to follow, remember that when you change one parameter's values, a different parameter will probably auto-change.

FIGURE 21-26   These objects have identical inside contours.

Contour Inside

With the exception of the 47 clowns that can get out of a Volkswagen, there is a real-world and mathematical limit to how many steps you can create a shape within a shape. For contours, if the offset spacing value you enter in the Offset box (on the Property Bar) exceeds the number of steps the distance allows, the Steps value is automatically reduced to fit. Figure 21-26 shows some results of applying inside contours to different objects; as you can see, compound paths produce quite elegant contour steps. Remember: open paths are not eligible for Inside Contour effects; it can't be done mathematically, and it can't be done in CorelDRAW.

Contour Outside

Choosing Contour Outside creates contours *around* your object, and yes, you can use an open path, as shown in Figure 21-27 with outside contouring. It creates an interesting effect you can use for designing everything from neon signs to expensive paperclips. The Steps value can be set as high as 999, and the Offset values travel within a range of 0.001 to 300 inches.

Open path

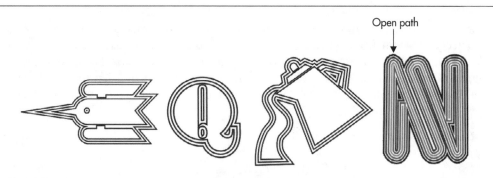

FIGURE 21-27   The same objects as shown in Figure 21-26 look a little different when Outside is chosen as the contour style.

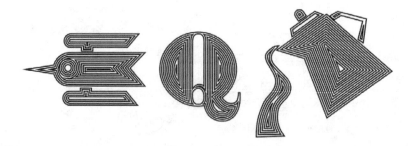

FIGURE 21-28   The To Center option creates contours to the center of an object while the number of steps is calculated by CorelDRAW.

Contour To Center

The To Center direction creates the contour inside the selected object, but it does so using as many steps as mathematically possible. The number of steps depends on the Offset value (editing the number of steps is not available)—in any case, your object is filled with a contour. This is a terrific option for illustrating game mazes—with a little editing after making a contour of a bicycle or a flower in a pot, you could fill a book with games like you see on children's menus in restaurants. Here, the Offset value is the only parameter that can be changed; the number of steps is calculated automatically. Figure 21-28 shows contours applied using the To Center option; as with the Inside option, open paths cannot take a To Center contour.

Setting Contour Colors

Controlling the progression of color between your original object and the colors of the Contour effect is important to create great illustrations; CorelDRAW is a wonderful drawing program, but *you* are the artist! You can set color in several different ways, specify a *nonlinear color rotation,* control pen and fill colors, and even set fountain fill colors for individual contour steps.

Color Rotation Options

A default contour creates fill and outline colors in a steady progression between the base object and the final contour (the End object if contours were blends). However, you can rotate these colors to create rainbow contours and other special effects. To do this, choose either Clockwise or Counterclockwise color, as shown here, which has the effect of applying fill and outline colors based on color positions located around a color wheel—red, orange, yellow…you get the idea!

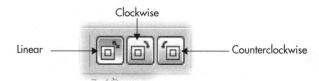

Outline Color

The Outline Color option, handsomely screen-captured here, sets the outline color of the last contour in the effect, meaning the colors change steadily from your original to the last contour object. If your object doesn't have an outline color applied, this option still displays Black as the default color, but no color will be applied to your contours. To set the outline color, click the Outline Color selector and choose a color.

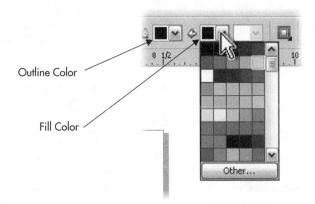

Outline Color

Fill Color

Fill Color

If you want to wow your audience, definitely play with Fill Color to create significant changes along the steps of a contour. If an object doesn't have a fill, although you can set a contour color, the contour will not have a fill. This creates an interesting effect if you have outline width and colors applied to the base object, but with no fill and no outline set for the base object to which you want to apply a contour, it's an exercise in artistic futility. To set the fill color, click the Fill Color selector and choose a color.

NOTE   *Although base objects cannot have a transparency effect in place when you use the Interactive Contour Tool, you can do some interesting things if you first create a contour, break it apart (CTRL+K), and then apply the Transparency effect to the group of objects that used to be a dynamically editable Contour. Try using Uniform transparency at about 90 percent in Xor mode on a group of 10 to 20 objects. Without a lot of preplanning, you can easily generate a color palette simply by experimenting (see Chapter 19).*

Creating Special Effects with Contours

Because Contour intermediate steps travel concentrically from the control object to the end of the effect, you can accomplish certain things that would take hours or perhaps not be possible using other tools and effects. For example, a Blend effect is simply the wrong choice of tool when you want interior shading in an object, because when you scale an irregularly shaped object (such as the letter *Q*), it scales disproportionately. As a result, when you blend, say, a *Q* to a smaller *Q* you've centered inside the larger *Q,* the intermediate blend objects scale different areas disproportionately. Therefore, a key to creating smoothly shaded objects is to use a Contour effect with many steps and a small Offset value. Here's an example recipe: with the Artistic Text Tool, type the letter **Q** (uppercase), choose a bold font such as Futura, use black as the Fill Color, and make it about 200 points in height. With the Interactive Contour Tool, choose Inside on the Property Bar, set the Offset to about 0.001", create about 150 steps, and choose white as the fill color. The result is a very smoothly shaded piece of artwork that will print beautifully with no banding, because 150 intermediate steps from black to white within relatively small objects is just about the upper limit for laser printers and most inkjet printers.

 Grayscale images—*those composed only of shades of black—are usually written to an image file format such as BMP and TIFF as 8-bit-per-pixel images. Eight bits of brightness values yield 256 possible shades from black to white, and this number is a good one to remember when you want to create smooth transitions with the Blend and Contour effects. In theory, you should see no banding in contour steps if you use 254 steps between a white and a black object of small size on your page. The greater the distance between Blend and Contour effect objects, the greater the chance you'll need to increase the number of steps, but 254 is a good bench value to begin your work with if a smooth transition is your goal.*

However, a smooth contour transition might not always be your artistic goal; by using no fill but only an outline width on objects, a small number of steps, and a relatively high Offset value, you can indeed design topographic maps, magnetic fields, and other illustrations in the technical vein. In Figure 21-29 at top is an example of the smooth contouring technique; the word "Denizen" appears twice, once with an Outside Contour effect from black center to white on the outside, and as a duplicate on top with an Inside Contour, from black to light gray on the inside. The illustration below the Contour effects is just an object with the top edge suggesting a landscape—created by using the Roughen Brush. The Contour objects are white lines, they have a high Offset value so they're clearly visible, and then the Effects | Add Perspective command was used to suggest Contour effects that have depth in the illustration.

Fountain Fill Color

Contour effects also support the use of certain fountain fills in linear, radial, conical, and square modes. If you've applied a fountain fill to your original object, the color fill properties of the contour group are also applied with the same fill type. If you've contoured an object that has a fountain fill, use the Property Bar to set the last color in the Contour fountain fill; if the fountain fill uses multiple colors, the Contour fountain fill ignores the transition colors. If an object doesn't include a fountain fill, the color selector on the Property Bar is unavailable.

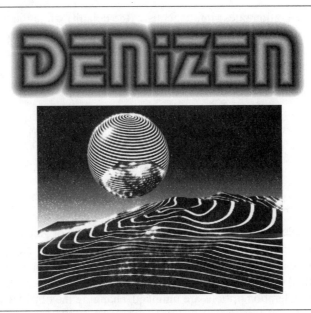

FIGURE 21-29 Make smoothly shaded Contour effects or make the effect obvious; the technique you choose depends on the illustration assignment.

Copying and Cloning Contour Effects

You can also copy and clone Contour effects to other objects, just as with blends as discussed earlier. To perform either operation, the effect you want to copy or clone must be in view on your screen at the same time as the object to which you want to copy or clone the effect. To copy an existing Contour effect to your selected object while using the Interactive Contour Tool, click the Copy Contour button on the Property Bar, and then use the targeting cursor to click an existing Contour effect. You can also use the Eyedropper and Paintbucket tools (discussed earlier). While using the Pick Tool, choose Effects | Copy Effect | Contour From, and use the same targeting operation. To clone a Contour effect to a selected object, use the Pick Tool and choose Effects | Clone Effect | Contour From, and target the existing effect.

Controlling Contour Acceleration

Just like blends, Contour Acceleration options have the effect of either increasing or decreasing the rate at which the contour group objects change shape (and color) as they progress between the control object and the final object. You can choose Object Acceleration and Color Acceleration options on the Property Bar when a Counter effect object is selected in the drawing window. When a default contour is applied, both these settings are at a default midpoint—the Contour objects change in color and size evenly.

Change both acceleration rates simultaneously (the default) while the two options are linked, or change them individually by clicking the Unlink Acceleration option, shown here.

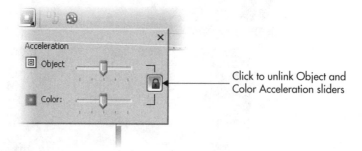

Click to unlink Object and Color Acceleration sliders

To access acceleration options, click the Object And Color Acceleration button in the Property Bar, and adjust the slider controls and/or choose the Unlink option. Moving sliders to the left of the center position reduces (or slows) the acceleration rate between the control object and the final contour in the effect. Moving sliders right increases the acceleration. While the two acceleration options are unlinked, changing the object acceleration affects only the progression of shapes in the contour group. Figure 21-30 shows the effects of increasing and decreasing acceleration.

When the Object Acceleration sliders are unlinked, changing the Color Acceleration affects only the change in progression of the fill and outline colors between the control object and the final contour in the effect, leaving the object shape acceleration unchanged.

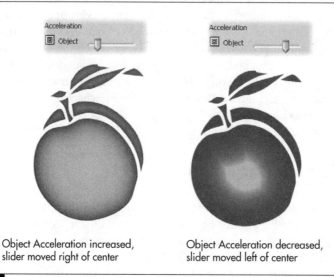

Object Acceleration increased, slider moved right of center

Object Acceleration decreased, slider moved left of center

FIGURE 21-30 Acceleration rates can dramatically change the look of an object that has a Contour effect.

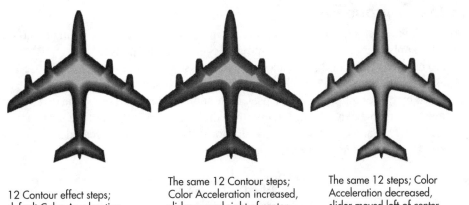

12 Contour effect steps;
default Color Acceleration

The same 12 Contour steps;
Color Acceleration increased,
slider moved right of center

The same 12 steps; Color
Acceleration decreased,
slider moved left of center

FIGURE 21-31 Acceleration rates are unlinked; you can increase and decrease the illustration's contrast by changing only the Color Acceleration.

Moving the sliders (or interactive markers) left or right increases or decreases acceleration between the control object and the final contour. Figure 21-31 shows the results of changing the Color Acceleration rates while unlinked from the Object Acceleration values.

TIP *Changing the Color Acceleration also affects the color properties applied to outline paths of objects.*

Using Contour Presets

Up to this point, you've learned about the effects of changing contour direction, steps, offsets, color rotation, and pen and fill colors of applied Contour effects. Next, it's only natural to save your efforts as presets to apply to other existing contours using the Presets options, as shown here:

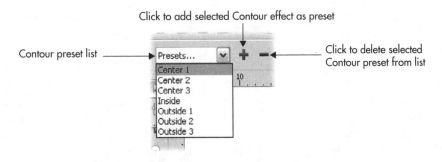

Click to add selected Contour effect as preset

Contour preset list

Click to delete selected
Contour preset from list

Contour presets are used in the same manner as other preset effects. Contour presets can be saved and quickly reapplied to different objects.

Using the Contour Docker

Although the Interactive Contour Tool is the most intuitive way of applying contours, you can still apply them using the old Contour docker as an alternative.

To open the Contour docker, shown next, choose Effects | Contour, or choose Window | Dockers | Contour (CTRL+F9). The Contour docker is organized into three separate areas accessed by clicking buttons for Steps, Color, and Acceleration, shown next. The docker's options are organized a little differently than on the Property Bar, but the same options are found here. One advantage to using the docker is that as with the Blend docker, you can choose all your options before applying them.

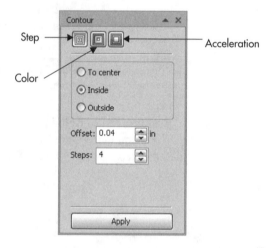

In this chapter you've seen where to find the options for controlling and customizing blends and contours, so you know where things are, but like operating heavy machinery:

- You don't take prescription medicines an hour before beginning.

- You turn the key and the real fun begins!

Dig into Blend and Contour effects; add shading to simple objects to make workaday illustration work an inspiring endeavor and to reap the reward of the automation that's possible within CorelDRAW. You can knock off 20 signs an hour using these effects instead of only two or three. Don't forget, either, that you can break these effects into groups (CTRL+K), ungroup the objects (CTRL+U), and rearrange the objects to suit your specific assignment. Blends and contours are one of the best ways to generate scores of similarly shaped objects, so fill your page with little drawing to make patterns, charts, you name it.

Chapter 22 continues with a survey of CorelDRAW effects, turning now to applying photographic qualities to your drawings through Lens Effects. Bring along some drawings you want to spruce up, and bring along your thinking cap. Specifically, your *Lens* cap.

You can groan now...

CHAPTER 22

Lens Effects and Transparency

L ens effects in CorelDRAW provide a method for quickly creating special effects and variations on your work, and for color correcting both vector and bitmap artwork. This chapter takes you through the slew of options available when you apply a Lens effect to a shape; the how-tos are quite simple, but the hard part is deciding what type of effect works best in your illustration. One of the best things about the Lens effect feature is that you can gain multiple returns on your single investment in drawing something—in an instant, you can create distorted, grayscale, tinted, darker, brighter versions of your original artwork, as you'll see shortly.

What's Behind a Lens Effect

Looking at your drawing with a lens effect object resting above it is like looking through a window or a magnifying glass. What you see through the lens effect object is influenced by the *properties* of the glass. For example, tinted glass in the real world makes objects in the distance appear darker—this phenomenon can be easily simulated with the Lens effect set to Color Limit and applied to a 50 percent black object.

The remarkable thing about Lens effects is that it doesn't matter whether a Lens effect object is over a vector drawing or over a bitmap—you'll get the same results. One of the more popular uses of this feature is to partially overlap a shape possessing a Lens effect over a drawing area, to see affected and original areas at once. In addition to putting a Lens effect shape over a drawing area, you can freeze the lens object, capturing whatever's underneath the lens, and then move the lens object around, retaining the original view within the object.

Using the Lens Docker

Later in this chapter the Interactive Transparency Tool is covered; this tool can create wonderful shading effects, and its function slightly overlaps some of the Lens effects features; let's start with the easier of the two effects—found under the Effects menu—which is simply called *Lens*.

The only way to apply a Lens in CorelDRAW X4 is through the Lens docker, opened by choosing Effects | Lens (ALT+F3). This docker, shown in Figure 22-1, follows the basic layout of all CorelDRAW dockers, but the options are unique to its function. The way to operate the Lens docker is to first have an object selected that's over a different object (or over several objects—vector or imported bitmap), to choose a lens type from the drop-down menu, and then to choose from different property options on the docker.

When an object is selected, the Lens docker preview window shows a thumbnail of what you're about to apply; with no objects targeted for the effect, the preview window looks similar to that in Figure 22-1. Options are detailed in following sections, but for right now, let's take the Lens docker out for a trial spin.

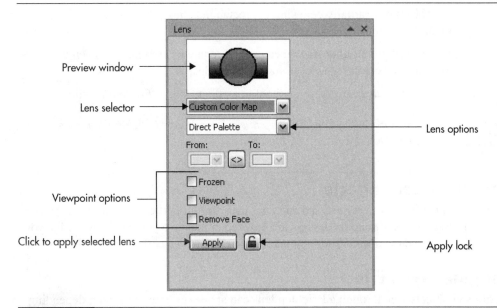

FIGURE 22-1 The Lens docker is where you customize effects to create a specific type of lens you need.

Working with a Lens Effect

1. Create a rectangle and then with the Interactive Fill Tool, click-drag to create a default Linear fountain fill from black to white. This rectangle will serve for this demonstration; you'll most certainly get better effects using artwork of your own!

2. Create an ellipse and with the Pick Tool arrange the ellipse so it partially overlaps the rectangle, to better see the creative possibilities of applying a Lens to the ellipse object.

3. With the ellipse selected, open the Lens docker (ALT+F3).

4. Choose Custom Color Map from the docker's selector drop-down list. Choose a deep blue from the From mini-palette, and then choose a bright green from the To mini-palette.

5. Click the Apply button. The Lens effect has remapped deeper shades in the rectangle to blues and lighter shades to greens. But areas of the rectangle not covered by the ellipse are still a black-to-white fountain fill.

6. Move the ellipse around a little to see how the Lens effect changes only those areas of the rectangle that the ellipse covers.

7. With the ellipse partially eclipsing the rectangle, click the Frozen box to put a check in it and then click Apply.

8. Move the ellipse around. As you can see, its contents are retained, even when you move the ellipse totally away from the rectangle.

9. Call your friends over and show them this effect. This is *fascinating* stuff!

 TIP   *The Apply lock on the Lens docker causes Lens effects to be applied immediately, with no need to click the Apply button.*

Exploring the Lens Effects

There are 11 different lens types, and each has different properties you set using the docker controls. Each lens type and its options are covered in detail so you can better judge your starting point when you want to dress up an illustration with a certain type of Lens effect.

Brighten Lens Effect

Colors in objects seen through a Brighten lens can appear brighter or darker, depending on the Rate you define in the num box. The Rate can be between 100 and –100; positive values brighten up underlying colors, while negative values cause them to darken, as shown in Figure 22-2. This is a handy effect when, for example, part of an illustration you've worked on for days looks under- or overexposed when you print it. The solution is to create (or copy) an object to use as the Lens and place it directly on top, perfectly aligned with the area that prints poorly. This saves you the time of recoloring several (perhaps hundreds) of original design objects.

Color Add Lens Effect

The Color Add lens fills the lens object with the color you choose by clicking the Color drop-down mini-palette, then combining all underlying colors in an additive fashion (see additive color models in Chapter 19). For example, if you were to create an object with a red-to-blue fountain fill, and then put a red Color Add lens object over it, the result would be that the red areas will look unaffected at all Rates, while the blue areas will move to magenta. This effect is good for adding a tint to isolated areas of an illustration and of imported bitmaps. Any color can be added within a range of 0 to 100 percent in increments of 5 percent. Higher values add more color; 0 adds no color at all.

Color Limit Lens Effect

The Color Limit lens produces an effect that looks like the opposite effect produced by Color Add. Color Limit decreases brightness in all underlying areas and tints, using the color you've chosen for the lens; the result is similar to staining a piece of cloth or wood, except for underlying colors that are the same or similar in hue to the lens object color. This can be quite useful,

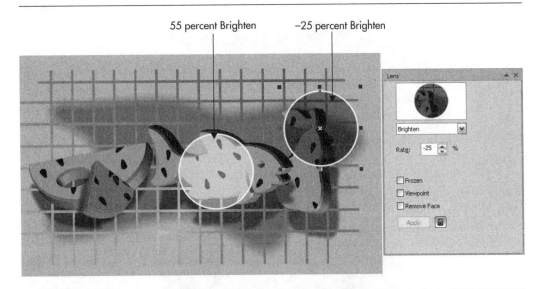

55 percent Brighten   **−25 percent Brighten**

FIGURE 22-2   Use the Brighten lens to correct the exposure in an area of a drawing or imported photograph.

---

for example, to highlight an object in a composition by de-emphasizing all other objects, as shown in Figure 22-3. At top you can see the original image of kitchen condiments; what you can't see are the colors of the liquids, so they are called out in the figure. At bottom, a red Lens set to Color Limit is placed above the image—the red wine doesn't change in brightness, but the other colors in the image become denser according to the amount of red in the underlying areas. The amaretto is increased in brightness a little (its color presence is limited) because brown contains a little red; the olive oil, however, becomes very dark because originally it contains very little red. The color can be anything you like; the rate has to fall within a range of 0 to 100 percent. A setting of 100 decreases the underlying colors that aren't the lens color to black (removing all color); a setting of 0 removes no color at all.

Custom Color Map Lens Effects

A Custom Color Map lens object looks at the original colors in the underlying objects—giving preference to brightness in its calculations—and then reproduces the design with the remapping colors you specify on the Lens docker. Usually, you want to choose a deep From color and a light To color; this tints and colorizes a drawing or bitmap in a traditional, stylized way. You can also remap your drawing colors in an untraditional way by using different hues with similar brightness values, and there are also Forward and Reverse Rainbow options. All of these are ideal for re-creating Fillmore West rock posters from the 1960s. Mapping is performed around the traditional color wheel—red travels to orange, then

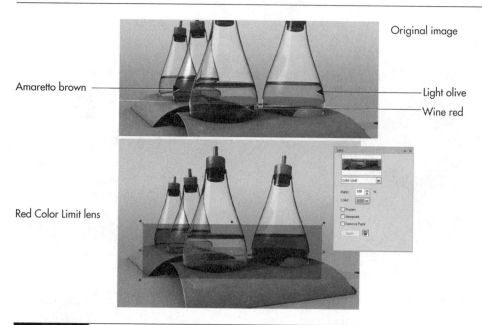

Original image

Amaretto brown

Light olive

Wine red

Red Color Limit lens

FIGURE 22-3 The Color Limit lens effect shown here limited all the reds in the image below the red lens rectangle.

to yellow, and so on—using either a direct or rotational direction. In Figure 22-4 you can see an original drawing, created by using PowerTRACE on a photograph. At bottom, a deep blue was defined as the From color and light yellow as the To color, which created a highly posterized finished illustration, very reminiscent of the style of many Russian Revolution posters—so much so that the text above the illustration says (more or less) "The People's Music!" To get the text to be legible against what is now a collection of color gradients, the Invert lens effect was used on the text; Invert is covered shortly in this chapter.

Mapping options consist of three palette-mapping choices:

- **Direct Palette** Choosing this option offers two colors (From and To) and maps the colors found in your objects evenly between the brightness values of colors found directly between these two around the color wheel.

- **Forward Rainbow** This option has the same effect as Direct Palette, but in this case, each of the object colors is mapped to *all* colors between your two chosen colors in a clockwise rotation. For example, if you choose red as the From color and green as the To color, instead of a blend between these two colors throughout your illustration, distinct areas of red, orange, yellow, and green are mapped with equal emphasis to the underlying design. Blue and purple are not included in the Color

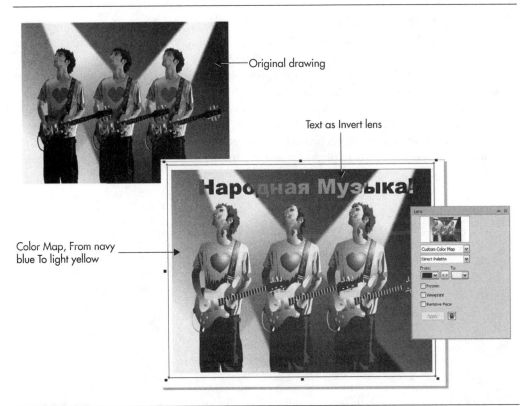

FIGURE 22-4   Color Map lens effects remap colors beneath the lens to a progression through the color wheel using a From color (usually a dark color) and a To color (usually a light color).

Map because on a color wheel these hues don't appear between the chosen red and green in this example. If you want the entire spectrum of the rainbow, you'd choose red as the From color and violet (purple) as the To color.

■ **Reverse Rainbow**   The Reverse Rainbow option has the effect of mapping the colors in your object to the RGB brightness values of all colors between your two chosen colors in a counterclockwise direction. If you choose this option after setting up Forward Rainbow colors, you'll get a chromatic inverse of Forward Rainbow color mapping, a highly solarized look, much like what developed film would look like if you had opened the back of the camera before rewinding the film.

TIP   *To swap your selected From and To colors quickly in the Lens docker while applying Custom Color Map Lens effects, click the small button located between the From and To color selectors.*

Fish Eye Lens Effect

A conventional camera "fish eye" lens is usually 18mm (compared with the standard 55mm) with a very wide angle of view—famous architectural photographs features 90° of vision and more. CorelDRAW's Fish Eye lens performs the virtual equivalent; you can produce exceptionally distorted artwork, which can be interesting if not an everyday effect in commercial design. Fish Eye is controlled by setting the rate of distortion within a range of 1,000 to –1,000 percent. The effect is so dramatic at maximum settings that the object shapes viewed through this lens can become unrecognizable. At lower rates, the effect is subtle while retaining a sense of drama and dynamism. Here is an illustration that actually uses some of the Lens effects and transparency covered later in this chapter.

Although it's a good illustration, let's say the fictitious client, Mr. Beefbarn, wants to "accentuate" his 1/16-pound all-beef special by plumping up the illustration for the advertisement. You can occasionally use an Envelope effect (see Chapter 20) to manually create a Fish Eye effect, but with groups of objects (the burger is made up of 138 objects, many of them blends) you always run the risk of unpredictably bent objects within a group. Instead, what you can do in a few mouse clicks is create a shape that fits over only the burger in the drawing, and then apply the Fish Eye. In Figure 22-5 you can see at left the result of an ellipse shape with the Fish Eye lens type defined, at a rate of 45%. The burger bulges toward the viewer, and Mr. Beefbarn is happy. At right a negative rate, –90 percent, is defined using the same lens object. The result is a leaner burger, which in today's health-conscious culture, works as well as the fat burger at left for advertising purposes.

Heat Map Lens Effect

The Heat Map lens is similar to the Color Map effect except the colors are predetermined (there are no specific color options). The effect simulates "black body" physics: a hypothetical object (in space) absorbs all light, and the presumption in this hypothesis is that the body is warm. With the Heat Map lens, colors in underlying objects on the warm side of the color

 Fish Eye, Rate at 45 percent

 Fish Eye, Rate at –90 percent

FIGURE 22-5 Two different Fish Eye lens effects settings are used to bloat and pucker the underlying drawing area.

wheel (red, orange, yellow) appear in shades of red or orange. Cool colors—green, blue, and violet—appear in shades of white, yellow, purple, blue, and light blue. By default, colors in the result composition tend to feature more warm than cool colors, but you can offset the color mapping by using the Palette rotation spin box. Figure 22-6 shows a drawing where the brown waffle cone is mapping to blues and violets (cool colors) with the wavy line Heat Map lens shape above it. In contrast, the orange and yellow spiral pattern in the background maps to red in the yellow areas, making a transition to violet where the spiral runs to orange and red. This is an effect that you really need to experiment with on your own, and you should scout down a lot of clients who have a need for simulated infrared photograph!

When you use the Palette Rotation spin box, values between 0 and 49 usually cause colors to appear warmer, and values between 50 and 100 cause colors to appear cooler.

Invert Lens Effect

The Invert lens applies color inversion to the colors of underlying objects. In this case, colors are directly mapped to colors found on the opposite side of a color wheel. Black areas change to white, light grays turn to dark grays, reds turn to greens, yellows turn to blues, and

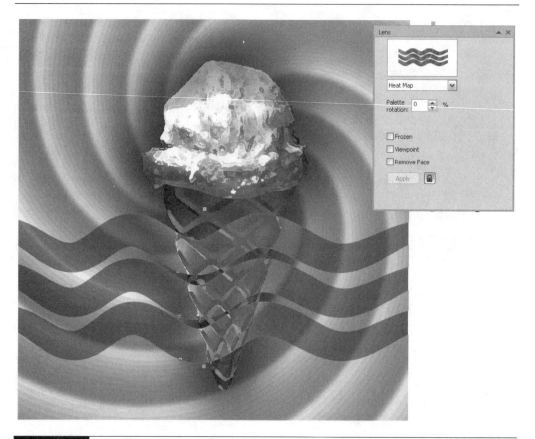

FIGURE 22-6   The Heat Map lens distorts the brightness values of objects beneath it, making all areas brilliant hues found in black-body physics.

so on. Figure 22-7 shows a creative use of Invert: this is one single illustration, but it appears to be a "day and night" composition because a rectangle placed over the left side of the drawings has the Invert lens effect.

Magnify Lens Effect

The Magnify lens produces a straightforward and predictable effect, but it can make underlying objects larger *or* smaller, depending on the settings you enter for the Rate value. The Rate can be set within a range of 0.1 to 100, where values between 1 and 100 cause increased magnification and values less than 1 cause reduced magnification. Figure 22-8 shows one of scores of creative possibilities for putting a magnifying glass in a drawing. In a nutshell, the Magnify lens is excellent for calling out details in a product: a gear, the fine print on a bottle, the exquisitely crafted detail in a wristwatch. In this figure, an ellipse was drawn over a title on the tabletop jukebox. The Magnify Amount is 3.5, and it's clear that

FIGURE 22-7   The Invert lens creates a photographic negative from the objects underneath.

the title is a fictitious one. However, you might not always want a Lens effect intruding on other areas of an illustration; the lens in this figure was frozen (explained shortly) and then moved so the audience can see both the illustration and the starring tune on the jukebox.

Tinted Grayscale Lens Effect

By default, the Tinted Grayscale lens converts the colors of underlying objects to grayscale values, which is terrific if you're into black-and-white photography, but you can use any color you like, thus tinting photos and drawings just by choosing a color from the color selector. It would be silly to show you a figure here of a Grayscale lens effect; you'll see the results yourself in your own work. Remember that digital images use the additive color model, so the lighter the lens color, the fainter the resulting composition will be. This might be an effect you want, however; try light grays and light warm browns to make new photographs look like they were taken in the 1940s.

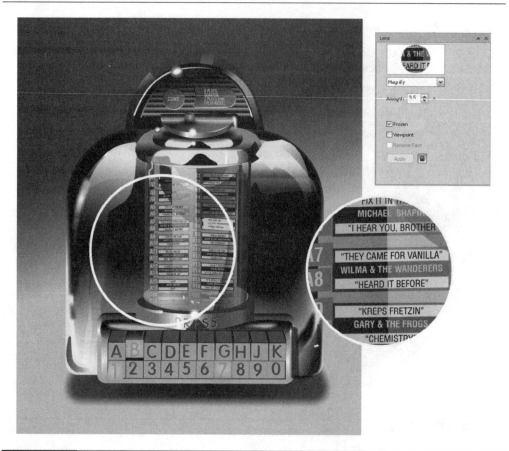

FIGURE 22-8 A Magnify lens effect rate of just 3.5 times enlargement is enough to make 5-point text in a full-page illustration completely legible.

Transparency Lens Effect

The Transparency lens effect is a simplified version of the effects that can be achieved using CorelDRAW X4's Interactive Transparency Tool. Blending modes are unavailable and the object itself becomes transparent—not the underlying objects—to varying degrees, based on the rate you set on the Lens docker. The Rate can be set within a range of 0 to 100 percent. A value of 0 applies no transparency, leaving the object opaque; a value of 100 percent applies the full transparency, making the object invisible. You can also specify a color to apply to the lens object using the color selector, which is the prime advantage of using the Lens instead of the Interactive Transparency Tool. You have an "either-or" choice when working with transparency; an object you make partially transparent with the Interactive Transparency Tool will lose its unique properties if you try to apply a Transparency lens to it—the Lens overrides the Transparency Tool. Figure 22-9 shows several duplicate groups of

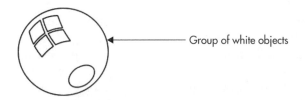

Group of white objects

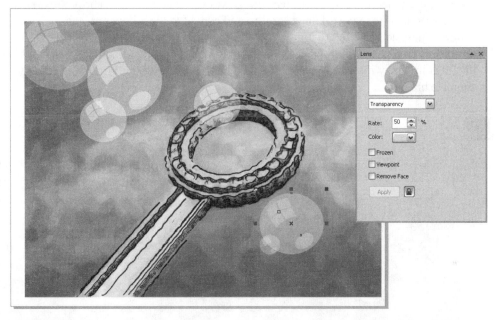

FIGURE 22-9 Put Transparency lens objects over each other to lessen the effect in certain areas.

objects set to different rates to disguise their identical features. As you can see, when a group accepts the Transparency, in this example at 50% Rate, overlapping objects create a progressively less transparent area. It's a neat effect, but limit yourself to two or three objects with the Transparent lens effect that overlap, because this effect is processor-intensive and can slow your creativity.

Wireframe Lens Effect

The Wireframe lens converts the color and outline properties of objects to specific colors; this is a very useful effect for pointing out the technical details in an illustration, much in the same way that artists who use modeling applications such as 3D Studio can view a wireframe of a 3D object and compare it with a photorealistic render of a 3D scene. You can set the outline and fill colors of objects beneath the lens to any uniform color you choose using the color selectors. The fill and outline colors of your objects are replaced with the selected colors, while outline properties—such as applied widths and line styles—are ignored to produce an outline of uniform width. In Figure 22-10 you can see the blend objects revealed in the illustration using the Wireframe lens, but there is something odd going on. The finished drawing of the burger has no outline width on any of the objects to produce the smooth shading, and therefore the wireframe view through the lens should show no outlines; yet this figure does. This was accomplished by first applying an outline width to the burger's blend objects; then the Wireframe lens effect was given to an ellipse above the drawing. The ellipse was then frozen (explained shortly) and copied to the Clipboard, and then the File | Revert command was used to remove the outline width on the burger. The frozen wireframe object was then pasted into the composition. For an interesting effect, try choosing blue as the fill color and white as the outline on the Lens docker with the Wireframe effect to simulate blueprints.

NOTE *The Wireframe lens doesn't work on bitmap images.*

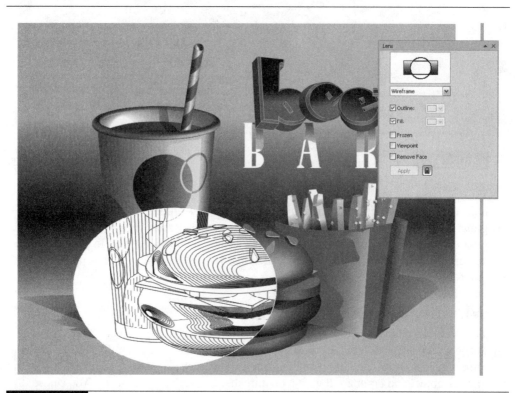

FIGURE 22-10   The Wireframe lens effect ignores original object fill colors and outline colors, producing a "technical" view of any drawing.

22

Using Lens Options

Only one Lens docker option, types of effects, has been discussed so far. You'll gain more control of your effects in a moment as the other options on the docker are explained in the following sections. Locking an effect, altering viewpoints, and controlling whether the page background is involved in an effect will open extra doors to this remarkable docker.

Using the Frozen Option

The Frozen option causes the view seen through any Lens effect to remain constant—even if the lens object itself is moved. This gives you the option to apply and freeze the lens object view and use it for other purposes. Behind the scenes, some complex calculations are being performed. A frozen lens effect object can actually be ungrouped to reveal a set of objects based on the lens you've applied. If the effect is applied above a bitmap, the result is often a complete copy of the image area, filtered, and can be exported as a bitmap.

After the Frozen option is chosen, the lens object can be ungrouped (CTRL+U). This action breaks the dynamic link between the lens object and the view of objects seen through it, and converts the effect to a collection of ungrouped vector and/or bitmap objects. Each of the objects representing the complete effect becomes a separate object, including the lens object, the page background, and the objects within the lens view. Figure 22-11 shows an example of an Artistic Text object with a black outline and a fountain fill viewed through an ellipse with the Invert lens effect applied. In this figure, the Frozen option was selected and applied, and the resulting effect is ungrouped to create several vector objects representing the complete effect. So if you ever need part of an effect as a nondynamic object for a composition, you now know the steps.

Changing a Lens Viewpoint

The Viewpoint option offers the chance to move a lens object but retain the view of the objects the lens was originally over. In effect, the Lens Viewpoint option lets you move a lens and keep the view inside the lens constant—like freezing a lens—but this option keeps the effect dynamic. When you check Lens Viewpoint on the docker, an Edit button appears. You can then click-drag interactively to reposition the viewpoint of the Lens effect either using your cursor (indicated onscreen by an X) or by entering numeric values in the X and Y page position boxes. Figure 22-12 shows the Viewpoint of a Fish Eye lens effect being edited.

 The view seen through a lens object is a function of object layering, which means that all objects layered below the lens object appear in the lens. While the Viewpoint is repositioned, you may find that an object might or might not appear visible. Arranging objects in back of the lens object causes them to be affected; arranging them in front of the lens object omits them from the view.

The default viewpoint position of a Lens effect is always the center of your object, but you can move it anywhere you like. After moving it, click the End button and then click the Apply button on the Lens docker to set the new position.

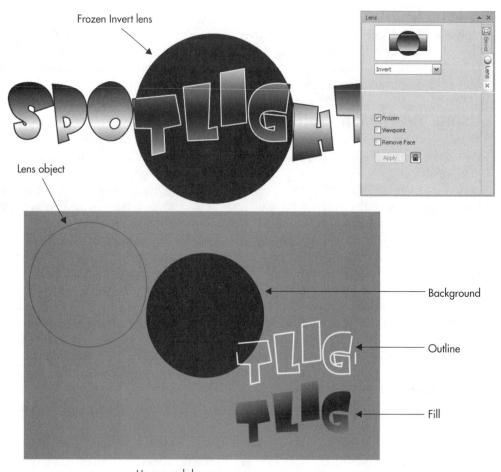

FIGURE 22-11   Each part of the Lens effect is rendered to a frozen object, which can be ungrouped.

Using the Remove Face Option

Remove Face is available for certain types of Lens effects and lets you specify whether other objects or the page background participate in the effect. By default, whenever a Lens effect is applied, the background—your page, which is usually white—is involved in the effect.

However, if the lens you are using alters colors—such as Custom Color Map—and you don't want your background to be changed within the view seen through the lens object, choosing this option leaves the background unaltered. As you can see here, the design idea is to remap only the objects under the lens; at top left, without Remove Face, the

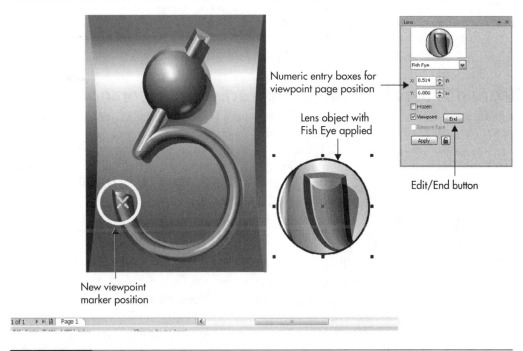

Numeric entry boxes for
viewpoint page position

Lens object with
Fish Eye applied

Edit/End button

New viewpoint
marker position

FIGURE 22-12   The Viewpoint of this Lens effect has been repositioned to alter the view seen
through the lens object.

background is tinted, but after Remove Face is applied at bottom right, the page background
is unaffected by the tinting effect.

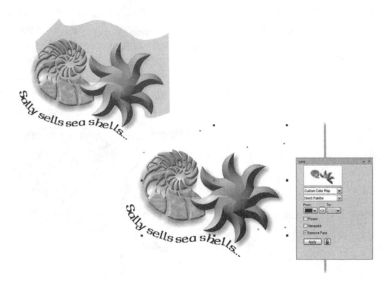

To copy a Lens effect quickly between objects, choose the object you wish to copy an existing Lens effect to, and then choose Effects | Copy Effect | Lens From. Using the targeting cursor that appears, click an existing Lens effect to copy its properties. When Lens effects are copied, edited viewpoints are also copied.

Clearing Things Up with the Interactive Transparency Tool

Transparency is an effect CorelDRAW users have leveraged for many years to illustrate scenes that have a very photorealistic look. The Interactive Transparency Tool—the focus of this section—is quite different in use and in the effect you achieve than the Transparency Lens. You have directions for transparency such as linear and radial, and also have various operators accessed from the Property Bar to set conditions for how a partially transparent object interacts with an object below it.

One thing is good to keep in mind when working with transparency in a design: this is the way you blend colors between objects. That's it; your work doesn't benefit from a totally transparent object—there has to be some influence from the object to which you apply transparency, and it's usually color. Therefore, an alternative and perhaps easier way to think about transparency is to think about color blending.

One of the keys to accomplishing amazing artwork using the Interactive Transparency Tool is the fill that a semitransparent object has; in addition to uniform fills, fountain and pattern fills can also take on transparency. You put fills and transparency together, and you're talking seriously sophisticated compositions! Another key lies in how you approach a drawing in which you plan to feature partially transparent objects. The best use of partially transparent objects is as an accent, an area here and there in a drawing to suggest a real-world object. To illustrate a real-world object such as a piece of jewelry, transparency plays a part—the gem in the jewelry, for example—but there will certainly be nontransparent objects in such a drawing. In short, use all the tricks and techniques you've learned in Chapters 1 through 21, and then apply transparency where the design areas call for it. In the illustration here, you can see what is today a fairly common button for a web page; it suggests glass. At left you can see a wireframe view; not a lot of objects went into a fairly convincing drawing of a glass button! With the Interactive Transparency Tool in combination with your own designer's eye, you can illustrate gases, smoke, fog, mist, and steam; you can also add reflections and highlights to your work to add detail, interest…and a touch of glass.

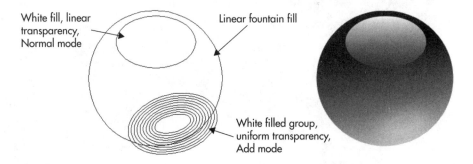

White fill, linear transparency, Normal mode

Linear fountain fill

White filled group, uniform transparency, Add mode

22

Photorealism and Transparency

It's important to understand that if photorealism is your goal, you'll most certainly use effects in combination with transparency: the real world has *clear* objects, not transparent ones. For example, if you want to illustrate a drinking glass, you would consider that glass bends light as light passes through it, glass is smooth and therefore reflects highlights, and glass casts shadows. As an example, Claude Rains in the 1930s classic film was *invisible*; he didn't cast shadows, and he didn't show highlights when he did his thing—if he did, he'd be called *The Clear Man,* not a very good movie title.

Transparency in CorelDRAW doesn't create highlights or reflections—this sort of thing you need to illustrate. The Interactive Transparency Tool is a tremendous helper, but cannot complete the artwork you have in mind. However, there's another property in real-world objects such as glass that the Interactive Transparency Tool does indeed imitate: tinting—you'll see shortly that an object with some transparency can cast a tint on objects it overlaps, depending on the operator used for blending the object to underlying objects and on its own color. For the discussions that follow, you'll need to remember only two terms and they're opposites. *Opacity* is the amount to which you can see an object; *transparency* is the amount you can't see an object. Therefore, 100 percent opacity is seen in a completely visible object, and 100 percent transparency can't be seen at all.

Using the Interactive Transparency Tool and Property Bar

The Transparency effects discussed next are applied using the Interactive Transparency Tool located in the Toolbox grouped with other interactive tools, as shown here:

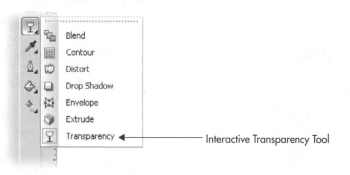

TIP   *When creating a transparency, you can set whether the fill and outline properties of objects are included in a Transparency effect. Choose All, Fill, or Outline using Property Bar options.*

While the Interactive Transparency Tool is chosen, the Property Bar displays all options to control the Transparency effect. These options, as shown here, are used together with any interactive markers surrounding the target object:

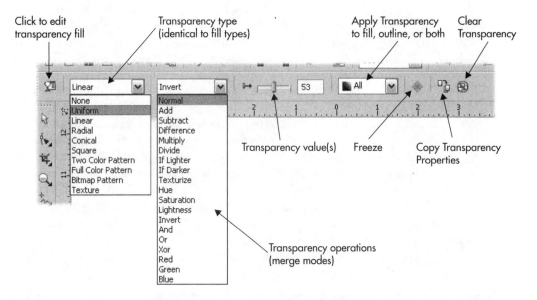

Click to edit transparency fill

Transparency type (identical to fill types)

Apply Transparency to fill, outline, or both

Clear Transparency

Transparency value(s)

Freeze

Copy Transparency Properties

Transparency operations (merge modes)

Often, the most rewarding way to discover and gain control over a feature in CorelDRAW or any program is to dive straight in. The following tutorial might seem a little challenging because an explanation of the transparency options is provided on-the-fly, sort of like getting directions *while* you're driving, but you might want the power of transparencies at hand *right now,* as we all do with valuable stuff! Follow along here to create a fairly realistic composition of a child's marble; transparency will take care of the shading and the highlights.

Creating a Dimensional Drawing Through Transparency

1. Create a circle (choose the Ellipse Tool and then hold CTRL while you drag). Give it a Bitmap Pattern fill by first choosing the Interactive Fill Tool; choose Bitmap Pattern from the Fill Type selector on the Property Bar, and then choose the first pattern from the Fill drop-down on the Property Bar, to the right of the Fill Type selector.

2. Press CTRL+C and then CTRL+V to put a duplicate of the circle directly above the original. Click the black color well on the Color Palette to give this duplicate a uniform black fill.

3. Choose the Interactive Transparency Tool. Choose Radial as the transparency Type from the Property Bar, and then choose If Darker from the Operations list on the Property Bar.

4. Click-drag the interactive marker, the black one that shows the start of the Radial transparency, and move it just a little toward 10 o'clock. Then click-drag the end marker (the white one) toward 4 o'clock until the shading this semitransparent object lends to the underlying bitmap-filled object creates the appearance of light coming into the scene from 10 o'clock. This is a classic *key lighting* effect used by photographers, so the composition should look a little photorealistic now. Refer to Figure 22-13, because you were promised directions while you're driving, and this figure is a roadmap!

5. Create a small, white circle, about a tenth the size of the circle. Fill it with white and then choose the Interactive Transparency Tool.

6. Set the transparency Type to Radial for the circle, and leave the Operations merge mode at the default of Normal.

7. The Radial type of transparency by default produces the opposite effect than the one desired here. This object should serve as a highlight on the child's marble; on the Color Palette, drag the black color well onto the end marker of the interactive transparency, and then drag white to the start marker.

8. Drag the end marker to just inside of the circle object; doing this ensures that the object is 100 percent transparent at its edges, creating a perfect highlight object. Put it at the upper left of the marble drawing, and consider this a frenetic tutorial well done!

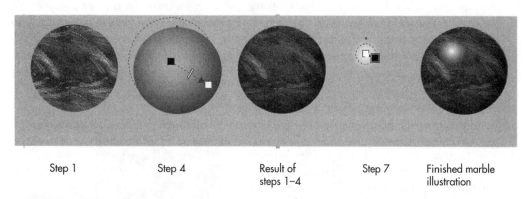

| Step 1 | Step 4 | Result of steps 1–4 | Step 7 | Finished marble illustration |

FIGURE 22-13   Use the Interactive Transparency Tool to create shading for simple objects that you want to look photorealistic.

Setting Transparency Properties

The preceding tutorial contains the steps used by professional illustrators to create an effect, however, it will increase your talents even more to understand what the fill types and operators do. In other words, your appetite might be whetted now, so prepare for an education *banquet*. The Property Bar options when the Interactive Transparency Tool is active will be your main resource for customizing a Transparency effect; as you grow more comfortable with the transparency feature, you'll probably ease into moving the transparency interactive markers above effects objects. There are nine transparency fill types (identical to regular object fills by category) and 19 available transparency operations (also referred to as "merge modes" and "blending modes" in Corel Painter and other graphics applications). Next up is the "good stuff" on what fills can offer as well as an explanation of the merge modes.

Setting Transparency Types

If you have experience with CorelDRAW's Interactive Fill Tool, you're 99 percent of the way to mastering the transparency fill types with the Interactive Transparency Tool. Because transparency isn't the same as an object's fill, the following sections take you through some unique properties. There are wonderful design potentials you can leverage by choosing your transparency type according to what you need to design.

Uniform Transparency

Uniform transparency is the default for objects to which you assign this trait; the object will feature a flat and even transparency value. The way this semitransparent object blends with underlying objects is completely predictable. For example, if you assign a red rectangle and then a blue rectangle with 50 percent (the default transparency amount) and overlap them, yep, you'll see violet in the intersection. Uniform transparency is set within a range of 0 to 100 percent using the slider control on the Property Bar. In this illustration, a white compound object is assigned 50 percent transparency and placed above a rectangle that has a bitmap fill. As a designer, you really need to play with the fill of underlying objects, the transparency amount of the top object, as well as the

transparent object's color. A Uniform fill will not win you a design award if you place the object on top of a uniform fill object! You need to work with the colors of your semitransparent object to create a successful effect; it took three tries to come up with this next drawing—finally, a dark background and a light transparent object provided the contrast to get the coffee illustration to read in a clear but subtle fashion.

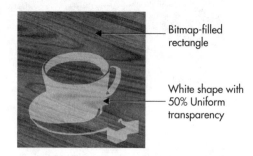

Bitmap-filled rectangle

White shape with 50% Uniform transparency

 TIP   *The Uniform transparency type has no control markers over the object as other types do.*

Fountain Fill Transparencies

Transparent objects that use any of the Fountain fill direction types are an exceptionally powerful tool for illustration, as you'll see in a moment. First, however, you really need to understand what's going on with a Fountain fill type transparency—on the surface, this transparency type makes a transition from one degree of opacity (let's use 100 percent opaque, for example) to a different degree of opacity, say 0 percent (completely transparent, invisible). What governs the degree of transparency at the start and end points are the control markers, not only their position relative to the object underneath but also *the brightness value* of the markers. Fountain fill transparencies are driven by *any of 256 shades from black to white.* Let's use the Linear transparency type; if you understand this type, all the others (Radial, Conical, and so on) will settle in your mind. By default, when you click-drag using the Linear transparency on an object, the start marker is white, indicating full opacity, and the end marker is black, indicating no opacity at all.

Here's Trick No. 1 in creating an elegant Fountain fill transparency that will be useful in your work. You can change the degree of opacity at the start and end points by using two methods and a combination of the two:

- Reposition the start and end markers. If you position the markers way outside of the object, the transition between full and no opacity will be gradual, and the outermost parts of the transparent object will be neither completely opaque nor completely transparent if you do this.

- Change the brightness; the markers can have any of 256 shades of black. Let's say you have the start and end markers exactly where you want them; you like the angle of the Fountain fill transparency. But you don't want, for example, the end (the black marker) to be 100 percent transparent. You click-drag 80 percent black from the Color Palette and then drop it onto the black end marker. The end of the transparency then becomes 80 percent transparent, not 100 percent.

Trick No. 2 when you want to create professional shading in a CorelDRAW composition is to choose the transparency object's color to influence (usually to tint) the objects below the transparency object. Here's a visual example in Figure 22-14: some black Paragraph Text is on the bottom of the drawing page. On top of it is a rectangle. At left, the rectangle is filled with white, and a Linear Fountain fill transparency is click-dragged from top to bottom. The text appears to be coming out of a fog. In the center, a 50 percent black fill is then applied to the rectangle and a different visual effect is achieved—the Paragraph Text still looks like it's in a haze, but more of it is legible toward the top. At right, black is the fill for the rectangle, and now the top of the text is as illegible as the white rectangle example, but a different artistic sense of drama has been achieved. Therefore, you now know two different methods for shading with transparency fills of the Fountain type: change the control markers and change the color of the transparency object.

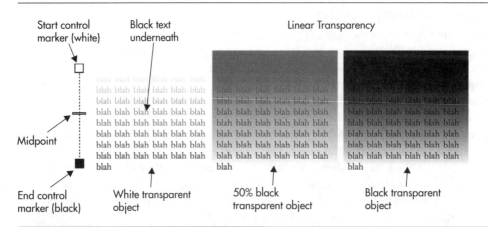

Start control marker (white)

Black text underneath

Linear Transparency

Midpoint

End control marker (black)

White transparent object

50% black transparent object

Black transparent object

FIGURE 22-14 Use the marker positions, the marker brightness values, and the color of a transparency object to create interesting effects.

Property Bar Options for Transparency Effects

Some CorelDRAW users prefer the hand-on controls of interactive markers, while others choose the precision offered by the Property Bar's numeric entry fields and sliders. Let's look at what is available on the Property Bar when the Interactive Transparency Tool is chosen and a target object is selected.

If no object is selected and you want to make any object partially transparent, the Interactive Transparency Tool is a selection tool in addition to controlling the interactive markers. With the tool selected, click once to select the object to which you want to apply transparency, and then click-drag to add and set the control markers.

Again, the controls for Transparency effects are almost identical to object fills. Here you can see the options available when the Linear transparency type is chosen.

Linear transparency selected

Angle

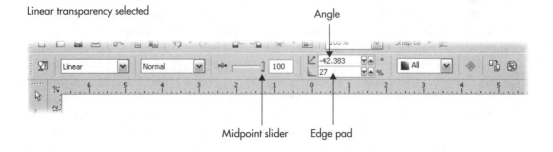

Midpoint slider   Edge pad

- **Midpoint slider**   This slider controls where the 50 percent point in a transparency is located. It does not indicate where an object is 50 percent transparency, but instead sets a relative 50 percent break point, because as mentioned earlier, you can set the start and end markers to any brightness value you like.

- **Angle**   When you click-drag, for example, a Linear transparency, you might not get the angle exactly the way you'd like it. Use this box to set an exact angle for the transition. A 90° setting runs a Linear fountain fill from transparent at bottom to opaque at top, and the angle measurement decreases as you travel clockwise.

- **Edge pad**   This increases or decreases the "speed," the contrast of the Fountain transparency. The highest value is 49, at which the transition is so abrupt you could shave yourself with the edge between the start and end opacity amounts.

TIP *By default, when you hold CTRL and drag a control marker for a Fountain type transparency, you constrain the angle you're setting in 15° increments. You can also straighten a crooked Fountain transparency you've manually defined by CTRL+click-dragging.*

Here is a practical example of a Linear transparency used in an illustration to imitate the Vista "glass icon" reflective look. In this illustration, the folder design has been copied and then mirrored horizontally. Then the Linear transparency is applied to the duplicate group of objects, from almost 100 percent opaque where it meets the original, to 100 percent transparent at the bottom. You can see that transparency is not only good for simulating glass but also for reflective objects.

Additional Fountain Transparency Types

You also have Radial, Conical, and Square Fountain transparency types at hand when you design something you need to look photorealistic. As shown in a previous tutorial, the Radial type Transparency effect is fantastic for making spectacular highlights—for example, brilliant but soft-edged highlights you commonly see when sunlight hits a highly polished metal or smooth plastic object. A Conical transparency is good to use when you need a pie-wedge-shaped area, and this, too, is good for simulating highlights and reflections. The Square transparency type might not prove to be useful on a day-to-day basis, but it's very easy to create soft-edged highlights to use as window panes and other right-angle geometric areas you want to visually emphasize.

In the illustration here, you can see a wireframe view of an illustration of a wrench. A custom-made Conical transparency was applied to the handle (explained shortly) to give it the effect of having been machine polished with a radial steel brush, a common and popular high-tech look. Several Radial transparency ellipses also give highlights to other areas, and the overall effect is that the wrench is brand new.

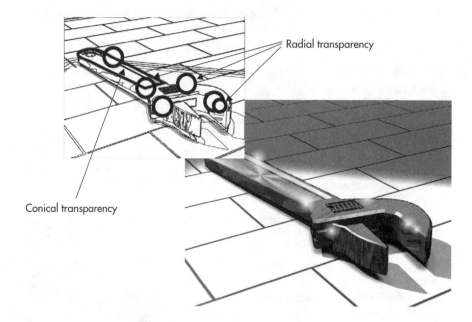

Radial transparency

Conical transparency

Before covering the bitmap type fills, which are listed below the Fountain transparency types on the Property Bar drop-down list, it's a good idea to take a side-step in this documentation to explain transparency operations. Also called merge modes and blend modes, *operations* have an additional effect on all objects that have a Transparency effect. Operations can get you out of a design predicament when a transparent object doesn't seamlessly blend with objects below it, and this quite advanced capability should be yours to tap into before getting any deeper into transparency types.

Using Transparency Operations (Merge Modes)

The Property Bar has a list of *modes* for you to set how your transparency colors interact with the colors of underlying objects. These options further the visual complexity of semitransparent objects, and their use is for professional-level illustration work; the more visually complex an illustration is, the better it mimics the visual complexity of the real world around us. For example, a red plastic drinking glass on a yellow tablecloth will show some orange through it due to the nature of colors that mix as light passes through the glass. However, the shadow cast by the nontransparent areas of the glass will not be the same shade of orange as the light we see through the glass, because light in the real world is subtractive, and the shadow in such a scene would be a deep, muddy orange, almost brown. The good news is that you don't have to calculate light properties or material properties when you illustrate to come up with something photorealistic—you first understand what the transparency operations do, and then you choose the one appropriate for your illustration!

Back to Boolean Math

The transparency operations are math-based, specifically Boolean math; the operations you use with the Shaping docker are Boolean math expressed geometrically—the Boolean operation with transparency is applied to color values instead of geometry.

To refresh a moment from Chapter 11, a Boolean operation is a set of rules that extends math beyond addition and subtraction; it's human language–based in its structure. For example, "Give me all those apples and all the peaches, but not the peaches that are smaller than my fist" is a reasonable request that unfortunately can't be expressed with the +, –, /, and * math operators alone. The apples and peaches command could, however, be expressed using Boolean operators; let X be apples, Y be all peaches, and let's call peaches smaller than your fist Y^1, a subset of all available peaches. The command would then be expressed as, "X and Y, but not Y^1."

This is valid math and this is what CorelDRAW's merge modes are doing when evaluating color combined with transparency. In the following section, for example, you'll hit the fairly mind-numbing option "XOR" as a merge mode. It's a Boolean operation and the title is meant for programmers. This is called an *exclusive OR function* in math (it excludes stuff), and it sets a condition with a CorelDRAW transparency that a result color is only seen if one of the two objects—the bottom object or the transparency object on top, but *not both* and *not neither* (it's clumsy English, but it's math-based English) has a unique color. For example, create a red ellipse and then put another red ellipse on top of it so it slightly overlaps. If the top transparency object has the XOR merge mode, the result you see in the overlapping areas is black, no result, because the operators in the math statement (the two ellipses) are identical. Change one of the other ellipse colors, and you'll see a new color in the areas where they overlap.

Whew! Got that? Admittedly, when you want advanced drawing features, you need to bite the bullet and understand why certain things work, but fortunately, you can always perform the "acid test." Choosing a merge mode based on, "This mode doesn't do anything for me; I'll try a different one" is a valid approach, but you'll learn more quickly and make fewer errors if you just understand that transparency modes are based on inclusive and exclusive statements, most of the time being no more complex than "Add this color to the color beneath except in areas where the brightness of the color underneath is greater than 50 percent."

The following definitions of merge modes describe the effect you can expect; let's use "source" as the top object that takes the Transparency effect; the "target" is one or more objects below the transparency object that are overlapped by the transparency object, and the "result" is the color you see in your drawing in the overlapping areas:

- **Normal** Normal merge mode is the default whenever a new Transparency effect is applied to an object. Choosing Normal at 50 percent opacity usually produces predictable color blends between the source and target objects; for example, a pure yellow object at 50 percent Normal opacity over a pure red object yields orange as a result in overlapping areas. Similarly and in traditional physical painting, a white source object produces a *tint* result over a pure color object (a pastel color), while a black source object produces a *shade* of the target object's color (if you're shopping for house paints, the salesperson will love this jargon). Normal merge mode does not produce particularly intense result colors—if you want to stain an object or create shadows, or bleach objects to produce highlights, move down this list—CorelDRAW has these modes.

- **Add** The Add(itive) mode applies transparency in a similar fashion to Normal mode, except it whitens and brightens the result—seriously! In English, there's a subtle but distinct difference between "plus" and "added to"; similarly, Additive mode moves the combined result of the target and source object colors in a positive direction in brightness value. The artistic result is good for adding subtle shading to composition areas; this is something painters through the centuries could not do without the added step of applying pure white, because inks and pigments use the real-world subtractive color model.

- **Subtract** This mode ignores the brightness value in the source object and is similar to mixing physical pigments. If you use Subtractive transparency mode on green and red objects and overlap then onto a target blue object, the result color will be black. Subtractive mode is great for creating photorealistic shadows, because in the real world, when objects are hidden by shadows, the result color is a subtractive process.

- **Difference** Remember color opposites on the color wheel? This is what Difference mode performs; it moves the result color to the difference (on the color wheel) between the source and target colors. For example, a red Difference transparency object over a yellow target object produces green areas. You'll see the Difference effect most clearly if you just put such an object over an empty area of the drawing page. A red difference object will cast cyan as the result on the page. This is a useful blending mode for creating dramatic lighting effects—for example, you can shine a Difference mode drawing of a shaft of theater spotlight on an object and get truly wonderful and bizarre lighting effects.

- **Multiply** Multiply always produces a darker result color from merging the source and target objects. Its effect is similar to using wood stain or repeatedly stroking a felt marker on paper. Several objects in Multiply mode, when overlapped, can produce black, and this is perhaps the best mode for artists to re-create real-world shadows cast on objects. If the source object's color is lighter than the target object, no change is the result.

■ **Divide**   The Divide mode produces only a lighter result color if neither the target nor source objects are black or white. Use this mode to bleach and produce highlights in a composition by using a light color for the transparency object such as 10 percent black. Also, if the source object is darker than the target object, no color change is the result.

■ **If Lighter**   If Boolean math could be accurately transcribed to street English, this mode would read, "If the color I'm over is darker than I am, lighten the result according to how much lighter I am than the target object. And if this color's lighter, don't make any result changes." This mode is useful for shading selective areas of a composition without affecting others, without reshaping the transparency object, and without the need for PowerClips.

■ **If Darker**   Similar in effect to Multiply mode, If Darker calculates the result color based on the following: If areas in the target object are darker, a color combination is the result. If the target area's the same color or lighter, there is no result color. It's particularly interesting to view the result when an If Lighter or an If Darker object is placed above a fountain-filled target object. You will see *clipping,* a hard edge where the fountain fill reaches a specific value such that the result color doesn't qualify to display a change. Try this mode when you need tinting and an abrupt end to the tinting process as the target object or objects grow lighter than the source object.

■ **Texturize**   This mode will not produce much of a change unless you fill the source object with a bitmap or pattern fill. However, for example, if you fill the transparency object with a bitmap fill, the result is a shaded and patterned area. This mode removes the hue and saturation from the bitmap fill, leaving only brightness values, in effect, making your target object a shaded version of the original, sort of like merging a grayscale photograph over an object. This is a useful mode when you do not want the target object to influence the result colors with any distinct hues, and you can use this mode to quickly build up texture and simulate real-world complexity in your composition.

■ **Hue**   The Hue merge mode changes the result color to the hue of the target color, without affecting saturation or brightness in the result. This mode is useful for tinting compositions, and the target object colors are ignored in the result.

■ **Saturation**   The Saturation merge mode can be used to remove color from the result; it's quite nice at making black-and-white photographs from color images. This mode ignores hue and brightness components in the result. Try using shades of black as the transparency object's fill. Highlight-saturated target and source objects will produce no change in the result.

■ **Lightness** The target object's lightness values are calculated ignoring hue and saturation. This is a great mode for brightening the result colors because the target object's colors are never changed, just the *lightness* (also called *value* and *brightness*).

■ **Invert** This creates a result color that is the chromatic inverse of the target color. You can occasionally reproduce the look of a color negative using this mode—it moves the result color to 180°, the opposite on the color wheel. Using Invert mode on the same colored target and source objects produces gray.

■ **AND, OR, and XOR** These are the operators discussed earlier in this section. The AND function includes similarity between the source and target objects; for example, two red ellipses that overlap and that both have the AND transparency merge mode appear not to be transparent at all, but instead display 100 percent red where they overlap. This is a useful mode when you want only a color result in overlapping areas, because AND creates no change outside of the overlapping result area. The OR operator is an exclusive operator; it excludes stuff. This is a good mode for clipping a color change, thus limiting it to only areas where the target and source objects overlap. You'll see nothing outside the overlapping areas when the target object has the OR operator. XOR is a fascinating math statement, based on something called a *truth table,* where certain conditions must be met to produce a result. However, you might not find use for this transparency mode unless you use more than two objects in a design area; if either or neither of the objects in an XOR operation are similar, you'll get no result color. This operation only works if there is one differently colored object in the color calculation operation.

■ **Red, Green, and Blue** Each of these merge modes filters out a respective (RGB) channel, and the native color of the source object is ignored. This is a useful transparency mode for color correcting photographs you import to CorelDRAW; for example, if you put a Green transparency mode object over a portrait, and then play with the amount of transparency on the Property Bar, you can sometimes correct for harsh indoor (particularly cheap fluorescent) lighting.

> **TIP** *CorelDRAW uses a Hue, Saturation, Brightness (HSB) color model for many of the merge mode operations to keep brightness a separate component for the resulting Transparency effect. In 24-bit imaging this means that there are 256 possible values for brightness, and as a consequence, occasionally you might see a harsh break point in a fountain-filled object beneath a transparency object in certain merge modes such as If Lighter and If Darker. This is because the math operation says, "Anything above or below 128 on the Brightness scale gets this effect." To avoid a clipped look when you work with transparency in different merge modes, try using a Fountain mode instead of Uniform, and try different start and end colors, ones other than pure white and black. Doing this forces the Boolean calculations to remap a Transparency effect, and the clipping, the break point in the resulting transparency design, might just disappear.*

Creating Multi-Stage Transparencies

You might find you need a transparency object that's more complex than the Fountain types offered on the Property Bar; for example, a lens flare can add a lot of photorealism to an illustration, and there doesn't appear to be this type on the Property Bar! CorelDRAW's Interactive Transparency Tool is extensible; you can engineer several transparency nodes on any of the "base" Fountain types. To create a multi-marker transparency, first apply a transparency to an object—use the Radial type to better follow this example of creating a lens flare.

Next, you drag shades of black alternating with white from the Color Palette and drop them onto the marker connector, as shown here. Remember, darker shades represent transparency, and lighter shades stand for opacity. You might want to reposition the new markers once you've added them; this is done by click-dragging with the Interactive Transparency Tool. If your drop point for a new marker isn't exactly over the marker connector (the blue dashed line), your cursor will turn into an international "no can do" symbol.

Radial transparency

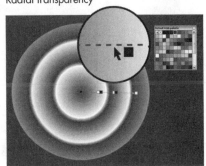

Drag color well shades onto marker connector

To complete the lens flare effect, you find a drawing or photograph that needs a lens flare, and then position several duplicates of the lens object shown in the previous illustration in a straight line—this is the way a photographic lens flare behaves. In this illustration, you can see that several lens flare objects are lined up; they overlap randomly and a Polygon shape has been added for some sparkle. The Polygon has a simple, two-node Radial transparency applied.

Pattern and Texture Transparencies

Pattern and Texture transparencies can add texture to object fill areas below the object, creating intricate detail, thus lending scene complexity that would take a great deal of time manually. The Transparency Type drop-down menu includes Two-Color Pattern, Full-Color Pattern, and Bitmap Pattern transparency types. With any of these selected for the transparency type, the Start transparency slider controls the percentage of transparency applied to brightness values in the chosen bitmap that lie above 126 on a brightness scale of 0–255 (256 shades); the End transparency slider controls the percentage of transparency applied to brightness values in the chosen bitmap that fall below 128.

Here you can see the options on the Property Bar when the Interactive Transparency Tool is chosen:

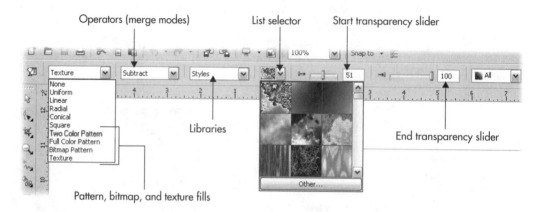

Operators (merge modes)   List selector   Start transparency slider

Libraries

Pattern, bitmap, and texture fills

End transparency slider

Figure 22-15 shows some variations on a theme; one drawing of a shirt yields a somewhat bizarre designer collection by changing the transparency types from two-color, to full-color, to two overlaid texture objects. This was done by first drawing the shirt and then creating an object that describes the outline of the shirt: one object, no shading. Notice how the shading on the shirt is evident when the bitmap fills are applied to the top object. The

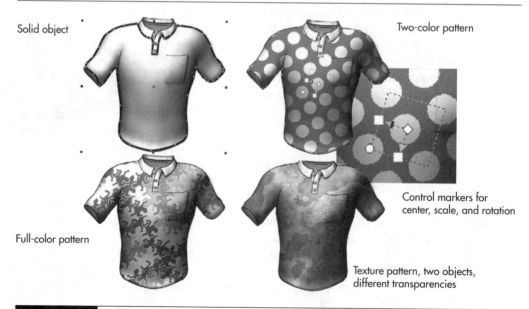

Solid object

Two-color pattern

Control markers for center, scale, and rotation

Full-color pattern

Texture pattern, two objects, different transparencies

FIGURE 22-15   Different patterns and textures are used for transparency, in different merge modes.

bottom-right tie-dyed shirt was created by duplicating the top object and then using two different texture fills and different object colors. You can indeed "stack" objects that have transparency. The interactive pattern fill markers appear around the object to indicate the dimensions, rotation, and center orientation of the applied bitmap tile; you can change them to come up with still more results from a single investment of time drawing an object.

 To edit the specific fill properties of a selected Transparency effect, click the Edit Transparency button in the Property Bar while the Interactive Transparency Tool is selected. This opens the Edit Transparency dialog, which gives you the opportunity to edit the current properties based on the corresponding fill type.

Applying Transparency to Fills and Outlines

You can apply transparency to the Fill, Outline, or All (both) properties of the object by using the drop-down selector in the Property Bar, shown here:

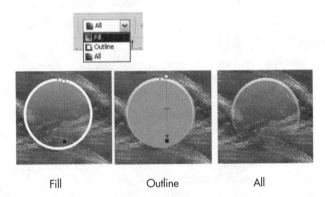

Fill   Outline   All

Using this option, you can control whether either or both object properties participate in the Transparency effect. This comes in very handy, for example, if you only want an object outline to be partially transparent to create a halo or other special effect in a composition. By setting an object to no fill, a wide outline, and then using a transparency type, you can hide parts of the outline without resorting to a destructive editing technique such as converting the outline to an object.

Using Transparency Freeze

Freezing a transparency object captures the composite of the object's properties combined with whatever was beneath the object before using the Freeze button on the Property Bar. This is a similar option to freezing a Lens effect and is useful for calling out an effect from an illustration: you can move a transparency object after freezing it (you might want to wear some insulated gloves) and present your audience with the effect in the frozen object plus an uncluttered view of the objects that were beneath it, shown next.

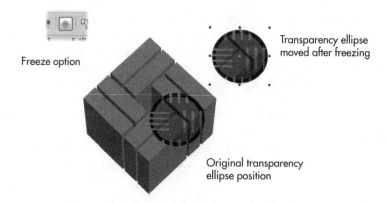

Freeze option

Transparency ellipse
moved after freezing

Original transparency
ellipse position

 TIP *Deactivating the Freeze option (without ungrouping it) returns a transparent object to its current and active state. This means if you freeze the object, move it, and then unfreeze it (thaw it?), its interior will display whatever is* currently *under it.*

Copying Transparency Effects

You can copy transparency properties to newly selected shapes by using the Copy Transparency Properties button in the Property Bar (shown next). This command is also accessible through use of command menus by choosing Effects | Copy Effect | Lens From and using the targeting cursor to click any transparent object. Here you can see the two-step procedure: a rectangle lies over the drawing and a transparency lens is targeted. By clicking the Copy Transparency button, you turn the cursor into a targeting cursor; then you click over the object that has transparency, and the selected object takes the transparency settings, including merge mode and any transparency pattern you might have applied.

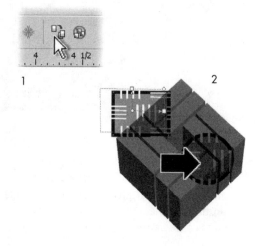

Hopefully you've seen through the figures in this chapter the ease and power of transparency objects and Lens effects. Together they represent the "bitmap side" of vector illustration work in CorelDRAW; you can shade drawing areas to faithfully represent glass, metal, reflections, highlights, and even a few things that don't exist in the real world.

To add to your repertoire of photorealistic effects, all you have to do is turn this page; Bevels, PowerClips, and shadow-making is next—CorelDRAW features that help you create drop shadows, cast shadows, soft-edged shadows, in essence, all the stuff that anchors a photorealistic object to its setting. We might even get into hand shadows: this is a bunny, here's an elephant, here's a gesture that baseball players make at the umpire…

CHAPTER 23

Embellishments: Bevels, PowerClips, and Shadows

When you need something more than distortions, blends, and contours, but your design doesn't require a full-blown 3D extrude look, elements of photorealism can push a design in your intended direction. This chapter takes a look at automated—and a few manual—techniques you can use to add shadows, an engraved look, and reflections and highlights to a composition.

Professional designers and illustrators often look for speedy ways to create a sense of depth in their layouts and drawings. For design and graphics, adding a sense of depth using drop shadows is one of the easiest ways to do this. CorelDRAW's drop shadows have become a favorite because they're so fast to create and easy to work with. You can create soft, transparent shadows in seconds and edit them to perfection with just a few quick clicks.

Using the Bevel Effect

If you've tried the Extrude effect on text to give a headline more punch and the result was stunning but illegible, you can still achieve a sort of 3D effect and retain the distinctness of an object via the Effects | Bevel docker. The Bevel docker offers two different types of engraving effect: Emboss and Bevel. The Emboss effect is an automated routine that creates duplicates of an object, offsets them, and gives them different colors to create the effect of, for example, a seal crimped onto a piece of paper like notary publics used to do. Although you can manually create this Emboss effect, the Bevel docker creates a dynamic, linked group whose color and position can change when you define different light intensities and light angles.

Figure 23-1 shows an example of a "before and after" using the Emboss effect. If you choose to use Emboss, it's a good idea to create a background for the object (because either the highlight or the shadow object might not be visible against the page background), and usually a color similar to the background will serve you well for the object color. You can

Original   Two offset duplicates
create the effect

FIGURE 23-1   The Emboss Bevel effect is performed by generating two duplicates of the object and offsetting them.

use any fill, including bitmaps and Fountain fills, for the object you want to emboss, but the resulting emboss objects will not feature the fill, but only solid (uniform) colors.

Here you can see the Bevel docker and the options you have while applying the Emboss effect.

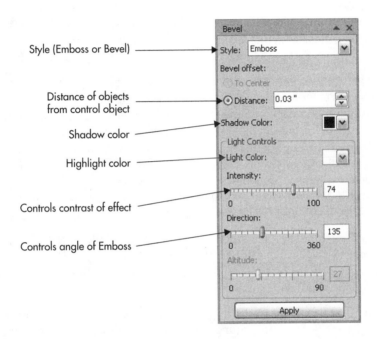

Emboss might not be the most sophisticated of all filters and effects, but it is effective, prints well, and the creation of an Emboss effect is fairly intuitive. Here's a rundown of what the options do on the Bevel docker in Emboss mode:

- **Bevel Offset-Distance**   (The To Center option is only available in Bevel mode.) This combination num box and spin box is used to set the distance of the duplicate objects from the original. You don't gain anything visually by setting a high value for an object; rather, this box is used to set a relational distance, depending on the size of the object to which you apply the Emboss effect. For example, a 4" object will look nice and embossed if you use a 0.09" Distance, but the effect looks a little phony at greater distances. On the other hand, an 8" object will probably not look embossed with a 0.09" Distance setting—0.16", however, scales the effect proportionately to the object and the emboss looks good. Use distance as a scaling factor. Also, distance does not auto-scale when you scale the control (parent) object. Therefore, if you need to resize an object, plan to redefine the Distance for the Emboss effect after you scale the parent object.

- **Shadow Color**   The color of the object has a direct influence on the color of the shadow object behind the control object. For example, if you create an Emboss effect with a blue object, the shadow object will be a dark blue, even if you set the color to black. You can neutralize the shadow color by defining the color opposite of the control object; for example, if you have a cyan circle, set the Shadow Color to red, the color complement of cyan. Regardless of what color you choose for the shadow object, the result color will always be duller than the color you define, because—well, it's a *shadow*! Shadow color is unaffected by the Intensity option.

- **Light Color**   This controls the color of the highlight object; it affects neither the control object's color, nor the color or brightness of the shadow object. Light color at full intensity displays the color you choose, and as you decrease intensity, the light color blends with the object color—light color does not depend on any object's color you might have beneath the effect. For example, if you set the control object's fill to red, the light color to yellow, and gradually decrease the light intensity, the highlight object's color will move from yellow to red. The exception to this behavior is if you use a bitmap or texture fill for the control object. As light intensity decreases, a bitmap-filled object's highlight color will move from its original color to white.

- **Intensity**   Use this slider to control the contrast of the Emboss effect. Although the shadow object's color is not affected by intensity, the highlight object's color is. High values display the highlight object's color most faithfully, while lower Intensity settings dull the highlight color and move its hue toward the control object.

- **Direction**   Use this slider to control the direction that light seems to cast on the emboss object(s). A Direction setting of 0° points the highlight at 3 o'clock, traveling counterclockwise. Therefore, if you need a highlight on an Emboss effect at 11 o'clock (a very classic lighting position), you'd set the Direction at about 160°. You can also use the number field to type in a value from 0 to 360 (both of which are the same angles) and then click Apply.

- **Altitude**   This option is reserved for the Bevel effect, covered shortly in this chapter.

Figure 23-2 shows three creative examples of using the Emboss effect; the fourth, at lower right, is an unsuccessful attempt, intended to show you the undesired result of setting the Offset value higher than is artistically correct.

Creating Soft Edge Bevel Effects

The other mode on the Bevel docker, Soft Edge, performs a lot more calculations than the Emboss effect and actually creates a bitmap image, masked by the control object, which can be dynamically adjusted. The Shadow Color, Light Intensity (and Color), and Direction options on the docker produce predictable results, much like those you get when using Emboss mode, but because the Soft Edge effect is generated to bitmap format, the results

Linear fountain fill,
135° direction,
0.03" offset

Multi-step Linear
fountain fill,
135° direction,
0.03" offset

Uniform fill,
283° direction,
0.03" offset

Uniform fill,
135° direction,
0.07" offset

FIGURE 23-2   Use different fills for the control object to create different looks in combination with the Emboss effect.

look more detailed, refined, and almost photorealistic in appearance. In addition to having an Altitude slider in this mode, you have To Center as an available option in the Bevel Offset field. Here's what it does and how To Center works.

All Soft Edge bevels are produced from the edge of a shape traveling toward its center. If, for example, you've created a circle that's 3" across and then type a Distance offset value in the num box in any amount smaller than 1.5", you'll see a dimensional, sloping bevel created inside the circle, with a flat top in the shape of the circle in its center. If, however, you type in a value greater than 1.5", the center of the object will bevel to a point, and the front face of the object is entirely lost. The reason this happens (you might or might not want this visual effect) is that the Bevel effect travels toward the interior of the shape, and half of the 3" diameter of this circle is 1.5". Just keep in mind the size of the shape to which you apply a Bevel to gain total control over the effect. If, on the other hand, you intend for the sides of the bevel to come to a point, you don't need to set values in the Distance field; you choose To Center, click Apply, and CorelDRAW creates the maximum width bevel, meeting at a point inside the shape. You can create interesting marine creatures such as a starfish by using the Polygon Tool to create the silhouette of a starfish, fill the object, and then To Center auto-creates a very lifelike composition.

TIP   *Although you can create a To Center bevel by increasing the Distance setting, it's not only much simpler to use the To Center option, but also less confusing. You can, for example, specify a 4" Distance in the Offset field to apply to a 1" object, but CorelDRAW limits the line to ½", even though you can enter such a mathematically impossible value in this field.*

Figure 23-3 shows two very different looks for the Bevel effect: at top a Distance has been set for the Offset, and at bottom To Center is chosen.

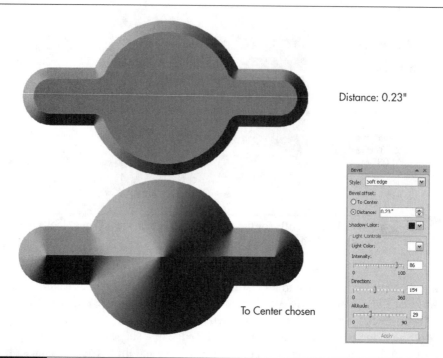

Distance: 0.23"

To Center chosen

FIGURE 23-3 Create intricate shapes that appear to have a steepled top by using the Soft Edge Bevel effect.

Shadow Color and Light Intensity

Much like the Emboss mode, the Shadow Color and Intensity in the Light Color field are great assets for shading the Bevel effect. By using similar Shadow and Light colors, you can decrease the visual contrast of the effect. For a very steep, dramatic effect, you use a very deep Shadow Color and a very light Light Color (black shadows and white lights produce the maximum, most visible effect). In this illustration at top, 60 percent black is used for the Shadow Color, and 20 percent black is used for the Light Color, to produce a very subtle yet visible Bevel effect. At bottom is the same object using the same light Direction, Altitude, and offset Distance, but black is used for the Shadow Color and white for the Light Color. You have further control over the bevel shading by setting the Light Color to white and then decreasing or increasing the Intensity by dragging the slider. In short, you have total tonal control over the bevel and can produce scores of very different looks using the same object.

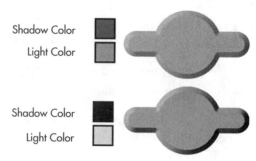

TIP *Objects with Bitmap fills will not show their fill when a Bevel effect has been applied. If you need, for example, to create a textured button with the Bevel effect, your best bet is to make a duplicate of the textured object, give the duplicate a Uniform (or Fountain) fill, apply the Bevel to the duplicate, and then with the duplicate over the textured object, use the Interactive Transparency Tool, uniform transparency. About 70 percent in Subtract mode seems to work fine in a variety of design situations.*

Altitude

Altitude determines the angle of the sun illuminating the Bevel effect…if the sun were actually *involved* in created the effect! Altitude is a simulation that does something a little different than Shadow and Light Color do to increase and decrease the contrast of the effect. At Altitude settings that approach 90°, you lessen the difference in brightness between the darkest and lightest areas in the Bevel effect. Think of a coin on the sidewalk at high noon; you can't really see the embossed president, queen, or other famous person on the coin because the bulges and recesses on the coin are fairly evenly lit. It's the same deal with the bevel Altitude setting; smaller Altitude amounts cast the hypothetical sun closer to the hypothetical horizon, and you get a lot more contrast on the bevel. The illustration here shows a 27° Altitude inclination at top and at bottom, a 73° value. Clearly, if you want the Bevel effect to produce the greatest visual impact with your work, you'll use a moderate Altitude value most of the time.

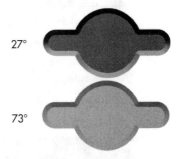

27°

73°

Because the Bevel effect has so many options, a tutorial is in order now to guide you through the steps to create a very popular commercial look, the 3D beveled logo. The fictitious steakhouse, GoodTymes, already has their logo, and although it's elegant, it's placed on a page to compete with an image of the $14.99 Thursday Special, and it doesn't separate very well against the background image in its current state.

DOWNLOAD

Download GoodTymes.cdr and open it in CorelDRAW.

Before you begin the steps, the gold lettering is in front of a deep brown shape that outlines the logo. This was done to help separate the finished beveled logo from the image on the bottom (locked) layer. The shaded areas of the finished logo will blend too easily into the image, spoiling the legibility of the logo. In your work, you can create your own separation barrier object by using the Contour Tool, set to Outside, one step, and then you need to break the contour shape apart from your logo (CTRL+K) because contour control objects are not valid for applying the Bevel effect.

Making a Fancy Beveled Logo

1. With the Pick Tool, select the gold object.

2. Choose Effects | Bevel to display the Bevel docker. Zoom into the logo to get a good look at the effect you'll apply and customize, as shown in Figure 23-4. Use your mouse's scroll wheel to zoom, and you can still have the Pick Tool selected.

3. Choose To Center as the Bevel Offset option, and then click Apply to apply the default settings to the gold logo. Although it's improved in appearance, you can do better; as shown in Figure 23-5, the direction of the lighting might be wrong—judging by the mug at right, the scene is lit from upper left. Additionally, the black Shadow Color makes the unlit areas of the Bevel effect go totally into shade, hides some of the lettering, and makes it hard to read.

4. Click the color swatch for Shadow Color; choose a warm brown to lighten up the shaded areas of the bevel.

5. Choose about 160° as the Direction. As covered in the Emboss effect section earlier, this angle puts the "lighting" for the effect at about 11 o'clock, the same as the way the image is lit in the background.

FIGURE 23-4 The logo is surrounded by an outer dark shape so the Bevel effect will look more pronounced and stand off from the background image.

FIGURE 23-5 Default setting for the Soft Edge bevel effect might not always provide you with the look you need in an assignment.

6. Increase the Altitude to about 50 percent. Doing this removes some of the contrast between the brightest and darkest areas of the effect.

7. You can click Apply now, and if you're not 100 percent pleased with the effect, try decreasing the Intensity. Less Intensity also reduces overall contrast, without changing the Direction or Altitude. See Figure 23-6.

8. Feel free to experiment with other settings! You might try using the Distance option instead of To Center. Pretend that this is your business, and you want a classy-looking logo so you can make this the ad for the *$24.99* Special!

FIGURE 23-6   Use less contrast on Bevel effects to allow the shape of the object to dominate the composition.

Here you can see one of several design possibilities for the advertisement. A catchy slogan was added below the beveled text. You might also want to add some text, and perhaps add a Bevel effect to it, for the lower-right corner of the file, where nothing really interesting is happening.

Soft Edge bevels, shadows, and everything else that looks like a bitmap-driven effect in CorelDRAW...are indeed bitmaps. Occasionally, you'll want some design flexibility and need to detach a bevel or a shadow from its control object; this is done by pressing CTRL+K...but don't do this yet. Bitmaps are created at the resolution specified in Tools | Options | Workspace | General, and the default bitmap size is intended for commercial printing: 300 pixels per inch (ppi). You might, however, want a smaller resolution, for example, for web work (72 ppi is the optimum). So the next time you want to work with a shadow or a bevel as a bitmap and not a dynamic effect, press CTRL+J, go to the General tab, set the resolution in the Rendering Resolution combo box, and then break the effect from the control object.

23

Using the Drop Shadow Effect

With the Interactive Drop Shadow Tool and the options available on the Property Bar when this is the active tool, you can create both shadows and glows, based on the shape of the target object (or group of objects). Although this section walks you through several variations, basically you have three different types of effects at hand when you use the Drop Shadow Tool, as shown in Figure 23-7.

- **Drop shadows**   This shadow type creates the impression that you're viewing an object from the front and that the object is basically lit from the front. Drop shadows are a popular effect; however, they don't always bring out depth in a composition, because the drop shadow suggests a face-front orientation of a scene—a viewpoint usually reserved for driver's license photos and wanted posters in the post office. However, drop shadows will indeed perk up a web page, because the audience expects a face-front orientation, since we all tend to face the front of our monitors.

- **Cast shadows**   This effect is sometimes called a *perspective shadow* in CorelDRAW. The effect suggests a shadow casting on the ground and diminishing in size as it travels to a scene's vanishing point. It visually suggests that the audience is looking *into* a scene from a perspective point, and is not looking *at* an object placed *on* a scene, as drop shadows tend to do.

- **Glows**   All effects created by the Interactive Drop Shadow Tool are dynamically updated bitmaps, and as such they can look soft as shadows do on overcast days; they can also be put into merge modes. Therefore, you take a blurry bitmap, put it in Multiply merge mode, and you have a re-creation of a shadow. However, if you take that same blurry bitmap, give it a light color, and then put it in Normal or Add merge mode, you have a glow effect! This is part of what CorelDRAW does when you use a Glow preset (covered later in this chapter), and you have a lot of manual control for creating a shady or glowing look that perfectly suits a piece of work.

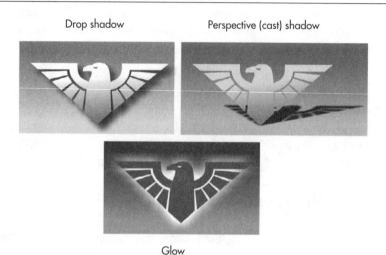

Drop shadow   Perspective (cast) shadow

Glow

FIGURE 23-7   The Drop Shadow effect can have perspective and can be used to light up a scene, not simply to make things cast shadows.

Like other effects in CorelDRAW, drop shadows maintain a dynamic link; any changes to the control object automatically update the shadow. A shadow's look—its position, color, opacity, and feathering—can be customized, plus you can manipulate the angle, stretch, and fade properties of shadows and glows.

Using the Interactive Drop Shadow Tool and Property Bar

The Interactive Drop Shadow Tool is about as hard to use as click-dragging, and after you click-drag to create a custom shadow, you'll see a series of Property Bar options. The tool is found in the Toolbox with other interactive tools.

NOTE   *A Drop Shadow effect is usually anchored to an object at a specific point. For example, after you click-drag to create a drop shadow, the shadow is apparently anchored to the object by the white marker, the beginning of the effect. It's not anchored, not if you understand that the effect has several anchor points, corresponding to nodes on the control object. If you click-drag just a little on the white marker, nothing happens, but if you click-drag toward a "snap point," a control node on the object, you'll find that you can convert a drop shadow to a cast (perspective) shadow and vice versa—the object's center is considered to be a control point as well. Shadows are anchored because you probably don't want your drop shadow to become detached from your object if you move the object. Losing your shadow is a privilege only to be enjoyed by vampires.*

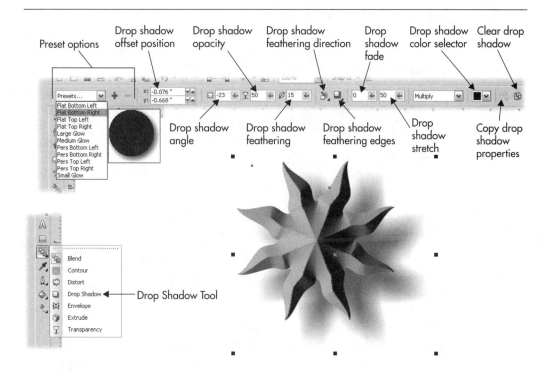

23

FIGURE 23-8   You might be a shadow of your former self after sifting through all the drop shadow options!

After an initial click-drag to add a drop shadow to an object, you'll notice the Property Bar lights up, and you now have a ton of options for refining what amounts to sort of a "default" Drop Shadow effect. Drop shadows can take one of two states: flat (drop) or perspective (cast). Depending on which state you use, the Property Bar options will change. Figure 23-8 handsomely illustrates a look at the Property Bar when applying a flat shadow.

Here's an introduction to shadow-making through a tutorial intended to familiarize you with the Property Bar options as well as with a little interactive editing. As with most of the effects in CorelDRAW, the onscreen markers for click-dragging to customize a shadow are very much like the markers for the Extrude fountain fill and other tool control handles.

Working the Property Bar and Shadow-Making Interactive Markers

1. Create an interesting object to which you want to apply a shadow, and finish applying its fill and outline properties. If you deselect it, this is okay—a click on the object with the Interactive Drop Shadow Tool selects it.

2. Choose the Interactive Drop Shadow Tool, and notice that your cursor changes to resemble the Pick Tool with a tiny Drop Shadow icon in its corner. If you don't do anything with the tool, the only option on the Property Bar is the Presets drop-down selector at the moment.

3. Click-drag from roughly the center of the selected object; continue holding down the mouse button so you can see some of the mechanics of this effect. Notice that a preview outline appears that matches your object. This indicates the position of the new shadow once you release the mouse button. Notice also that a white marker has appeared in the center of the object, and that another marker has appeared under the cursor as you drag it. A slider control has also appeared at the midpoint of a dotted guideline joining the two markers.

4. Release the mouse button and boing!, a drop shadow appears. This is a default shadow, colored black, and it has default properties.

5. Drag the slider control on the guideline between the two square-shaped markers toward the center of your original object. This reduces the shadow's opacity, making it appear lighter and allowing the page background color—and any underlying objects—to become more visible.

6. To change the shadow color, click the color selector on the Property Bar and then select a color. Notice that the color is applied; you can do some wild stage-lighting stuff by choosing a bright color for the shadow, but the opacity of the shadow remains the same.

7. Drag the white marker to the edge of one side of the original object. Notice the shadow changes shape, and the marker snaps to the edge. This action changes a drop shadow to a perspective shadow.

8. Using Property Bar options, change the default Feathering value to 4, and then press ENTER. The shadow edges are now more defined. Increase this value to a setting of 35, and notice that the shadow edges become blurry; you've gone from a sunny day shadow to an overcast day shadow.

9. Click the Fade slider control and increase it to 80. Notice that the shadow now features a graduated color effect, with the darkest point closest to the original object becoming a lighter color as the effect progresses further away from your object. This is not only a photorealistic touch, but it also helps visually integrate a shadow into a scene containing several objects.

10. Click the Drop Shadow Stretch slider and increase it to 80. The shadow stretches further in the direction of the interactive marker, and you've gone from high noon to almost dusk in only one step.

11. Click a blank space on the page to deselect the effect, or choose the Pick Tool, and you're done. Take a break and hang out in the shade for a while.

To launch quickly into the editing state of an existing Drop Shadow effect while using the Pick Tool, click the shadow once to display Property Bar options, or double-click the shadow to make the Interactive Drop Shadow Tool the current tool.

Manually Adjusting a Drop Shadow Effect

After the Drop Shadow effect is applied, you'll notice the interactive markers that appear around your shape. You'll see a combination offset position and color marker joined by a dotted line featuring an Opacity slider. If you're new to interactive controls, this illustration identifies these markers and indicates their functions.

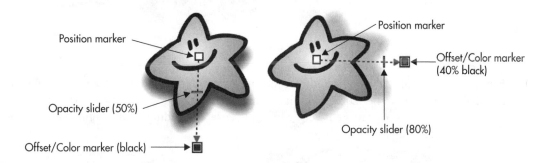

 To change a selected drop shadow's color, click-drag any color well from the onscreen Color Palette onto the shadow's Color marker.

Using Flat Drop Shadow Options

Flat shadows also feature opacity and feathering options, both of which dramatically affect the appearance of the shadow. Opacity can be set interactively using the slider control, while either option may be set by using the slider controls available in the Property Bar while the shadow is selected, as shown to the right.

The following definitions explain the use of these controls:

- **Controlling Shadow Opacity**   The Opacity slider controls shadow transparency; the bitmap that represents a shadow can be set to a uniform opacity value between 0 (transparent) and 100 (opaque) percent.

- **Adjusting Shadow Feathering**   *Feathering* is the falloff at the edges of the bitmap shadow. New shadow effects are applied with a feathering value of 15 percent. The feathering value may be set between 0 and 100 percent. Increasing the feathering value extends the edge of the shadow outward, creating a larger bitmap. Feathering can be adjusted only by using the Property Bar Feathering slider.

Here you can see a shape applied with different feathering values, but with identical offset and opacity values.

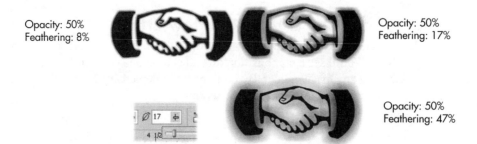

Opacity: 50%
Feathering: 8%

Opacity: 50%
Feathering: 17%

Opacity: 50%
Feathering: 47%

Feathering Direction

Feathering direction can be adjusted by choosing Average (the default), Outside, Middle, or Inside from the Feathering Direction selector on the Property Bar, as shown next. You can thin out a drop shadow or make it very wide and dense, depending on the option you choose.

Feathering
Direction button

Copying and Cloning Drop Shadow Effects

You can copy or clone from existing shadows quickly when the need arises. At least one Drop Shadow effect must be in view, and one object must be selected. To copy a drop shadow to a selected object, choose Effects | Copy Effect | Drop Shadow From, and then use the targeting cursor to specify the shadow. Alternatively, you can use the Interactive Drop Shadow Tool to select an object, and then click the Copy Drop Shadow Properties button on the Property Bar. Yet another way to duplicate a shadow effect is to sample the shadow with the Eyedropper Tool. You choose this tool, and then choose Drop Shadow from the Effects drop-down on the Property Bar. You click a shadow, then hold SHIFT to toggle to the Paintbucket Tool, and then click over the object that you feel needs a drop shadow.

Cloning a Drop Shadow effect is accomplished slightly differently. When an effect is applied through cloning, the master clone effect object controls the new effect. Property changes made to the master effect will immediately be applied to the clone. To clone a Drop Shadow effect, choose Effects | Clone Effect | Drop Shadow From. Again, use the targeting cursor that appears to target the existing Drop Shadow effect you want to clone by clicking directly on the drop shadow portion of the effect.

Feathering direction sets the feathering in relation to the edges of the shadow. The shape of feathering edges corresponds to the control object's shape. The following descriptions explain the purpose of each of these options:

- **Average**   By default, Average is used whenever a new drop shadow is created. Average has the effect of feathering the shadow to an even shape, centered over the corresponding outline shape of your original object.

- **Inside, Outside**   These two options have the opposite effect of each other. Each one limits the feathering effect applied to a shadow to the inner or outer edges as those edges correspond to the shape of your original object. If the Inside option is applied to a shadow layered directly behind your original (there is no offset value), however, the shadow is then completely hidden from view. The previous illustration was only possible by manually offsetting the Inside Feathering direction by using the shadows control markers.

- **Middle**   Choosing the Middle option has the effect of applying the feathering equally to both sides of the control object's shape.

Choosing Inside, Outside, or Middle feathering offers a slight, but visible, additional level of control over a shadow's appearance.

Feathering Edges

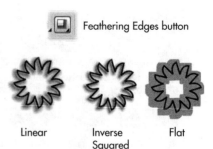

Feathering Edges button

When Inside, Middle, or Outside feathering options are selected, you can control the appearance of the edges of the feathering by using the Feathering Edges button shown next. By default, when a new shadow is applied, the feathering is set to Average. Feathering is created concentrically by spreading pixels beyond the outline of an object.

Linear   Inverse   Flat
              Squared

With different feathering edge options, you can choose a style that is slightly different from normal concentric—linear—pixel spreading. These additional options include Squared, Inverse Squared, and Flat edge feathering and are defined here:

- **Linear**   This setting (the default) creates an even-edge effect for the feathering style applied.

- **Squared, Inverse Squared**   When using either of these options, the most noticeable difference appears when using Outside as the feathering direction and when viewing convex shapes. Squared feathering edges spread pixels perpendicular to and away from the original object path shape, while Inverse Squared has the opposite effect. Usually, the visual result is a feathered shadow that looks sharper than when you use Linear.

- **Flat**   Flat edges aren't feathered at all but instead appear as uniform flat color, much the same as using a uniform fill color or using the Contour effect.

Using Drop Shadow Presets

Drop shadow presets follow the same options as other effects and can be saved and reapplied and deleted from the list on the Property Bar. Use these following steps if you're not familiar with CorelDRAW presets:

1. Start by selecting an object using the Pick Tool. Then choose the Interactive Drop Shadow Tool.

2. Choose a saved Drop Shadow effect from the Preset List. The properties of the shadow are immediately applied, and its current effect properties are displayed on the Property Bar.

3. To save an existing shadow as a Preset, click to select the shadow portion of an applied shadow effect and click the Add Preset (+) button. The Save As dialog opens. Enter a new name for your new shadow Preset in the File Name box and click Save. Your drop shadow preset is added to the Preset List.

4. To delete a saved drop shadow preset, select it from the Preset List selector and click the Delete Preset button (–) in the Property Bar. The saved preset is immediately deleted.

Shadows as Glow Effects

CorelDRAW X4's Drop Shadow effect is not limited to making shadows; if you think about it, a blurry bitmap can also represent a glow effect by using a different merge mode and color.

By default, whenever a new shadow is created, black is automatically the applied color. You can reverse this effect by applying light-colored shadows to dark-colored objects arranged on a dark page background or in front of a darker-colored object. Here you can see a black compound path (the cartoon light bulb) on top of a Radial fountain filled rectangle (black is the end color and 30 percent black is the start color at center) with a light-colored shadow effect applied. The result is a credible glow effect; there are also Glow Presets on the Property Bar when you use the Interactive Drop Shadow Tool to give you a jump-start on creating glows.

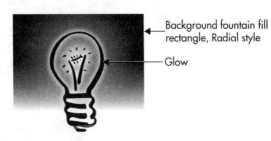

Background fountain fill rectangle, Radial style

Glow

The following section uses the Drop Shadow effect in a novel way: control objects do not have to be visible while a drop shadow is visible. Therefore, you can float a drop shadow, or a glow, in your design and treat it like a dynamically adjustable bitmap in a composition. For example, to create a soft area glow, create the control shape, apply a glow, and then choose the Interactive Transparency Tool from the Toolbox. Select the control object, choose Uniform transparency mode on the Property Bar, and then set the object opacity to 0 percent.

PowerClipping Your Way to Advanced Design Work

Using CorelDRAW's PowerClip (on the Effects menu) is a terrific and indispensable alternative to performing permanent (destructive) edits to an object, part of which you want to hide. Unlike the Shaping operations, a PowerClip consists of a container object and the object you want to put into the container. Areas of the contained object that fall outside of the container object are not visible; you can place objects behind the container, edit the position of the contained object—you have a wealth of design options after you learn this feature.

Mastering DRAW's PowerClip Feature

Here is a practical example of CorelDRAW's PowerClip effect; this illustration has an extruded heart shape (see Chapter 25 on the Extrude effect) and *two* arrow shapes. At top in this illustration, you can see two PowerClip container objects because they have a dashed outline. The top arrow is a complete arrow, as is the arrow on the bottom, but because the arrows are clipped to the boundary of these container objects, you can see neither the right side of the top arrow, nor the left side of the bottom arrow. Visually, it looks as though one single arrow is piercing the heart (an odd sign of love, but it's traditional). At bottom in this illustration, the dashed outlines have been removed from the container objects and the illusion is complete. The arrow objects are not edited in any way and can be changed and repositioned in the container objects (and removed from the containers) at any time.

You can download "Heart and arrow.cdr"—a practice file—and "Heart and Arrow finished.cdr" to get a better idea of how a PowerClip effect is created.

You can create as many levels of clipping as you need. PowerClip containers can be nested—one filled container is placed into another container, and so on—making successive levels of clipping as you need. Each container can have its own contents, creating a hierarchy.

One of the most powerful uses of PowerClips is clipping a photo or other bitmap image to a container object, as the following tutorial leads you through. It's often difficult or completely impractical to manually trim a photograph, and the Trim and other Shaping operations are permanent; they delete portions of an imported bitmap. However, with PowerClips, you can put an image inside a container and achieve the same "peekaboo" effect.

A PowerClip Composition

Let's suppose you have a need for a fancy, glossy chrome button for a web page. Artists frequently illustrate chrome looks, but this requires a lot of skill and is largely unnecessary if you understand PowerClips and have a photo of a slightly distorted horizon.

Download Environments.zip and then extract the zip file's contents to a location on your hard drive that'll be easy to locate later. In addition to a file you'll use in the following tutorial, this zip archive also contains three other environment images for you to use in your own PowerClip adventures. The finished tutorial composition also can be found in this archive.

NOTE *The environment bitmap images were created from renders performed in Carrera and Vue, modeling applications. The rendered images were then distorted to a fish-eye perspective using the Pinch/Punch bitmap filter, available within both CorelDRAW and PHOTO-PAINT. You can create environment images of your own for PowerClips using an ordinary digital camera, a good scene with a visible horizon, and this 3D filter.*

Here are the steps to creating a PowerClip illusion and in the process building a fairly photorealistic metal reflecting button. Be sure to read the previous sections if you haven't already, because this button will need a glow effect to complete its look.

 ## Creating a Photorealistic Button with PowerClips

1. Create a new document with landscape orientation, and then click the Import button of the Property Bar.

2. Choose Environment04.jpg in the Import dialog, click Import, and then just click on the page to place it at its original size.

3. Choose the Rectangle Tool from the Toolbox. Because this environment image is much wider than it is tall, the button you'll create will be a lozenge shape.

4. Click-drag a rectangle inside the environment image and then fill it with blue. Right-click the *X* color well on the Color Palette to give the rectangle no outline width.

5. With the Shape Tool, click-drag the upper-right control node downward until you've made the corners of the rectangle so rounded that the shape is now a lozenge.

6. Duplicate the lozenge shape; you'll need a spare copy to complete the look of the metal button.

7. With the Pick Tool, select the image underneath the blue lozenge, and then choose Effects | PowerClip | Place Inside Container, as shown in Figure 23-9. Your cursor turns into a targeting cursor, and you now click the blue lozenge shape: the environment image is now contained within the blue lozenge shape. Contained objects are usually auto-centered within the container shape; this is good in this example—repositioning contained objects is covered later in this chapter.

8. Put the duplicate shape over the PowerClip container. Choose the Interactive Transparency Tool, choose Uniform as the transparency style from the Property Bar, about 50% Opacity, and then choose Multiply as the merge mode. As you can see in Figure 23-10, the effect looks terrific, but needs just a little shading now.

9. With the Rectangle Tool, create a smaller rectangle to serve as a highlight for the button design. Fill it with white, remove the outline (width), and make a lozenge shape using the Shape Tool exactly as you did in step 5. Put this object, centered, toward the top of the blue lozenge.

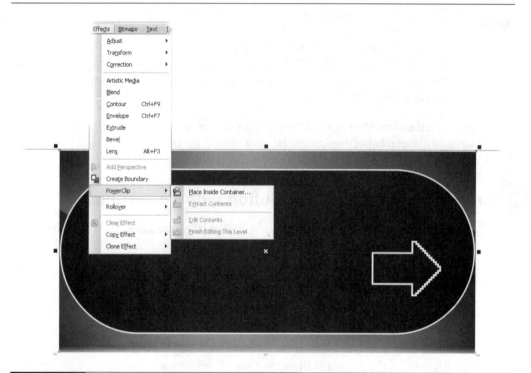

FIGURE 23-9 The cursor is a targeting device to choose the container for the object to be clipped.

10. With the Interactive Transparency Tool, click-drag, beginning at about 11 o'clock on the white lozenge, to just below the shape, releasing the mouse button at about 4 o'clock. As you can see in Figure 23-11, you've created a simple highlight that looks far from simple!

FIGURE 23-10 Tint the button by adding a shape on top in Multiply Transparency merge mode.

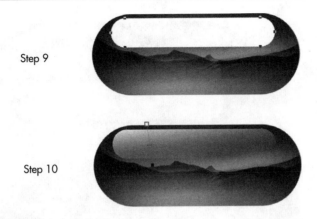

Step 9

Step 10

FIGURE 23-11   Add some gloss to the button by creating a semitransparent shape on top.

11. Create another lozenge shape, and then choose the Interactive Drop Shadow Tool. Choose Large Glow from the Presets list on the Property Bar, and then choose a medium blue from the drop-down color picker on the Property Bar.

12. Choose the lozenge and not its glow, choose the Transparency Tool, choose Uniform as the style on the Property Bar, and then give the object 0 percent opacity. Add some text to the button, and you now have something like the button in Figure 23-12.

Interactive Clipping and Positioning

You don't have to go the menu route to clip an object to a container if you have a little skill with a mouse or any input device that has a right-click feature. Creating PowerClips interactively involves a *right* mouse button click-drag, and the following tutorial walks you through the steps. Additionally, the next steps show you how to adjust the position of a contained object relative to its container, so you have exactly the areas you want peeking through.

DOWNLOAD

Download Postcard.zip and then extract the contents to a place on hard disk that's easy to locate. The zip archive contains all the elements you'll need to work through the creation of a vintage postcard.

The following set of steps is an excursion into Pop Art; one of the more popular visual effects seen on postcards from the 1950s was the "peekaboo" scenery poking through bold text naming the state or city. This was an expensive process to create, which required patience and talent, neither of which is necessary once you're comfortable working with PowerClips! By default, contained objects are centered in the PowerClip container, and this

Step 11

Step 12

FIGURE 23-12 Bitmap images within a PowerClip container can provide a sumptuous background for your foreground vector drawings.

tutorial (and probably your own work) doesn't call for this auto-positioning, so the first thing to do is press CTRL+J to display the Options dialog. Click Workspace and then Edit. Uncheck Auto-Center New PowerClip Contents, as shown here:

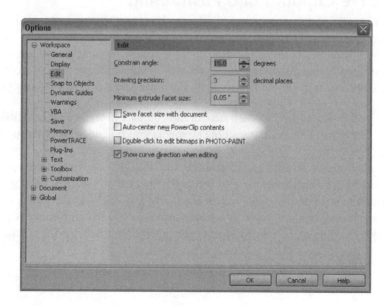

If you want to enable this option, you know where to find it in the future. It's time now to visit sunny Florida, vintage-postcard style. Open Postcard.cdr now: the black text is on an unlocked layer, and some of the characters are a single combined path, so putting images inside the letters will be a fairly simple task.

 ## PowerClipping Images to Text

1. Click the Import button on the Property Bar, and then choose Florida.jpg from your hard drive; click Import and then before you import it, click-drag to scale the image to a little larger than the "DA" in "FLORIDA," the combined path the image will clip to.

2. With the Pick Tool move the image so you can see its future container, and then right-click and hold on the image; drag it to on top of the "DA" object and you'll see (as shown in Figure 23-13) that your cursor is now a crosshair—this is CorelDRAW's way of notifying you that you will put the selection inside the object beneath it as a PowerClipped object. Release the right mouse button and a pop-up menu appears; choose PowerClip Inside and the image now peeks through the "DA" in the postcard.

Crosshair cursor

FIGURE 23-13   Dragging and dropping objects into PowerClip containers is quicker than using the Effects menu.

3. Click the Import button and then choose Oranges.jpg from your hard drive; click Import and then scale the image by click-dragging over the "ORI" black lettering in the composition.

4. Repeat step 2 with the oranges. Now let's say you don't like the positioning of the oranges as they peek through the lettering. One way to edit the position of the oranges image is to right-click over it and then to choose Edit Contents. The link is still active between the contained image and its container, and your editing is in a temporary "space" in CorelDRAW. Edit Contents is also available on the Effects menu, but easier still is to CTRL-click the image to go to Editing mode.

5. You can now position and scale the image relative to a blue outline that's a proxy for the container while in Editing mode. If you click the image (or any object you use) while it's selected, you put the object into Rotate/Skew mode. When you're finished editing the position (and scale and rotation angle), click the Finish Editing Object button above and to the left of the vertical document scroll bar in the drawing window, as shown in Figure 23-14. You can also CTRL-click on a blank area of the page to let CorelDRAW know that you've finished editing.

6. Bring in the toucan.jpg image and repeat step 4. You will probably want to edit the contents of the container to get the toucan's eye and beak aligned with the "FL" object for the best composition.

7. You're done! Print a few copies, put them in your suitcase, make sure you have enough stamps for postcards, and you're outta here! Figure 23-15 shows the finished postcard.

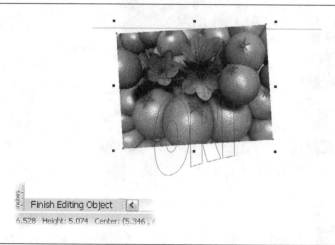

FIGURE 23-14 Edit the position of the contained object so only the areas you want revealed lie within the outline of the PowerClip container.

FIGURE 23-15   Make sure you use bold typefaces when you want images to PowerClip peek through.

 Although the text in this tutorial was broken into curves, you can use Artistic Text as editable text as a PowerClip object. And yes, you can edit the text at any time without breaking the link between the contained object and the container.

PowerClip Lock Options

By default, all new PowerClip contents are locked to their container object; when you move, rotate, and scale the container, the contained object remains relative to the container. However, after an object becomes a PowerClip content object, you *can* change its relationship to the container through the locking and unlocking options. You right-click over the PowerClip object, and then choose Lock or Unlock from the pop-up menu. This can be a terrific part of a design technique to be able to shuffle the container relative to the contents, but it can also create misaligned contents unintentionally, so be careful how you use this feature.

PowerClip content-locking options are available only through the pop-up menu when you right-click; the Lock Contents To PowerClip option can be toggled on or off. This particular option is available only from the pop-up menu when right-clicking an existing PowerClip object on the document page.

This chapter has shown a lot of non-special effects; effects that aren't supposed to "wow" your audience, but rather PowerClips, shadows, and bevels speak of a quiet elegance that strikes the viewer on a subliminal level. It's well worth your time to become proficient with these effects for future times when you need a touch of photorealism in a drawing, something that strikes the audience without hitting them over the head. Chapter 24 takes you into another area of photorealism, that of perspective, as you'll soon see how to make 2D drawings into 2-and-a-half—and quite possibly, 3D—works of art.

PART VII

Creating the Illusion of 3D Objects

CHAPTER 24

Working with
Perspective

The quality of optical perspective was first documented by Leonardo da Vinci and used in his technical drawings to give an accurate sense of depth to those 2D (two-dimensional) pieces. Perspective in drawings can be calculated today by CorelDRAW and other applications, and this chapter takes you through a definition of perspective, how to use CorelDRAW's Perspective effect, and how to feature the quality of perspective in your work to produce lifelike illustrations. If you want your audience to be drawn *into* your work and not simply to stare at it, consider adding some perspective…so your *audience* will see it, too!

The Optical Principle of Perspective

We've all witnessed the effect of perspective; for example, you make sure a train isn't coming, and then you stand on the tracks and look into the horizon. Apparently, the train tracks converge as they vanish at the horizon. Naturally, the tracks don't actually converge, or it would be difficult to drive a train on them. This is an optical illusion that demonstrates the very real optics of the human eye. Any object that has parallel sides (a milk carton, most tables) when viewed at an angle other than straight-on will look as though its parallel sides converge at a point somewhere in the distance. This point, whether you can see it on train tracks or imagine it by mentally extending the parallel lines, is called the *vanishing point,* and CorelDRAW's Perspective effect offers an onscreen marker for moving a shape's vanishing point.

Depending on the angle upon which you view an object—let's use a cube as an example—you can see one, two, or three sides of the cube. When you draw a cube, face front, in CorelDRAW, you've drawn a square; there is no perspective, and it's not a very visually interesting representation. If you can see two faces of the cube, you're viewing from a perspective point; the object is said to have *one-point perspective.* Naturally, you can't see more than three sides of a cube at one time, but when you do see all three front-facing sides, this is called *two-point perspective.* It's very visually interesting to pose an object (or draw one) using two-point perspective, and CorelDRAW can help you set up an object for two-point as well as one-point perspective.

What Is Normal?

Before getting into the wildly distorted perspectives you have available in CorelDRAW, it's probably a good idea to cover what the human eye normally sees with respect to perspective. In your design work, you might occasionally want to portray an object in "normal" perspective—learn how to do this, and you can increase and exaggerate perspective quite easily.

It's simple to calibrate and measure a camera lens when compared with measuring what the human eye sees, because the human eye is in constant motion, and there's a brain behind the eyes that interprets and occasionally *mis*interprets the optical signals it receives.

However, three things come into play that determine the appearance (including the apparent perspective) when using your eye or your eye through a lens:

- **Distance of lens from subject**   In CorelDRAW you might be surprised when you copy a perspective setting to a new object—depending on the perspective, the object might grow or shrink in dimensions. Not to fret; this is covered later in this chapter—perspective changes the apparent distance of objects. Because you're drawing on a flat plane in a CorelDRAW document, the program scales objects according to their perspective to simulate depth in a composition.

- **Field of view**   There is no field of view setting in CorelDRAW's Perspective effect, but in the real world, this property affects how distorted an object looks and is related to focal length. Humans have anywhere from 140° to 180° field of view, but much of this is peripheral vision, not truly in focus, and the consensus is that we usually use about 40° normal field of view.

- **Focal length**   Focal length is the distance between a lens and the imaging surface and is proportional to field of view: as one changes, so does the other. This property is the most responsible for the distorted or undistorted appearance of objects. It's generally conceded that humans have a focal length of 50–55mm. As this relates to CorelDRAW, to simulate short focal lengths (such as a camera's fish eye lens), the vanishing points for the Perspective effect are quite close to the object. As focal length increases, a telescopic effect is achieved, and the perspective of an object is lessened. For example, if you wanted to simulate a 500mm telescopic camera lens in CorelDRAW, the vanishing points for the perspective on the object would be clear off the page, probably in the parking lot somewhere!

This illustration of a child's toy block was rendered to a fairly accurate representation of what a normal human eye would see, from a two-point perspective. The focal length is 50mm and the field of view is about 40°. The lines you see along the parallels of the block indicate the direction of the vanishing points: a normal lens on the child's block puts the vanishing points off this page.

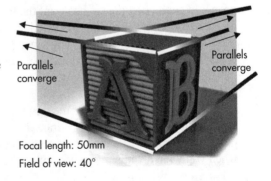

Getting a Perspective on Perspective

Now that you understand what a "normal" lens does to perspective, let's take a look at a few abnormal (but artistic and creative) perspectives, beginning with no perspective and working

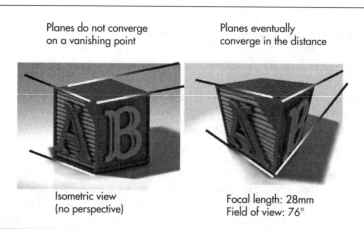

Planes do not converge
on a vanishing point

Planes eventually
converge in the distance

Isometric view
(no perspective)

Focal length: 28mm
Field of view: 76°

FIGURE 24-1   Examples of isometric views and a fairly wide-angle view of the same object.

our way up. In Figure 24-1 you can see at left an *isometric* view (also called an "orthographic" view) of the kid's block; regardless of the term, it's unrealistic because the parallels of the cube do not converge. Isometric views of objects are quickly accomplished in CorelDRAW by putting an object into rotate/skew mode (clicking once and then a second time), and then skewing the object by click-dragging a middle control handle. Isometric views are completely the province of computer graphics and geometry. They don't exist in the real world with human eyes, but they are useful in illustration to put equal emphasis on all visible sides of an object. For example, if you want your client to read the side panel of a proposed cereal box design but want the box posed to show more than one side, you'd use an isometric view (occasionally called "isometric perspective"). At right you can see the same kid's block using a wide-angle perspective. In CorelDRAW such an illustration is accomplished by putting the vanishing points outside of the drawing page. It's exaggerated mostly because the human eye does not have a field of view as large as 76°, that is, the view is not entirely in focus.

Figure 24-2 goes way over the top; the vanishing points are quite close to the object, and the resulting perspective is very dramatic, unrealistic, and unsuitable for presenting a product design. As you read through this chapter, you'll learn that there are some occasions when you want a vanishing point on the drawing page and other occasions when you want perspective of the "normal" human-eye type.

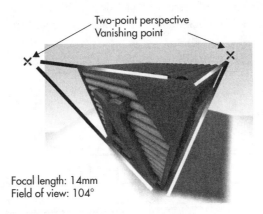

Two-point perspective
Vanishing point

Focal length: 14mm
Field of view: 104°

FIGURE 24-2   Vanishing points that are close to objects suggest an extremely distorted perspective.

Experiments in Perspective

It's a lot more fun and rewarding to experiment with the Perspective effect than it is to read about it. The operations are fairly simple and straightforward, and you'll probably get ideas for future illustrations just by playing with it! Single objects and object groups can be put in perspective; you can change the angle of a perspective shape (or group) by click-dragging any of the four control corners or by click-dragging the vanishing point(s), which changes two of the four control corners at once. Let's begin with a simple perspective, performed on an object that will immediately, visually give you a reference for what's going on: a 12×12-cell Graph Paper object. The Perspective effect displays subdivisions in red dotted lines on top of the object you're manipulating, which provides good visual feedback; with a Graph Paper object, you'll see exactly how the grid corresponds to the visual changes in the graph paper cells.

Creating One-Point Perspective

1. Press D, the keyboard shortcut for the Graph Paper Tool. On the Property Bar, set the number of columns to 12 and the number of rows to 12.

2. Hold CTRL while you click-drag to constrain the Graph Paper object to a square. Make the object fairly large, about 7" is good. Because the Perspective effect can appreciably shrink one or more sides of an object, it's a good design practice to create objects that are a little exaggerated in size.

3. Choose Effects | Add Perspective, as shown here. It might not be obvious, depending on the color of the selected object, that it now has control handles around it. Notice that your current tool has changed to the Shape Tool. The Shape Tool is used during Perspective creation. Additionally, if you intend to edit a Perspective effect while

you're working on a different area of a design, all you need to do is choose the Shape Tool and then click on an object that's in perspective.

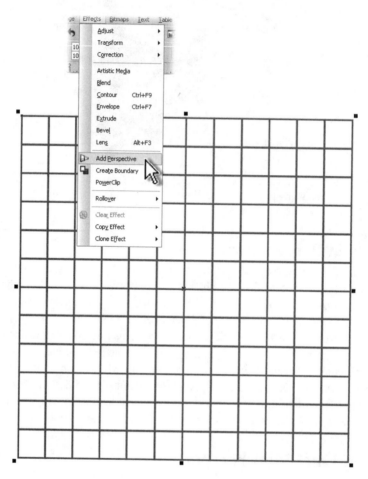

4. Click the top-right handle of the Perspective Effect box surrounding the Graph Paper object. Hold CTRL to constrain the movement of your cursor to the first direction in which you drag, and then drag down to about the second or third cell in the right column, as shown here. You've created a Perspective effect on the object, as you can see the cells align more or less with the effect's red-dotted overlay reference, and a vanishing point appears directly to the right.

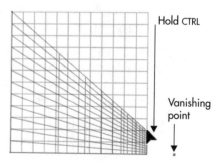

24

5. Click-drag the vanishing point up and then down as long as this is an experiment and not playing for points. Notice what happens: you've defined one-point perspective—this is the right side of a hypothetical cube, and one-point perspectives have only one vanishing point. So the left side of the object is anchored; it doesn't change with the perspective change.

6. Click-drag the vanishing point left and right. The left side is still anchored, and what you're doing is making the hypothetical box's right side deeper and shallower, extending to and from an imaginary horizon on the page.

7. Save this document; you'll work with it in a moment, so don't close it. This is only the beginning of the experiment with suggesting depth in a 2D document!

There has to be a practical use for what you've just learned; adding one-point perspective to a Graph Paper object by itself is about as exciting as watching grass grow. Here you can see the result of grouping some text with the Graph Paper object before applying the Perspective effect. It's a simple drawing and it certainly could use some embellishment, but the point here is that one-point perspective can establish a *ground plane* for a dimensional composition—a ground has been suggested in this illustration by the effect, the "scene" has depth, and the illustrator obviously can't read signs.

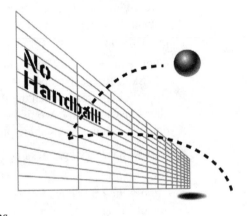

Working with Two-Point Perspective

Any 2D drawing can be made by the Perspective effect to look as though it extends into space, as you proved in the previous tutorial. However, it's time to up the stakes and create a *second* vanishing point. This will make this Graph Paper object look as though it occupies space, suggesting visually that the grid recedes away from the page, and that its depth is traveling in a direction. This is going to be fun; by the end of the following steps, you'll have created a great high-tech, sci-fi background you can use in several design situations.

Creating a 3D Ground Plane

1. With the graph-paper document you saved in the previous tutorial open, choose the Shape Tool and then click on the object to reveal its Perspective effect control handles and the vanishing point you defined.

2. Click-drag the top-right control handle up and toward the center of the object, until you see a second vanishing point marker at about 12 o'clock on the page. You might

want to zoom out to better see the second vanishing point, because it will initially be defined quite far away from the object. Use your mouse scroll wheel to zoom whenever you have a drawing or editing tool chosen; scrolling toward you zooms the window view out, and scrolling away from you zooms it in. Here you can see how the Graph Paper object should look now. Notice also that because this two-point perspective is so extreme, the graph-paper outlines are actually curved to accommodate the severely distorted perspective. This is not an

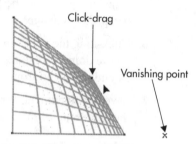

optical illusion (the lines are indeed curved now), but it does mimic the human eye's perception of parallel lines viewed at exceptionally wide angles.

3. Choose the Pick Tool, and with the Graph Paper object selected, click on it to put it into Skew/Rotate transformation mode. Rotate the object about 45° counterclockwise— stop click-dragging when the Property Bar reports that you've rotated the object by about this amount. It would be difficult to change the orientation of the object by only changing the vanishing points' positions.

4. Choose the Rectangle Tool and then click-drag a rectangle to cover the Graph Paper object.

5. Choose the Interactive Fill Tool, and then click-drag from top to bottom on the object so the top is black, fading to white at the rectangle's bottom.

6. Choose the rectangle with the Pick Tool, and then press SHIFT+PAGE DOWN to put the rectangle on the back of the drawing page, behind the Graph Paper object.

7. Choose the Graph Paper object, and then right-click the white color well on the Color Palette. Then double-click the Outline Pen swatch on the Status Bar to open the Outline Pen dialog.

8. Type 4 in the Width field, and then click OK to apply this width. You're done and your composition will look like the illustration here.

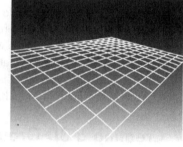

| NOTE | *The Outline properties of an object possessing the Perspective effect do not diminish in width along with the shape of the object. If you need outlines to follow a perspective, you need to first convert the outlines to objects: press CTRL+U, for example, to ungroup a Graph Paper object, and then choose Arrange | Convert Outline to Object (CTRL+SHIFT+Q).* |

Copying Perspective and Creating a 3D Scene

Like many of the features in CorelDRAW, a perspective can be copied from an object and applied to a different object, by use of the options on the Property Bar. Being able to instantly copy and match perspective between objects in a composition can turn the entire drawing into a 3D celebration, as the following tutorial guides you through.

Download Cocopelli celebration.cdr and open it in CorelDRAW.

The little cocopelli characters will make a nice part of a composition as you'll angle them using the Perspective effect in the steps to follow, but you can use an illustration of your own if you prefer. The concept is to get all four objects in the scene facing left by copying one instance of the Perspective effect, and then you'll embellish the composition a little to give the drawing true depth.

> **NOTE** *"Cocopelli" is the name given to ancient stone drawings by Native Americans in the New Mexico area. The character is a sprite associated with trickery, travel, and trade, usually depicted playing a woodwind instrument similar to a flute.*

Perspective Scenes via Copying

1. Select the left object on the page, and then choose Effects | Add Perspective.

2. Click the top-right control handle on the object, and then drag a little up and to the right. Then click-drag the bottom-left control handle, and drag up and to the right until the object is facing left in perspective, as shown in Figure 24-3. You will not see the vanishing points on the page because this perspective is not dramatic or severely distorted.

FIGURE 24-3   Create just enough perspective to give the shape some dimension.

3. While the Shape Tool is still the current tool, click on the first (purple) cocopelli guy. Then choose Effects | Copy Effect | Perspective From. Click over the object at left that has perspective, as shown here, and the second object adopts the perspective of the first.

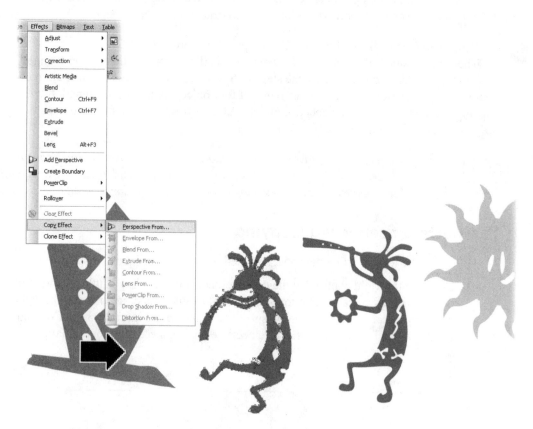

4. Repeat step 3 until all the objects have the same perspective.

5. Create a Graph Paper object, and then give it a medium-gray fill and a white outline. Put it to the back of the illustration.

6. Put the graph paper in perspective to make a ground plane. Next, drag the top-left control handle to the right, and then drag the top-right control handle to the left until you see a vanishing point just above the Graph Paper object. This object will not and should not be in the same perspective as the cocopelli characters, but instead its perspective should be very distorted, suggesting a horizon at the characters' waist level.

7. Create a second Graph Paper object, fill it with medium gray, and give its outline a white property exactly like you did with the first object in step 5. Put it to the back of the drawing (SHIFT+PAGE DOWN).

8. If you haven't already read Chapter 23 on shadows, here are the simple steps to "grounding" the cocopelli characters on the graph paper below them: click any of the foreground objects, and then choose the Interactive Drop Shadow Tool from the Effects group of tools on the Toolbox.

9. Choose Pers. Top Right from the Presets drop-down on the Property Bar. With your cursor, click-drag the black control marker for the shadow down and to the right until the shadow looks correct.

10. Repeat step 9 with the three other foreground objects, or more easily, click an object that has no shadow with the Interactive Drop Shadow Tool; then click the Copy Drop Shadow Properties button on the Property Bar, and click on the first shadow (not the object casting the shadow) you defined. Your scene should look like Figure 24-4 now.

The preceding tutorial might have been a bit of a workout, but look at what you've accomplished. Often, the effect you seek is accomplished through the use of a *combination* of CorelDRAW features. Unfortunately, there is no "create a complete piece of artwork" tool in version X4!

 Any object that has the Perspective effect can be quickly put into editing mode when the Pick Tool is the current tool by double-clicking the object.

FIGURE 24-4 With the Perspective effect and the use of a few drop shadows, you can build a virtual diorama.

Mirroring Perspective Control Handles

There will be occasions in your design work when you need to add perspective or adjust the existing perspective of an object so that the perspective is symmetrical. This is accomplished by holding CTRL+SHIFT while you click-drag a perspective control handle. In Figure 24-5 you can see that this technique is a convenient way to set up perspective for a bowling alley.

Pre-Visualizing Designs in Perspective

Often you'll design something such as a pattern and want to see what it will look like as a garment, gift wrap, or some other physical piece of art before you pay to have the design printed; this is called *pre-visualization* (preVis), and you can do this in CorelDRAW with the Perspective effect. In the following example, you'll create a simple gift-wrap pattern; then, using Perspective, you'll virtually wrap a package. The package is provided for you as an image on layers in a CorelDRAW document.

Download A present.cdr and open it in CorelDRAW. The image of the present is locked on the bottom layer, and the bow is locked on the top layer. A middle, editable layer should be the current layer in the file. Use Window | Dockers | Object Manager if necessary to ensure that you're working on the gift-wrap layer before beginning.

Let's use CorelDRAW's Artistic Media Tool to create the gift wrap for the present in the following steps. After completing the tutorial, you can use a design of your own with this file in the future.

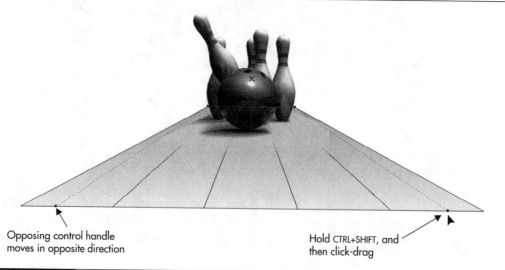

Opposing control handle
moves in opposite direction

Hold CTRL+SHIFT, and
then click-drag

FIGURE 24-5 Create symmetrical perspective by holding CTRL+SHIFT while you drag a control handle.

Pre-Visualizing a Design on a Product

1. With the Rectangle Tool (the present is roughly square), hold CTRL to constrain the rectangle to a square, and then click-drag a square that is approximately the same height as the facing side of the package image. This is a template for the gift-wrap design you'll create.

2. Choose the Artistic Media Tool from the Pen Tool group on the Toolbox. Then choose the Sprayer button on the Property Bar. You can use any preset you like; the bubbles preset is shown in the following figures.

3. Make a few strokes over the rectangle until you've approximated a pleasing pattern for the gift wrap, as shown in Figure 24-6.

4. Select the strokes with the Pick Tool, and then press CTRL+K to break Artistic Media strokes into groups of objects. Delete the control paths, and then group all the groups of objects.

5. Put the rectangle (the square) at the top of the page (SHIFT+PAGE UP). Select the grouped groups of the pattern and the rectangle, and then choose Intersect on the Property Bar. You now have a pattern that's perfectly proportioned for the face of the package. It only needs the right perspective now.

6. Choose Effects | Add Perspective. With the Shape Tool, drag, one at a time, the control handles for the effect to match the four corners of the face of the present, as shown here.

FIGURE 24-6 Create a pattern within the rectangle you drew.

7. Duplicate the pattern and then use the Shape Tool to edit this duplicate (which also has the Perspective effect applied) so it matches the four corners of the top side of the present. Because the bow is on the top layer, you're actually adding the top pattern in perspective below the bow so it looks optically correct.

8. Repeat step 7 to create the left panel of the pattern on the present. This will not look perfect because of the paper flaps on the image of the present—certain areas of the pattern need to be hidden—but this is fine work for the moment. After you read Chapter 23 on PowerClips, you'll be able to hide the areas outside of the present's flaps. This finished pre-visualization provides you and your client with a view of the goods you've designed, as they will appear from the customer's point of view, and perhaps this is the best "perspective" effect of all, as shown here.

You've seen in this chapter how to take a drawing, several objects, and even a complete design, and put a 3D spin on it. Perspective effects can help a client visualize what a design should look like when projected into real space, and at the very least the Perspective effect is a fun and quick method for embellishing a drawing that needs a "certain something" to lift it off the page. Chapter 25 takes you into a more complete visualization of 3D within a 2D drawing as you explore the Extrude effect in CorelDRAW. Bring along what you know about vanishing points now, and bring along an object or two that you want to add another side—literally—to!

CHAPTER 25

Extruding Objects

Although CorelDRAW is a 2D vector drawing application, the Extrude feature can be used on shapes to automatically create a third dimension, one of depth. Depending on the elegance of the target object and how you pose the object and light it, extruded objects can open up a whole new world of design opportunities and extend your style of illustration to present your audience with scenes they can step right into! This chapter takes you through the rich feature set of the Interactive Extrude Tool, demonstrates some creative possibilities for its use, and gets your head around the initial challenges of navigating 3D space in CorelDRAW.

How Extrude Works

CorelDRAW X4's Extrude effect examines the geometry of an object, which can be a single or a compound path (two or more combined paths). Then, with your input, it creates extensions to all path segments, which are dynamic objects, that suggest the path segments recede into the distance to a vanishing point. (See Chapter 24 on perspective vanishing points.) An example of the Extrude effect applied to different shapes, including compound paths, is shown in Figure 25-1.

When an Extrude effect is applied to an object, the original becomes a *control object,* and the Extrude effect objects become a dynamically linked group. Any editing you then perform on the properties of the control object, such as fills and edits to the outline of the control object, are immediately updated in the linked extrude group. The extrude group itself can also be edited in ways that increase the intricacy and photorealism of the effect; you can change the depth, color, lighting, and rotation of the Extrude effect.

Be aware that both lighting and the control object's geometry have an impact on how many extrude group objects are created. Although you don't usually need to concern yourself with how many objects are dynamically created to make an extrude, the sheer number of objects can slow down redraws of your page when you have, for example, hundreds of objects in the extrude group. When CorelDRAW creates an extrude group, it calculates lighting (when you

FIGURE 25-1　Examples of the Extrude effect applied to different objects

use lighting, covered later in this chapter) and creates extrude group objects based on curved path segments in the control object. Here you can see a star-shaped control object with lighting; the object has a Radial fountain fill, and it's an interesting design in Enhanced view. At right, the page is viewed in Wireframe, and 48 objects are grouped in the Extrude effect.

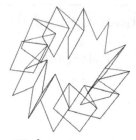

Extrude on straight path shape, with lighting, Enhanced view

Wireframe view, 48 extrude group objects

Here, a much more complex control object is used for an extrude. It not only is a compound path, but its path segments are curved. In Wireframe view it's evident that the Extrude group is composed of more objects than the star-shaped extrude. No lighting is used in the Extrude effect, which in turn limits the number of extrude group objects CorelDRAW has to create, and it is a fairly interesting design.

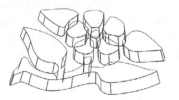

Extruded object with flat fill

Wireframe view, 118 extrude group objects

Lighting is now applied to the flower-shaped control object, and as you can see here, the number of extrude control objects created to represent the curved paths with added lighting is an order of magnitude more. This information is by no means a warning to limit the intricacy of extrude objects you design, but rather a point of information if you own a video card with lots of RAM and suddenly find you're getting slow screen redraws. CorelDRAW does not use Fountain fills to shade an extrude group when you apply lighting. As the lighting is cast on the sides of an extruded shape, curved segments in a control object require that many extrude group objects are created, each with different fill properties, to suggest highlights and shadows.

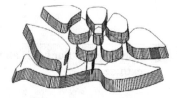

Extrude on curved path shape, with lighting, Enhanced view

Wireframe view, 890 extrude group objects

Choosing and Applying an Extrude Effect

Extrude can be applied interactively using the Interactive Extrude Tool, located in the Toolbox with other interactive tools, or you can choose from the Presets list to instantly create a 3D object.

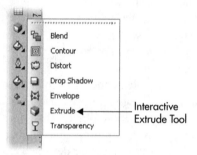

While you're using this tool, the Property Bar provides all the extrude options for setting the properties of the effect. Browse the Property Bar options as shown in Figure 25-2. Options are grouped into areas for saving your applied extrusions as Presets, controlling the shape, depth, vanishing point position, rotation, lighting, color, and bevel effects.

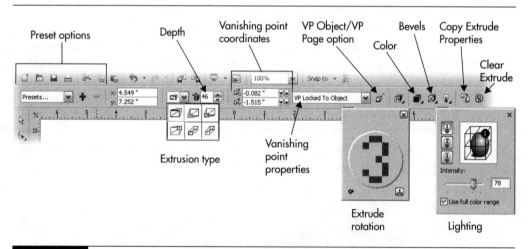

FIGURE 25-2   The Property Bar holds all the options for defining and saving the look of an extrude.

Navigating the Interactive Markers

When you decide to manually extrude a shape, interactive markers appear around the resulting object after you perform the first step in an extrude: you click-drag on the face of the object you want to be the control object. The interactive markers offer you control over the position, depth, and vanishing point position for the 3D object. You'll be creating a 3D object by hand in the following tutorial, so it's good now to familiarize yourself with the elements that surround a 3D extruded shape, as shown in Figure 25-3.

As mentioned earlier, you can apply a Preset extrude effect to receive a 3D version of a shape in lightning time; however, you might want hands-on control over the creation of an Extrude effect. Follow this tutorial to get a handle on what some of the Property Bar options do to an Extrude effect; in no time, you'll be able to "sculpt" whatever you envision as a scene that has objects with depth.

Getting Deep with the Interactive Extrude Tool

1. Create an object to be the control object for the extrude. A rectangle will produce results that make the relationship between the face of the object and the sides very clear, but not very artistic (unless you're into Cubism). Try a Star shape for more dramatic extrude results. Give the shape a fill (a Fountain fill will produce a stunning effect), and give the outline a contrasting color such as white so you can visually track where the extrude objects are created.

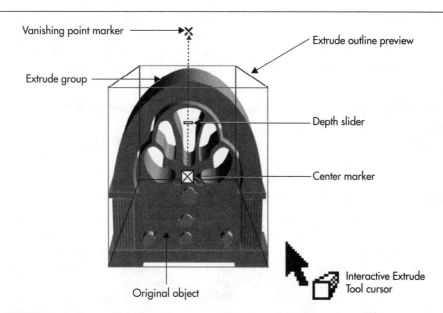

Vanishing point marker

Extrude outline preview

Extrude group

Depth slider

Center marker

Interactive Extrude Tool cursor

Original object

FIGURE 25-3 These control handles are used after an object is initially extruded to change the appearance of the extrude.

2. Choose the Interactive Extrude Tool, and your cursor takes on a novel appearance. When held over your object, the cursor indicates a start extrude position by using a tiny shape with a direction line below the arrow.

3. Drag from the center of your object outward in any direction, but don't release the mouse button. The control object is now surrounded by interactive markers, including a preview outline of the resulting extrude group (the front of the object is bound by a red outline, and the back of the 3D shape is bound by a blue outline) and an X symbol. The preview indicates the length and direction of the Extrude effect; the X symbol you're dragging is the *vanishing point*. As discussed in Chapter 24, a vanishing point is a geometric indicator of where parallel lines on a surface would converge at the horizon if the surface actually were to extend into the horizon.

4. Drag the vanishing point symbol around the page; not only does the preview outline change, but more importantly, the view on the 3D object also changes. When the vanishing point is above the control object, you're looking down on the object; similarly, you move your view to expose the side of an object in direct correlation to the position of the vanishing point.

5. As you dragged with the Interactive Extrude Tool, you defined both the direction of the 3D object and the depth. Try dragging the Depth slider toward and then away from the control object. Notice how you first make the extrude a shallow one, and then a deeper one, all the while the sides extend in the direction of the vanishing point.

6. Click outside of the object, and the extrude operation is complete. However, because extrude is a dynamic effect, you can change the appearance of the extrude at any time in the future by double-clicking either the extrude group or the control object with the Pick Tool to once again display the interactive handles.

Using the Interactive Extrude Tool and Property Bar

Like other effects, extrusions can be set using the Property Bar. Using the Interactive Extrude Tool, you'll encounter one of several cursor states. Let's take a look at the different cursors and what they indicate in the following sections.

Interactive Extrude Tool States

The Interactive Extrude Tool cursor, shown here, changes appearance based on what it's over in your document. When the cursor is held over an object that can be extruded, the cursor features a start symbol. If an object cannot be extruded, the cursor features the international "No" (⊘) symbol. Most shapes you draw with the Pen tools except Artistic Media can be extruded. If you have your heart set on extruding Artistic Media strokes, the strokes need to be first broken from the control path (CTRL+K); bitmaps cannot be extruded at all (but the 3D Effects on the Bitmaps menu can be used). You can only extrude one object at a time: you'll get the "No can do" cursor if you select more than one object and then try to use the tool. Grouped objects cannot be successfully extruded, and you do not get a warning cursor—only the bottommost object in the group will be extruded, and the group remains a group.

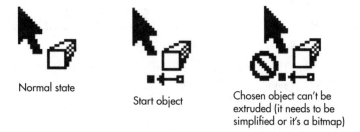

Normal state

Start object

Chosen object can't be extruded (it needs to be simplified or it's a bitmap)

Setting Extrusion Shape

The Extrusion Type selector, shown next, offers six different shape types with which you can control both direction of the extrude and whether you need wide-angle, small perspective, or totally isometric (no perspective) 3D objects. Depending on the type you choose, your extrusion can extend toward the back or front relative to the control object. Choosing a front style causes the vanishing point to project from the front of your object; choosing a back style does the opposite. Because you're working with geometric solids, when you choose a back style, the direction of the extrude will looked mirrored, although in wireframe view it's clear that the object inverted itself, its back side projecting forward instead of into the distance. Icons in the selector indicate each shape type, with the darkened outline indicating your original object. Here are the icons with callouts and examples of each style.

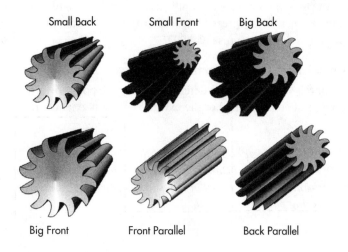

| Small Back | Small Front | Big Back |
| Big Front | Front Parallel | Back Parallel |

- **Small Back** This option (the default setting) causes the extrusion and vanishing point to be layered behind your original object. Small Back is perhaps the most commonly applied extrusion type.

- **Small Front** This causes the extrusion and vanishing point to be layered in front of your original object.

- **Big Back** This option causes the extrusion to be layered behind your original object, while the vanishing point is in front.

- **Big Front** This causes the extrusion to be layered in front of your original object, while the vanishing point is in back.

- **Back Parallel** This option causes the extrusion to be layered behind your original object so that the extruded surfaces appear parallel to the original surfaces. When this option is selected, the vanishing point sets the depth of the extrusion, while the actual depth option is unavailable. No vanishing point is involved using this style.

- **Front Parallel** This causes the extrusion to be layered in front of your object so that the extruded surfaces appear parallel to the original surfaces. When this option is selected, the vanishing point sets the depth of the extrusion, while the actual depth option is unavailable. No vanishing point accompanies this extrusion style.

Setting Extrude Depth

Extrude Depth is based on the distance between the control object and the vanishing point. You will get different appearances using the same Depth value but different styles, and Extrude Depth can be set as high as 99. Figure 25-4 shows a shallow and a deep extrude, using two different Depth values but the same Extrude style. You can control object depth manually by dragging the interactive depth slider on top of the object, or enter values in the num box on the Property Bar (press ENTER after typing a value; the spin box controls update the object without the need to press ENTER).

Setting Vanishing Point Properties

The direction of the vanishing point determines only the point toward which objects diminish; it does not control whether the extruded portion extends from the front or back of the object.

| NOTE | *Vanishing points can be set on four of the six extrusion styles: Small Back, Big Back, Small Front, and Big Front. The sides of the extruded portions created in the Front Parallel or Back Parallel types never converge; these are isometric views, and no vanishing point is involved.* |

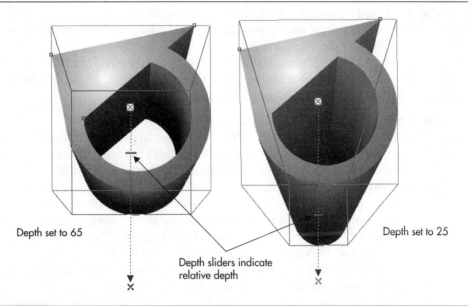

Depth set to 65

Depth set to 25

Depth sliders indicate
relative depth

FIGURE 25-4   Go for the subtle—or the dramatic—by changing the Depth setting on the
Extrude effect control object.

Using the Property Bar options shown here, you can lock an extrusion's vanishing point,
copy vanishing points from an existing extrusion, and share vanishing points between
extruded objects.

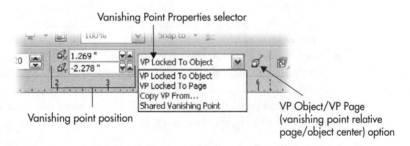

Vanishing Point Properties selector

Vanishing point position

VP Object/VP Page
(vanishing point relative
page/object center) option

Here are the definitions of the various ways vanishing points can be set and shared
between different extruded objects:

■   **Locking to the object**   Choosing the VP Locked To Object option (the default
setting) fixes the vanishing point to a position relative to the object, regardless of
where the original extruded object is positioned.

- **Locking to the page** VP Locked To Page offers the option to tack the vanishing point to your page, forcing the extrusion to diminish toward a fixed page position, no matter where the original object is moved. Try this out to see for yourself the worth of this setting: lock the vanishing point of an extruded object to the page, and then move the object; you'll see that the sides of the extrude dynamically update to always show the correct perspective of the object.

- **Copying VP from** This command is among the other options on the drop-down selector. Copying a vanishing point lets you set up several extruded objects on a page, and in a few clicks the objects all appear to be facing the same direction, at a common point of view from the audience's perspective. Immediately after you choose Copy VP From, your cursor changes to a vanishing point targeting cursor (a really, really large arrow), which you use to target any other extruded object on your document page, with the goal of copying its vanishing point position. For this command to be successful, you must have at least one other Extrude effect applied to an object and in view. After the vanishing point has been copied, the Property Bar indicates the object's vanishing point as VP Locked To Page, meaning that the vanishing point can no longer be repositioned.

- **Sharing vanishing points** Choosing Shared Vanishing Point enables you to have multiple objects share the *same* vanishing point, but you must have applied at least an initial Extrude effect to your objects before attempting to use this command. Immediately after you choose this option, your cursor changes to a vanishing point targeting cursor, which signifies that you now target any other extruded object for the purpose of creating a common vanishing point position for multiple objects. This creates a similar effect to copying vanishing points, but the overall effect is that every object on the page is in the same scene. The objects are positioned in different areas, but it's one big, visually integrated scene. Shared Vanishing Point can be repeated for as many objects as you like. When multiple objects share a vanishing point, they can be repositioned anywhere on your document page, and the perspective on the 3D object updates to maintain the relationship of a common vanishing point. Figure 25-5 shows the results of setting up a shared vanishing point arrangement with four objects. The figure has been retouched (you can't view more than one vanishing point at a time) to show the converging point for all the objects' sides, their depth aspect.

- **Setting a relative position for vanishing points** The VP Object/VP Page option in the Property Bar enables you to toggle the measurement state of object vanishing points. While the option is inactive (meaning the button is not depressed), the vanishing point position boxes enable you to specify the vanishing point relative to your page origin—a value determined either by the lower-left corner by default or by the zero markers on your ruler origin. While the option is active (meaning the button is depressed), the center of your currently selected object is used as the measurement value, which changes according to the object's page position.

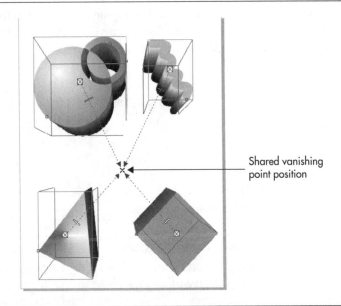

Shared vanishing
point position

FIGURE 25-5 These four objects share the same vanishing point, applied using the Shared Vanishing Point command.

Setting 3D Rotation

Until now, the extrudes you've created and read about have been based on the control object facing you; this is a good beginning point in your 3D experience, but it's not the most visually interesting of poses for your 3D objects. You can rotate extruded objects; the extrude group follows and aligns perfectly with the control object, and you have two ways to perform 3D extrude rotations: via the Property Bar and with the interactive control handles. To rotate an object, naturally you have to have an extrusion already in place in your document; let's begin with the precise, noninteractive method of rotation you access through the Property Bar when the Extrude Tool is chosen and an object is selected.

The Rotation pop-up menu offers a proxy box that you use by click-dragging on the "*3*," as shown next. As you drag, a very faint yellow line appears on the "*3*", indicating the current rotation of the object and the proposed new rotation once you release the mouse button. You might not always get the exact look you need using this technique because of the position of the object's vanishing point—your experience can be similar to levering an object seesaw-fashion when the pivot point (the fulcrum) is 15 miles away! To alleviate this imprecision, you can click the toggle button labeled in the illustration below to move to a number field display of the X, Y, and Z rotational values (see following sidebar). The value fields have spin box controls that increase and decrease the values by 10; you probably want to enter values manually, because a single degree of rotation can be quite significant, considering only 100 of them are in this pop-up box. If at any time you've gotten too deep in this 3D rotation stuff, clicking the "undo" curved arrow icon on the lower left of the selector, shown here, resets all rotation values to zero.

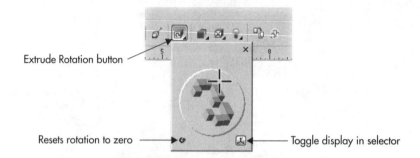

Extrude Rotation button

Resets rotation to zero

Toggle display in selector

Using the Interactive Rotation Tools

You don't have to use the rotation pop-up box on the Property Bar to rotate an extruded object: you can define a degree of rotation along the X, Y, and Z axes of any object by click-dragging the object directly. To do some manual rotation, the object needs to be extruded and first put into Editing mode—you can double-click on the extrude group of objects with the Pick Tool to put the object into Editing mode, and then a second click exposes the control handles shown here. Before you leap in, read on for an explanation of what the interactive controls do and what you do with them to achieve the desired result.

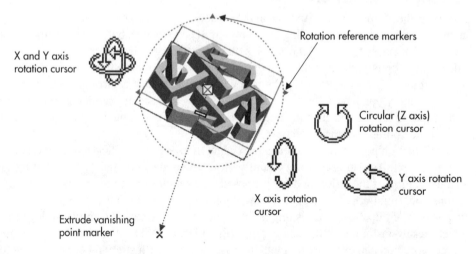

Rotation reference markers

X and Y axis rotation cursor

Circular (Z axis) rotation cursor

Y axis rotation cursor

X axis rotation cursor

Extrude vanishing point marker

NOTE   *While either Back Parallel or Front Parallel is selected, Extrude Rotation controls are unavailable; parallel extrusions have no vanishing point, so there's nothing to pivot with. Also, when the vanishing point is locked to the page, Extrude Rotation cannot be performed.*

Rotational Directions in 3D Space

The creative rewards of knowing how to extrude and rotate objects in CorelDRAW require that you learn how to navigate in 3D space as you would in any professional modeling program such as Luxology modo or Cinema 4D. Directions in space are measured much the same as on a CorelDRAW page: positive X values (measuring width) move to the right, positive Y values (height) travel bottom to top, and the values of depth (Z) travel from back to front. Rotation direction travels positive in a counterclockwise direction, and this might take some familiarization to better use your time. Fortunately, you have an excellent mnemonic device at hand, literally, *your right hand.*

Modeling usually uses the right-hand coordinate system: stand in front of a mirror if you don't want your hand to cramp, face your palm upwards, and then extend your forefinger to your right. This is the X measurement of 3D space, and X rotation travels counterclockwise around your forefinger. Now point your middle finger straight up to indicate the positive motion along the Y axis. The rotation of an object along Y is also counterclockwise. Point your thumb at yourself. Z motion travels toward you, and rotation along Z is counterclockwise, following the curl of your fingers.

Therefore, when you want to rotate a CorelDRAW extruded object so its top is leaning toward you, this is the X axis, your forefinger. You enter positive values in the X field in the pop-up box. If you want the left side of the extruded object to face you, this is your middle finger, and you enter positive Y values in the pop-up box, as shown in this illustration.

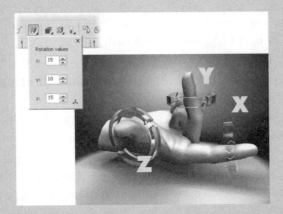

Overall, the best teacher is experience, particularly with manipulating your view of a 3D object in CorelDRAW. Set aside some quality time, and you might even be pleasantly surprised by some of your errors!

Rotating an Extrude Effect

Because a rotated extrude is usually more visually interesting than a face-front view, the following tutorial will come in handy when you've extruded an object that has some built-in visual interest. Extrude something interesting now, and let's take the manual, interactive rotation feature out for a spin.

Putting a New Spin on an Extruded Object

1. With the Pick Tool, double-click the extrude group or the control object to expose the editing handles. Alternatively, you can use the Interactive Extrude Tool to select the object, and it's immediately put into Editing mode.

2. Single-click the *extruded* portion a second time. The interactive rotation markers appear, and circular guides surround the effect. The inside and outside areas of this circular area determine the tool's cursor state.

3. Move the cursor outside of the green dashed circle, and notice that it changes to the rotation cursor. This cursor is used to rotate the face of the object, the Z axis, counterclockwise and clockwise. Dragging right and down creates a clockwise rotation, and left and up rotates the face of the object counterclockwise.

4. Move the cursor inside the green dashed circle area, and it changes to the X/Y axis rotation cursor. Using this cursor is a lot like using an onscreen trackball; you just drag in any direction to simultaneously rotate the X and Y axes of the extrude object. It's fun, you can see the vanishing point move to reflect the new aspect of the object, and it's also not as precise as it could be when you only want to, for example, rotate the object along the top-to-bottom (Y) axis.

5. Release the mouse button for a moment and then hold CTRL. Then click-drag upward (downward is okay, too); you're now constraining rotation to the X axis of the object.

6. Release the mouse button again and then hold CTRL. Now click-drag left or right; you're constraining rotation to the Y axis of the object and not touching the X axis rotation.

7. When the amusement has worn thin or your task is accomplished, click a blank space on the document page way outside of the interactive rotational cursor area to deselect the effect. The cursor returns to the normal extrude cursor state. You've just completed manually rotating the Extrude effect.

After an Extrude effect has been rotated, you can still adjust the extrude depth of the effect, but not the vanishing points.

Adding Lights

Adding lighting to an extruded object can spell the difference between an effect and a piece of artwork that truly attracts a viewer with its realistic appearance; many of the figures in this chapter use the Lighting option. To access the lighting controls, click the Extrude Lighting button on the Property Bar while an Extrude effect is selected, as shown here:

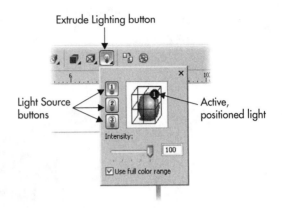

Working with the Options in the Lighting Control Window

Three independent light sources can be activated, positioned, and adjusted for intensity and for whether all the control object's colors are used in the extrude group (the Use Full Color Range option). These lights are unidirectional; they can be positioned, but not aimed as you would a real flashlight or spotlight. Light intensity is set on a light-by-light basis between 0 and 100 percent by using the slider control when each is selected. One of the nice things about setting up light intensity and position is that response is immediate—there is no Apply button and your object's light changes as you make changes in the control window.

When you first open the Extrude Lighting control window, all lights are inactive. To activate a light, click one of the three Light Source buttons—the numbering is for your reference; it's just a label. There is nothing special about light 3 versus light 1, for example, in any of its properties. Once a light button is clicked, a circle with the light's number inside appears in the front, upper-right position on a 3D grid surrounding a sphere, which represents the extrude object (see Figure 25-6). The lights themselves aren't visible on the drawing page, but the lighting effect you define displays highlights and shaded areas on your extrude object, particularly evident when the sides of the control object are curved. The light sources can be posed by adding them to the grid and then dragging them—there are 14 possible positions for lights; some of the positions can create very interesting "edge lighting" on your object.

Every time you activate a new light, it appears on the grid in the default position of front, top, right. This means if you click to activate two or three Light Source buttons in succession without first moving them, you'll stack them on top of each other and wind up with one extremely intense light source on the object. If this happens, simply drag the individual lights to reposition them at different points.

A *selected* light is shown as a black circle in the preview; unselected lights are shown as white circles. Lights set to brightness levels less than 100 percent appear in shades of gray. As these light sources are dragged around the 3D grid, they automatically snap to line-intersection points on the grid. You cannot position lights at the back-mid-center or back-center-bottom position, but this is not really a creative limitation, because lights in these positions would not significantly contribute to the shading of the extrude shape.

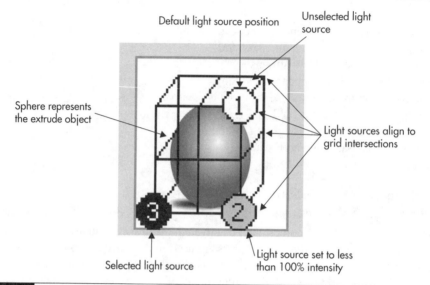

Default light source position

Unselected light source

Sphere represents the extrude object

Light sources align to grid intersections

Selected light source

Light source set to less than 100% intensity

FIGURE 25-6 The 3D grid represents light positions relative to the selected extrude object.

> **NOTE** *There is no option to set the color of lights; all lights cast white. If you want a spotlight effect, read Chapter 22 on Lens effects for techniques on shading objects with color.*

Adding and Editing Extrude Lights

The following tutorial obliges you to put on your stagehand cap as you work the lights in a scene, adding them to the extrude object's properties and learning how to position them and turn the wattage up and down.

 ## Working with Extrude Light Options

1. Create a color-filled object and apply an Extrude effect to it.

2. Using the Interactive Extrude Tool, click the Extrude Lighting selector in the Property Bar to open the light source option.

3. Click the Light Source 1 button, and a light source symbol appears in the upper-right-front corner of the grid, shown as a black circle numbered *1*. The Intensity slider becomes active; Light Source 1 is now active, and the colors of your Extrude effect are altered (brightened and possibly a little washed-out) to reflect the new light's contribution to the Extrude effect.

4. Drag the symbol representing Light Source 1 to a different position on the 3D grid; notice how the coloring of the effect changes in response to the new lighting position.

5. With Light Source 1 still selected, drag the Intensity slider to the left approximately to the 50% position, and notice how the color of the object becomes darker and more saturated.

6. Click the Light Source 2 button to activate it. Notice that it appears in the same default position as the first light source, and the symbol representing Light Source 1 is gray, indicating that it is not selected and it is not at 100 percent Intensity. When an unselected light is at 100 percent Intensity, the symbol is white. Drag Light Source 2 to a different grid position—in classic scene lighting, a secondary light of, say, 50 percent of the main light's intensity, is usually positioned directly opposite the main light to make objects look rounder, deeper, and overall more flattering with more visible detail than using only one light source.

7. Click the activation buttons for Light Sources 1 and 2 to toggle them off, and the color of the extrude object returns to its original state. To finish editing lights, click anywhere outside the Extrude Lighting selector.

> **TIP** *Occasionally in your design work, you might like the perspective you've created for the face of an extrude object, but might not need the extruded side in the extrude group of objects. You can remove an Extrude effect from an object and keep its perspective and position on the page by clicking on the extruded portion of the effect and choosing Effects | Clear Extrude. You can also use the Interactive Extrude Tool by clicking the Clear Extrude button in the Property Bar. The control object of an extrude that has been rotated cannot be restored to its original perspective, but if you have not rotated the control object, Clear Extrude restores your object to its unchanged original dimensions.*

Controlling Light Properties

Two additional options available when you're using lighting have the following effects on your extrusion:

- **Lighting intensity**   As mentioned in the previous tutorial, the Intensity slider determines the brightness of each light. While a light is selected, the range can be set between 0 and 100 percent; higher values cause brighter lighting.

- **Full color range**   Below the Intensity slider you'll find the Use Full Color Range option, which directs your display to use the full *gamut* of colors when coloring the surfaces of your original object and its extruded portion. *Gamut* is the expressible range of colors available to CorelDRAW, which depends on the color mode (see Chapter 19) of the original object and the extrusion. When working in CMYK process or RGB color, you might find the shading on an object to have too much contrast; the lighting might look too harsh and might create washed-out surfaces. The remedy then is to uncheck Use Full Color Range; the gamut of colors is then limited, and the dynamic range of available colors becomes narrower. You just might wind up seeing areas that are hidden in deeply shaded zones when Use Full Color Range is checked.

Using a Narrow Gamut for Spot Colors in an Extrude

If your original shape and/or the extruded portion uses spot colors, the Use Full Color Range option might help you get where you want to go. Deselecting it has the effect of limiting the color variations caused by light sources to only those percentages of the spot colors defined in both your original object and its extruded portion. Unfortunately, deselecting this option limits color depth and diminishes the effects of the lighting you apply, but it results in a print-legal spot color tint, as opposed to the normal color space of RGB that you see onscreen. This means that if your objects are filled with spot color, you should consider unchecking the Use Full Color Range check box.

Setting Extrude Color

In addition to shading an extrude group using lighting, you can further embellish and draw out photorealistic qualities by using Color options for the extrude. You might need to perform some technical illustration with extrude objects, and you might need cross-hatching in addition to lighting, for example. This is when you turn to the Color option on the Property Bar; you have three different ways to shade an extrude group: object fill color, solid color, or color shading (much like a Fountain fill transition from one color to a different color).

Let's begin left to right on the Color control window; below you can see callouts for the various modes you can use with Color.

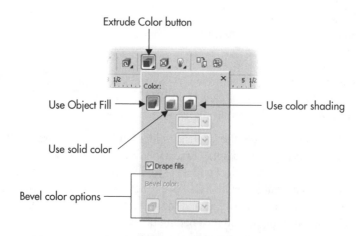

Extrude Color button

Use Object Fill

Use color shading

Use solid color

Bevel color options

You can achieve effects that range from flat, technical illustrations to highly polished metallic surfaces—which actually can work on their own without the need for lighting the object—and it all depends on the choices you make on the Color control window:

■ **Using an object's fill**   The Use Object Fill option is the most straightforward to use, but it does not automatically create any sort of shading—if you choose to use the default object fill and the object is filled with a uniform color, it's usually a good idea to give the control object an outline width whose color contrasts against the object fill color. When Object Fill is selected, the Drape Fill option also becomes available (and is selected automatically). Drape Fill is discussed shortly; here is an example of a fountain-filled control object, with and without Drape Fill.

Radial Fountain fill control object, Use Object Fill

Radial Fountain fill control object, Use Object Fill, Drape Fill

■ **Choosing your own solid fill**   Choose Use Solid Color to set any uniform color to the extrude portion of your effect, regardless of the fill type currently applied to your object. The secondary color option becomes available only when Use Color Shading is selected.

| TIP | *If an object has no outline width/color applied, it might be difficult to see the edges between the original and extruded portions. Applying an outline to your original object will help define the edges of overall composition.* |

■ **Using color shading**   Choose Use Color Shading to add depth by using your object's color as the From color and black (by default) as the To color. If the object to which you've applied your Extrude effect is already filled with a Fountain fill, Use Color Shading is selected automatically. Visual separation between the extrude group objects and the suggestion of depth is easy to create using Color Shading.

Extrude color applied with Use Solid Color option

Extrude color applied with Use Color Shading option

■ **Draping your object's fill over the Extrude effect** *Draping,* as used in CorelDRAW's Extrude effect, means, "treat each extrude group object's fill as a unique item." Say, for example, you have a patterned piece of cloth and you drape it over a coffee table: you will see discontinuity in the pattern as each angle of the folds of cloth travels in different directions in 3D space. Similarly, draping creates discontinuity in a pattern and fountain fill you apply to both the control object and the extrude group of objects, as shown in Figure 25-7. At left, with Drape Fills enabled, the polka dot shape (with some lighting applied) truly looks dimensional, even though the two-color bitmap fill doesn't change perspective (bitmap fills do not take on the rotation angle of extrude objects; they're always face forward). At right, with Drape Fills turned off, the pattern proceeds across the object and the extrude group of objects in a continuous pattern, as though it's *projected* on the surface of the shape instead of *being* the surface of the shape.

■ **Using bevel color** This option becomes available only if you've applied the Bevel effect to an extruded shape. Bevel options are located on the Bevels selector in the Property Bar (covered in the next section). This is an important option to enable when your object and its child extrude group have a fountain or bitmap pattern fill. The effect of enabling Drape Fill does to the bevel edges what Drape Fill does to the extrude group—it breaks up the pattern continuity, which in turn makes the overall object more realistic in appearance.

 To detach an Extrude effect, right-click the extrude group and choose Break Extrude Group Apart. This breaks the link between your original and its effect portion, making it a separate group that can be further broken down using the Ungroup command (CTRL+U). The result is that the control object adopts the perspective of the Extrude effect; you can independently edit all objects for color and outline properties, and do some editing to manually increase the realism of your composition—some examples are shown at the end of this chapter. This is a destructive edit, be forewarned, and the only way to reverse the process is via the Undo docker or by pressing CTRL+Z.

With Drape Fills
Pattern is
discontinuous
(looks realistic)

Without Drape Fills
Pattern is continuous
(looks hokey)

FIGURE 25-7 The Drape Fills options can make or break the realism you're trying to illustrate.

Speak of the Bevel!

Bevels in the real world are the flattened edges where two planes meet on furniture to give it an ornamental look, to make the furniture safer for kids romping around the living room, and to make furniture more expensive. Similarly, the Bevel option in CorelDRAW's Extrude effect creates new objects, in perspective, that join the face and sides of an extrude object.

Bevel effects are built to put a cap on the front end of the control object. Therefore, if an extrude is defined using a style that projects from front to back, the bevel is created as a group of objects facing you. However, if you choose the Small Front style, the bevel will go to the back face of the object, and without rotating the object the bevel will be hidden from view. Bevel shape is based on the angle and depth defined using the Bevel selector, shown here:

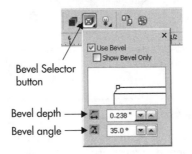

- **Using bevels**   The Use Bevel option causes the Bevel effect to become active and makes the remaining options in the control window become available. Bevel effects can be used only after an Extrude effect has been applied.

- **Showing bevels only**   You might not want the extruded side but only the Bevel effect of an object to be visible; this is a quick and easy way to make a fancy, engraved headline from Artistic Text. Click the Show Bevel Only check box, and the extrude for the selected object is hidden, but can be restored at any future time by unchecking this box. You can rotate an object that has a Bevel effect, but the extrude parts are hidden. However, you must do this through the Rotation pop-up box on the Property Bar—interactive control handles will not appear around an extrude object that's not visible once the object has been deselected.

- **Setting bevel shapes**   The Bevel Depth and Bevel Angle options can be defined by entering values in the corresponding fields on the Bevel pop-up on the Property Bar; you can also click-drag in the proxy window to interactively define the angle and depth. Bevel Depth can be set between 0.001 inch and 1,980 inches. Bevel Angle may be set to a maximum of 89°. Shallow angles of less than 30° often provide the best visual results. At significant depths, you might get self-intersections in the bevel because control objects that have sharp curves along the path segments are difficult for the Bevel effect to reconcile mathematically. Figure 25-8 shows the results of applying a Bevel effect with and without an Extrude effect involved.

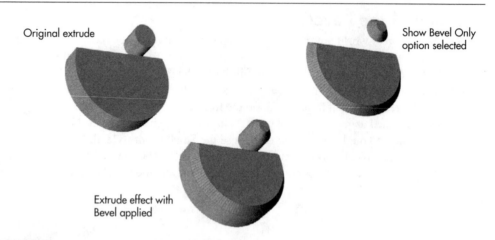

Original extrude

Show Bevel Only
option selected

Extrude effect with
Bevel applied

FIGURE 25-8 The shape of a bevel is determined by Bevel Depth and Bevel Angle.

Using Vector Extrude Presets

You might spend an hour or two creating the exact Extrude effect you've envisioned, and naturally it would be nice to save the parameters you've defined to later apply them to other objects. When the Extrude Tool is active, you have an area on the Property Bar for applying factory-designed Presets as well as for saving and ditching presets, as shown in Figure 25-9.

Extrude Presets are used the same way as all other CorelDRAW Presets. You can save and reapply them to any object that qualifies for the effect (in other words, no Artistic Media, bitmaps, or objects that have an incompatible effect already in place). If you've never

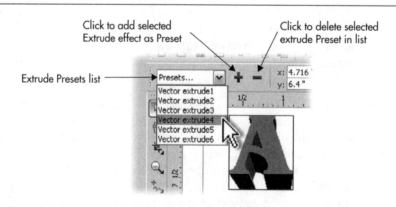

Click to add selected
Extrude effect as Preset

Click to delete selected
extrude Preset in list

Extrude Presets list

FIGURE 25-9 Use these options to save your extrude properties as Presets.

used extrude Presets or any other Preset options before, do not pass "Go," collect your wits, and move on to the following tutorial.

Working with Extrude Preset Options

1. Select an object and then choose the Interactive Extrude Tool.

2. Using the Property Bar, choose an Extrude effect from the Presets list. The properties of the Extrude effect are immediately applied, and its properties are shown on the Property Bar.

3. To save an existing extrude as a Preset, select the extrude group (not the control object), and then click the Add Preset (+) button. The Save As dialog opens. Enter a name for your new Preset in the File Name box, then click Save, and your extrude Preset is added to the Presets list.

4. To delete an extrude Preset, while no object is selected, choose the preset from the Presets list and then click the Delete Preset button (–) in the Property Bar. The saved Preset is immediately deleted, and there is no Undo command for this operation.

Using the Extrude Docker

If you're a longtime CorelDRAW user, you may have grown accustomed to applying Extrude effects using a docker; new users will probably find the interactive editing methods and the options on the Property Bar to be more convenient to access, but the Extrude docker is available via Window | Dockers | Extrude. The Extrude docker is organized into five areas: Camera (referring to shape), Rotation, Light, Color, and Bevels, as shown here.

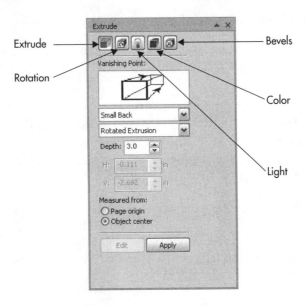

25

Copying and Cloning Extrude Effects

As with other effects in CorelDRAW X4, you can copy or clone from existing extrusions. Neither operation requires the Interactive Extrude Tool; both are accomplished by using menu commands.

When copying an Extrude effect, at least one Extrude effect must be in view, and at least one object must be selected. To copy an Extrude effect, choose Effects | Copy Effect | Extrude From. The cursor becomes a targeting cursor (the large right-facing arrow guy). Use this cursor to indicate to CorelDRAW the extrude portion of an existing Extrude effect to copy all applied extrude properties. If you're using the Interactive Extrude Tool, you can also copy the effect by clicking the Copy Extrude Properties button on the Property Bar and then clicking to target an existing extrusion.

Cloning an Extrude effect produces a slightly different result. When an effect is applied through cloning, the master clone effect object controls the new effect. Any changes made to the master are immediately applied to the clone. Any changes made to the clone properties will override the properties applied by the master, with any unchanged effect properties maintaining a perpetual link to the master clone effect. For example, if you change the depth of a clone, depth is no longer linked to the master object, but rotation, bevel, and other properties you didn't change are still linked from clone to master. To clone an Extrude effect, you must have created at least one other Extrude effect and have this object in view. You must also have at least one object selected onscreen.

To clone an Extrude effect, choose Effects | Clone Effect | Extrude From. Your cursor becomes a targeting cursor. You then click on the existing Extrude effect you want to clone by clicking directly on the extrude group portion of the effect.

Although these options are organized differently from the Property Bar, all the options are there. Using the docker method for extruding objects lets you choose extrude settings before applying them.

Controlling Extrude Complexity Using Facet Size

You might have noticed how the curves and shading are applied with the Use Color Shading option. Smooth curves and shading require complex calculations and produce a large number of extrude group objects to maintain curve smoothness. The smoother the curve and shading, the better the display and print quality.

When CorelDRAW X4 creates an extrusion, the smoothness of curves and the number of objects used to create shaded extrusion fills are controlled by a value called a *facet*. Facet size can be increased or decreased to control curve smoothing and object count. This is what Facet Size is and does, so right now would be a good time to reveal where this option is *located!*

The option itself is named "Minimum Extrude Facet Size" and has a range between 0.001 inch and 36 inches—the default is 0.05 inch. To access it, choose Tools | Options (CTRL+J) to open the Options dialog, and click Edit in the tree directory, as shown here.

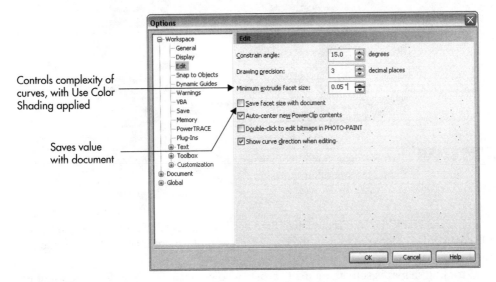

25

In Options, you can also choose Save Facet Size With Document to avoid the need to change the facet size each time your document is reopened. Higher facet values cause extrude curves to display and print less smoothly; lower values increase the smoothness of extruded curves but significantly increase display and printing times; Figure 25-10 shows a Minimum Facet size of 1" and a shape that has a lot of curved segments and lighting that needs to be rendered using a correspondingly high number of extrude facets.

FIGURE 25-10   This Extrude's Minimum Facet Size is too high; the extrude edges, as they change color to reflect the lighting, are very obvious.

Minimum facet size set to 0.001 inch; facets are nearly invisible

Wireframe view

FIGURE 25-11   Extrude facet smoothness is proportional to the number of facets needed to create the smooth impression.

In Figure 25-11, the Minimum Facet Size has been reduced to a fraction of an inch; the little cocopelli guy looks extruded, the curved edges look smooth, and the wireframe view shows why.

Extruding shapes is something many artists who compete with you for jobs might not be able to offer, especially if they don't own CorelDRAW! However, it's probably not a career-enhancer to use the Extrude effect (or any other effect) as a substitute for your own talent as a designer. Use Extrude with good judgment. Use it when you're in a design rut and need that certain something to perk up a piece, and don't let yourself get branded as the Extrude King or Queen (it even *sounds* rude!).

As a bonus for completing this chapter, you can download "Extrude examples.cdr," a page of novel uses in a design assignment for the Extrude effect. The text has been converted to curves, and the effects are live in this document, so you can use the Copy Extrude From command to sample and apply any of these effects to objects you've drawn.

DOWNLOAD

In Figure 25-12 you can see the file, and an explanation of what was done and why will give you some ideas of your own based on the principles behind the novel use of the effect.

■ The Artistic Text spelling out "DRAMATIC" is not a "straight" extrude, but instead it was created by extruding the first character and then rotating it. Then the Extrude effect was copied to every other character via the Copy Extrude From button on the Property Bar. Finally, the Rotation pop-up was used in Numerical Value mode to rotate the characters progressively by about 10° difference to create an arc of text instead of a somewhat flat and planar treatment of this flashy headline.

FIGURE 25-12 Four examples of strange and inspired use of the Interactive Extrude Tool

- The suntan lotion bottle takes advantage of the fact that an extrude doesn't have to face forward; the *side* of the rounded rectangle is exposed to view to represent the bottle, a circle was extruded to make the cap, and similarly, you see the extrude group edge more than you do the control object circle. When you extrude something, you're dealing with a 3D object, and it's up to you, the artist, to decide which side of the 3D shape is the most visually interesting. The label on the bottle was created by using the Perspective effect, covered in Chapter 24.

- The little tin-roof hut is another example of using the extruded sides instead of the face of the extrude to convey an artistic idea. The roof is a squiggle created with the Bézier Pen Tool, and then the outline was converted to a shape (CTRL+SHIFT+Q) to extrude (you can't really extrude open paths). The shed itself is a compound shape, and the chimney is an extruded circle, rotated along its X axis so it's almost at a 90° angle to the roof.

- The glass cubes were made from extruded rectangles, but they were then simplified (CTRL+K), and the three faces hidden by the original extrude were drawn in by hand (using Snap To Objects for precision). The Extrude effect does not create back-facing facets. Then transparency was applied in Linear style, at different amounts to allow the back faces to show in certain areas and remain hidden in others.

The real lesson here is that the Extrude effect can sometimes be a jumping-in point for an idea, and not necessarily the finished product. When you break the extrude group from the control object, you're free then to manually edit all the objects to arrive at *exactly* the design you had in mind.

This concludes Part VII of your adventures, but obviously you still have some pages remaining under your right thumb. You're going to get up to your knees in pixels in the next few chapters; no, not those crunchy gherkin things—we're talking *digital photography*, retouching, color correction, all the stuff you'd expect was only possible in a paint program. But you can do extensive image editing and some pretty amazing photographic special effects *right within CorelDRAW,* as you'll shortly witness for yourself.

PART VIII

Thinking Outside the (Tool)Box

CHAPTER 26

Bitmap Boot Camp: Working with Photographs

A time will come when you'll want to set aside the Bézier Pen Tool and the Fountain fill—your layout for a brochure, for example, is all done, and now you want to add a photograph of your product—front page and center. The good news is that CorelDRAW can import just about any bitmap file from your camera, a scan of a photo, a painting you created in PHOTO-PAINT, an image you snagged of your client's website—you name it, and you can crop, rotate, and perform enhancements on it right within CorelDRAW. This chapter takes you through the structure of pixel-based images (AKA "bitmaps"): how you can get them to print well, what you can and cannot do with them, special properties, and the difference between this type of graphic and the one you're more accustomed to, vector artwork. Then you'll work with some photographed and created bitmap images to learn how to do some basic—and some fairly advanced—image editing and enhancing.

Putting a photo into a CorelDRAW document isn't very rewarding unless it's a really *good* photo, and you feel confident it will print well. This chapter delivers the goods on the whats, whys, and whens for bitmap importing, finessing, and integration to make your documents come alive and communicate.

The Properties of a Pixel-Based Image

Many of us take the structure of a pixel-based image for granted, without a lot of concern over its structure. We take a photograph with our megapixel camera, we copy the image to hard disk as a JPEG, we email it, and that's the end of the story.

However, if you want to *do* something with a digital image, such as incorporate it into a flyer, crop it, resize it, or put something else into it within a CorelDRAW composition, this is only the *beginning* of the story of pixel-based images and their manipulation. Without a cursory understanding of how pixel-based images are structured, you won't be able to successfully do as many things as you'd like to with them in CorelDRAW. Therefore, the following sections dig a little into what goes into a pixel-based image, so you can get more out of them as covered in the rest of this chapter.

Pixel Artwork vs. Vector Artwork

Although there are two fundamentally different types of graphics you can work with on a personal computer—vector graphics and pixel graphics—actually 100 percent of what you see onscreen is a *pixel-based graphic.* Your computer monitor has no easy way to display vectors as vectors, so even when you work with paths in CorelDRAW, what you're seeing onscreen is a pixel-based representation that CorelDRAW draws to your screen on-the-fly. This truth is not presented to confuse you, but rather to get you thinking more about pixels as an art form and as a tool.

Vector artwork, the kind of art you create in CorelDRAW, is *resolution independent,* a term you'll hear a lot, particularly if you're around programmers. Resolution independent means that the art you create in CorelDRAW can be scaled up and down, rotated and distorted every which way, and it still retains focus and its structural integrity. Vector artwork can be boiled

Artifacts and Anti-Aliasing

It's possible to take resolution-dependent bitmap images and make them larger, artificially increasing the size (and the saved file size) of the final image. However, you can't do this directly in CorelDRAW by dragging a selection handle, and you probably shouldn't once you discover the way. When a computer application is commanded to add pixels to an image, it has no real way of telling what color pixels should be added to the photograph. Not CorelDRAW, not Adobe Photoshop, no application except those lame forensic computers you see on TV can intelligently, artistically, or accurately add, for example, detail to a photo of a mailbox so the address instantly becomes crisp and legible.

What you get when you perform any "make this photo larger" command is "fake resolution"; the program averages pixel colors neighboring the original pixels to create more, similarly colored pixels. This can often lead to *artifacting,* what we commonly describe as "there's some junk in the upper left of this photo near my aunt's face." Artifacting can be introduced to a digital photograph at any stage of photography: your camera didn't write the file correctly, the image became corrupted when you copied it to your hard drive, and/or you tried to enlarge a resolution-dependent image. The cure for the last reason here is, don't resample important images; instead, print a copy of the image at its original size and see how it looks. From there, increase its size, check for visible artifacts in your print, and if there's visible corruption, go back to your original or seriously consider reshooting the image.

One of the methods CorelDRAW, PHOTO-PAINT, and other programs that can import bitmaps use to lessen and occasionally eliminate visible artifacting from resampling a photo is called *anti-aliasing,* and you have some control over this method, discussed later in this chapter. Anti-aliasing is a math calculation that performs averaging in a resulting photo that's been altered in areas where there is visual ambiguity (some of the pesky pixels are traveling under an alias). For example, suppose you could photograph a checkerboard plane that extends from your feet way out to the horizon. You look down toward your feet and clearly see black squares and white squares. You look at the horizon, and you do not see clear edges of the black and white squares: actually you'll see a lot of gray, as your mind blends black and white together because your eyes don't have photoreceptors fine enough to resolve the very distant black and white squares. Similarly, our computers cannot reconcile black and white areas in a digital image that are smaller than the size of the pixels in the image, so when you resample the image, they create—inaccurately—little black and white squares where they shouldn't be. The inaccuracy means the black and white squares are traveling as an *alias* and presenting themselves falsely.

(Continued)

Anti-aliasing comes to the designer's rescue by *averaging* pixel colors when you resample such a checkerboard photo, or any photo. The anti-aliasing technique examines, in this example, areas that include both a white square and a black one, understands that both colors can't be assigned to only one pixel, and so writes a blend of colors—gray—to the new pixel color value. At left in this illustration, you can see some unwanted patterning toward the horizon—this image was not anti-aliased when it was resampled to produce a larger image. At right, the same image was resampled using anti-aliasing; at 1:1 viewing, you can see the smooth transition as the checkerboard extends into the distance—and the close-up shows the result of good anti-aliasing (some applications anti-alias poorly)—gray is substituted for black and white when it's a toss up for a single pixel color.

Aliased image   Anti-aliased image

down to a direction a path travels in, the width of its outline, its fill color—regardless of how complex you make a drawing, it can be explained and saved to file in math terms. And because math can be divided and multiplied without discarding the values you put into an equation, you understand that scaling a vector drawing doesn't change its core values. $150 \times 2 = 300$, for example, is an equation that results in twice the 150 value, but the 150 value isn't really altered to produce a result of 300.

Pixel-based graphics, on the other hand, are *resolution dependent.* This means that a finite number of pixels goes into what you see onscreen, and it cannot be increased or decreased without making a visible, fundamental change to the structure of such a graphic. Pixel-based images are fragile compared with vector artwork; until you understand the term *resolution,* it's quite possible to irrevocably damage a pixel-based image, throwing it out of focus or adding artifacting (explained in a moment). However, the positives of pixel images outweigh the negatives: while it's very easy to take a snapshot, it's quite hard to draw (using vectors) something that looks exactly like a photograph. Pixel-based images can have depth of field, exposure, a source of scene lighting, and other properties; although many talented artists have created CorelDRAW pieces that look almost like a photograph, many of us cannot invest the time and talent to "make photographs" using CorelDRAW. Fortunately, this chapter shows you the easy way to make your CorelDRAW more photographic in nature: you just import a photograph!

Bytemaps and Pixels

Programmers and users alike are accustomed to calling a pixel-based image a *bitmap.* However, the term "bitmap" is a little like the term "dial phone." Telephones haven't had dials in nearly two decades, and similarly, a bitmap—literally a map of bits of information—is inadequate to describe a pixel-based image, but "bitmap" is used as the term for non-vector graphics in this chapter anyway. We're comfortable with the term, the term is described in the next paragraph, and "bitmap" is shorter to write than "pixel-based image"!

Let's say you have onscreen a JPEG fresh off your camera. What are you seeing? Of course, you're probably seeing a friend or relative, but what you're *really* seeing is a finite number of placeholders for color—the number of placeholders for color is so large that your mind integrates the placeholders into a familiar image. That's the "map" part of the term "bitmap"; this map could also be called a "mesh," a "grid," or a "canvas." All the bitmap images you take with a camera or paint in a paint program are composed of information units all lined up in a grid. You don't *see* the grid (or the *map* part of a bitmap); it's only a figurative thing, intangible—it's the *structure* for the visual information. The finer the grid, the less likely you are to see the individual color elements, instead of your mind blending the elements into a photograph. The "bit" part of the term "bitmap" is actually a *byte* of color information: a bit of information can only have two possible values (usually on or off); the graphics that artists work with today have a byte (8 bits) of information per color channel with which to express a color value. The term bitmap was coined in the days when a monitor could truly only display a color or no color; thus the term bitmap, and the term has stuck with us for more than 30 years.

To extend this explanation further, this unit of information lodged in a map is called a *pixel,* short for *pic*ture *el*ement, the smallest unit of color you can see in a bitmap image. A pixel is only *a placeholder for a color value*; it is *not* a unit of measurement, and it doesn't even have to be square (digital movie cameras take rectangular-proportioned movie pixels), and it has no fixed size. Other things a pixel is *not* include:

- **A dot**   Occasionally even professionals will lapse into describing the resolution of a digital image in dots per inch. This is okay if they're using the term "dot" as slang to mean a pixel, but this is confusing jargon. Printers print dots of toner and other pigment onto a surface (usually paper); a 1,200 dpi printer, for example, renders 1,200 dots of toner per inch of paper, but it is not rendering 1,200 pixels per inch of toner! In fact, a 1,200 dpi laser printer is incapable of rendering 1,200 pixels per inch (ppi). A pixel is *not* a dot of toner or ink, nor is a dot of ink equal to a pixel—pixels alone have no size.

- **A screen phosphor or LED**   Pixels that make up an image do not correspond 1:1 to whatever the elements on your monitor are made of. With high-quality images, there are many more pixels per inch than there are light units (phosphors, LEDs, and so on) on your screen. This is why CorelDRAW and paint programs such as PHOTO-PAINT and Adobe Photoshop offer zoom tools, so you can get a better look at image areas, mapping small amounts of pixels to your screen, which has a finite number of light-emitting elements. As resolution is discussed later in this chapter, it's good to know that the most frequently used resolution for web graphics is 72 ppi (pixels per inch). Therefore, if the resolution of an image is also 72 ppi, this means that when you view it at 100 percent viewing resolution, what your screen's light-emitting elements are mapping corresponds 1:1 to the image resolution. This means you're viewing a bitmap graphic exactly as the creator of the bitmap intended it.

■ **Any sort of ratio** The measurement we commonly use in bitmap evaluation is pixels per inch, which is a ratio, like mph is a ratio—miles (one unit) per hour (a different unit). A pixel is a unit, but not a ratio, and therefore if someone says they have an image that's 640 by 480 pixels, they've told you how many pixels are in the image, but not its resolution and not its size. A pixel is a unit, and needs to be contextualized—for example, 120 pixels per inch, or 300 pixels per centimeter—before the unit becomes meaningful and useful to a printer or designer. If you told friends you were driving your car down the Autobahn at "200 miles," they probably wouldn't be impressed because you haven't contextualized this unit into something meaningful such as a measurement. But "200 miles per hour" tells your friends something—that they probably don't want to ride with you!

Color Depth

In addition to being color value placeholders, pixels also have "depth," not "depth" as we'd measure a swimming pool, but rather a color "density." For example, GIF images have a maximum color depth of 256 unique values; grayscale images have a brightness depth of 256 shades.

Because 256 unique colors can't truly express the beauty we capture with a digital camera (even dull scenes can contain tens of thousands of unique colors), programmers decided early on in the digital imaging game to structure high-quality images into components, the most common structure being red, green, and blue, like your computer monitor is based on the RGB color model. We usually call these three components *color channels*: by adding the brightness values of these three channels together, we get the composite view of digital photos and other bitmaps. Channels are a very efficient method for storing bitmap color information—in contrast, GIF images store image colors as explicit color table values, and this is one of the reasons why GIF images are limited to 256 unique colors. By assigning the red, green, and blue color channels in a bitmap image an 8-bit per channel color capability, this equals 2^8, meaning the red, green, and blue channels can each have one of 256 possible brightness values with which to contribute color to the RGB composite image. Eight bits per channel times three color channels adds up to 24-bit images—BMP, PNG, TIFF, TGA (Targa), and Photoshop PSD being the most common file formats that can hold this color information. So, 24-bit images have a maximum unique color capability of 16.7 million colors.

However, color depth doesn't stop at 24-bit (8 bits per channel); although monitors today can only display 24-bit image depth, the camera manufacturers anticipate that this will change soon, with the advent of high dynamic range (HDR) displays and higher-definition monitors. Today, many of the middle-range digital cameras can write photos to the Raw file format, whose specifics vary from manufacturer to manufacturer as do the file extensions, but happily CorelDRAW can import most digital camera Raw files. Raw files (as covered later in this chapter) are "unprocessed film": they contain exposure settings, f-stops, and other camera data, but they also provide a lot of flexibility and leeway when you import such an image. CorelDRAW has a little utility called Camera Raw Lab where you can color-correct, change image exposure—all after the photo was taken. You can do this because Raw images can contain 16 bits per color channel, to offer a 48-bit image—more than 281 trillion possible colors…indeed this would require a very large crayon box.

Consider it a given that because CorelDRAW can handle such mega-information and has some very good processing tools for imported bitmap images, the compositions you create using bitmaps along with vector designs will print splendidly. Now it's time to discuss image resolution as it relates to outputting your work.

Resolution and Resolution-Dependent Images

As mentioned earlier, resolution is expressed as a fraction, a ratio between units (pixels) and space (inches, usually). As you'll see later in Table 26-1, a few image file types such as PSD and TIFF can store image resolution information, and this is good. For example, let's say you need to inkjet-print a brochure, and the front page needs a photograph. A photograph of insufficient resolution is going to print lousily, pure and simple. However, if the photographer saved the digital photo to PSD, TIFF, PNG, or Raw camera file format (and knows about image resolution), you can import the image and know before you print whether the image needs to be resized or not (resizing is covered later in this chapter). The rule is that an image's resolution should be in the neighborhood of your printer's resolution. Therefore, let's say that you've imported a photo and you know (by looking at the Bitmap page of Object Properties, covered in detail later in this chapter) that it's 4" wide, 3" tall, and 250 pixels per inch in resolution. Your next move is to check the printer manufacturer's documentation: although manufacturers tend to tap dance around specific printer resolutions, a good working guide is that an inkjet prints about one-third of the stated overall resolution on the box. If the box says the inkjet is a "720 dpi enhanced resolution," disregard the hype about "enhanced" and cut to the chase: a 720 dpi (dots per inch, not pixels per inch) inkjet can render about 240 pixels per inch. Therefore in this example, you can indeed faithfully print this 4×3" image with no loss in image detail.

There is a way to tell the resolution of image file formats that cannot hold resolution information, so don't worry if you have a bunch of JPEG images you want to use in a composition you need to inkjet-print. As you progress through this chapter, working tutorial files will demonstrate what you want to do and when.

Resolution vs. Image Size

Another digital-image reality that makes many designers pull their hair out is that image resolution is inversely proportional to dimensions: this is another cold and hard fact about bitmap resolution. When you make an image larger in dimensions, its resolution decreases. Now, viewing resolution and image resolution display the same thing onscreen, but changing *viewing resolution*—zooming in and out of an image—is nondestructive, whereas changing *image resolution* is destructive editing and often irreversible. Here's an example that

32×32-pixel icon
viewed at 1:1,
72 ppi resolution

32×32-pixel icon
viewed at 10:1,
7.2 ppi resolution

32×32-pixel icon
viewed at 20:1.
Pixels are clearly visible

FIGURE 26-1 With resolution-dependent bitmaps, the larger the image, the fewer pixels
per inch.

demonstrates the resolution-dependence properties of bitmaps. Figure 26-1 shows a desktop
icon; it's 32×32 pixels, and the largely adopted resolution convention is that screen pixels
are 72 per inch. At 1:1 viewing resolution, this icon looks fine, but when you zoom into it
to 10:1 viewing resolution, it begins to look coarse. The same thing would be visible if you
actually were to change the resolution of the image. Bitmap images are resolution dependent;
the pixels you capture of a scene with a camera can't be added to later to increase detail—no
application can guess what the extra detail and extra pixels would be. In Figure 26-1 you can
see an extreme enlargement of the icon, and the pixels are so clearly visible that you can't
make out what the design is!

The lesson here is that to take advantage of the unique property of bitmap images—
that they accurately portray a photographic scene—you need to take a photo that is high
resolution—3,264 pixels × 2,448 pixels is average for an 8-megapixel camera, a little larger
than 10×8 at 300 ppi. CorelDRAW can resize an image; for example, this same 8-megapixel
image could also be expressed as 20 × 15 at 163 ppi without changing any visual information.
CorelDRAW can also resample an image, and this is the destructive type of editing; you
change pixels when you resample, so generally it's a good idea to resize and only resample
as a last resort when adding photos to a CorelDRAW composition.

Importing Bitmaps into a Document

As a CorelDRAW user, you have at your fingertips a vast collection of bitmap import filter
selections. Although import commands are discussed in Chapter 3, some of the import options
apply specifically to bitmaps and are explained here; you'll definitely find them useful if your
work requires photographs and graphics from the Web. Table 26-1 does not list the bitmap types
CorelDRAW can import the way that the Files Of Type drop-down list does in the Import dialog.
Although it's terrific to have a billion different file types available for import, particularly if you

Bitmap Type	File Extension
Adobe Photoshop	PSD*
JPEG and JPEG 2000 bitmaps	JPG, JP2, JFF, and JTF
Adobe Portable Document File	PDF
TIFF bitmap	TIF*
Portable Network Graphic	PNG*
Targa bitmap	TGA
Raw image file format	CRW, CR2 (Canon); MRW (Minolta); NEF (Nikon); ORF (Olympus); DNG (Adobe); PTX (Pentax); ARW, SRF, SR2 (Sony)
Corel PHOTO-PAINT	CPT
CompuServe bitmap	GIF
GIF Animation	GIF
Windows bitmap	BMP
Kodak PhotoCD bitmap	PCD*
Painter 5/6	RIFF
Frame Vector Metafile	FMV
WordPerfect graphic bitmap	WPG
Corel (and Micrografx) Picture Publisher	PPF, PP4, and PP5
Kodak FlashPix Image	FPX
Lotus Pic	PIC
Macintosh PICT	PCT
MACPaint bitmap	MAC
OS/2 bitmap	BMP
PC Paintbrush bitmap	PCX
Scitex CT bitmap	SCT, CT
Wavelet Compressed bitmap	WVL
Windows bitmap	DIB/RLE
Computer graphics metafile	CGM
CALS compressed bitmap	CAL

TABLE 26-1   CorelDRAW X4's Importable Bitmap Formats

26

have legacy file formats, you'll probably only use a handful of image types in everyday work. Therefore, the table lists the most common file types first; more exotic and legacy file formats appear toward the bottom of this table. The asterisk after the file extension indicates that a file type can retain resolution information; this is a capability—it doesn't necessarily mean the person who saved the file actually saved resolution information.

Importing a bitmap is a straightforward operation; more experienced users know that you can simply drag and drop an image file from a folder window into CorelDRAW's drawing window, but let's review the dialog box process first. Choose File | Import (CTRL+I) or click the Import button in the Standard Toolbar to open the Import dialog (see Figure 26-2).

Choose your bitmap format from the Files Of Type menu. By default, the Import dialog is set to import the Full Image. If the cropping and resolution of the image you're importing are needed, choose the option from the selector list, and then click the Import button to proceed with the operation.

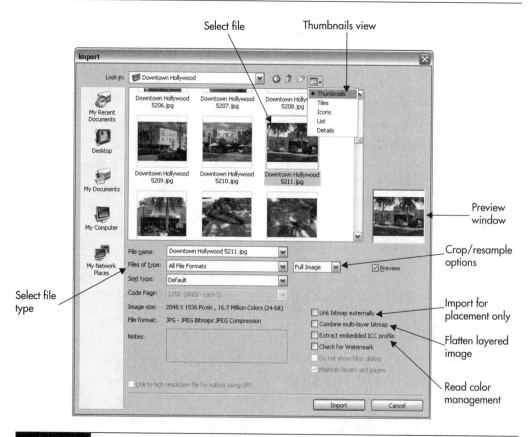

FIGURE 26-2   The Import dialog lets you choose to crop before importing, and other options can help you flatten layered images and retain color profiles.

Here you can see what appears onscreen after you've chosen Crop from the Import selector list and then click Import; you have selection handles that you create a crop area with, and you click-drag inside the crop area to reposition the crop. You can also use the numeric entry fields to specify a precise crop area; however, there's an easy manual way to refine a cropped image after it's been placed on a page. Note that when you import, you import a copy of the original file, and when you crop, there is no way to un-crop the placed image later.

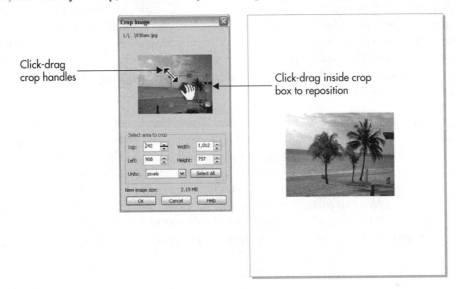

Click-drag crop handles

Click-drag inside crop box to reposition

26

As mentioned earlier, it's not a good idea to resample an imported image so it's larger than the original, but scaling it so it's smaller usually works just fine. It's easier for an application to discard pixels than for it to think up additional ones. If you choose Resample from the drop-down selector and then click Import after selecting an image, you'll get the following dialog. Note that in this illustration the imported file size is smaller than the original; the image is to be resampled down (not up), and life is good.

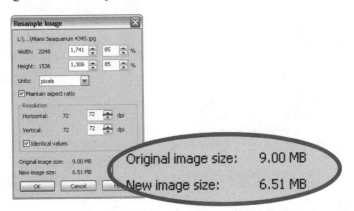

After the Import dialog closes, your cursor will change to an import cursor that has two functions: with it you specify the upper-left corner of your new bitmap using a single-click, which in turn imports the image onto a document page at its original size—whatever dimensions by whatever resolution. Pressing ENTER instead of using a mouse click imports the image to the center of the page.

You can also specify a proportional width and depth for the imported image using a diagonal click-drag action. After you specify the size this way, the bitmap is imported and automatically resized to closely fit the defined area with the original proportions of the bitmap preserved. As you drag, the cursor inverts and a preview of the image's bounding box appears, showing the space the new image will occupy, as shown in Figure 26-3. While importing during either operation, the original filename and the image dimensions are displayed beside the cursor.

 Bitmap images can't be edited at the pixel level directly in CorelDRAW. For example, if your cousin Flossie's mascara is a little runny in the photo, this is an isolated photo problem area, and you need to use a bitmap editing application to make the makeup look better. Not to worry, Flossie: you can open Corel PHOTO-PAINT X4 by clicking the Edit Bitmap button on the Property Bar or by right-clicking the bitmap and then choosing to edit it from the context menu. Naturally, you need to know how to use PHOTO-PAINT's tools, but there are several good books out there on image editing; image retouching is not within the scope of this book. After editing, you will return to

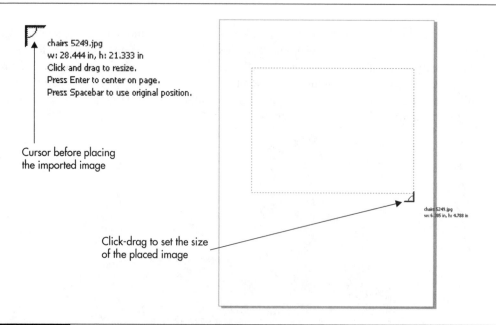

FIGURE 26-3   Click-dragging the Import cursor defines a size for your imported file.

CorelDRAW X4 when you click Corel PHOTO-PAINT's Finish Editing button on its Property Bar. However, as you'll soon see, you can do just about anything else in CorelDRAW with bitmaps, including special effects filtering, overall color and tone corrections, rotations, resizing, and custom cropping.

This illustration shows the drag-and-drop method for importing images. CorelDRAW examines the type of bitmap; naturally when you use this method, cropping and other Import dialog features are overridden.

Other Import Dialog Options

On the right side of the Import dialog (shown in Figure 26-2) are options you might not use on a daily basis, but it's good to know what they do!

- **Link Bitmap Externally** If you want to position an image and keep the saved CDR file size small, you can choose to create a link to the file instead of actually placing a copy in your design. The disadvantages to doing this are that the original image could be edited by someone else, thus potentially spoiling your CorelDRAW design, and that occasionally people misplace images, which breaks the link in the CorelDRAW document so the image will not display in your work. Also, if you choose the external link option, you cannot resample or crop the image before importing it—but you can manually crop the placed copy of the photo using the Shape Tool (discussed later in this chapter).

- **Combine Multi-layer Bitmap**   This option flattens special image types that contain layers. PHOTO-PAINT and Adobe Photoshop (among other programs) can write a file that has image layers, just as you can create layers in a CorelDRAW composition. Choosing this option makes this special image type into a "normal" image, such as a JPEG photo from your camera.

- **Extract Embedded ICC Profile**   Your copy of Windows has color management profiles in Windows\System32\spool\drivers\color and CorelDRAW, and other applications use these color profiles (they have the .ICC file extension) when applications embed this information in a bitmap image file to tell other applications and your printer how to display and render the image: brightness, how much contrast, how broad a color range, and other aspects of the image. ICC profiles help ensure color consistency from the screen to the application to the printer. To save and use this color management information, check this option's box before you click Import.

- **Check For Watermark**   This is a copyright-holder insurance feature. You check this option if there's any doubt about the legal rights to use the image; there are utilities available for putting a visible—and often invisible—watermark on digital images. The most common watermark is Digimarc, a service available to use in CorelDRAW (at an additional fee), which adds subtle noise to an image as a method for placing a watermark. Metadata is also written into the header of the file (which is not visible in the image), and a copyright symbol will appear to the left of a filename on its title bar when a watermarked image is imported.

Working with Raw Images

Camera Raw is the next generation of high-fidelity imaging; it's affordable, most cameras you *don't* buy at a drugstore can write a Raw file format, and as with any comparatively new technology, there's a small learning curve we'll tackle in this section.

A Raw image is similar to an unprocessed physical piece of camera film; although it contains a lot of data about exposure, light temperature, f-stop, lens, and other conditions, the Raw image does *not* have locked data about pixel colors. Raw offers the ultimate in flexibility—if the light was too low or the wrong temperature, you can adjust for these and other flaws through CorelDRAW's Camera Raw Lab. The Camera Raw Lab appears after you choose to import a Raw camera image; a Raw image cannot be placed in a CorelDRAW composition before it passes through the Lab (even if you choose not to do anything to the image). Depending on your camera settings, you'll most likely be working with a 48-bit image, 16 bits per channel; this offers a color space of several trillion unique colors and is part of the reason why Raw images can be adjusted to make dramatic lighting changes while retaining high image fidelity.

Working with the Camera Raw Lab

Working with the Raw Lab in CorelDRAW is an experience you won't want to miss. If you don't have a Raw image handy or if your camera cannot take Raw file format images, you can download the example image of a historic factory.

Because no two manufacturers could agree on a file extension, a Raw image could have .CRW, .DNG, or scores of other extensions. The good news is that CorelDRAW doesn't care about the file extension—you just choose Raw-Camera RAW from the Files Of Type drop-down list in the Import dialog, and then navigate to the location of a Raw image, in the following example, Future factory.dng. The *better* news is that CorelDRAW can import Raw images from a *three-page list* of manufacturers—just short of photos on a View-Master reel, you're assured that CorelDRAW can import most Raw files.

Let's dig right into the features and options available to you when you import a Raw image; follow these steps and guidelines to import the image, and then perform minor processing enhancements. There's nothing truly wrong with the image, but this tutorial is instead an opportunity to gain hands-on experience with the Camera Raw Lab features.

Raw Image Color Correction

1. Choose File | Import, or click the Import button on the Property Bar.

2. Choose All File Formats from the Files Of Type drop-down list, and then choose Future factory.dng from the folder you downloaded the file to. Now you need to tell CorelDRAW's import filter that the image you chose is a Raw file; choose Raw-Camera Raw now from the Files Of Type box. Click Import or press ENTER.

3. The Camera Raw Lab interface appears. The very first thing to do is to check the properties of this unprocessed photograph. The Properties tab of the interface tells the day and date of the photo, the camera, whether or not flash was used, aperture, and ISO-equivalent film speed. If you're familiar at all with cameras, the info shown here will give you a clue to what, if anything, needs adjusting in the image. For example, at ISO 50 at an f-stop of 4.0, the image probably doesn't require sharpening—the depth of field looks good and the Properties tab confirms this. Also, because a flash wasn't used, when you get to the Color tab, you can rule out Flash as a choice from the White Balance options.

4. The Detail tab has a slider for sharpening the image as well as sliders for reducing Luminance Noise and overall Color Noise. This photo doesn't require these enhancements. The Hints area at the bottom of the tab is a handy context-sensitive reminder of what each slider does, and before you take your next Raw image, it's good practice to "get it right in the camera." You'll get less noise in a photo generally if you set your camera to slower ISO speeds. The ISO of 50 in this example image produced very little visible noise (similar to grain in traditional physical film), but an ISO setting of say, 400, for the camera that took this photo would indeed have required noise reduction using the Detail sliders.

5. Click the Color tab; here's where the fun begins. Follow the callout letters in Figure 26-4 to guide you through which features do what.

   ■ The *A* area is for rotating the Raw image before placing the copy into your CorelDRAW document. Raw camera data can also include portrait and landscape orientation, so you might never need to use these buttons if your camera saved orientation info.

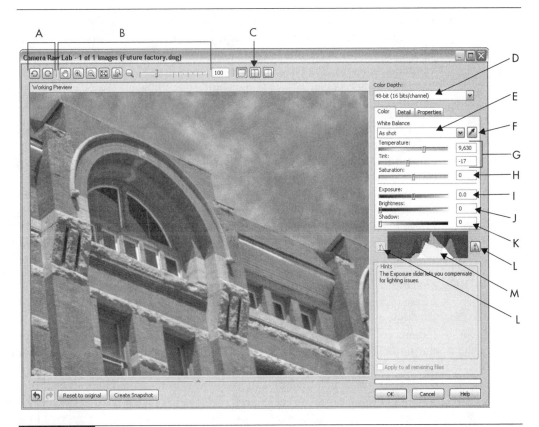

FIGURE 26-4   Use the Raw Lab to color- and tone-correct high-quality digital images.

■ *B* marks your navigation tools for previewing the image. From left to right you have tools for panning the window (you click-drag when your cursor is inside the preview window), zoom in and out, Fit To Window, 100 percent (1:1) viewing resolution, and finally a slider to zoom your current view in and out.

■ *C* marks the split pane view (shown in the previous illustration) so you can compare the original image to any corrections you make.

■ *D* marks the Color Depth. You'd be ill-advised to change this from 48-bit, because only a high-depth image can be adjusted extensively without taking on banding and color clipping (explained shortly). The only reason you'd choose 24-bit from the selector list is if the image were flawless and you wanted to get down to work by placing it in your document and saving space on your hard disk.

- *E* marks the White Balance selector. You have many choices that influence the color casting of the Raw image. Ideally, you want the placed image to be casting neutral; the grays in the image contain no hues, and the photo looks neither too warm nor too cold. You have selections such as Tungsten, Cloudy, and other lighting conditions that influence the color cast of images. "As Shot" is the default setting, and this image appears to be fine As Shot.

- *F* is the White Balance eyedropper tool, used to define a completely neutral area in the preview window to better set and possibly neutralize color casting. The cursor for this tool gives you an RGB readout of the current area in the preview photo; this is the true color over a pixel, and not the "ideally neutral color." You click over an area you believe *should* contain equal amounts of red, green, and blue components (R:64, G:64, B:64, for example), and this action remaps the image to reflect the color casting in the image based on where you clicked. Although it's a useful tool, you might not have a photo that contains a perfectly white or a perfectly neutral gray area; if this is the case, don't use this tool.

- *G* marks color Temperature and Tint, perhaps the least intuitive of Raw digital image properties. The values in the Raw Lab's color Temperature controls run from low at the left of the slider (cools down warm images) to high at right (warms cool images). The temperature controls, specifically values you enter in the numeric field, are *not* degrees of Kelvin; they are correction values only for you to refer to and compare with other settings and other images. However, it *is* correct to *think* of color temperature in general as measured in degrees Kelvin. You might want to "uncorrect" a perfect image to make it warmer or colder: try setting the color Temperature for this image to 10,000 to warm the sky a little and to accentuate the brick red of the building. The Tint slider is the color complement of the color Temperature control; a neutral temperature displays a band on the Tint slider from magenta at left to green at right. You always use Tint after you've set Temperature because Tint varies according to temperature.

- *H* is the Saturation control, which is mostly self-explanatory—it's used to compensate for dull photographs (you increase Saturation) or for overly colorful images (you de-saturate by dragging to the left with the slider).

- *I* marks the Exposure control. Exposure is not the same as, for example, the brightness/contrast controls on a TV set or the Levels command in image editing applications. Exposure is the *total light that falls on a scene,* and it's set when you take a picture by setting the ISO value. Therefore, it's always a good idea to double-check the info in the Properties tab: if the ISO is a low value and the picture looks dark or muddy, then Exposure is probably the Color option that needs adjusting.

■ *J* marks Brightness, which you should play with only after setting the best Exposure. If you drag Brightness to the right with this image, you'll see that the upper ranges of the image become brighter, but not the shadow areas. So you use this slider to bring out detail in the midranges in an image without ruining the deeper tones.

■ *K* is the Shadows slider, and this option is used only to make deeper areas more pronounced without affecting the midtones and highlights. Shadows might also be called "contrast"; dragging the slider to the right does indeed create a difference between the lighter and darker areas of the overall image.

■ *L* marks both the Shadow and Highlights clipping regions. These two buttons that frame the histogram (*M*) will display a bright red color overlay in the preview window in areas where the brightest brights have fallen out of range (they can't be accurately displayed onscreen, and they can't be accurately printed); and deepest shadows will display a green-tinted overlay. If you see a tint in areas, this means that the Shadows, the Exposure, or the Saturation adjustments you've made are too intense. The solution is to choose lesser values for any of these options until the tint disappears in the preview window.

■ *M* is the histogram of the current photograph. A *histogram* is a visual representation of how many pixels of what color are located at what brightness in the image. A well-toned image will have a lot of color pixels in the mid-region of the histogram—this is where the most visual detail is apparent in digital photographs. If the histogram shows too many pixels—for example, in the lower regions there's a hump in the histogram curve toward the left—it means your image needs less Shadow or more Exposure.

6. Once you've made your adjustments, you click OK, and you're then presented with a loaded cursor for placing and scaling the imported image, as discussed earlier in this chapter.

TIP *To import more than one digital image at a time, hold SHIFT while clicking to select contiguous files, or hold CTRL while clicking to select noncontiguous files in the Import dialog. For different file types, set the Files Of Type option to All File Formats. As multiple files are imported, the cursor indicates the file information for each image being placed.*

Integrating a Photograph into a Layout

In this section you'll take some of what you've learned in previous sections, combine it with some new techniques covered here, and the result will be a color-corrected photograph as the centerpiece of a travel brochure design. Most of the work has been done for you in Travel brochure.cdr; the steps you'll learn put it all together as a complete solution for your next brochure need. As far as the graphics go, it's simple stuff that's covered in Chapter 14 on text and Chapter 17 on object fills. All the text and graphics have been converted to curves—DF Ancestor, a Bitstream typeface, was used for the primitive drawings.

Working in the Image Adjustment Lab

For "normal" photographs—photos in JPEG, TIFF, and file formats other than Camera Raw, you have under the Bitmaps menu in CorelDRAW a fairly comprehensive Image Adjustment Lab to make practically every global adjustment (but not local pixel adjustments) you'll find in PHOTO-PAINT. This makes it very easy to photo-correct imported bitmaps and to integrate them into a composition without ever leaving CorelDRAW; better still, the features are almost identical to those in the Camera Raw Lab.

Let's work through a mock assignment: a 5×7" travel brochure has been created in Brochure.cdr for you to download along with Cabana 5106.jpg, the image for the cover of the brochure.

The following tutorial covers features in the Adjustment Lab, but it's only one of a three-part assignment, with image transformations covered after this tutorial, and finally a tutorial on how to export a completed design for use as a web graphic. Here's how to add a little more punch to an image.

DOWNLOAD

Adjusting a JPEG in the Lab

1. Open Travel brochure.cdr. Choose the Object Manager docker by choosing Window | Dockers | Object Manager. Click the "put the photo on this layer" title on the Object Docker to make it the current layer (the background and graphics layers are locked).

2. Choose File | Import (CTRL+I) and then choose Cabanas 5106.jpg from the location where you downloaded it. Click Import.

3. Your cursor is loaded with the image now, and it's much larger than the place for it within the layout, so you'll scale the image as you place it. First, click an insertion point to the lower right of the primitive couple dancing (about 10 o'clock in the design), and then while holding the left mouse button, drag down to about the "*a*" in "Mololai." You've scaled the image to more or less fit on the front cover, as shown in Figure 26-5. With the Pick Tool, move the image if it's not placed to suit your artistic eye.

4. Right-click over the image and then choose Properties. On the Object Properties docker, click the Bitmap tab (the far right button). Remember the discussion about image resolution? Let's suppose you were going to send this brochure out for commercial printing. As you'll see later in Chapter 28 (where printing specs are covered), commercial presses need images of 266 to 300 ppi for printing. As you

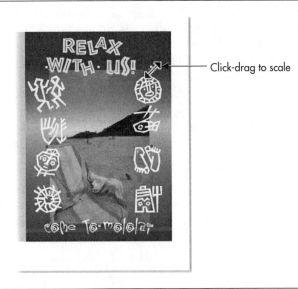

Click-drag to scale

FIGURE 26-5 Scale the imported image as you place it in the design.

can see here, the resolution of the image is higher than this, so you can rest assured that the brochure will print without artifacting or other problems. However, the photo is a little *duller* than it could be, as shown here.

5. With the photo selected, choose Bitmaps | Image Adjustment Lab.

6. In Figure 26-6 you'll see a lot of the same navigation controls as you did in the Camera Raw Lab. However, there are slightly different features for color and tone adjustments here. The dullness of this photo is due to poor tone distribution, not Saturation: always shoot for tone correction for exposure, and then work on the color if necessary. *A* marks Auto Adjust, a one-step routine that adds contrast to an image; let's skip this feature—automated routines don't give "one of" assignments the custom attention they need, and you don't learn anything from automated routines. *B* marks the White Point eyedropper tool, used to define in the preview window the lightest area that should be in the picture. Click in the center of a cloud in the image to see if the Lab adjusts the other tones and snaps up the image.

■ *C* marks the Black Point eyedropper, which redefines the darkest point in the image based on where you click in the preview window. Try clicking toward the base of the mountains, and see if this adds contrast to the image.

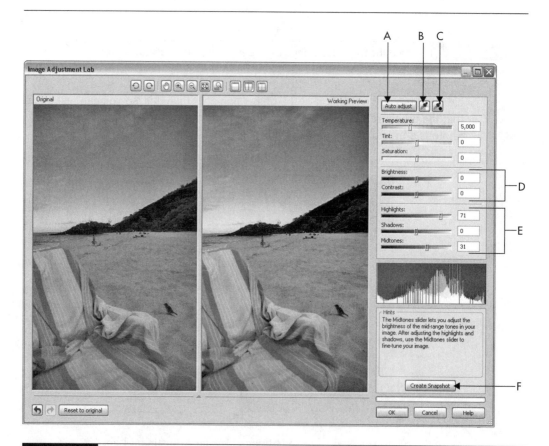

FIGURE 26-6   Color and tone correction can be performed on photographs with CorelDRAW.

- *D* marks the Brightness and Contrast sliders. They basically do what you'd expect; they're like the controls on a television set, but as with a TV set, brightness and contrast don't always make an image better. Skip these controls for this assignment.

- *E* marks the area the professionals use to snap up a photo: Drag the Highlights slider to about 71; this brightens the brighter areas in the image without affecting the midtones or shadow areas. Now drag the Midtones slider up to about 31 to open up darker regions to provide image detail without messing up the Shadows region, which is fine as is.

7. Finally, click the Create Snapshot button (*F*). This creates an entry on the Undo docker in case you want to reverse a correction after exiting the Lab. Also, within a single session of the Adjustment Lab, a Snapshot will appear at the lower left of the interface, and you can create several color corrections, save a snapshot, and then compare versions for the one you like the best. Click OK and your adjusted image is now placed in the layout.

Photo Transformations

If you need to do something dramatic to a photo, such as bowing the image so it looks as though a fish-eye lens was used, you have these options:

- Put an object over the photo, and then use Lens effects, covered in Chapter 22. You might not get exactly the effect you want with a Lens, and the advantage to this method is that the change isn't made directly to the photo—a Lens effect can be deleted at any time, restoring the normal appearance of objects beneath it.

- Use the effects such as Bitmaps | 3D Effects | Pinch/Punch. The whole gamut of effects found on the bottom of the Bitmaps menu is covered in Chapter 27.

Minor transformations such as moving, scaling, and rotating a photo are easy to accomplish by direct manipulation in CorelDRAW. However, skewing, perspective, and other dramatic alterations cannot be accomplished directly—CorelDRAW is a vector program, and it's amazing it can do the advanced stuff you're read about up to this point, but it's not a bitmap editing program.

Because this brochure has a light touch with the placement of the text and graphics—objects are rotated and sized as though a child composed the piece—it would be in keeping if the photograph were rotated a little, too. This is done exactly as you transform vector objects in CorelDRAW (see Chapter 8 for thorough documentation); follow these steps to put a spin on the placed, color-corrected photograph.

Rotating a Photograph in a CorelDRAW Composition

1. With the Pick Tool, click the photo to select it. You should see black square markers at the boundary of the photograph.

2. Click the photo again; you should see curved, double-arrow markers replace the square ones. This means the photo is in Rotation/Skew mode—but the center markers (at 12, 3, 6, and 9 o'clock) are skew handles. Although the border of the photo can be skewed, the visual content of the photo will remain the same, sort of like rotating a picture frame, but without the picture rotating. This is okay; the goal is to rotate the image, and this operation works in CorelDRAW.

3. Drag a corner handle left or right until the photo looks more integrated into the cover design, as shown in Figure 26-7; about 10° will do the trick. You can tell the degree of rotation on the Property Bar—a 10° clockwise rotation would make the Angle Of Rotation field read 350 before you release the mouse button.

Exporting Your Composition to Bitmap Format

One of the terrific things about designing using a computer application is that you can repurpose a good design. A good design such as the front cover of this travel brochure can yield several different uses from only one investment in time—and from knowing how to export the design.

Although CorelDRAW is a vector drawing program, it can create a bitmap copy of photographs, a bitmap from photos combined with vectors, and also it can export vector art only—text, graphics, anything is fair game. When vectors are copied out of CorelDRAW as bitmaps, a process called *rasterizing* is performed; CorelDRAW examines the vector artwork at the size and resolution you specify and then uses anti-aliasing (unless you specify no anti-aliasing) to create a bitmap that looks as good as what you see onscreen in your CorelDRAW document.

Let's say you want to feature the front cover of this brochure on your website. This narrows your export choices down to GIF, PNG, and JPEG (see Chapter 29 for more details on web content creation and exporting). PNG images are typically larger than a JPEG equivalent, so let's export only the front page, with the background, the color-corrected photo, and the overlaid text and graphics on the top layer, to a small JPEG image.

Click, click a second time, and then drag the rotation handle

FIGURE 26-7 You can scale, move, mirror, and rotate photographs in a composition.

Saving a Bitmap Copy of Your CorelDRAW Composition

1. CorelDRAW will write the JPEG to the dimensions of the outermost object, and you don't need the back cover (it hasn't been designed yet); unlock the background and the Text and glyphs layers by clicking the "no" symbol over the Pencil icon on the Object Manager for these two layers.

2. With the Pick Tool, marquee-select only the front cover objects by click-diagonal dragging over them. Start your selection outside of the objects, and release the mouse button at the opposing corner, outside of the objects. Objects by default aren't selected unless you select all of them. The Status Bar should tell you that 12 objects are selected across multiple layers.

3. Click the Export button on the Property Bar.

4. In the Export dialog, choose JPG-JPEG Bitmaps as the Save As Type from the drop-down list. Check the Selected Only check box, type a name in the File Name field, use the directory pane to choose a location for the export, and then click Export.

5. You want the Resolution of the image to be 72, the same as a monitor's resolution, so type this value in the Resolution field. A good web graphic, one that's legible and helps sell a product or service, should be at least 400 pixels measured by the greater of its dimensions, but probably not larger than 700 pixels in height, so the audience members don't have to scroll their browser window to see the complete image. Type **500** in the Height field. Maintain Aspect Ratio is checked by default; it's a good idea to leave it checked (images get distorted otherwise), and the width value decreases in proportion automatically. Check Anti-aliasing to keep the glyphs and headline smooth, and then if the dialog looks like this illustration, click OK, and you're on to the following (and last) dialog. Yes, the image in the design is going to be resampled, but as mentioned earlier, it's okay to make a large photo smaller—CorelDRAW has the resampling recipe down pat to create a small but crisp copy of the photograph.

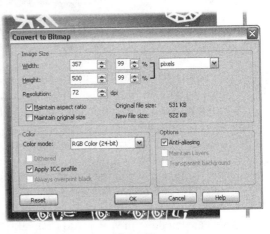

6. In the JPEG Export dialog, you can now set the compression amount for the exported bitmap. Click the Optimize check box to maximize the fidelity of the export while keeping the file size small. Usually, a 10:1 compression ratio keeps an exported image looking good as a JPEG while keeping the file size small. Small is

the name of the game on the Web, but JPEG compression discards original data, so too much compression yields a poor export for photographs. Choose 10 as the Compression value, and then click the Preview button.

7. Click-drag in the Original preview window to pan your view to different areas of the design. If certain areas of your own design export look like they're acquiring artifacting in the right Result preview pane, back off on the compression amount or increase the Smoothing slider just a little. Smoothing helps disguise JPEG artifacting, but at the price of losing image focus. Don't check Progressive—this option allows a dial-up connection audience to view your image on the Web as streaming data (it builds up as the image loads), but as you can see here, the estimated saved file size is less than 64K. A dial-up connection can usually download up to 55 kilobits per second; you divide that by 8 because the file is measured in bytes and not bits, and we're talking about 8 seconds for a dial-up to see the image. That's the worst-case scenario. Click OK and you're done!

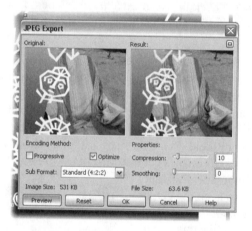

If you're feeling a little jazzed after reading this chapter, get a friend to pat you on your back, because you deserve it. You've taken a serious detour in your "CorelDRAW is a drawing program" education and vaulted right into the arena of design professionals who integrate photos and vector artwork on a daily basis. You now know how to scale an image, to check to see whether its resolution is sufficient to pull a good print, to color-correct both Raw images and regular ones, and how to export your work so friends you'd like to send an email attachment to can see it without necessarily owning CorelDRAW—and the composition is Web-worthy, to boot.

This is not the complete story of CorelDRAW and bitmaps. You'll want to do things as special as you do with vectors, so Chapter 27 is devoted to special effects, converting bitmap art to vector, and there's this little thing called *alpha channels* that there wasn't room to cover in this introductory chapter. Bitmaps can have transparent areas, so you can "float" a bitmap to create extraordinary and sophisticated compositions. Read on and see how to create exactly the effect you need for tomorrow's assignment at work.

CHAPTER 27

Image-ination: Advanced Photography Techniques

Because people seldom photograph an object or a scene that contains exactly the elements they want to feature in a composition, the field of retouching has thrived since the day a professional had something to sell using a photograph! This is why professionals trim photographs, and so can you, using the CorelDRAW features covered in this chapter. As objects, photographic areas that have been carefully cut out can be composited with other photos and vector shapes to add a whole new dimension to your posters, flyers, and fine art. Additionally in this chapter, Corel PowerTRACE, part of CorelDRAW, is demonstrated; you'll learn how to create a vector copy of a bitmap so you can scale and rotate it, edit it, and never lose details or resolution as bitmap images are prone to do.

This is fun, intriguing, advanced stuff; composite work is your next stop, and all the images you'll need to run through the tutorials can be downloaded.

Cropping a Placed Photograph

You can perform two types of cropping on placed photos: destructive (permanent) and nondestructive (you can undo what you've done). The Crop Tool on the Toolbox performs destructive cropping. Unless you press CTRL+Z to undo a crop you don't like, you're stuck with your crop, and no exterior areas to the image remain that you can expose later. Some users prefer this; you'll learn both methods in this section. To crop a photo involves several steps:

1. You define the area you want to crop by click-diagonal dragging the Crop Tool from one corner to the opposite corner.

2. You can redefine the crop by click-dragging the resulting bounding-box markers. The corner markers scale the proposed crop area proportionately, while the center markers are used to resize the proposed crop area disproportionately.

3. You can rotate the crop box, which is handy if you want an artistic crop or just want to straighten a horizon in the photo. To do this, you first click inside the image; doing this puts the crop area into Rotate mode. You then drag on a corner double-headed arrow marker to rotate the crop. This doesn't rotate the photo itself, but rather the crop area.

4. You double-click inside the crop area to finish the crop. Figure 27-1 shows the elements you work with onscreen to crop a bitmap image.

 To quickly see the resolution of a placed bitmap image, use the Bitmap tab on the Object Properties docker, displayed at any time by pressing ALT+ENTER. Because bitmap size varies inversely to image resolution, the Bitmap tab will not accurately report the absolute dimensions of a cropped bitmap, but the Details tab of this docker will.

 Download Miami Seaquarium 4417.jpg to use for some of the cropping experiments in this chapter.

Crop Tool

Scale crop box
disproportionately

Click-drag

Rotate crop box

Scale crop box
proportionately

FIGURE 27-1   The Crop Tool eliminates the exterior image areas of your defined crop area.

Nondestructive Cropping

In a nutshell, if you want to hide an area of a photo and not delete it as you do with the Crop Tool, you use the Shape Tool. Try this out with the Miami Seaquarium 4417.jpg image by following the steps in the informal tutorial coming up.

Using the Shape Tool to Crop

1. Create a new (default-sized) document with landscape orientation. Place the image of the Amazon Macaws in a new document by clicking the Import button on the Property Bar and then selecting the image from the location you downloaded it to. With the loaded cursor, click-diagonal drag to place the image so it fills most of the page.

2. Choose the Shape Tool. Notice that the photo, which is still selected, now has control node markers at each corner. These markers behave and operate exactly like control nodes for vector shapes.

3. Just for the fun of it, click a node to select it, and then drag it toward the center of the image. This is not what the pros call an "expert crop," but you've just learned something that will come in very handy in your future work. When you drag a node inside of the outside dimensions of a placed photo, the two sides that meet at this node hide areas of the photograph. Press CTRL+Z to undo this, and we'll now perform a more practical crop.

4. Click-drag so that you've marquee-selected two neighboring nodes; they can make up a horizontal or vertical edge of the photo. For this experiment it makes no difference.

5. Use the keyboard arrows to nudge the nodes toward the center of the image. Hold SHIFT to super-nudge the nodes if you like. This is how you can nondestructively crop a placed photo; nudge the nodes in the opposite direction now—you've hidden and then unhidden one dimension of the photograph.

6. With two nodes selected, hold CTRL and then drag the nodes toward the center of the photo. The CTRL key constrains movement so the edge you're cropping remains parallel to the dragging page.

Masking Through Nondestructive Cropping

Go to the head of the class if you've already figured out that you can *add* control nodes to a placed photograph with the Shape Tool! CorelDRAW "sees" a bitmap as an object that has a fill—specifically a bitmap fill. Therefore this object can be shaped and reshaped by adding nodes and also by changing the segment property between nodes. The following sections take you through some advanced bitmap editing to trim around a photograph so it becomes a floating object in a composition.

Trimming Away Unwanted Image Areas

What you'll learn in this section goes way beyond the simple cropping of an image. You're going to trim the background away from an image of a bust of classical composer Johann Sebastian Bach, put a new background behind the bust, and by the end of this section, you'll have designed a concert poster. There are two nondestructive methods for removing the background from a photo's subject, and both techniques are described in this section. The elements of the poster have already been created for you, and by working through the tutorials, you'll see how to make a design with elements in front of and behind each other, just like you do with vector shapes, but we're talking *photographs* here.

Download Concert poster.cdr, JS Bach.tif, and Bach 4 part Chorale.cdr to use in the following tutorials.

DOWNLOAD

To begin at the beginning of this poster design (call it an overture), you need to create a new document (portrait orientation, default page size) and then place the image of Bach—a little smaller than the page size, but he can be scaled at a later time when needed—to then use the Shape Tool to trim the background out.

Background Removal, Technique 1

1. Click the Import button on the Property Bar, and then in the Import dialog, locate JS Bach.tif, select him, and then click Import.

2. Your cursor is loaded with the image: click-drag, as shown in Figure 27-2, and then release the mouse when the cursor reports that the height for the placed image will be about 9 inches.

Click-diagonal drag to size and place

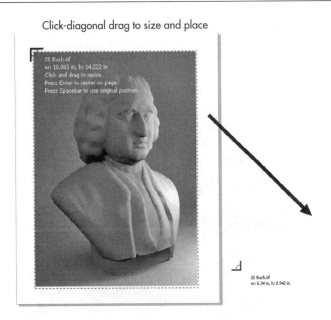

JS Bach.tif
w: 10.083 in, h: 14.222 in
Click and drag to resize.
Press Enter to center on page.
Press Spacebar to use original position.

JS Bach.tif
w: 6.34 in, h: 8.942 in

FIGURE 27-2   Scale and place the image by click-diagonal dragging your loaded cursor.

Click-drag

3. Choose the Shape Tool. Begin by clicking the top-right node of the image, and then click-drag it toward the center of the image until the top and right edges touch the bust of Bach, as shown here. Clearly, you're not going to get where you want to go with only four control nodes, because the geometry of the bust is far from perfectly rectangular. This is okay; you'll add nodes to the outline of the image in the following step.

4. With the Shape Tool, click a point on the outline of the photo where there should be a change in direction of the line; Bach's powdered wig near his forehead is a prime area. Now, either press the keyboard plus (+) key, or click the Add Node button on the Property Bar to add a node. While you're in the vicinity of Bach's forehead, several additional points will be needed. A quick way to add points in-between existing points is to repeatedly click a point and press the + key.

5. Click-drag points so they visually coincide with the vertices of Bach's wig. It's okay if the lines between the nodes hide areas you want exposed.

6. Click on a straight line segment that should curve away from the photo. Then click the To Curve button on the Property Bar. The segment can now curve; click-drag the segment away from the photo, as shown here, until you can see Bach's locks.

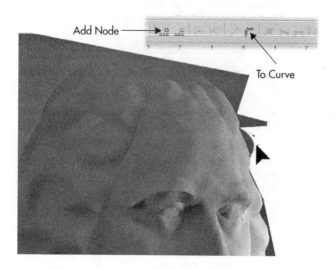

7. That's it; all it takes now is about a half hour of your time to work around the profile of the bust, hiding areas and creating curve segments where needed. Yes, it's a lot of work; so is putting on a tuxedo or gown to go and collect an industry award for outstanding design work (*prompt, hint, encouragement!*).

A good thing to do once you've trimmed away the non-essential Bach, because the default color of the page is white, is to put a colored vector shape behind your work to check your edge work. As you can see here, the example looks pretty good; a rectangle was created, filled, and then rotated, and then SHIFT+PAGE DOWN is pressed to put the rectangle to the back of the page's layer.

If you'd like to confirm the fact that the editing you performed is nondestructive, take the Shape Tool and marquee-select several control nodes. Then drag them away from the center of the photo, as shown here. Then press CTRL+Z to undo this nondestructive *and unwanted* edit!

27

Boolean Operations as a Trimming Technique

It takes an equal amount of effort, but it might be easier to visualize the nondestructive photo-trimming process by drawing the outline of the image object you want to isolate and then use the Shaping commands to "slice" out the area you want to use. If you have Bach trimmed now, you don't have to follow this tutorial, but *do* read the steps because you might find this technique easier than editing the control nodes.

Background Removal, Technique 2

1. Using the Pen Tool with which you're the most comfortable and experienced, draw a silhouette around the object you want to isolate in the photo, as shown in Figure 27-3. It usually helps if you choose a contrasting outline color as you progress; you right-click, in this example, white on the Color Palette after you've begun tracing. Choosing outline and fill colors *after* you've begun drawing a shape avoids triggering the attention box asking whether all new objects should get a white outline.

2. After you've closed the shape, choose Arrange | Shaping | Shaping to display the docker for performing an Intersect Boolean operation. You could use the Property Bar shaping buttons to perform this, but the Property Bar shaping buttons by default leave a copy of the target and source objects after the operation, a minor hassle to clean up later.

3. Select the object you just drew. Choose Intersect from the drop-down selector, and then uncheck both "Leave Original" boxes if they are checked. Click Intersect With, click the region of the photograph that is outside of the white outline you just drew, and you're home free, as shown in Figure 27-4.

FIGURE 27-3   Draw an outline that tightly matches the shape of the object you want to trim.

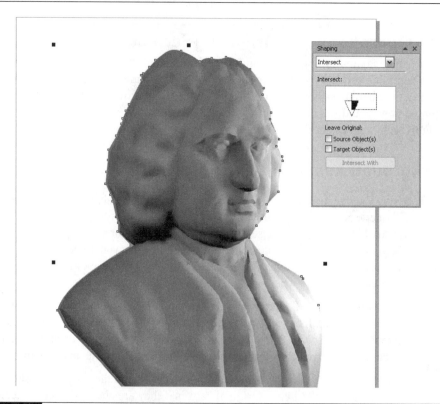

FIGURE 27-4   Use the Intersect Shaping command to remove all regions of the photo outside of the shape you drew.

Creating the Composition

Creating the poster is going to be fun. Much of the work has been done for you, but if you read Chapter 8, you already know how moving and scaling objects is done. What you'll see in the Concert poster.cdr file are two image objects: the background night scene is locked on the bottom layer, and the gold title is an *alpha-channel masked image,* something covered a little later in this chapter. It's also the first and *last* time Fette Fraktur should be used as a headline font!

Work through the following steps to duplicate your Bach trimming work to the concert poster document (a dedicated unlocked layer is active, so duplicating takes only one step). Then you'll add a vector shape to the composition to create an air of elegance...it's a piece of *chorale* sheet music, actually, not an *air.*

Composing a Design Using Vector and Image Shapes

1. Open Concert poster.cdr, and then choose Tile Vertically from the Window menu.

2. Hold CTRL and then drag your trimmed bust of Bach into the Concert poster window, as shown in Figure 27-5. This duplicates your work; it doesn't move it. You can save and then close your Bach image as a CDR file now.

3. Click the Import button on the Property Bar, and then choose the Bach 4 part Chorale.cdr file from your hard drive. Click Import; your cursor is now loaded with the imported file, and you can click anywhere to place it at its original size.

4. With the music notes selected, click the white color well on the Color Palette to create the effect shown here.

5. Choose Window | Dockers | Object Manager. Click-drag the title "Group of 100 Objects" (the music notes), and then release the mouse button when the title is below the "JS Bach.tif" object.

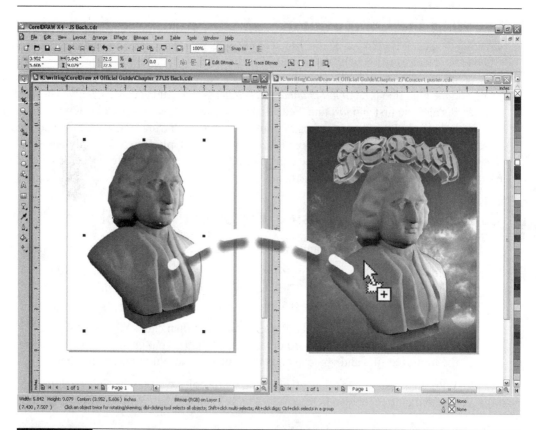

FIGURE 27-5   Duplicate your work into the Concert poster.cdr window.

6. Let's make the music sort of swell behind its composer. Choose the Interactive Envelope Tool from the Effects group on the Toolbox. Choose Envelope 4 from the Presets list on the Property Bar. This is a good base envelope you can customize now.

7. With the Shape Tool, one at a time click the control nodes that bound the music notes, and then drag the top ones up a little and the bottom ones down a little. Use your artistic eye and Figure 27-6 to guide you. Bach's compositions are stirring; the music notes should visually reflect this.

8. A time and place for this concert would help sell it; read Chapter 14 if you haven't done so already for good text-composition techniques. As you can see in Figure 27-7, the completed poster looks handsome, and most of its visual success is because you now know how to isolate an important subject from a fairly boring background.

FIGURE 27-6   Shape the music so it appears to extend around the bust toward the audience, as music really does…

FIGURE 27-7   When you can move image objects around on a page as easily as vector shapes, new design opportunities open up to you.

Working with Alpha Channels and Image Transparency

The following sections explain how some professions trim subjects out of their image backgrounds, why certain file types are imported with transparency, and what transparency really means in your CorelDRAW work. You take a brief excursion into Corel PHOTO-PAINT because when you bought CorelDRAW, you also bought a bitmap editing program that can shave hours off your photo composition work in CorelDRAW!

Image Information Channels

Usually, digital photographs that come straight off your camera, when they're not specially encoded Raw files, are JPEGs or TIFFs. Both JPEG and TIFF images are arranged using color channels red, green, and blue that in combination make up all the colors you see. However, because these images are arranged using channels (of color), mathematician and artist Dr. Alvy Smith discovered that TIFF images had a structure that would allow the coding of *additional* channels into such a file format. The additional channels could be used to map information that has nothing to do with image color; they're called *alpha channels,* and the original use of an alpha channel was to tell the application importing the file, "Wherever there's a black pixel in the alpha channel, don't display anything in the corresponding red, green, and blue channels." This is, of course, an oversimplification, but the result is that TIFF file format images and currently several other file formats can hold information that tells CorelDRAW and other programs to display transparency in certain areas of the image.

Don't get a headache yet; this stuff gets even better and more useful in your work! The Bach image you trimmed earlier in this chapter can actually become an image with transparency information; you just export it to TIFF file format, and in the Convert To Bitmap dialog, you check the Transparent Background check box. However, exporting a composition to bitmap file format with transparency might not be as important to your work as getting an image *into* CorelDRAW with transparency, and that's why a little trip to PHOTO-PAINT can't hurt right now.

A photo of a scarecrow is shown in several of the following figures (you can see it in the color section as well). Although it's a nice if somewhat unremarkable image, the important quality lies in the fact that every strand of straw and the dozens of holes in the straw hat are masked. They disappear when this photo is brought into CorelDRAW or some other application that can read transparency information.

You can download Scarecrow.png and import it into CorelDRAW to see how refined the edges are around the transparency.

Let's say you want to take an image of similar visual complexity to this scarecrow image, because you want to pose the scarecrow against a cornfield. Your first step is

Layer Transparency vs. Alpha Channel Masking

There is only a *technical* difference between images that have transparency on layers and images where areas drop out due to alpha channel masking. For the designer, there is no apparent difference in the transparent quality between a PNG that has transparency and a TIFF image with transparency-masking information.

As you travel down the road of professional digital design work, you'll discover that a TIFF image and occasionally a Photoshop PSD file will present the importing application with the choice between showing or not showing the alpha channel information. You can use the Bitmap Color Mask feature in CorelDRAW, for example, to *remove* the alpha channel information in an imported TIFF file (you click Show Colors on the docker). However, a PNG with transparency does not have an alpha masking channel, but instead is structured around a single layer where pixels are opaque, transparent, or partially transparent. With PNG files, there *is* no background image; this is the fundamental difference between alpha masked images and layered images with transparency.

Of less importance is that as an information channel—and alpha does not necessarily have to be keyed to transparency—it can be used as anything the host application wants to use it for, although in 99 percent of your imaging adventures "alpha equals transparency." Applications such as Corel Painter and Adobe Photoshop can use alpha channel information to make certain areas on the image look bumpy, or blurred, or distorted…an alpha channel is just an information channel.

preparation when you shoot the photo—you make sure that the background is as nearly a solid color as possible, as evenly lit as possible. Why? Because both CorelDRAW and PHOTO-PAINT can select photo areas based on color and then auto-mask them. In the illustration below, the original scarecrow image (a JPEG file off a digital camera) is imported to PHOTO-PAINT. The scarecrow was photographed in front of a cyan seamless sheet of construction board; cyan was used because no color in the scarecrow is remotely similar to this cyan color. Here's how the cyan was masked out of the photo:

1. Mask | Color Mask displays the docker for choosing image colors you want to drop out.

2. Click a color slot, check its box, and then with the Eyedropper Tool, click over the most common color in the image you want masked. Doing this displays areas you haven't selected as being masked; you want the inverse of this, the *scarecrow and*

not the background to be selected, but this is how you do it. Then click additional color slots, and add areas that you want masked but that aren't. Here you can see the scarecrow almost completely unselected (masked).

3. Then click OK, and a selection marquee now shows the selected area, the cyan background. Click the Inverts A Mask button on PHOTO-PAINT's Property Bar, and the scarecrow and scores of little holes in the geometry are now selected.

4. Choose Object | Create | Object:Cut Selection, and then delete (or hide) the bottom layer of a two-layer image. Here you can see that a little manual work is needed because most but not all of the cyan background has been removed, but again there's no simpler way to cut out a background of the enormous complexity of this scarecrow.

5. Once the image layer has been cleaned up using the Eraser or other tool, the background is deleted via the Objects docker, and you use File | Save As, and PNG is fine in this example for a single-layer image with transparency.

Figure 27-8 shows an example layout featuring the now trimmed and exported scarecrow against a field of corn with a similarly corny headline. Therefore, you're only a few hours' worth of practice and only five PHOTO-PAINT steps away from the ability to compose bitmap and vector scenes such as this one when you've set up your photography with the right solid background color.

Using CorelDRAW's Bitmap Color Mask

On the Property Bar, whenever a bitmap image is selected, you have the Bitmap Color Mask docker button on the Property Bar. This docker can help mask areas of a placed bitmap, although it's a less robust feature than found in PHOTO-PAINT. Here's the deal: if you have, for example, an image completely surrounded by pure white, you can remove the white background by hiding this color value. Similarly, if you have an image with a background whose color is not remotely similar to colors in the foreground person or object in the photo, the Bitmap Color Mask docker can successfully hide the background, too. What the Bitmap

FIGURE 27-8   Photo-illusions are a snap to create with images that have transparent areas.

Color Mask docker cannot do is distinguish between subtle variations in differing hues. For example, if you have a maroon background with a pink foreground object you want clipped out, no can do. Maroon contains heavy concentrations of tone in its red color channel, and so does pink, although to a lesser extent. The Bitmap Color Mask *looks at colors in channels* in an image; unless you're trying to mask a GIF indexed color image (a file structure that doesn't use color channels, but instead uses a color index), your recourse is to use PHOTO-PAINT or to manually trim the image using the methods described earlier.

However, lots of professionals receive "object against pure white" photos every day—and now you will, too, to experiment with in the following tutorial.

Download Beach.png and Beach ball.png.

Here's a quick little tutorial that shows how to auto-mask images such as Beach ball.png for easy compositing work in CorelDRAW.

Removing White from Around a Subject

1. Import the Beach.png image to a new document. This is the background for the composition.

2. Import the Beach ball.png image. PNGs don't necessarily have to have a transparent background—clearly, this one doesn't. It's up to a designer to determine (and edit) a PNG file to contain transparency. Place it anywhere you like for the moment. As shown in Figure 27-9, the white area around the beach ball thwarts its integration into the beach scene.

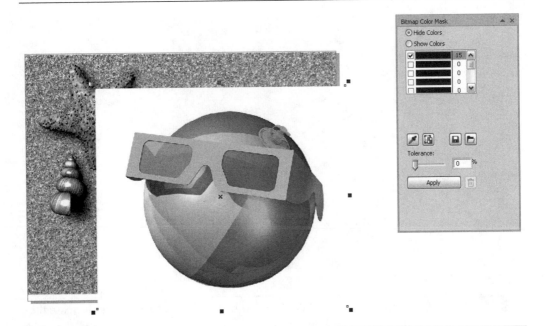

FIGURE 27-9 An image without a transparent background can't be successfully melded into a composition.

3. With the beach ball image selected, click the Bitmap Color Mask button on the Property Bar.

4. Click the check box to the left of the first black color swatch. This is the first color you'll mask in the beach ball image.

5. Choose the Eyedropper Tool, and then click over a white area on the beach ball image. Click Apply. The white has become masked—invisible—and you can now use the Pick Tool to move and scale the beach ball so it becomes part of the background scene.

6. Let's try a little more scene integration by adding a slight shadow behind the ball. This also demonstrates how the image mask allows CorelDRAW effects to be placed behind it. Choose the Drop Shadow Tool from the Effects group of tools, and then choose Flat Bottom Right from the Presets list on the Property Bar.

7. Well, oops! It appears that there is some fringing between the ball and its shadow, an unwanted width of white background pixels from the original image. With the Pick Tool, click and make sure the beach ball image and not the drop shadow is selected; then drag the Tolerance slider up to about 35 and click Apply. As you can see in Figure 27-10, the beach ball looks like it's part of the scene. The reason the off-white glasses aren't masked is because they aren't pure white like the background

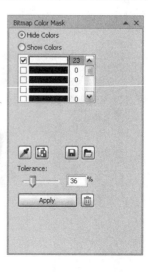

FIGURE 27-10 Use the Tolerance slider on the Bitmap Color Mask docker to increase the mask of the color you chose.

is—but if you set a higher Tolerance, the glasses will indeed drop out of the composition. As a little independent experiment, try clicking the second check box, and then with the Eyedropper Tool, click over a red area of the image and see what disappears. To undo this move, all you need to do is uncheck the red swatch's check box on the docker and then click Apply.

Working with Partial Transparency

Both alpha channel transparency and image layer transparency offer more than simply 100 percent opaque or 100 percent transparent areas. With 24-bit images, you can have 256 levels of opacity in any area of the image, and this leads to some fascinating visual effects you can create. You'll work shortly with an image that has semitransparent areas, but right now it's time to learn how to build semitransparent areas into an image that has none but should have them.

DOWNLOAD

Download Bob's Beer.png and Bob's background.cdr.

The Bob's Beer.png file has a transparency (a mask) around its exterior, so the bottle from a fictitious microbrewery can be placed and moved freely around Bob's background.cdr or any file you choose. However, the bottle is an image of dark green glass. Glass is not opaque, but instead allows some light—and in this example, some of the background—to show through.

The following tutorial shows you how to trim away the top quarter of the bottle, the most transparent part, the part with no beer in it; then you'll see how to make this area only partially opaque so some of the striped background shows through. And to top it off, you'll see how to build a cast shadow from the bottle onto the "ground" in the composition.

Creating a Photorealistic Glass Effect

1. Open Bob's Background.cdr, and then click the Import button and choose Bob's Beer.png; it's a domestic beer, but you'll import it anyway. Click Import and then with the loaded cursor, click-diagonal drag until the bottle is placed in the image as shown here.

2. With a Pen Tool (the Bézier pen works fine in this example), create a shape that describes the top part of the glass, from the fill line to the bottle's lip, staying slightly inside the edge of the beer bottle so the edge is not part of the trimming operation you'll perform in a moment. You should fill the shape after creating it to better see what you're doing in the following steps—any color is fine.

3. Select the shape but not the bottle. Choose Arrange | Shaping | Shaping to display the Shaping docker. Choose Intersect from the selector drop-down list, and then check Leave Original Target Object(s). Click the Intersect With button, and then click on the bottle. The shape is deleted because it's the Source Object, and you didn't choose to leave it. Apparently the bottle has not changed, but there is a perfect cutout duplicate of the top of the bottle resting on top of an unchanged bottle; you're halfway there—you need to trim away part of the bottle using the new intersect shape now.

4. Click on the top of the bottle to select the product of the Intersect operation in step 3 (don't worry; it's hard to see that it's a separate object). Choose Trim from the Shaping docker's drop-down list, check Leave Original Source Object(s), and uncheck Leave Original Target Object(s). Click the Trim button and then click on the bottle, and the

beer bottle is now actually two separate pieces. See the following illustration for the docker settings for steps 3 and 4. Now it's on to transparency.

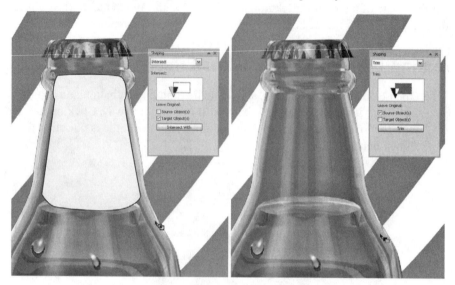

5. Select the top part shape, and then choose the Interactive Transparency Tool from the Effects group of tools on the Toolbox. Choose Uniform from the selector drop-down on the Property Bar, and then drag the Opacity slider on the Property Bar to about 31 percent. As you can see here, your editing work resulted in quite a convincing illustration. You can see the stripes in the background peeking through semitransparent glass; the stripes are even tinted a little from the green of the object on top of it.

6. Here's the piece de resistance: with the bottle selected and not the semitransparent piece, choose the Drop Shadow Tool. On the Property Bar, choose Pers. Top Right from the Presets selector drop-down list.

7. Click-drag the end marker of the shadow so the shadow ends closer to the bottle. Then, because the bottle should be casting a deep green (not black) shadow, drag a deep green from the Color Palette, and drop it on the end marker, as shown here. Kentucky Green works in this example.

8. The area you trimmed in step 4 is not part of the shadow—there's a hole in the shadow where there should be a lighter green, because a shadow cast by green glass through beer would be a little darker than a shadow cast through green glass alone. No problem; you draw a fill shape for the missing part of the shadow as shown here, fill the shape with green, and then give it about 50 percent Uniform Transparency.

Adding Transparency to Transparency

In addition to using semitransparency, you'll often have the need to fade an object's opacity across an area; the following tutorial shows a fanciful example of a ghost rock guitarist who should fade from 100 percent transparency up to his native semitransparency at the top of the compositing.

Download Phantom of the Rock Opera.png and Festival seating.png.

What you will learn by doing is how to use the Interactive Transparency Tool's style and merge mode to apply a fancy effect to an image that already natively has regions of transparency, opacity, and semitransparency. The ghost was created in a modeling application using a special material that created varying levels of opacity, and you'll riff on this property by following these steps.

Using Transparency Styles and Merge Modes on a Bitmap

1. In a new document, landscape orientation, click the Import button on the Property Bar, and then import Festival seating.png. Make the image fill the page (its original dimensions are a little larger than the default CorelDRAW page size of 8.5×11").

2. Click the Import button and then import Phantom of the Rock Opera.png. Use the click-diagonal drag technique to scale the little fellow as you place him so he fits within the height of the document.

3. With the ghost selected, choose the Interactive Transparency Tool, and then click-drag, beginning at the ghost's neck, releasing the mouse button where his ankles would be if he had ankles. As you can see (pun intended) by varying the transparency, Linear style, you've created quite an astounding special effect. Go call Spielberg and tell him you'll compete against ILM for his next blockbuster.

4. Try changing the merge mode for this transparency to Add, from the drop-down selector on the Property Bar, which currently highlights the Normal mode. Add mode accentuates the underlying deep reds of the background image mostly because the ghost guitarist is almost pure white. Check out Figure 27-11, and check into Chapter 22 if you haven't already, to learn what other things you can do with the Transparency feature.

FIGURE 27-11 Linear and all other styles of transparency can be applied to bitmaps, even those bitmaps that contain some native transparency.

Bitmaps to Vector Art: Using PowerTRACE

You've seen in this chapter and in Chapter 26 how you can export both vector art and bitmaps to bitmap file format, but once in a while you'll need to go the other way: taking a bitmap and making vector art from it. Many design professionals are faced daily with clients who want to use their logo for a truck sign or a high-resolution print ad, when all they can provide the designer is a really pathetic GIF copy from their web page. GIF images are notorious for jaggy aliased edges because the file format is limited to 256 unique colors, and original designs and photographs usually contain thousands of colors. Part of the problem arises when an application brute-forces the original design's colors down to a limited GIF color palette; not only aliasing appears but also *dithering,* a patterning of alternating pixel colors an application performs to "fake" the colors that cannot be included in the limited GIF color palette.

Fortunately, designers don't have to reconstruct logos by hand—Corel PowerTRACE is quite an accurate utility that often produces a vector equivalent of a placed bitmap that requires no hand-tweaking afterward. What PowerTRACE does is simple: it creates a vector version of the selected bitmap. *How* PowerTRACE does this is a lot more complicated to explain: in a nutshell, PowerTRACE examines the bitmap based on the criteria you specify in the dialog and then seeks edges in the bitmaps that show a clear and marked difference in color and/or brightness between neighboring pixels. PowerTRACE then creates a vector line at this neighboring region, continues to create a closed path (with the Centerline option chosen, it creates open paths), and fills the path with the closest color match to the pixels inside the area it creates. The following sections take you through the operation of PowerTRACE and offer suggestions on settings and when and why you'd use this handy feature.

Download Lousy Graphic.gif (it lives up to its name) and SilverSpoon.png, and download and install Candid.ttf.

Bitmap Conversion for Repairs

Lousy Graphic.gif is an exaggerated example of bad design and bad execution—whoever exported this design as a GIF should have thought twice. Fountain fills simply do not render well to GIF file format because of all the transition colors; they exceed in number the maximum number of solid colors the GIF file format can accommodate, and the smart designer goes with the more flexible PNG file format for the Web. In Figure 27-12 you can see the flaws in this GIF image, the concept notwithstanding.

All said and done, let's say this is your client's logo, and they want it full-page size at 300 ppi in TIFF file format to print on the cover of the corporate annual report. After you're done laughing yourself silly, you turn to CorelDRAW and follow these steps to auto-trace the lousy graphic and then see what needs to be done to restore the unusable Fountain fill.

Jaggy aliased edges

Dithered colors

FIGURE 27-12 Sometimes a bitmap needs tracing as a restoration method.

PowerTRACE to the Rescue

1. In a new document, click the Import button on the Property Bar, and then choose Lousy graphic.gif. With your cursor loaded, just click on the page to place it at its original size.

2. With the graphic selected, click the Trace Bitmap button on the Property Bar to reveal the drop-down list—choose Outline Trace | Line Art. The reason you'd choose Line Art in this example instead of "Logo" (hey, this is a logo, right?) is because the Logo setting would generate a lot of "false detail," detail that's not visually a part of the logo. By choosing Line Art, you ensure that PowerTRACE will not labor for minutes on end trying to reconcile all the dithered pixels in the Fountain fill in the original logo. Instead, it's going to generate a posterized approximation of the Fountain fill area; the Fountain fill needs to be re-rendered by hand, and by choosing Line Art, you'll only have a few unwanted objects to delete after the trace instead of hundreds.

3. Set the Smoothing slider to about 60; this prevents PowerTRACE from laboring over sharp turns in its path creation based on neighboring pixels whose colors abruptly change. Smoothing will also produce fewer objects; you need to consider the visual content of the bitmap before you set up tracing options: this logo clearly has very few unique solid colors and very few sharp turns and twists in its geometric content.

4. Uncheck Delete Original Image; you probably want to compare it to the trace. Usually, Remove Background is a good option, but is not relevant in this example because the GIF logo has a transparent background. Check Group Objects By

Color—doing this will make it a lot easier to delete the attempt at reproducing the Fountain fill. If your screen looks like the illustration here, click OK and let PowerTRACE do its thing.

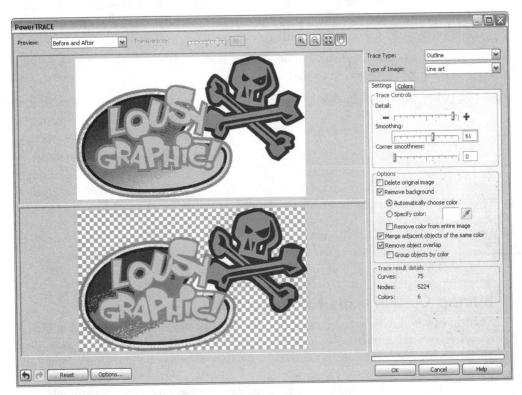

5. A group of objects is created directly over the original bitmap. With the Pick Tool, move the vector group away from the bitmap original.

6. Ungroup the group (CTRL+U). Subgroups will be in the vector trace, but for the moment you're all set to do a little manual editing. With the Shape Tool, it's probably a good idea to sharpen some of the corners of the yellow text; the vector curves are a little soft in areas where it was hard for PowerTRACE to discern between the background fill and the text. For example, the *A* in "GRAPHIC" is missing a node at top left; you first ungroup (CTRL+U) the bluish-purple outline subgroup.

7. With the Shape Tool, click the smooth contour adjacent to the bluish-purple outline at the top left of the deep yellow *A*. Press the keyboard + key to add a node, and then click To Cusp on the Property Bar to set a cusp property for the new node. Then you drag the node handles to sharpen the corner of the *A*.

8. Delete all the objects that make up the background Fountain fill; there should be no more than three of these shapes, in groups and as individual objects. With the Bézier Pen Tool, draw the approximate original shape. Then with the Interactive Fill Tool, drag a Linear style fill to match the angle you see in the GIF original. Drag a deep blue from the Color Palette, drop it onto the start fill marker, and then drag a deep yellow onto the end color marker.

9. Press CTRL+A to select all, CTRL+G to group, delete the original GIF image, and then scale the vector group to page size.

10. Click the Export button on the Property Bar. Choose TIFF (per the client's request) from the Save As Type drop-down in the Export dialog, give the file a name, check Selected Only, click Export, and you're on to the Convert To Bitmap dialog.

11. Set the Image size to 100 percent if this is not the default value, set the Resolution to 300, check Transparent Background (whoever is laying out the report might appreciate the alpha transparency so they can composite the artwork against a background), and then click OK.

 TIP *To get superfluous objects out of a finished PowerTRACE very quickly, use Edit | Find And Replace | Find Objects, and set the criteria for the search to specific unwanted colors. Then you can delete all the selected objects at once.*

Bitmap Conversions for Alterations

Sometimes you'll want to use PowerTRACE not to resurrect a lousy graphic, but instead to rework an existing logo that's in bitmap format. Suppose SilverSpoon.png, a good, clean graphic, is the logo for a caterer that was bought out yesterday by Phil Greasy, and Phil likes the logo but wants the name changed to…you guessed it. You use similar settings for PowerTRACE to make a vector conversion of the logo, but this is a prime example of "knowing your fonts" (covered in Chapter 13). A lot of times it's a futile endeavor to trace typography in a logo: it's much easier and provides cleaner results just to recast the text using the same or similar font.

The original logo's text was cast in Motter Fem; if you don't own it, this is okay. Install Candid.ttf through the Start menu | Control Panel | Fonts before you begin the tutorial. Candid is not a complete typeface; it's missing punctuation marks and numbers, and it was created after the Candy font by URW. It's very close in look to Motter Fem, and Candy is a great packaging design font you might seriously consider purchasing for your collection— Candid is a hastily cobbled knockoff whose purpose is solely to get you through the techniques in the following steps.

 ## Reworking a Logo Using Vectors

1. In a new document, import SilverSpoon.png. Place it on the page at actual size just by clicking on the page with the loaded cursor. As you can see, the logo has no dithering and no aliased edges. Therefore, the PowerTRACE can be set for less

smoothing and greater precision. As you can see here, the logo has no transparent background, but because you'll trace it, you can automatically delete its white background, a little perk for your client.

27

2. Click the Trace Bitmap button on the Property Bar; choose Outline Trace | Clipart. Your choices for tracing styles go from simple at top to more complex as you move down the list. This logo will benefit most from a Clipart-style trace due to its relatively high color fidelity and overall smoothness.

3. Set the Detail to a fairly high value such as 92 percent with the slider. Set Smoothing at about 25; the logo is already fairly smooth and will not benefit from the averaging PowerTRACE would make in defining paths.

4. Check Remove Background. Choose Group Objects By Color, and then take a look at the Trace Results details field, as shown in Figure 27-13. About 163 objects will be produced; this seems right if you tally up all the individual areas in the original bitmap. If this number ever seems too low, try increasing the Detail slider. Click OK now.

5. You will want to delete two groups: the group of white lettering that spells "Silver," and the red outline around "Silver." This will leave a hole in the design because PowerTRACE doesn't draw layers of objects—it only draws what it "sees."

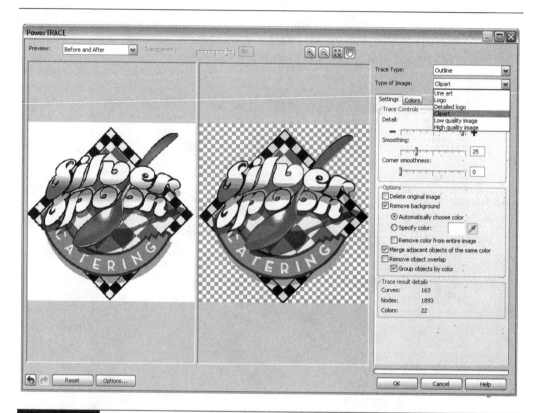

FIGURE 27-13   The higher the quality of image you import, the higher the tracing style should be.

6. With the Text Tool, type **Greasy**, and then apply Candid from the Font selector drop-down on the Property Bar.

7. Apply a white fill to the text, and then choose a 2-point outline by using the Outline Pen group on the Toolbox.

8. Choose the Envelope Tool from the Effects group on the Toolbox, and then choose Envelope 6 from the Presets selector on the Property Bar. You might want to massage the result of this preset by click-dragging its control nodes with the Shape Tool because it's close to the original text arc but not exactly the same. If your design looks like Figure 27-14 now, you're in good shape with only a step or two to go.

9. Create rectangles that match the color of the missing checkerboard in the logo, rotate them to the correct diamond-shaped orientation as the original logo, position them accordingly for your patchwork, and then send them to the back of the page by pressing SHIFT+PAGE DOWN.

FIGURE 27-14   Replace the text in the original design using a similar font choice.

10. You can embellish the revised logo by adding a drop shadow to the new owner's name, as it appears in the original logo, and you can smooth out the posterized edges on the spoon by overlaying an object that uses a Fountain fill using the same colors. But as you can see here, the new logo is pretty faithful to the original, and with the help of PowerTRACE it took ten steps. Think of how many steps and lost nights of sleep you'd have without an auto-tracing utility!

This chapter has shown you how to work with bitmaps in almost the same way as you work with vector art in CorelDRAW. Both vectors and bitmaps can happily coexist in a single document. You can shuffle and rearrange objects as if they were made of the same digital materials, and you do need bitmaps in your work when you're trying to convey any sense of photorealism. Naturally, you're anxious to print all this great stuff you've done up 'til now, so that's what Chapter 29 holds for you: how to output like a pro, and get everything you designed onscreen using CorelDRAW to look the same way when rendered as ink on paper.

CHAPTER 28

Printing: Professional Output

Print is *not* dead! It's alive and well, thank you, in almost every enterprise, and outputting your work so your clients can hold it in their hands is just as much an art as designing a piece in CorelDRAW. This chapter takes you through *professional* output—CorelDRAW's features that extend *beyond* the now-familiar File | Print command—and what it takes from CorelDRAW and you to make every dot of ink on a page look exactly like every pixel you designed on the screen.

The good news is that CorelDRAW X4's print engine is organized into several well-defined and easy to understand areas for setting printer hardware parameters, previewing your print selection, and using various other options to enhance your finished printed work. In this chapter, you'll learn to set options from beginner to advanced levels in all of these areas.

Printing a Document to a Personal Printer

Let's suppose that you want to print a "one of," perhaps to show to your boss or coworkers as a proof of concept, or for personal pleasure, or to see if everything is arranged on the page correctly before packing off a copy to a commercial press. If your artwork is for black and white (you used no color, but only shades of black in the design), you'll probably print to a laser printer. Laser printers don't really have any color-critical settings, so you're probably as ready to go as you'd be if you were printing a text document. If you're printing to an inkjet, most of today's inkjet circuitry does an automatic conversion from RGB color space and the color ink space (usually CMYK, although many affordable printers use six inks), and again, you really don't have to jump through any hoops if you've designed a document that uses RGB, LAB, or CMYK color spaces to define the colors you filled objects with.

Here's a tutorial that covers the basics for outputting your work to a personal printer. Before you begin, make sure on the Object Manager docker that the layers you want to print are visible and that printing is enabled for the layers; a tiny red international "no" appears on layer properties that are disabled—you click on the "no" symbol to enable the layer property.

Printing Single- and Multiple-Page Documents

1. Open the document you want to print, and then choose File | Print (CTRL+P), or click the Print button on the Standard Toolbar. Any of these actions opens the Print dialog, shown in Figure 28-1. An attention box might pop up over the Print dialog if your default printer's page orientation is different from your CorelDRAW document's orientation. If you get this box, click Yes, particularly if you only have one printer attached to your PC. The printer's page orientation is adjusted; this does nothing to your CorelDRAW document.

2. In the General tab, choose your printer from the Name drop-down menu, and then click Properties to set any printer properties such as the print material page size, orientation, and so on. Keep in mind that any special features specific to your printer might override any CorelDRAW-specific features, in particular, color management (discussed later in

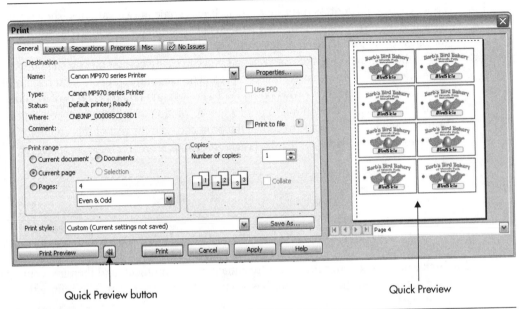

Quick Preview button

Quick Preview

FIGURE 28-1 Clicking the Quick Preview button in the Print dialog expands it to show a preview window enabling you to review your document before you print it.

this chapter). In general, it's not a good idea to allow CorelDRAW to color-manage your document as you print it at the same time you have a color management feature enabled on your printer. Two color management systems will contend with each other, and what you see onscreen will *not* be what you get in your print.

3. Click the Quick Preview button to expand the dialog to show a preview window if you'd like to check the document for position on the printable page. A dashed line appears in the preview window, indicating document areas that are close to or that go over the printable page margin. If you see this, you might want to cancel the print operation and rework your page. Alternatively, you can click the Layout tab and then check Fit To Page, although doing this scales the objects in your document (so forget about the CD label you want to print fitting perfectly on a physical CD).

4. If you have more than one document open in CorelDRAW, you can choose which document to print by clicking the Documents radio button in the Print Range area; make certain that all documents you want to print have the same portrait or landscape orientation before printing, or you're inviting a headache. In a multi-page CorelDRAW document, choose the page(s) you want to print from the Print Range area, and then enter the print quantity in the Number Of Copies box.

5. Before you click Print, check to see whether there are any Issues on the Issues tab. If the tab reads "No Issues," proceed to step 6 and collect $200. However, if there's an

issue, you should address it (or them) first. Issues come in two varieties: showstoppers, indicated by a triangular traffic sign with an exclamation mark, and trivial stuff, indicated by an info (*i*) icon. A common example of trivial stuff is printing blank pages; the Issues tab will inform you, and you can easily correct this by changing the Pages value in the Print Range area of the General tab. Showstoppers require careful reading of the explanation provided on the Issues tab; the remarks and explanations are quite clear—such as attempting to print a low-resolution image to a high-resolution printer—and your best bet is to cancel the print and read the rest of this chapter…and save paper and ink. Here's what the Issues icons look like:

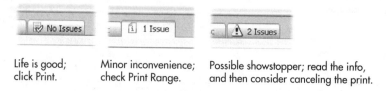

Life is good;   Minor inconvenience;   Possible showstopper; read the info,
click Print.   check Print Range.   and then consider canceling the print.

6. Click Print, go get your favorite refreshment, wait a moment, and then get your print once the racket of the print heads has stopped (laser printer users can ignore this last comment).

The Quick Preview deserves a little more coverage here. After clicking the Quick Preview button, you're shown a preview window and page browsing controls (see Figure 28-2). While

FIGURE 28-2 Use the buttons on the bottom of the dialog to more easily choose what pages you'd like to print.

you're previewing, a right-click offers invaluable commands from the pop-up menu to Show Image, Preview Color, Preview Separations, and to toggle the view of Rulers. When you want to print a multi-page CorelDRAW file, you can quickly turn pages in Quick Preview to make sure you're printing within page boundaries and that all the pages contain what it is you want to print. To print the preview page at the current settings, choose Print This Sheet Now from the pop-up menu.

Setting Print Options

The tabbed areas of the Print dialog more or less follow from left to right a progression from personal printing options to more ambitious endeavors such as printing separations for process *color composite* (commercial) printing. Some of the areas on the tabs are device dependent and appear only after CorelDRAW X4 evaluates your printer's capabilities; Use PPD (PostScript Printing Description), for example, is dimmed on the General tab until you've chosen a printer that is PostScript capable. This is why selecting your printing device must be your first step in printing from CorelDRAW. Depending on the printer defined, you'll see tabbed areas for General, Layout, Separations, Prepress, PostScript, Misc, and Issues.

Setting General Options

The General tab of the Print dialog, shown in Figure 28-3, offers control over some of the most common printing options.

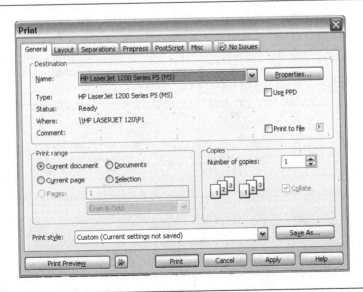

FIGURE 28-3   Use the General tab of the Print dialog to set the most basic printing options.

28

Here's a description of what each option in the General tab controls:

- **Destination** This area represents the feedback provided by the printer driver used to your selected printer showing the Name, Type, Status, Where, and Comment information. Direct, network, or spooler printers are indicated according to their connection status. If CorelDRAW cannot find a printer connected directly or remotely (through a network) to your computer, you'll need to pay a visit to the Windows Start menu | Printers And Faxes, and then choose Add A Printer by clicking this item in the Printer Tasks area. The good news is that this is a wizard-style process and that Windows ships with just about every conceivable print driver for popular makes and models. You might be prompted for a specific print driver, so it's a good idea to have the manufacturer's disk handy or to download the latest drivers from their website. Clicking the Properties button provides control over printer-specific properties and output material sizes. Choosing Use PPD lets you assign a PostScript Printer Description file; checking this box displays the Open PPD dialog, where you locate and then select an appropriate PPD file. Unless you're already familiar with what Print To File does, don't check this box in your everyday printing; see "Saving a Print File" later in this chapter.

- **Print Range** This area contains options to select pages from the file you have maximized in the drawing window—or from *any* document you have open in CorelDRAW—it can be minimized, and you can print it as long as it's open. Choose Current Page to print the page currently in view in your CorelDRAW document, or enter specific page numbers in the Pages box. If you go into the Print command with one or more objects selected in your document, the Selection option becomes available, so you can print *only* your selection; this is quite handy for printing only a part of your document without rearranging or hiding objects, or for changing your document before printing. If you have more than one document open, choosing the Documents option displays a list of the open documents, so you can choose which document to print. Choose Even and/or Odd from the drop-down menu to print only certain pages. By default, both Even and Odd pages are printed.

- **Copies** This area has two options for setting the Number Of Copies to print either collated or not. When Collate is chosen, a picture appears indicating the effect of collating. Collating is a great timesaver when you want to publish a multi-page presentation and don't need the hassle of reordering pages as they come out of the printer.

| TIP | *To print contiguous (consecutive) pages of a document, in the Print Range area's Pages box, enter the page numbers separated by a hyphen (for example, type **6-8** to print pages 6, 7, and 8). To print noncontiguous pages, for example, pages 6, 8, and 16, type commas between specific page numbers—**6, 8, 16** in this example. You can also combine these two conventions to print both contiguous and noncontiguous pages by separating each entry by a comma. For example, entering **6-8, 10-13, 16** will print pages 6, 7, 8, 10, 11, 12, 13, and 16.* |

Using Print Styles

Print styles remove the repetitive task of setting up the same (or similar) printing parameters by letting you choose to save all the selected options in the Print dialog in one tidy print style file. If your printing options have already been saved as a style, open the Print Style drop-down menu on the General tab of the Print dialog, and choose the style from the list. By default, all print styles are saved in a folder named Print Styles, located in *(Boot drive letter):*\Documents and Settings*Your User Name*\Application Data\Corel\CorelDRAW Graphics Suite X4\User Custom Data\Print Styles.

To create a style that includes all the settings you have currently selected, follow these steps:

1. On the General tab, click Save As to open the Save Settings As dialog, shown here. As you can see, this dialog includes a Settings To Include tree directory listing the categorized print options and check boxes according to current settings.

2. Click to select the options you want to save with your new style, enter a unique name for your style, and then click Save to store the settings, after which they are available from the Print Style drop-down list.

Saving a Print File

Print To File goes back to the days of DOS, and today you'd be hard-pressed to use this option more than twice in your career. However, Print To File is supported in CorelDRAW, and you might want to generate this huge, text-based PostScript file for a couple of reasons:

- If you're handing the document over to a third party to print because you don't have a specific printer hooked up to your computer, and you don't want them editing the document in any way. Print To File files are text-based printing instructions; they contain no graphics as graphics, so they are nearly impossible to edit using a graphics application.

- If (and this is a big "if") someone has specifically requested a Print To File document because they like the intellectual challenge of decoding the PostScript printing instructions to reconstruct the graphic using Ghostscript or a similar PostScript deciphering program.

Throughout the history of PC printing, printing to file served a valuable purpose. It enables someone who doesn't own CorelDRAW to print your CorelDRAW file; a dozen years ago, high-resolution printers such as Linotronics imagesetting devices were the only game in town when you wanted coffee table–book printing quality. If a service bureau that owned the device didn't own CorelDRAW, you printed to file. Today there are alternatives to making a CorelDRAW document portable for a service bureau to render, but if Print To File is a client's mandate, here are the steps you need to use:

1. Choose the Print To File check box in the General tab of the Print dialog, and then choose from four options in the adjacent flyout menu. Choose For Mac if the file is to be printed from a Macintosh system. Choose Single File (the default), Pages To Separate Files, or Plates To Separate Files to set how the files are prepared. Single File creates one, usually huge, print file for the entire printout. Pages To Separate Files creates separate files for each page. The Plates To Separate Files option creates a single file to represent each page *and* each of the color separations you've chosen to print if your printing destination is to CMYK process color printing.

2. Click Print to start creating the print files, and the Print To File dialog will open, where you choose a destination for the PRN file.

You then copy the PRN file to removable media and take it to the party who will print the file; alternatively, many service bureaus offer ftp upload sites for getting files to them. Printing to file is only available if your target device is a PostScript printer, because Adobe's PostScript technology is the only real standard for offset printing today, and it is the only common device printing language that can be expressed in a plain text file. Traditionally, before artists use Print To File, they have a target device's print driver installed—this is done just like you install a printer in Windows, except you're only installing a *device driver* and *not* the physical printer itself. Service bureaus like to provide you with their print drivers because if you write a Print To File using an incompatible driver, you're left with a job the service bureau can't print, and you've wasted time and hard disk space.

Also, if the CorelDRAW file you print to file contains fonts, you either need to convert all text to curves (which significantly increases the saved PRN file's size), or you need to include the typefaces on the disk you give to the service bureau, which is a thorny legal issue. Users give service bureaus digital typefaces all the time, but according to most font licenses, this isn't legal. On the other hand, you cannot depend on a service bureau or commercial press house to have exactly the same font as the one you used—if a high-resolution printer reads a Print To File and cannot find the typeface on its operating system, chances are you'll get a beautiful high-resolution print that uses Courier instead of your typeface.

In short, before you send out work for printing:

- Find a service bureau that owns CorelDRAW and save yourself some headaches.

- Failing that, find a service bureau that accepts Acrobat PDF documents (more on this later in this chapter).

- Export a copy of your CorelDRAW to Illustrator file format. It might not export perfectly, and certain CorelDRAW-specific effects will not translate, but Windows and especially Macintosh service bureaus are likely to own a copy of Illustrator.

- Use Print To File.

Choosing a Layout

Options on the Layout tab give you the control to set how the page is laid out on the printing material you've loaded into your rendering device. Although the options are set to defaults for the most common print tasks, you can customize options in each area.

Setting Image Position and Size

Image Position And Size options control the position of the layout of each page. These settings will override settings you've defined in Printer Properties (your system's printing preferences, which aren't related to CorelDRAW). The following options are available:

- **As In Document**   This option (the default) leaves the current layout unchanged.

- **Fit To Page**   Choose this to enlarge or reduce your page layout to fit exactly within the printable area for your selected output material size. Understand that choosing this option immediately ruins as a print any precise measurements you've created in your file. For example, if you've labored on a fancy spine design for a presentation booklet that's 12" high, CorelDRAW will scale the design for print to the maximum dimension of your media, such as an 8½×11" sheet of paper. If you run into this problem, hang on and check out the Print Tiled Pages option covered shortly.

- **Reposition Images To** Choose this option to change the position of images as they print relative to how they're arranged on your CorelDRAW page. By default, images are automatically positioned to Center Of Page on your printing material. However, you can align images to the top, left, right, and bottom corners of the printing material page size—a very convenient way to save paper and to make trimming a printed piece easier. Using this option, you can also individually specify the position of images on each page of a multi-page document differently by choosing a document page number from the Settings For Page menu. Use the Position, Size, and Scale Factor boxes to enter specific values. Unlocking the horizontal/vertical lock by clicking the nearby lock icon gives you the opportunity to set horizontal and/or vertical Scale Factor separately for nonproportional scaling, although you might not want a distorted print.

- **Imposition Layout** *Imposition* is the orientation and position of multiple pages to create a book signature—pages are ordered and rotated so that a commercial press can print a large page, and then the pages can be trimmed and bound so the book looks like a finished product. If you intend to print to high-resolution output, this option must be set exactly according to the specifications given to you by the printing service or other vendor you are using. It's always wise to talk with press operators (or their boss) before an expensive print job, because the owners of the press know the characteristics of it better than you do. Clicking the Edit button opens a preview feature, where you can customize the imposition requirements; you can rotate pages, move gutters, and even reorder pages at the last minute. However, Imposition Layout is also an important feature even if you're home printing a single copy of a booklet from your inkjet printer. Here you can see a four-page booklet; a template was *not* used to set up the file, and yet by choosing Booklet from the Imposition Layout drop-down, you ensure that the pages will indeed be printed in book fashion.

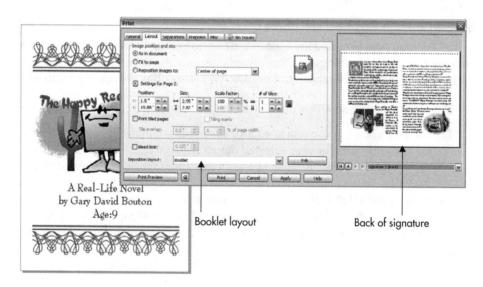

Booklet layout

Back of signature

Tiling Your Printed Document

Often you'll need to print a piece that is much larger than the maximum output size of a personal printer: a bake sale banner, for example, or other display that exceeds even the output dimensions of today's wide-format inkjet printers. This need calls for using the Print Tiled Pages option. After printing, you get a utility blade, a metal ruler, some adhesive, and a cutting surface, and you're in business. The options for setting how each tile is printed are as follows:

- ■ **Print Tiled Pages**   Choose this option to print pages in portions. Once selected, the # (Number) Of Tiles, Tiling Marks (you want to use Tile Overlap if you use this, to avoid showing the marks in your finished project), and Tile Overlap options are available. The # Of Tiles option lets you print your document in vertical or horizontal tiles, up to 24 portions for each. Setting the Tile Overlap option gives you control over how much image portion is repeated around the edges of each tile, based on unit measure or a percentage of the original page width. By default, Tile Overlap is set to 0 inches.

- ■ **Tiling Marks**   Choose this to have crop-style marks print around your tiles, making it easier to realign the tile pages when you put the tiles together.

- ■ **Tile Overlap**   This option adds an extra printed portion around each tile to make it easier to align the tiles for your large sign. Overlap can be set from 0 through 2.125 inches.

- ■ **% Of Page Width**   Use this to specify the tile overlap as a percentage of the page size between 0 and 25 percent.

- ■ **Bleed Limit**   Choosing this check box lets you use a portion of the area surrounding your document page. For example, if certain objects overlap the page border of a document, this option lets you print a portion outside the limits of the page. Bleed Limit can be set within a range of 0 to 40 inches, the default of which is a standard 0.125 inch.

The illustration here shows dashed lines (which would not be in the finished banner) where the single sheets tile in the bake sale banner, only one of scores of needs for tiling a print when your budget prohibits extra-extra-large-format prints.

Printing Separations

If you know what color separations are and you work at a commercial printer, this next section is for you. If you *hire* a commercial printer when you have a color job, and only have a working understanding of process color and separations, read on to learn a little more, but *don't* provide a commercial press operator with your own color separations! CorelDRAW creates terrific color separation work, but you really need to output to a high-resolution (expensive, you don't buy them at a department store) imagesetting device that can render to film or other reproduction medium. You need to know as much about the printing characteristics of a printer as you do about color separations to prepare your own job for printing presses—for example, trapping margin of error, undercolor removal, ink characteristics, and other factors. You probably wouldn't practice brain surgery on yourself— similarly, don't do your own separations ("seps") if you're inexperienced in the field of standard web-offset printing.

If you're a silk screener or know a commercial press inside-out, when Print Separations is selected in the Separations tab of the Print dialog, you have control over how each ink color prints; see Figure 28-4.

Choosing Separation Options

Here is the rundown on your color separation options as shown in the dialog in Figure 28-4:

- **Print Separations In Color** This option is available only if the printer you've defined is a color printer such as a personal inkjet, which prints a simulation of a coated printing plate, each plate reproduced in its respective color. This option is sometimes used for printing progressive proofs, checking registration, and checking

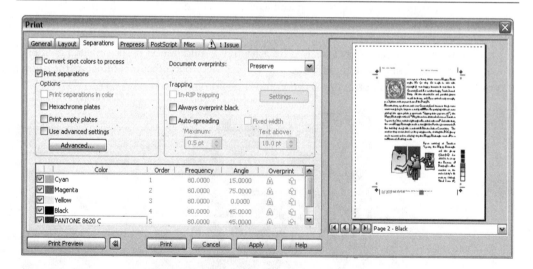

FIGURE 28-4 Use the Separations tab options to specify ink colors and trapping preferences.

color accuracy. Understand that if you use this option on a personal inkjet printer, you'll print several pages, each containing a single color; this could use a lot of ink, particularly if your CorelDRAW is dense with colored objects! Printing separations in color results in a good test for separations, but it's nothing you would want to frame and hang in the den later.

- **Hexachrome Plates** Hexachrome printing is a more involved (and more expensive) alternative to printing CMYK four color, but it offers higher quality and color accuracy. If you're doing a color separation to hand over to a commercial printer, it's a good idea to check to see whether the company can handle a Hexachrome job. Process color uses four ink colors (cyan, magenta, yellow, and black), while Hexachrome involves six, usually adding orange and green to the process. Choosing Hexachrome Plates offers the option to convert all colors in your document to the Hexachrome color model, resulting in six potential color separations. When the Hexachrome Plates option is selected, you can also choose High Solid Ink Density, which causes high ink density to be used when 100 percent color values are printed.

- **Convert Spot Colors To Process** Choosing this option is often a wise choice in non-color-critical printing, when you can't afford to print a fifth plate using a spot color. This option converts non-CMYK colors such as fixed-palette, spot-ink colored objects to the closest process color equivalent when printing. You can usually get away with this if your spot color *is not* a special ink, such as a metallic. Letting CorelDRAW convert a metallic, fluorescent, or other specialty spot ink to process will dull the final print job; the results will look amateurish at best.

- **Print Empty Plates** While unchecked (the default), this option causes pages without any objects to be skipped during printing, enabling you to avoid printing blank pages. To include the blank pages, activate this option. This can save you time, for example, if you only have a spot color on one page but not others in a multi-page document.

Frequency and Angle and Overprint Options

When separations are selected to print, the ink colors used in your document are listed at the bottom of the Separations tab. Each ink includes options for choosing if and how they will be printed. You'll see a series of columns that show how each ink color is set to print, with its color reference, ink color name, screen frequency, screen angle, and overprint options. The inks will ultimately print in order from top to bottom as you see them on the list.

First, *don't* change the frequency or line angle unless you're a professional—the default values are standard among the printing community. To change the Frequency and/or Angle of a specific ink color, click directly on the value and then enter a new value. To change overprinting properties of a specific ink color, click directly on the overprint symbols for text and/or graphic objects to toggle their state. The following list explains what each of these options controls:

- **Order** Use the selector for each ink to set the order in which separations are printed based on the number of available ink colors.

- **Frequency**   This option sets the output resolution in lines per inch (lpi); high-resolution imagesetters that speak PostScript organize dots for printing into lines. A typical line frequency for high-quality printing is 133 lpi, which results in color process prints of 2,500 dots per inch and higher. In comparison, a home laser printer, the 1,200 dpi variety, is only capable of rendering 80 lines per inch—you would not get magazine-quality prints using 80 lpi for color separations. Screen frequency values are automatically set to the default values of the imagesetter or printer selected on the General tab. Screen frequency values are also controlled by settings in the Advanced Separation Settings dialog.

- **Angle**   This option sets the angle at which the rows of resolution dots align. When separating process color inks, the following standard default screen angles are set automatically: Cyan = 15°, Magenta = 75°, Yellow = 0°, and Black = 45°. When separating fixed palette ink colors such as Pantone, Toyo, DIC, and so on, all colors are set to the default 45° value. You occasionally need to check the Issues tab when custom inks are used for spot-color plates to ensure that the spot plate is not at the same or even similar angle to the process plate screen angles. Change the angle if necessary; an incompatible spot-color screen angle can result in moiré patterning in your print, an effect similar to laying a screen window on top of another one at a certain angle.

- **Overprint**   Click directly on the symbols for text (the *A* symbol) and/or objects (the page symbol) to set whether text and/or objects for each ink are printed. Both states toggle on or off when clicked.

> **NOTE**   *If you've used two (or more) spot-ink colors in your document, these inks will separate at the default 45°. Consult with your print vendor for the correct screening angles for overlapping fixed-palette, spot-ink colors.*

The Use Advanced Settings option is always dimmed unless you have a PostScript printer selected. When it's enabled, advanced settings will override settings in the Separations tab. Clicking the Advanced button displays the Advanced Separations Settings dialog, shown in Figure 28-5.

Here's what the options in this dialog control:

- **Screening Technology**   This selector drop-down contains scripts for specific printing technologies such as Agfa and Linotronic imagesetting devices. When Standard Defaults is used as the Screening Technology, other options are set according to settings for your specific printer driver, accessed through Properties on the General tab.

- **Resolution**   This sets the output resolution of your printed material, the default value of which is set according to the Screening Technology selected. A service bureau or your print vendor will know the specifics.

- **Basic Screen**   This option sets the resolution as measured in lines per inch of the screens rendered in your output material. Check with your print vendor for the exact setting needed.

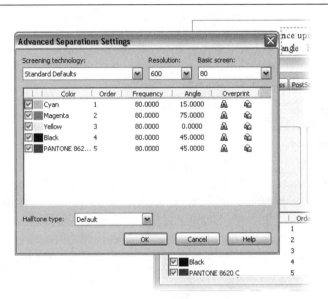

FIGURE 28-5   Choosing options in the Advanced Separations Settings dialog will override
settings in the Separations tab.

- **Halftone Type**   The Halftone Type selector is used to set the shape of the actual
  dots that compose the screens in the final output. Using this drop-down menu, you
  can choose to use such shapes as the default (Dot), Line, Diamond, Elliptical,
  Euclidean, Lines, Grid, Microwaves, Rhomboid, and Star. If you're just getting into
  commercial printing, anything other than a dot halftone shape is either used because
  the print press pulls better prints, or because you really know what you're doing and
  want to create an effect in the finished print job. Microwaves, for example, is a
  special effect that sounds interesting, but you would have to have already seen the
  effect on a printed sample before choosing it, and then you do a short run to see
  whether the example produces the same effect in your own piece. On the other hand,
  Elliptical and Star shapes can be used to sharpen the output of a print, and therefore
  are more of an enhancer than an effect.

Setting Trapping Options

Trapping involves either spreading or overprinting portions of colored objects to avoid printing
inaccuracies, the most common one being paper white showing at the edge between two color
objects. Overprinting causes one ink color to print over another, resulting in two layers of
ink—it's a technique used to work around precise ink alignment. You can set the overprinting
of fills and outlines applied to objects directly in your document; you cancel out of the Print
dialog and return to the open document. Then with the Pick Tool, right-click one or more
objects, and choose Overprint Fill or Overprint Outline from the pop-up menu options.

Overprinting can be set in three ways: directly in your document for each object, in the Separations tab using either fill or outline ink overprinting options, or using automated trapping. Where options have been set manually in your document or for each ink color, overprinting operates on a three-level hierarchy, which creates a condition where one overprinting setting overrides another one as follows:

1. When printing, the objects in the drawing are first examined for any selected fill and/or outline overprinting properties. Applying overprint properties directly to an object in a drawing overrides all other overprinting functions.

2. Next, ink color overprinting options are examined. If an ink color is set to overprint and no object fill or outline overprint properties are applied, the ink color overprints the objects beneath it. Ink colors can be set to overprint specifically for objects and/or text, including both Artistic and Paragraph Text objects.

3. Finally, the trapping options you have chosen in the Separations tab of the Print dialog are examined. If no other options are set, the automatic settings are used.

Automatic trapping and overprinting options in the Separations tab have the following effects on how colors in your document are printed:

■ **Preserve Document Overprints**   This option (enabled by default) preserves the overprint options applied directly to your drawing objects, regardless of the settings selected elsewhere. If Preserve Document Overprints is not selected, any trapping options set in this dialog override any fill or outline overprinting properties applied to objects in your drawing.

■ **Always Overprint Black**   When this option is selected, all objects that have color tints between 95 and 100 percent black will overprint underlying ink colors. Usually, you want black to overprint; black is the key plate for all the fine details, particularly necessary if you're using a bitmap image in part of your design.

■ **Auto-Spreading**   This option causes CorelDRAW X4's print engine automatically to create an overprinting outline of identical ink color around objects where they overlap other ink colors. When the option is selected, you can set the Maximum width of the spread within a range of 0 to 10 points (0.5 point is the default, a little wider than a hairline). Automatic width values vary according to the difference between the color being overprinted and the underlying color. Choose Fixed Width to set the Auto-Spreading width of the outline to a constant width regardless of this color difference. When Auto-Spreading is selected, choosing the Text Above option makes CorelDRAW ignore text sizes below a certain size; small text is often distorted by the spread effect. Choose a size between 0 and 200 points; the default is 18 points.

In-RIP Trapping Settings

If your output device is equipped with its own In-RIP trapping software, you can use this option. The term *RIP* stands for *raster image processor,* the process of converting mathematical chunks of information to a map of where dots of ink go on the page to represent what you see onscreen. Many high-end imagesetters are equipped with internal software with which certain In-RIP trapping makes the whole trapping process faster and more efficient.

This option is dimmed unless the output device defined on the General tab is PostScript compatible, PostScript 3 is selected in the PostScript tab, and Print Separations is *disabled* in the Separations tab. With the feature enabled, click the In-RIP Trapping option, and then click the Settings button to open the In-RIP Trapping Settings dialog, shown in Figure 28-6.

Here you'll find an ink listing similar to the one in the Separations tab, plus other options for setting these items:

- **Neutral Density** This is a value based on an ink color's CMYK equivalents, ranging from 0.001 to 10.000. Default values often work, or the value can be set according to advice from your print vendor. Most third-party ink swatches list the neutral density values for each ink color.

- **Type** You choose the Type for an individual ink by clicking its type in the top list to reveal an options drop-down. Although Neutral Density is the default for Image Trap Placement, this option becomes available when you have a specialty ink defined for a spot plate, such as a spot varnish. You can choose from Neutral Density, Transparent, Opaque, or Opaque Ignore. Opaque is often used for heavy nontransparent inks such as metallic inks, to prevent the trapping of underlying colors while still allowing trapping along the ink's edges. Opaque Ignore is used for heavy nontransparent inks to prevent trapping of underlying color *and* along the ink's edges.

- **Trap Width** This option controls the width of the overlap value, where due to imprecise printing tolerances and ink impurities, a plate's ink might spread. This used to be known as "choking" (choking compensates for spreading); the term has fallen into disuse.

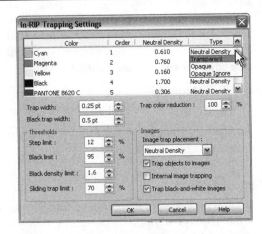

FIGURE 28-6   If your output device is equipped with In-RIP Trapping, these options are available.

- **Black Trap Width**   This option controls the distance that inks spread into solid black, or the distance between black ink edges and underlying inks. It is used when the amount of black ink reaches the percentage specified in the Black Limit field (in the Thresholds area).

- **Trap Color Reduction**   Use this option to prevent certain butt-aligned colors (areas on different plates that meet one another) from creating a trap that is darker than both colors combined. Values smaller than 100 percent lighten the color of the trap.

- **Step Limit**   This option controls the degree to which components of butt-aligned color must vary before a trap is created, usually set between 8 and 20 percent. Lower percentages increase sensitivity to color differences and create larger traps.

- **Black Limit**   This value controls the minimum amount of black ink required before the value entered in the Black Trap Width field is applied.

- **Black Density Limit**   This option controls the neutral density value at, or above, the value at which the In-RIP feature considers it solid black. To treat a dark spot-color as black, enter its Neutral Density value in this field.

- **Sliding Trap Limit**   This value sets the percentage difference between the neutral density of butt-aligned colors at which the trap is moved from the darker side of the color edge toward the centerline. Use this option when colors have similar neutral densities to prevent abrupt shifts in trap color along a Fountain fill edge, for example.

- **Trap Objects To Images**   Choosing this option lets you create traps between vectors and bitmaps.

- **Image Trap Placement**   This option sets where the trap falls when trapping vector objects to bitmap objects to either Neutral Density, Spread, Choke, or Centerline in this option's drop-down list. Neutral Density applies the same trapping rules used elsewhere in the printed document. Using this option to trap a vector to a bitmap can cause uneven edges because the trap moves from one side of the edge to the other. Spread produces a trap in areas where bitmaps meet vector objects. Choke causes vector objects to overlap the bitmap (the bitmap is choked). Centerline creates a trap that straddles the edge between vectors and bitmaps.

- **Internal Image Trapping**   This option creates traps *within* the area of a bitmap, which is useful when very high contrast and posterized images are part of a design.

- **Trap Black-And-White Images**   Choosing this option performs trapping between vectors and black-and-white (monochrome) bitmaps.

Setting Prepress Options

The term *prepress* is used to describe the preparing of film for various printing processes. Choosing the Prepress tab displays all options controlling how your printing material will be produced, and which information is included on the page, as shown in Figure 28-7.

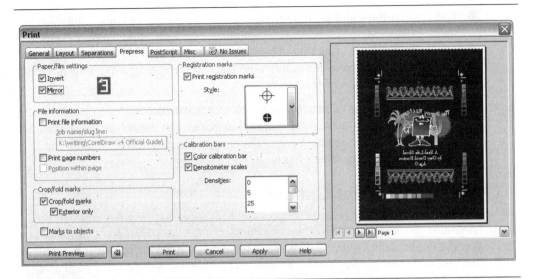

FIGURE 28-7   Use these options to control how your output is produced and to add prepress information and markings.

Here's what the options in the Prepress tab offer:

- **Paper/Film Settings**   These two options specify negative/positive printing and on which side of the film the light-sensitive emulsion layer appears. Choose Invert to cause your output to print in reverse; choose Mirror to cause the image to print backward. Ask the press operator or service bureau which way their imagesetter is set up for film.

- **Print File Information**   A Job Name/Slug Line text box is printed on each separation, to better visually identify each printed sheet. The path and filename of your document is used by default, but you can enter your own information. Choose Print Page Numbers to print page numbers as defined in your CorelDRAW document; choose Position Within Page to print this information *inside* the page boundaries—outside is the default.

- **Crop/Fold Marks**   Crop marks help locate your document's page corners; fold marks indicate folds for a specific layout. Choose Crop/Fold Marks to print these markings. While this is selected, you can also choose Exterior Only to cause the marks to print only outside the page boundaries on your printing material, which produces a more polished final presentation. Both options are selected by default.

- **Registration Marks and Styles**   Registration marks help to align each separation plate; the film print is used to make the plate, and the plates need to be precisely aligned when your piece is printed, or you get a "Sunday Funny Pages" finished output. Choosing Print Registration Marks (selected by default) includes these marks on your output. Use the Style selector to specify a specific mark shape; the selector includes a preview of both positive and negative versions.

- **Calibration Bars and Densitometer Scales**   These two options enable you to include color calibration bars and densitometer scales outside the page boundaries of your printed material. Calibration bars are useful for evaluating color density accuracy by printing a selection of grayscale shades that may be used for measuring the density—or blackness value—of film or paper output.

- **Marks To Objects**   Choosing this option causes whichever prepress marks are currently selected to be included with your output to print around the entire arrangement of objects on each document page. These appear regardless of whether the Crop/Fold Marks option is selected to print.

Choosing PostScript Options

None of the above information on separations and advanced trapping features will be meaningful if your chosen output is not to a PostScript device. If you don't currently see the PostScript tab, shown in Figure 28-8, you need to define a different print driver. Options in this tab area offer control over PostScript options that use a specific type of page description language, Level 2, Level 3, the type of device, and so on.

You set the following options on the PostScript tab:

- **Compatibility**   In most cases, the printer and the PPD (PostScript Printing Description) file you choose are automatically set with the Compatibility option, which determines which PostScript features the output device is capable of handling. Older printers may be limited to PostScript Level 1 or 2 technology; most new models are compatible with Level 3. If you're unsure which to choose, check out the manufacturer's FAQ area on their website or the physical printer documentation.

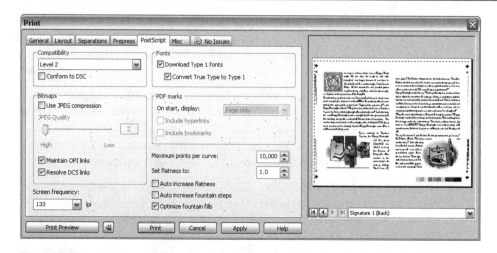

FIGURE 28-8   These options will become available if your selected printer is PostScript compatible.

- **Conform To DSC** Document Structuring Convention (DSC) is a special file format for PostScript documents. It includes a number of comments that provide information for *postprocessors*. Postprocessors can shuffle the order of pages, print two or more pages on a side, and perform other tasks often needlessly performed by humans.

- **Bitmaps** Selecting Level 2 or 3 PostScript-compatible printers offers you the option of using the Use JPEG Compression option to reduce printing time if you have bitmap images in your document. When this option is selected, the Quality Factor slider is available for setting the quality of the bitmaps being printed. Keep in mind that JPEG is a *lossy* compression standard, some of the original image information is discarded, quality is compromised, and at high compression settings, a photograph can take on visual noise.

- **Maintain OPI Links** This option preserves links to server-based bitmap images, provided you have imported temporary low-resolution versions using the Open Prepress Interface (OPI) option when you created your CorelDRAW document. Using OPI, you can store high-resolution bitmap images in a printer's memory, and work temporarily with an imported low-resolution version. When your document is printed, the lower-resolution version is swapped with the higher-resolution version. By default, this option is selected.

- **Resolve DCS Links** Desktop Color Separation (DCS) technology is similar to OPI; you use placeholders in your document that have links to digitally separated images for use in process or multi-ink printing. When this option is enabled, the linked images automatically replace the placeholder images at print time. By default, this option is selected. If this option is not selected, a prompt will appear while the document is being printed, so you can relink the files manually through directory boxes.

- **Screen Frequency** This selector is where you set the Screen Frequency for your output, which can also be set in the Separations tab while setting Advanced Setting options. Remember: dots per inch is *not* the same value as lines per inch. A typical high-resolution lpi value is 133, and you really need to know before printing what your intended output device is capable of rendering. A good rule of thumb for bitmap images is the *Times Two rule*; if your intended output is 133 lpi, for example, a bitmap in your design should be 266 pixels per inch for optimal rendering.

- **Fonts** PostScript printing devices can print both Type 1 and True Type fonts. Type 1 fonts are often preferred because the font data is written in PostScript language. CorelDRAW's options let you control which fonts are used during printing. It's more reliable to download the fonts to the printing device; this speeds printing and produces better-looking text. To enable this feature, select Download Type 1 Fonts. If this option is disabled, fonts are printed as curves, which can take a lot of printing time when you have a lot of text on a page. When you select the Download Type 1 Fonts option, the Convert True Type To Type 1 option becomes available (and selected by default).

28

- **PDF Marks**   If your document is being prepared for printing as a composite to an Adobe PDF distiller, these options become available. You can specify how your PDF file initially displays when viewed in Adobe Acrobat Reader or a third-party reader by using options in the On Start, Display selector. Choose Page Only, Full Screen, or Thumbnail view. You can also choose whether to Include Hyperlinks and/or Include Bookmarks in the resulting PDF file. If you're preparing a PDF to send to a service bureau for high-resolution output, don't use hyperlinks; they mess up the appearance of your printed piece, and let's get real—how does your intended audience click on a piece of paper to visit a website?

- **Maximum Points Per Curve**   This setting lets you define how complex curves are rendered when printed, the default of which is fixed at 10,000 nodes per curve. The limit may be set within a range of 20 to 20,000 nodes per curve. The more nodes per curve, the more complex your printing will be, but the smoother, for example, your text will look. Here's the deal: printers don't render curves like you see CorelDRAW render curves to your screen. Instead, curves must be defined as straight vectors connected by nodes—the more nodes along a curve in your document, the closer the rendered design looks to a truly curved shape.

- **Set Flatness To**   The Set Flatness To setting is used to set the flatness limit to a value between 0.20 and 100.0. The Auto Increase Flatness feature has the effect of increasing the flatness of complex objects by a factor of 2 until the object prints. Increased flatness will cause the printing of curves to be less smooth. Flatness is related to the Maximum Points Per Curve option, discussed above.

- **Auto Increase Flatness**   This option lets you simplify the printing of curves by decreasing the number of straight vector lines that describe the curve. This option can be used as a last resort if you run into problems printing highly complex shapes in your CorelDRAW document, usually a printer memory problem, as in *not enough* memory.

- **Auto Increase Fountain Steps**   This option makes the print engine examine your document for opportunities to increase the number of fountain steps in an effort to avoid Fountain fill banding. *Banding* is the visible effect of not having enough sequential steps in a Fountain fill; you see bands of gradually changing color instead of a smooth transition from one object area to another. Increasing the number of steps that describe a Fountain fill will cause Fountain fills to appear smoother, but it will also increase printing complexity and output time.

- **Optimize Fountain Fills**   This option works in reverse of the previous option by setting the print engine to *decrease* the number of fountain steps set for objects in your document to the number of steps your printer is capable of reproducing.

Miscellaneous Printing Options

The Miscellaneous (Misc) tab has a mix of options ranging from color profile and proofing, to bitmap handling, as shown in Figure 28-9.

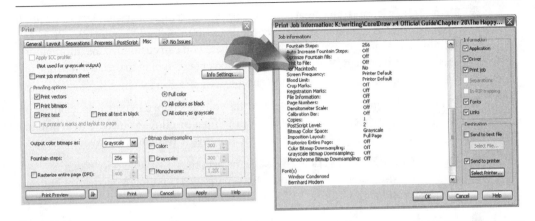

FIGURE 28-9 The Misc tab features a potpourri of options for specifying proofing and bitmap colors.

Here's what these options offer control over:

- **Apply ICC Profile** This option is available only when printing to a color printer; it lets you print using a color profile. An ICC (International Color Consortium) profile contains specific color data used to reproduce colors more faithfully as compared with your monitor view of the document. ICC profiles are all about color space: for example, sRGB (Stokes RGB, also somewhat derisively called *Small* RGB) is a profile used to conform to Internet standards that Microsoft and Hewlett-Packard also support big-time. If you wanted to print an image you downloaded from the Web in JPEG file format, the chances are good it was created using the sRGB color profile. Therefore, to print it as closely as possible to how you see it on your monitor, you'd use the sRGB color profile. The Apply ICC Profile option enables Corel's Color Manager while printing. Be aware that you should use only *one* color management system during the printing process. If your printer uses its own color management system, you should *disable* this feature—two color management systems operating at the same time is equivalent to two wheels on your car traveling in their own directions...you get nowhere. Objects in your document that are filled with process color (any color you chose from the Palettes tab in Uniform fill, and CMYK-based colors) do not use color management, and no color corrections are performed on them while printing because their color composition is fixed to a specific printing color space. If your printer is a color printer and separations are not selected, the profile displayed in this field is the profile selected in Corel's Color Manager Composite profile. To open the Color Manager, choose Tools | Color Management *before* you choose to print a document.

28

- **Print Job Information Sheet**   Select this option to include a summary of all printing options you have selected. Clicking the Info Settings button opens the Print Job Information dialog, shown in Figure 28-9, where you can customize the information sheet format if needed. You can also use options in this dialog to create a separate text file and/or immediately print the info sheet.

- **Proofing Options**   Proofing options offer you the chance to create specialized output specifically for checking your output prior to final printing. You can toggle printing of vectors, bitmaps, text, or color options, and/or toggle printer's and layout marks.

- **Output Color Bitmaps As**   This selector becomes available only when a composite is selected to print (not color separations) and lets you specify how color bitmaps print using CMYK, RGB, or Grayscale.

- **Fountain Steps**   This setting controls the number of overall fountain steps used in printing fountain-filled objects. Fountain steps can be set within a range of 2 to 2,000 steps. For proofing purposes, reducing this value speeds up printing time.

- **Rasterize Entire Page (DPI)**   While Rasterize Entire Page is selected, you can quickly proof a document by printing entire pages as low-resolution bitmaps. Resolution can be set within a range of 72 (low screen resolution) to 600 dpi (fairly high).

- **Bitmap Downsampling**   To lower the resolution of bitmaps only, use these options. You can individually set the resolution of Color, Grayscale, and/or Monochrome (black *or* white, not black *and* white, similar to fax quality) images from 10 to 9,999 dpi.

CorelDRAW X4's Printing Issues Tab

The process of verifying that every last detail in your document will print as expected is often called *preflight,* and the good news is that the Issues tab is your flight attendant. CorelDRAW X4 examines the contents of your document and the printing options you've selected and then compares them to the capabilities of your selected printer and your selected output material. Printing snafus are found automatically and flagged by warning symbols as shown in the first illustration in this chapter. Figure 28-10 is the Issues tab, which is divided into two sections; with Print Preview turned on, it's both documented and visually obvious what this proposed print has going against it.

The top half of the Issues dialog lists the preflight issues detected with a brief explanation. The bottom half explains the causes, identifies the exact problems, and offers suggestions and recommendations for correcting them.

The Issues feature will not prevent you from printing your document. If you want, you can deactivate the feature by selecting the found issue in the upper portion of the tab and choosing Don't Check For This Issue In The Future at the bottom of the tab. This disables

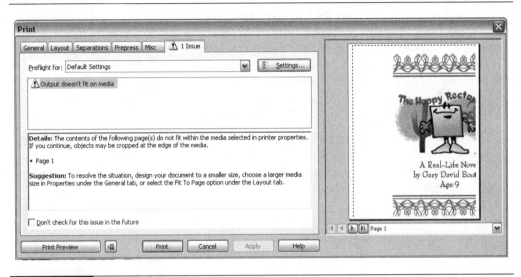

FIGURE 28-10   If CorelDRAW X4 anticipates printing problems, they'll be explained in this dialog.

the detection of the issue in the Preflight Settings dialog, shown next. Clicking the Settings button opens this dialog, which also lets you save and load current settings for future use.

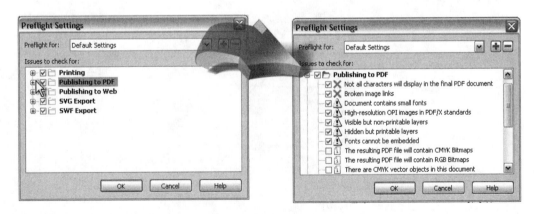

Previewing Your Printed Document

CorelDRAW X4's Print Preview feature provides a very good way of viewing your document and performing minor touchups, and it's fully integrated with CorelDRAW X4's print engine. To open the Print Preview feature, click the Print Preview button from within the Print dialog. Print Preview also is available in the File menu.

Print Preview (see Figure 28-11) is a separate application window and includes its own command menus, toolbars, Property Bar, Status Bar, and Toolbox. When Print Preview is open, CorelDRAW is still open in the background. You'll also find that nearly all of the options that can be set while viewing your document in the Print Preview window are available, except they provide a higher level of control.

Browsing and Viewing Previews

The first thing you'll want to do in Print Preview is examine how your printed pages will look. Across the bottom of the Print Preview window, you'll find page controls, shown next, so you can browse each printed page. Use the arrow buttons to move forward or backward in the sequence, or click a page tab to display a specific page. As you do this, you'll discover

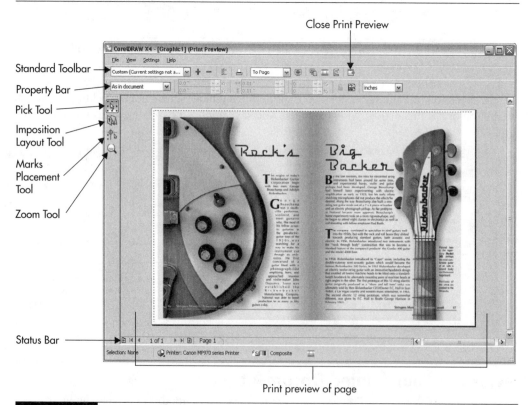

FIGURE 28-11 Print Preview is a program within a program, with its own interface, tools, shortcuts, and commands.

each printed page is represented—including individual ink separation pages for each page in your document when you're printing separations.

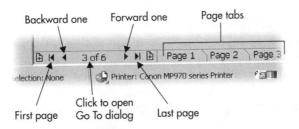

You can view your pages in a number of different ways based on output mode, color, and object type. To change view modes, choose one of the following from the View menu:

- **Show Image**   Choosing this lets you hide the display of page contents to speed screen redraw times when you've got a lot of objects on a specific page.

- **Preview Colors**   Choose this to access three basic previewing states. Auto (Simulate Output) shows each page's color according to your selected options and your printer's capabilities. If your chosen printer driver does not print in color, you'll see only grayscale color on your pages. To override this, choose either Color or Grayscale, which forces a specific view.

- **Preview Separations**   Choose Preview Separations to access three basic states. Auto (Simulate Output) displays separations according to your printer driver and selected print options. If Separations are not selected to print, only a composite is shown, and vice versa. You can override this by choosing either Composite or Separations to force a specific separation display state.

- **Printable Area**   This varies from printer to printer; the *printable area* is the physical area that the printer can render onto a page. Choose this option (selected by default) to show a dotted line representing the maximum extent to which the printer can render.

- **Render PostScript Fills**   Use this option to have PostScript fills display as they will print. Deactivating this option can free up system resources when viewing documents where you used a lot of PostScript filled objects.

- **Show Current Tile**   This option highlights individual tiles as you hover your cursor over them when previewing, and it's useful when printing large documents in sections onto small output material (*tile printing,* covered earlier in this chapter). To use tile printing from within Print Preview, choose Settings | Layout to open the Print Options dialog to the Layout tab, and then click to activate the Print Tiled Pages option.

Print Preview has keyboard shortcuts to access specific Print dialog areas, including these:
General (CTRL+E)
Layout (CTRL+L)
Separations (CTRL+S)
Prepress (CTRL+M)
Miscellaneous Options (CTRL+O)
Preflight (CTRL+I)

Print Preview Tools and the Property Bar

The key to using Print Preview to its fullest is learning where all the options are located, what each tool does, and what print properties are available while using each. There are four tools on the Toolbox—the Pick Tool, Imposition Layout Tool, Marks Placement Tool, and Zoom Tool—each of which is discussed in the sections to follow. The Standard Toolbar, shown next, contains printing options, viewing options, and shortcuts you can use to open print-related dialogs.

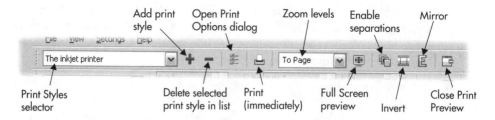

First is the Print Styles selector, which is used to choose all printing options according to a saved set of print parameters. As with other CorelDRAW X4 Preset features, you can select, save, delete, or modify print styles in the selector. Choose an existing Print Style, use the current unsaved settings on the current print job, or choose Browse to show the Open dialog so you can work with a saved Print Style. To delete a selected Print Style, click the Delete (–) button. To save a Print Style, click the Add (+) button (or use the F12 shortcut) to open the Save Settings As dialog. Use the Settings To Include options to specify which print options to save with your new style, and click Save to add the Print Style to the selector.

The remaining options in the Standard Toolbar have the following functions, many of which are covered earlier in this chapter:

- **Print Options** This option opens the Print Options dialog.

- **Print button** This option immediately sends the document to the printer using the current options. Use CTRL+T as a shortcut.

- **Zoom Levels** Select a predefined zoom level from the list to change the view magnification level.

- **Full Screen Preview button**   This option is self-explanatory. Press ESC to return to Print Preview. You can also use CTRL+U as a shortcut.

- **Enable Color Separations button**   This option sends the printing of color separations to the output device using color selected in the Separations tab of the Print Options dialog.

- **Invert button**   This option inverts the printed image to print in reverse. This is for film using an imagesetting device, but can also provide an amusing special effect (and use a lot of ink!).

- **Mirror button**   This option flips the printed document to print backward to set emulsion orientation on imagesetting devices. You can also use this to print to T-shirt transfers.

- **Close Print Preview button**   Pressing this (or using the ALT+C shortcut) returns you to the current CorelDRAW X4 document.

Pick Tool Property Bar Options

The Pick Tool in Print Preview is used in much the same way it's used in the drawing window; with it you select and move (by click-dragging) whole pages. While the Pick Tool and objects on a page are selected, the Property Bar features a variety of printing options, shortcuts, position settings, and tool settings, as shown here:

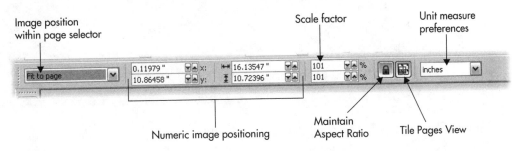

Many of these options are for positioning and scaling the contents of whole pages in relation to the printed output page size that your printer is currently set to use. You can click-drag to move whole pages or enter numeric values in Property Bar boxes. Click-dragging the page object control handles lets you scale the objects interactively.

Imposition Layout Tool Property Bar Options

The Imposition Layout Tool provides control over the print layout. Only certain imagesetters are capable of printing multiple pages in signature formats, so it's best to check with the person doing your print job before making changes using the Imposition options.

When the Imposition Layout Tool is selected, the preview is changed to display imposition-specific properties. This tool has four separate editing states, each of which is chosen on the Edit Settings selector. Options accessible on the Property Bar while Edit Basic Settings is selected, shown here, give you control over imposition layout options. Choosing Edit Page Placements, Edit Gutters & Finishing, or Edit Margins from this selector displays a set of imposition options for each state.

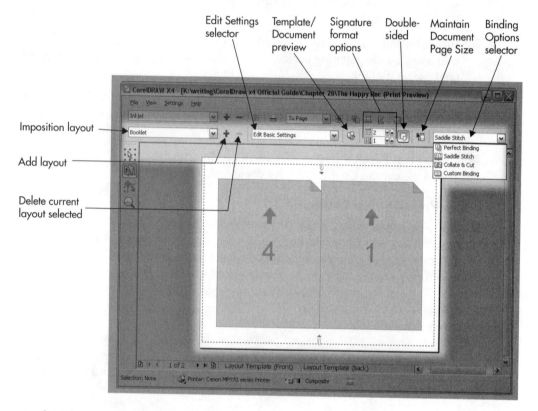

Marks Placement Tool Property Bar Options

The Marks Placement Tool lets you alter the position of crop and fold marks, registration marks, color calibration bars, printing information, and Density Scale positions. When the Marks Placement Tool is selected, the Property Bar features options for positioning and printing certain mark types, as shown in Figure 28-12.

To view or position crop and fold marks, click-drag the top, bottom, or sides of the rectangle defining their position, or enter values in the Property Bar boxes. To change the position of other marks you have selected to print with your document page, choose the Marks Placement Tool and drag directly on the marks.

Zoom Tool Property Bar Options

The Zoom Tool in the Print Preview window is used much the same way as the Zoom Tool in CorelDRAW X4, so you can increase or decrease the view of your Print Preview. Many of the functions of the Zoom Tool are performed interactively or by using hot keys. While the

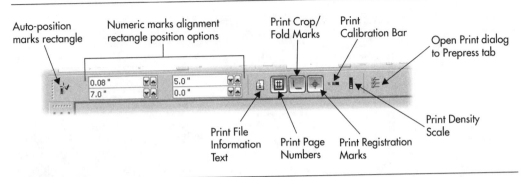

Auto-position marks rectangle

Numeric marks alignment rectangle position options

Print Crop/Fold Marks

Print Calibration Bar

Open Print dialog to Prepress tab

Print File Information Text

Print Page Numbers

Print Registration Marks

Print Density Scale

FIGURE 28-12 While the Marks Placement Tool is selected, the Property Bar features these options.

Zoom Tool is selected, the Property Bar features all Zoom options and magnification commands, as shown here:

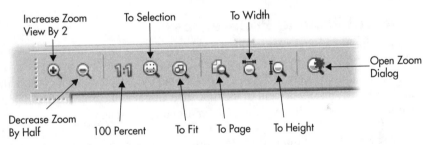

Increase Zoom View By 2

To Selection

To Width

Open Zoom Dialog

Decrease Zoom By Half

100 Percent

To Fit

To Page

To Height

You can also change Zoom settings by choosing View | Zoom (CTRL+Z) to open the Zoom dialog to choose among all Zoom Tool functions. Use shortcuts to change your view magnification while using Print Preview's Zoom Tool: Zoom Out using F3, Zoom To Page using SHIFT+F4, Zoom To Selection using SHIFT+F2, and Zoom To Fit using F4.

TIP | *Print Preview doesn't have an Undo command; to reset options quickly, close and then reopen Print Preview. Click the Close button in the Standard Toolbar to return to either your CorelDRAW X4 document or the Print Options dialog.*

Setting Printing Preferences

Once you're familiar with the ocean of printing options, what your output device is capable of, and what you want from a specific print job, Printing Preferences can be your one-stop shop for most of the items covered in this chapter. Choose Settings | Printing Preferences (CTRL+F is the shortcut) while in the Print Preview window to open the Printing Preferences dialog, shown in Figure 28-13. Preferences are subdivided into General, Driver Compatibility, and Preflight options. To change any of the options, click a Setting title; a drop-down selector appears, and then you make your change.

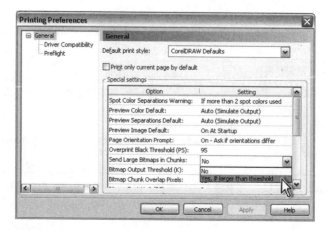

FIGURE 28-13   The Printing Preferences dialog offers comprehensive control over output settings.

General Printing Preferences

Options in the General tab provide control over fonts, crop mark color, driver banding, and so on, and they set the parameters for potential preflight issues or warning dialogs that appear before and during printing. These options are set by default to the highest fault tolerance for most printing jobs; 99 percent of the time your prints will come out fine if you don't change the settings. Here's a list explaining the most common states:

- **Spot Color Separations Warning**   This option lets you control the warning state while printing color separations. The warning can be set to appear if more than one, two, three, or any spot colors are used in the document being printed.

- **Preview Color Default**   This option sets the initial color display of your printed document when the Print Preview window is first opened. Choose Auto (Simulate Output), Color, or Grayscale.

- **Preview Separations Default**   This option sets the initial color display of your separations when the Print Preview window is first opened. Choose Auto (Simulate Output) or Composite.

- **Preview Image Default**   This controls whether your document image is automatically set to show when the Print Preview window first opens. Choose On At Startup (the default) or Off At Startup.

- **Page Orientation Prompt**   The Page Orientation Prompt may be turned On or Off using this option. While On, the warning may be set to Ask If Orientations Differ (the default), and when it's set to Off, you can choose Always Match Orientation or Don't Change Orientation.

- **Overprint Black Threshold (PS)**   During overprinting, CorelDRAW X4 sets a default value for overprinting black objects only if they contain a uniform fill of 95 percent or more black. The Overprint Black Threshold setting can be changed using this option, so you can further customize the global overprinting function. The threshold limit can be set between 0 and 100 percent black.

- **Send Large Bitmaps In Chunks**   This option works in combination with the Bitmap Output Threshold setting and can be set to the default Yes, If Larger Than Threshold (referring to the Bitmap Threshold value), or No.

- **Bitmap Output Threshold (K)**   When printing to non-PostScript printers, this option lets you set a limit on the size of bitmaps, as measured in kilobytes, sent to the printing device. By default, this value is set to the maximum, but you can set it to specific values within a range of 0 to 4,096 (the default). This is a good option to change if your non-PostScript printer doesn't have a lot of memory and you're pulling prints that are unfinished due to lack of RAM for processing the image.

- **Bitmap Chunk Overlap Pixels**   If a printing device has insufficient memory or another technical problem processing very large bitmap images, you can have CorelDRAW tile sections of such a bitmap. The Overlap value is used to prevent seams from showing between "chunks" of the large image. When you're printing to non-PostScript printers, this option lets you define the number of overlap pixels within a range of 0 to 48 pixels. The default is 32 pixels.

- **Bitmap Font Limit (PS)**   Usually, font sizes set below the Bitmap Font Size Threshold preference are converted to bitmap and stored in a PostScript printer's internal memory. This can be a time-consuming operation that usually increases the time your document takes to print. You can limit the number of fonts to which this occurs, forcing the printer to store only a given number of fonts per document. The default setting here is 8, but it can be set anywhere within a range of 0 to 100. Unless your document is a specimen sheet of all the fonts you have installed, 8 is a good number to set this option to.

- **Bitmap Font Size Threshold (PS)**   Most of the time CorelDRAW X4 converts very small sizes of text to bitmap format when printing to PostScript printers, such as 4-point legal type on a bottle label. This option lets you control how this is done, based on the size of the font's characters. The default Bitmap Font Size Threshold is 75 pixels, but it can be set within a range of 0 to 1,000 pixels. The actual point size converted to bitmap varies according to the resolution used when printing a document. The threshold limit will determine exactly which font sizes are affected. For example, the equivalent font size of 75 pixels when printing to a printer resolution of 300 dpi is roughly 18 points, while at 600 dpi it's about 9 points. The higher the resolution, the lower the point size affected. A number of provisions determine whether these controls apply, including whether the font has been scaled or skewed, and whether Envelope effects, Fountain or Texture fills, or print scaling options such as Fit To Page have been chosen.

28

- **Composite Crop Marks (PS)**   This is a useful feature for setting the pen color of crop marks either to print in black only or in process (CMYK) color, making the crop marks print to every color plate during process color separation printing.

- **PostScript 2 Stroke Adjust (PS)**   The PostScript Level 2 language has a provision particularly useful for graphics programs such as CorelDRAW. Stroke Adjust produces strokes of uniform thickness to compensate for uneven line widths due to the conversion of *vector* artwork to *raster* printed graphics, which is what all printers do. The PostScript 2 Stroke Adjust option *should not* be used for older printers that are not compatible with PostScript Level 2 or Level 3 technology. Most recently manufactured printing devices are at least PostScript Level 2 compatible. If you are not sure what level your printing device is, leave this setting Off or consult the docs that came with the device.

- **Many Fonts**   This controls a warning that appears if the document you're printing includes more than ten different fonts. If you're new to CorelDRAW and are experimenting with all the cool fonts that came on the CD, your file can easily exceed this limit. If your printer's memory and/or your system resources are capable of handling large numbers of different fonts, consider increasing this value. The Many Fonts warning option can be set within a range of 1 to 50 fonts. Tangentially related to this option is a creative design issue: very few professionals use more than ten different typefaces in a design; five can express an idea using text quite well in most situations.

- **Small Fonts**   This controls a warning that appears if the document you're printing includes fonts below a 7-point size threshold by default. The Small Fonts warning option can be set between 3 and 18 points. Resolution plays an important part in rendering small point size typefaces, as does the design of the characters within the font. For example, a 1,200 dpi laser printer can render 4-point Helvetica quite legibly, less so with a serif typeface such as Times Roman because the serifs at this size are about equal to insect parts. Choose a simple, sans serif font for extremely small font sizes. Do not expect a perfect rendering of a very small typeface, because the dots of ink or toner cartridge can only render a finite number of dots to represent very small text.

- **Render To Bitmap Resolution**   This option by default is set to Automatic, which causes bitmaps to be output at the same resolution as vector objects and text in your document. To specify the resolution of bitmaps to be printed at lower or higher resolutions than the rest of the document, choose specific settings within a range of 150 to 600 dpi.

Driver Compatibility

The Driver Compatibility area, shown in Figure 28-14, provides control over specific driver features for *non-PostScript* printers. Choose a Printer from the drop-down menu, and then choose specific options in the dialog to make changes. Clicking Apply saves and associates your changes with the selected driver.

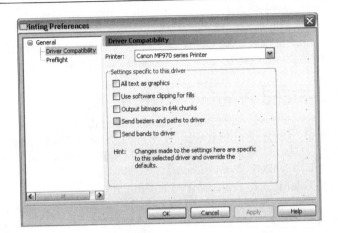

FIGURE 28-14   Use the Driver Compatibility options to specify how non-PostScript printers handle specific object types.

28

Printing Issues Warning Options

You can customize issues found by CorelDRAW X4's built-in preflight feature using options in the Preflight page of the Printing Preferences dialog (CTRL+F), which can be accessed only from within Print Preview by choosing Settings | Printing Preferences and clicking Preflight in the tree directory, as shown in Figure 28-15.

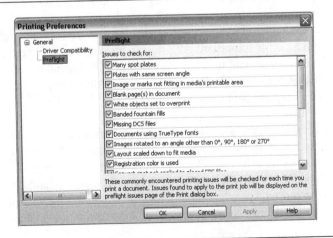

FIGURE 28-15   Preflight options let you control how and when detected printing issues appear.

This is a comprehensive list covering specific issues ranging from mismatched layout sizes to spot colors with similar names. Use the check box options in the list to activate or deactivate each option, or use the Don't Check For This Issue In The Future option, located at the bottom of the Issues tab of the Print Options dialog when an issue is discovered.

Corel's Double-Sided Printing Wizard

You can create booklets and other double-sided printed documents on your personal printer by using the Double-Sided Printing Wizard. You can access this feature independently of CorelDRAW by choosing Start | Programs | Corel Graphics Suite X4 | Duplexing Wizard or by pressing CTRL+D while in Print Preview.

This wizard is fairly self-explanatory and straightforward to use. When a driver is set to use the duplex printing feature, the Manual Double-Sided Printing dialog displays when CorelDRAW's print engine starts to print, asking whether you want to print on both sides of a printed page. For specific page-insertion directions, you'll find an option that will print an instruction sheet to show you which way you should reinsert the sheet of paper after printing the first side.

To prevent the Manual Double-Sided Printing dialog from appearing, disable the duplex printing feature by running the Duplexing Setup Wizard and selecting Disable when asked. To access the Disable option, you must run the wizard by choosing Start | Programs | Corel Graphics Suite X4 | Duplexing Wizard.

Using the Prepare for Service Bureau Wizard

CorelDRAW X4 provides a wizard that collects all the information, fonts, and files required to display and print your documents correctly if you don't own an imagesetter or other high-end output device and need to send your document to press.

Corel has a service bureau affiliate program, and service bureaus approved by Corel can provide you with a profile to prepare your document with the Service Bureau Wizard. This profile can also contain special instructions that a service bureau needs you to follow before sending your files. Check with your vendor to see whether it is a Corel Approved Service Bureau (CASB). If it's not, and your printing need is a do-or-die situation, see the following sidebar on PDF files.

To launch the wizard, choose File | Prepare For Service Bureau. From there, the wizard guides you through a series of question-and-answer pages that gathers the information you need to upload or put on a disk to deliver to a printer or service bureau. When you finish the process, all necessary files are copied to a folder you define, and optional documents specifying your required output are included, depending on your wizard option choices. Figure 28-16 shows the succession of wizard dialogs from the beginning to the end of the process.

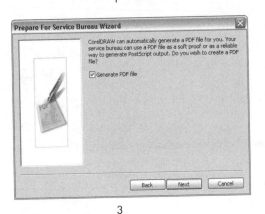

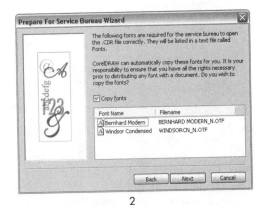

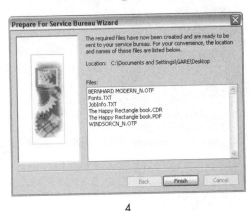

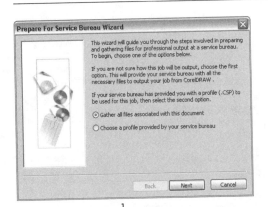

28

FIGURE 28-16   In four steps your files are prepared for sending to a service bureau.

When in Doubt, PDF It

Because printing is an art in and of itself, it's an unrealistic expectation for you, the designer, to be well acquainted with an expensive piece of machinery, an equally expensive process, and all the parameters that need to be known to ensure the best quality output. Fortunately, the Acrobat PDF file format is the best hedge to date for anything short of an ironclad guarantee that a print job will turn out as you want it to. When CorelDRAW writes a "soft proof" PDF file as part of the Prepress Wizard process, what you're getting can, under certain circumstances, be used as the file a commercial printer or service bureau uses to make printing plates. Naturally, your

(Continued)

preferred option is to find a Corel Approved Service Bureau, but in a rush, this might be like finding size 14 shoes in exactly the color and style you desire at the first store you pull into.

When CorelDRAW writes a PDF document, vector shapes are preserved as vectors—they are *not* transformed into bitmap images—so object outlines and text will print crisply. Any bitmap images are written to PDF at their original resolution in CMYK, print-ready color space, and although by default any bitmaps are written as JPEGs, the amount of lossy compression is usually visually negligible. When you're using typefaces in a document, the Prepress Wizard embeds a subset of the characters used directly into the PDF file (when a font is coded to allow font embedding—some commercial fonts disable this), and any Fountain fills you might have used print smoothly because PostScript Level 2 and later support gradient fills.

The only disadvantage to using a PDF as your press-ready document is that last-minute touchups and corrections are difficult. If the press or service bureau owns Adobe Illustrator, the document can be opened as editable, and most of the time it opens accurately. Overall, the PDF that you can choose to be written during the Prepress Wizard process can serve as a visual guide for the press operator, and it's a valuable part of an alternative strategy if your local service bureau is a little backward and doesn't own a copy of CorelDRAW.

Print Merge

Print Merge gives you the design and business opportunities to merge database information with specific fields of your CorelDRAW documents at print time, to print personalized documents with only a click or two. If you create mailing labels, short runs targeted at a specific audience, and marketing documents, this feature will be invaluable. By creating special fields, you can merge specific database information into your document and set properties such as color, font style, and so on. This feature also lets you use ODBC Data Sources from database management systems that use Structured Query Language (SQL) as a standard.

Follow these steps when you need to create a Print Merge:

1. Choose File | Print Merge | Create/Load Merge Fields. Choosing this command opens the Print Merge Wizard, and you either create a database from scratch or choose an existing one.

2. If you need to create a custom merge document, choose the Create New Text option and then click Next. Create fields for your custom database by entering unique names in the Text Field and/or Numeric Field, shown in Figure 28-17, and then click

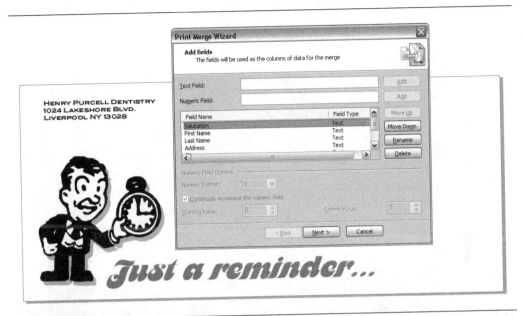

| **FIGURE 28-17** | Create your custom database fields by typing in the Text and/or Numeric Field box and then click Add. |

the Add button. As you build your field list, you can change the order of the fields by clicking to highlight a field in the Field Name list, and then clicking the Move Up and Move Down buttons. You can also edit the fields you've created by using the Rename and Delete buttons to change or remove a selected field. Choose the Incremental Field Data option while a field is selected in the list to number each entry in the field automatically. If you need numeric data, enter the value in the Numeric Field; when this option is used, new fields display, letting you specify the numeric sequence of your data and formatting. You can also choose the Continually Increment The Numeric Field box to save time making your field entries. Once your list is created, click Next to proceed.

3. The next page of the wizard, shown in Figure 28-18, gets you right into building your database by entering values to build sets of field entries. To begin a new entry, click the New button, and then fill in the fields with the appropriate data; click the spreadsheet-like box to highlight it, and then type your entry. You can quickly revise an entire field by highlighting it and then pressing DELETE or BACKSPACE. To delete an entire record, make sure it is the only one with a check to the left of it, and then click the Delete button. Browse your database entries using the navigation buttons, or search for specific entries by clicking the Find button. Once your database is complete, click Next to proceed.

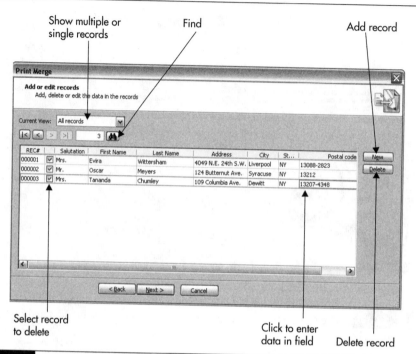

Show multiple or single records   Find   Add record

Select record to delete   Click to enter data in field   Delete record

FIGURE 28-18   Use this page of the wizard to begin building your field entry sets.

4. The final wizard page is where you save your database to reuse and update in the future. Choose the Save Data Settings As box, and then browse your hard drive for a location to save the file in Windows Rich Text Format, Plain Text, or File With A Comma Used As A Delimiter (CSV Files). You probably also want to save the Incremental field data to make looking up a record easier in the future. Click Finish to exit the wizard and automatically open the Print Merge Toolbar, shown here:

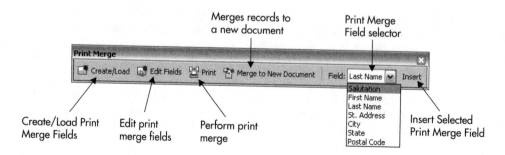

Merges records to a new document   Print Merge Field selector

Create/Load Print Merge Fields   Edit print merge fields   Perform print merge   Insert Selected Print Merge Field

5. By default, the toolbar opens with your newly created database open and the individual fields it includes listed in the Print Merge Field selector. To load your fields from a different database, click the Create/Load Print Merge Fields button to relaunch the Print Merge Wizard.

6. By inserting fields, you're creating a link from entries in your database to insertion points in your document. To insert a field into your document, make a selection from the Print Merge Field selector, and then click the Insert Selected Print Merge Field button to activate the Insert Tool cursor. Use the cursor to define an insertion point in your document with a single click. As you insert a field, a code appears in your document with the name of the field bracketed, such as <Street Address>. Repeat your insertion procedure for each field you want to include in your print merge operation, or deactivate the Insert Tool by clicking the Insert Selected Print Merge Field button.

7. The print merge fields can be formatted as Artistic Text, so you can apply any properties associated to Artistic Text to the field text to format it as you would like it to appear when printed. This includes color, alignment, font, size, style, and so on. Fields can be inserted as stand-alone text objects, inserted into Paragraph Text, or simply typed using the same code format.

8. Once your fields have been placed and formatted, the print merge document is all set up, and you might want to click the Merge To New Document button to proof the different pages with the data entered. When it comes to merging your printed document with the Print Merge feature, you must use the Print button *on the Print Merge Toolbar,* not CTRL+P. Alternatively, choose File | Print Merge | Perform Merge. Doing so immediately opens the Print dialog, where you proceed with printing using your print option selections.

9. To edit print merge fields and records, click the Edit Fields button in the Print Merge Toolbar, or choose File | Print Merge | Edit Merge Fields. This opens the Print Merge Wizard, where you begin the process again or choose an existing database to edit. Choosing Existing Database in the wizard causes the next page, shown in Figure 28-19, to offer options for choosing a data File (in TXT, CSV, or RTF format), or an ODBC Data Source. Use the data File option to open an existing database file containing the information you want to merge. Use the ODBC Data Source option and the Select ODBC Data Source button to open an existing data source.

This chapter has shown you where the print options are for both PostScript and non-PostScript output, how to check for errors and correct them before you send your CorelDRAW file to an output device, and how to make your work portable so someone with more expensive

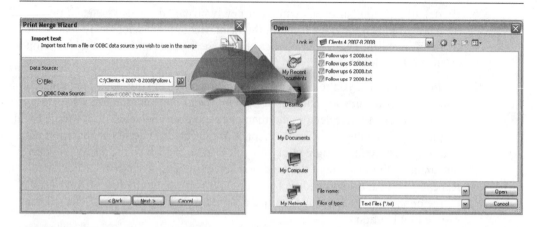

FIGURE 28-19   Use features in this dialog to specify a text-formatted data file or link to an ODBC driver.

equipment than mere mortals own can print your work to magazine quality. But this is only half the story of CorelDRAW output. Take a trip to the following chapter, where output for the Web is explored; you'll want companion pieces up on your website in addition to printed material. Regardless of whether you put dots of ink on a page or broadcast pixels to a screen 10,000 miles away, today it's called *publishing* your work.

CHAPTER 29

Basic HTML Page Layout and Publishing

Whether it's for personal pleasure or selling your wares, the Web is your connection between your ideas and your business and social contacts. It's far less expensive than other publication media such as television and print, and the really great thing about it is that it's *hot*. The good news is that you don't have to be a rocket scientist to get media up on your website using CorelDRAW, and the better news is that once you've designed a piece for print, it's practically ready to go on the Web. Create once, publish many times!

In this chapter you learn about the many tools and features at your disposal in CorelDRAW for optimizing your work for the Web, and about how to create special web graphics such as rollover buttons that turn your art into interactive art.

Web Page Navigation Buttons and Hotspots

What makes the Web a *web* are the links that connect each page to other pages. The World Wide Web is engineered by connecting *this* bit of this page to that bit of *that* page on the same site—or on any other website in the world. The engine that performs all this interconnecting magic is actually the text-based *hyperlink*. Although text-based hyperlinks are the foundation of the Web, text links are about as attractive as a foundation, and the links themselves often are just a bunch of letters and numbers that mean something to a computer, but mean nothing to a human.

However, if you put a graphic face on a link—perhaps one that changes as a visitor hovers or clicks on it—you have a web page that speaks of your talent. You also get a chance to provide nonverbal communication, the sort that plays to a worldwide audience, many of whom might not speak your native tongue. With a graphic, you can clearly point out that Area X is a link and not part of your text message. Using a graphic also gives you the opportunity to provide a visual clue about where the link goes. Consider the humble shopping cart: a great many people in this world now know that clicking on a shopping cart button takes them to a page that has something to do with buying something. That's a pretty all-encompassing message using only a few pixels!

Creating and applying attractive, well-thought-out navigational aids to a web page are a must in this competitive cyberworld. The following sections take a look at how you can use CorelDRAW's tools in combination with your skills and ingenuity to create web pages worth a thousand words.

CorelDRAW's Internet Toolbar

You'll find that several web tools and resources are located throughout CorelDRAW, but the *central* location for many of these resources is the Internet Toolbar. Here's a look at the toolbar; you choose Window | Toolbars | Internet or right-click any visible toolbar, and then choose Internet from the pop-up menu. The buttons on this toolbar are dimmed unless you have an object or two on the current drawing page; now is a good time to create a few button-shaped graphics for tutorial steps you can follow a little later.

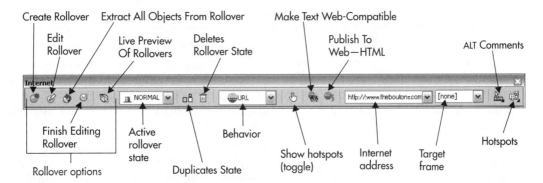

> **TIP**   *When an object is selected with the Pick Tool, you can right-click to choose Effects | Rollover | Create Rollover, and then choose Effects | Rollover | Edit Rollover (or Edit Rollover from the context menu) to define rollover states.*

29

From the Internet Toolbar you can apply web-specific properties to objects, such as hyperlinks, rollover effects, and image maps. *Hyperlinks* are links to existing web pages (or to bookmark links applied to objects in your CorelDRAW document). *Rollovers* are objects that can change their appearance and perform an event in response to a visitor's cursor action over the object. *Image maps* are objects that have one or more linked areas to web page destinations. Rollovers are unique object types (that this chapter shows you how to make); however, hyperlinks can be applied to *any* single object or to specific characters in a Paragraph Text object.

The Internet Toolbar provides a convenient hub for applying nearly all Web object properties. Many of these properties can also be found and applied elsewhere in CorelDRAW, but it's more convenient to use the toolbar. Making your graphics actually perform the duties you've assigned to them (by applying web properties) requires that a matching piece of HTML code is added to the web page HTML. CorelDRAW will write this code for you when you export your Corel document. You *will* need to provide the HTML along with the graphic to your client or to the webmaster to make the interactive graphics you've created do what they're supposed to do. In the sections to follow, you'll learn what options are available, and where they are.

Creating Rollover Buttons

Almost any object you draw can be made into a rollover that reacts to cursor actions, so you can liven up your published document with simple animated effects and hyperlinks. *Cursor actions* are events such as when a user holds or passes a cursor over the object, or clicks the object by using a mouse.

When you're creating rollovers, three basic states can be defined: Normal, Over, and Down. The *Normal state* sets how an object appears in its "static" state—when the cursor is not over or clicked on the object on the web page. The *Over state* sets the appearance of the object whenever a cursor passes over it. The *Down state* sets how the object appears when being clicked. By varying what the graphic looks like in these states, you can create interesting visual effects and give your users meaningful feedback related to their cursor movement.

This is fun stuff and deserves a tutorial. The following steps show how to animate an object or several selected objects that will serve as the finished rollover button. Although the button will react to cursor actions when you've completed the tutorial, the actions will not link to anything; linking a button is covered later in this chapter—let's concentrate on the *art* for the button first. For this example, let's suppose you want a button that tells the visitor that something is for sale: a button with a *$* symbol plays in several countries, or use a currency symbol of your preference in this example. To continue the concept here, the action a visitor would take would be to click to buy the item; therefore when visitors hover their cursor over and/or click the button, the button should change to a different look. In this example it will change its text from a *$* symbol to an official-looking "SOLD" message. Yep, as ambitious as this might sound, all you need to do is to follow these steps...

Creating Different Looks for Rollover States

1. Create a button object, make it as fancy as you like (Effects | Emboss works well), but keep the size of the button to approximately the size you'd want it on your web page—under an inch is fine for this example. Then with the Text Tool type $ and give the symbol a fill color that contrasts with the button color.

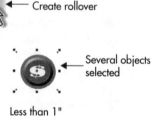

2. Select all the objects (CTRL+A), and then click the Create Rollover button on the toolbar to let CorelDRAW know this is going to be a rollover button once you've finished, as shown here.

3. With the object now defined as a Rollover object, all the states on the Active Rollover State selector display the same group of objects you selected...and it's time to create a change now. Click the Edit Rollover button to enter the editing state, as shown here, and then choose Over from the selector list.

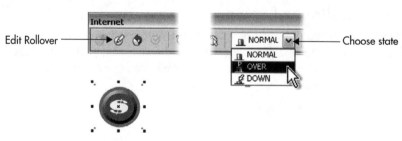

4. Edit your button; in the illustration below, the embossed circle has actually been replaced with a Polygon object. You *can* replace objects, change the fill, do just about anything you like because this editing state is not a "normal" page view in CorelDRAW's drawing window. Some tricky stuff is going on behind the scenes, and if you choose to delete a shape and replace it now, you haven't really deleted it. You remove an object from a state's *view*, in this case from the Over state, but in the Normal state all your original objects are still there. Similarly, delete the *$* and then with the Text Tool type **SOLD** in an interesting font.

Replacement objects

5. For the sake of testing all these features, let's suppose that the Over state, the SOLD button, is also good for the Down state, the state that occurs when the visitor clicks the button. By default, the Normal state is assigned to all three available states when you first made the collection of objects a rollover button. First, click on the Rollover State selector and choose Down; a view of the Normal state objects appears.

6. Trash the contents of the Down state by clicking the Delete State trashcan button.

7. Choose Over from the selector, and then click the Duplicates State button. The Over state now duplicates the following unassigned state (Down).

8. Mission accomplished! Click the Finish Editing button (shown here) and save this file to CDR file format.

Finish editing rollover

9. Oh, yeah, you want to see your creation *in action*! CorelDRAW will preview your interactive button right on the drawing page. Click the Live Preview Of Rollovers button; before you move your cursor over the button, it should look like it did when you set it to Normal—your original group of objects. Move your cursor over the button, and it should show the Over state, as it will in the Down state (when you click the button) because you duplicated Over to Down in the tutorial. After previewing the effect, click the Live Preview Of Rollovers icon again to deactivate the live preview, because live drawings can get a little disconcerting.

DOWNLOAD

Rollover.cdr is available for you to look at and take apart to better see the wealth of creative possibilities in your own work. This setup has three different states, and when you click the button, it changes shape and sort of squishes away from you. Just about any edit you can perform on objects, including totally replacing them, can be used in a Rollover button.

The Internet Toolbar also has other rollover-related commands to objects, as follows:

■ **Edit Rollover**   This was covered earlier, but you should know that even after you think you're finished, rollovers can be edited a week or a year from now.

■ **Extract All Objects From Rollover**   This is a destructive edit! Think about this command twice before you undo all your rollover work. Depending on the replacement objects you've built into a rollover, use this button to view and edit everything CorelDRAW has hidden while the document was a rollover. The objects will be stacked on top of each other, so you will have to change the stack order or drag them apart to see them.

 Rollover buttons can't be edited while the Live Preview Of Rollovers option is on. To edit any button, first disable this option by clicking on the button. You can turn on Live Preview again when you finish editing the button.

■ **Duplicates State**   Covered briefly in the tutorial, this button is used to copy the Normal state to Over and Down states if you have deleted them using the command button, discussed next.

■ **Deletes Rollover State**   This deserves a little more quality time here: while editing any rollover state, you can delete the object(s) representing it by clicking this button. After a state has been deleted, there will be no object to represent it, so the rollover state will appear blank. If needed, use the Duplicates State button to create an exact copy of the Normal state back into a blank state to avoid the need to re-create the object(s) used for this state. If you've deleted a state, be sure to set the Active Rollover State list back to Normal, or your button will be blank during an action when it's put up on a web page.

You've just created a three-step rollover button! It is an interesting graphic effect, and sometimes you might want to use it just the way it is—a sort of graphic hide-and-seek game. Most of the time, however, you'll want something additional to happen; you want the action of clicking on the link to activate a hyperlink, and the user to be taken to the link's destination. The destination can be a bookmark location on the current page, like the top or bottom of the page, or the destination might be another web page or URL location altogether. How to make the rollover or any other element do something is presented in the following section.

Setting Internet Object Behavior

While any individual object or rollover state is selected, you can set its behavior as a Web object to either a URL or an Internet bookmark using options in the Behavior selector on the Internet Toolbar, shown here.

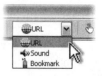

 Unfortunately, the capability to link to a sound does not work properly in CorelDRAW X4. However, if you want to link a sound to a rollover button, it's easily done in Corel PHOTO-PAINT: mp3s and WAV files are valid objects PHOTO-PAINT can tag. You can also tag a rollover event to a media file manually in an HTML editor, if you have experience speaking the language of HTML code.

Adding URL Behavior

You can apply hyperlinks to any object using this option. For example, Corel's URL is http://www.corel.com. Internet addresses must be preceded with the correct Internet protocol prefix (such as *http://, https://,* or *ftp://*). For example, if you're linking to www.corel.com, the format must be http://www.corel.com. You can also use a "mailto" protocol to link to an email address, such as by entering **mailto:*someone@somewhere.com***. This is a great way to get, for example, a potential client to write to you. By default, the *http://* protocol is automatically added to precede your URL, but you can edit it as needed.

To set a URL as the behavior for your Web object, click to select the object, and use the Behavior selector on the Internet Toolbar to specify the URL. With this option selected, type the actual URL in the Internet Address box, pressing ENTER to apply the address link. Once a URL has been applied, the Internet Toolbar displays other options. Here are the URL-specific things you can define:

- ■ **Target Frame**   Use this option to specify an optional browser window location for the new page to open into. Unless you specify differently using this drop-down, the page that is called by the assigned URL address will open in the current browser window, replacing the page that contained the link. This produces the same results as the Default [None] setting in the Target Frame list. Choosing the _blank option from the list causes a new web browser window to open to display the linked page.

If your web page uses frames for its display, you can specify where in the frameset the new content will open. Choosing _self opens the new URL to the same frame where the Web object is located. The _top option opens the new URL in the full body of the window, and all frames are replaced with a single frame containing the new document. The _parent option opens the new document in the current frame's Parent frameset. You can also enter custom frame names by typing them in the Target Frame combo box.

> **NOTE**   *Frame-based web pages cannot be searched by most search engines such as Google's, and onscreen readers for the visually impaired cannot read the contents of frames. Think very carefully if you choose a frame-based web document, and consider the audience you might lose and annoy.*

- ■ **ALT Comments**   Use this option to add ALT (alternative) text to your Web object. ALT text is a text description that is displayed either until the Web object downloads or while your web user's cursor is held over the object. It is both polite and professional to add meaningful ALT Comments text to all graphics for accessibility reasons. Because page reading software usually prefaces the reading of ALT text with an announcement of what kind of object the ALT text belongs to, such as a graphic or a hyperlink, don't repeat the link URL or enter the words "graphic" or "link." Instead describe the function or content the link leads to, for example, "Home Page," or "CorelDRAW Forums," or "send email to this terrific guy or gal." If you don't enter ALT comments for an URL, reading software will probably read or spell out the URL to your visitor; this is not a considerate way to treat visitors to your site.

■ **Hotspots** A hotspot in a graphic can be a great way to create one graphic and yet tag several different areas to different links. Once you've entered a link for an object, click on this icon to choose whether an object's shape or its bounding box will define the clickable area. Choose either Object Shape or Bounding Box Of Object in the selector, as shown. You can choose the Cross-hatch and Background colors if the currently set colors are difficult to distinguish from other colors in your document. These don't show on your published web page; they're only a visual convenience while you work in CorelDRAW.

■ **Show Hotspot** This option in the middle of the toolbar can be toggled on or off, and it can activate or deactivate the display of the crosshatch pattern, which indicates hotspots applied to Web objects, shown here.

Adding Bookmark Behavior

Assigning a bookmark to a graphic object is a method you can use to provide a convenient way for users to navigate between web pages on your site. For example, you could use a bookmark if you wanted your audience to be able to click on a button or other link and return to the first page of your site from another page in your site. This is a two-step process. In the first part of the process, you define a fixed location to which one or more URL links can point. The fixed location is an anchor or bookmarked object. The second step in the process would be to create a button or text link elsewhere that points to the object's bookmark. Let's walk through the process.

Creating Bookmark Links

1. Select an object that you want to serve as the anchor or bookmark, for example, a graphic at the top of your first page. The object that is bookmarked *must be a graphic, not text.*

2. From the Behavior drop-down list in the Internet Toolbar choose Bookmark.

3. In the Internet Bookmark box enter a descriptive name for the bookmark, such as "Home page" or "bottom of page 4" and press ENTER, as shown in Figure 29-1.

4. Select another object or button or piece of Paragraph Text on the same page or on another page in your document. This is the object that when clicked upon will take your user to the object you previously bookmarked.

5. From the Behavior drop-down list on the Internet Toolbar, choose URL.

6. From the Internet Address drop-down list, choose the Bookmark name you gave to the object in step 3. For example, if "Home page" was the bookmark name you used, you would see an entry like this: _PAGE1#Home page, as shown in Figure 29-2.

You can also enter a fully qualified URL in the Internet Address field to link to the bookmark. The URL would take the form of the web page's address, followed by a pound (#) sign and then the bookmark name. For example, a website's home page is usually named index.html. So a bookmark named "picture" on the index.html page would be typed in as http://www.mysite/index.html#picture.

29

and that's about all you really need to do until the next time.

HOME

FIGURE 29-1   A Bookmark object can be on any page of a multi-page document you want to publish as a website.

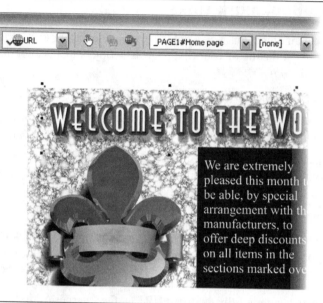

FIGURE 29-2 Use the target for the Bookmark you find on the Internet Address drop-down selector.

If you are not familiar with how to write valid HTML hyperlinks and link anchor names or IDs (called bookmarks in CorelDRAW), consult your favorite HTML manual or the World Wide Web Consortium (W3C) page on Links and Anchors at http://www.w3.org/TR/html4/struct/links.html#h-12.2.1

Web Properties and the Object Properties Docker

You can use the Object Properties docker, shown in Figure 29-3, an alternative to using the Internet Toolbar. While you can apply many of the same settings from here, Rollovers cannot be created from this docker. To open the Object Properties docker to display Web object properties for a selected object, choose Window | Dockers | Properties, or press ALT+ENTER. With the Object Properties docker open, click the Internet (Globe icon) tab.

Using the Bookmark Manager Docker

Use the Bookmark Manager docker to view, name, and apply preexisting bookmarks to objects. To open the Bookmark Manager docker, shown in Figure 29-4, choose Window | Dockers | Internet Bookmark Manager.

Purely for convenience, this docker automatically lists the currently applied bookmarks and includes commands for linking, selecting, and deleting existing bookmark links. The bookmarks themselves can only be created using the Bookmarks option from the Behavior

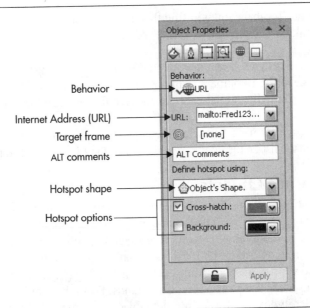

Behavior

Internet Address (URL)

Target frame

ALT comments

Hotspot shape

Hotspot options

FIGURE 29-3   The Object Properties docker provides an alternative way of applying common Internet properties to objects.

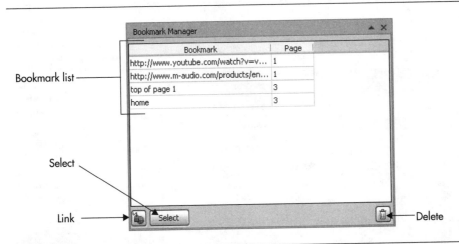

Bookmark list

Select

Link

Delete

FIGURE 29-4   The Bookmark Manager docker provides a convenient way for you to manage bookmarks applied to objects.

selector in the Internet Toolbar. You will find this docker most useful if you are trying to find a particular bookmarked graphic in a multi-page document that contains a lot of bookmarked items.

To find a bookmark in your document, open the Bookmark Manager and click to choose the bookmark's name in the Bookmark column. Then click the Select button to locate the bookmarked object. You will automatically be taken to the page, and the bookmarked object will be selected.

To create a link to a bookmark, first select the object to which you want to link a bookmark, click the link name in the list on the docker, and then click the Link Command button.

Inserting Internet Objects

Tucked away inside CorelDRAW X4 is the ability to insert form elements like text entry boxes and radio buttons into a CorelDRAW document that you could use to build a form for a web page. Included in the Internet Object category along with form building are tools to insert a Java Applet or to embed a file. If this is something you really, truly *need* to do, you will have to add it to your Workspace from the Options dialog (CTRL+J). In the Options menu click on Workspace | Customization | Commands. From the drop-down choose All (Show All Items). Scroll down to Insert Internet Objects, and then click-drag the command onto the Internet Toolbar or other convenient locations, as shown in Figure 29-5. Click OK to close the Options dialog. You can change the name and value options associated with any

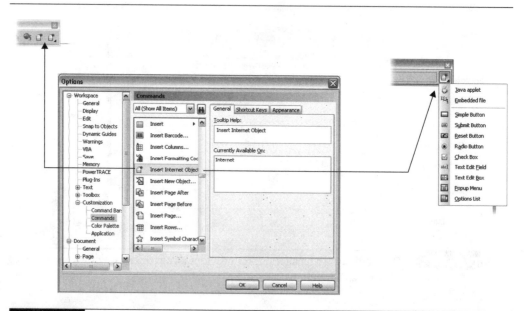

FIGURE 29-5 Drag the Insert Internet Objects button to the Internet Toolbar for easy future access.

selected Internet Object you have added to your document by using this command from the Object Properties docker (ALT+ENTER).

Inserting a Java Applet or an Embedded File Internet Object requires that you have the applet or file available to upload to your server. All other Internet objects require *scripting*— a type of programming—to transfer data from your web page to your web server. You should contact your web page host to learn more about the scripts that they allow to operate on their server. Your web host should also be able to help you locate (or provide you with) free scripts for use in your web pages. Once you find an acceptable script for use with your objects, you can enter its Internet location using the Object Properties dialog.

Setting Web Page Properties

Each page in your document can have different web-specific properties applied to it such as the Page Title and HTML filename, and other metadata such as Author, Classification, Description, or Keywords. To apply these properties, use the Page tab of the Object Properties docker (ALT+ENTER), shown in Figure 29-6, when no objects are selected. Type the values you want in the text fields, and they will be included when you export your page as an HTML file.

Assigning a Document Page a Title

Enter a title for your web page in the Page Title box. The page title will be used to name your exported web page in the title bar of the browser window used to view the page. If

	29

FIGURE 29-6   Use these options to apply web-specific properties to the pages in your document.

you're using frames, only the title of the main frames page will appear, although you may title other pages for your own reference. If no title is entered here, your document page numbers are used in place of a text title.

Giving Your Document Page an HTML Filename

Each page of your exported web document must feature a unique HTML filename, which must end with either .HTM or .HTML as the file extension to be recognized as a web page document. The HTML File box lets you provide a unique name. If no filename is entered here, your document page numbers are used instead, followed by the .HTM extension. Ask your webmaster which extension you should use. Websites hosted on Windows servers usually use .HTM, while websites hosted on Unix or Linux use .HTML. Additionally you should make all of your filenames and extensions lowercase for maximum compatibility with Web standards.

Entering Page Information

The Object Properties docker Page tab is a convenient place to enter page information. Information entered in the Author, Classification, Description, and Keywords boxes here is entered as metatag information in your web page, making it easier for search engines to locate and catalog the page content. When entering this information, keep the following in mind:

- **Author** Use the Author label to identify yourself in your web page's HTML code. You may also include information about yourself, but be careful about entering your email address. Entering your email address here makes it visible not only to people who look at your source code, but also to spambots that harvest email addresses, which *will* increase the amount of spam that lands in your inbox.

- **Classification** Use this to enter any additional metatag information to assist search engines in categorizing the information on your web page. Classifications determine whether a web page contains adult or general audience content.

- **Description** The Description portion of a web page is the summary seen by your viewers when they locate your page via a search engine. Entire websites and chapters of books have been devoted to writing good descriptions. One of the most important things to remember when writing your description is to keep it relatively brief (a two-sentence maximum is a good idea). Anyone who has used a search engine has seen descriptions that cut off in mid-paragraph. The reason is that each search engine allows only a predetermined amount of space for description metatags. Once you go over the search engine's allotted space, the remainder of your description tag is simply ignored.

- **Keywords** *Keywords* are the words used to match your page to words entered in a search engine. When a search engine goes through its database of web pages, those pages containing keywords that match the words being searched for are displayed in the search results. *Don't* be tempted to add popular words that do not relate to your page. It will hurt your web ranking when the sham is eventually discovered.

Applying a Page Background

If the background of your web page design calls for something other than white, you'll need to apply a unique background color or tiling background pattern. Page background is applied using the Page Setup pane of the Options dialog (CTRL+J), shown in Figure 29-7. To access this dialog quickly, click to expand the listing under Document, and then click Page | Background in the tree directory to view the available options.

Although it might seem logical to create a separate background object for your page and to apply your background properties to it, this can cause problems when it comes time to export your page. The Background should be chosen in this dialog as No Background (the default), a Solid color, or a saved Bitmap.

Choose Solid to access the color selector for choosing a uniform color. Choose Bitmap and click the Browse button to select a bitmap image as the tiling background. You'll find a collection of Corel's saved bitmap files in your Program Files\Corel\Corel Graphics Suite X4\Custom Data folder under Textures (saved in TIF format) or Tiles (saved in CPT format). Or you can use your own custom background or tile. Most web page bitmap backgrounds are files saved in the JPG or GIF format; PNG files are infrequently used because of lingering browser incompatibility issues.

29

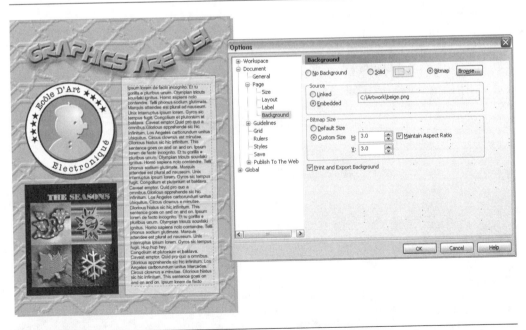

FIGURE 29-7   Use these options to apply color or tiling bitmap backgrounds to your web document pages.

While Bitmap is selected and a bitmap file has been specified, the Source and Bitmap Size options in the dialog become available. The Source option lets you link to and embed the bitmap with your document, but it has no bearing on how exported web pages are created. The Bitmap Size options let you to use either Default Size (the inherent size of the original bitmap) or a Custom Size as the size. By default, the Print And Export Background option is selected, which should remain so to be included as one of your web page elements.

Publishing Web Documents

The Publish To The Web command is used to export your CorelDRAW X4 document to web page file format. To access this command, choose File | Publish To The Web | HTML or click the Publish To Web–HTML button in the Internet Toolbar. Both open the same Publish To The Web dialog, shown in Figure 29-8, which has options for you to set exactly how your web page content will be exported. The tabbed dialog looks like and is arranged similarly to CorelDRAW's Print Options dialog.

You'll find everything you need to save your web page and images. You can also use options to upload your page and the image content to a web server. The dialog itself is divided into six option areas ranging from General to Advanced. You can also view a detailed Summary of the exported content and any web export preflight issues that CorelDRAW detects. Use the Browser

FIGURE 29-8   You can use these options for total control over how your page content will be exported.

Preview button to check the appearance of your web page. The sections that follow provide a close look at all the options available.

Setting General Options

Use the General tab to set options such as the destination folder for your exported files. You can specify a separate subfolder for your graphics or remove the default subfolder name (images\) to have the graphics saved in the same folder as your HTML document. To give the graphics subfolder the same name as the HTML document, select Use HTML Name For Image Sub-Folder.

As for the HTML Layout Method area, the best choice for the majority of users is the HTML Table (Most Compatible) method. If you're using the export filter only to export the HTML code for an image map (rather than for an entire web page), you should select Single Image Width Image Map.

Examining Web Page Details

The Details tab, shown next, provides information regarding exactly what you selected for export and what the exported file(s) will be named. If you want, you can apply unique page titles and/or HTML filenames to your exported web pages by clicking the existing fields and typing in the current names.

Reviewing Web Images

The Images tab, shown in Figure 29-9, provides a detailed list of the images that will be exported and their default filenames. For a thumbnail preview of each image, click the Image Name. To change the type of format to which an image is exported, click the field adjacent to the Image Name under the Type heading.

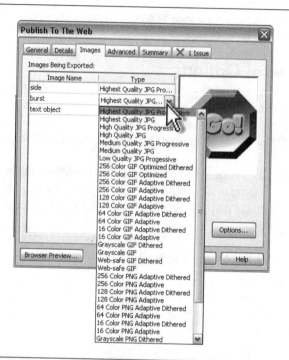

FIGURE 29-9 The listing shown in this tab provides you with invaluable details on how each of your web images will be exported.

To change the default settings used for each type of exported image, click the Options button to access the Options dialog Image page, shown in Figure 29-10. This dialog is where you choose an export format for GIFs, JPEGs, and PNGs. You can also choose Anti-Alias and Image Map options. Choosing the Anti-Alias option will ensure that your images don't have a rough, jagged edge. Choosing Client for the Image Map is the best because client image maps provide faster interaction with your user than do server image maps.

Setting Advanced HTML Options

The Advanced tab provides options for maintaining links you may have made to external files, including JavaScript in your HTML output, and for adding cascading style sheets (CSS) information in your web page. If you're using rollovers, be sure to choose the JavaScript option.

Browsing the Web Page Export Summary

The Summary tab, shown in Figure 29-11, provides information on the total size of your web page and how long it will take users to download your page at various modem speeds. The information is then itemized for each HTML page and image, so you can see if something in particular (such as a large image) might cause an unnecessarily long download time.

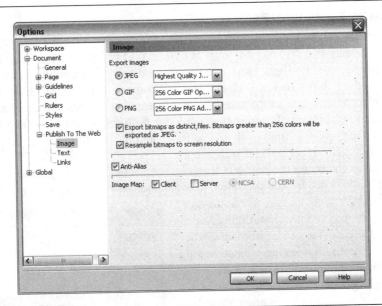

FIGURE 29-10 Using these options, you can globally set how each web image format will be handled.

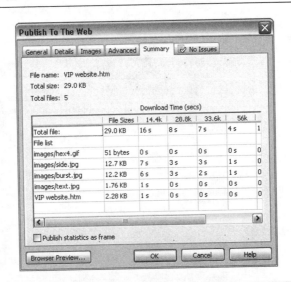

FIGURE 29-11 The information in this page helps you to measure download times against connection speeds for each of your web pages.

Preflight Web Issues

The Issues tab—shown in Figure 29-12, where an object that's off the web page has been flagged—detects and displays potential HTML export problems by using a series of preflight conditions. Preflight issues are found and displayed according to the options set throughout the Publish To The Web dialog, most commonly regarding issues surrounding color model use, text compatibility issues, and image size and resolution. The top portion of the dialog tab lists any found issues, while the bottom portion offers suggestions for correcting the problems. Images should be RGB, and the resolution for graphics should be 72 pixels per inch (dpi or ppi) for web images.

To change the issues the preflight feature detects, click the Settings button to open the Preflight Settings dialog, and then click to expand the tree directory under Issues To Check For, shown here. You can also use options in this dialog to Add (+) saved preflight issue sets or to Delete (–) existing issue sets in the list. HTML preflight rules are a function only of the web document HTML that you are exporting. If you have, for example, more than three issues flagged, it's often a good idea to make a mental note of the problems, cancel out of the Publish To The Web dialog, and then manually correct the issues in your drawing.

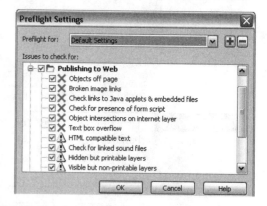

FIGURE 29-12   Use this page to troubleshoot problems and to resolve them before exporting.

Setting Web Publishing Preferences

CorelDRAW X4 gives you complete control over your personal web publishing preferences by enabling you to set Publish To The Web options. These options enable you to predetermine many of the settings used when your documents are exported to HTML format, as described earlier. To access these options, open the Options dialog (CTRL+J), click to expand the tree directory under Document, and click Publish To The Web, as shown here.

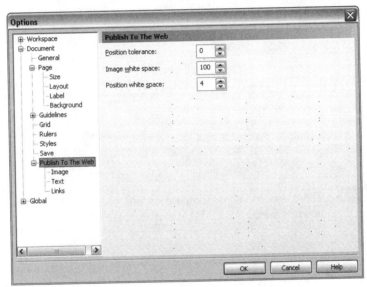

When this Options page is selected, you'll see three options for setting conditions under which object position and white space are handled when your web page is exported:

- ■ **Position Tolerance**   Here you can specify the number of pixels that text objects can be nudged to avoid creating very thin rows or narrow columns when the page is converted to HTML during export. Position Tolerance can be set within a range of 0 (the default) to 100. Increasing this value adds extra space.

- ■ **Image White Space**   Here you specify the number of pixels an empty cell may contain before being merged with an adjacent cell to avoid unnecessary splitting of graphic images.

- ■ **Position White Space**   This option controls the amount of white space to be added to simplify your exported HTML document.

Image Handling

To set the default settings controlling how images are exported, open Options and click Document | Publish To The Web | Image, as shown in Figure 29-13. Specify the default file format for images as JPEG, GIF, or PNG, including additional options for each. Using JPEG

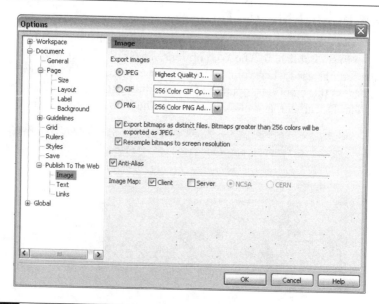

FIGURE 29-13 These options let you globally set how your default web image file formats are handled during the HTML export process.

image formats, choose from one of seven preset compression types. Using GIF, you may choose from one of a dozen palette types varied by color depth and dithering properties. Using PNG, choose from one of 14 palette types also varied by color depth and dithering properties.

Because all objects you draw in CorelDRAW are vector in their makeup, while most web graphics are in bitmap format, there is no real "perfect" file format to optimize file size and maintain palette color depth while preserving image quality levels for all the object types you can create in CorelDRAW X4. However, two key options provide you with a way of setting export conditions for most object types:

- **Export Bitmaps As Distinct Files**   Choose this option (the default) to set the export condition of bitmaps that have more than 256 colors as JPEG, leaving bitmaps with color depths of 256 or less to be exported as GIF. If this option is not selected, all bitmaps are exported according to your default image format preference.

- **Resample Bitmaps To Screen Resolution**   Choosing this option scales all exported bitmaps automatically to a screen resolution of 72 pixels per inch.

Specifying Web Text Export Options

To set the defaults controlling how text is exported, open the Options dialog and click Document | Publish To The Web | Text, shown in Figure 29-14.

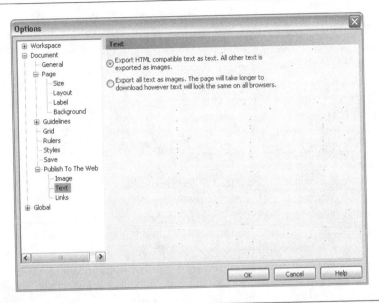

FIGURE 29-14 This dialog features options for globally setting default handling of your exported HTML text.

Here's what the three web-specific text options control:

- **Export HTML Compatible Text As Text**   CorelDRAW determines what text should remain text and what text would be better exported as an image. When you use this option, CorelDRAW exports your text as HTML text if HTML can be used to reproduce the text properly. If the text contains something HTML cannot reproduce, such as a special fill, CorelDRAW converts the text to an image and saves it according to your image-handling guidelines.

- **Export All Text As Images**   This option should be used with caution because it converts all your text into bitmap images. Although this allows for perfect text reproduction, it also adds significantly to download time and can present design challenges. Additionally, web readers can't read text cast as a bitmap, nor can they use search engines. If you have an important message you want everyone to be able to read, export the text as text.

HTML Link Colors

Choose the color of normal hyperlinked, visited, and unvisited text links in your exported web page using the Links page in the Options dialog. To access this page, open the Options

Making Your Text Web-Compatible

Before you start formatting a document for publishing to the Web, it's important to make your text Web compatible. Choosing Text | Make Text Web Compatible (available on the pop-up menu when you right-click over Paragraph Text) changes the text properties such as intercharacter spacing and Fountain fills to be compatible with the Web. This command also removes fancy effects such as character rotation. This conversion process makes it easier to edit your Corel HTML export in an HTML editor. The command is also available from the pop-up menu when you right-click with the Pick Tool on text.

Artistic Text must be converted to Paragraph Text before it can become web-compatible. You right-click with the Pick Tool over Artistic Text, and then choose Convert To Paragraph Text from the pop-up menu (or press CTRL+F8). CorelDRAW does not change your font when it makes text web compatible, and most web browsers handle only five or six different font styles. Therefore, if you make, for example, Paragraph Text set in Palatino 24-point web compatible, CorelDRAW won't change anything, but your text as displayed on a web page won't be in Palatino; instead it will be in the Web's closest match, Times Roman.

dialog (CTRL+J), and click Document | Publish To The Web | Links. The three selectors, as shown, let you choose a color for each link condition.

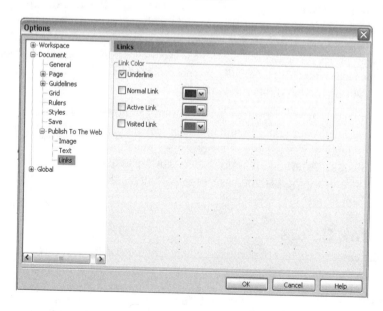

Choose the Underline option (selected by default) to display links using underlining. The Normal Link color selector enables you to set the color appearance of text applied with URL or Bookmark links as they appear in your web page document. The Active Link option sets color conditions of the link while your web page user is actively clicking a link. The Visited Link option sets the color of links that have already been visited. Unless the background of your web page is an unusual color, it's best to leave these link colors at their default because you and many visitors are accustomed to these colors; we all tend to subliminally understand what the link colors represent.

Web Image Optimizer

Using the Web Image Optimizer, you can specify how images will be optimized and how CorelDRAW vector graphics will be converted to bitmaps when exported for HTML pages. To open this feature, choose File | Publish To The Web | Web Image Optimizer. Using the options in the dialog (see Figure 29-15), you can compare up to four different scenarios at a

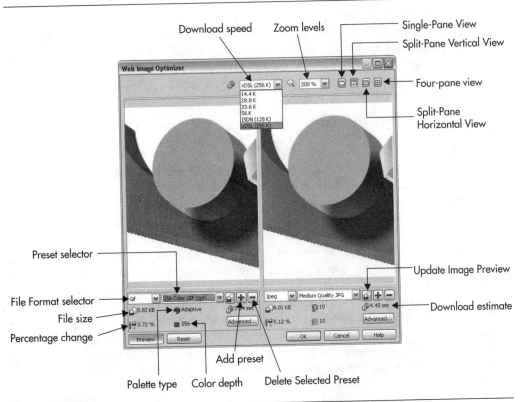

FIGURE 29-15 The Web Image Optimizer can be used to compare web image formats to evaluate quality and file sizes when publishing to HTML.

time using GIF, JPEG (JPG), JPEG 2 Standard (JP2), JPEG 2 Codestream (JPC), PNG8, and PNG24 bitmap formats. JPEG 2 Standard and Codestream refer to JPEG 2000 file formats. The majority of web browsers today do not support the display of images in the JPEG 2000 format, so stick to saving your images in GIF, JPEG, or PNG formats.

Choosing Web Image Optimizer Settings

The Web Image Optimizer features options to set the pane preview state, zoom levels, and download speed. Each preview pane has its own further options that can be set independently for comparing different settings. Here's what each of the options offers control over:

- **Download Speed**   This selector pretends it's the connection speed of your intended audience so you can optimize a photo or a graphic, and compare image quality to the time it might take to download to a web browser. Download speed can be set to 14.4K, 28.8K, 33.6K, 56K, ISDN (128K), or xDSL (256K), ranging from slowest (dial-up) to fastest (ISDN and cable modem) and measured in Kbps (Kilobits per second).

- **Zoom Levels**   Use this to set the view magnification of all panes in the dialog between 25 and 1600 percent. You can also use Zoom/Hand Tool functions directly within the preview panes in the same manner as other bitmap filter effect dialogs. A single click zooms in, a right-click zooms out, and a click-drag action enables you to pan within the pane preview. However, most of your audience will be viewing your graphics at 100 percent, so this is just a convenient way to better proof potential problem areas in your graphic.

- **Pane Preview Buttons**   Use these buttons to choose single, vertical split, horizontal split, or four-pane view.

In each of the pane previews, you can choose a different format for comparison. Begin by choosing a format from the File Format selector.

The Preset selector lists the available presets associated with each format. You can choose a preset, or click the Advanced button to access additional file format options. The Advanced button opens different export filter dialogs, depending on which file format is selected. For example, when an image is selected, clicking the Advanced button opens the Convert To Palette dialog, where you can apply smoothing and dither the image down to a very limited color palette to really make the GIF image small in file size.

Before choosing a format, the File Format selector defaults to Original, and the preview pane provides statistics such as file size, dimensions, and the current time required for an image to download (in seconds) at your selected Download Speed. As you choose File Format and/or Preset options, the information provided and the image preview are constantly updated, as long as the Preview button at the bottom of the dialog is selected (depressed).

Information displayed includes file size reduction based on percentage of the original image size, the palette type used, and a color depth value, as shown here:

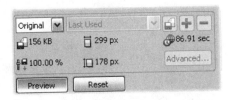

If you choose to use the Advanced settings for a specific file format type and you intend to use these often, you can save them using the Preset options. Here's a scenario that takes advantage of the usefulness of saving a preset: suppose you have a lot of images that will go against a white background. You want to use the PNG file format's masking feature to keep the files small in download size/time and to be able to arrange the text and graphics on the page tightly. Eliminating excess pixels surrounding a graphic is one of the many uses for image transparency. Your workflow would go something like this:

1. Select a graphic on the page, and then choose File | Publish To The Web | Image File Optimizer.

2. Choose PNG 24 from the File Format drop-down selector, and then click Advanced.

3. If your image is a bitmap that already has transparency masking, you can click the Masked Areas button and you're good to go. However, if you've chosen a vector shape (or group of shapes), choose the Image Color option, and then either choose white from the color selector or use the Eyedropper Tool to choose the page white area in the left (Original) preview window. Then click Preview, and the areas that'll be transparent when you export the PNG image will show as a black and white checkerboard in the Result preview pane.

4. Click OK. In the Web Image Optimizer dialog, click the + button to display the Web Preset Name dialog. Give the preset a name that's easy to remember, and then click OK.

5. Click OK in the Web Image Optimizer dialog, and then in the Save Web Image To Disk directory box, save your image.

6. Here's the timesaving part: Choose another shape or image on your web page, and then choose File | Publish To The Web | Image File Optimizer.

7. Click the File Format selector drop-down, and then choose the preset you saved in step 4 from the Preset selector drop-down list. Then just export the graphic. The process is visually summarized in Figure 29-16.

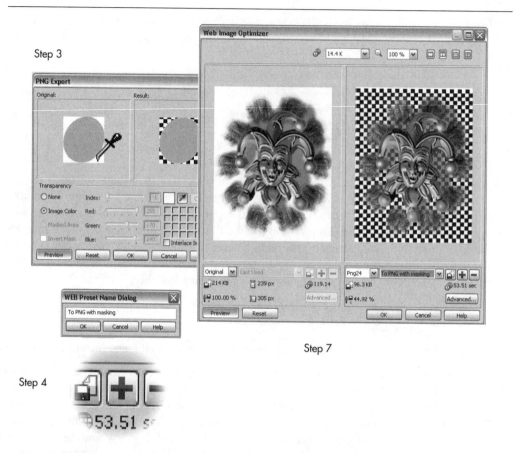

Step 3

Step 7

Step 4

53.51 se

FIGURE 29-16   Save time on repetitive tasks by saving your options as a preset.

Saving a Transparent GIF Using the Web Image Optimizer

The GIF (Graphics Interchange Format, introduced by CompuServe in 1987) file format is still used a lot on the Web today; although restricted to 256 possible colors, GIF images can often be saved to a file size smaller than the more color-capable JPEG and the lossless compression PNG. One of the charms of the GIF file format is that you can define one transparency value (not a mask, and not more than one color) to make a button or small graphic appear to float on your web page.

Get out a graphic you think would make a good button or banner, and follow these steps to learn how GIFs with a transparent background are built.

Making a Transparent GIF Image

1. Select the object(s) that you want to export.

2. From the File menu choose Publish To The Web | Web Image Optimizer.

3. Click on the Split-Pane Vertical View icon. Both panes show the Original image. Choose GIF from the File Format selector in the right pane. Choose a preset from the Preset selector. For example, choose 256 Color GIF Adaptive or any other preset that makes your image look good in the preview.

4. Click Advanced to open the Convert To Palette dialog.

5. In the Convert To Palette dialog make any adjustments you deem necessary. Even if you don't need to make any further adjustments, you need to come to this dialog so that you can get to the next dialog, the GIF Export dialog, where transparency is set.

6. Click on OK and the GIF Export dialog opens. If you click OK, by default the image will export without transparency. But in this example you *do* want to set a transparent drop-out color, so choose the Image Color option in the Transparency section of the dialog.

    You can now choose the color you want to drop out by moving the Index slider, by entering the number the color occupies in the palette, by clicking on the color in the palette display, or by using the Eyedropper Tool (the recommended method).

7. Click on the Eyedropper Tool, and then move your cursor, which changes into an eyedropper, over the left image pane labeled "Original." Click on the color you want to be transparent; then click on the Preview button. All instances of the color you clicked on in the image now show in the Result pane as a filled white and black checkerboard pattern. If you like the results, click OK. If not, click Reset and try choosing a different color.

8. You are returned to the Web Image Optimizer dialog. Click OK to close that dialog, and then open the Save Web Image To Disk dialog. Choose where you want to save your image, give it a name, and be sure that GIF – CompuServe Bitmaps is in the Save As Type selector. Click Export and you are done.

Using the Web Connector Docker

The default page of the Web Connector docker (Window | Dockers | Web Connector) is used to quickly launch your Internet browser and go to Corel.com and Coreldraw.com. Once there you can take advantage of free online resources such as CorelDRAW updates and service packs, access Newsgroups, find a Corel Approved Service Bureau, shop at the Corel Store, or get Corel Technical Support. You must have an active Internet connection open to use the Web Connector docker.

The Web Connector docker can also be used as a web browser that displays pages within CorelDRAW, and it works just as you would expect Internet Explorer to work. Buttons at the top of the docker, shown in Figure 29-17, are used to control what you see in the docker window, to open bookmarked pages, to stop or refresh the docker content, or to print the current page. A selector below these buttons enables you to view the current page URL or to recall previously typed URL addresses for viewing.

To browse to a website from this docker, enter an address in the URL Address box. You can easily navigate to websites that you have saved as Microsoft Internet Explorer Favorites, by clicking on the Favorites icon. CorelDRAW reads the contents of your Favorites folder and displays the links in a list. If you're using the Web Connector docker to view typical web pages, you'll likely need to enlarge the docker's size by dragging the edge of the docker window toward the center of the screen.

One creative use for the docker is its capability to be copied from: you can highlight text and click-drag it right onto a drawing page. Also, where graphics are directly linked to a page, you can click-drag a graphic from a web page onto your drawing page. It should go without saying that copying other people's graphics for your own use is called "appropriation"

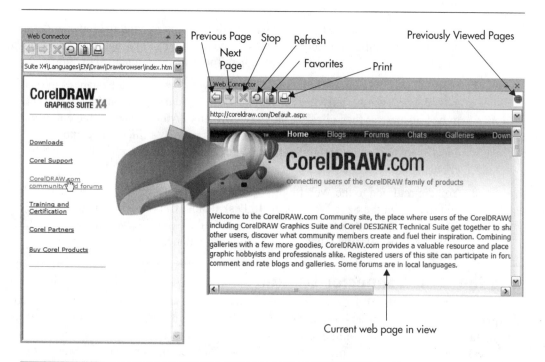

FIGURE 29-17   Use these buttons to control how you view the Web Connector docker contents.

in polite circles and other things in less-polite communities! However, if a client, for example, wants a vector copy of their logo, you can snag a copy from their website, use PowerTRACE, and the only time you'll need to leave CorelDRAW is to email the client the finished work and to bill them.

This chapter has shown you how to take just about any media on a CorelDRAW page, be it a drawing, a photo, or text, and make your design compatible as a web page. With links, your web page connects you to a community and keeps you connected with business associates, friends, and potential customers you haven't even met yet. Chapter 30 moves into a different area for the ambitious designer: how to save your efforts for use on creative work while optimizing your time by letting CorelDRAW automate rote tasks. Even some *complex* tasks using Visual Basic for Applications are covered in the next chapter. If you have some programming skills, you're going to love the stuff CorelDRAW offers. And if you have no scripting or programming skills, you're going to learn the essentials.

CHAPTER 30

Automating Tasks and Visual Basic for Applications

B oth seasoned macro programmers and designers who don't know a macro from a macaroon will benefit from this chapter on CorelDRAW's macro and VBA (Visual Basic for Applications) programming features. Novices can use the macro recording feature in CorelDRAW to create simple macros to automate repetitive tasks in CorelDRAW; if you're ambitious, you can also build macros to design very complex artwork—you'll see later in this chapter an example of a background design generated through a simple macro you can program. If you don't fancy yourself the programming type, you'll also see in this chapter how to install and use macros and mini-programs that have been written by third-party programmers.

It's easy to assign VBA macros that you've written yourself or downloaded from the Web to toolbar buttons, menus, and shortcut keys in CorelDRAW. You can insert macros right into CorelDRAW's interface in the places where they're handy. If you put macros to work, you can turbo-charge your workflow, making your hours much more efficient and streamlined.

With VBA, you can tweak or supplement CorelDRAW's features to meet your exact (and perhaps unique) needs. This news is very exciting when you realize that Visual Basic is *not* limited to working solely within CorelDRAW. VBA can be used to integrate work that takes place, and data that is exchanged, between CorelDRAW and PHOTO-PAINT... *and* most other Corel products, including the WordPerfect Office Suite. Your VBA automation possibilities expand beyond the Corel universe of products to include many other applications such as Microsoft Office and Autodesk's AutoCAD to name but two.

Learning all the ins and outs of VBA, an application in its own right, can fill its *own* book (and it does), and mastering CorelDRAW's Object Model is not a small topic, either. Everything you would need to know to master VBA control of CorelDRAW cannot be completely documented in this one chapter, but a novice *can* get started using VBA macros by reading the information here. You'll learn how to build your own simple macros, and if you're so inclined, there is plenty of VBA documentation on the Web and in other reading. If you're a programmer, use this chapter as a quick brushup with pointers to CorelDRAW-specific VBA information and implementations.

What's Possible with VBA?

You can build simple macros from the ground up that perform everyday tasks, such as creating a rectangle or an ellipse shape. Other operations that aren't a challenge to program move and resize objects on the page, change object colors, rotate, extrude, and do almost anything you would normally do in CorelDRAW by click-dragging and using menu commands.

VBA, more precisely, *CorelDRAW's Object Model,* gives developers control over most aspects of CorelDRAW through programmed code. Using VBA, you can record and write small, ten-line programs that perform specific tasks. You can then assign macros to a button, a menu, or a shortcut key in CorelDRAW for easy access. Alternatively, you can build mini-applications of many hundreds or thousands of lines of code for performing complex tasks that are otherwise difficult or impossibly time-consuming to execute with a mouse and keyboard alone.

To really get a handle on CorelDRAW VBA, you'll want to refer to these Acrobat documents: The CorelDRAW X4 Programming Guide for VBA.pdf, The CorelDRAW VBA Object Model.pdf, *and* The PP VBA Object Model.pdf *(information for PHOTO-PAINT). These guides can be found in the Program Files\ Corel\CorelDRAW Graphics Suite X4\Programs\folder; you can also access them from Windows' Start menu\ All Programs | CorelDRAW Graphics Suite X4 | Documentation | CorelDRAW X4 Programming Guide for VBA PDF.*

What's New in Version X4

The big news here for programmers (beginners most likely won't immediately benefit from this new feature) is the addition of Corel Query Language (CQL) to your toolset. You can use CQL in your VBA to search for objects, including text that has specific properties such as shape, fill, outline, color, and other properties. See page 90 of *The CorelDRAW X4 Programming Guide for VBA.pdf* for more information on the query expression syntax and the operators that are available.

If you are a programming wizard, you'll be pleased to know that Corel continues to make new additions to the CorelDRAW Object Model. An object module shows the parent and child relationship of objects (features) that you can control using VBA. You can get a visual overview of the CorelDRAW Object Model by taking a look at the *CorelDRAW VBA Object Model.pdf* file in the Program Files\Corel\CorelDRAW Graphics Suite X4\Programs\ folder. It can also be found via Windows' Start menu | All Programs | CorelDRAW Graphics Suite X4 | Documentation.

Upgrading VBA Macros from Version X3 to X4

Most VBA macros written for CorelDRAW X3 should work in CorelDRAW X4 without any modifications. Copy the GMS files from one folder to another. However, some macros might fail to work because of minor changes to the Object Model, or because they explicitly reference the CorelDRAW X3 object instead of referencing the CorelDRAW object. If a macro doesn't run, you'll have to edit it using the Macro Editor (ALT+F11).

The GMS files are usually stored in the Program Files\Corel\CorelDRAW Graphics Suite X4\Draw\GMS folder. If you don't have access to this folder, you should find the GMS files in C:\Documents and Settings*UserName*\Application Data\Corel\CorelDRAW Graphics Suite X4\User Draw\GMS.

Working with Existing Macros

CorelDRAW ships with some macros. The Internet is a great place to find macros, and you may even be given a document that contains macros that a colleague created. So how do you get them to work?

Installing an Existing Macro

Macros are distributed as single project files in the GMS (global macro) file format. They may also have accompanying "helper" files. For example, you might download a macro in a zip archive, and then extract and copy the included files into your GMS folder; or the developer may have packaged the macro with an install program that will automatically put the GMS file and any related files in the correct place for you.

The other way to obtain a macro is to receive it embedded in a CorelDRAW drawing; the CDR file format can hold onto a macro, a very convenient way to share macros. When you open a CDR file that has a macro embedded in it, a Security Warning dialog appears, asking if you want to Disable Macros, Enable Macros, or get More Info, as shown here.

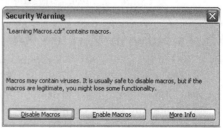

If you've received the document from a trusted source, in other words, from a coworker and *not* as an email attachment with a subject line telling you you've won a lot of money, and you think that you will need to use the macros contained in the document, you *should* choose to Enable Macros. But if you're unsure, choose Disable Macros. Disable Macros does what it says, but you can use the Macro Editor to view the macros so you can determine if they are safe and you want to use them, as shown here. To use a macro you've chosen to disable, close the CorelDRAW file, reopen the file, and then choose Enable Macros.

Nothing suspicious, the embedded macro is okay

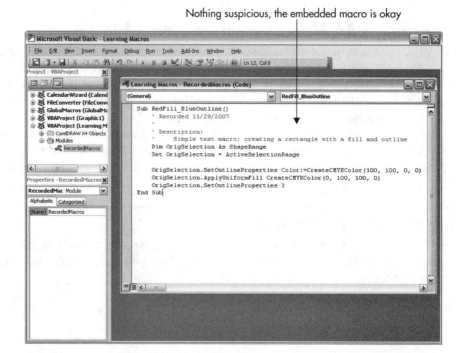

Running an Existing Macro

To run a macro, choose Tools | Macros | Run Macro to bring up the CorelDRAW X4 Visual Basic for Applications dialog. From the Macros In drop-down list, choose the VBA Project that contains the macro you want to run. Any macros stored in the VBA Project file you chose are displayed in the Macro Name field. If the macro was created entirely in the VB Editor and not recorded, this macro will be displayed at the top of the list. Recorded macros you've created will appear later in the list, and the name of the macro will appear as RecordedMacros.*MacroNameYouGaveYourMacro*. Select the macro you want to run from the Macro Name list, and then click on the Run button.

If the macro was created by programming, it might pop up a dialog or interface for you to set options for what the macro will do, or for where in the document the macro will perform its task. If no interface is provided, the macro will probably perform its actions in the active document. Some macros may only work if there is an active selection in the document at the time you run the macro, so if nothing appears to have happened (an extrude, a move, a color change, for example), try selecting an object and then run the macro again.

CorelDRAW comes with very useful CalendarWizard.gms and FileConverter.gms project files that are VBA macro-based mini-applications. You really owe it to yourself to open a new file and run these macros; the Calendar Wizard alone can shave hours off designing a custom calendar for business or the home. However, it's not difficult to make your *own* macro; you know best what your own automation needs are. Don't be intimidated by lines of seemingly incomprehensible code: *recording* a macro is the easiest way to create a macro, and it's the topic of the following sections.

Global vs. Local Projects

When you make your own macro, you have a choice of making it a *local* or *global* macro. If you want to make the macro you're recording available for use only in the current open document, you store it locally in the document. However, if you want the macro available whenever you use CorelDRAW—or you want to share the macros with others—you need to create a new VBA project and store the project file in the GSM folder. It is *not* a good idea to store your macro work in any of the projects that Corel has provided, or in those from third-party developers, because you could accidentally overwrite a global macro. Make your own project file for your work and back it up regularly.

> **NOTE** *Project files are not created in CorelDRAW or in the VBA Editor. To create a project file, close CorelDRAW and open a text editor such as Notepad. Open a new file in Notepad and* without typing anything in the file, *save it to the Program Files\Corel\ CorelDRAW Graphics Suite X4\Draw\GMS folder. When saving it, give it a filename that contains only letters, numbers, and underscores—no spaces. Be sure to give the file a .GMS file extension, for example,* MyMacroProjects_1.*gms. Note that no spaces are in this example filename because no spaces are allowed in Visual Basic. Restart CorelDRAW, and MyMacroProjects_1 will appear in the Save Macro dialog as one of the places you can save the macro.*

30

Recording a Macro

You might have recorded a macro in other programs before; if so, you won't find the process very different here in CorelDRAW—it's quite easy. Macros can be recorded using the Macros Toolbar, which contains VCR-like controls for starting, pausing, and stopping the macro recorder. Or you can skip the recorder, and make a macro by performing your actions and then saving your macro using the Undo docker. Both methods produce similar results.

Here is a walk-through on recording a macro using the Macros Toolbar.

 The macro recorder can only perform simple operations on text such as rotations and scaling—you cannot record a macro, for example, to enter text, change case, and other operations that involve typing. Macro recording only works with simple shapes. If you need to do something to text, you will have to enter the text and then convert it to curves before you start recording your macro. The recorder also doesn't work well with other complex objects, so you may have to break things apart and ungroup them before they can be part of a recorded macro.

 ## Recording a Macro: Filling a Page with Confetti

1. Open a new document. This is the document where you'll perform the actions that make up the macro. Save the file as **Confetti macro.cdr**.

2. With the Ellipse Tool, create an ellipse that's about an inch wide. Then fill it with a color on the Color Palette, give it a 4-point outline width by using the Property Bar, and then assign the outline a color. The colors you choose will be written to the macro, and when you run the macro, these colors will be used; choose colors that appeal to you! Leave the object selected for the following steps.

3. Right-click on any of the toolbars at the top of the application window. From the pop-up menu choose the Macros Toolbar. The Macros Toolbar is shown in Figure 30-1. The Tools | Macros commands can be used to record a macro, but it's easier to use the Macros Toolbar.

4. Click on the red Start Recording button on the Macros Toolbar to open the Save Macro dialog, as shown in Figure 30-2.

5. In the Macro Name field enter a name for your macro. It must start with a letter and contain only letters, numbers, and underscores. The Visual Basic programming language allows no spaces. Click on the icon in the Save Macro In field that represents the project or file in which you want the macro saved. In these steps you'll save locally in the current document; click the VBAProject (Confetti macro.cdr) icon. Write any notes about the purpose of the macro, the date, the version number of the macro, or any other useful information about the macro in the Description section. Click OK and you're now recording.

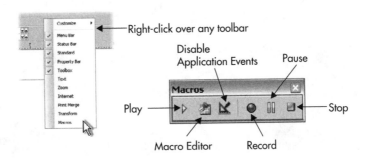

FIGURE 30-1 Use the Macros Toolbar much in the same way you use any onscreen or even physical recording device. The buttons are labeled with universal symbols.

6. With the Pick Tool, click-drag the ellipse to a different location on the page; then before releasing the left mouse button, right-click to drop a copy of the ellipse.

7. Scale the duplicate ellipse to about 50 percent, and then recolor it.

8. Marquee-select both ellipses; then repeat step 6.

30

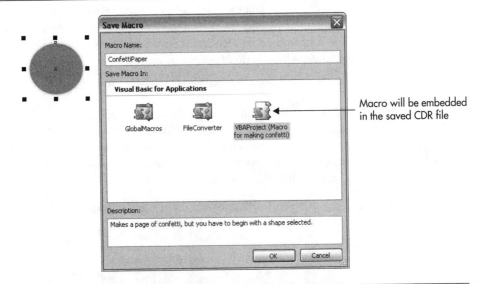

FIGURE 30-2 Click the icon for where you want to save the macro you'll record, and write project notes for yourself and others.

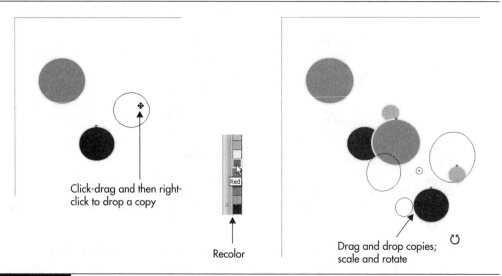

Click-drag and then right-click to drop a copy

Recolor

Drag and drop copies; scale and rotate

FIGURE 30-3 Start recording, make some transformations that might be tedious in the future to repeat, and then stop recording. You now have a local macro.

9. Repeat steps 6 and 7; you're populating the page with different-colored, different-sized ellipses. The beauty of this macro is that in the future you don't have to repeat these steps! Additionally, when you marquee-select multiple ellipses, try rotating the group as you reposition them by clicking within the group as they're selected to put the bounding box for the group into Rotate/Skew transformation mode. In Figure 30-3, you can see the steps used in this example macro.

10. Finally, click the Stop Recording button on the Macros Toolbar.

Now try deleting all the objects on the page, and then create a polygon or a rectangle. Select it and then run the macro you just created. Your recipe is the same, but you're using a different ingredient, as shown here. This is a simple macro, but you can see the potential for incredible time-savings with macros and a little headwork before you begin recording. Because the macro was saved in this document, it is only available for use in this document.

Recorded macro result

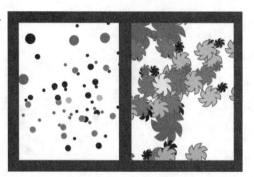

Macro applied to a different object

If you later decide that you want to use a macro that is stored in a user document with other files, you can use the Macro Editor to copy the macro into other VBA Project documents.

Saving Undo Lists as VBA Macros

Lists of Undo Actions can be saved as a VBA macro from the Undo docker as an alternative to recording them. To open the Undo docker, choose Window | Docker | Undo, shown here after several actions have been applied to an object.

The list that you see contains the available actions that you can undo or redo using Edit | Undo and Edit | Redo for the active document; Undo and Redo are also registered on the Undo docker when you use these buttons on the Standard Toolbar. The last-action highlight indicates the last action you performed, which is also the action that will be undone if you choose Edit | Undo. If you choose Edit | Repeat, the highlighted item will be repeated, if it's repeatable. Clicking any action in the list undoes or redoes any actions between it and the last action highlighted on the docker.

If you click the Save List to a VBA list button on the Undo List docker (the floppy disk icon), the list of commands starting at—but not including—File | New and up to the selected command will be saved to a VBA macro. Clicking the Save List button opens the Save Macro dialog. Choose a suitable name, project, and description, and then click OK.

The Clear Undo List button removes *all* Undo and Redo items in the list, an action that in itself *can't* be undone. If you clear the list, you will not be able to undo anything already done in CorelDRAW. However, if you want to save an undo list as a macro, clearing the list before you perform your actions is a good idea, because it removes all the other actions that you don't want included in your macro.

Playing Back Recorded or Saved Macros

To play back a macro that comes with CorelDRAW, a third-party macro, or any valid macro that you have written yourself, click the Play button on the VBA Toolbar, or choose Tools | Macro | Run Macro. You will be presented with the CorelDRAW X4 Visual Basic For Applications Macros dialog, where you can choose the macro you want to run.

Choose the correct project in the Macros In list, and then select the macro you want to run in the Macro Name list. Then click the Run button.

Writing a Macro

Creating macros by recording is easy, but unfortunately a lot of things cannot be accomplished by recording and can be done only through programming. Therefore, a *taste* of programming language and programming possibilities using VBA is covered in the following sections.

Programming Term Definitions

Programming, in a nutshell, is less art and much more science. The English language can state ideas ambiguously, and therefore it's important to understand a few VBA keywords. Some of the following definitions are subtle, but they make the discussion easier as you progress through these sections.

 You'll find a more complete explanation of terms in the CorelDRAW VBA *Programming Guide, opened by choosing from Window's' Start menu | All Programs | CorelDRAW Graphics Suite X4 | Documentation | CorelDRAW X4 Programming Guide for VBA.pdf.*

- **Project**   Projects group together related *modules* and *forms* into a single file. Project files are stored as separate files with the extension .GMS.

- **Module**   A module is a VBA document that contains the individual macros. Modules can be *normal* modules, *class* modules (not discussed here), or *forms*.

- **Form**   A form is a window that contains the user interface for your macro. Forms are also known as dialogs and can contain buttons, boxes, options, text input areas, static text, drop-down lists, and more.

- **Shape**   *Shape* is the term used for any object in a CorelDRAW drawing—many people call them objects, but *object* means something different in VBA.

- **Object**   Objects have a special meaning in VBA: *object* in VBA is the general name for any aspect of CorelDRAW that can be named and programmed, such as Shape, Layer, Page, or Document, and dozens of other items.

- **Object Model**   The Object Model is the "wiring" between VBA (or any other programming language) and the CorelDRAW document—without the Object Model it is simply not possible for you to control the shapes in the document, or even the document's other settings. The Object Model gives everything an object name so that you can get a reference to anything and then modify it.

- **Member**   Objects are usually made from smaller objects called *members*. Members can be sub-objects, properties, and methods. As an analogy, a car is an object, but it has an engine and four wheels that are sub-objects.

- **Property**   One aspect of objects is that they have *properties*. A property is a characteristic of an object, such as size, position, or color. You can access these properties with VBA.

- **Method**   A method is a task that the object can perform when you tell it to: "Resize yourself to three inches wide," "Move one inch to the right," "Rotate 10 degrees," "Group with the other shapes," "Delete yourself." Methods are often called *member functions*.

■ **Macro, Sub, Function, and Procedure** All these mean, in a general sense, the same thing: a block of code that has a clearly defined start point and end point. We use the word "macro" as a general term for "sub," "function," "method," or "program," although its original meaning is "a collection of keystrokes." A *sub*, or subroutine, is a piece of code that performs some task, and then returns control to the object that called it. A *function* is a piece of code that performs a task and then returns a value to the object that called it. You can see that subs and functions are basically the same things, but a function returns a value (a number or text), and a sub does not. (Note that this is different from languages like C++ or Java, in which all procedures are functions and always return a value, even if it is just zero.)

Introducing the VBA Editor

The VBA Editor is written by Microsoft and licensed to Corel for inclusion in CorelDRAW. This means that while the CorelDRAW Object Model is the responsibility of Corel, the VBA Editor is solely Microsoft's. The big advantage here is that the VBA Editor is mature, refined, and first class, as it derives so much from Microsoft's long line of software development tools. Another advantage is the fact that VBA is a variant of Visual Basic, so anyone with VB experience will be able to use VBA without additional learning. And if you are just starting out, what you learn here will give you a leg up when working with VBA or Visual Basic in other programs.

The VBA Editor includes many features designed to assist the programmer, including the following:

■ **Syntax Check** This feature checks each line as you type it and immediately identifies any problems it finds by marking the code with red.

■ **Auto List Members** A list of all valid members of an object pops up, from which you can choose one, or you can type it yourself.

■ **Auto Indenting and Formatting** The Editor tidies up your code and automatically formats the code to maintain a uniform look, which makes it easier to read and debug.

■ **Color Coding** The editor colorizes the code according to whether the words are reserved keywords (blue), remarks (green), errors (red), or normal code (black); the colors can be customized.

■ **Form Designer** You can quickly design powerful custom forms (dialogs) for your macro's user interface containing any of the standard controls, such as buttons, lists, text-entry boxes, and labels.

You'll discover many other useful features of the VBA Editor once you start using it.

TIP *Although CorelDRAW uses "VBA," the editor is borrowed from full Visual Basic, and is known as the "Visual Basic Editor" or "VB Editor."*

30

The VB Editor Layout

The VB Editor has three main areas: menus and toolbars, dockers, and code and form-designer windows. These are shown in Figure 30-4.

The most important window in the VB Editor is the code window, as this is where you do most of your hands-on programming. The code window is a text-editor window where your code is listed, and where you can enter new code and edit existing code. The next most important window is the Project Explorer, which helps you to navigate among all the modules and components of your open projects. The Properties window is also important, particularly if you are editing forms.

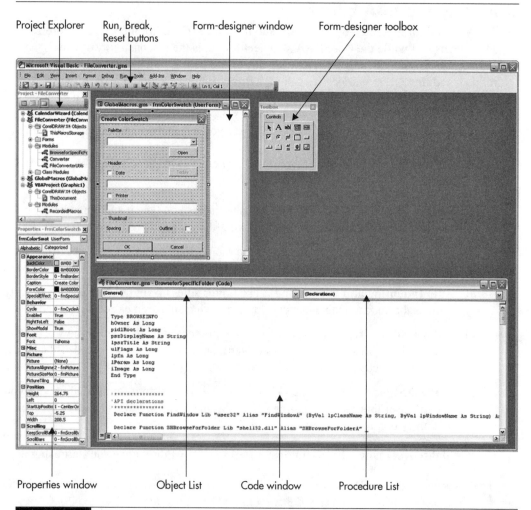

FIGURE 30-4 Window layout of the VB Editor

The final powerful feature of the VB Editor is the Object Browser. This is a fundamental tool you can use when you decide to start programming by hand, rather than just recording macros.

Each of these parts of the VB Editor is described in the following sections. A more thorough description is presented in Corel's *CorelDRAW VBA Programming Guide.* Also, any good general VBA book will provide additional detail.

The Project Explorer

The Project Explorer shown in Figure 30-4 can be switched on by choosing View | Project Explorer or by pressing CTRL+R. It lists all the loaded projects (GMS files) and all the modules that they contain separated into folders. It is simple to use the Project Explorer to keep your VBA code organized.

You can perform various filing operations within the Project Explorer, including creating new modules, importing and exporting modules, and deleting modules. These are explained next:

- **Opening Modules and Forms** You can open a module or form simply by double-clicking it in the Project Explorer, or by right-clicking and choosing View Code from the pop-up menu. Forms have two parts—the visual controls and the code. Double-clicking displays the controls; right-clicking and choosing View Code displays the code. Or, you can press F7 to open the selected module or form.

- **Creating New Modules and Forms** Right-click on a project you want, and choose either Insert | Module or Insert | Form. The new module or form will be added to the appropriate subfolder. You can name the module or form in the Properties window, and the naming convention is the same as for naming macros (no spaces or special characters).

- **Exporting** Right-click the module or form that you want to export, and choose Export File from the pop-up menu. This is a simple way to share small parts of your work with other people.

- **Importing** Right-click anywhere within the project you want to import a module or form into, and choose Import File from the pop-up menu.

- **Deleting Modules** You can delete a module or form by right-clicking it and choosing Remove from the pop-up menu. This actually removes the module from the project file; so, if you want to keep a copy of it, you must export it first.

The Code Window

The VB Editor code window has several interesting features: the main code entry area, the Object List, and the Procedure List, as shown in Figure 30-4. The *code window* shows the code from a single module, a class module, or a form, although you can have as many code windows as you like open at the same time. Press CTRL+TAB to cycle through the windows, or choose a window from the window list at the bottom of the Window menu.

30

The Object List at the top of the code window lists the available objects for that module. If a module is displayed, only one object—the "(General)" object—appears. If a form's code window is open, all the form's controls (buttons, labels, text boxes, list boxes, and so on) will be listed as well as (General). The Procedure List names the available procedures for the selected object. For most modules, this is merely a list of all the subs and functions. (VBA records macros as subroutines, which it identifies with the keyword "Sub.") Basically, these two lists give you a table of contents for zooming around large modules. Some modules can grow to several hundred—or even thousands—of lines in length, so such assistance is welcome.

The Object Browser

The Object Browser is a central tool for programming CorelDRAW. The Object Browser shows you how every object, member function, and property within CorelDRAW fits together—and it shows you the exact syntax you must use (the exact words and variables). To start the Object Browser, shown in Figure 30-5, choose View | Object Browser, or press F2.

In the Object Browser, the Classes list at the lower left shows object types, or classes, that exist within CorelDRAW. Each class may exist as a sub-object of CorelDRAW's main *Application* object, or it may be a sub-object of a sub-object. The list to its right shows the Members of the selected class, including all of its properties, methods (subs and functions), and events (not many). The bottom area of the window shows the member's definition,

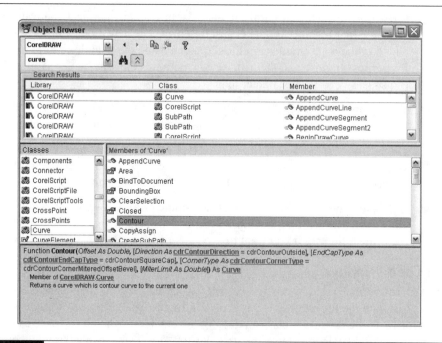

FIGURE 30-5   The Object Browser provides insight into CorelDRAW's Object Model.

including its parameters. You can click any green words in this area, and you will be taken straight to the definition for that item.

The Object Browser is a powerful tool, and once you are familiar with VBA, you'll find it quick to use the Object Browser to find a particular definition.

The Object Browser also offers a search button (the Binoculars icon) to help locate the definition you are looking for. Clicking on any item in the Search Results window takes you to that object's definition. Figure 30-5 illustrates a search for "curve," and you can see in the Search Results pane that Curve is defined as an Object Class with AppendCurve as a Member.

Auto Syntax Check

An Auto Syntax Check occurs every time you leave one line of code to move to a different line. The VB Editor reads the line that you just moved from and checks the *syntax,* or the code you just typed. If any obvious errors are found—perhaps you missed a parenthesis, or the word "Then" from an If statement—that line will be highlighted in red.

In its default state, the VB Editor will use a pop-up message box to tell you about every error. Choose Tools | Options in the VB Editor and disable the Auto Syntax Check option: the line will still be highlighted in red, but you won't get any obtrusive messages.

Auto List Members

Each object in VBA has a set of associated members—properties and functions that the object "owns." With Auto List Members enabled in the VB Editor's Options dialog (Tools | Options), when you type a dot or period (.) after a valid object name, that object's member properties and functions pop up in a scrolling list. You can choose one of the properties from the list by scrolling down to it and clicking it, or by selecting it and pressing TAB.

If you want to use this feature on a new line, right-click and choose List Properties/ Methods, or press CTRL+SPACEBAR.

Form Designer

The Form Designer is used for designing objects called *forms.* Every dialog consists of a form—a blank panel on which you can place buttons, check boxes, text boxes, title bars, lists, groups, labels, and other controls. Forms are effectively empty dialogs—until you put controls in them.

To design a good, easy-to-use form takes practice. Because this chapter only introduces the basics of VBA, and because forms are usually used only in complex macros and applications, designing forms is not covered here. However, if you need to design a form, keep the following points in mind:

■ **Keep It Simple**   There's nothing worse than a form that is too intricate or overly clever. Keep your forms simple. Use only necessary controls.

■ **Make It Usable**   If you make the form illogical and difficult to use, you and your users will be unhappy and unimpressed. A usable, logical layout is important.

- **Use a Model of What Has Been Done Before**   You can learn a lot from professional applications. Look at what makes a good form and what makes a bad one—learn from the professionals.

- **Pay Attention to Detail**   When you have finished designing the layout of a form, check the details of each control's properties carefully. Make sure every control has an AcceleratorKey. At least the most important controls should each have a ControlTipText. Make sure that the TabIndex order is logical and straightforward.

Recording and Playing Macros

The quickest way for any new programmer to learn how to program CorelDRAW, or any VBA-enabled application, is to record a few actions using the VBA Recorder and then to examine the code. While it is recording, the VBA Recorder converts your actions into logical VBA code—you might not always get the result you expected, but that in *itself* is a good lesson to learn...and accept!

Experienced programmers can also benefit from recording macros: CorelDRAW is vast, and finding the exact function or property name to do whatever it is you are trying to do can take some time. Developers often record the action they need to program, and then look at the code that the recorder creates, which tells them what they need to know. They delete the recorded macro, but might use some of that code in their own custom macro or program.

In a nutshell, the VBA Recorder records what it sees you doing. However, it often interprets your actions in roundabout ways. For example, if you create a shape and then fill it, the recorder does not realize that each action occurs on the same shape; it adds extra, unnecessary code that does the job, but not as efficiently as if you were to hand-code it.

Customizing Macros into the User Interface

If you record or write macros that you use regularly, you might find it handy to assign them to a toolbar button, a menu, or a shortcut key in CorelDRAW. This puts your macros at your fingertips, and this is where you can use macros to optimize your workflow, saving you time and money. Only macros that are stored in macro project files (files with .GMS file extensions) in the GMS folder can be assigned to toolbars, menus, or shortcut keys.

To customize your workspace and assign macros to buttons, menus, or shortcuts, open the Options dialog (CTRL+J), and from the tree on the left choose Customization | Commands to open the Command section of the Options dialog. From the drop-down box choose Macro. Select the macro you want to add to the interface from the scroll box. Enter a description or the macro name in the Tooltip Help field. Then either give the selected macro a Shortcut assignment from the Shortcut Keys tab, or click-drag the macro from the scroll box and drop it on the toolbar or menu in the location that you want the macro to appear in the interface. Figure 30-6 shows a user-recorded macro dragged to the Standard Toolbar area, where it then becomes a single button on a new toolbar. In the Appearance area of Customization | Commands you can even draw an icon or choose an imported icon to represent your macro button (otherwise it will be confusing after you put several custom macros with the same default icon on a toolbar).

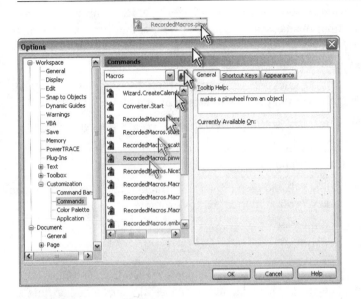

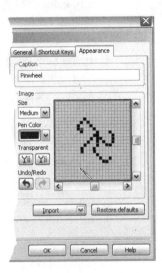

FIGURE 30-6   Assign a macro to a shortcut key, or put it on a toolbar as a button.

30

Looking at the Macro Code

If you are at the beginning of the learning curve for programming CorelDRAW, a useful exercise is to record a few macros and see how they work and what the code looks like.

Before you start to program in VBA, let's examine a VBA macro that you'll create in the following section. The term *macro* in this context means "a series of recorded commands that imitate the user's actions." A macro can be run (*executed*) any number of times, and the result should be the same every time.

Recording Creating New Shapes

You can look at any macro, but it will be easier to understand how the code is written if you start with something very simple you record yourself. So start by recording a drawing of a rectangle, about two inches wide by one inch high. Here are the steps to record and save this action.

Creating a Macro for a Rectangle

1. Open a new document and then, first thing, save it with the name **Learning Macros.cdr**. Naming the file first makes it easier to find, run, and edit the macro later.

2. Click the Record button on the Macros Toolbar, or choose Tools | Macros | Start Recording.

3. Give the macro an obvious name, such as **DrawRectangle**. Remember: don't use any spaces or punctuation; the name must start with a letter and can *only* contain the characters A–Z, a–z, 0–9, and _ (underscore). You'll be reminded with an attention box if you don't type a valid macro name.

4. In the Save Macro In section, click VBAProject (Learning Macros)—the recorded macro will be stored in the current document instead of in a global project file.

5. Type in a brief description, such as **Simple test macro; creating a rectangle**.

6. Click OK. Don't be fooled by the lack of activity at this point—VBA will record every action that you take from now until you stop.

7. Choose the Rectangle Tool (F6), and then draw a 2×1" rectangle in the approximate center of the page; accuracy is not important in this example.

8. Choose Tools | Macros | Stop Recording or press CTRL+SHIFT+O or click Stop Recording on the Macros Toolbar.

That's it; you can now play back the macro to create a new rectangle each time at the same position as the original. This is not the endgame, however—the goal is to generate a few macros you can view to gain an understanding of what's written in the macro document.

Let's quickly make another macro. You'll use these simple macros as a basis for your work in the rest of this chapter. You will *write* a macro that performs functions that cannot be captured by the macro recording process.

With the rectangle from the preceding section selected, record the application of a 3-point-thick blue outline and a Uniform red fill; call this macro **RedFill_BlueOutline**. Stop the recording. Create a different shape, select it, and run this macro: the red fill and blue outline are applied to the new shape.

The lesson you are about to work through is an example of how you can record *approximately* what you require as a macro, and then through a little text editing, modify the macro later.

Solving Macro Needs with VBA

Now you'll take a look through the code that you recorded a few sections ago. Shortly you'll optimize the RedFill_BlueOutline macro. Then you will create an advanced macro, using the optimized RedFill_BlueOutline as the foundation. This advanced macro will apply the fill and outline to the selected objects. However, it will apply the fill *only* to those objects that *have a fill already*, and it will apply the outline part *only* to those objects that *have an outline already*. This will demonstrate how a little VBA programming can be a more powerful resource than the Find and Replace in CorelDRAW when it comes to automating your work.

Viewing Macro Code

To view the VBA code that CorelDRAW created when it recorded your macro, you need to open in the Macro Editor, also called the Microsoft Visual Basic Editor, the project in which the macro is stored. Open the Macro Editor by pressing ALT+F11, or click on Macro Editor on the Macros Toolbar. Look for "VBAProject (Learning Macros)" in the Project Explorer pane on the left side of the editor window. Each open document that has a macro stored in it, as well as the global macro project files that are stored in the GMS folder, is listed here.

Expand the listing for the VBAProject (Learning Macros). Click on the plus button to expand the Modules entry. Under the Open The Modules section you will see a listing, RecordedMacros. Each time you record a macro in this document, it is added to the RecordedMacros module. Double-click on the RecordedMacros entry in the tree listing, and a document window opens to the right, with the name of the VBAProject file, Learning Macros - Recorded Macros (Code) on the title bar. This document window contains the actual programming code that you recorded that makes the macro work.

Taking a Look and Understanding the DrawRectangle Code

In the Learning Macros - Recorded Macros (Code) window you just opened, you should see the following code. Note that the underscore character is used to break the lines to fit within this book's width, this is valid to actually write in code, and using underscores is also legitimate in Visual Basic code.

```
Sub DrawRectangle()
    '' Recorded 11/28/2007
    ''
    '' Description:
    ''      Simple test macro; creating a rectangle
    Dim s1 As Shape
    Set s1 = ActiveLayer.CreateRectangle(2.240205, 6.824638, 4.25, 5.81974)
    s1.Fill.ApplyNoFill
    s1.Outline.SetProperties 0.006945, OutlineStyles(0), CreateCMYKColor(0, 0, 0,
100), ArrowHeads(0), ArrowHeads(0), cdrFalse, cdrFalse, cdrOutlineButtLineCaps,
cdrOutlineMiterLineJoin, 0#, 100, MiterLimit:=45#
End Sub
```

Here's what the lines mean:

- **Sub DrawRectangle()**   This is the name you gave your macro. The word Sub tells VBA that this is the beginning of a *subroutine*. The parentheses here are empty, but sometimes they have programmer code, but never in a recording.

- **'**   Wherever you add an apostrophe, VBA completely ignores the rest of the text on the line after the apostrophe. The green text is *comment information* (notes to you or a coworker, for example) that is ignored by VBA.

- **Dim s1 As Shape**   Dim is short for *dimension*; it reserves enough space in memory for the *variable* called s1, which is of type Shape. *Variables* are containers for something that is not known until the program is running. For example, if you ask the user his or her name, you won't know the result until the program is run and asks the question; the answer would be stored in a *string* or text variable.

30

Variables of the type Shape are not shapes in themselves; they are a *reference* to a shape. It's more or less like a shortcut in Windows to the CorelDRW.exe file: you can have many shortcuts (references) to the same EXE file, but they are all *forward* links. The CorelDRW.exe file knows nothing of the shortcuts until one of them passes a command along the reference. Shape variables act the same: the shape to which s1 later refers is not bound to s1; s1 is only a *forward reference* to that shape.

- **Set s1 = ActiveLayer.CreateRectangle …** This actually creates the rectangle. The first four parameters are the left, top, right, and bottom coordinates of the rectangle, in inches from the bottom-left corner of the page. You use Set each time the reference stored in s1 is changed from one shape to a different shape.

- **s1.Fill.ApplyNoFill** This line states that the Fill property of s1 is set to *no* fill.

- **s1.Outline.SetProperties 0.006945, OutlineStyles(0), CreateCMYKColor(0, 0, 0, 100), ArrowHeads(0), ArrowHeads(0), cdrFalse, cdrFalse, cdrOutlineButtLineCaps, cdrOutlineMiterLineJoin, 0#, 100, MiterLimit:=45#** This last line is shown as several lines in this book, but is (and should be entered as) one line in the VB Editor. This describes the outline properties that have been assigned. In this line of code you can see that the outline width is 0.006945, the OutlineStyles(0) means that it is a solid line, **CreateCMYKColor** is set to black, and other property assignments follow. The settings that are listed here correspond to the settings that are in effect in Outline Pen dialog settings.

- **End Sub** This closes the Sub again, and control passes back to the object that called the Sub, which could be VBA, CorelDRAW, or another Sub or function. It tells VBA to stop here.

Characters that appear in blue are *reserved keywords,* which are special to VBA; you cannot use these words as variable or procedure names. Characters that appear in green are comments or remarks; VBA ignores these completely. Characters that appear in red are lines with syntax errors—VBA cannot understand your fractured VBA "grammar." All other characters appear in black.

Here are some important things to note:

- Recorded macros are created as enclosed subs, starting with a Sub statement and ending with an End Sub statement.

- Variables are dimensioned before you use them. This means that you have to name a variable and set aside memory for it (*dimension* it) before you can do anything with it. You are basically listing the "players" that will be participating in the program.

■ You use `Set` to set a variable to reference that object. If the variable is a simple variable—if it just holds a number or a string (text) and not a reference to another object—you do not need the `Set` statement.

If you right-click `.CreateRectangle` and select Quick Info from the pop-up menu, the definition for the `.CreateRectangle` method is displayed, and you can see from the parameter names the meanings of each parameter.

If you have a look at the `Layer` class in the Object Browser, you will see quite a few members of `Layer` that start with `Create`. These are the basic VBA shape-creation procedures. Therefore, if you wanted an ellipse, you'd use `CreateEllipse`; for a polygon, you would use `CreatePolygon`; or for some text, you would use `CreateArtisticText`.

> **NOTE** *Although you can program the creation of Artistic Text, you cannot record it using CorelDRAW's Macros Toolbar.*

Analyzing RedFill_BlueOutline

For this macro, you recorded two distinct actions. So, the code is longer and has more parts to it:

```
Sub RedFill_BlueOutline()
    '' Recorded 4/1/2008
    '' Description:
    ''     Simple test macro; creating a rectangle with a fill and outline
    Dim OrigSelection As ShapeRange
    Set OrigSelection = ActiveSelectionRange
    OrigSelection.ApplyUniformFill CreateCMYKColor(0, 100, 100, 0)
    OrigSelection.SetOutlineProperties Color:=CreateCMYKColor(100, 100, 0, 0)
    OrigSelection.SetOutlineProperties 0.041665
End Sub
```

■ **Sub RedFill_BlueOutline()**   This line declares the beginning of the macro and the name you assigned it. The three lines that follow as before are comment lines that hold useful information for you, but are not part of the code that performs any work.

■ **Dim OrigSelection As ShapeRange**   This first line of the program code declares (dimensions) the term `OrigSelection` to be a `ShapeRange`. A `ShapeRange` is a special VBA term that means a collection of shapes.

■ **Set OrigSelection = ActiveSelectionRange**   Here the reference `OrigSelection` is set to the object `ActiveSelectionRange`, which is a reference to all the selected objects in the active window.

- ■ **OrigSelection.ApplyUniformFill CreateCMYKColor(0, 100, 100, 0)**   This line sets the fill of the selected shape or shapes to a Uniform fill using the CMYK Red.

- ■ **OrigSelection.SetOutlineProperties Color:= CreateCMYKColor(100, 100, 0, 0)**   CMYK Blue is the color specified here for the selected shape(s) outline.

- ■ **OrigSelection.SetOutlineProperties 0.041665**   Here is where the width (in inches) of the 3-point-wide outline is specified.

- ■ **End Sub**   This is the end marker for this and all macros.

The next refinement to make is that the outline width as recorded in the macro code is in *inches,* regardless of the fact that in the CorelDRAW application window you set the width in *points.* This is because CorelDRAW's default document units in VBA are inches, and you want to set the VBA document units to points, and then set the outline width to 3 points.

To make this change, you'll edit the macro in the VB Editor, and not by making changes to settings in CorelDRAW and re-recording.

Place your cursor in front of the last program line (`OrigSelection.SetOutlineProperties 0.041665`), and press ENTER to create a space where you can insert an additional line of code. Insert your cursor in the blank line you made, and type in this new line of code:

```
ActiveDocument.Unit = cdrPoint
```

Then, in the next line, change .041665 to **3** so that the line now reads:

```
OrigSelection.SetOutlineProperties 3
```

The macro should look like this now:

```
Sub RedFill_BlueOutline()
    '' Recorded 4/1/2008
    ''
    '' Description:
    ''      Simple test macro; creating a rectangle with a fill and outline
    Dim OrigSelection As ShapeRange
    Set OrigSelection = ActiveSelectionRange
    OrigSelection.SetOutlineProperties Color:=CreateCMYKColor(100, 100, 0, 0)
    OrigSelection.ApplyUniformFill CreateCMYKColor(0, 100, 100, 0)
    ActiveDocument.Unit = cdrPoint
    OrigSelection.SetOutlineProperties 3
End Sub
```

CorelDRAW supports lots of different units, including millimeters, centimeters, meters, feet, points, pixels (whose size is determined by the property `Document.Resolution`), and picas that you can set in your macros using this technique.

Extending RedFill_BlueOutline

Let's now take the basic RedFill_BlueOutline macro and add some extra code now. The fill is applied to the selected shapes that already have fills, and the outline is applied to the selected shapes that already have outlines, but neither is applied to those shapes that have neither one nor the other. To do this, you'll add two fundamental programming methods: the *loop* and the *decision*.

First, however, you should know about a powerful feature in VBA: the *collection*.

Collections

VBA provides the programmer with a strong method of handling many similar objects as one object—a collection. Say that you have selected ten shapes in CorelDRAW, and you run a script that starts like this:

```
Dim shs as Shapes
Set shs = ActiveSelection.Shapes
```

The variable shs is dimensioned as type Shapes. The Shapes type is a type of collection of many Shape objects. Think of it as a container that can hold many references to similar objects. The type Shape (singular) means *anything drawn in CorelDRAW*, so the *collection* of Shapes contains lots of references to Shape—to items drawn in CorelDRAW. Collections are a particular type of *array*. If you have done any programming before, you're already familiar with arrays.

Here's the payoff: once you've set a reference to a collection of shapes, you can reference each shape in the collection individually by using a loop, which is what you'll do next. The other advantage to referencing is that you do *not* need to know the size of the collection at any time; VBA does all of that for you. If the user doesn't select anything, the result of the operation is an empty collection. On the other hand, if the user selects 1,000 objects, you will get one collection of 1,000 shapes. The chore of always having to know exactly how many shapes are selected has been taken over by VBA, so you can get on with some clever coding.

Looping

A *loop* is a piece of code that is run, run again, and rerun until a condition is met or until a counter runs out. The most useful loop to us is the For-Next loop, of which there are two types: basic For-Next and For-Each-Next.

The basic For-Next loop might look something like this:

```
Dim lCount as long
For lCount = 1 To 10
    MsgBox ""Number"" & lCount
Next lCount
```

This loop counts from one to ten, displaying a message box for each number.

The For-Each-Next loop comes into its own *when dealing with collections,* however. The purpose of a collection is to allow the programmer to reference the collection without knowing what is inside. Thus, to step through all the shapes in the collection, the following code is used:

```
Dim shs as Shapes, sh as Shape
Set shs = ActiveSelection.Shapes
For Each sh in shs
    '' We will add our own code into this loop
Next sh
```

 This loop code is a fundamental algorithm when programming CorelDRAW. It is strongly recommended that you become very familiar with it, because you will need to use it often.

Note the `Dim` line: You can dimension more than one variable on a single line by separating each variable with a comma. With large modules that have tens of variables, this helps to keep down the module length.

This code loops through all the shapes in the collection, and you can replace the remark line with your *own* code—of as many lines as needed. Each time the `For` line is executed, `sh` is set to the next shape in the collection. A programmer can then access that shape's members within the loop by referencing `sh`. For example, the following code sets the width of each shape to two centimeters:

```
Dim shs as Shapes, sh as Shape
Set shs = ActiveSelection.Shapes
ActiveDocument.Unit = cdrCentimeter
For Each sh in shs
    sh.SizeWidth = 2
Next sh
```

Because this code operates on each shape, one shape at a time, the size will be set relative only to that shape and not to the selection, so each shape will now be two centimeters wide. But the selection's width will still be approximately the same.

Now it's time to move to making decisions, and then to put loops and decisions together.

Decision Making—Conditionals

Decision making is what really sets programming apart from macros. Macros in their original sense are little pieces of "dumb code." Macros do not make decisions; they just perform a series of actions without any understanding of what they are doing. However, as soon as you introduce decision making, a macro becomes a *program.*

Decisions in VBA are made using the If-Then-Else construction: *If* (something is true) *Then* (do this), or *Else* (do that). The conditional statement—the "something"—must be able to return the answer True or False, but VBA is very tolerant. For example, you could write code in this way:

```
If MsgBox (""Do you want to hear a beep?"", vbYesNo) = vbYes Then Beep
```

As long as the Yes button is clicked, you will hear a beep. In this case, the result of the test in the conditional statement was True or False: The button clicked either *was* the Yes button (True), or else it *was not* the Yes button (False).

The statement does not have to reside all on one line, and usually you would not write it so. Instead you might write it something like this:

```
If sShape.Type = cdrEllipseShape Then
    MsgBox ""Ellipse""
Else
    MsgBox ""Some other shape""
End If
```

As with most things in VBA, what is opened must be closed; don't forget to add an `End If` statement. You don't always have to supply an `Else` if it's not necessary, but it is a good programming technique.

Notice also that you can use Boolean operators—such as AND, OR, NOT, and XOR—to combine results from two or more conditional statements.

Conditional Loops—Putting It All Together

Now you know how to assign an outline and a fill (RedFill_BlueOutline), and you've looked at looping through collections (For-Each-Next). You should also have a fairly good idea about decision making (If-Then-Else). The trick is to put all of this together, so that you can apply the fill and the outline based on whether each object already has a fill or an outline.

Most of the code already exists for you in the previous code. The only missing part is a reliable decision-making routine for this particular instance. What you and your soon-to-be program need to determine for each shape are the following:

- *Does it have a fill?*   If it does, *then* apply the new fill; *else* do nothing to the fill.

- *Does it have an outline?*   If it does, *then* apply the new outline; *else* do nothing to the outline.

Fortunately, determining an object's outline is simple: The `Shape.Outline.Type` property returns either `cdrOutline` or `cdrNoOutline`. All that needs to be done is to ask whether the outline type is `cdrOutline`.

Determining whether a shape has a fill is slightly trickier: ten different fill types are possible, including Uniform, Fountain, PostScript, Pattern, and so on. Instead of asking, "Does the shape have a fill?" and having to ask it for all the different types, it is easier to ask, "Does the shape *not* have a fill?" and invert the answer, as in "Is the shape's fill *not* of type `cdrNoFill`?" For this, you use the greater-than and less-than symbols together (<>), which means, not-equal-to.

Put all this together and here is the resulting code:

```
Sub Apply_RedFill_BlueOutline()
    Dim dDoc as Document
    Dim sShapes As Shapes, sShape As Shape
    Set dDoc = ActiveDocument
    dDoc.BeginCommandGroup ""Apply Red Fill & Blue Outline""
    dDoc.Unit = cdrPoint
    Set sShapes = ActiveSelection.Shapes
    For Each sShape In sShapes
        If sShape.Fill.Type <> cdrNoFill Then
            sShape.Fill.UniformColor.RGBAssign 255, 0, 0
        End If
        If sShape.Outline.Type = cdrOutline Then
            sShape.Outline.Color.RGBAssign 0, 0, 255
            sShape.Outline.Width = 3
        End If
    Next sShape
    dDoc.EndCommandGroup
End Sub
```

This code steps through the collection of selected shapes, one at a time. It first asks, "Does the shape have a fill type that is not `cdrNoFill`?" and applies the new fill if the condition is true. Then it asks, "Does the shape have an outline?" and applies the new outline if it does.

In the code above, notice that before `End Sub` there's `EndCommandGroup`, which deserves an explanation here. The `BeginCommandGroup` and `EndCommandGroup` methods put together all the commands in between into a single `Undo` statement in CorelDRAW, with the name that you specify. After running this macro once, there will be an item on CorelDRAW's Edit menu called Undo Apply Red Fill & Blue Outline, which, when selected, will remove all of the commands between the `BeginCommandGroup` and `EndCommandGroup` statements.

Developing from Scratch

Developing solutions from scratch requires experience and planning—experience with using CorelDRAW's Object Model, and a plan of what the solution is supposed to achieve. Most of all, it requires *planning*. Given sufficient clarity and completeness in the plan, usually the code for the solution is a simple step.

For very large projects, it is better to break the solution into small, self-contained chunks that you can develop independently of the rest and test in isolation—testing that the code does do what you expect is important and is far simpler with small chunks of code than with whole projects in a single bite.

Where to Go for More Information

Using VBA to perform automation in CorelDRAW is a lengthy topic that extends well beyond this book. You now have a good understanding of how to record your own macros and how to play them back. That alone should be quite useful in future simple automation needs. However, it's important to understand that you can do a lot more with VBA than just record a few keystrokes and mouse clicks.

To attain a proficiency with VBA in CorelDRAW, two areas of expertise and knowledge will lead to productivity—CorelDRAW's Object Model and VBA. You'll find a lot more information about all of the VBA Editor and command syntax in the VBA help files. Also, CorelDRAW's help files contain plenty of information on Visual Basic for Applications, and the Object Browser is also a great place to go for more information on the Object Model. Here are plenty of other places to get help.

Newsgroups and Forums

Corel offers a large number of newsgroups and support forums for their products. You can find details on how to access Corel's newsgroups by going to Corel's website at www.corel.com. Navigate to the Community area and then click on Newsgroups in the Menu Bar for details about Corel's newsgroups. If you prefer to use web-based forums, go to www.coreldraw.com and on the page's Menu Bar, click Forums.

You can seek help freely via the newsgroups and forums, and because lots of people use only the newsgroup *or* the forum, it is a good idea to *check out both* when you have a question. The forums and newsgroups are filled with postings from knowledgeable, friendly professionals who are usually eager to jump in and lend you a hand.

Corel Websites

Corel has several websites that offer information for users. The most relevant site for articles about CorelDRAW is coreldraw.com. You'll find free macros and other materials in the Downloads section that Corel engineers and users have posted.

If you are looking for information on what third-party developers have whipped up to enhance CorelDRAW, check out the Third-Party Tools section from the Partners tab at www.corel.com.

Visual Basic Websites

Many excellent websites have information on how to program with Visual Basic, and some deal with Visual Basic for Applications. Because VBA is a pared-down version of Visual Basic, you can use the Visual Basic websites as an excellent learning resource.

To find other informational websites, use the Yahoo Toolbar, if you installed it, or your favorite Internet search engine to locate some VB sites. Then browse them and any other sites they link to.

30

APPENDIX
Shortcut Keys

Align Commands	Keypresses	Description
Align Left	`L`	Aligns selected objects to the left
Align Right	`R`	Aligns selected objects to the right
Align Top	`T`	Aligns selected objects to the top
Align Bottom	`B`	Aligns selected objects to the bottom
Align Centers Horizontally	`E`	Horizontally aligns centers of selected objects
Align Centers Vertically	`C`	Vertically aligns centers of selected objects
Center To Page	`P`	Aligns centers of selected objects to page center

Distribute Commands	Keypresses	Description
Distribute Bottom	`Shift` + `B`	Distributes selected objects to the bottom
Distribute Centers Horizontally	`Shift` + `E`	Horizontally distributes centers of selected objects
Distribute Centers Vertically	`Shift` + `C`	Vertically distributes centers of selected objects
Distribute Left	`Shift` + `L`	Distributes selected objects to the left
Distribute Right	`Shift` + `R`	Distributes selected objects to the right
Distribute Spacing Horizontally	`Shift` + `P`	Horizontally distributes space between selected objects
Distribute Spacing Vertically	`Shift` + `A`	Vertically distributes space between selected objects
Distribute Top	`Shift` + `T`	Distributes selected objects to the top

Document Display	Keypresses	Description
Full-Screen Preview	`F9`	Displays a full-screen preview of the drawing
Refresh Window	`Ctrl` + `W`	Forces a redraw of the drawing window
Toggle Display	`Shift` + `F9`	Toggles between the last two used view qualities
Show Nonprinting Characters	`Ctrl` + `Shift` + `C`	Shows nonprinting characters

Open/Close Dockers	Keypresses	Description
Contour	`Ctrl` + `F9`	Opens or closes the Contour docker
Envelope	`Ctrl` + `F7`	Opens or closes the Envelope docker
Graphic and Text Styles	`Ctrl` + `F5`	Opens or closes the Graphic and Text Styles docker
Lens	`Alt` + `F3`	Opens or closes the Lens docker

Open/Close Dockers	Keypresses	Description
Linear Dimensions	`Alt` + `F2`	Opens or closes the Linear Dimensions docker for assigning linear-dimension line properties
Object Properties	`Alt` + `Enter`	Opens or closes the Object Properties docker
Position	`Alt` + `F7`	Opens or closes the Position docker
Rotate	`Alt` + `F8`	Opens or closes the Rotate docker
Scale and Mirror	`Alt` + `F9`	Opens or closes the Scale and Mirror docker
Size	`Alt` + `F10`	Opens or closes the Size docker
Insert Symbols and Special Characters	`Ctrl` + `F11`	Opens or closes the Insert Character docker
View Manager	`Ctrl` + `F2`	Opens or closes the View Manager docker
Symbols Manager	`Ctrl` + `F3`	Opens or closes the Symbols Manager docker

Clipboard & Object Editing Commands	Keypresses	Description
Copy	`Ctrl` + `C`	Copies selection to the Clipboard
Copy	`Ctrl` + `Insert`	Copies selection to the Clipboard
Cut	`Ctrl` + `X`	Cuts selection to the Clipboard
Cut	`Shift` + `Delete`	Cuts selection to the Clipboard
Delete	`Delete`	Deletes selected object(s)
Duplicate	`Ctrl` + `D`	Duplicates selected object(s) to offsets
Paste	`Ctrl` + `V`	Pastes the Clipboard contents into the drawing
Paste	`Shift` + `Insert`	Pastes the Clipboard contents into the drawing
Redo	`Ctrl` + `Shift` + `Z`	Reverses the last Undo operation
Repeat	`Ctrl` + `R`	Repeats the last operation
Undo	`Ctrl` + `Z` or `Alt` + `Backspace`	Reverses the last operation

File Commands	Keypresses	Description
Export	`Ctrl` + `E`	Exports pages or objects to selected file format
Import	`Ctrl` + `I`	Imports (or links) content into your document
New Document	`Ctrl` + `N`	Creates a new drawing
Open	`Ctrl` + `O`	Opens an existing drawing
Print	`Ctrl` + `P`	Prints the active drawing

A

File Commands	Keypresses	Description
Save	Ctrl + S	Saves the active drawing
Save As	Ctrl + Shift + S	Opens the Save As dialog
Exit	Alt + F4	Closes CorelDRAW X4

Fill and Effects Dialogs	Keypresses	Description
Open Fountain Fill dialog	F11	Specifies fountain fills for objects
Uniform Fill dialog	Shift + F11	Opens dialog for specifying uniform color fills
Color Balance	Ctrl + Shift + B	Opens dialog for changing color balance
Brightness/Contrast/Intensity	Ctrl + B	Opens dialog for changing color brightness, contrast, and/or intensity
Hue/Saturation/Lightness	Ctrl + Shift + U	Opens dialog for changing hue, saturation, and/or lightness

Find & Replace Using Text Tool	Keypresses	Description
Find Text	Alt + F3	Opens the Find dialog
Format Characters	Ctrl + T	Opens the Character Formatting dialog

Font Formatting Commands Using Text Tool	Keypresses	Description
Bold	Ctrl + B	Changes the style of text to bold
Font List	Ctrl + Shift + F	Shows a list of all the available/active fonts
Font Weights	Ctrl + Shift + W	Shows a list of all the available/active font weights
Italic	Ctrl + I	Changes the style of text to italic
Small Caps	Ctrl + Shift + K	Changes all text characters to small capital letters
Underline	Ctrl + U	Changes the style of text to underline
Decrease Font Size	Ctrl + NUMPAD 2	Decreases the font size to previous point size
Font Size	Ctrl + Shift + P	Shows a list of all the available/active font sizes
HTML Font Size	Ctrl + Shift + H	Shows a list of all the available/active HTML font sizes
Increase Font Size	Ctrl + NUMPAD 8	Increases font size to next point size
Next Font Combo Size	Ctrl + NUMPAD 6	Increases font size to next setting in Font Size List

Font Formatting Commands Using Text Tool	Keypresses	Description
Previous Font Combo Size	`Ctrl` + NUMPAD `4`	Decreases font size to previous setting available in Font Size List
Change Case	`Shift` + `F3`	Changes the case of selected text
Convert Text	`Ctrl` + `F8`	Converts text (Paragraph to Artistic, or vice versa)
Align to Baseline	`Alt` + `F12`	Realigns selected text to its original baseline

Grid, Guides, & Snapping	Keypresses	Description
Snap To Grid	`Ctrl` + `Y`	Snaps objects to the grid (toggle)
Dynamic Guides	`Alt` + `Shift` + `D`	Toggles the view of dynamic guides
Snap To Objects	`Alt` + `Z`	Toggles snapping to objects using current modes

Object Groups & Combine Commands	Keypresses	Description
Break Apart	`Ctrl` + `K`	Breaks apart the selected object
Combine	`Ctrl` + `L`	Combines the selected objects
Convert Outline To Object	`Ctrl` + `Shift` + `Q`	Converts an outline to an object
Convert To Curves	`Ctrl` + `Q`	Converts the selected object to a curve
Group	`Ctrl` + `G`	Groups the selected objects
Ungroup	`Ctrl` + `U`	Ungroups the selected objects or group of objects

Object Nudge Commands	Keypresses	Description
Nudge Down	`↓`	Nudges downward
Nudge Left	`←`	Nudges to the left
Nudge Right	`→`	Nudges to the right
Nudge Up	`↑`	Nudges upward
Super Nudge Down	`Shift` + `↓`	Nudges downward by the Super Nudge factor
Super Nudge Left	`Shift` + `←`	Nudges to the left by the Super Nudge factor
Super Nudge Right	`Shift` + `→`	Nudges to the right by the Super Nudge factor
Super Nudge Up	`Shift` + `↑`	Nudges upward by the Super Nudge factor
Micro Nudge Down	`Ctrl` + `↑`	Nudges downward by the Micro Nudge factor
Micro Nudge Left	`Ctrl` + `←`	Nudges to the left by the Micro Nudge factor

A

Object Nudge Commands	Keypresses	Description
Micro Nudge Right	Ctrl + →	Nudges to the right by the Micro Nudge factor
Micro Nudge Up	Ctrl + ↑	Nudges upward by the Micro Nudge factor

Options	Keypresses	Description
Text Options	Ctrl + F10	Opens the Options dialog with the Text options page selected
Workspace Options dialog	Ctrl + J	Opens the dialog for setting CorelDRAW options

Object Ordering	Keypresses	Description
Back One	Ctrl + Pg Dn	Places selected object(s) back one position in the object stacking order
Forward One	Ctrl + Pg Up	Places selected object(s) forward one position in the object stacking order
To Back of Layer	Shift + Pg Dn	Places selected object(s) to the back of layer
To Front of Layer	Shift + Pg Up	Places selected object(s) to the front of layer

Object Outline Pen	Keypresses	Description
Open Outline Color Dialog	Shift + F12	Specifies outline color of objects
Open Outline Pen Dialog	F12	Specifies outline pen properties for objects

Document Navigation	Keypresses	Description
Next Page	Pg Dn	Go to the next page
Previous Page	Pg Up	Go to the previous page

Select All	Keypresses	Description
Objects	Ctrl + A	Selects all objects in the entire drawing

Styles	Keypresses	Description
Graphic and Text Styles	Ctrl + F5	Opens or closes the Graphic and Text Styles docker

Text Formatting Using Text Tool	Keypresses	Description
Bullet Text	`Ctrl` + `M`	Toggles current bullets for Paragraph text object
Center Justify	`Ctrl` + `E`	Changes the alignment of text to center alignment
Convert Text State	`Ctrl` + `F8`	Converts Artistic Text to Paragraph Text or vice versa
Apply Drop Cap	`Ctrl` + `Shift` + `D`	Applies/removes a Drop Cap effect for text object (toggle)
Edit Text	`Ctrl` + `Shift` + `T`	Opens the Edit Text dialog
Force Justification	`Ctrl` + `H`	Changes alignment of text to force last line full alignment
Format Character	`Ctrl` + `T`	Formats the selected text characters
Full Justify	`Ctrl` + `J`	Changes the alignment of text to full alignment
Horizontal Text	`Ctrl` + `,`	Changes the text to horizontal direction
Left Justification	`Ctrl` + `L`	Changes the alignment of text to left alignment
No Justification	`Ctrl` + `N`	Changes the alignment of text to have no alignment
Right Justification	`Ctrl` + `R`	Changes the alignment of text to right alignment
Vertical Text	`Ctrl` + `.`	Changes the text to vertical (toggle)

Text Editing & Cursor Moves Using Text Tool	Keypresses	Description
Delete character to right	`Delete`	Deletes character right of cursor
Delete word to right	`Ctrl` + `Delete`	Deletes word right of cursor
Cursor down one frame	`Pg Dn`	Moves cursor down one frame
Cursor down one line	`↓`	Moves cursor down one line
Cursor down one paragraph	`Ctrl` + `↓`	Moves cursor down one paragraph
Cursor left one character	`←`	Moves cursor left one character
Cursor left one word	`Ctrl` + `←`	Moves cursor left one word
Cursor right one character	`→`	Moves cursor right one character
Cursor right one word	`Ctrl` + `→`	Moves cursor right one word
Cursor up one frame	`Pg Up`	Moves cursor up one frame
Cursor up one line	`↑`	Moves cursor up one line
Cursor up one paragraph	`Ctrl` + `↑`	Moves cursor up one paragraph
Cursor to start of frame	`Ctrl` + `Home`	Moves cursor to start of frame

A

Text Editing & Cursor Moves Using Text Tool	Keypresses	Description
Cursor to start of line	Home	Moves cursor to start of line
Cursor to start of text	Ctrl + Pg Up	Moves cursor to start of text
Cursor to end of frame	Ctrl + End	Moves cursor to end of frame
Cursor to end of line	End	Moves cursor to end of line
Cursor to end of text	Ctrl + Pg Dn	Moves cursor to end of text
Select all text	Ctrl + A	Selects all text in Paragraph Frame or Artistic Text object
Select character to left	Shift + ← ↓ ↑	Selects character to left of cursor
Select character to right	Shift + →	Selects character to right of cursor
Select down one frame	Shift + Pg Dn	Selects text downward by one frame
Select down one line	Shift + ↓	Selects text downward by one line
Select down one paragraph	Ctrl + Shift + ↓	Selects text downward by one paragraph
Select up one frame	Shift + Pg Up	Selects text upward by one frame
Select up one line	Shift + ↑	Selects text upward by one line
Select up one paragraph	Ctrl + Shift + ↑	Selects text upward by one paragraph
Select word to left	Ctrl + Shift + ←	Selects word to left of cursor
Select word to right	Ctrl + Shift + →	Selects word to right of cursor
Select to start of frame	Ctrl + Shift + Home	Selects text to start of frame
Select to start of line	Shift + Home	Selects text to start of line
Select to start of frame	Ctrl + Shift + Pg Up	Selects text to start of frame
Select to end of frame	Ctrl + Shift + End	Selects text to end of frame
Select to end of line	Shift + End	Selects text to end of line
Select to end of text	Ctrl + Shift + Pg Dn	Selects text to end of frame

Text Tools	Keypresses	Description
Change Case	Shift + F3	Changes the case of selected text
Show Nonprinting Characters	Ctrl + Shift + C	Shows nonprinting characters such as spaces, tabs, returns, and line feeds
Spell Check	Ctrl + F12	Opens the Spell Checker; checks the spelling of the selected text
Style List	Ctrl + Shift + S	Shows a list of the document text styles
Text Options	Ctrl + F10	Opens the Options dialog to the Text page

Toolbox Tool Selection	Keypresses	Description
Artistic Media Tool	`I`	Draws curves and applies Preset, Brush, Spray, Calligraphic, or Pressure Sensitive effects to the strokes
Ellipse Tool	`F7`	Draws ellipses and circles; double-clicking the tool opens the Toolbox tab of the Options dialog
Eraser Tool	`X`	Erases part of a graphic or splits an object into two closed paths
Toggle Eyedropper & Paintbucket	`Shift`	Holding this modifier toggles between Eyedropper and Paintbucket tools while either is selected
Freehand Tool	`F5`	Selects the Freehand Tool
Graph Paper Tool	`D`	Draws a group of rectangles; double-clicking opens the Toolbox tab of the Options dialog
Hand	`H`	Pans around the drawing by clicking and dragging using this tool
Interactive Fill Tool	`G`	Adds a fill to object(s); clicking and dragging on object(s) applies a fountain fill
Mesh Fill	`M`	Converts an object to a Mesh Fill object
Polygon Tool	`Y`	Draws symmetrical polygons; double-clicking opens the Toolbox tab of the Options dialog
Rectangle Tool	`F6`	Draws rectangles; double-clicking the tool creates a page frame
Shape Tool	`F10`	Edits the nodes of an object; double-clicking the tool selects all nodes on the selected object. Hold `Alt` + `Shift` to activate marquee-style node selecting
Smart Drawing Tool	`Shift` + `S`	Creates typical CorelDRAW objects by sketching. Hold `Shift` while sketching to erase.
Spiral Tool	`A`	Draws spirals; double-clicking opens the Toolbox tab of the Options dialog
Text Tool	`F8`	Adds text; click on the page to add Artistic Text; click and drag to add Paragraph Text
Toggle Pick State	`Ctrl` + `Spacebar`	Toggles between the current tool and the Pick Tool

Visual Basic	Keypresses	Description
Open VBA Editor	`Alt` + `F11`	Launches Visual Basic for Applications Editor

A

Workspace	Keypresses	Description
Display Property Bar	Ctrl + Enter	Selects the Property Bar and highlights the first visible item that can be tabbed to

Zoom & Pan	Keypresses	Description
Navigator	N	Brings up the Navigator window allowing you to navigate to any object in the document
Hand Tool	H	Pans around the drawing by clicking and dragging using this tool
Pan Down	Alt + ↓	Pans the drawing downward
Pan Left	Alt + ←	Pans the drawing to the left
Pan Right	Alt + →	Pans the drawing to the right
Pan Up	Alt + ↑	Pans the drawing upward
View Manager	Ctrl + F2	Opens or closes the View Manager docker
Zoom One Shot	F2	Enables you to perform a zoom action; then returns to the last-used tool
Zoom Out	F3	Zooms out
Zoom To All Objects	F4	Zooms in on all objects in the drawing
Zoom To Page	Shift + F4	Displays the entire printable page
Zoom To Selection	Shift + F2	Zooms in on selected objects only

INDEX

CorelDRAW®
GRAPHICS SUITE X4

The legendary power of CorelDRAW® Graphics Suite is all around.

With extensive file compatibility and powerful automation and customization features to optimize your workflow, CorelDRAW Graphics Suite is the graphics solution of choice for the engraving, awards and recognition, and vinyl-cutting industries. The suite's ease of use, compatibility and value has appealed to professionals in these industries for years, and the latest version is

packed full of features that will help make your
workflow easier than ever.

Experience it for yourself! Upgrade today at
www.corel.com/officialguide

Don't own a previous version? Get started for free
at **www.corel.com/officialguidetrial**

© 2008 Corel Corporation. All rights reserved. 06/08 JB#469-08